Translated Texts for Historia

300–800 AD is the time of late antiquity
transformation of the classical world, the beginnings of Europe and of Islam, and the evolution of Byzantium. TTH makes available sources translated from Greek, Latin, Syriac, Coptic, Arabic, Georgian, Gothic and Armenian. Each volume provides an expert scholarly translation, with an introduction setting texts and authors in context, and with notes on content, interpretation and debates.

A full list of published titles in the **Translated Texts for Historians** series is available on request. The most recently published are shown below.

History and Hagiography from the Late Antique Sinai
DANIEL F. CANER, with contributions by SEBASTIAN BROCK, RICHARD M. PRICE and KEVIN VAN BLADEL
Volume 53: 346pp., ISBN 978-1-84631-216-8

Orosius: Seven Books of History against the Pagans
Translated with introduction and notes by A. T. FEAR
Volume 54: 456pp., 2010; ISBN 978-1-84631-473-5 cased, 978-1-84631-239-7 limp

The Chronicle of Pseudo-Zachariah Rhetor: Church and War in Late Antiquity
Translated by GEOFFREY GREATREX, with ROBERT PHENIX and CORNELIA HORN; introductory material by SEBASTIAN BROCK and WITOLD WITAKOWSKI
Volume 55: 2010; ISBN 978-1-84631-493-3 cased, 978-1-84631-494-0 limp

Bede: On the Nature of Things and On Times
Translated with introduction and notes by CALVIN B. KENDALL and FAITH WALLIS
Volume 56: 371pp., 2010, ISBN 978-1-84631-495-7

Theophilus of Edessa's Chronicle
Translated with introduction and notes by ROBERT G. HOYLAND
Volume 57: 368pp., 2011, ISBN 978-1-84631-697-5 cased, 978-1-84631-698-2 limp

Bede: Commentary on Revelation
Translated with introduction and notes by FAITH WALLIS
Volume 58: 343pp., 2013, ISBN 978-1-84631-844-3 cased, 978-1-84631-845-0 limp

Two Early Lives of Severos, Patriarch of Antioch
Translated with an introduction and notes by SEBASTIAN BROCK and BRIAN FITZGERALD
Volume 59, 175pp., 2013, ISBN 978-1-84631-882-5 cased, 978-1-84631-883-2 limp

The Funerary Speech for John Chrysostom
Translated with an introduction and notes by TIMOTHY D. BARNES and GEORGE BEVAN
Volume 60, 193pp., ISBN 978-1-84631-887-0 cased, 978-1-84631-888-7 limp

The Acts of the Lateran Synod of 649
Translated with notes by RICHARD PRICE, with contributions by PHIL BOOTH and CATHERINE CUBITT
Volume 61, 476pp., ISBN 978-1-78138-039-0 cased

Macarius, *Apocriticus*
Translated with introduction and commentary by JEREMY M. SCHOTT and MARK J. EDWARDS
Volume 62, 476pp., ISBN 978 1 78138 129 8 cased, ISBN 978 1 78138 130 4 limp

For full details of **Translated Texts for Historians**, including prices and ordering information, please write to the following: **All countries, except the USA and Canada:** Liverpool University Press, 4 Cambridge Street, Liverpool, L69 7ZU, UK (*Tel* +44-[0]151-794 2233, Email janmar@liv.ac.uk, http://www.liverpooluniversitypress.co.uk). **USA and Canada:** Turpin Distribution, www.turpin-distribution.com

Translated Texts for Historians
Volume 63

Khalifa ibn Khayyat's *History* on the Umayyad Dynasty (660–750)

by CARL WURTZEL
prepared for publication
by ROBERT G. HOYLAND

Liverpool
University
Press

TTH

First published 2015
Liverpool University Press
4 Cambridge Street
Liverpool, L69 7ZU

British Library Cataloguing-in-Publication Data
A British Library CIP Record is available.

ISBN 978 1 78138 174 8 cased
ISBN 978 1 78138 175 5 limp

Typeset by Carnegie Book Production, Lancaster
Printed by BooksFactory.co.uk

CONTENTS

For my mother Dora Wurtzel and to the memory of my father Samuel A. Wurtzel whose love and support enabled me to complete this work

FOREWORD

Islamic historians tend to assume that the Muslim histories they work with are merely compilations of material culled from numerous earlier sources with no deliberate purpose or focus.[1] For that reason, Islamicists very rarely compose studies on a single author or a single text, and they seldom consider the character and program of the histories they use to write on specific topics and events. Only the most major of authors, like al-Tabari (d. 310/923) and al-Mas'udi (d. 345/956),[2] have been the subject of a monograph, while the rest languish in relative obscurity. It seemed to me worthwhile, therefore, to make available Carl Wurtzel's excellent unpublished doctoral dissertation (Yale University, 1977), which provides a translation and evaluation of the Umayyad portion of the *History* of Khalifa ibn Khayyat, as an example of how one can reveal interesting insights into the aims and methods of a medieval Muslim historian. Khalifa certainly drew upon earlier sources, but, as Wurtzel demonstrates, he selected, edited, and shaped these excerpts, and in the process produced his own distinctive take on events. Furthermore, as the earliest extant work of Muslim historiography, Khalifa's *History* is crucial to an understanding of the emergence of this discipline in the framework of Islamic civilization, and his choice of an annalistic format brings to light its links to the Syriac chronicle tradition, which was still flourishing at this time.[3] It is to be hoped that this publication will encourage translations of other examples of early Arabic historical writings and more studies dedicated to specific Muslim historical texts.[4]

Robert Hoyland (17 November 2014)

1 Hoyland, "History and Fiction in Classical Arabic Literature."

2 Kennedy; Shoshan; Shboul. Note that in this volume dates will usually be given in *hijra* form (lunar years counting from AD 622) and Christian/Common Era form (AD/CE).

3 Noted in Hoyland, "Arabic, Syriac and Greek Historiography."

4 As yet, there are no published monographs on the ninth-century histories of Ibn 'Abd al-Hakam, al-Ya'qubi, al-Baladhuri, or al-Dinawari, though I have recently supervised doctoral dissertations in this vein; see Bonner; Lynch.

PREFACE

The *Ta'rīkh* (*History*) of Khalifa b. Khayyat, who died c. 240/854–855, is the oldest complete annalistic history in Arabic with a comprehensive treatment of the rise, expansion, and internal turmoil of the Arab-Islamic empire. It is of interest in several respects. As a very old historiographical document, it has intrinsic value as a source charting the development of Islamic historiography. The importance of an early work such as Khalifa's lies also in its value as a check against the accounts of later historians, who in some cases may have embellished or distorted historical narratives to suit their own purposes. In addition, Khalifa's work may serve to counter the pronounced anti-Umayyad tenor found in the works of most of the historians of the later ninth century and thereafter.

Although Khalifa's reports are frequently very brief, his *Ta'rīkh* does contain some unique and detailed information. There is valuable material in the accounts of the raiding expeditions – particularly in Armenia and the Caucasus, the Maghrib, Anatolia, and India – and certain of the Kharijite rebellions and civil wars. Another unique feature of the *Ta'rīkh* is the comprehensive, detailed listing of the names of governors, judges, secretaries, and other administrative officials who served during the reign of each caliph.

The body of the present study is a translation of the section on the Umayyad dynasty. Khalifa's life, and his religio-political attitudes (insofar as they can be ascertained), his approach to historical writing, the sources for his *Ta'rīkh*, and the influence – with regard to methodology and content – of Khalifa's work on that of later Muslim writers of history are treated in the introduction. It is hoped that this study will contribute something to our understanding of certain aspects of Islamic historiography.

The translated portion of the *Ta'rīkh*, covering the years 41/661 to 132/750, represents just over a half of the text of the entire work, 167 pages (pp. 118–284) of a manuscript of 336 pages. This corresponds to pages 234–625 in the printed edition of Zakkar. The Umayyad period in Khalifa's *Ta'rīkh* is particularly useful for researchers because of a number of unique sources that Khalifa uses, and his markedly different view of that period.

In contrast to some other genres of Arabic literature, such as poetry, philosophy, and certain religious writings, most Arabic historical writing, Khalifa's included, offers comparatively few linguistic difficulties. It is hoped, however, that the translation and commentary will prove useful to Arabists as well as non-Arabists. For the latter, the translation may provide an insight into the history of the Umayyad period, as told in the words of an early Arab historian. They will find that the somewhat unusual emphasis Khalifa places on certain of the conquests and internal rebellions, the lively dialogue through which some accounts are related, the vivid first-person narrative style of other accounts, and his lack of interest in the 'Alid Shi'a, give his work a refreshing change of pace to the customary histories of the Umayyads. Scholars whose interests lie primarily outside the field of Islamic history, but upon whose work the Islamic empire of the years 661–750 has some bearing, may also find the translation and notes pertinent. This applies in particular to students of Armenian, Caucasian, Byzantine, North African, and Indian history. Arabists may find that the translation and annotations illuminate certain otherwise obscure passages, and resolve some textual problems. Because of the features of Khalifa's *Ta'rīkh* enumerated above, the work has been, since its publication in 1967, a heavily utilized source for students of early Islamic history. It is hoped that the translation and annotation may make Khalifa's text accessible to a much wider audience.

Acknowledgement

This book was originally written as a Ph.D. dissertation at Yale University in the Department of Near Eastern Languages and Literatures under the expert guidance of Prof. Franz Rosenthal.

ABBREVIATIONS

Aghānī – Abu l-Faraj al-Isbahani, *Kitāb al-Aghānī*
Amari – M. Amari, *Biblioteca Arabo-Sicula*
Ansāb – al-Baladhuri, *Ansāb al-ashrāf*
BGA, I – al-Istakhri, *Masālik al-mamālik*
BGA, II – Ibn Hawqal, *al-Masālik wa-l-mamālik*
BGA, III – al-Muqaddasi, *Aḥsan at-taqāsīm*
BGA, V – Ibn Faqih al-Hamadhani, *al-Buldān*
BGA, VI, 3–183 – Ibn Khurdadhbih, *al-Masālik wa-l-mamālik*
BGA, VI, 184–266 – Qudama, *Kitāb al-kharāj*
BGA, VII, 1–229 – Ibn Rustah, *al-A'lāq an-nafīsa*
BGA, VII, 231–373 – al-Ya'qubi, *al-Buldān*
BGA, VIII – al-Mas'udi, *at-Tanbīh wa-l-ishrāf*
Dh. – adh-Dhahabi, *Ta'rīkh al-Islām*
Din. – ad-Dinawari, *al-Akhbār at-ṭiwāl*
Dunlop – D. M. Dunlop, *The History of the Jewish Khazars*
EI – *Encyclopaedia of Islam*
EI2 – *Encyclopaedia of Islam,* new edition
Fihrist – Ibn an-Nadim, *al-Fihrist*
Futūḥ – al-Baladhuri, *Futūḥ al-buldān*
GAL – C. Brockelmann, *Geschichte der arabischen Litteratur*
GAS – F. Sezgin, *Geschichte des arabischen Schrifttums*
IA – Ibn al-Athir, *al-Kāmil fī t-Ta'rīkh*
IAH – Ibn 'Abd al-Hakam, *Futūḥ Miṣr wa-akhbāru-hā*
Ibn 'Asakir – *Ta'rīkh madīnat Dimashq*
Ibn 'Asakir, *Tahdhīb* – The old abbreviated edition of his *Ta'rīkh madīnat Dimashq*
Ibn Hajar – Ibn Hajar al-'Askalani, *Tahdhīb al-tahdhīb*
Imāma – al-Imāma wa-s-siyāsa
'Iqd – Ibn 'Abd Rabbihi, *al-'Iqd al-farīd*
Isāba – Ibn Hajar al-'Askalani, *al-Iṣāba fī tamyīz as-ṣaḥāba*
Istī'āb – Ibn 'Abd al-Barr, *al-Istī'āb fī ma'rifat al-aṣḥāb*

Jarḥ – Ibn 'Abi Hatim, *al-Jarḥ wa-t-ta'dīl*
Kh. – When followed by a page number, Kh. = edition of Zakkar. When a second page reference follows in parentheses, the second number refers to the edition of al-'Umari. When no number follows Kh., it means that the citation is found in both editions.
Ma'ārif – Ibn Qutayba, *Kitāb al-ma'ārif*
Minorsky – *Ḥudūd al-'ālam*
Murūj – al-Mas'udi, *Murūj adh-dhahab*
s.v. – *sub verbo* or *sub voce*; refers to an entry in a dictionary or encyclopedia
Tab. – at-Tabari, *Ta'rīkh ar-rusul wa-l-mulūk*
Tanbīh – al-Mas'udi, *at-Tanbīh wa-l-ishrāf*
Ṭbq. – Zakkar's edition of Khalifa's *Ṭabaqāt*
trans. – translated or translation
U – al-'Umari's edition of Khalifa's *Ta'rīkh*: page numbers placed within {}
'Uyūn – Ibn Qutayba, *'Uyūn al-akhbār*
al-Ya'qubi – al-Ya'qubi, *at-Ta'rīkh*
Z – Zakkar's edition of Khalifa's *Ta'rīkh*: page numbers placed within []

In the footnotes, some references are given in abbreviated form, but these can be easily located in the bibliography at the end of the book, where full publication details are given.

Transliteration and Dates

Since Translated Texts for Historians is intended to cut across disciplinary boundaries and reach a broad audience, we have simplified the transliteration of the original text of Carl Wurtzel. In particular proper names are rendered without any diacritical marks; however, words that are not proper names, which are not so readily recognisable, are given with full diacritical marks. Dates are usually given in both *hijra* form (counting from AD 622) and Christian/common era form (AD/CE) in that order [comment of the editor, Robert Hoyland; henceforth indicated by the initials RGH].

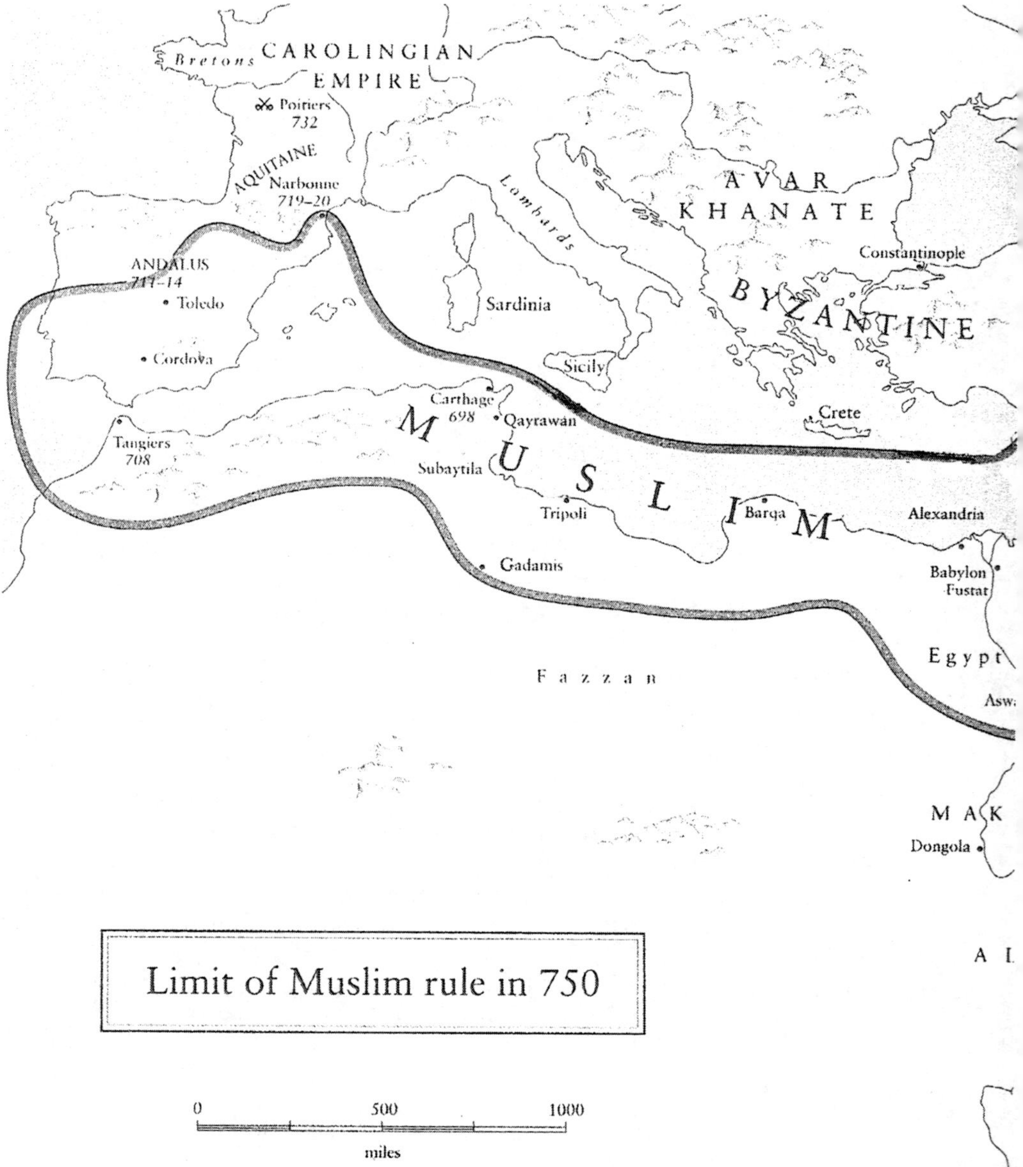
Bretons
CAROLINGIAN EMPIRE
Poitiers 732
AQUITAINE
Narbonne 719–20
Lombards
AVAR KHANATE
Constantinople
BYZANTINE
ANDALUS 711–14
Toledo
Cordova
Sardinia
Sicily
Crete
Carthage 698
Qayrawan
Tangiers 708
MUSLIM
Subaytila
Tripoli
Barqa
Alexandria
Gadamis
Babylon
Fustat
Egypt
Fazzan
MAK
Dongola
Limit of Muslim rule in 750
0
500
1000
miles

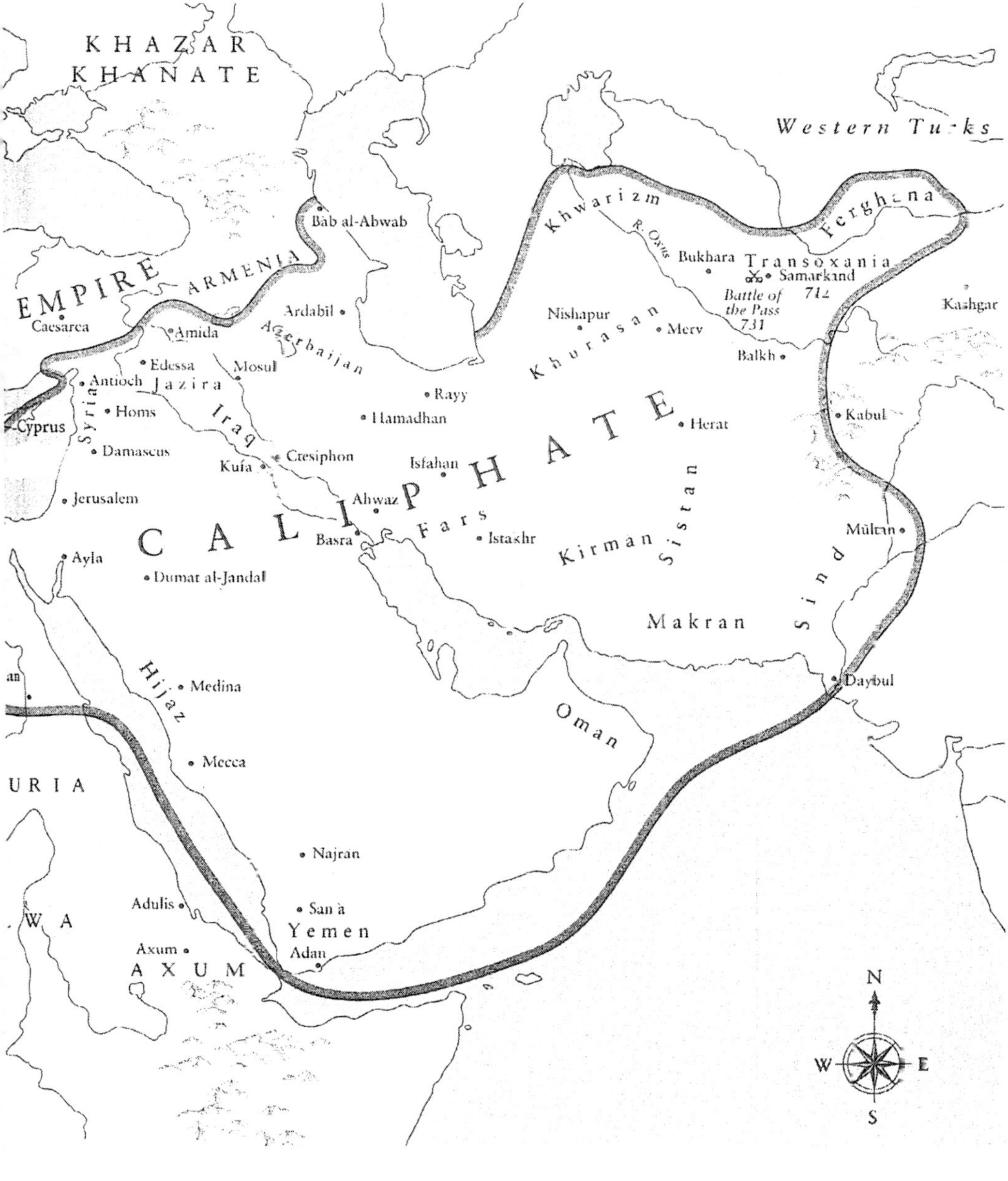
KHAZAR
KHANATE
Western Turks
EMPIRE
ARMENIA
Bab al-Abwab
Caesarea
Amida
Ardabil
Azerbaijan
Edessa
Mosul
Antioch
Jazira
Cyprus
Syria
Homs
Damascus
Iraq
Ctesiphon
Kufa
Jerusalem
Rayy
Hamadhan
Isfahan
Ahwaz
Basra
Fars
Istakhr
CALIPHATE
Khwarizm
R. Oxus
Bukhara
Transoxania
Samarkand
712
Battle of
the Pass
731
Ferghana
Kashgar
Nishapur
Khurasan
Merv
Balkh
Herat
Kabul
Sistan
Kirman
Makran
Sind
Multan
Daybul
Ayla
Dumat al-Jandal
Hijaz
Medina
Mecca
URIA
Oman
Najran
Adulis
San'a
Yemen
Adan
Axum
AXUM
WA
N
W
E
S

INTRODUCTION

1. Khalifa's Life

Nothing is known about Khalifa's birth. He was no doubt born in Basra, and from the indication about his age given by adh-Dhahabi in his *Siyar a'lām an-nubalā'*, it was probably around the year 160/776–777. The earliest dates of death among his teachers and authorities also suggest that he could not have been born much later than this year.

Similarly, nothing is known of Khalifa's early education. Since both his father and grandfather were traditionists,[1] it may be inferred that his family was concerned about education and that there was a scholarly atmosphere in his home. He was probably exposed to reading, writing, and a religious education early in life. Basra during Khalifa's lifetime was a center of culture and creativity in the fields of philology, poetry, tradition, Qur'ān study, genealogy, and history.[2] Khalifa's education probably included study in all or most of these fields. He must have taken a particular interest in the Qur'ān, the sayings of Muhammad (*ḥadīth*s), history, and genealogy, since he eventually wrote books concerned with these subjects. There is no explicit evidence that Khalifa ever traveled outside his native Basra, at least for any extended period. There is no mention of any travel in the biographical notices, although such information is customarily included in biographical accounts; nor is there any mention of Khalifa in al-Khatib al-Baghdadi's *Ta'rīkh Baghdād*. It is possible that he was summoned to Baghdad, and went there, to stand trial for anti-Mu'tazila views.[3] As for his domestic situation, all we know is based on his teknonym (*kunya*),

1 The term "traditionist" is used by Islamicists to refer to those who collected, studied, and taught the religio-legal sayings (traditions or *ḥadīths*) transmitted from the Prophet Muhammad [RGH].

2 On the cultural atmosphere of Basra during the lifetime of Khalifa (and al-Jahiz), see Pellat, *Le Milieu basrien*.

3 Cf. below. The Mu'tazila were adherents of a theological school that favored the use of rational thought and inquiry to elucidate the nature of God and the world [RGH].

Abu 'Amr. Although "honorary" teknonyms are not unknown, it may be assumed that Khalifa had at least one wife, and a son, whose name was 'Amr.

Khalifa was probably a relatively prominent member of the community in Basra. He lived through the caliphate of al-Ma'mun (198–218/813–833) and his two successors, al-Mu'tasim (218–227/833–842) and al-Wathiq (227–232/842–847). Al-Ma'mun initiated a policy of official recognition of the Mu'tazila sect and persecution of its opponents, and the policy was continued under the regimes of his two successors. Basra was a particular hotbed of Mu'tazilism. Khalifa was apparently an opponent of Mu'tazilism, which made him – in the eyes of the Mu'tazilite caliphs and their supporters, at least – an enemy of the government.

In his *Akhbār al-quḍāt* (*History of the Judges*), Waki' relates an anecdote in which Khalifa is mentioned. The anecdote concerns a judge, Ahmad b. Riyah, who became judge of Basra in 223/837–838. A complaint was lodged by the Mu'tazilites against Ibn Riyah, who was ordered to appear in court (perhaps in Baghdad) to defend himself against the charges of his Mu'tazilite opponents. He appeared, according to Waki', accompanied by some prominent Basrans (*wujūh ahl al-Baṣra*), among whom were Abu r-Rabi' az-Zahrani,[4] Husayn b. Muhammad adh-Dhari',[5] and Khalifa b. Khayyat. The charges against Ibn Riyah, that he had been persecuting the Mu'tazilites, were not proven, and the case was dismissed.[6] Waki''s text is hard to understand, but if this interpretation of the story is correct, it would seem that Khalifa may have been summoned to court as part of a sweep operation instigated by the Mu'tazilites to cleanse the city of their opponents, and actually was a defendant himself, along with the judge and the other individuals mentioned.

It might be enlightening to compare the different positions of Khalifa and al-Jahiz, the leading creative writer and thinker of the time, whose religio-political outlook and attitude toward the government were quite different from Khalifa's. Al-Jahiz was born about the same year as Khalifa, in 160/776–777, and, like Khalifa, was a native of Basra. Born into a poor household, al-Jahiz gravitated toward intellectual pursuits. He became a leading proponent of Mu'tazilism, and defender of the 'Abbasids. His

4 Sulayman b. Dawud, d. 234/848–849 (adh-Dhahabi, *Tadhkirat al-ḥuffāẓ*, II, 49; Ibn Hajar, IV, 190).

5 D. 247/861–862 (Ibn Hajar, II, 366).

6 Ahmad b. Abi Du'ad, an important Mu'tazilite jurist (EI2, I, 271) was Ibn Riyah's chief adversary, according to Waki'.

brilliant and innovative writings came to the attention of the high officials and the court at Baghdad, and al-Jahiz spent much of his life courting the rich and powerful. Khalifa, on the other hand, was undoubtedly of orthodox religious persuasion, and may have sympathized with a school of Umayyad defenders, the Nabita, criticized by al-Jahiz. The Nabita, in the words of C. Pellat, "were opposed to the Mu'tazilites and to the 'Abbasids, championed the Umayyads, [and] sided with the Hanbalites."[7]

The celebrated orthodox jurist Ahmad b. Hanbal, an approximate contemporary of Khalifa and al-Jahiz, was severely persecuted by the 'Abbasid authorities, as were his supporters, for his opposition to the official Mu'tazilism and his insistence on teaching the so-called orthodoxy. Khalifa and Ibn Hanbal received traditions from a number of the same authorities, and Ibn Hanbal's son, 'Abdallah, is named as one of Khalifa's students. These facts show Khalifa as basically of orthodox religious outlook, and possibly in the Hanbalite camp. The contrast in outlook between Khalifa and al-Jahiz gives some indication of the range of opinions and attitudes that was to be encountered in Basra in their lifetimes.

The earliest scholar who offers a date for Khalifa's death is al-Mutayyan, who died in 297/909–910. Al-Mutayyan gives the year 240/854–855, and is quoted only by very late writers, adh-Dhahabi and Ibn Hajar being the earliest. Ibn Khallikan offers three dates. His own choice seems to be *Ramaḍān* 230/May–June 845. However, Khalifa's *Ta'rīkh* records events through the year 232/846–847, and his *Ṭabaqāt* contains the notice of at least one person whose death was as late as 236/850–851.[8] The second date, 240, is given on the authority of Ibn 'Asakir. The third date, 246/860–861, Ibn Khallikan takes from an unnamed source. In reference to Ibn Khallikan, or others now unknown, adh-Dhahabi maintains in his *Siyar a'lām an-nubalā'*, that the year 246 is incorrect. Again in the *Siyar*, without naming any source for the information, adh-Dhahabi claims that Khalifa reached (or surpassed) the age of 80 (*kāna min abnā'i th-thamānīn*). Since the oldest authority, Mutayyan, gives the year 240, and that year is accepted by the majority of the later writers, it is convenient to accept it as the year of Khalifa's death.

7 Pellat, *The Life and Works of Jahiz*, 13. Al-Jahiz wrote an essay criticizing the Nabita, entitled "an-Nabita," which was translated by Pellat in *Annales de l'institut d'études orientales* 1952.

8 See *Ṭbq.*, 577, #1964, s.v. Hudba b. Khalid.

The Sources for Khalifa's Biography

The following, in chronological order, are the sources for information on Khalifa's life and works:

1. Khalifa himself, in his *Ta'rīkh* and *Ṭabaqāt*, and the information supplied by the transmitters of the works, his students, Baqi b. Makhlad[9] (d. 276/889), and Abu 'Imran Musa b. Zakariyya' at-Tustari.[10]

2. Abu l-Hasan 'Ali b. 'Abdallah al-Mada'ini[11] (d. 234/849). His alleged remarks about Khalifa are quoted by al-'Uqayli, Ibn 'Adi, adh-Dhahabi, and Ibn Hajar.

3. 'Abd ar-Rahman b. Rusta (d. c. 246/860–861). He offers an anecdote in which Khalifa is mentioned. It is quoted by Abu sh-Shaykh 'Abdallah b. Hayyan al-Ansari (d. 369/979) in his *Ṭabaqāt al-muḥaddithīn bi-Iṣbahān*, which, still in manuscript, is quoted by al-'Umari in the introduction to his edition of the *Ta'rīkh* (17).

4. Muhammad b. Isma'il al-Bukhari (d. 256/869–870), *at-Ta'rīkh al-kabīr*, II, I, 176, #652. He had personal contact with Khalifa, and transmitted traditions received from him.

5. Muslim b. al-Hajjaj al-Qushayri[12] (d. 261/874–875). His remarks, from his *al-Kunā wa-l-asmā'*, are cited but not quoted by al-'Umari in the introduction to his edition of the *Ta'rīkh* (13). The passage deals with Khalifa's name, but its exact contents are not made clear by al-'Umari's citation.

6. Abu Hatim Muhammad b. Idris ar-Razi[13] (d. 277/890–891). He is said to have related traditions from Khalifa. His remarks are quoted by his son, Ibn Abi Hatim, in the latter's *al-Jarḥ wa-t-ta'dīl* (I, II, 378).

7. Abu Ja'far Muhammad b. 'Abdallah al-Hadrami al-Kufi, called al-Mutayyan[14] (d. 297/909–10). He is cited by adh-Dhahabi and Ibn Hajar for the date of Khalifa's death.

9 EI2, I, 956; GAS, I, 152.

10 Cf. adh-Dhahabi, *Mīzān*, III, 210; adh-Dhahabi, *al-Mushtabih fī r-rijāl*, I, 77; al-'Umari, introduction to his edition of Khalifa's *Ṭabaqāt*, 65ff.

11 GAS, I, 108.

12 GAS, I, 136.

13 GAS, I, 153.

14 GAS, I, 163.

8. Waki‘ Muhammad b. Khalaf[15] (d. 306/918–919), *Akhbār al-quḍāt* (II, 175), offers an anecdote in which Khalifa is mentioned.

9. Abu Ja‘far Muhammad b. ‘Amr al-‘Uqayli[16] (d. 322/933–934). His remarks in his *ad-Ḍu‘afā’* are cited but not quoted by al-‘Umari, in the introduction to his edition of the *Ta’rīkh* (19). The passage seems to be an alleged quotation from ‘Ali b. al-Mada’ini. A similar passage is also found quoted by Ibn Hajar, quoting Ibn al-Mada’ini.

10. ‘Abd ar-Rahman b. Abi Hatim[17] (d. 327/938–939), *al-Jarḥ wa-t-ta‘dīl* (I, II, 378, #1728).

11. Muhammad b. Hibban al-Busti[18] (d. 354/965). His opinion of Khalifa in his *ath-Thiqāt* is quoted by as-Sam‘ani and Ibn Hajar.

12. ‘Abdallah b. ‘Adi al-Jurjani[19] (d. 365/976). His remarks appear in his *al-Kāmil fī ḍu‘afā’ ar-rijāl*, and are quoted by Zakkar in the introduction to his edition of the *Ta’rīkh* (pages d–h), and the *Ṭabaqāt* (pages j–d).

13. Ibn an-Nadim (d. 385/995), *al-Fihrist* (trans., 559; Fluegel, 232).

14. Abu l-Fadl Muhammad b. Tahir b. al-Qaysarani[20] (d. 507/1113), *al-Jam‘ bayna kitābay Abī Nasr al-Kalābādhī wa-Abī Bakr al-Iṣbahānī fī rijāl al-Bukhārī wa-Muslim* (I, 126, #495).

15. Abu l-Qasim ‘Ali b. al-Hasan b. ‘Asakir[21] (d. 571/1176). His *Mu‘jam mashāyikh al-a’imma as-sitta* is quoted by Ibn Khallikan.

16. Abu Bakr Muhammad b. Khayr al-Ishbili,[22] (d. 575/1180), *Fahrasat mā rawā-hu ‘an shuyūkhi-hi* (225 and 230).

17. ‘Abd al-Karim b. Muhammad as-Sam‘ani (d. 582/1186), *al-Ansāb* (392b, s.v. al-‘Usfuri)

18. ‘Izz ad-Din b. al-Athir, (d. 630/1233), *al-Lubāb fī tahdhīb al-ansāb* (II, 140, s.v. al-‘Usfuri).

15 GAS, I, 376.
16 GAS, I, 177.
17 GAS, I, 178.
18 GAS, I, 189.
19 GAS, I, 198.
20 GAL, S, I, 603.
21 GAL, S, I, 566; on the work mentioned, see GAL, S, I, 567, #8.
22 GAL, I, 499.

19. Ibn Khallikan (d. 681/1282), *Wafayāt al-a'yān* (II, 243, #219; trans., I, 492).

20. Shams ad-Din Muhammad b. Ahmad adh-Dhahabi (d. 748/1347), *al-'Ibar* (I, 432); *Mīzān al-i'tidāl* (I, 665, #2561); *Tadhkirat al-ḥuffāẓ* (II, 21); *Ṭabaqāt al-ḥuffāẓ* (part II, 9 [eighth *ṭabaqa*, #22]); *Siyar a'lām an-nubalā'*, quoted by Zakkar in the introduction to his edition of the *Ta'rīkh* (h–w), and the *Ṭabaqāt* (d–h).

21. 'Imad ad-Din Isma'il b. 'Umar b. Kathir (d. 774/1372), *al-Bidāya wa-n-nihāya* (X, 322).

22. Abu l-Khayr al-Jazari[23] (d. 833/1430), *Ghāyat an-nihāya* (I, 275, #1241).

23. Ibn Hajar al-'Asqalani (d. 852/1448), *Tahdhīb at-tahdhīb* (III, 160, #104).

24. Safi ad-Din al-Khazraji[24] (d. 923/1517), *Khulāṣat tahdhīb al-kamāl fī asmā' ar-rijāl* (90).

25. Abu l-Fallah b. al-'Imad[25] (d. 1089/1678), *Shadharāt adh-dhahab* (II, 94).

The following nineteenth- and twentieth-century writers have included brief notices on Khalifa in their works:

1. F. Wuestenfeld, *Die Geschichtschreiber der Araber* (19, #57)
2. Isma'il Pasha al-Baghdadi, *Hadiyyat al-'ārifīn* (I, 350)
3. 'Umar Rida al-Kahhala, *Mu'jam al-mu'allifīn* (IV, 108)
4. Muhammad b. Ja'far al-Kattani, *ar-Risāla al-mustaṭrafa* (139)
5. Khayr ad-Din az-Zirikli, *al-A'lām* (II, 361)
6. F. Rosenthal, *A History of Muslim Historiography* (392 n. 6)
7. F. Sezgin, *Geschichte des arabischen Schrifttums* (I, 110)

Major biographies, utilizing practically all the available source material, have been written in Arabic by A. D. al-'Umari and S. Zakkar, and appear in the introductions to their respective editions of the *Ta'rīkh*. Zakkar's

23 GAL, S, II, 274.
24 GAL, S, I, 606.
25 GAL, S, II, 403.

biography also appears, in slightly different form, in the introduction to his edition of the *Ṭabaqāt*. An abridged and modified version of Zakkar's biography, in English, is in the second edition of the *Encyclopaedia of Islam* (III, 838).

Long as the preceding list is, little is known about Khalifa's life. The fact that he was not only an historian but also a *ḥadīth* scholar accounts for the existence of most of the biographical notices devoted to him. All of them are brief, and most give no more than his name, a list of some of his teachers and students, the year of his death, a pronouncement or anecdote concerning his trustworthiness as a transmitter of traditions, and in some cases a comment about his erudition as an historian and genealogist. Of the medieval scholars, the most well-rounded biographies of Khalifa are those by Ibn Khallikan, adh-Dhahabi, in his *Mīzān al-i'tidāl* and *Siyar a'lām an-nubalā'*, and Ibn Hajar. These are basically compilations of earlier notices on Khalifa, with Ibn Khallikan and adh-Dhahabi adding their own comments on his merits. Ibn Khallikan, adh-Dhahabi, and Ibn Hajar had a first-hand acquaintance with Khalifa's work, since they quote from both his *Ta'rīkh* and his *Ṭabaqāt* elsewhere in their own books.

His Name and Ancestry

The sources which may be considered most reliable with respect to Khalifa's name and ancestry are his students, Musa at-Tustari, Baqi b. Makhlad, and al-Bukhari. Curiously, there is some lack of agreement among them. At-Tustari records his teacher's name as Khalifa b. Khayyat, with the *nisba* ash-Shaybani adh-Dhuhli,[26] the *kunya* Abu 'Amr, and the *laqab* Shabab.[27] Al-Bukhari omits the *nisba* ash-Shaybani adh-Dhuhli, but adds al-'Usfuri, and indicates the name of his grandfather and great-grandfather, giving his name as Khalifa b. Khayyat b. Khalifa b. Khayyat. In his recension of the *Ta'rīkh*, Baqi cites his teacher only as Khalifa or Khalifa b. Khayyat, his name appearing as Khalifa b. Khayyat b. Khalifa b. Khayyat on the title page. Ibn Sa'd, who died in 230/844–845 and is the oldest writer to mention Khalifa, refers to him simply as Khalifa b. Khayyat.[28] Ibn al-Athir mentions

26 The first page of the *Ṭabaqāt* has al-Bahili rather than adh-Dhuhli. Shayban b. Duhl was a descendant of the tribe of Bakr b. Wa'il (cf page 8 and note 29 below).

27 A *nisba* is a name that denotes affiliation (to a place, tribe, profession, etc.); a *kunya* is a teknonym (father/mother of + name of eldest child), and a *laqab* is a descriptive name (a cognomen or nickname) [RGH].

28 Ibn Sa'd, VII, 75 (cf. note 177 below).

Khalifa's alleged tribal affiliation, not under his biographical entry on him in the *Lubāb*, but under the entry "ar-Raqashi" (*al-Lubāb*, I, 473), as an incidental item of information. According to Ibn al-Athir, Khalifa was a descendent of Shayban b. Dhuhl b. Tha'laba b. 'Ukaba b. Sa'b b. 'Ali b. Bakr b. Wa'il.[29] Khalifa himself could have offered information on his genealogy, but did not; although he subdivides many of the "generations" in his *Ṭabaqāt* according to tribal affiliation and residence, he does not do so for the eighth generation (*ṭabaqa*) of Basrans, in which his grandfather is included.

As-Sam'ani, followed by Ibn al-Athir in his *al-Lubāb* and Ibn Khallikan, explains the significance of the *nisba* al-'Usfuri, and indicates the correct spelling and vocalization. The designation al-'Usfuri pertains to one who is involved in some way – such as a merchant – with *'uṣfur* (safflower), which, the authors explain, is used to produce a substance for dyeing cloth red.[30] Ibn Khallikan indicates the spelling and vocalization of Khalifa's nickname, Shabab,[31] on whose significance his (unnamed) sources are said to differ.

His Immediate Forebears

The sources for information on Khalifa's grandfather are the following:

1) *Ṭbq.*, 535, #1871

2) Kh., 651, 670

3) al-Bukhari, *at-Ta'rīkh al-kabīr*, II, I, 175, #646

4) Ibn Abi Hatim, in *al-Jarḥ wa-t-ta'dīl*, I, II, 378, #1727

29 The genealogy of Bakr b. Wa'il is traced to Asad b. Rabi'a b. Nizar b. Ma'dd b. 'Adnan (cf. W. Caskel in EI2, I, 962, s.v. Bakr b. Wa'il; cf. *Ma'ārif*, 92–100).

30 The Arabic *nisba* was frequently passed down through the generations, like our surnames. Khalifa's forebears may have long since left the *'uṣfur* business, and neither Khalifa, his father, nor his grandfather *necessarily* had anything to do with *'uṣfur*. On the other hand, it is possible that Khalifa, his father, or his grandfather had a family *'uṣfur* business. It cannot be determined whether Khalifa was a professional teacher and author, or the degree to which, if at all, he earned his living in the marketplace.

31 Shabib, given by Ibn an-Nadim as Khalifa's *laqab*, is to be dismissed as an error. The readings "Sayyar" and "Yasar" found in al-Azdi's *Ta'rīkh al-Mawṣil* (see index) are scribal errors, as is the reading "Sabab," on page 11 of Abu Bakr al-Maliki, *Riyāḍ an-nufūs*. "Shayban," mentioned by adh-Dhahabi, *Ta'rīkh al-Islām*, V, 224, l. 8, may also be a scribal error for Shabab.

5) Ibn Hibban, *Mashāhīr 'ulamā' al-amṣār*, 157, #1239

6) as-Sam'ani, *al-Ansāb*, 392b, s.v. al-'Usfuri

7) Ibn al-Athir, *al-Kāmil fī t-ta'rīkh*, VI, 50

8) Ibn Khallikan, *Wafāyāt al-a'yān*, II, 244, sub-#35 (trans., I, 492)

9) Ibn Hajar, *Tahdhīb*, III, 161

The sources for information on Khalifa's father are the following:

1) al-Bukhari, *at-Ta'rīkh al-kabīr*, II, I, 209, #771

2) Abu Hatim, quoted in *al-Jarḥ wa-t-ta'dīl*, I, II, 405, #1853

In the *Ṭabaqāt*, Khalifa gives his grandfather's name as Abu Hubayra Khalifa b. Khayyat. Al-Bukhari, adds the *nisba* al-'Usfuri, and, quoting an unidentified source named Muslim, gives the additional *nisba* al-Laythi. Ibn Hibban and as-Sam'ani give both al-'Usfuri and al-Laythi. Khalifa's grandfather was a traditionist of some note. He is listed by his grandson in the latter's *Ṭabaqāt*, in the eighth *ṭabaqa* of Basrans, where the date of his death is given as *Rajab* 160/April–May 777.[32]

Khalifa's father, Khayyat b. Khalifa b. Khayyat, was also a traditionist. His son does not list him in his *Ṭabaqāt*, although it dates to as late as 236/850–851 – when his father can be assumed to have been dead (although it is not impossible that in 236, when Khalifa was about 76, his father was still alive) – are included therein. It would seem, however, that his father was in no way a prominent scholar. Al-Bukhari and some later writers name Khayyat b. Khalifa as one of the authorities from whom Khalifa related traditions. He is cited once by his son in the latter's *Ta'rīkh* as the authority for a report from Khalifa's grandfather.[33] It is possible, but pure conjecture, that Khalifa's father was more a businessman than his own father and son, and devoted most of his time to the family *'uṣfur* business.

32 Khalifa says that his grandfather died in the same month as Shu'ba (b. al-Hajjaj), who, Khalifa indicates, died in *Rajab* 160 (*Ṭbq*., 535).

33 Kh., 651.

Those from Whom and to Whom he Transmitted Historical Accounts

Most of the biographical notices on Khalifa include a list of some of the authorities from whom he transmitted traditions, and a list of those who learned traditions from him. Many of those listed as his authorities are quoted by Khalifa in his *Ta'rīkh* or *Ṭabaqāt* with the expression *ḥaddatha-nī*, *ḥaddatha-nā*, or the like, indicating personal contact with the authority. The following is a list of individuals who are not cited as authorities in the translated portion of the *Ta'rīkh*, but from whom Khalifa is said to have related traditions. Names preceded by an asterisk are cited as authorities by Khalifa elsewhere in the *Ta'rīkh* or the *Ṭabaqāt*, or are quoted by Khalifa as authorities for traditions preserved by al-Bukhari.

1. *Yazid b. Zuray'[34] (d. 3 *Shawwāl* 182/17 November 798)
2. *Khayyat b. Khalifa, his father
3. *Artat b. al-Husayn al-Bunani[35]
4. Bakkar b. 'Abdallah al-Basri[36]
5. *Shu'ayb b. Hayyan[37]
6. *Mu'adh b. Hani' al-Basri[38] (d. 209/824–825)
7. *Mu'tamir b. Sulayman[39] (d. 10 *al-Muḥarram* 187/8 January 803)
8. *Durust b. Hamza al-Basri[40] (d. between 170/786 and 200/816)
9. Unays b. Sawwar al-Jarmi[41]
10. *Abu Yahya Bakr b. Sulayman al-Aswari (al-Uswari?)[42]

34 *Ṭbq.*, 541; *Tadhkirat al-ḥuffāẓ*, I, 236; Ibn Hajar, XI, 325; cf. GAS, I, index.

35 Al-Bukhari, *at-Ta'rīkh*, I, II, 58; *Jarḥ*, I, I, 327. He is not mentioned by Khalifa in the *Ta'rīkh* or *Ṭabaqāt*, but is cited by Khalifa as the authority for a *ḥadīth* of the Prophet quoted by al-Bukhari, *at-Ta'rīkh*, I, II, 154.

36 Al-Bukhari, *at-Ta'rīkh*, I, II, 121.

37 Al-Bukhari, *at-Ta'rīkh*, II, II, 225; *Jarḥ*, II, I, 343.

38 Al-Bukhari, *at-Ta'rīkh*, IV, I, 367; Ibn Hajar, X, 196.

39 *Ṭbq.*, 541; Ibn Hajar, X, 227; adh-Dhahabi, *Tadhkirat al-ḥuffāẓ*, I, 245.

40 *Jarḥ*, I, II, 438. He is cited by Khalifa as the authority for a *ḥadīth* of the Prophet quoted by al-Bukhari, *at-Ta'rīkh*, II, I, 230. Cf. Ibn Hajar, III, 209f.

41 *Jarḥ*, I, I, 335. He is not mentioned by Khalifa in the *Ta'rīkh* or *Ṭabaqāt*.

42 *Jarḥ*, I, I, 387.

11. Marzuq b. Maymun an-Naji[43]

12. *Bishr b. al-Mufaddal[44] (d. 187/802–803)

13. Sufyan b. 'Uyayna[45] (d. 198/813–814)

14. *Abu Dawud Sulayman b. Dawud at-Tayalisi[46] (d. 204/819)

15. Ja'far b. Sulayman[47] (d. 178/794–795)

16. *Khalid b. al-Harith[48] (d. 186/802)

17. Muhammad b. Abi 'Adi[49] (d. 194/809–810)

18. *Muhammad b. Sawa'[50] (d. 187/802–803)

19. *Yahya b. Sa'id al-Qattan[51] (d. 198/813–814)

20. *Ziyad b. 'Abdallah al-Bakka'i[52] (d. 182/798–799)

21. *Ghassan b. Mudar[53] (d. 184/800–801)

22. Isma'il b. Umayya[54]

23. Kahmas b. Minhal[55]

43 *Jarḥ*, IV, I, 265. He is not mentioned by Khalifa.

44 *Ṭbq.*, 541; al-Bukhari, *at-Ta'rīkh*, I, II, 84; *Jarḥ*, I, I, 336; adh-Dhahabi, *Tadhkirat al-ḥuffāẓ*, I, 284; Ibn Hajar, I, 458.

45 *Ṭbq.*, 718; GAS, I, 96. He is quoted in the *Ta'rīkh*, not directly, but from intermediaries who received the information from Sufyan and passed it on to Khalifa.

46 GAS, I, 97; *Ṭbq.*, 571.

47 *Ṭbq.*, 540; adh-Dhahabi, *Tadhkirat al-ḥuffāẓ*, I, 222; Ibn Hajar, II, 95. He is quoted once in the *Ta'rīkh*, but with an intervening link. Of the scholars from whom Khalifa is alleged to have learned, and for whom dates are available, Ja'far b. Sulayman is the oldest – perhaps too old for Khalifa to have studied with him in person. He is named as Khalifa's teacher only by adh-Dhahabi. Perhaps he misread the name Mu'tamir as Ja'far?

48 *Ṭbq.*, 542; adh-Dhahabi, *Tadhkirat al-ḥuffāẓ*, I, 284; Ibn Hajar, III, 82.

49 Muhammad b. Ibrahim (*Ṭbq.*, 544; adh-Dhahabi, *Tadhkirat al- ḥuffāẓ*, I, 297; Ibn Hajar, IX, 12).

50 *Ṭbq.*, 543; Ibn Hajar, IX, 208.

51 *Ṭbq.*, 542; adh-Dhahabi, *Tadhkirat al-ḥuffāẓ*, I, 274; Ibn Hajar, XI, 216; cf. GAS, I, index.

52 *Ṭbq.*, 402; Ibn Hajar, III, 375.

53 Ibn Hajar, VIII, 247. He appears in the translated portion of the *Ta'rīkh* as an indirect source for Khalifa, and elsewhere in the *Ta'rīkh* as a direct source.

54 He is listed only by Ibn Hajar in his biographical entry on Khalifa, and is unidentified.

55 Ibn Hajar, VIII, 451.

24. *'Awn b. Kahmas b. al-Hasan[56]

25. *Mu'adh b. Mu'adh al-'Anbari[57] (d. 196/811–812)

Al-Jazari names two authorities from whom Khalifa allegedly learned Qur'ān recitation (*al-qirā'a*), but this seems to be misinformation based on mistaken identities.[58]

The great majority of the authorities in the preceding list were natives of, or resided in, Basra. Most of the authorities whom Khalifa quotes in his *Ta'rīkh* were also Basrans.[59] It is thus clear that Khalifa acquired the bulk of his learning from his Basran teachers and colleagues, "the Basrans in general" (*'āmmat al-Baṣriyīn*), in the words of as-Sam'ani.

Two of Khalifa's teachers, Bishr b. al-Mufaddal and Yazid b. Zuray', are described by Ibn Sa'd as having 'Uthmani sympathies.[60] The 'Uthmaniyya were those who felt that the caliph 'Uthman had been the most suitable and deserving candidate for the office of the caliphate, that is, to serve as successor to Muhammad as leader of the Islamic community. The 'Uthmanis decried the murder of 'Uthman, and held that vengeance should have been demanded and exacted for it. In some cases, the 'Uthmaniyya extended their support for 'Uthman to support for his kinsmen, Mu'awiya and his successors of the Umayyad house.[61] It is possible that Khalifa was particularly influenced by his two 'Uthmani teachers, and may have been an adherent of the 'Uthmaniyya himself.[62]

His Students

The following is a list of the individuals named in the biographical notices as Khalifa's students. For the first four there is actual evidence of personal contact with Khalifa.

56 He is quoted by Khalifa in the translated portion of the *Ta'rīkh*, so his name does not belong in this list. See introduction, page 34, below.

57 *Ṭbq.*, 544; adh-Dhahabi, *Tadhkirat al-ḥuffāẓ*, I, 297; Ibn Hajar, X, 194.

58 He names Warqa' b. 'Umar, and Abu 'Amr b. al-'Ala'. Al-Jazari seems to have been confusing Shabab (Khalifa) with Shababa (b. Sawwar al-Fazari). Cf. al-Jazari, II, 359; cf. Ibn Hajar, IV, 300, where Warqa' is named as one of Shababa's teachers, and Ibn Hajar, IX, 113, where Shababa is named as one of Warqa''s students.

59 Cf. page 31, below.

60 Ibn Sa'd, VII, 289, 290.

61 On the 'Uthmaniyya in Basra, see Pellat, *Le Milieu basrien*, 188–194.

62 On Khalifa's attitude toward the Umayyads in his *Ta'rīkh*, see page 24, below.

1. Al-Bukhari. He quotes traditions which he learned from Khalifa, in both his *aṣ-Ṣaḥīḥ* and his *at-Ta'rīkh al-kabīr*[63]

2. Baqi b. Makhlad. He transmitted the extant recension of the *Ta'rīkh*, and a recension, now lost, of the *Ṭabaqāt*[64]

3. Abu 'Imran Musa b. Zakariyya' at-Tustari. He transmitted the extant recension of the *Ṭabaqāt* and a recension, now lost, of the *Ta'rīkh*[65]

4. Abu Hafs 'Umar b. Ahmad b. Ishaq al-Ahwazi. He transmitted a now lost recension of the *Ṭabaqāt*[66]

5. Abu l-'Abbas al-Hasan b. Sufyan an-Nasawi,[67] (d. 303/916)

6. Abu Ya'la Ahmad b. 'Ali al-Mawsili[68] (d. 307/919–920)

7. 'Abdallah b. Ahmad b. Hanbal[69] (d. 290/903)

8. Abu Zur'a 'Ubaydallah b. 'Abd al-Karim ar-Razi[70] (d. 264/878)

9. Abu Hatim ar-Razi (d. 277/890–891)

10. Abu Ya'la Zakariyya' b. Yahya as-Saji[71] (d. 307/919–920)

11. 'Abdallah b. 'Abd ar-Rahman ad-Darimi[72] (d. 255/869)

12. Ya'qub b. Shayba[73] (d. 262/875)

63 In his introduction to the *Ta'rīkh*, 18, al-'Umari notes that Khalifa is quoted 18 times in the *Ṣaḥīḥ*. See, for example, IV, 498 (*tawḥīd*, 55). Ibn al-Qaysarani remarks that Khalifa is quoted for one *ḥadīth* by al-Bukhari, which is in the section on *ad-da'awāt*. Khalifa is quoted in *at-Ta'rīkh al-kabīr*, I, II, 154, and II, I, 230. There may be other examples of which I am unaware. Ibn Khallikan observed that al-Bukhari quoted traditions from Khalifa in both the *Ṣaḥīh* and *at-Ta'rīkh al-kabīr*. Ibn Sa'd has preserved some *ḥadīth*s compiled by Khalifa (see 40f., below).

64 Cf. al-Ishbili, 225.

65 Scattered portions of it are preserved in the works of Ibn 'Asakir and adh-Dhahabi (cf. section V, 39ff., below).

66 Portions of it are preserved in the *Ta'rīkh Dimashq* of Ibn 'Asakir (cf. al-'Umari, in the introduction to his edition of Khalifa's *Ṭabaqāt*, 65ff.).

67 GAS, I, 169.

68 GAS, I, 170

69 GAS, I, 511.

70 GAS, I, 145.

71 Cf. GAS, I, 549; Ibn al-Athir, *al-Lubāb*, I, 520; Rosenthal, 436 n. 5, and 593.

72 GAS, I, 114.

73 GAS, I, 144.

13. Harb b. Isma'il al-Kirmani[74] (d. 280/893)

14. Abu Bakr b. Abi 'Asim[75] (d. *Rabī'* II 287/April 900)

15. Ahmad b. 'Ali al-Abbar[76] (d. 15 *Sha'bān* 290/14 July 903)

16. Ibrahim b. 'Abdallah b. al-Junayd al-Khuttali[77] (d. 260/874)

17. 'Abdallah (b. Muhammad) b. Najiya[78] (d. 301/914)

18. Tamtam Muhammad b. Ghalib[79] (d. 283/896)

19. Muhammad b. Musa al-Harashi[80]

According to al-Jazari, the following studied Qur'ān recitation with Khalifa:

20. Ahmad b. Ibrahim b. 'Uthman al-Warraq[81]

21. Al-Mughira b. Sadaqa[82]

His Works

The earliest writer to make reference to a book by Khalifa is Ibn Abi Hatim, who, quoting his father, mentions a *Musnad* (*Collection of ḥadīths*). Ibn 'Adi, who died in 365/976, is the earliest writer to mention Khalifa's two extant books, the *Ta'rīkh* and the *Ṭabaqāt*, and he perhaps alludes to the *Musnad* when he says that Khalifa knew many *ḥadīths*. In the *Fihrist*, Ibn an-Nadim ascribes five books to Khalifa:

1. *At-Ṭabaqāt* (*The Generations*)

2. *At-Ta'rīkh* (*The History*)

3. *Ṭabaqāt al-qurrā'* (*The Generations of the Qur'ān Readers*)

74 Adh-Dhahabi, *Tadhkirat al-ḥuffāẓ*, II, 170; cf. GAS, I, 507.
75 Ahmad b. 'Amr an-Nabil (adh-Dhahabi, *Tadhkirat al- ḥuffāẓ*, II, 193).
76 Ibn al-Athir, *al-Lubāb*, I, 17; adh-Dhahabi, *Tadhkirat al-ḥuffāẓ*, II, 192.
77 GAS, I, 645.
78 Adh-Dhahabi, *Tadhkirat al- ḥuffāẓ*, II, 239.
79 Ibn al-Athir, *al-Lubāb*, I, 181; adh-Dhahabi, *Tadhkirat al- ḥuffāẓ*, II, 172.
80 Ibn Hajar, IX, 482.
81 Al-Jazari, I, 34.
82 Al-Jazari, II, 305.

4. *Ta'rīkh az-zamnā wa-l-'urjān wa-l-marḍā wa-l-'umyān* (*The History of the Chronically Ill, the Lame, the Diseased, and the Blind*)[83]

5. *Ajzā'u l-Qur'ān wa-a'shāru-hu wa-asbā'u-hu wa-āyātu-hu* (*The Thirtieths, Tenths, Sevenths, and Verses of the Qur'ān*)

The fourth and fifth titles are not mentioned elsewhere in the literature on Khalifa. Zakkar identifies the *Ṭabaqāt al-qurrā'* of Ibn an-Nadim's list with the extant *Ṭabaqāt*, but he seems to have overlooked the first title on the list.[84] The Turkish bibliographer Hajji Khalifa lists two works by Khalifa, the *Ta'rīkh* and another he calls the *Ṭabaqāt ar-ruwāt*, which no doubt should be identified with the extant *Ṭabaqāt*.[85] Both of Khalifa's extant works have been edited and published.[86]

Khalifa and his Works in the Estimation of Medieval Scholars

In general, the earliest writers discuss Khalifa's merits as a *ḥadīth* scholar only. Later writers also mention his accomplishments in the fields of history and genealogy.[87] The earliest scholar allegedly to express an opinion of Khalifa's work is Ibn al-Mada'ini, who is quoted by Ibn 'Adi on the authority of Muhammad b. Ja'far al-Matiri[88] and of Muhammad

83 For perhaps a similar example of this – to modern western tastes, at least – rather bizarre genre, cf. *Ma'ārif*, 578ff., which contains classified lists of persons who suffered from various diseases or defects, or who had unusual physical characteristics. Cf. adh-Dhahabi's classification of the types of historical works, as quoted by as-Sakhawi, in Rosenthal, 390, item number 25: The history of the blind, invalid, deaf, mute, and hunchbacked.

84 EI2, III, 838b. On several occasions Ibn Hajar, quoting Khalifa, mentions that the latter listed the individual under discussion among the *qurrā'* of Basra (cf., e.g., Ibn Hajar, IV, 16, and Ibn Hajar, XII, 129). However, there is no evidence that Ibn Hajar used a book that was different from the extant *Ṭabaqāt*.

85 *Kashf aẓ-ẓunūn*, II, 129, and IV, 138.

86 The *Ṭabaqāt* was edited independently by S. Zakkar, Damascus, 1966, and A. K. al-'Umari, Baghdad, 1967. On the printed editions of the *Ta'rīkh*, see section VI, 47f., below.

87 It should be pointed out that in Khalifa's time any learned individual was a *ḥadīth* scholar and transmitter (cf. R. Guest, introduction to al-Kindi, 37, paragraph 2). Until adh-Dhahabi, in the eighth/fourteenth century, Khalifa is nowhere called an historian. He is said to have been learned in historical matters (e.g., *kāna 'āliman bi-ayyām an-nās*, *kāna 'ārifan bi-t-tawārīkh*, and the like), but only beginning with adh-Dhahabi is he called an historian. The word adh-Dhahabi uses is *akhbārī*. It would be interesting to know when the modern word for historian, *mu'arrikh*, is first attested in Arabic literature. It is not in *Lisān al-'Arab*. Cf. Rosenthal, 11ff.

88 D. *Ṣafar* 335/September 946 (Ibn al-Athir, *al-Lubāb*, III, 152).

b. Yunus al-Kudaymi,[89] who alleged that he heard Ibn al-Mada'ini say, "If Shabab had not transmitted *ḥadīth*, it would have been better for him." Ibn 'Adi, however, discounts the validity of this quotation, and avers that Ibn al-Mada'ini would not have said such a thing about Khalifa. Ibn 'Adi himself praises Khalifa as a distinguished historian, genealogist, and *ḥadīth* scholar. Ibn al-Mada'ini is also quoted by al-'Uqayli and Ibn Hajar as calling Khalifa "a tree which bears *ḥadīth*." It is not clear whether this was intended as praise for the abundance of *ḥadīth*s Khalifa knew and transmitted, or whether it was meant to call attention to his alleged unauthorized transmission or distortion of *ḥadīth*s.

Abu Hatim ar-Razi criticizes Khalifa as a weak *ḥadīth* scholar, but the reason he gives for this judgment, as related by his son in the *Jarḥ*, is not quite clear. Ibn Abi Hatim relates that when one of his own teachers, Abu Zur'a ar-Razi, recited *ḥadīth*s he had transmitted on Khalifa's authority, he (Ibn Abi Hatim) erased them, apparently since his father had said Khalifa was weak. On the other hand, Khalifa's reliability as a *ḥadīth* scholar is vouched for by the fact that the eminent al-Bukhari quotes *ḥadīth*s he learned from his teacher, Khalifa, in both his *Compendium of Sound Traditions* (*aṣ-Ṣaḥīḥ*) and his *Great History* (*at-Ta'rīkh al-kabīr*).[90]

Later scholars, beginning with Ibn Hibban, and including Ibn 'Adi, Ibn al-Athir, Ibn Khallikan, adh-Dhahabi, Ibn Kathir, and al-Khazraji, express high praise for Khalifa's accomplishments as an historian and genealogist. Ibn 'Abd al-Barr considered Khalifa among the eminent scholars of history, biography, and genealogy on whose works other scholars, including himself, relied for their information.[91] In addition to his own laudatory comments, Ibn al-Athir acknowledged the conflicting opinions among the early authorities with respect to Khalifa's trustworthiness as a transmitter. Testimony to Khalifa's distinguished place in the spheres of historiography and biography-genealogy is given most compellingly by the large number of writers who quote his *Ta'rīkh* and *Ṭabaqāt*, and the frequency and extent to which some of these writers quote his works.

89 D. *Jumādā* I 286/May–June 899 (Ibn al-Athir, *al-Lubāb*, III, 31; adh-Dhahabi, *Tadhkirat al-ḥuffāẓ*, II, 175). Adh-Dhahabi quotes several authorities who considered al-Kudaymi less than completely truthful, some calling him an outright liar. Ibn 'Adi also expresses a very low opinion of al-Kudaymi.

90 Cf. note 63, above. On the technical details of the nature of al-Bukhari's reliance on the *ḥadīth*s he received from Khalifa, see al-'Umari's introduction to the *Ta'rīkh*, 18.

91 *Istī'āb*, 20 and 22.

2. Khalifa's Approach to the Writing of History

The Place of the Annalistic Method in the Early Period of Muslim Historiography

The basic forms of the early stages of Islamic historiography have been thoroughly discussed by Franz Rosenthal in the third chapter of his *History of Muslim Historiography*. The oldest form was the *khabar* history, which dealt with an individual event, such as a battle or series of battles, or some significant events in the life of an individual or in the history of a place. The section in the *Fihrist* which covers historians is filled with the titles of *khabar* monographs, almost all of which are now lost, although portions of some were incorporated into the works of later historians. The titles of these *khabar* works indicate works of very limited scope, such as "The Battle of the Camel," "The Fortifications of Ibn az-Zubayr," and "Yazid b. al-Muhallab and his Murder at al-'Aqr," to name several attributed to Abu Mikhnaf. The character of the *khabar* works was, in the words of Professor Rosenthal, that of "the vividly told short story [with a] preference for situation and color as against sober facts."[92] The sources for the authors of the *khabar* monographs consisted of innumerable oral traditions attributed to individuals relating their experiences in raiding expeditions and civil wars, reporting memorable quotations and speeches by, and anecdotes about, famous people, and pertinent poetry. Another source probably consisted of government records and documents. A third source was genealogical information preserved by traditionists.

Later, historians attempted to compile more comprehensive histories. A need was felt for a unified treatment of the history of the Islamic empire in a single work utilizing and synthesizing the diverse material from many different sources. To this end, several historiographical forms were developed.

The familiar dynastic arrangement divided the course of past events by the reigns of rulers, which enabled the author to link, and present in a single unified work, accounts concerning many different unrelated events occurring over a period of time. The oldest complete extant Arabic histories arranged according to the dynastic method are those of ad-Dinawari and al-Ya'qubi, who flourished about half a century after Khalifa. The historical section of Ibn 'Abd Rabbihi's *'Iqd* is arranged according to the reign of each caliph, as is the *Murūj adh-Dhahab* of al-Mas'udi.

92 Rosenthal, 67.

The authors of *ṭabaqāt* and genealogical works were also able to utilize unrelated *akhbār* and diverse traditions and information in a single long work. The *Ṭabaqāt* of Ibn Sa'd, for example, is a series of individual biographies which were related only in their arrangement according to the generation and residence of the biographees. Events were treated only as they pertained directly to the subject of each individual biography. The *Ṭabaqāt* is not a unified history of the empire (nor was it meant to be), although it does preserve diverse traditions pertaining to an extended period of time.

In his *Ansāb al-Ashrāf*, al-Baladhuri made an attempt to synthesize a huge amount of miscellaneous historical data into a unified work. The lifetime of each biographee serves as a unifying factor for the data, and the individual biographies are tenuously linked by the kinship of their subjects. The *Ansāb* treats the significant events that took place during the lifetime of each major biographee, even when those events did not directly involve the biographee.[93] In its concentration of the bulk of the historical material under the biographies of important leaders and rulers, al-Baladhuri's *Ansāb* bears a superficial resemblance, in part, to the dynastic works. In his *Futūḥ al-Buldān*, al-Baladhuri limited the material, as the title indicates, to traditions pertaining to the Islamic conquests. The accounts of events are arranged by region, in chronological sequence.

The origins of the annalistic method are not known with certainty, but the oldest known complete extant Arabic history of the Islamic empire, the *Ta'rīkh* of Khalifa b. Khayyat, is arranged annalistically. In the annalistic arrangement, diverse, unrelated traditions are connected through their common relationship to a beginning point in time reckoning, which in the case of Islam was the year of Muhammad's *hijra*, his flight from Mecca to Medina in 622. The annalistic historians narrowed to the period of a single (lunar) year, the common denominator by which the occurrence of otherwise unrelated events were linked. The picture of events given was, as it were, brought into sharper focus with respect to the date of events' occurrence, and with respect to the chronological relationship between different events.

Khalifa's *Ta'rīkh* opens with an introductory section in which the author discusses the various dating systems (*ta'rīkh*) that were known, and the origins of the Islamic system thereof, and gives a brief account of the birth of the Prophet. The remainder of the book is arranged chronologically,

93 Cf. Goitein, introduction to vol. V of the *Ansāb al-ashrāf*, 12 and 14.

beginning with the year 1/622–623 and ending with the year 232/846–847, approximately eight years before the death of the author. Each chapter is devoted to the events of one particular year. Otherwise unrelated events which occurred in the same year are linked by the introductory phrase "in it" (*fī-hā*), that is, "in this year …," which precedes the account of each event. Sometimes the year is specifically mentioned (e.g., "In the year 96 …"). Khalifa will divide up the account of, say, a raiding expedition, which may have lasted two or more years, and place portions of the original account under different chapters of his *Ta'rīkh*. The same narrative might be found in al-Baladhuri's *Futūḥ al-buldān*, where the entire expedition is recounted as a complete episode, in one, two, three, or more consecutive paragraphs.

The system does not always work, but the exceptions are insignificant. Occasional reports extend to the future, and a future year is mentioned for later occurrences. For example, it might be mentioned that a person under discussion would later die in a certain year, or that a certain commander later returned from a raiding expedition in a certain year. Sometimes a date in the past might be mentioned. This is usually found in the customary recapitulation of governors and administrators given at the end of the reign of each caliph. Sometimes Khalifa's information on exact dates fails him, and he reverts to a technique of the dynastic histories, stating that an event took place not in a specific year, but during the governorship or reign of a specific person, whose term in office extended over many years. Superimposed on the otherwise almost purely annalistic arrangement is a vestige of the dynastic arrangement. The year of the commencement and close of the reign of each caliph is marked by mention of his maternal lineage, and the place of his birth or death. There follows after the death of each caliph a detailed list of the governors, judges, frontier commanders, secretaries, and attendants who served during his reign, and a list of prominent individuals who died during it.[94]

The annalistic *ta'rīkh* was quite a successful development in that it eventually came to be employed by many other Muslim historians. Important histories which follow this method (allowing for certain individual modifications and idiosyncrasies) were written by at-Tabari, al-Azdi, Ibn al-Athir, adh-Dhahabi, Ibn Kathir, Ibn Taghribirdi, and others.

94 The close of the tenures of the governors of Iraq are likewise marked by lists of the governor's aides, guards, secretaries, and deputies, and the prominent individuals who died during his term of office.

Khalifa's Purposes in Writing his *Ta'rīkh*

Khalifa probably intended his work to be a sort of outline, or convenient handbook, in which historical data were presented for the sake of determining a date for every important event in the history of Islam. Although Khalifa was an early pioneer in the writing of history in the annalistic arrangement, he was probably not the first to do so. Yet his *Ta'rīkh* may be considered an early experiment in a relatively new form of historical writing. Because of the newness of the technique, Khalifa may have been hesitant to fill in the outline with too many details, and thus presented only what he considered the barest essentials of the historical data he encountered in his sources. Still, he presents enough vivid first-hand descriptions of events to make his own work readable and more than just a dry list of facts. The *Ta'rīkh* contains many reports which quote alleged participants in the actual events, and are told in the first person. In some cases, such accounts are able to convey the mood of certain situations more dramatically than ordinary third-person narratives can.[95] His own most important purpose, however, was to fix the dates of events. A reader wanting more information on subjects mentioned could go back to the original sources.

There is evidence that Khalifa extracted only a bare skeletal outline from some long reports which are offered in longer versions by at-Tabari. These accounts deal particularly with events in Khurasan, and most of the examples are reports compiled by al-Mada'ini, from whom Khalifa received much material, and whom Khalifa cites frequently in the *Ta'rīkh*. Many of the reports in question can be broken down sentence by sentence, and each sentence can be matched in corresponding reports related by at-Tabari, frequently word for word, or nearly so. At-Tabari's version may extend over several pages, yet Khalifa extracted only enough material from the common original source to fill a paragraph or two with the essential facts.[96] Another technique employed by Khalifa for the sake of brevity was

95 This is a stylistic feature, and has no bearing on the factual accuracy of the report.

96 Cf. the following passages in the translation: 125(c), 230(a), 230(b), 232(c), 233(b), 235(a), 253(c), 254(e), 255(a), 277(a), 291(a), 304(a), 307(e), 338(d), 340(a), 340(b), 340(c). Cf. the following passages and their parallels in the *Kitāb al-Aghānī*: 375(b), 376(a), 377(a), 388(a), 389(c), 391(b), 391(d), 391(e), 392(b). We should, however, be on guard against possible elaborations and interpretations provided in the fuller accounts of at-Tabari and others, which may have been added by intermediary transmitters of the material. In such cases, Khalifa's version may reflect the letter or spirit of the original account more precisely than the seemingly more complete versions of the later historians. Cf. G. Rotter, "Zur Ueberlieferung einiger historischer Werke Mada'inis in Tabaris Annalen," 117ff.

to combine information contained in the accounts of two or more different sources and credit all of the sources.

There are sections in the *Ta'rīkh* in which the author is relatively long-winded and retains a considerable amount of detailed information from the original sources. It is possible that, despite his main intention of providing a brief sketch of Islamic history, Khalifa felt that the information available to himself on certain matters was not readily available elsewhere, and that he had an obligation to preserve the material *in toto*, or nearly so, in his own otherwise highly abridged work.

The Contents of the *Ta'rīkh*

Slightly less than half of the *Ta'rīkh* is devoted to the Umayyad era.[97] This was a period of increasingly distant conquests on the fringes of the empire, and a time of frequent internal turmoil as the result of civil wars waged between opposing social, religious, and political factions within the empire. Stories about these events were told, and retold, and passed on from father to son, and from teacher to pupil. In Khalifa's time there must have been innumerable such accounts in circulation. Some had been conveniently compiled in *khabar* monographs, others remained part of the stock-in-trade of traditionists. The authors of comprehensive histories, such as Khalifa, selected from the available accounts only that information they considered relevant for their purposes. In spite of its great scale, at-Tabari's *Ta'rīkh* has less to report, or is even silent, on certain events which Khalifa includes. For the Umayyad period, at-Tabari emphasizes the political and military events in Iraq and Khurasan, and the activities of the 'Alid-'Abbasid Shi'a. In his *Ansāb al-Ashrāf*, al-Baladhuri emphasizes the internal conflicts in Iraq and the Hijaz – the civil wars, and the activities of the Kharijites and the Shi'ites; in his *Futūḥ al-Buldān*, he is concerned with the external conquests.

Although Khalifa seems to have truncated, and severely abridged, many of the narratives he presents, his work is in general more well rounded than many of the other histories in its coverage of events throughout the Umayyad empire. Nevertheless, certain emphases can be perceived in the contents of the *Ta'rīkh*. For the Umayyad period, Khalifa's general emphasis is on the raiding expeditions and conquests, the civil wars, and the activities of

97 Approximately a third is devoted to Muhammad and the first four caliphs, and approximately 15 per cent to the 'Abbasid period.

the Kharijites. The activities of the 'Alids are almost completely ignored. Despite a tendency to extreme abbreviation of some reports, certain events are pursued to a depth and degree not encountered in other sources. Khalifa gives strong coverage of events in the Caucasus, Sijistan, Sind, and the Maghrib, places which tend to be ignored by at-Tabari. Khalifa's information on certain events in these regions matches, and in some instances exceeds, the information given in parallel accounts in the works of al-Baladhuri, al-Ya'qubi, and Ibn 'Abd al-Hakam. With respect to the Kharijites, Khalifa gives information on several Kharijite rebellions ignored or only briefly touched upon by at-Tabari, and sometimes provides information lacking in al-Baladhuri's account.[98] It is noteworthy that Khalifa and al-Baladhuri utilized certain sources for information on the Kharijites which were not used by at-Tabari.[99]

The *Ta'rīkh* also reproduces several notable speeches, such as those of Yazid III, and the Kharijite Abu Hamza, as well as excerpts from others, and a number of interesting alleged quotations of a variety of individuals. There is also a certain amount of poetry, some of which has not been found elsewhere.[100] Expectedly, Khalifa showed much interest in accounts of strange occurrences.[101]

Khalifa's training as a biographer and genealogist is apparent throughout the *Ta'rīkh*. Each chapter concludes with a list of the prominent individuals – traditionists, theologians, and Companions of the Prophet – who died during that year. Sometimes the births of prominent individuals are given too. Khalifa also frequently gives lists of prominent individuals who participated, or were killed, in the raiding expeditions, and those who participated, or were killed, in the internal rebellions and civil wars, or who were executed by the authorities. Sometimes these lists are broken down by family and tribal affiliation. One list, that of those killed in the battle of the Harra, requires 22 pages in Zakkar's edition. Khalifa's concern with genealogy is also shown by his frequent references to relationships among

98 Cf. the account of Qurayb and Zahhaf (Kh., 260ff.). There are Kharijite rebellions covered by at-Tabari that go unmentioned or are not given much attention by Khalifa.

99 Cf. the information about ar-Rayyan an-Nukri (Kh., 358, 360, 391), and Dawud b. an-Nu'man (Kh., 348).

100 I have not been able to trace the following verses: Kh., 279; Kh., 362 (1st verse in trans., 2nd verse in text); Kh., 375; Kh., 473 (4th verse); Kh., 576 (6th verse of the poem).

101 Cf. the accounts of the conquest of the city of Jalula' in the Maghrib (Kh., 247f.), Yazid b. al-Muhallab's treatment of the prisoners of Jurjan (Kh., 424f.), the founding of Kairouan (Kh., 247), and Maslama b. 'Abd al-Malik's treatment of the inhabitants of Hayzan (Kh., 505), to cite several examples.

individuals, noting fathers, cousins, aunts, and uncles, and frequently giving a long enumeration of an individual's ancestors. It would seem that Khalifa was highly influenced by his concern with genealogy, and was unable to separate completely the purposes of *ṭabaqāt* and *ta'rīkh* writing.[102]

Finally, a word may be said about Khalifa's very detailed lists of governors and administrators. While many of the names of governors, commanders, and administrators may be found elsewhere, such as in the works of al-Ya'qubi, at-Tabari, Ibn al-Athir, al-Baladhuri, al-Jahshiyari, and Ibn 'Abd Rabbihi, Khalifa's method of systematically enumerating all the officials, by region and in chronological order, at the close of each caliph's reign, is very convenient for reference purposes. This arrangement is another indication that Khalifa intended his work to be a ready handbook of historical data. There are many otherwise unknown names included in the lists.[103] One well-known fact which the lists of administrators confirm is that the caliphs tended to surround themselves with non-Arab *mawālī* who were employed in sensitive capacities, serving as chamberlains, secretaries, treasurers, bookkeepers, and keepers of the official seal.

In short, the themes that are common to the histories of Khalifa and the other early historians are military and political in character. The discussion of cultural events and developments was, for the most part, left to other genres of literature. In Khalifa's work in particular, there is little mention of matters not pertaining to military operations – internal or external – or political developments and changes. Khalifa does not dwell on the intrigue, conspiracies and counter-conspiracies, betrayals, tribal rivalries, and personal jealousies with which the works of al-Baladhuri, at-Tabari, and some other early writers are filled; his narratives are straightforward statements of (alleged) facts, with little attempt to explain the underlying causes for the course events took.

102 The combination *ta'rīkh-ṭabaqāt* was adopted to different extents by al-Azdi, Ibn al-Athir, adh-Dhahabi, and many other later writers of history. At-Tabari avoided obituary lists for the most part.

103 Khalifa's lists are a valuable supplement to the information in Zambaur's *Manuel de généalogie*, any revision of which will have to take Khalifa's information into account.

3. Khalifa's Religio-Political Attitudes in the *Ta'rīkh*

General Impressions

Khalifa's *Ta'rīkh* is generally free from expressly stated editorial opinions by the author or his sources, and from reports containing subjective comments – either positive or negative – about individuals or groups. The general impression is one of detached neutrality and objectivity in dealing with the data available to Khalifa concerning most events and subjects. Although a small number of reports express subjective opinions in the *Ta'rīkh*, they are not as frequent or as intense as in the works of some other writers whose works contain frequent expressions of value judgments. For many of the early historians, things are either black or white, with no shades of grey. A typical account in some works might include a statement that an individual under discussion was either the most generous man of his age, learned, pious, fearless in battle, and a defender of widows and orphans, or that he was the most depraved man of his generation, addicted to wine, song, and women, a violator of widows, and robber of orphans. Such comments, with extremely few exceptions, are not to be encountered in Khalifa's work, and then only in far less severe language. Descriptions of events and individuals are presented in the *Ta'rīkh* in a straightforward, detached manner, even when reported by an avowed eye-witness or participant, who it might be supposed had personal opinions and emotions about the subject. In only one instance, it seems, does Khalifa express an outright negative editorial comment, when he adds the phrase "May God not have mercy on him, and may he curse him" upon reporting the death of Muslim b. 'Uqba.[104] Maledictions such as this abound in the works of some other writers.

His Attitude toward the Umayyads

The generally negative image given to many of the Umayyad caliphs and their lieutenants in the majority of the early historical works (which formed the basis of the material used by later historians) has often been discussed by modern students of Islamic history and historiography.[105] Many of the Umayyad caliphs are described with bitterness and hostility. Yazid I,

104 Kh., 320.

105 Cf. Wellhausen, *Arab Kingdom*, introduction, especially xiv–xv; Nicholson, *A Literary History of the Arabs*, 194; Gibb, *Studies*, 36; Lewis, *The Arabs in History*, 64; Petersen, "'Ali and Mu'awiya," 157f., and 163ff.; Dixon, 1.

Yazid II, and al-Walid II, to name three outstanding cases, are described as playboys who ignored their religious duties, and are accused of being addicted to frivolous occupations, such as playing games, drinking, unlawful relations with women, and of committing various heinous crimes.

Khalifa, on the other hand, offers no such accusations or verbal abuse, and makes no mention of any such traits in connection with the Umayyad caliphs or their lieutenants. Where does the truth lie? Probably in between, but closer to Khalifa's non-committal picture. The earliest historians whose works are extant lived under the 'Abbasid caliphs, who came to power by destroying the Umayyads. Naturally, they had to be careful what they said about the government in power. They owed some sort of allegiance to it, and were expected to denigrate its enemies. This, however, was probably not an important cause for the literary mistreatment the Umayyads suffer at their hands.[106] From the quantity of material most of the early historians devote to the activities of the 'Alid Shi'a, and the generally extremely sympathetic attitude toward the 'Alids and their partisans, it seems that most of the early historians were Shi'ites themselves, or Shi'a sympathizers, or at least reflect predominantly pro-Shi'a sources. This may be of greater significance for their harsh treatment of the Umayyads. The Shi'ites were bitterly opposed to the Umayyads and their memory because, among other things, they believed that the Umayyads, beginning with 'Uthman, had usurped the caliphate, which rightfully belonged to 'Ali and his descendants, and that the Umayyads persecuted and murdered the 'Alids and their partisans.

On the other hand, if Khalifa actually had Umayyad sympathies, he might have had a desire to conceal any mention of depravity supposedly displayed by the Umayyads;[107] and there is probably at least a kernel of truth in the accusations widely directed against most Umayyad rulers, of neglect of religious duties and love of worldly pleasures, of excessive autocracy and cruelty displayed by some of them and their lieutenants. In these respects, the Umayyads were probably no worse than the 'Abbasids. Yet, as H. Gibb has noted, the 'Abbasids "were able to satisfy Muslim feeling to a degree never attained by the Umayyads." To understand this difference in attitude toward the Umayyads and the 'Abbasids we must, says Gibb,

> free ourselves from the habit of the Arabic chroniclers to view the historical process in terms of personal action, without consideration of the relevant

106 Cf. Margoliouth, 16f.; Goitein, introduction to volume V of the *Ansāb al-Ashrāf*, 15f., and 23f.

107 Cf. pages 2–3 and 12, and 2f., above.

> circumstances within which individuals acted and by which their action was circumscribed ... The Umayyads were, so to speak, the victims of a dialectical process within Islamic society, a process of self-criticism by which its political ideals were gradually adumbrated; but since the society itself lacked the means or the will to define them and to articulate them in a political system, it tried to evade its own responsibilities by fastening the blame for its failure on the Umayyads, as convenient scapegoats.[108]

A few examples will illustrate the different impressions of the Umayyads given by at-Tabari and al-Baladhuri on the one hand, and Khalifa on the other. In the first three of the following examples the difference lies merely in what Khalifa's text lacks. They constitute an argument *ex silentio*, and as such are not very convincing. But there are so many such examples that a pattern emerges of a hostile attitude toward the Umayyads on the part of other historians, and a lack of such in Khalifa:

1. In at-Tabari's version of the battle against the Umayyad forces in Jurjan, Qahtaba b. Shabib, the commander of the Musawwida (the pro-'Abbasid forces), who were attacking Jurjan, is quoted as addressing his Khurasani troops with the following statements: "Do you know against whom you are battling? Against those who burned God's House." (This is a reference to the burning of the Ka'ba, probably caused accidentally by Ibn az-Zubayr's own people, during the siege of Mecca by the Syrians in 64/683–684). "Your fathers' lands were taken over by the basest community [the Umayyads and their lieutenants] on the face of the earth. They appropriated your fathers' lands by force, took [your fathers'] wives for themselves, and enslaved their children [i.e. you] ... You will now take vengeance and regain what is rightfully yours."[109]

2. In at-Tabari's account of the murder of al-Walid II, the victim asks his murderers why they are killing him after he had raised their stipends and supported their poor. He is told that it was not to avenge themselves on him for anything, but because he engaged in forbidden activities, drank wine, took women forbidden to him by Islamic law, and did not take God's will seriously.[110]

3. In the account of at-Tabari, Ibn 'Atiyya, the commander of the Umayyad

108 Gibb, *Studies*, 36.

109 Tab., II, 2004f.

110 Tab., II, 1799f. Khalifa's account does, however, have one of the murderers exclaim, "Kill the sodomite the way sodomites should be killed!" (Kh., 549).

forces which defeated Abu Hamza in the Hijaz, is ludicrously made to utter blasphemous statements. Abu Hamza, upon meeting the Umayyad army on the battlefield, and in order to test them before battling them, asks their commander, Ibn ‘Atiyya, what he thought about the Qur’ān. Ibn ‘Atiyya is quoted as answering, “We put it at the bottom of a sack!” Then, asked what he had to say about the money that belongs to orphans, Ibn ‘Atiyya is alleged to have replied, “We take their money, and violate their mothers!”[111]

4. Other writers frequently refer to Ziyad, Mu‘awiya’s governor over Iraq, as Ziyad b. Abihi, Ziyad the son of his father, which cast doubt on his parentage. Mu‘awiya had recognized him as his own half-brother, and Ziyad called himself Ziyad b. Abi Sufyan, which he liked to be called by others.[112] This is the only name by which he is known in Khalifa’s *Ta’rīkh*.

5. There is an interesting variation in Khalifa’s version of an account in which someone other than his father speaks out in defense of Yazid b. Mu‘awiya. Called upon to pledge allegiance to Yazid, Ibn az-Zubayr, the anti-caliph in the Hijaz, says to the messengers sent by Yazid, “Are you ordering me to pledge allegiance to a man who drinks wine, neglects his prayers, and goes hunting?” One of the messengers, Hammam b. Qabisa, retorts, “Your words more aptly describe yourself than him [Yazid]!”[113]

In the same report, apparently from the same source, as reported by al-Baladhuri, Hammam makes no retort in defense of Yazid.[114]

Although Khalifa’s work is almost, though not totally, free of anti-Umayyad traditions and invective, there is also very little that could be interpreted as positively pro-Umayyad other than by inference. A tradition reported by al-Muhallab b. Abi Sufra, in which he stated an opinion that ‘Abd al-Malik b. Marwan was highly qualified for, and worthy of, the caliphate, as a good Muslim and a prominent man, was added to Khalifa’s *Ta’rīkh* by Baqi b. Makhlad.[115] Perhaps the material most blatantly favorable to the Umayyads in Khalifa’s book is a verse by Jarir in praise of the caliph Yazid b. ‘Abd al-Malik and the “purity of the origins” of his sovereignty.[116]

111 Tab., II, 2013.

112 On the significance to Ziyad of being recognized as the son of Abu Sufyan, cf. Abbot, 189f.

113 Kh., 317.

114 *Ansāb*, IV-B, 19f.

115 Kh., 330.

116 Kh., 481.

Khalifa adds the phrase "May God have mercy on him" after mentioning the death of Umayyad caliphs, with the exception of 'Umar II,[117] and does not add the phrase "May God curse him" after mentioning the Umayyads.[118]

A sustained narrative as told from the point of view of the Umayyad side is found in Khalifa's account of the events pertaining to Qahtaba's march against Iraq, the siege of Wasit, the truce, and the murder of Ibn Hubayra, which is based primarily on reports from a certain Bayhas b. Habib, who apparently was an officer in Ibn Hubayra's army.[119] Although his reports relate the events as witnessed from the side of the Umayyads, they are neutral with respect to subjective judgments. He does, however, make one or two unfavorable references to the opposition, some of whom he refers to as "louts" or "barbarians" (*'ulūj*), who are accused of violating the terms of the truce between Ibn Hubayra and Abu Ja'far.[120]

Khalifa makes no comment when dealing with the fall of the Umayyad dynasty and the rise to power of the 'Abbasids. The account of Abu l-'Abbas's receipt of the pledge of allegiance, and the defeat, flight, and death of Marwan II, is given without any change in tone. Khalifa reproduces no part of Abu l-'Abbas's alleged inaugural speech, and only a fragment of the speech of Dawud b. 'Ali, versions of which appear in at-Tabari and are full of nasty comments about the Umayyads. Dawud b. 'Ali, for instance, refers to Marwan II as "the enemy of God and caliph of Satan."[121] In connection with the demise of the Umayyad dynasty, Khalifa offers a report whose narrator states that he saw the head of Marwan II fixed on a pole in front of the mosque in Kufa, and "thus the hopes of the supporters of the Umayyads were crushed."[122] The fact that Khalifa ushers in the 'Abbasid dynasty with no literary fanfare, does not refer to them as the "Blessed Dynasty" or as members of the House of the Prophet, but only gives the dismal statement, "thus the hopes of the supporters of the Umayyads were crushed" is, I think, significant with respect to his attitude toward the two dynasties.

Even with the occasional hints, and rare pro-Umayyad remarks, it is not so much a pro-Umayyad attitude that emerges in Khalifa's *Ta'rīkh* as

117 E.g., Kh., 277, with reference to Mu'awiya, and Kh., 533, with reference to Hisham.

118 It should be noted that the works of other historians are not totally devoid of accounts depicting the Umayyads in a positive light. Cf., e.g., al-Ya'qubi, II, 283. See also the references given in note 106, above.

119 Cf. page 35, below.

120 Kh., 609.

121 Tab., III, 32.

122 Kh., 612.

the author's brevity and his lack of gratuitous denigrating remarks and information not relevant to an objective description of the course of events. The possibility must be considered that at least some of the anti-Umayyad comments and stories, as they appear in the works of at-Tabari and others, were later additions to, and embellishments of, older, less hostile traditions.

His Attitude toward the 'Alids and 'Abbasids

Perhaps in no other single respect is Khalifa's subject matter and that of the other early and later historians so divergent as in their coverage of the activities of the 'Alid Shi'a during the Umayyad period. While at-Tabari, al-Baladhuri, and many other historians devote a disproportionately large amount of space to the activities of the 'Alids and their partisans, there is a dearth of information concerning them in Khalifa's *Ta'rīkh*. He seems to have deliberately ignored them, apparently considering their activities insufficiently important to relate in detail. In a sense, Khalifa was right. In contrast to the Kharijites, who achieved a certain measure of fleeting success in their rebellions, Shi'ites rarely achieved much in the way of tangible results except to become martyrs for their cause. Khalifa's coverage of the rebellion and death of al-Husayn b. 'Ali consists of little more than a list of those who died with him, and some information on their genealogies. Of the rebellion of Hujr b. 'Adi, nothing is said but that he and some of his comrades were put to death by Mu'awiya. The revolt of al-Mukhtar is barely mentioned. Of the rebellion of Zayd b. 'Ali, Khalifa tells only that he was killed in Kufa in 122/739–740. The reports on these subjects require scores of pages in the works of at-Tabari and al-Baladhuri, and much space in the works of many other writers.

Khalifa does, however, include at least two clearly pro-'Alid traditions in his *Ta'rīkh*. One is a statement by al-Farazdaq that "the people's hearts" were with al-Husayn b. 'Ali.[123] Another is a statement by al-Hasan al-Basri praising al-Husayn's family.[124]

With respect to the rebellion of 'Abdallah b. Mu'awiya, his connection with, and initial support by, the Shi'ites is reported by Khalifa, but the episode is related in its aspect as a temporarily successful rebellion against the Umayyads, not as a movement of specifically Shi'ite inspiration.

123 Kh., 281.
124 Kh., 285.

Probably very early in ʻAbbasid history, the year 100/718–719, which marked the beginning of the second Islamic century, came to be considered the year of the birth of the ʻAbbasid revolt. Therefore, beginning in the year 100 we find that historians such as at-Tabari give regular reports every few years detailing the progress of the ʻAbbasid propaganda campaign and conspiracy in Iraq, the Hijaz, and Khurasan. This information is totally ignored by Khalifa, who makes practically no mention of the ʻAbbasid movement until the appearance of Abu Muslim in 129/746–747, and he makes no explicit connection between him and the ʻAbbasids. This may be an indication that, at least in the eyes of earlier observers such as Khalifa, Abu Muslim's movement began more as an independent, homegrown Khurasani movement than as one controlled or inspired by a distant conspiratorial clique, as the reports in at-Tabari and others would have us believe.

His Attitude toward Kharijites and Other Rebels

Among the events given much attention by Khalifa are some of the insurrections by Kharijites and others. Despite the detailed treatment he gives the activities of some of the Kharijites, on the whole Khalifa betrays no pronounced sympathy or antipathy for them. For example, he recounts the atrocities committed by Qurayb and Zahhaf, and quotes a verse in praise of the "noble deeds" of Dawud b. an-Nuʻman, with no editorial comment.[125] With respect to the rebellion of Ibn al-Ashʻath, Khalifa does reveal a degree of sympathy for the many prominent people who joined Ibn al-Ashʻath in his revolt against al-Hajjaj.[126]

4. The Sources for the Umayyad Section of Khalifa's *Ta'rīkh*

Since a fair amount of material for the Umayyad period in the *Ta'rīkh* was added by Khalifa's student, Baqi b. Makhlad, it seems convenient to divide this heading into two divisions: Khalifa's sources, and Baqi and his sources.

125 Kh., 260–264, and 348. Khalifa does include a statement attributed to Mirdas b. Udayya, another Kharijite, harshly critical of the bloodthirstiness of Qurayb (Kh., 264).

126 See, for example, the statement concerning those who had fallen and those who escaped (Kh., 372).

Khalifa's Sources

Khalifa frequently, although not always, cites the source or sources for his information. Sometimes the *isnāds* are incomplete, but it is not possible to determine with certainty whether Khalifa dropped the *isnād* and just named his own direct source, or whether the source had failed to cite the names of the transmitters. As was also done by other writers, Khalifa sometimes combines information relating to the same topic from two or more sources, citing the sources and their *isnāds*, and separating the different sources by the word *wa-* (and). An adequate description of the process by which traditions and books were transmitted is given by R. Guest in the introduction to his edition of al-Kindi (15–16, and 37ff.), and by C. Torrey in the introduction to his edition of Ibn 'Abd al-Hakam (3–4).

Khalifa used the works of some well-known authors, as well as material from less famous, and some wholly unknown compilers of historical information. The following, in alphabetical order, are the direct sources for the Umayyad section of the *Ta'rīkh*, with a summary of each authority's contributions and, where information is available, titles of books Khalifa may have used. Of those for whom biographical information has been found, all but three – 'Abd al-'Aziz b. 'Imran, Abu Nu'aym, and Ibn al-Kalbi – were Basrans by birth or residence. An asterisk before a name indicates that Khalifa had personal contact with the authority, signaling the contact by citing the authority at least occasionally with the expressions *ḥaddatha-nī* ("he told me"), *sami'tu* ("I heard"), and the like:

1. *'Abd al-A'la b. 'Abd al-A'la[127] (d. 189/804–805). He is quoted once for a version of the celebrated story of the founding of Kairouan by 'Uqba b. Nafi'.

2. 'Abd al-'Aziz b. 'Imran[128] (d. 197/812–813). He gives the ages of several caliphs at the time of their death.

3. *'Abd ar-Rahman b. Mahdi[129] (d. 198/814). His material includes traditions in praise of those who revolted with Ibn al-Ash'ath, and quotations from the son of 'Umar b. al-Khattab and another unnamed Companion, who urge

127 *Ṭbq.*, 542; adh-Dhahabi, *Tadhkirat al-ḥuffāẓ*, I, 272; Ibn Hajar, VI, 96.

128 *Ṭbq.*, 692; Ibn Hajar, VI, 350.

129 *Ṭbq.*, 571; adh-Dhahabi, *Tadhkirat al-ḥuffāẓ*, I, 301; Ibn Hajar, VI, 279; *Ma'ārif*, 5[illegible]3; cf. GAS, I, 488.

moderation and a wait-and-see attitude with respect to the caliphate of Yazid b. Mu'awiya.

4. *'Abdallah b. al-Mughira. He transmitted information he had received from his father, and is quoted numerous times in the *Ta'rīkh*. Most of his information concerns names and dates pertaining to the administration of Iraq. He also relates a tradition in praise of Qutayba b. Muslim, and a description of Abu l-'Abbas as-Saffah on the day of his inauguration and again a week later. From the type of data conveyed by 'Abdallah b. al-Mughira, it may be presumed that his father, al-Mughira, may have served in some official capacity in the administration of Iraq, and may have utilized government records. 'Abdallah b. 'Umar b. 'Abd al-'Aziz, who served as governor over Iraq during the last years of the Umayyads, had a secretary named al-Mughira b. 'Atiyya, who might have been 'Abdallah's father.[130]

5. *Abu 'Asim ad-Dahhak b. Makhlad[131] (d. 212/828). He gives the alleged text of a sermon by 'Abd al-Malik.

6. Abu dh-Dhayyal Zuhayr b. Hunayd.[132] His reports pertain to certain events in Khurasan in the late Umayyad period, Qahtaba b. Shabib, and the rout and death of Marwan II. He does not name his sources.

7. *Abu l-Hasan al-Mada'ini[133] (d. between 215/830 and 235/850). His information concerns 'Alid genealogical data, Kharijite activities in Iraq and the Hijaz, al-Hajjaj's treatment of those who rebelled with Ibn al-Ash'ath, accounts of raiding expeditions in Jurjan and Khurasan, and miscellaneous additional material. Among the many titles attributed to him in the *Fihrist*, Khalifa might have used any of his numerous books on the conquests in Khurasan, Sijistan, and India, *The Invasion of Jurjan and Tabaristan*, *The Khawārij*, and *Account of al-Hajjaj and his Death*. A number of reports for which Khalifa does not name his source may be attributed to al-Mada'ini on the basis of parallel reports given by at-Tabari.[134] Much of Khalifa's information on the raids and conquests in Khurasan, Sijistan, and India may derive from al-Mada'ini's works, whose sources are given in about a third of his citations.

130 Cf. al-Jahshiyari, 70 and 39.

131 *Ṭbq*., 545; Ibn 'Asakir, *Tahdhīb*, VII, 24; adh-Dhahabi, *Tadhkirat al-ḥuffāẓ*, I, 333; Ibn Hajar, IV, 450; cf. GAS, I, index, s.v. Abu 'Asim.

132 Ibn Hajar, III, 353.

133 EI, III, 81; GAS, I, 314.

134 Cf. note 94, above.

8. *Abu Khalid Yusuf b. Khalid as-Samti[135] (d. 190/805–806). He is cited numerous times in the *Ta'rīkh*, and received much of his information from a certain Abu l-Bara' an-Numayri, and from a certain Abu l-Khattab. Abu Khalid's reports pertain to the expeditions in Armenia and the Caucasus, battles against the Khazars, raiding expeditions in North Africa and the Mediterranean islands, and internal turmoil in North Africa. Much of Abu Khalid's information is unique to Khalifa, and lacks parallels in other sources. He does not indicate the source for his information on the Maghrib.

9. *Abu Nu'aym al-Fadl b. Dukayn[136] (d. 219/834). He is cited as an authority for the date of death of several prominent individuals.

10. *Abu 'Ubayda Ma'mar b. al-Muthanna[137] (d. 209/824–825 or 210/825–826). He is quoted numerous times in the *Ta'rīkh*. His information pertains to the activities of the Kharijites in Iraq and Bahrain, the conquests of Muhammad b. al-Qasim in Sind, and data concerning the martyrs of Karbala'. Among the many works ascribed to him in the *Fihrist*, the following might have been used by Khalifa: *al-Baṣra*, *The Khawārij of Bahrain and al-Yamama*, and *Warriors of the Nobles*. His sources are rarely named.

11. *Abu l-Yaman Mu'alla b. Rashid an-Nabbal.[138] He relates an account of Sinan b. Salama's raid against al-Qiqan. Although the report is narrated in the first person, he does not name his source. His grandmother, Umm 'Asim,[139] a concubine (*umm walad*) of Sinan b. Salama (who might have been Abu l-Yaman's grandfather), was probably his source.

12. *Abu l-Yaqzan 'Amir b. Hafs,[140] also known as Suhaym b. Hafs (d. 190/805–806). He is cited many times, throughout the *Ta'rīkh*. His contributions treat a wide variety of subjects, and include entertaining anecdotes and poetry, accounts of Kharijite revolts, battles, expeditions in India and North Africa, and other topics.[141] He rarely names his sources. The only

135 *Ṭbq.*, 543; Ibn al-Athir, *al-Lubāb*, I, 560; Ibn Hajar, XI, 411; cf. GAS, I, 417, 936.

136 GAS, I, 101; EI2, I, 143.

137 EI2, I, 158; cf. GAS, I, index.

138 Ibn Hajar, X, 237.

139 Ibn Hajar, XII, 473.

140 GAS, I, 266.

141 There are several reports in the *Ta'rīkh al-Islām* and the *Ta'rīkh Dimashq* which appear to have been quoted from Khalifa's *Ta'rīkh,* and which are attributed to Abu l-Yaqzan, although he is not named as the authority in the extant *Ta'rīkh*. These attributions – the texts

books ascribed to him by Ibn an-Nadim deal with genealogical subjects, but the author states that "He had a knowledge of historical traditions, genealogies, heroic deeds, and scandals, and was accurate in what he quoted about them."[142]

13. *Al-'Ala' b. Burd b. Sinan. He was the son of Burd b. Sinan, a confidant of Yazid III, and relates the experiences of his father at Yazid's deathbed.

14. *'Ali b. 'Abdallah.[143] He relates some information pertaining to the rebellion of Ibn al-Ash'ath.

15. *'Amir b. Salih b. Rustam[144] (d. 182/798–799). He gives a list of the prisoners taken by al-Hajjaj among the followers of Ibn al-Ash'ath, and quotes an anti-Hajjaj poem.

16. *'Amr b. 'Ubayda. His reports are attributed to Qaza'a, a freedman of Nasr b. Sayyar, and pertain to the retreat and death of Nasr b. Sayyar in Khurasan, and the fate of his family and followers at the hands of Qahtaba b. Shabib. They include some anecdotes and poetry.

17. *Ashhal b. Hatim[145] (d. 208/823–824). He transmits a remark allegedly made by 'Abdallah b. 'Amr concerning Mu'awiya and Yazid.

18. Al-Asma'i[146] (d. 215/830–831). He transmits a quotation attributed to ash-Sha'bi, who was explaining to al-Hajjaj his participation in the revolt of Ibn al-Ash'ath. He also quotes the son of 'Umar II on his father's age at the time of his death.

19. *'Awn b. Kahmas b. al-Hasan.[147] He quotes his father, who describes his experiences in Sind with Muhammad b. al-Qasim.

20. *Bakr b. 'Atiyya. He relates two reports from 'Awana which deal with the expeditions of Musa b. Nusayr in North Africa and Spain, and a report from his father on the raising of the head of Marwan II in front of the mosque in Kufa.

---

are identical – probably represent minor differences in the recensions of Baqi and at-Tustari. Cf. the following passages: 164(a), 175(b), and 176(b).

142 *Fihrist* (trans.), 204.

143 Unidentified.

144 Ibn Hajar, V, 70.

145 Kh., 771; Ibn Hajar, I, 360.

146 'Abd al-Malik b. Qurayb (GAL, I, 104; EI2, I, 717).

147 Al-Bukhari, *at-Ta'rīkh al-kabīr*, IV, I, 18; Ibn Hajar, VIII, 173.

21. Bayhas b. Habib. He was apparently an officer in the army of Ibn Hubayra during the last years of the Umayyad caliphate, and was close enough to Ibn Hubayra, or important enough, to have accompanied him (or at least he claimed he did) when he went to visit Abu Ja'far after the truce had been made.[148] His reports form a long narrative from the year 130/747–748 to 132/749–750 covering the rise of Abu Muslim, the advance of Qahtaba b. Shabib from Khurasan toward Iraq, the retreat of the Umayyad forces, the death of Qahtaba, the siege at Wasit, the truce, and the murder of Ibn Hubayra. Khalifa does not indicate that he had personal contact with Bayhas. However, Khalifa received several episodes of Bayhas's narrative directly from a certain Muhammad b. Mu'awiya. Perhaps Bayhas had compiled his experiences in a book of memoirs, which was introduced to Khalifa by Muhammad b. Mu'awiya.

22. *Bishr b. Bashshar/Yasar (?). He gives the number of cavalry troops (100,000) on the side of Marwan II at the battle of the Zab.

23. *Ghundar Muhammad b. Ja'far[149] (d. 193/808–809). His reports are transmitted from Shu'ba b. al-Hajjaj and 'Abd al-Malik b. 'Abd al-'Aziz b. Jurayj. Those from the former pertain to the revolt of Ibn al-Ash'ath, while the traditions of the latter concern Ibn az-Zubayr and the siege of the Ka'ba.

24. *Al-Hasan b. Abi 'Amr. He gives some data on the martyrs of Karbala'.

25. *Hatim b. Muslim.[150] He is cited numerous times in the *Ta'rīkh*. His reports are mostly brief statements giving the ages of the Umayyad caliphs when they died, and the length of their reigns. He also quotes verses by Kuthayyir 'Azza in defense of the Muhallabids, and gives some information on the terms of peace agreements in Tabaristan and Jurjan, one of which involved Yazid b. al-Muhallab.

26. Hisham b. Muhammad al-Kalbi[151] (d. 206/821–822). He is cited numerous times in the *Ta'rīkh*. Most of his reports are brief statements pertaining to the raiding expeditions against the Byzantines in each year. He does not name his sources.

148 Kh., 609.

149 *Ṭbq.*, 544; Kh., 752; *Ma'ārif*, 513; adh-Dhahabi, *Tadhkirat al-ḥuffāẓ*, I, 276; Ibn Hajar, IX, 96.

150 *Jarḥ*, I, II, 257; Ibn Hajar, II, 130.

151 GAS, I, 268.

27. *Isma'il b. Ibrahim b. Ishaq ash-Shu'ayrawi al-'Ataki. He is one of Khalifa's most important sources for extended and entertaining narratives, which include anecdotes, poetry, and quotations. His reports treat events in Syria, al-Jazira, and Iraq, and include information about the conspiracy against, and murder of, al-Walid II, the text of Yazid III's speech, information on the revolt of 'Abdallah b. Mu'awiya, long and valuable accounts about the Kharijites in al-Jazira and Syria, and anecdotes about the battle of Qudayd. He usually names his sources, most of whom are unknown. Since Khalifa frequently refers to him as "Isma'il," it is possible that some of the reports I have attributed to him should be ascribed rather to Isma'il b. Ishaq (cf. below), or vice versa.

28. *Isma'il b. Ishaq. See the remarks above, under Isma'il b. Ibrahim. It might even be that Isma'il b. Ibrahim and Isma'il b. Ishaq were the same person; perhaps Khalifa sometimes confused the names of Isma'il's father and grandfather. His contribution consists of material pertaining to the Kharijites. He offers a report concerning the demise of Shayban b. 'Abd al-'Aziz al-Yashkuri, and a long narrative concerned with Abu Hamza in the Hijaz, including a version of his famous sermon and the battle between Talib al-Haqq (an epithet meaning Seeker of the Truth) and Ibn 'Atiyya in the Yemen, and the death of Ibn 'Atiyya. His material on Talib al-Haqq, Abu Hamza, and Ibn 'Atiyya is very similar (although somewhat abridged) to the version of al-Mada'ini in the *Kitāb al-Aghānī* (XX, 97–114), and without doubt derive from a common source.

29. Isma'il b. Sinan.[152] He transmits a prediction made by the prognosticator 'Abdallah b. 'Amr concerning Ibn az-Zubayr and Yazid I.

30. *Muhammad b. 'Abdallah al-Ansari[153] (d. 215/830–831). He offers a report from Ibn Jurayj concerning Ibn az-Zubayr and the siege and burning of the Ka'ba.

31. *Muhammad b. Mu'adh.[154] He gives a brief report concerning Ibn al-Ash'ath.

32. *Muhammad b. Mu'awiya. He transmits several reports from Bayhas b. Habib (see above). He also offers a report, from a certain Sufyan, giving some data on the martyrs of Karbala'.

152 Al-Bukhari, *at-Ta'rīkh al-kabīr*, I, I, 358.

153 *Ṭbq*., 545; adh-Dhahabi, *Tadhkirat al-ḥuffāẓ*, I, 337; Ibn Hajar, IX, 274.

154 Ibn Hajar, IX, 462.

33. *Sahl b. Yusuf al-Anmati[155] (d. c. 190/805–806). He reports an anecdote concerning Iyas b. Mu'awiya, a judge of Basra.

34. Salm b. Qutayba[156] (d. 201/816–817). He names one of the casualties of the battle of az-Zawiya.

35. *Shihab (unidentified). He relates a report from 'Abdallah b. al-Mughira concerning the bloody aftermath of the revolt of Yazid b. al-Muhallab.

36. *Sulayman b. Harb[157] (d. 224/838–839). He relates – on the authority of Hammad b. Zayd – the dying utterances of one of the casualties of the battle of az-Zawiya.

37. *Umayya b. Khalid[158] (d. c. 200/815–816). He relates several traditions concerning the revolt of Ibn al-Ash'ath. His sources are Hammad b. Zayd, Shu'ba b. al-Hajjaj, and 'Awana b. al-Hakam.

38. *'Uthman b. 'Uthman.[159] He relates several miscellaneous traditions concerning the leader of the pilgrimage in one year, the name of a governor over Medina, and a quotation attributed to the caliph 'Umar II.

39. *Wahb b. Jarir b. Hazim[160] (d. 207/822–823). He is cited numerous times in the *Ta'rīkh*. His information pertains to the conflicts between the Umayyads and the Medinese, and the activities of Kharijites in Basra. Most of his material was conveyed to him by his father, Jarir b. Hazim,[161] and some by Juwayriya b. Asma'[162] and several other sources. In most cases, full *isnād*s are given.

40. *Al-Walid b. Hisham al-Qahdhami[163] (d. 222/836–837). He is cited frequently in the *Ta'rīkh*. His material consists of lists of administrators and other data pertaining to the governorship of Iraq, caliphs' death dates, and certain other miscellaneous information. Most of his information was

155 Ibn Hajar, IV, 259.

156 *Ṭbq.*, 572; *Jarḥ*, II, I, 266; Ibn Hajar, IV, 133.

157 *Ṭbq.*, 574; *Ma'ārif*, 526; adh-Dhahabi, *Tadhkirat al-ḥuffāẓ*, I, 355; Ibn Hajar, IV, 178.

158 Ibn Hajar, I, 370.

159 Ibn Hajar, VII, 137.

160 *Ṭbq.*, 572; *Ma'ārif*, 502; adh-Dhahabi, *Tadhkirat al-ḥuffāẓ*, I, 307; Ibn Hajar, XI, 161; cf. GAS, I, 311.

161 D. 170/786–77 (GAS, I, 310).

162 D. 173/789–790 (GAS, I, 94).

163 *Ṭbq.*, 576; al-Jahiz, I, 61; as-Sam'ani, 443a (= Ibn al-Athir, *al-Lubāb*, II, 243); adh-Dhahabi, *Mīzān al-i'tidāl*, III, 276.

conveyed to him by his father, Hisham b. Qahdham, who received it from his father, Qahdham b. Sulayman, who had been secretary of finance for Yusuf b. 'Umar when he was governor over Iraq.[164]

41. *Yahya b. Muhammad al-Ka'bi. He gives the ages of al-Walid I and al-Walid II at the their death. His information was conveyed to him by 'Abd al-'Aziz b. 'Imran.

Baqi b. Makhlad's Additions to the *Ta'rīkh*

Baqi b. Makhlad[165] (201–276/816–889), a native of Córdoba and a prominent *ḥadīth* scholar, journeyed to the east to pursue his studies. Khalifa b. Khayyat was one of his teachers in Basra, and he eventually returned to Spain with the *Ta'rīkh* and the *Ṭabaqāt*. Before returning to Spain, Baqi had also gone to Damascus to study, where he seems to have learned and preserved some unique Syrian traditions pertaining to the raids against the Byzantines, and certain information and anecdotes about Mu'awiya and other Umayyad caliphs. Much of Baqi's material deals with the Maghrib and raids in the Mediterranean. His contributions to the *Ta'rīkh* are found from the year 58/677 through the year 75/694–695, excluding 62 and 63, and one item in the year 231/845–846. The beginning of Baqi's additions, and the resumption of Khalifa's text, are frequently noted in the text of the *Ta'rīkh*, and always in the translation.

Baqi acquired his material from the following sources:

1. *Yahya b. 'Abdallah b. Bukayr[166] (d. 231/845–846). Baqi indicates that he attended sessions at which Yahya b. 'Abdallah b. Bukayr's works were read out loud, presumably by his students.[167] Ibn Bukayr received his information from al-Layth b. Sa'd[168] (d. 175/791–792), a native of Egypt. The latter's sources are not named. The material consists of data pertaining to the leader of the pilgrimage, and events in Egypt and the Maghrib.

2. *Muhammad b. 'Abdallah b. Numayr[169] (d. 234/848–849). His material

164 Kh., 556; cf. al-Jahshiyari, index.

165 See note 9, above.

166 Ibn Hajar, XI, 237; R. Guest, introduction to al-Kindi, 24f.; C. Torrey, introduction to Ibn 'Abd al-Hakam, 6; cf. GAS, I, 460.

167 Cf. R. Guest, introduction to al-Kindi, 16.

168 GAS, I, 520.

169 Adh-Dhahabi, *Tadhkirat al-ḥuffāẓ*, II, 24; Ibn Hajar, IX, 282; cf. Rosenthal, 520 n. 2.

supplies general information relating to the Umayyads, the Hijaz, Syria, and some obituary notices.

3. *Bakkar b. ʻAbdallah[170] (born 185/801–802). Baqi uses the expression *kataba ilayya*, indicating that the information he received from Bakkar was in written form. The source was Muhammad b. ʻA'idh ad-Dimashqi[171] (d. 233/847–848 or 234/848–849), who received the material from ʻAbd al-Aʻla b. ʻAbd al-Aʻla, Muhammad b. ʻUmar al-Waqidi, Ismaʻil b. ʻAyyash[172] (d. 182/798–799), al-Walid b. Muslim ad-Dimashqi[173] (d. 194/809–810), and a certain Marwan b. Muhammad. Bakkar's material pertains to the raids against the Byzantines and to the Umayyad caliphs. The material compiled by him suggests the preservation of remnants of a Syrian school of historical tradition.

5. The Use of Khalifa's *Ta'rīkh* by Later Writers

A large part of Khalifa's *Ta'rīkh* was incorporated into the works of later writers. Ibn ʻAbd Rabbihi, al-Azdi, Ibn ʻAbd al-Barr, Ibn ʻAsakir, adh-Dhahabi, and Ibn Hajar quote Khalifa extensively in their own works, directly from the *Ta'rīkh*. Furthermore, much material in *an-Nujūm az-zāhira* of Ibn Taghribirdi, and the *Ta'rīkh al-khulafā'* of as-Suyuti can be traced to Khalifa, probably through the *Ta'rīkh al-Islām* of adh-Dhahabi. In addition to the authors and works cited below, future research may reveal other books that quoted Khalifa's *Ta'rīkh*.

The *Ta'rīkh* is known to have been transmitted by two of Khalifa's students, Abu ʻImran b. Musa b. Zakariyya' at-Tustari and Baqi b. Makhlad al-Qurtubi, in independent recensions. At-Tustari's version was used by Ibn ʻAsakir, who indicates it in the *isnād*s when he quotes Khalifa, and most likely by adh-Dhahabi, in whose *Ta'rīkh al-Islām* none of Baqi's additions is included among the copious and varied quoted material. Also, slight differences between adh-Dhahabi's quotations and the extant recension of Baqi are sometimes apparent, indicating that Baqi may have

170 Ibn ʻAsakir, X, 228f.

171 GAS, I, 301.

172 *Ṭbq.*, 811; Ibn ʻAsakir, *Tahdhīb*, III, 39; adh-Dhahabi, *Tadhkirat al-ḥuffāẓ*, I, 233; Ibn Hajar, I, 321; cf. GAS, I, 301.

173 GAS, I, 293.

omitted some information retained by at-Tustari.[174] On the whole, however, the recensions of Baqi and at-Tustari must have been practically identical, since the passages quoted by Ibn 'Asakir duplicate almost literally the same passages in Baqi's version. Baqi's recension was used by the Spaniards Ibn 'Abd Rabbihi and Ibn 'Abd al-Barr, who indicate it in their works.[175] The other Spaniards who are known to have quoted Khalifa – Abu Bakr al-Maliki and Abu Bakr b. al-'Arabi – probably also used Baqi's recension. The Spanish bibliographer Ibn Khayr al-Ishbili (d. 575/1180) lists Khalifa's *Ta'rīkh* in his catalogue, indicating Baqi's recension.[176]

In his edition of the *Ta'rīkh*, al-'Umari has indicated passages which were taken from Khalifa in the works of most of the writers listed below, but he has done so only when Khalifa is cited *by name* by the author. In the course of the translation below I note many more passages taken from Khalifa (indicated in the footnotes), but which the authors of the later works did not specifically attribute to him, and which were thus left out by al-'Umari. In many cases it can be proved that a particular passage or passages are from Khalifa when two or more unrelated reports appear in the same order as in the original. In certain instances it is, of course, possible that a writer took his information from a common source that is now lost rather than from Khalifa, but I think that if there are any such passages listed below or in the translation, they are very few.

1. Ibn Sa'd, who died ten years before Khalifa, in 230/844–845, is the only earlier writer I am aware of who quotes Khalifa. A passage in volume VII (75f.) of his *at-Ṭabaqāt al-kubrā* corresponds, with the same *isnād*, but slight differences in the text to pages 100 of Zakkar's edition of the *Ta'rīkh* and 85 of al-'Umari's (cf. pages 114 of Zakkar and 96 of al-'Umari). Ibn Sa'd also quotes Khalifa seven other times,[177] but the passages are not found in the *Ta'rīkh*. These quotations, including the one found in the *Ta'rīkh*, may have been taken from Khalifa's *Musnad* (*Collection of Traditions*), rather than from his *Ta'rīkh*, since they relate the words and activities of the Prophet. In each case, Ibn Sa'd uses the expression *ukhbirtu 'an Khalīfa b. Khayyāṭ* ("I was informed on the authority of Khalifa b. Khayyat"), which would seem to indicate that Ibn Sa'd did not have personal contact with Khalifa,

174 Compare Dh., III, 343, l. 4f., and Ibn 'Asakir, *Tahdhīb*, III, 150, l. 15, with Kh., 336, l. 12 = trans., 175(b). Cf. note 141, above.

175 Cf. *'Iqd*, IV, 95; *Istī'āb*, 22.

176 *Fahrasat mā rawā-hu*, 230.

177 *At-Ṭabaqāt al-kubrā*, VII, 76–78, and 87.

but either learned the traditions from one of Khalifa's students, or from a written copy of his *Musnad*.

2. At-Tabari cites Khalifa once for an account about al-Mansur sending al-Mandi on an expedition to ar-Rayy in the year 141/758–759 (Tab., III, 136), which does not appear in the extant version of the *Ta'rīkh*. At-Tabari's indirect (*dhukira 'an*) source for the passage is a certain Ahmad b. al-Harith,[178] who indicates that he received the information from Khalifa in the course of personal contact with him. While at-Tabari and Khalifa used certain material from common sources, such as Wahb b. Jarir, al-Mada'ini, Ibn al-Kalbi, and others, at-Tabari seems either not to have known of Khalifa's book, or, more likely, he may have considered it too sketchy and obscure to be of much use to him since he had access to many detailed, comprehensive monographs for the material he was interested in. It is possible, nevertheless, that Khalifa's *Ta'rīkh* was among the works which inspired the style and arrangement of at-Tabari's own work, even though it is unlikely that he utilized the information it contained.

3. Ibn 'Abd Rabbihi quotes numerous passages from the *Ta'rīkh* in his *al-'Iqd al-Farīd*. The passages cover a variety of subjects, but most are concentrated in the section on the history (*akhbar*) of the caliphs, in volume IV of the *'Iqd*. Some poetry, anecdotes, and speeches are included in the material. The lists of secretaries and administrators given for each caliph were also probably taken, at least in part, from the *Ta'rīkh*. The borrowed passages range in length from a sentence or two, to several pages. They are for the most part very close to Khalifa's text, and reproduce it practically word for word. In a few instances there is some paraphrase, summarization, or recombination of the material. Khalifa is occasionally cited by name as the source. In at least one instance (*'Iqd*, IV, 95), Baqi b. Makhlad is cited as the transmitter of Khalifa's information. There is also a passage (*'Iqd*, I, 50) perhaps mistakenly attributed to Khalifa that does not appear in the surviving version of the *Ta'rīkh*.

4. Al-Azdi, the author of the *Ta'rīkh al-Mawṣil*, relied to a great extent upon information derived from Khalifa's *Ta'rīkh*. The *Ta'rīkh al-Mawṣil*

178 This Ahmad b. al-Harith is mentioned only one other time in at-Tabari's *Ta'rīkh*. He is not named in any of the biographical sources as one of Khalifa's students. Perhaps he is Ahmad b. al-Harith b. al-Mubarak al-Khazzaz, an historian of Baghdad who died in 231/845–846 (*Fihrist*, trans., 227–229, and index). He is quoted several times by al-Azdi in his *Ta'rīkh al-Mawṣil*.

(which is not really a history of Mosul, at least for the years 101/719 to 132/750, but a general history of the empire, with some stress on internal affairs, and some biographical information on prominent Jazirans), quotes many passages taken from Khalifa, usually citing the source as Khalifa b. Khayyat, or Shabab, and once as Shabab al-'Usfuri.[179] The author uses the expression *ḥuddiththu 'an*, "I was told (or informed) on the authority of," when citing Khalifa. Al-Azdi's quotations are not restricted to any particular subject matter. In many cases they are close to the original, and almost verbatim, but frequently, they are at least partially paraphrased. Sometimes they are greatly abridged, and sometimes they seem to have been combined with material from other sources.

5. Abu Bakr al-Maliki's *Riyāḍ an-nufūs* includes a passage (I, 11)[180] which combines portions of material in Khalifa's *Ta'rīkh* (164 and 165 in Zakkar's edition, and 134 and 135 in al-'Umari), dealing with a raid in the Maghrib in the year 17/638–639. Al-Maliki cites his source as the *Ta'rīkh* of Sabab[181] al-'Usfuri.

6. Abu sh-Shaykh al-Ansari quotes a passage from Khalifa in his *Ṭabaqāt al-muḥaddithīn bi-Iṣbahān* (I, 32), which corresponds to pages 167 in Zakkar's edition and 136 in al-'Umari's). This reference was noted by al-'Umari in his edition of the *Ta'rīkh* (136 n. 2).

7. Abu Nu'aym Ahmad b. 'Abdallah al-Isbahani (d. 430/1039) quotes Khalifa in his *Dhikr akhbār Iṣbahān* ([Leiden, 1931], I, 61), corresponding to page 167 in Zakkar's edition of the *Ta'rīkh* and 136–137 in al-'Umari's. These passages were noted by al-'Umari in his edition of the *Ta'rīkh* (137). In his *Ḥilyat al-awliyā'* ([Cairo, 1351/1932], II, 37), Abu Nu'aym cites Khalifa quoting a passage which does not appear in the extant version of the *Ta'rīkh*. This reference was noted by al-'Umari in his edition of the *Ta'rīkh* (187).

179 In the printed edition of the *Ta'rīkh al-Mawṣil*, Shabab appears as "Sayyar," and Shabab al-'Usfuri as "Yasar al-'Usfuri" (see al-Azdi, index). The Arabic spellings of these three names are very similar in appearance, especially if written or read carelessly or hastily. The manuscript of the *Ta'rīkh al-Mawṣil* seems to be filled with similar misspellings of many other names and has many grammatical mistakes as well. The editor, 'Ali Habiba, corrected many, but not all, of the mistakes.

180 This reference was noted by Franz Rosenthal in *A History of Muslim Historiography*, 392 n. 6.

181 The printed edition has an initial *sīn* rather than *shīn*.

8. Ibn 'Abd al-Barr utilized Khalifa's *Ta'rīkh* as a source for his *al-Istī'āb fī ma'rifat al-aṣḥāb*. A Spaniard, Ibn 'Abd al-Barr, used the recension of the *Ta'rīkh* brought to Spain by Baqi b. Makhlad. In the preface to his *al-Istī'āb*, the author lists his sources, among whom is Khalifa b. Khayyat. He states that he read Khalifa's work in two recensions (one of which might have been the *Ṭabaqāt* rather than the *Ta'rīkh*), although both derived from Baqi b. Makhlad.[182] Neither of the recensions corresponds to the ones listed by Ibn Khayr al-Ishbili in the sixth/twelfth century.[183]

9. Abu Bakr b. al-'Arabi cites Khalifa once, on page 172 of his *al-'Awāṣim min al-qawāṣim*. Ibn al-'Arabi has two paragraphs dealing with the battle of Siffin and the arbitration of the representatives of 'Ali and Mu'awiya. The two paragraphs are an abridged paraphrase of certain information in 216–220 of Zakkar's edition of the *Ta'rīkh* and 173–176 in al-'Umari) Concerning the subject under discussion, Ibn al-'Arabi says, "What is correct about that is what the *imāms*, such as Khalifa b. Khayyat and ad-Daraqutni[184] say about it ..." This reference was noted by Zakkar in the introduction to his edition of the *Ta'rīkh* (page ḥ) and of the *Ṭabaqāt* (page z).

10. Ibn 'Asakir quotes Khalifa frequently in his *Ta'rīkh Dimashq*. He utilized the recension of at-Tustari, whose name is cited before Khalifa's in practically every instance. The passages are very close to the extant version, and only rarely subjected to any paraphrasing or abridgement. Khalifa is also cited several times in the *Ta'rīkh Dimashq* for information which does not appear in the extant recension of his *Ta'rīkh*. These passages may indicate that at-Tustari's recension was more complete than Baqi's.

11. Yaqut quotes Khalifa three times in his *Mu'jam al-buldān*.[185] It is not impossible that Yaqut quotes Khalifa elsewhere in his *Mu'jam* without citing him as the source of the passage. One possibility is a poem of nine verses appearing at II, 744, which is arranged in the same order as Khalifa's order of the verses, which appear on page 166(a) of the translation. Versions of the poem appear in several other sources, with different numbers of verses, or different verse order.

182 *Istī'āb*, 22.

183 Cf. *Fahrasat mā rawā-hu*, 230 (the *Ta'rīkh*), and 225 (the *Ṭabaqāt*).

184 'Ali b. 'Umar, d. 385/995 (GAS, I, 206).

185 Compare this to the well over 100 citations of al-Baladhuri by Yaqut (index).

12. It is probable, but not certain, that Ibn al-Athir utilized Khalifa's *Ta'rīkh* for certain information found in his *al-Kāmil fi t-ta'rīkh*. If the parallel passages in the following list were not taken by Ibn al-Athir from Khalifa, they at least derive from a common source. Most of the passages do not appear in at-Tabari. When they are found in the works of al-Baladhuri (from whom Ibn al-Athir is known to have taken material), the versions of Ibn al-Athir and Khalifa are much closer to each other than either is to al-Baladhuri. The quoted passages include narratives pertaining to Mu'awiya and 'Abd al-Malik, some poetry, and reports on the raids against the Byzantines and in the Maghrib. Almost half pertain to the expeditions in the Caucasus and the Khazar wars.

13. An-Nawawi quotes Khalifa in his *Tahdhīb al-asmā' wa-l-lughāt*, and names Khalifa in the preface of the book as one of his sources.[186]

14. Ibn Khallikan used Khalifa's *Ta'rīkh*, and quotes it in several places.

15. Adh-Dhahabi quotes extensively from the *Ta'rīkh* in his *Ta'rīkh al-Islām*. In the preface to that work, adh-Dhahabi listed his sources, mentioning among them the *Ta'rīkh* and the *Ṭabaqāt* of Khalifa b. Khayyat.[187] The *Ta'rīkh al-Islām*, like Khalifa's *Ta'rīkh*, is arranged annalistically, although the vast bulk of the book, at least for the Umayyad period, is composed of biographies arranged alphabetically by decade of death.[188] Scarcely any of the chapters for the years between 41/661 and 132/750 in adh-Dhahabi's work are unaffected by Khalifa's *Ta'rīkh*. The material ranges from the bare mention of the leader of a pilgrimage or the year of someone's death, to entire pages lifted word for word. Some of the chapters in the *Ta'rīkh al-Islām* are simply abridgements of the corresponding chapters in Khalifa's *Ta'rīkh*. The quoted passages are often close to the original, but frequently adh-Dhahabi abridged or paraphrased the material. Khalifa is frequently cited by name as the authority for quoted material, but in many cases Khalifa is shown to be the source by the occurrence of several unrelated reports in the same order in the *Ta'rīkh al-Islam* as they are in Khalifa's book. The quoted material is used in both the biographical

186 It is quoted by as-Sakhawi, and translated by Rosenthal, 448.

187 Dh., I, 15. A portion of adh-Dhahabi's preface, 13–17, as quoted by as-Sakhawi in his *I'lān*, has been translated by Rosenthal in *A History of Muslim Historiography*, 391–393.

188 Khalifa sometimes uses a decade system to record the deaths of prominent persons when he did not know the exact year of their death. For example, he says, "Between the year 70/689–690 and 80/699–700, the following died: …" See, e.g., trans. pages 141 and 173.

sections of the *Ta'rīkh al-Islām* and the annalistic section. One feature to be noted is that unusual place names, or sections whose reading or interpretation is unclear, are sometimes omitted by adh-Dhahabi. Thus, while he can occasionally be used to clarify a dubious reading in Khalifa's work, he is often of no help. Certain data in Khalifa's text must have been as unclear to the historian of the fourteenth century as they are to us.

I have not done a systematic study of the material taken from Khalifa appearing in adh-Dhahabi's *Siyar a'lām an-nubalā'*. Khalifa is mentioned many times in the index to each of the published volumes. In the annotations in his edition of the *Ta'rīkh* al-'Umari has indicated the passages in the *Siyar* which cite Khalifa by name as the source. Most of the passages pertain to the date of death of prominent individuals.

16. Ibn Kathir quotes Khalifa in his *al-Bidāya wa-n-nihāya*. In the annotations to his edition of Khalifa's *Ta'rīkh*, al-'Umari has indicated passages quoted by Ibn Kathir where he cites Khalifa by name as the source. I have not checked Ibn Kathir systematically for quotations from Khalifa. It is possible that this would reveal more passages, for which Khalifa is not cited by name as the source, and which thus were left out by al-'Umari. Elsewhere in his *al-Bidāya*, Ibn Kathir lists Khalifa among the dead of the year 240/854–855, and calls him "an eminent historian" (*aḥad a'immat at-ta'rīkh*).[189]

17. Ibn Hajar quotes Khalifa extensively in his *Tahdhīb at-Tahdhīb*, mostly as an authority for the dates of death of prominent scholars, and for the dates of other events, such as battles, or the beginning or end of a judge or governor's term of office. The bulk of the data appears in Khalifa's *Ṭabaqāt* as well as in his *Ta'rīkh*. Ibn Hajar cites both works by name in his *Tahdhīb* (e.g., II, 62, l. 4). Ibn Hajar also quotes Khalifa in his *al-Iṣāba fī tamyīz as-ṣaḥāba*. The passages are indicated by al-'Umari in his annotations.

18. Although Ibn Taghribirdi cites Khalifa by name only about half a dozen times in the Umayyad section of his annalistic history *an-Nujūm az-zāhira*, it is clear that a large part of that section of his work derives from Khalifa's *Ta'rīkh* through adh-Dhahabi's *Ta'rīkh al-Islām*. A comparison of the texts of Ibn Taghribirdi and adh-Dhahabi for the Umayyad years shows that much of the *Ta'rīkh al-Islām* was incorporated into *an-Nujūm az-zāhira*. Thus, much of Khalifa's material, taken by adh-Dhahabi directly from his *Ta'rīkh*, passed into the work of Ibn Taghribirdi. It is interesting that

189 *Al-Bidāya wa-n-nihāya*, X, 322.

the latest of these historians was the first to be published and utilized by western scholars, who though they did not realize the fact, had access – through Ibn Taghribirdi – to passages and data from Khalifa's *Ta'rīkh*.

19. As-Suyuti does not, so far as I am aware, cite Khalifa by name in his *Ta'rīkh al-khulafā'*, but many passages are attributable to the latter's *Ta'rīkh*. Rather than using Khalifa's book first-hand, as-Suyuti, like Ibn Taghribirdi, may have used adh-Dhahabi's *Ta'rīkh al-Islām*, or perhaps some other work, from which he took passages derived from Khalifa's *Ta'rīkh*. The material in the *Ta'rīkh al-khulafā'* which is traceable to Khalifa includes the alleged texts of certain utterances of several Umayyad caliphs, anecdotes and biographical information about the caliphs, and the names and dates of places raided and conquered during the reign of each caliph. Examples are the account of Mu'awiya undertaking the pilgrimage in 51/671 in order to persuade the Hijazis to pledge allegiance to his son Yazid (Jarrett, 199f.), the speech of Yazid III, and deathbed anecdote about him (Jarrett, 257f.).

In addition to these users of Khalifa, al-'Umari has found that Ibn Makula, in his *al-Ikmāl*, cites the *Ta'rīkh*s of Khalifa b. Khayyat and at-Tabari as the sources for a passage which does not appear in the extant version of either Khalifa's or at-Tabari's *Ta'rīkh*. Al-'Umari has also found that Abu l-Faraj al-Isbahani cites Khalifa b. Khayyat Shabab al-'Usfuri as a link in an *isnād* for information which is not in the extant version of the *Ta'rīkh*. Both passages are quoted by al-'Umari on pages 521–523 of his edition of the *Ta'rīkh*.

A NOTE ON THE TWO PRINTED EDITIONS OF THE *TA'RĪKH*

The two printed editions of Khalifa's *Ta'rīkh*, each divided into two volumes but with continuous pagination, were edited independently by Suhayl Zakkar (Damascus, 1967) and Akram Diya' al-'Umari (an-Najaf, 1967). Both were used for the present translation: the pagination for Zakkar's edition is indicated in square brackets [], while the pagination for al-'Umari's is indicated in curved brackets {}. The manuscript was not seen.[190] Zakkar's is the technically more attractive edition. The text is a model of clarity, well designed, and spread out in a generous 798 pages. Zakkar also provided each of the two volumes of his edition with a table of contents, which is lacking in the edition of al-'Umari. Al-'Umari's text is cramped into 520 pages, and is often awkwardly laid out. However, his edition has an index of the poetry quoted in the *Ta'rīkh*, which is lacking in Zakkar's edition, and an extremely useful separate index of the individuals mentioned in the *isnād*s. Zakkar's index lacks many references to most of the individual transmitters in the *Ta'rīkh*. Both editions would have benefitted by having each chapter's year indicated in the upper margins, as is done in the Dar al-Ma'arif and Leiden editions of at-Tabari's *Ta'rīkh*.

Both editions usually note the occurrence of marginal explanations, corrections, and other annotations in the manuscript. Zakkar has generally left readings of names of places and persons as they appear in the text of the manuscript, indicating with a footnote a correction supplied in the

190 The only known surviving manuscript of the *Ta'rīkh* is in the General Library in Rabat, Morocco, #199q. It comprises 336 pages written in Maghribi script, and is dated 477/1085 or 479. Rosenthal inspected the manuscript briefly, and expressed the opinion that, contrary to the much older date of copying indicated therein, it seemed to have been written in the thirteenth or fourteenth century (*A History of Muslim Historiography*, 71f.). Brockelmann was unaware of it, and Khalifa is not mentioned in his GAL. The manuscript is listed by Sezgin, GAS, I, 110. Since I have not had the opportunity to inspect the manuscript, I refrain from making any comments about it. Al-'Umari and Zakkar provide detailed descriptions and sample photographs of the manuscript in their editions of the *Ta'rīkh*.

margin of the manuscript, or his own, if necessary. Al-'Umari, on the other hand, frequently inserts the marginal corrections into the body of the text, whether or not these corrections are right or wrong. There are occasional variations in the reading of the more unusual names of persons and places. Otherwise, the texts of both editions are practically identical, so that we can be assured that they accurately reflect the reading of the manuscript.

Both editors' introductions merit great praise, and have been highly useful to me in preparing the present study. Al-'Umari's annotations were also very helpful in calling attention to many of the later writers who quote from the *Ta'rīkh*.

CONVENTIONS

The following conventions are employed in the translation and annotations:

1. In the *isnāds*, the symbol < means that the individual to the left of the symbol received the information from the individual to the right. When personal contact is indicated by the expressions *qāla lī*, *ḥaddatha-nī*, and the like, the relator (i.e., the *subject* of the verb) has an asterisk preceding his name.

2. When Khalifa names his source for a particular report or piece of information, the material is in a single paragraph following the name of the source or the *isnād*. A new paragraph indicates that the information no longer derives from the previously indicated source.

3. The extent of parallel passages is indicated in footnotes.

4. An asterisk preceding a reference to a parallel passage in another work indicates that the passage was taken from Khalifa's *Ta'rīkh* essentially unchanged. An asterisk within parentheses means that the user significantly abridged or paraphrased the passage or combined it with information from other sources.

5. If a parallel passage was not taken from Khalifa, but both derive from a common third source, the reference to the parallel passage is given with no symbol preceding it.

6. When the name of the source for a parallel passage is cited by the author of the later work, that name appears in parentheses immediately following the page reference to the passage; for example: Tab., II, 1477 (al-Mada'ini).

7. If a parallel passage appears also in Khalifa's *Ṭabaqāt*, the citation of the parallel is preceded by the symbol #. This occurs almost exclusively with death dates.

8. If a parallel passage was not taken from Khalifa, and does not appear to derive from a common third source, but the parallel is deemed

useful for comparative purposes, the reference to it is preceded by the abbreviation cf.

9. Words and phrases in brackets within the body of the translation were added by the translator.

TRANSLATION

{187}[234] The Year 41/661–662

This was the Year of Accord.[1]

Al-Hasan b. ʿAli b. Abi Talib and Muʿawiya reached an agreement. Meeting in Maskin,[2] in the Sawad, near al-Anbar, they made peace with each other, and al-Hasan b. ʿAli surrendered [his claims on the caliphate] to Muʿawiya. That was in *Rabīʿ* II/August or *Jumādā* I 41/September 661.[3]

The caliphate of al-Hasan b. ʿAli lasted seven months and seven days.[4] He retained his father's governors. Al-Mughira b. Shuʿba forged a document of appointment in the name of al-Hasan, and led the pilgrimage in 40/661.[5] Al-Hasan died in Medina in 49/670–671. Saʿid b. al-ʿAs, then governor over Medina, recited the prayers for him. Al-Hasan died at the age of 46. He was born in Medina in 3/624–625. His mother was Fatima, the daughter of the Prophet.

The people united in support of Muʿawiya, whose mother was Hind bint ʿUtba b. Rabiʿa b. ʿAbd Shams b. ʿAbd Manaf.

{188} When Muʿawiya entered Kufa, ʿAbdallah b. Abi l-Hawsaʾ revolted against him in an-Nukhayla.[6] Khalid b. ʿUrfuta al-ʿUdhri,[7] an ally[8] of the Banu Zuhra, was sent against him by Muʿawiya, with a force of Kufans. Ibn Abi l-Hawsaʾ was killed in *Jumādā*[9] 41/September–October 661, [235] according to Abu ʿUbayda and Abu l-Hasan.[10]

1 The Arabic is *sanat al-jamāʿa*. Although *jamāʿa* generally means "community," its meaning can, as here, verge on "consensus" or "accord." Adh-Dhahabi, II, 208 explains that the year 41 was called "the Year of *al-jamāʿa*" because in that year the Community agreed upon one caliph, Muʿawiya (*li-jtimāʿ al-umma ʿalā khalīfa wāḥid*). Wellhausen defines *jamāʿa* as "the unity of Muhammad's Congregation" (*Arab Kingdom*, 56) and "the uniting of the congregation of Muhammad under one sceptre" (ibid., 111).

2 BGA, V, 198, 199; VI, 7, 98, 235, 237; VII, 104; VIII, 38; Yaqut, IV, 529; Wellhausen, *Arab Kingdom*, 104.

3 From "This was the Year …" cf.* Dh., II, 208, l. 3 (Khalifa).

4 From "This was the Year …" cf. Tab., II, 8f.; **ʿIqd*, IV, 361.

5 From "Al-Mughira b. Shuʿba forged …" cf. Tab., II, 4.

6 EI, III, 951.

7 *Ṭbq*., 268; Ibn Saʿd, IV, 355; Ibn Hajar, III, 106.

8 The Arabic is *ḥalīf*. On the institution of *ḥilf*, see EI2, III, 388.

9 The account in the *Istīʿāb*, taken from Kh., has *Jumādā* I.

10 I.e. Maʿmar b. al-Muthanna and ʿAli b. Muhammad al-Madaʾini. See also Introduction, pages 33 and 32. From "When Muʿawiya entered Kufa …" cf. *Ansāb*, IV-A, 138f.; **Istīʿāb*, 435, l. 3 (Khalifa); (*) Dh., II, 209, l. 5.

Abu 'Ubayda and Abu l-Hasan:
When Ibn Abi l-Hawsa' was killed, Hawthara b. Dharra'[11] revolted. Mu'awiya dispatched 'Abdallah b. 'Awf b. Ahmar against him, with 1,000 [troops]. Hawthara was killed in *Jumādā* II 41/October 661.[12]

Abu 'Ubayda and Abu l-Hasan:

In this year, Sahm b. Ghalib al-Hujaymi revolted with al-Khatim al-Bahili, whose name was Ziyad b. Malik,[13] near the Bridge of Basra. 'Ubada b. Qurs al-Laythi,[14] a Companion of the Prophet, was killed. 'Abdallah b. 'Amir went out against them.[15] Sahm and al-Khatim requested safety, which he granted them, but he killed a number of their companions.[16]

Abu 'Ubayda:
{189} Sahm b. Ghalib also killed Sa'd, a *mawlā* of Qudama b. Maz'un.[17]

In this year, 'Amr b. al-'As, who was governor over Egypt, appointed 'Uqba b. Nafi' al-Fihri – 'Amr's cousin on his mother's side – over Ifriqiya.[18] He went as far as Libya.[19] and Maraqiya.[20] [The inhabitants] submitted, but

11 In the *Ansāb*, Hawthara's father's name is read as *Wadā'*, which in Arabic script is almost identical to *Dharrā'*. Cf. Wellhausen, *Religio-Political Factions*, 35 n. 7.

12 From "When Ibn Abi l-Hawsa' ..." cf. *Ansāb*, IV-A, 139f.

13 Al-Baladhuri and at-Tabari give his name as Yazid.

14 *Ṭbq*., 65; Ibn Sa'd, VII, 82.

15 Ibn 'Amir was governor over Basra. On Ibn 'Amir see EI2, I, 43.

16 From "In this year, Sahm ..." cf. *Ansāb*, IV-A, 147f.; Tab., II, 15f. and 83f.; **Istī'āb*, 809.

17 From "Sahm b. Ghalib also killed ..." cf. *Ansāb*, IV-A, 148. The term *mawlā* is often translated as client or freedman; it refers to those who attached themselves via a patron-client relationship to a member of the Arab conquest society; often he/she converted and was subsequently manumitted, becoming a freedman/freedwoman [RGH].

18 On the geography of Ifriqiya, see EI2, IV, 1049.

19 Cf. BGA, V, 7, 74; VI, 82, 91, 155; VII, 339.

20 Cf. BGA, VI, 91; VII, 339; VIII, 21. R. Guest places Maraqiya west of Lubiya on his map of "The Abbaside Empire" in his edition of al-Kindi's *Governors and Judges*. Cf. Yaqut, IV, 477.

then rebelled.[21] He conducted another raid against them in the same year, killing [many], and taking captives.[22]

[Mu'awiya] appointed 'Abdallah b. 'Amir b. Kurayz as governor over Basra, Marwan b. al-Hakam over Medina, and 'Abd ar-Rahman b. Khalid b. al-'As b. Hisham [236] b. al-Mughira over Mecca.[23] Some say it was al-Harith b. Khalid b. Hisham.[24] Later, he consolidated [the administration of Medina, Mecca and] at-Ta'if under the governorship of Marwan b. al-Hakam.

In this year, Mu'awiya made a truce with the Byzantines.[25] 'Utba b. Abi Sufyan b. Harb led the pilgrimage.[26]

In this year, al-Hajjaj b. Yusuf was born.

[237] The Year 42/662–663

In this year, ['Abdallah] b. 'Amir sent 'Abd ar-Rahman b. Samura to Sijistan.[27] He was accompanied on that raiding expedition by al-Hasan

21 Kh. uses a number of different words with the meaning "revolt" or "rebel." *Kharaja*, literally "go out," is found most frequently, and is used in connection with almost all the so-called Kharijite rebellions. *Intaqaḍa* (e.g., Kh., 328) and *naqaḍa* (used without a direct object; e.g., Kh., 287, l. 8) are used in connection with the rebellion of inhabitants of a conquered territory. *Naqaḍa* implies abrogation of a treaty. The use of *kafara* as, e.g., in the present instance, implies a reversion to unbelief in the principles of Islam. When *kafara* is found, it might be assumed that the inhabitants had at least nominally converted to Islam in the course of the conquest. The word *kufr* ("unbelief") was used by the caliph 'Abd al-Malik and his governor, al-Hajjaj, in describing those who participated in the rebellion of Ibn al-Ash'ath (cf. Kh., 365). *Khala'a* ("repudiate," "depose") is frequently used by Kh. in relating the rebellions of governors and generals, as well as other individuals, and the inhabitants of cities. During the period of the 'Abbasid revolution, the verb *sawwada* is used by Kh. and other writers with the meaning "join the revolution of the Musawwida": (e.g., Kh., 610). Cf. also the usage by at-Tabari of the verb *bayyaḍa* with the meaning of "rebel against the Musawidda" (e.g., Tab., III, 52).

22 From "In this year, 'Amr b. al-'As ..." cf. **Istī'āb*, 1075f.; IA, III, 419.

23 The only reference to him I have found is several lines of poetry ascribed to him in Tab., II, 1031.

24 Ibn 'Asakir, *Tahdhīb*, III, 437.

25 From "In this year, Mu'awiya made a truce ..." cf. al-Ya'qubi, II, 285.

26 *Istī'āb*, 1025; Dh., II, 231.

27 EI2, I, 86.

b. Abi l-Hasan,[28] al-Muhallab b. Abi Sufra,[29] and Qatari b. al-Fuja'a.[30] He conquered Zaranj[31] and [other] districts of Sijistan.[32]

{190} 'Uqba b. Nafi' conducted a raiding expedition in Ifriqiya. He conquered Ghadamis,[33] killing [many] and taking captives.[34]

Ibn 'Amir appointed Rashid b. 'Amr al-Judaydi as commander over the frontier of al-Hind.[35]

Abu Khalid < Abu l-Khattab:
Rashid remained there carrying out raids. He penetrated deeply into Sind.[36]

In this year, Habib b. Maslama al-Fihri[37] died in Armenia.[38] The following died in the beginning of Mu'awiya's caliphate: Safwan b. Umayya,[39] 'Uthman b. Talha,[40] [and] Rukana b. 'Abd Yazid.[41] The following died when Mu'awiya first came to power: Abu Burda b. Niyar[42] [and] Rifa'a b. Rafi'.[43]

'Anbasa b. Abi Sufyan b. Harb led the pilgrimage.[44]

28 He is commonly known as al-Hasan al-Basri. EI2, III, 247; GAS, I, 591.

29 EI, III, 640.

30 EI2, IV, 752; GAS, II, 350.

31 EI, IV, 1218; Bosworth, index.

32 From "In this year, ['Abdallah] ..." cf. *Futūḥ*, 396; **Istī'āb*, 835 (Khalifa); *Dh., II, 209, l. 181; **Iṣāba*, II, 393 (Khalifa).

33 EI2, II, 991.

34 From "'Uqba b. Nafi' ..." cf. IAH, 194, l. 7; **Istī'āb*, 1076; IA, III, 419.

35 On the terms al-Hind and Sind and their geographical significance, see S. Maqbul Ahmed in EI2, III, 404ff.

36 From "Ibn 'Amir appointed ..." cf. *Futūḥ*, 433; *Dh., II, 209, l. 20.

37 EI2, III, 12.

38 From "In this year, Habib b. Maslama ..." cf. #Ibn 'Asakir, *Tahdhīb*, IV, 35 (Khalifa). More generally, *Ṭbq.*, 54; Ibn Sa'd, V, 449; Ibn 'Asakir, VI, 427; Ibn Hajar, IV, 424.

39 Safwan b. Umayya taken from #Ibn 'Asakir, *Tahdhīb*, VI, 428 (Khalifa) and 432 (Khalifa); #Ibn Hajar, IV, 425 (Khalifa).

40 *Ṭbq.*, 32; Ibn Sa'd, IV, 447; Ibn Hajar, VII, 124.

41 *Ṭbq.*, 21; *Istī'āb*, 507; Ibn Hajar, III, 287.

42 *Ṭbq.*, 261; *Istī'āb*, 1608; Ibn Hajar, XII, 19.

43 *Ṭbq.*, 220; *Istī'āb*, 497; Ibn Hajar, III, 281.

44 *Ṭbq.*, 583; *Jarḥ*, III, I, 400; Ibn Hajar, VIII, 159. U reads 'Utba b. Abi Sufyan. In Arabic script the two names are practically identical. Although some later writers may have been somewhat confused between 'Anbasa and 'Utba b. Abi Sufyan (e.g. Ibn Hajar, possibly), two separate individuals – brothers of Mu'awiya b. Abi Sufyan – seem to have existed. Cf. Tab., index; *Ma'ārif*, 344–345; Ibn Hazm, 111f.

[238] The Year 43/663–664

In this year, 'Abd ar-Rahman b. Samura conquered ar-Rukhkhaj[45] and Zabulistan[46] in the province of Sijistan.[47]

'Uqba b. Nafi' al-Fihri raided and conquered districts in the Sudan.[48] He conquered Waddan,[49] which is in the territory of Barqa. All of these [places] are in Ifriqiya.[50]

Busr b. Artat[51] conducted a winter expedition in the land of the Byzantines.[52]

Mu'awiya appointed 'Abdallah b. Sawwar al-'Abdi over Mukran.[53]

In this year, the following died: 'Amr b. al-'As, in Egypt, on *Yawm al-Fiṭr* (1 *Shawwāl*)/6 January 664; according to some, he died in 42 – Muhammad b. Maslama al-Ansari[54] and 'Abdallah b. Salam.[55]

Marwan b. al-Hakam led the pilgrimage.

{191}[239] The Year 44/664–665

In this year, Ibn 'Amir conquered Kabul[56] Abu Qatada al-'Adawi[57] was killed in Kabul. According to some, the one who was killed was Abu Rifa'a al-'Adawi.[58] Among those taken prisoner at Kabul were the following:

45 Ancient Arachosia. See Bosworth, index; Minorsky, 346.

46 Cf. Minorsky, 345f.; Bosworth, index.

47 From "In this year, 'Abd ar-Rahman b. Samura …" cf. *Futūḥ*, 396; (*) Dh., II, 210, l. 3.

48 "The Sudan" here probably refers to the land south of the coastal area.

49 BGA, II, 44, 45; V, 79; VI, 87; VII, 345.

50 From "'Uqba b. Nafi' al-Fihri raided …" cf. IAH, 194f.; **Istī'āb*; 1076; IA, III, 419; *Dh., II, 210, l. 4.

51 EI2, I, 1343.

52 From "Busr b. Artat conducted …" cf. al-Ya'qubi, II, 285; cf. Tab., II, 27; Ibn 'Asakir, X, 7 (Khalifa); (*) Dh., II, 210, l. 5.

53 From Mu'awiya appointed …" cf. *Futūḥ*, 433. For Mukran, see EI, III, 174.

54 *Ṭbq.*, 185; *Istī'āb*, 1377; Ibn Hajar, IX, 454.

55 'Abdallah b. Salam taken from #Ibn 'Asakir, *Tahdhīb*, VII, 448 (Khalifa).

56 Kabul was apparently conquered by 'Abd ar-Rahman b. Samura for Ibn 'Amir. Cf. *Futūḥ*, 396; cf. Bosworth, 19.

57 Khalifa may possibly have been confusing al-'Adawi with Abu Qatada al-Ansari, who died in 54/673–674 according to most accounts. Cf. Kh., 232; *Ṭbq.*, 224; Ibn Hajar, XII, 204.

58 From "In this year, Ibn 'Amir conquered Kabul…" cf. (*) Dh., II, 210, l. 8; *Ibn Hajar, XII, 96 (Khalifa). For Abu Rifa'a al-'Adawi, see *Ṭbq.*, 89; *Istī'āb*, 1657; Ibn Hajar, XII, 96.

Makhul ash-Sha'mi;[59] Salim b. 'Ajlan al-Aftas;[60] Kaysan, the father of Ayyub b. Abi Tamima as-Sakhtiyani;[61] Nafi',[62] a *mawlā* of Ibn 'Umar;[63] [and] Mihran, the father of Humayd at-Tawil.

In this year, al-Muhallab b. Abi Sufra raided al-Hind.[64] He marched to Qandabil,[65] then he reached Banna[66] and '-l-'-h-w-'-n/'-l-'-h-w-'-z,[67] which are at the foot of the mountain of Kabul. A number[68] [of people] confronted them, but God put them to rout. The Muslims filled their hands with booty and departed unharmed.[69]

[240] The business between Mu'awiya and Ziyad occurred in this year.[70]

Ibn 'Amir went on an official visit to Mu'awiya, leaving Qays b. al-Haytham as-Sulami[71] as his lieutenant over Basra.[72]

Ibn al-Kalbi:
'Abd ar-Rahman b. Khalid[73] conducted a winter expedition in the land of the Byzantines.[74]

Mu'awiya b. Abi Sufyan led the pilgrimage.

59 D. 113/731–732 (GAS, I, 404).

60 D. 132/749–750 (*Ṭbq.*, 823; Azdi, 139f.; Ibn Hajar, III, 481).

61 The son, Ayyub, died in 132 (GAS, I, 87).

62 D. 118/736–737 (*Ṭbq.*, 641; *Jarḥ*, IV, I, 451; Ibn Hajar, X, 412; cf. GAS, I, index).

63 From "Among those taken prisoner …" cf. (*) Dh., II, 210, l. 11 (Khalifa).

64 From "In this year, al-Muhallab …" cf. *Dh., III, 307, I. 19 (Khalifa).

65 EI2, IV, 534.

66 Banna (?) is mentioned only by al-Baladhuri (*Futūḥ*, 432; quoted by Yaqut, I, 747), according to whom it is between Multan and Kabul. There is a modern city called Bannu (cf. EI 2, I, 1020) in Pakistan, situated between Multan and Kabul. Perhaps there is some association between the ancient and modern cities. (Ibn al-Athir, [IA, III, 446] also quotes *Futūḥ*).

67 *Futūḥ*: *al-Ahwār*. Perhaps Lahore is intended. Cf. Minorsky, 246f.

68 *Futūḥ*: *al-'adūw* ("the enemy").

69 From "In this year, al-Muhallab …" cf. *Futūḥ*, 432; (*) Dh., II, 210.

70 Mu'awiya publicly recognized Ziyad as the son of his (Mu'awiya's) own father, Abu Sufyan. For an example of the importance to Ziyad of being addressed as the son of Abu Sufyan, cf. Abbot, 189f. At-Tabari and other writers frequently refer to Ziyad as Ibn Abihi, "son of his (unknown) father." Khalifa never uses anything but Ziyad or Ziyad b. Abi Sufyan.

71 *Ṭbq.*, 465; *Jarḥ*, III, II, 105.

72 From "Ibn 'Amir went …" cf. Tab., II, 68f.

73 EI2, I, 85.

74 From "'Abd ar-Rahman b. Khalid conducted …" cf. al-Ya'qubi, II, 285; Tab., II, 67.

[241] The Year 45/665–666

In this year, Mu'awiya dismissed Ibn 'Amir from the governorship of Basra, and appointed al-Harith b. {192} 'Amr al-Azdi, who arrived at the beginning of the year/March–April 665. Mu'awiya [soon] thereafter dismissed him and appointed Ziyad, who arrived in Basra in the month of *Rabī'*/May–July 665. He killed and gibbeted Sahm b. Ghalib al-Hujaymi, who had revolted near the Bridge of Basra.[75]

Ibn 'Amir sent 'Abdallah b. Sawwar al-'Abdi [on a raiding expedition]. He conquered Qiqan,[76] and acquired booty.[77] He brought back horses whose progeny is the Qiqani workhorse. Then he went [to Syria], leaving Kuraz b. Abi Kuraz al-'Abdi[78] as his lieutenant. He went to Mu'awiya, who returned him to his command,[79] and dismissed Ibn 'Amir.

Mu'awiya b. Hudayj conducted a raiding expedition in Ifriqiya.[80] He camped at a mountain where it rained on him. [Because of that] it was called Jabal al-Mamtur.[81]

Marwan b. al-Hakam led the pilgrimage.

In this year also, 'Abd ar-Rahman b. Khalid b. al-Walid conducted a winter campaign in the land of the Byzantines.[82]

Mu'awiya b. Abi Sufyan sent Mu'awiya b. Hudayj on a raiding expedition. He reached [242] F-ḥ-ṣ/M-ḥ-ṣ-n[83] and took some captives, but did not conquer any city or fortress. Then he returned.

In this year the following died: Zayd b. Thabit and Salama b. Salama b. Waqsh.[84]

Marwan b. al-Hakam led the pilgrimage.

75 From "In this year, Mu'awiya dismissed ..." cf. (*) Dh., II, 210; from "He killed and gibbeted Sahm b. Ghalib al-Hujaymi ..." cf. *Ansāb*, IV-A, 148; cf. Tab., II, 83f.

76 Cf. Minorsky, 373, where Qiqan is tentatively identified with Kizkanan (modern Kalat in Pakistan).

77 From "Ibn 'Amir sent ..." cf. al-Ya'qubi, II, 273; (*) Dh., II, 210.

78 U: *H-z-'-z*, b. Abi Kuraz al-'Abdi. He is unidentified.

79 From "Ibn 'Amir sent ..." cf. *Futūḥ*, 433.

80 From "Mu'awiya b. Hudayj conducted ..." cf. *Dh., II, 210.

81 From "Mu'awiya b. Hudayj conducted ..." cf. **Istī'āb*, 1414. The meaning of Jabal al-Mamtur is "The mountain of the one upon whom rain has fallen."

82 From "In this year also ..." cf. al-Ya'qubi, II, 285; Tab., II, 81.

83 Cf. al-Fahs al-Abyad (Kh., 530). A final *alif* would have been expected if Fahs or *M-ḥ-ṣ-n* were being used as a common noun.

84 *Ṭbq.*, 176; *Istī'āb*, 641.

[243] The Year 46/666–667

In this year, Mu'awiya dismissed 'Abd ar-Rahman b. Samura from his command over Sijistan, and appointed ar-Rabi' b. Ziyad b. ar-Rabi' al-Harithi.[85] The Turks took up arms. The Kabul Shah gathered an army and marched against the Muslims, expelling them from Kabul. They overwhelmed Zabulistan and {193} Rukhkhaj, and advanced as far as Bust,[86] where ar-Rabi' b. Ziyad confronted them. God put Zunbil[87] to rout, and ar-Rabi' pursued him to Rukhkhaj.[88]

Ibn al-Kalbi:
Abu Hakim Malik b. 'Abdallah[89] conducted a winter campaign in the land of the Byzantines.[90]

According to others, it was Malik b. Hubayra al-Fazari[91] [who wintered in the land of the Byzantines].[92]

'Utba b. Abi Sufyan b. Harb led the pilgrimage.

[244] The Year 47/667–668

In this year, 'Abdallah b. Sawwar al-'Abdi raided Qiqan. The Turks gathered an army against him. 'Abdallah b. Sawwar and most of that force were killed, and the polytheists took control of Qiqan.[93]

Ibn al-Kalbi:
Malik b. Hubayra conducted a winter campaign in the land of the Byzantines.[94]

Abu 'Abd ar-Rahman al-Qayni conducted a winter campaign in Antioch.[95]

85 D. 53/672–673 (*Ṭbq.*, 479; Tab., II, 161; Ibn Hajar, III, 243.

86 EI2, I, 1344.

87 Kh. Has *R-t-b-y-l*. *Zunbīl* is the generally accepted reading of this title (cf. Wellhausen, *Arab Kingdom*, 231 n. 3; Minorsky, 345; Bosworth, 34–36.

88 From "In this year, Mu'awiya dismissed ..." cf. *Futūḥ*, 397; (*) Dh., II, 211.

89 *Ṭbq.*, 256; *Istī'āb*, 1353; Dh., II, 315.

90 From "Abu Hakim Malik b. 'Abdallah ..." cf. al-Ya'qubi, II, 285; Tab., II, 82.

91 *Ṭbq.*, 164; *Istī'āb*, 1361; Ibn Hajar, X, 24.

92 From "it was Malik ..." cf. al-Ya'qubi, II, 285; cf. Tab., II, 82.

93 From "In this year, 'Abdallah b. Sawwar al-'Abdi raided Qiqan ..." cf. *Futūḥ*, 433; al-Ya'qubi, II, 278; *Yaqut, IV, 217 (Khalifa); *Dh., II, 211.

94 This sentence parallels al-Ya'qubi, II, 285; Tab., II, 84.

95 This sentence parallels Tab., II, 84.

Ruwayfi‘ b. Thabit al-Ansari[96] went on a raiding expedition from Antabulus.[97] He entered Ifriqiya, and departed in the same year.[98]

‘Anbasa b. Abi Sufyan led the pilgrimage.

[245] The Year 48/668–669

In this year, Mu‘awiya dismissed Marwan b. al-Hakam from the governorship of Medina, and appointed Sa‘id b. al-‘As.[99]

Abu l-Yaqzan:
When ‘Abdallah b. Sawwar was killed, Mu‘awiya wrote to Ziyad: “Find a man suitable for the frontier of al-Hind, and send him there [as commander].” Ziyad sent Sinan b. Salama b. al-Muhabbaq al-Hudhali.[100]

Ibn al-Kalbi:
Abu ‘Abd ar-Rahman al-Qayni conducted a winter campaign in Antioch again in this year.[101]

{194} According to others, it was Ibn Mukraz, of the Banu ‘Amir b. Lu’ayy [who conducted the winter campaign].

Sa‘id b. al-‘As led the pilgrimage.

[246] The Year 49/669–670

In this year, Ziyad killed al-Khatim al-Bahili the Kharijite, of the Banu Wa’il, in Basra. [Al-Khatim’s] name was Ziyad b. Malik.[102]

*One of the sons of Sa‘id b. Salim[103] < his father:
Qutayba b. Muslim was born on the day al-Khatim was killed, and that was in 49/669-670.

96 *Ṭbq.*, 750; *Istī‘āb*, 504; Ibn Hajar, III, 299.

97 I.e., the province of Pentapolis, which contained the cities of Barqa, Cyrene, Ptolemaita, Arsinoe, and Berenice.

98 From “Ruwayfi‘ b. Thabit al-Ansari …” cf. IAH, 110; (*) *Istī‘āb*, 504; *Dh., II, 211.

99 This sentence parallels *Dh., II, 211. For Sa‘id b. al-‘As, see EI, IV, 66.

100 From “When ‘Abdallah b. Sawwar was killed …” cf. *Futūḥ*, 433; al-Ya‘qubi, II, 278; **Istī‘āb*, 658 (Abu l-Yaqzan); *Dh., II, 211; *Ṭbq.*, 453; *Istī‘āb*, 657; Ibn Hajar, IV, 241.

101 This sentence parallels al-Ya‘qubi, II, 285; Tab., II, 85.

102 This sentence parallels *Ansāb*, IV-A, 148f.; cf. Tab., II, 83f.; (*) Dh., II, 211.

103 Z: Sa‘id b. Salm. Perhaps this is Sa‘id b. Salim al-Qaddah (Ibn Hajar, IV, 35).

During the governorship of al-Mughira b. Shu'ba over Kufa, Shabib b. Bajra al-Ashja'i revolted. Al-Mughira dispatched Kuthayyir b. Shihab al-Harithi [against him] and he killed him in Azerbaijan.[104]

Abu 'Ubayda:
Shabib b. Bajra, who had been present at an-Nahrawan, revolted against al-Mughira b. Shu'ba in Kufa, at Dar ar-Rizq,[105] and was killed.[106]

Ibn al-Kalbi:
Malik b. Hubayra conducted a winter campaign in the land of the Byzantines.[107]

According to others, Fadala b. 'Ubayd al-Ansari[108] conducted the winter campaign.[109] 'Abdallah b. Mas'ada[110] conducted a winter expedition by land.

Sa'id b. al-'As led the pilgrimage.

In this year, al-Hasan b. 'Ali b. Abi Talib died,[111] God's mercy upon him.

{195}[247] The Year 50/670–671

In this year, al-Mughira b. Shu'ba died in Kufa in *Sha'bān*/August–September 670. He designated his son, 'Urwa, to succeed him. According to some, he designated Jarir b. 'Abdallah.[112]

Mu'awiya appointed Ziyad over Kufa and Basra, and consolidated [the administration of] Iraq under his governorship. Ziyad dismissed ar-Rabi' b. Ziyad al-Harithi from [his command over] Sijistan, and appointed

104 From "During the governorship of al-Mughira b. Shu'ba …" cf. *Ansāb*, IV-A, 141; cf. al-Ya'qubi, II, 262; *Dh., II, 211.

105 *Ansāb*, IV-A, 141 has al-Quff (cf. Yaqut, IV, 153f.). There is a Dar ar-Rizq in Basra (BGA, V, 191) but I have not found references to one in Kufa. Perhaps it was the site of the *dīwān* office.

106 This sentence parallels *Ansāb*, IV-A, 141; al-Ya'qubi, II, 262; *Dh., II, 211.

107 This sentence parallels Tab., II, 86; *Dh., II, 211f.

108 D. 59/678–679 (*Ṭbq.*, 195; *Istī'āb*, 1262; Ibn Hajar, VIII, 267).

109 This sentence parallels al-Ya'qubi, II, 285; cf. Tab., II, 86; *Dh., II, 212.

110 *Istī'āb*, 987; Dh., III, 39.

111 Note on al-Hasan b. 'Ali b. Abi Talib's death parallels #Dh., II, 220 (Khalifa is named as a source, but the year 50 is given).

112 From "In this year, al-Mughira b. Shu'ba died …" cf. (*) Dh., II, 212; *Ṭbq.*, 257; *Istī'āb*, 236; Ibn Hajar, II, 73.

'Ubaydallah b. Abi Bakra to the post.[113] He ordered him to put to death the *hirbidhs*,[114] and to extinguish all the [ritual] fires from [Iraq] to Sijistan.[115]

In this year, Mu'awiya sent 'Uqba b. Nafi' to Ifriqiya. He founded Kairouan, and remained there for three years.[116]

*'Abd al-A'la b. 'Abd al-A'la[117] < Muhammad b. 'Amr b. 'Alqama[118] < Yahya b. 'Abd ar-Rahman b. Hatib:[119]
When 'Uqba b. Nafi' conquered Ifriqiya, he stood at [the site of] Kairouan, and said three times, "Inhabitants of the valley! We [Muslims] shall take up residence here, if God is willing. So depart!" We saw reptiles come forth from underneath every rock and tree, and eventually disappear [from] inside the valley. Then he said, "Settle here, in the name of God."[120]

Maslama b. Mukhallad,[121] commander in Egypt,[122] sent Mu'awiya b. Hudayj[123] on a raiding expedition. He obtained prisoners, and returned safely.

{196} Abu Khalid:
Maslama b. Mukhallad sent Mu'awiya b. Hudayj on a raiding expedition. [248] Mu'awiya b. Abi Sufyan wrote to Marwan b. al-Hakam, his governor over Medina: "Send 'Abd al-Malik b. Marwan with a corps of Medinese to the Maghrib." So 'Abd al-Malik set out, and entered Ifriqiya with Mu'awiya b. Hudayj. Mu'awiya b. Hudayj sent him in command of mounted troops against Jalula'[124] in the Maghrib. He set up mangonels

113 From "Mu'awiya appointed Ziyad..." cf. *Dh., II, 212; from "Ziyad dismissed ar-Rabi' ..." cf. *Futūḥ*, 397.

114 The *herbadh* (Arabic *hirbidh*; plural *harābidha*) was a priest in the Zoroastrian religious hierarchy. Cf. Frye, *The Heritage of Persia*, 209 and 274 n. 26; Bosworth, 5–6.

115 From "He ordered ..." cf. the passage from the anonymous *Ta'rīkh-i Sīstān* translated by Bosworth in *Sīstān under the Arabs*, 24.

116 From "In this year, Mu'awiya sent 'Uqba ..." cf. **Istī'āb*, 1076 (Khalifa); *an-Nawawi, I, III, 421 (Khalifa); *Dh., II, 212.

117 D. 189/804–805 (*Ṭbq.*, 542; Ibn Hajar, VI, 96).

118 D. c. 143/760–761 (*Ṭbq.*, 677; Ibn Hajar, IX, 375).

119 D. 104/722–723 (*Ṭbq.*, 604; Ibn Hajar, XI, 249).

120 From "When 'Uqba b. Nafi' conquered Ifriqiya ..." cf. IAH, 196; cf. *Futūḥ*, 228; cf. Tab., II, 93f.; **Istī'āb*, 1076; cf. Yaqut, IV, 213; *Dh., II, 212; *Dh., III, 50.

121 *Ṭbq.*, 218; Ibn Hajar, X, 148; Ibn Taghribirdi, I, 132.

122 Instead of the more common *walī miṣr*, Kh. here has *amīr bi-miṣr*. Cf. A. A. ad-Duri, in EI2, I, 438, s.v. *amīr*, and EI2, I, 435, s.v. *'āmil*.

123 *Ṭbq.*, 163; Ibn Hajar, X, 203.

124 BGA, II, 60; V, 79; VI, 87; al-Bakri, *Description*, 31ff.; Yaqut, II, 107. De Slane identifies Jalula' with the Oppidum Usaletanum of antiquity (Ibn Khaldun, I, 307 n. [illegible]).

and besieged the inhabitants.[125] [Then] Mu'awiya b. Hudayj wrote to him, [ordering him] to depart. So he departed. [But] the walls [of Jalula'] had been weakened and fell down. [So] he set out with the people, and returned [to Jalula']. He killed the fighting men, and took the women and children as captives.[126] Ibn Hudayj sent an army, which encamped at a city.[127] The inhabitants sought to surrender to him peacefully. He acceded, and departed in 51/671–672.

Yazid b. Mu'awiya conducted a raiding expedition in the land of the Byzantines. He was accompanied by Abu Ayyub al-Ansari.[128]

In this year, Mu'awiya called upon the Syrians to pledge allegiance to his son, Yazid b. Mu'awiya, which they did.[129]

'Abdallah b. 'Amir conducted a winter campaign in the land of the Byzantines.

In this year, Rashid b. 'Amr al-Judaydi was killed in al-Hind.[130]

{197} Yazid b. Mu'awiya led the pilgrimage after he had returned from the land of the Byzantines.

In this year, the following died: Abu Ayyub al-Ansari, in the land of the Byzantines;[131] 'Abd ar-Rahman b. Samura, for whom Ziyad recited the prayers; Abu Musa[132] in Kufa; al-Hakam b. 'Amr al-Ghifari[133] in Khurasan; Rashid b. 'Amr al-Judaydi in al-Hind; al-Mughira b. Shu'ba.

Ar-Rabi' b. Ziyad al-Harithi, sent by Ziyad, arrived in Khurasan. He raided Balkh, which had been retaken[134] [and held by the enemy] after

125 From "Maslama b. Mukhallad sent Mu'awiya ..." cf. (*) Dh., III, 277f. (Khalifa); (*) Ibn Kathir, IX, 63 (Khalifa).

126 From "Maslama b. Mukhallad sent Mu'awiya ..." cf. IAH, 193f. Kathir, IX, 63 (Khalifa).

127 U: the city.

128 From "Yazid b. Mu'awiya conducted ..." cf. Tab., II, 86; (*) Dh., II, 212; (*) Ibn Kathir, VIII, 229 (Khalifa); Khalid b. Zayd (EI2, I, 108).

129 From "In this year, Mu'awiya called ..." cf. *Dh., II, 213.

130 This sentence parallels *Futūḥ*, 433.

131 Note on the death of Abu Ayyub al-Ansari parallels #Ibn 'Asakir, *Tahdhīb*, V, 37 (Khalifa).

132 Note on the death of Abu Musa parallels #Ibn Hajar, V, 363 (Khalifa). See also 'Abdallah b. Qays al-Ash'ari (EI2, I, 695).

133 *Ṭbq.*, 72; *Istī'āb*, 356; Ibn Hajar, II, 436.

134 The verb used here, *ughliqat*, literally means "was closed, shut." The transitive verb *aghlaqa* is the opposite of *fataḥa*, "to open," which is the word commonly used by historians with the meaning "conquer," particularly in connection with fortresses and cities, many of which had walls and gates which were actually opened in the course of the conquest. The verb *aghlaqa* possibly came to be used analogically to express the opposite of *fataḥa*, in the

al-Ahnaf[135] [had conquered it]. The inhabitants made peace with ar-Rabi‘, who then proceeded to raid Quhistan,[136] which he conquered by force.[137]

[249] Al-Walid b. Hisham < his father < his grandfather; and ‘Abdallah b. Mughira < his father:
[The administration of] Iraq was consolidated under [the governorship of] Ziyad in 50/670–671.

Chief of Police: in Basra, ‘Abdallah b. Hisn, of the Banu Tha‘laba b. Yarbu‘; [and] in Kufa, Shaddad b. al-Haytham al-Hilali.

Finance Secretary[138]: Zadhan Farrukh.

Secretar[ies] for Correspondence: ‘Abd ar-Rahman b. Abi Bakra[139] [and] Jubayr b. Hayya.[140]

[Ziyad's] Chamberlain: Mihran, his *mawlā*.

[Ziyad] died at the age of 53.

In this year, ‘Amr b. al-Hamiq al-Khuza‘i[141] was killed in Mosul by ‘Abd ar-Rahman b. ‘Uthman ath-Thaqafi, the paternal uncle of ‘Abd ar-Rahman b. Umm al-Hakam.[142]

Yahya b. ‘Abd ar-Rahman < Ibn Lahi‘a[143] < *Bukayr b. ‘Abdallah b. al-Ashajj[144] < Sulayman b. Yasar:[145]
We raided Ifriqiya with Ibn Hudayj.[146] He gave us half of the booty after

---

sense of a city being shut (again) to the Arabs by the enemy. Cf. De Goeje's glossary, p. 79 of the introduction to the *Futūḥ*, *sub radice gh-l-q*.

135 Al-Ahnaf b. Qays (EI2, I, 303) had conquered Balkh in 30/650–651 (Kh., 174). Cf. EI2, I, 1001a (s.v. Balkh).

136 EI, II, 1108ff.; Minorsky, 326f.

137 From "Ar-Rabi‘ b. Ziyad al-Harithi, sent ..." cf. Tab., II, 156 (al-Mada'ini); *Dh., II, 212.

138 Arabic: *kātib al-kharāj*. On the *kharāj* see EI, II, 902; Løkkegaard, index; Dennett, passim.

139 *Ṭbq.*, 483; Ibn Hajar, VI, 148; Ibn Sa‘d, VII, 190.

140 *Ṭbq.*, 484; Ibn Hajar, II, 62.

141 *Ṭbq.*, 235; Ibn Hajar, VIII, 23. For details of his killing, see Tab., II, 127f., and *Aghānī* XVI, 6f.

142 This sentence parallels Tab., II, 127f. (Abu Mikhnaf); cf. *Aghānī*, XVI, 6f.; (*) *Istī‘āb*, 1174; #Ibn Hajar, VIII, 24 (Khalifa).

143 ‘Abdallah, d. 174/790 (EI2, III, 853; GAS, I, 94). The individual who received this account from Ibn Lahi'a cannot be Yahya b. ‘Abd ar-Rahman b. Hatib, who died in 104 (cf. note 119).

144 D. 122/739–740 (GAS, I, 405).

145 D. 104/722–723 or 110 (*Ṭbq.*, 618; Dh., IV, 120; Ibn Hajar, IV, 228; Ibn Sa‘d, V, 174).

146 This sentence parallels **Istī‘āb*, 1414, l. 18.

the [customary] fifth [designated for the central authority, had been set aside].[147]

{198} In this year, Ziyad appointed Sinan b. Salama b. al-Muhabbaq over the frontier of al-Hind, after Rashid had been killed.[148]

*Abu l-Yaman an-Nabbal:[149]
We raided Qiqan with Sinan, and were confronted by a great number of the enemy. Sinan said, "Rejoice! You will attain one of two [good] things: Paradise or booty."[150] Then he took seven stones, and stood in battle position against the people. He said, "When you see me attack, you attack." When the sun reached the center of the sky, he threw a stone in [250] the faces of the people, and praised God. Then he threw the stones one by one until only the seventh remained. When the sun passed from the center of the sky, he threw the seventh. Then he said, "*Ḥā-mīm*, they will not be protected!"[151] He praised God, and attacked, and we attacked with him. [The enemy] fled from us and we [pursued them] a distance of four *parasang*s, killing them. We came to people who had taken refuge in a fortress. They said, "It was not you who killed us. We were killed by men whom we do not see among you now, who were riding piebald horses and were wearing white turbans." We said, "This is God's victory,"[152] and returned. We had only one casualty among us.[153] We said to Sinan, "You stood in battle position against the people until, when the sun sank in the sky, you attacked them." He said, "The Prophet used to do the same thing."[154]

Mu'awiya led the pilgrimage.[155]

147 From "We raided Ifriqiya with Ibn Ḥudayj ..." cf. IAH, 193, l. 5.

148 This sentence parallels *Futūḥ*, 433; *Istī'āb*, 658 (Khalifa); (*) Dh., III, 252; *Ibn Hajar, IV, 241 (Khalifa).

149 Mu'alla b. Rashid (Ibn Hajar, X, 237).

150 From "We raided Qiqan with Sinan ..." cf. *Dh., II, 213.

151 Cf. Qur'ān 41:16 and 44:4. *Sūra*s 41 and 44 are among those which begin with the cryptic letters *ḥā'-mīm*. Adh-Dhahabi quotes a tradition that the Prophet said, "If you attack (an enemy) at night, let your motto be '*Ḥā-mīm*, they shall not be helped!'" (Dh., III, 307, l. 15; cf. Wensinck, VI, 460). Al-Baladhuri reports that the motto of 'Abdallah b. Khazim, a governor over Khurasan, was "*Ḥā-mīm*, they shall not be helped!" (*Futūḥ*, 414). Cf. *Futūḥ*, glossary, 30; cf. Lane, 638a.

152 *Naṣr Allāh* is also a Qur'ānic expression. Cf. Qur'ān 2:210, for example.

153 From "We said, 'This is God's victory' ..." cf. (*) Dh., II, 213.

154 This is an allusion to the *ḥadīth* discussed in note 151.

155 Cf. Kh., 248, where it is stated that Yazid b. Mu'awiya led the pilgrimage in this year.

{199}[251] The Year 51/671–672

In this year, Mu'awiya b. Abi Sufyan put to death Hujr b. 'Adi b. al-Adbar,[156] along with Muhriz b. Shihab,[157] Qabisa b. Dubay'a b. Harmala al-Qaysi,[158] and Sayfī b. Fusayl,[159] of the Rabi'a. In this year, Ka'b b. 'Ujra died.[160]

In this year Mu'awiya had the people pledge allegiance to Yazid.

*Wahb b. Jarir b. Hazim < *my father < *an-Nu'man b. Rashid[161] < az-Zuhri[162] < Dhakwan, a *mawlā* of 'A'isha:
When Mu'awiya resolved to designate his son Yazid as heir apparent, he went on the pilgrimage. He proceeded to Mecca with about 1,000 men. When he neared Medina, Ibn 'Umar, Ibn az-Zubayr, and 'Abd ar-Rahman b. Abi Bakr departed. When Mu'awiya arrived in Medina, he mounted the pulpit and praised God. Then he mentioned his son, Yazid, and said, "Who is more worthy of this position of authority than him?"[163] Then he departed, and went to Mecca. After having completed the ritual circumambulation, he entered his house and sent for Ibn 'Umar. 'He recited the *shahāda*, then said, "Ibn 'Umar, you used to tell me [252] that you did not want to spend one dark night without a caliph. I am warning you not to split the staff of the Muslims, and not to strive to cause the destruction of their commonwealth." When he had finished speaking, Ibn 'Umar spoke. He praised God, and said, "There have been caliphs before you who had sons. Your son is no better than their sons. They did not have in mind for their sons what you have in mind for your son. But rather, they left it to the Muslims to make whatever choice they knew[164] to be best. You are warning me not to split the staff of the Muslims, and not to strive to cause the destruction of their commonwealth. I have not been one to do that. {200} I am a member of the Muslim Community. If the Muslim Community agrees on something,

156 EI2, III, 545. Cf. Wellhausen, *Religio-Political Factions*, index.

157 Cf. Tab., index; *Aghānī*, XVI, 8.

158 Cf. Tab., index; *Aghānī*, XVI, 8, 10; Wellhausen, *Religio-Political Factions*, 99.

159 On the death of Sayfī b. Fusayl cf. *Ibn 'Asakir, *Tahdhīb*, VI, 459 (Khalifa); Tab., index; *Aghānī*, XVI, 7, 8; Dh., II, 293; Ibn 'Asakir, *Tahdhīb*, VI, 458.

160 Note on the death of Ka'b b. 'Ujra parallels #Ibn Hajar, VIII, 436 (Khalifa); *Ṭbq.*, 306; *Istī'āb*, 1321; Dh., II, 313; Ibn Hajar, VIII, 435.

161 Ibn Hajar, X, 452.

162 Muhammad b. Muslim b. 'Ubaydallah, d. 124/741–742 (EI, IV, 1239; GAS, I, 280).

163 From "When Mu'awiya resolved …" cf. Ibn A'tham, IV, 235, l. 11. Also *Dh., II, 259f. and as-Suyuti, 196f. (= Jarrett, 199f.) begin in the same place and run for several more lines. The end is marked below.

164 Z: *'amilū*; U and the parallels: *'alimū*.

then I am with them." Then he said, "God have mercy on you," and Ibn 'Umar left.[165] Then Mu'awiya sent for 'Abd ar-Rahman b. Abi Bakr. He recited the *shahāda* and began to speak. But 'Abd ar-Rahman b. Abi Bakr interrupted him and said, "You would have us entrust you to God in the matter of your son. But we shall not do that. You must refer this matter to a council of the Muslims, or else we shall convene one against you."[166] Then Mu'awiya jumped up and said, "Oh God, protect me from him as you wish!" Then he said, "Take it easy, man. Do not rely upon support by the Syrians. I am afraid that they will kill you first, unless I make it known this evening that you have pledged allegiance. Afterwards, do whatever seems proper to you."[167] Then he sent for Ibn az-Zubayr, and said, "Ibn az-Zubayr, you are a sly fox who emerges from one den only to enter another. You have turned to those two men, breathed in their nostrils, and convinced them to alter their opinions." Ibn az-Zubayr then spoke, saying, "If you have grown weary of the caliphate, resign and give us your son, and let us pledge allegiance to him. Can't you see that if we were to pledge allegiance to both you and your son [we would then have a problem]? Which of you would we listen to? Which of you would we obey? We shall never give the pledge to both of you at one time."[168] Then he rose. [253] Mu'awiya went and mounted the pulpit. He praised God and said, "We have found what the people say is wrong. They claimed that Ibn 'Umar, Ibn az-Zubayr, and Ibn Abi Bakr as-Siddiq did not pledge allegiance to Yazid. But they complied, and did pledge allegiance to him." But the Syrians said, "No! We will not be satisfied until they pledge allegiance in public. If they do not, we will cut off their heads!"[169] But Mu'awiya said, "Calm down. God be praised!

165 From "He recited the *shahāda* ..." cf. Ibn A'tham, IV, 242, l. 10.

166 U: *la-nu'īdanna-hā 'alay-ka jadh'atan*; Z: *la-n-f-ranna-hā 'alay-ka jadh'atan*; cf. Lane, 396b.

167 From "Then Mu'awiya sent for 'Abd ar-Rahman b. Abi Bakr ..." cf. Ibn A'tham, IV, 241, l. 12.

168 From "He recited the *shahāda* ..." cf. *Imāma*, I, 197; from "Then he sent for Ibn az-Zubayr, and said 'Ibn az-Zubayr, you are a sly fox ...'" cf. Ibn A'tham, IV, 243, l. 8.

169 Beheading was probably the most popular method of execution in those days, having the virtues of convenience, efficiency, and seemingly relative painlessness. The idea of beheading connotes much greater barbarity and terror to us now than it did to the Arabs of the seventh and eighth centuries, for whom beheading held the same associations as shooting or hanging hold for us. Of course, it would be ludicrous to translate "behead" as "shoot" or "hang," even though the psychological associations are equivalent. In the following pages the translation "behead" will occasionally be translated as "kill" or "execute." The literal meaning of the Arabic will be given in the notes.

How quick the people are to harm Quraysh! I do not want to hear this kind of talk from anyone after today."[170] Then he descended from the pulpit. The people said, "Ibn 'Umar, Ibn az-Zubayr, and Ibn Abi Bakr as-Siddiq pledged allegiance while denying it, but the people say, 'On the contrary, you did pledge allegiance.'" Mu'awiya departed, and returned to Syria.[171]

*Wahb < *my father < Ayyub[172] < Nafi':[173]
{201} Mu'awiya delivered a sermon in which he mentioned Ibn 'Umar, saying, "If he does not pledge allegiance, I will kill him." 'Abdallah b. 'Abdallah b. 'Umar went out to his father and, having traveled to Mecca in three [nights], he informed him. When he did so, Ibn 'Umar wept. The news reached 'Abdallah b. Safwan,[174] who went to Ibn 'Umar and said, "Did that man say such a thing in his sermon?" He answered, "Yes." Ibn Safwan asked, "What do you intend to do? Do you intend to fight him?" Ibn 'Umar said, "Ibn Safwan, it is better to be patient."[175] Ibn Safwan said, "If that is his intention, I shall certainly fight him." Mu'awiya went to Mecca and encamped at Dhu Tawa.[176] 'Abdallah b. Safwan went out to him and asked, "Are you the one who claims you will kill Ibn 'Umar if he does not pledge allegiance to your son?" He answered, "Would I kill Ibn 'Umar? I certainly would not do that."[177]

Wahb b. Jarir < *Juwayriya b. Asma' < some Medinese *shaykh*s:
'When Mu'awiya was near [254] Mecca, as he was leaving Marr,[178] he said to the captain of his guard, "Do not allow anyone to travel with me unless I myself give him a mount." So he went out traveling alone until, when he found himself in the middle of al-Arak,[179] al-Husayn b. 'Ali came upon him. He halted and said, "Greetings and welcome to the grandson of the

170 From "Mu'awiya went and mounted the pulpit ..." cf. Ibn A'tham, IV, 248, l. 1; *'Iqd*, IV, 372, l. 9–17.

171 From "When Mu'awiya resolved to designate his son Yazid as heir apparent ..." cf. *Dh., II, 259f.; as-Suyuti, 196f. (= Jarrett, 199f.).

172 Possibly Ayyub b. Abi Tamima as-Sakhtiyani (see note 61).

173 Probably the *mawlā* of 'Abdallah b. 'Umar, d. 118/736–737 (see note 62, above).

174 D. 73/692–693 (*Ṭbq.*, 591; *Jarḥ*, II, II, 84; Dh., III, 176; Ibn Hajar, V, 265).

175 Cf. Qur'ān 12:18.

176 Cf. *Futūḥ*, 49, 51; BGA, VII, 314; Tab., II, 1199; Yaqut, III, 553f.; *Aghānī*, index.

177 From "Mu'awiya delivered a sermon ..." cf. (*) Dh., II, 260; (*) Dh., III, 184.

178 Marr is also known as Batn Marr and Marr az-Zahran (cf. *Futūḥ*, 16; BGA, I, 20; III, 105, 106; VI, 131, 187; VII, 178; Yaqut, I, 667; IV, 493).

179 Al-Bakri, *Mu'jam*, I, 134; Yaqut, I, 182.

Prophet and master of the Muslim youth. Let us have a mount for Abu 'Abdallah[180] to ride!" A horse was brought, which he mounted.

Then 'Abd ar-Rahman b. Abi Bakr appeared. [Mu'awiya] said, "Greetings and welcome to the *shaykh* and master of the Quraysh, the son of the Truthful One[181] of this community. A mount for Abu Muhammad!"[182] A horse was brought, which he rode. Then Ibn 'Umar appeared. [Mu'awiya] said, "Greetings and welcome to the companion of the Prophet, the son of al-Faruq, and master of the Muslims." He called for a mount for him, which he rode. Then Ibn az-Zubayr appeared. [Mu'awiya] said to him, "Greetings and welcome to the son of the disciple of the Prophet, the son of as-Siddiq, and son of the paternal aunt of the Prophet."[183] Then he summoned a mount for him, which he rode. Then he set out accompanied only by them, and traveled until he entered Mecca. Then they were [regularly] the first to enter and the last to leave [Mu'awiya's house].[184] Every day he gave them gifts and treated them with generosity.[185] He made no mention to them of his intentions, until he had finished the pilgrimage rituals, and his baggage had departed.[186] Upon approaching the Ka'ba, he made his camels kneel. The people turned to each other {202} and said, "People! Do not be deceived. Surely he has not dealt with you as he has because of his love for you or his generosity toward you. He has only done what he has done because he wants something. So prepare an answer for him." They approached al-Husayn and said, "You, Abu 'Abdallah." But he said, "There is among you the *shaykh* and master of the Quraysh. He has more right to speak." They said, "You, Abu Muhammad" to 'Abd ar-Rahman b. Abi Bakr. He said, "I am not the right one either. But you have in your midst a companion of the Prophet, the son of the master of the [255] Muslims, namely Ibn 'Umar." They said to Ibn 'Umar, "You." He said, "I am not your leader.

180 I.e., al-Husayn b. 'Ali.

181 Siddiq, an epithet applied to the first caliph, Abu Bakr.

182 I.e., Ibn Abi Bakr.

183 Ibn az-Zubayr was actually the grandson of Abu Bakr as-Siddiq, whose daughter Asma' was Ibn az-Zubayr's mother. Ibn az-Zubayr's paternal grandmother was Safiyya bint 'Abd al-Muttalib, the paternal aunt of the Prophet. In addition to these blood relationships, the Prophet was also the uncle of Ibn az-Zubayr through marriage to 'A'isha, Ibn az-Zubayr's maternal aunt, and he was Ibn az-Zubayr's great uncle through marriage to Khadija bint Khuwaylid, the sister of Ibn az-Zubayr's paternal grandfather, al-'Awwam.

184 For an unrelated example of the use of the expression *awwal dākhil wa-ākhir khārij*, cf. *'Iqd*, IV, 204.

185 Z: *la-hum fī-hi ḥabā' wa-karāma*; U: *la-hum fī-hī ḥubban wa-karāma*.

186 From "When Mu'awiya was near Mecca ..." cf. Ibn A'tham, IV, 239, l. 13.

Appoint Ibn az-Zubayr to speak. He will protect you." They said, "You, Ibn az-Zubayr." He said, "Yes. If you give me your solemn pledge that you will not oppose me, I will protect you from that man." They said, "You have [our word on] that." The chamberlain came out, and permitted them to enter. Mu'awiya spoke. He praised God and said, "You know my behavior toward you, my blood relationship to you, my forgiveness toward you, and my tolerance of what you have done. Yazid, the son of the Commander of the Faithful, is your brother and your paternal cousin, and thinks most highly of you. I want you to address him as caliph, for you are the ones who install and remove caliphs, and collect taxes and distribute the funds. One does not interfere with you in this respect." But the people remained silent. He asked, "Are you not going to answer me?" But they remained silent. He turned to Ibn az-Zubayr and said, "Come here, Ibn az-Zubayr. You are the one who speaks for the people." [Ibn az-Zubayr] said, "Yes, Commander of the Faithful. We shall let you choose from three alternatives. The one you select shall be according to your desire." [Mu'awiya] said, "Fine. Tell me what they are." [Ibn az-Zubayr] said, "If you wish, you may do what the Prophet did. If you wish, you may do what Abu Bakr did, and he was the best member of this community after the Prophet. Or, if you wish, you may do what 'Umar did, and he was the best member of this community after Abu Bakr." [Mu'awiya] said, "Fine. What did they do?" [Ibn az-Zubayr] said, "The Prophet died without designating or authorizing anyone as his successor. The Muslims agreed upon Abu Bakr. So you may wish to desist from this affair until God decides it, and the Muslims then make a choice for themselves." [Mu'awiya] said, "But today there is no one among you like Abu Bakr. Abu Bakr was a man nobody {203} would oppose. I have no faith in you to overcome your differences of opinion." [Ibn az-Zubayr] said, "You have indeed spoken the truth. We do not wish you to leave us in charge of this community. [256] Do what Abu Bakr did." [Mu'awiya] said, "Fine. What did Abu Bakr do?" [Ibn az-Zubayr] said, "He selected a man of a distant branch of the Quraysh, who was neither one of his father's sons nor one of his nearer relatives, and he designated him as his successor. So you may wish to consider any man at all of the Quraysh, who is not of the Banu 'Abd Shams, and be satisfied with him."[187] [Mu'awiya] said, "Fine. What is the third alternative?" [Ibn az-Zubayr] said, "That you do what 'Umar did." [Mu'awiya] asked, "What did 'Umar do?" [Ibn az-Zubayr] said, "He put the matter in the hands of a council composed of six members of the Quraysh,

187 Dh., II, 262, l. 1: *fa-narḍā bi-hi.*

among whom were none of his sons or brothers, or members of his family." [Mu'awiya] said, "Do you have anything else to suggest?" [Ibn az-Zubayr] said, "No." [Mu'awiya] said [to the others], "And what about you?" They said, "Nor do we." [Mu'awiya] said, "As for [your answer] 'No,' I would like to submit to you that one who gives warning is excused.[188] Any of you who wanted to do so has been able to come up to me and call me a liar in public, and I have tolerated this of him. I am about to speak. If I speak truly, then my veracity is to my credit. If I speak falsely, then my lies will be held against me. I swear to you by God that if any of you utters one word in reply to me during my speech, he will not receive a word in response before I obtain his head. Let no man look out for anyone but himself." Then he summoned the captain of his guard and said, "Station two men from your guard corps to watch over every one of these people. If anyone should utter one word in reply to me while I am delivering my speech, either truthfully or falsely, have the two men strike him with their swords." Then he went out and they went out with him. He mounted the pulpit, praised God, and said, "These individuals are the leaders of the Muslims, and the best of the Muslims.[189] We cannot act independently of them, and we cannot carry out any plans except after consulting with them. They have pledged allegiance to Yazid, the son of the Commander of the Faithful, and have recognized him as heir apparent. So pledge allegiance, in the name of God." They confirmed it by shaking hands. Then [Mu'awiya] mounted his camel and departed. The people confronted them,[190] and said, "You made claims and declarations. But when you were made content and given gifts, you acted [in accordance with Mu'awiya's wishes]." They responded, "We did not do that." [The people] asked, "What prevented you from replying to the man when he lied?"[191] Then the Medinese and the people pledged allegiance, and [Mu'awiya] departed for Syria.[192]

188 From "Mu'awiya spoke. He praised God ..." cf. Ibn A'tham, IV, 245, l. 11 to 247, l. 6.

189 This sentence parallels Ibn A'tham, IV, 248, l. 3.

190 I.e. Al-Husayn b. 'Ali, Ibn 'Umar, Ibn az-Zubayr, and Ibn Abi Bakr.

191 From "The people confronted them ..." cf. Ibn A'tham, IV, 249, l. 4.

192 From "When Mu'awiya was near Mecca ..." (*) *'Iqd*, IV, 371, l. 9–372, l. 20; IA, III, 509ff.; cf. IA, III, 508f., which seems to be a distorted version; *Dh., II, 260ff.

{204}[257] *‘Abd ar-Rahman b. Mahdi < *Sufyan[193] < Muhammad b. al-Munkadir:[194]
When Yazid b. Mu‘awiya received the pledge of allegiance, Ibn ‘Umar said, “If he is good, we will be satisfied. If he proves to be an affliction, we will endure it patiently.”[195]

*‘Abd ar-Rahman < *Abu ‘Awana[196] < Dawud b. ‘Abdallah al-Awdi[197] < Humayd b. ‘Abd ar-Rahman:[198]
We went to see one of the Prophet’s companions when Yazid b. Mu‘awiya was designated successor. He asked, “Are you saying that Yazid is not the best member of Muhammad’s Community, and that he is not the most learned and most illustrious in the Community?” We said, “Yes.” He said, “I agree with you. But I truly think it is better when the Community of Muhammad is in agreement than when it is divided. Imagine a door which, if the Community of Muhammad tried to enter it, would be wide enough for them. Would one man, then, be unable to enter it?” We said, “No.” He said, “Imagine that every member of the Community of Muhammad were to say, ‘I will not shed my brother’s blood, or take my brother’s property. Would they be able to do this?” We answered, “Yes.” He said, “That is what I am telling you.” Then he said, “The Prophet said, ‘Modesty results in nothing but good.’”[199]

Isma‘il b. Sinan[200] < *Hammad b. Salama[201] < Ya‘la b. ‘Ata’[202] < his uncle:
I was with ‘Abdallah b. ‘Amr[203] when Yazid b. Mu‘awiya sent him to ‘Abdallah b. az-Zubayr. I heard ‘Abdallah b. ‘Amr say to Ibn az-Zubayr, “Know that I have found it written in the book[204] that you will be both

193 Perhaps Sufyan b. Sa‘id ath-Thawri, d. 162/778–779 (EI, IV, 500; GAS, I, 518).

194 D. 136/753–754 (*Ṭbq.*, 670; *Jarḥ*, IV, I, 97; *Ma‘ārif*, 461; Dh., V, 155; Ibn Hajar, IX, 473; cf. GAS, I, 65).

195 From “When Yazid b. Mu‘awiya received …” cf. *Dh., II, 260.

196 Al-Waddah b. ‘Abdallah, d. 176/792–793 (*Ṭbq.*, 539; *Ma‘ārif*, 503f.; Ibn Hajar, XI, 116).

197 Ibn Hajar, III, 191.

198 Possibly Humayd b. ‘Abd ar-Rahman al-Himyari, died in the eighties (*Ṭbq.*, 487; Ibn Hajar, III, 46). At-Tabari quotes a tradition from al-Himyari < Dawud b. ‘Abdallah al-Awdi < Abu ‘Awana (Tab., I, 1818).

199 Cf. Wensinck, I, 542 (*al-ḥayā’ lā ya’tīka illā bi-khayr*).

200 Abu ‘Ubayda al-Basri (al-Bukhari, *at-Ta’rīkh al-Kabir*, I, I, 358).

201 D. 167/784 (*Ṭbq.*, 537; *Ma‘ārif*, 503; *Fihrist* (trans.), 549; Ibn Hajar, III, 11; cf. GAS, I, 109, 406).

202 D. c. 120/737–738 (*Ṭbq.*, 726; Ibn Sa‘d, V, 520; Ibn Hajar, XI, 403).

203 ‘Abdallah b. ‘Amr b. al-‘As, d. 65/684–685 (GAS, I, 84).

204 I.e., foreordained, destined. ‘Abdallah b. ‘Amr was credited with the ability to foretell

tormentor [258] and tormented, and that you will claim the caliphate for yourself, although you are not [the rightful] caliph. I find {205} Yazid b. Mu'awiya to be [the rightful] caliph."[205]

Ashhal[206] < *Ibn 'Awn[207] < Muhammad < 'Uqba b. Aws as-Sadusi[208] < 'Abdallah b. 'Amr b. al-'As:
The king of the Holy Land is Mu'awiya, and his son [also].[209]

In 51/671 Mu'awiya b. Abi Sufyan led the pilgrimage.

Fadala b. 'Ubayd al-Ansari conducted a winter naval campaign in the land of the Byzantines.[210]

In this year, the following died: 'Amr b. Hazm al-Ansari;[211] Jarir b. 'Abdallah al-Bajali;[212] Sa'id b. Zayd b. 'Amr b. Nufayl;[213] Maymuna,[214] the wife of the Prophet; Ka'b b. 'Ujra al-Ansari.

In this year, az-Zuhri[215] was born.[216]

---

the future. According to Ibn Qutayba, he was able to read Syriac (*Ma'ārif*, 287). According to at-Tabari, he had read "the books of Daniel" (*kutub Dāniyāl*; Tab., II, 399). The Biblical Book of Daniel, much of which is in Aramaic (of which Syriac is a dialect), was considered a source of prophetic information by the Arabs (cf. Rosenthal, *History of Muslim Historiography*, 112, and EI2, II, 112, s.v. Dāniyāl). Cf. also the report by adh-Dhahabi about a Jew who "read books" (*qara'a l-kutub*) and prognosticated the fall of the Umayyads (Dh., III, 278, l. 3).

205 From "I was with 'Abdallah b. 'Amr …" cf. *Dh., III, 91.

206 Ibn Hatim al-Jumahi, d. c. 208/823–824 (Ibn Hajar, I, 360).

207 Perhaps 'Abdallah b. 'Awn, d. 151/768–769 (*Ṭbq.*, 528; Ibn Hajar, V, 346).

208 *Ṭbq.*, 471; Ibn Hajar, VII, 237.

209 This sentence parallels (*) Dh., III, 91.

210 This sentence parallels al-Ya'qubi, II, 285; Tab., II, 111.

211 For the notice of the death of 'Amr b. Hazm al-Ansari cf. #Ibn Hajar, VIII, 20 (Khalifa); *Ṭbq.*, 202; *Istī'āb*, 1172; Dh., II, 309; Ibn Hajar, VIII, 20.

212 For the notice of the death of Jarir b. 'Abdallah al-Bajali cf. #Ibn Hajar, II, 74 (Khalifa).

213 For the notice of the death of Sa'id b. Zayd b. 'Amr b. Nufayl cf. #Ibn Hajar, IV, 34 (Khalifa); *Ṭbq.*, 49; *Istī'āb*, 614; Dh., II, 285; Ibn Hajar, IV, 34.

214 For the notice of the death of Maymuna cf. *an-Nawawi, I, II, 356 (Khalifa); *Dh., II, 325 (Khalifa); EI, III, 146.

215 See n. 162 above.

216 This sentence parallels *Dh., V, 147 (Khalifa); *Ibn Hajar, IX, 450 (Khalifa).

[259] The Year 52/672

In this[217] year, ‘Ubaydallah b. Abi Bakra made peace with [the] Zunbil with respect to Kabul and its environs, for a tribute of 1 million *dirhams*.[218]

Sa‘id b. al-‘As led the pilgrimage.

Busr b. Artat conducted a winter campaign in the land of the Byzantines. He was accompanied by Sufyan b. ‘Awf az-Zuhri.[219]

{206} In this year, the following died: Abu Bakra,[220] for whom Abu Barza al-Aslami[221] recited the prayers, in Basra; ‘Imran b. Husayn,[222] in Basra.

[260] The Year 53/672–673

In this year, Ziyad b. Abi Sufyan died in Kufa. He designated Samura b. Jundub[223] as governor over Basra, and ‘Abdallah b. Khalid b. Asid[224] as governor over Kufa. Mu‘awiya dismissed ‘Abdallah b. Khalid and appointed ad-Dahhak b. Qays al-Fihri to [the post].[225]

[Mu‘awiya] dismissed ‘Ubaydallah b. Abi Bakra from [his post in] Sijistan and appointed ‘Abbad b. Ziyad.[226] ‘Abbad raided Qandahar,[227] and reached Bayt adh-Dhahab.[228] The people of al-Hind raised an army

217 See n. 87.

218 This sentence parallels *Futūḥ*, 397; *Dh., II, 262.

219 From “Busr b. Artat conducted …” cf. al-Ya‘qubi, II, 285; Tab., II, 157 (two versions); *Ibn ‘Asakir, X, 7 (Khalifa); Dh., II, 290; Ibn ‘Asakir, *Tahdhīb*, VI, 191. These writers have al-Azdi rather than az-Zuhri.

220 For the notice of the death of Abu Bakra cf. #Dh., II, 329 (Khalifa); Nufay‘ b. al-Harith ath-Thaqafi (EI2, I, 111).

221 Nadla b. ‘Abdallah, d. c. 64/683–684 (*Ṭbq.*, 241; *Istī‘āb*, 1610; Dh., II, 328; Ibn Hajar, X, 446).

222 *Ṭbq.*, 234; *Istī‘āb*, 1208; Dh., II, 306; Ibn Hajar, VIII, 125.

223 *Ṭbq.*, 112; Tab., index; *Istī‘āb*, 653; Dh., II, 290; Ibn Hajar, IV, 236.

224 Cf. *Ma‘ārif*, 195, l. 11; Ibn Hazm, 91; Zambaur, *Manuel de généalogie*, index.

225 This sentence parallels (*) Dh., III, 22 (Khalifa).

226 This sentence parallels (*) Dh., III, 189, (Khalifa); (*) Ibn Hajar, V, 93 (Khalifa); Bosworth, 43–45; EI2, I, 5; Ibn ‘Asakir, *Tahdhīb*, VII, 218; Ibn Hajar, V, 93; Dh., III, 260.

227 EI2, IV, 535.

228 Bayt adh-Dhahab may refer to a shrine in the city of Multan. Cf. *Fihrist* (trans.), 829; Idrisi, 51, 96, and 149; Gabrieli, 288; cf. EI, III, 721, s.v. Multan.

against him. He battled them, and God put the people of al-Hind to rout. He remained as governor over Sijistan until Mu'awiya died.[229]

'Abd ar-Rahman b. Umm al-Hakam[230] conducted a winter campaign in the land of the Byzantines.[231]

Mu'awiya appointed 'Ubaydallah b. Ziyad over Khurasan.[232]

In this year, Yazid b. al-Muhallab was born.[233]

Ziyad died at the age of 53.

It is said that in this year 'Abd ar-Rahman b. Abi Bakr as-Siddiq died.

{207} During the governorship of Ziyad over Iraq, there occurred the affair of Qurayb and Zahhaf, who were maternal cousins.

[261] *Wahb b. Jarir < my father < Jarir b. Zayd:[234]
Qurayb and Zahhaf revolted during the governorship of Ziyad. There were 70 men involved. That was in the month of *Ramaḍān*. They came upon the Banu Dubay'a while they were in their mosque. [On their way] they confronted one of them, whose name was Ru'ba b. al-Mukhabbal, and killed him.[235]

Wahb < my father < *az-Zubayr b. al-Khirrit[236] < Abu Labid:[237]
On the night he was killed, Ru'ba b. al-Mukhabbal spoke earlier that evening about something he had reported previously. He said, "If I have told the truth, may God make me a martyr before I reach home."[238] They came upon him that night before he reached his house, and killed him. Then they went to the mosque of the Banu Qutay'a.[239]

Wahb < *my father < Qatan al-Azraa[240] < one of their *shaykh*s
We were standing in the mosque, when suddenly they were at the doors of the mosque. They were uttering the slogan "Judgment belongs to God

229 From "[Mu'awiya] dismissed 'Ubaydallah b. Abi Bakra …" cf. *Futūḥ*, 397 and 434; Ibn 'Asakir, *Tahdhīb*, VII, 219, l. 2; *Dh., II, 263; (*) Dh., IV, 17.

230 Cf. *Ṭbq.*, 786.

231 This sentence parallels Tab., II, 157; *Dh., II, 263.

232 This sentence parallels *Dh., II, 263; *Dh., III, 44 (Khalifa).

233 This sentence parallels *Ibn Khallikān, VI, 306 (Khalifa).

234 U: *Jarīr b. Yazid.* Ibn Hajar, II, 72.

235 From "Qurayb and Zahhaf revolted …" cf. al-Mubarrad, 581; *Dh., II, 262f.

236 Ibn Hajar, III, 314.

237 Limaza b. Zabbar (Ibn Hajar, VIII, 457).

238 From "On the night he was killed …" cf. *Dh., II, 263.

239 This sentence parallels *Ansāb*, IV-A, 151, l. 10.

240 Unidentified.

alone."[241] They turned against the people in the mosque to kill them. The people jumped over the partitions and ran for the doors. A man ascended the minaret and began to call, "Cavalry of God, mount up and ride!"[242] They went up after him, and killed him.[243] Only after everyone in the mosque had fled or been slain did they go out into the street, shouting, "Judgment belongs to God alone!" A man of the Banu Qutay'a went out the door of his house and found himself face to face with them as they passed his door. One of them struck him with his sword the moment he stuck his head out [the door], and cut off his chin. He went back in, and closed the door. He had just recently been married. His wife went to him and bandaged him with a veil of hers which was dyed [red] with [extract of] Brazilwood.[244] It healed, and he recovered.

{208} Qatan:
I saw him. His mouth was twisted [because of the injury to his chin].[245]

[262] [Qatan:]
That man also told me about them.

[Qatan:]
They went on. A man from the neighborhood approached them with a sword in his hand. Some people looking down on him from the roofs of the houses called out to him, "Oh so-and-so! Watch out for the Harurites!" One of them said, "We are not the Harurites. We are the guard." So the man felt safe, and continued on until they came upon him and killed him.[246] They proceeded until they entered the mosque of the Ma'awil, and killed everyone in it Then they went out to the dwellings of the Banu 'Ali.

*Wahb < *my father < *Jarir b. Zayd:
They went to the dwellings of the Banu 'Ali, who came out to battle them.

241 The Arabic verb is *ḥakkamū*. The Kharijites are sometimes referred to as *al-Muḥakkima*, 'those who utter the slogan, *lā ḥukma illā li-llāh* ("Judgment belongs to God alone"). Cf. Wellhausen, *Religio-Political Factions*, index s.v. *taḥkīm*.

242 For the use of this expression in connection with other events, cf. *'Uyūn*, I, 117; Tab., II, 284, 919, 1318.

243 From "We were standing in the mosque ..." cf. *Ansāb*, IV-A, 151, l. 10; (*) Dh., II, 263.

244 The meaning may perhaps be rather "... a veil [*khimār*] which seemed to have been dyed [red] with Brazilwood dye [because of the blood it absorbed]." On the *khimār* cf. Dozy, 169f. On Brazilwood (*baqqam*), cf. Idrisi, 130.

245 From "A man of the Banu Qutay'a ..." cf. *Ansāb*, IV, IV-A, 151, l. 9 (a one-line summary).

246 From "They went on ..." cf. al-Mubarrad, 581, l. 16.

They were bowmen, and shot arrows at them until they killed them all.[247] In the morning, we went out – we were youths – and behold! They had been gibbeted at Hafr as-Sa'diyin. A young woman came with a large bowl filled with money. She saw them and said, "Peace to you, for all that you have steadfastly endured. How wonderful is the reward in Paradise!"[248] She was seized and gibbeted with them.[249] It is as if I see her [even now] with the money, and nobody paying any attention to it. Qurayb and Zahhaf were maternal cousins.

*Wahb < *Ghassan b. Mudar[250] < *Sa'id b. Yazid:[251]
Qurayb and Zahhaf revolted while Ziyad was in Kufa and Samura [b. Jundub] was in Basra. They went out one night and encamped at the cemetery of the Banu Yashkur. But [263] the Mudarite Kharijites did not show up. They said to one another, "We should separate." They said, "Each one of you is known in the place from which he came. You will be pursued to your houses and killed." That was in the month of *Ramaḍān*. There were 70 men among them. {209} They approached and came upon the Banu Dubay'a. They came to one of their *shaykh*s, whose name was Habkan.[252] When he saw them, he said, "Welcome, Abu sh-Sha'tha'," thinking that [one of them) was Ibn Hisn,[253] the chief of police. They killed him.[254] They separated in the mosques of al-Azd. One group went to the Banu 'Ali while another group went to the mosque of al-Ma'awil. Sayf b. Wahb and some of his companions attacked them with shield and lance. He could hit a man and lift him off the ground. Whoever came to him he killed. The youths of the Banu 'Ali and the Banu Rasib attacked Qurayb and Zahhaf with arrows. Qurayb said, "Is so-and-so in this crowd?" – referring to 'Abdallah b. Aws at-Tahi, the paternal uncle of Tawq. Aws had competed with him before that. They answered, "Yes." He said, "Then let him come forward for a duel." 'Abdallah b. Aws killed him, and took his head.[255]

247 From "They went to the dwellings of the Banu 'Ali ..." cf. al-Mubarrad, 582, l. 1; *Dh., II, 263.

248 Cf. Qur'ān 13:24.

249 From "In the morning, we went out ..." cf. *Ansāb*, IV-A, 152, l. 6.

250 D. 184/800–801 (Ibn Hajar, VIII, 247).

251 Al-Azdi, d. before 131/748–749 (*Ṭbq.*, 522; Ibn Hajar, IV, 100).

252 *Ansāb*, Tab.: *Ḥakkāk*.

253 'Abdallah b. Hisn was Ziyad's chief of police in Basra (Kh., 249).

254 From "They approached and came upon the Banu Dubay'a ..." cf. *Ansāb*, IV-A, 151, l. 8.

255 From "Qurayb and Zahhaf revolted ..." cf. Tab., II, 90f. (abridged).

[Sa'id b. Yazid:]
Ziyad came from Kufa with Mas'ud b. 'Amr.[256] Ziyad was vigorously upbraiding him,[257] saying to him, "You did and you did [?]." Mas'ud said, "That is not true." Ziyad said, "Did a companion of the Prophet lie?" Then he said, "Tahiyites, if you had not killed them [the Kharijites], I would send you to jail."[258] The Banu 'Ali claimed that they had killed them, while the Banu Rasib claimed that they had killed them. They said, "The arrows will determine whether it was us or them." They found that the arrows of the Banu 'Ali were more numerous among the slain.

Sa'id b. Yazid:
Qurayb and Zahhaf were the first of the Harurites to revolt after [the battle of] an-Nahrawan.[259] Qurayb was of the Banu Iyad, and Zahhaf was of the Banu Tayyi'. They were maternal cousins.[260]

{210} Wahb < *Ghassan b. Mudar < *Sa'id b. [264] Yazid:
Abu Bilal[261] said, "Qurayb – may God not accept him![262] I swear, I would rather fall from heaven to earth than do what he did," referring to indiscriminate massacring.[263]

Wahb < my father:
Ziyad was severe in dealing with the Harurites after the revolt of Qurayb and Zahhaf. He killed them, and ordered Samura [b. Jundub] to kill them. He killed many of them.[264]

Abu 'Ubayda:
Zahhaf, a Ta'i, and Qurayb, an Iyadi of the [Banu] Iyad b. Sud, revolted. They

256 Mas'ud was the leader of the Azd in Basra. Cf. Wellhausen, *Arab Kingdom*, index.

257 It is not clear whether he was upbraiding Mas'ud or 'Abdallah b. Aws (cf. Tab., II, 91). The meaning of this sentence, and that of the dialogue in the following sentences, is rather vague. This portion – among others – was eliminated in Tab.'s version of the passage.

258 From "Ziyad came from Kufa ..." cf. Tab., II, 91 (abridged).

259 EI, III, 836. On the battle, cf. Wellhausen, *Religio-Political Factions*, index; Brunnow, 169f.

260 From "Qurayb and Zahhaf were the first ..." cf. Tab., II, 91.

261 Mirdas b. Udayya (EI, III, 514; Wellhausen, *Religio-Political Factions*, index, s.v. Abu Bilāl).

262 Abu Bilal is punning on Qurayb's name. The Arabic is *Qurayb – lā qarrabahu llāh*.

263 From "Abu Bilal said ..." cf. *Ansāb*, IV-A, 151, l. 6; al-Mubarrad, 581f. Tab., II, 91. See also *Isti'rād*, the killing of men, women, and children who did not agree with the Kharijites, was practised by some of the so-called Kharijites. On *Isti'rād* cf. Wellhausen, *Religio-Political Factions*, 41, 47, 51; C. Pellat, in EI2, IV, 269.

264 From "Ziyad was severe ..." cf. Tab., II, 91; *Dh., II, 263.

killed Ru'ba b. al-Mukhabbal. Then they killed Jabir b. Ka'b al-Judaydi. They beat Bukayr b. Wa'il at-Tahi on his arm and he warded [them] off.[265]

Abu 'Ubayda:
Ziyad was riding when he was joined by Shaqiq b. Thawr,[266] Hajjar b. Abjar,[267] and 'Abbad b. Husayn al-Habati.[268] They had wounded Shaqiq in the forehead, and had knocked down Hajjar b. Abjar. Shaqiq had rescued him.[269] It was claimed that Ziyad told the Banu 'Ali, "If they escape, you will receive no stipend from me." So the warriors battled them, and the women and children pelted them from the roofs of the houses, until they were killed.[270]

Sa'id b. al-'As led the pilgrimage.

[265] The Year 54/673–674

In this year, Mu'awiya dismissed Sa'id b. al-'As from [the governorship of] Medina, and appointed Marwan b. al-Hakam to the post.[271] Marwan appointed Mus'ab b. 'Abd ar-Rahman b. 'Awf[272] as judge.

'Ubaydallah b. Ziyad led a raiding expedition in Khurasan. He crossed the river[273] to Bukhara on camel, and was the first Arab to cross the river

265 This sentence parallels *Ansāb*, IV-A, 151, l. 11; cf. *Ansāb*, IV-A, 152, l. 17.

266 D. 64/683–684 (Ibn 'Asakir, *Tahdhīb*, VI, 333; Dh., III, 18; Ibn Hajar, IV, 361.

267 *Ṭbq.*, 327; Ibn Sa'd, VI, 231; Ibn 'Asakir, *Tahdhīb*, IV, 84; cf. Wellhausen, *Religio-Political Factions*, 30.

268 *Ma'ārif*, 414; Tab., II, 453; Ibn al-Athir, *al-Lubāb*, I, 275.

269 From "They had wounded Shaqiq ..." cf. *Ansāb*, IV-A, 151, l. 13.

270 From "Ziyad told the Banu 'Ali ..." cf. Tab., II, 91.

271 This sentence parallels Tab., II, 164; (*) Dh., II, 264.

272 D. 64/683–684 (*Ṭbq.*, 585; *Ma'ārif*, 237ff. Dh., III, 82; Tab., index).

273 The *Amū Darya* (Oxus) is meant.

to Bukhara.[274] He conquered Zamin[275] and half of {211} Baykand,[276] which are part of Bukhara.[277]

Mu'awiya dismissed Samura b. Jundub from [the governorship of] Basra and appointed 'Abdallah b. 'Amr b. Ghaylan ath-Thaqafi,[278] who remained in office for six months. Mu'awiya appointed ad-Dahhak b. Qays [al-Fihri] as governor over Kufa.[279]

Muhammad b. Malik conducted a winter campaign in the land of the Byzantines.[280]

Marwan b. al-Hakam led the pilgrimage.

In this year, Maslama b. Mukhallad sent Khalid b. Thabit al-Fahmi[281] on a raiding expedition in the [266] Maghrib, and ordered him to leave Abu l-Muhajir Dinar,[282] of the Ansar, as his lieutenant. He set out, leaving Abu l-Muhajir to take his place.

*Hatim b. Muslim:
When ad-Dahhak b. Qays was governor over Kufa, he sent Masqala b. Hubayra ash-Shaybani[283] to Tabaristan.[284] He made peace with the

274 On the various traditions associated with the conquest of Bukhara, cf. Gibb, 17ff.; R. N. Frye in EI2. I, 1293 s.v. Bukhara.

275 *Zāmīn* is mentioned frequently in the first six volumes of BGA. Cf. Zambaur, *Münzprägungen*, 131. In their parallel accounts, the following variations occur: *R-'-m-d-y-n* (*Futūḥ*); *Rāmīthan* (Tab. cf. *Rāmīthana*, BGA, I, 307, note b, 310; II, 360; III, 267, note c; cf. Yaqut, II, 739.

276 Baykand is mentioned frequently in all volumes of BGA. Cf. also Yaqut, I, 797; LeStrange, 463; Gibb, 18; Frye, *Bukhārā*, 11, 13, 179; Minorsky, 352, and index s.v. Paykand. Tab., II, 169 also has the unusual expression "and half of Baykand" (*wa-niṣf Baykand*).

277 From "'Ubaydallah b. Ziyad led a raiding expedition ..." cf. *Futūḥ*, 410f.; al-Ya'qubi, II, 281; Tab., II, 169; *Dh., II, 264; *Dh., III, 44 (Khalifa).

278 Dh., III, 267.

279 This sentence parallels *Dh., III, 22 (Khalifa).

280 This sentence parallels cf. al-Ya'qubi, II, 285; Tab., II, 163.

281 Kh.: al-Fihri. Cf. IAH, 231; Kindi, 15; Ibn 'Asakir, *Tahdhīb*, V, 29f.

282 Ibn 'Abdallah an-Nahudhi (Cf. as-Sam'ani, 573b = Ibn al-Athir, *al-Lubāb*, III, 250; IAH, 197ff.).

283 Cf. *Futūḥ*, 335f.; *Ma'ārif*, 403; *Aghānī*, index.

284 This sentence parallels *Futūḥ*, 335; cf. *Ma'ārif*, 403; cf. Tab., II, 1322; (*) Dh., II, 264.

inhabitants against payment of 500,000 *dirhams*, with a weight of five [*mithqāls*],[285] 100 *ṭaylasāns*,[286] and 300 head [of slaves].____________.[287]

In this year, the following died: Hakim b. Huzam,[288] Makhrama b. Nawfal,[289] Abu Qatada,[290] Huwaytib b. 'Abd al-'Uzza[291] of the Banu 'Amir b. Lu'ayy, Thawban,[292] [and] Sa'id b. Yarbu' al-Makhzumi.[293]

[267] The Year 55/674–675

In this year, Mu'awiya dismissed 'Abdallah b. 'Amr b. Ghaylan from the governorship of Basra and appointed {212} 'Ubaydallah b. Ziyad to the post. He remained in office until [Mu'awiya] died, and was retained by Yazid.

Sufyan b. 'Awf conducted a winter campaign in the land of the Byzantines.[294] Yazid b. Shajara ar-Rahawi[295] conducted a raiding expedition,

285 I.e. each *dirham* weighed 5/10ths of a *mithqāl*, which was standard in Tabaristan (*Futūḥ*, 465–66). On the standard and variant weights of the *dirham*, see G. C. Miles in EI2, II, 319, s.v. *dirham*.

286 On the *ṭaylasān*, a kind of mantle, cf. Dozy, 278ff. and 254ff; Hitti, *History of the Arabs*, 334.

287 The phrasing of the final sentence of this report is ambiguous, and is translatable in several different ways, none more meaningful than another. In the version of Masqala's raid as reported by al-Baladhuri (*Futūḥ*, 335) and at-Tabari (Tab., II, 1322), there is no indication that Masqala conquered anyone, but rather that his army, himself included, was trapped by the enemy in a mountain pass and annihilated. Perhaps Khalifa confused this expedition with a later one against Tabaristan led by Yazid b. al-Muhallab in 98/716–717 (cf. Kh., 424). In that campaign, Yazid sent Hayyan an-Nabati, who had been a *mawlā* of Masqala b. Hubayra (*Futūḥ*, 337), to reach an agreement with the Isbahbadh of Tabaristan. The name in the present account which is pointed by both U and Z as *B-y-r-k* might possibly be Nayzak (Nezak Tarkhan), a prominent leader of the inhabitants of Khurasan (cf. Shaban, *'Abbasid Revolution*, index s.v. Nesak; Tab., II, 1222 ff.).

288 On the notice of the death of Hakim b. Huzam cf. #Ibn Hajar, II, 448 (Khalifa). See also *Ṭbq*., 31; *Istī'āb*, 362; Dh., II, 277; Ibn Hajar, II, 447.

289 GAS, I, 259.

290 Cf. note 42.

291 On the notice of the death of Huwaytib b. 'Abd al-'Uzza cf. *Ibn Hajar, III, 67 (Khalifa). See also GAS, I, 261.

292 Abu 'Abdallah, a *mawlā* of the Prophet (*Ṭbq*., 15; *Ma'ārif*, 147; Dh., II, 273; Ibn 'Asakir, *Tahdhīb*, III, 378; Ibn Hajar, II, 31).

293 *Ṭbq*., 47; *Istī'āb*, 626; Ibn 'Asakir, *Tahdhīb*, VI, 178; Dh., II, 289; Ibn Hajar, IV, 99.

294 This sentence parallels Tab., II, 171 (al-Waqidi).

295 *Ṭbq*., 171; *Ma'ārif*, 448; *Istī'āb*, 1577; Ibn Hazm, 412, 413. Rahawi is the vocalization given by Ibn al-Athir, *al-Lubāb*, I, 483. See also *Ṭbq*., 783.

in the course of which he was killed. According to some, he was not killed in this raid, but some time later.[296]

Marwan b. al-Hakam led the pilgrimage.

In this year the following died: Sa'd b. Malik;[297] Abu l-Yasar.[298]

Abu l-Hasan:
Zayd b. Thabit died in this year.

[268] The Year 56/675–676

In this year, Mu'awiya dismissed 'Ubaydallah b. Ziyad from the governorship of Khurasan, replacing him with Sa'id b. 'Uthman b. 'Affan. Sa'id set out on a raiding expedition, accompanied by al-Muhallab b. Abi Sufra, Talha b. 'Abdallah b. Khalaf[299] – [known as] Talha at-Talahat – Aws b. Tha'laba of the Banu Taym Allat, and Rabi'a b. 'Isl al-Yarbu'i. When he raided Samarqand, the Sughdians[300] went out to battle him, but he forced them back into their city. They made peace with him, and gave him pledges.[301]

Mas'id b. Abi Mas'ud conducted a winter expedition in the land of the Byzantines. According to some, it was Junada b. Abi Umayya[302] [who wintered in the land of the Byzantines].[303]

Al-Walid b. 'Utba b. Abi Sufyan led the pilgrimage.

In this year, the following died: Ishaq b. Talha b. 'Ubaydallah,[304] in Khurasan; Juwayriya bint al-Harith,[305] the wife of the Prophet.

296 From "Yazid b. Shajara ar-Rahawi ..." cf. Tab., II, 173; (*) *Istī'āb*, 1577; *Dh., II, 264.

297 Sa'd b. Malik = Sa'd b. Abi Waqqas (EI, IV, 29).

298 Ka'b b. 'Amr (*Ṭbq.*, 225; *Istī'āb*, 1776 and 1322; Dh., II, 339; Ibn Hajar, VIII, 437 and XII, 281).

299 Ibn Hajar, V, 17; Ibn Asakir, *Tahdhīb*, VII, 65.

300 EI, IV, 473.

301 I.e., human hostages. Cf. Tab., II, 179, where it is stated that among the "pledges" were 50 sons of the important people of the city. Cf. also Tab., II, 1423, and Ibn A'tham, IV, 198. From "In this year, Mu'awiya dismissed 'Ubaydallah ..." cf. Tab., II, 178f. (al-Mada'ini); *Dh., II, 264f; from "When he raided Samarqand ..." cf., *Ibn Asakir, *Tahdhīb*, VI, 155, l. 7 (Khalifa).

302 D. 80/699–700 (*Ṭbq.*, 255; *Istī'āb*, 249; Dh., III, 146; Ibn 'Asakir, *Tahdhīb*, III, 408; Ibn Hajar, II, 115.

303 From "Mas'id b. Abi Mas'ud conducted ..." cf. al-Ya'qubi, II, 285; cf. Tab., II, 173.

304 Kh.: Ishaq b. Yahya b. Talha b. 'Ubaydallah (*Ma'ārif*, 232, l. 12; Ibn 'Asakir, *Tahdhīb*, II, 441).

305 *Istī'āb*, 1804; Dh., II, 275; Ibn Hajar, XII, 407.

{213}[269] The Year 52/676–677

In this year, Mu'awiya dismissed ad-Dahhak b. Qays from the governorship of Kufa, and appointed 'Abd ar-Rahman b. Umm al-Hakam to the post.

In this year, Mu'awiya b. Abi Sufyan sent Hassan b. an-Nu'man al-Ghassani[306] to Ifriqiya. The Berbers whom he encountered made peace with him, and he imposed the *kharāj* on them.[307] He remained commander there until Mu'awiya died.

Mu'awiya dismissed Marwan b. al-Hakam from the governorship of Medina and appointed al-Walid b. 'Utba b. Abi Sufyan, who served as governor until Mu'awiya died. He appointed al-Walid b. Zama'a al-'Amiri as judge of Medina. Mu'awiya dismissed Sa'id b. 'Uthman from the governorship of Khurasan and appointed 'Abd ar-Rahman[308] b. Ziyad.[309]

'Abdallah b. Qays[310] conducted a winter expedition in the land of the Byzantines.[311]

In this year, the following died: 'A'isha, the Mother of the Faithful; Abu Hurayra.[312]

Al-Walid b. 'Utba b. Abi Sufyan led the pilgrimage.

[270] The Year 58/677–678

Khalifa:

In this year, Malik b. 'Abdallah conducted a winter campaign in the land of the Byzantines.[313] {214} Yazid b. Shajara ar-Rahawi conducted a raid, in the course of which he and his companions were killed.[314]

Al-Walid b. 'Utba b. Abi Sufyan led the pilgrimage.

306 EI2, III, 271.

307 From "In this year, Mu'awiya b. Abi Sufyan sent Hassan ..." cf. *Dh., III, 151 (Khalifa).

308 Kh.: 'Ubaydallah b. Ziyad, but cf. Zambaur, *Manuel de généalogie*, 47.

309 This sentence parallels *Futūḥ*, 413; cf. *Ma'ārif*, 347, l. 15; cf. Tab., II, 189.

310 Cf. Ibn Hajar, V, 364, #627.

311 This sentence parallels al-Ya'qubi, II, 285; Tab., II, 180; *Dh., II, 265.

312 On the notice of the death of Abu Hurayra cf. #Ibn Hajar, XII, 266 (Khalifa). See also EI2, I, 129; cf. GAS, I, index.

313 This sentence parallels al-Ya'qubi, II, 285; Tab., II, 181.

314 This sentence parallels al-Ya'qubi, II, 285; Tab., II, 181 (al-Waqidi).

In this year, the following died: ‘Ubaydallah b. al-‘Abbas b. ‘Abd al-Muttalib;[315] ‘Uqba b. ‘Amir al-Juhani.[316]

Baqi[317] < *Ibn Bukayr < al-Layth:
In 58, there took place the expedition against Rhodes by Akdar[318] and Sa‘id b. Yazid, as did the expedition of Malik al-Abjar[319] in Ifriqiya. In this year, [Mu‘awiya] dismissed Marwan from his governorship over the Medinese and appointed al-Walid b. ‘Utba.

Baqi < *Bakkar b. ‘Abdallah < Muhammad b. ‘A’idh < *al-Walid < *Yazid and others:
[271] In 58, ‘Amr b. Murra[320] conducted a winter campaign in Badhandun.[321] Al-Husayn b. Numayr[322] conducted the summer campaign against the Byzantines.

Khalifa and al-Layth:
Al-Walid b. ‘Utba b. Abi Sufyan led the pilgrimage.

{215}[272] The Year 59/678–679

Khalifa:
In this year, Abu l-Muhajir Dinar conducted a raiding expedition and attacked Qartajanna.[323] They battled, and the dead and wounded on both sides were many. When night separated them, the Muslims withdrew and encamped at a mountain facing Tunis. Then they returned to battle them again. They made peace with them on condition that they evacuate

315 On the notice of the death of ‘Ubaydallah b. al-‘Abbas b. ‘Abd al-Muttalib cf. #*Istī‘āb*, 1010 (Khalifa); #an-Nawawi, I, I, 312 (Khalifa); #Dh., III, 282 (Khalifa); #Ibn Hajar, VII, 20 (Khalifa).

316 On the notice of the death of ‘Uqba b. ‘Amir al-Juhani cf. #*Istī‘āb*, 1073 (Khalifa); #Ibn Hajar, VII, 243 (Khalifa). See also *Ṭbq.*, 266; *Istī‘āb*, 1073; Dh., II, 306; Ibn Hajar, VII, 242.

317 The remainder of the material in this chapter was added by Baqi b. Makhlad.

318 Cf. IAH, 191: al-Akdar b. Humam; cf. al-Kindi, 26, 43, 45–46: al-Akdar b. Hammam b. ‘Amir al-Lakhmi, killed in the middle of *Jumādā* II 65/January 685; cf. al-Ya‘qubi, II, 306, l. 5 (MS Akdar emended by the editor to Ukaydir).

319 U: Malik b. al-Abjar. Unidentified.

320 Al-Juhani (*Ṭbq.*, 264; *Isti‘āb*, 1200; Dh., II, 310; Ibn Hajar, VIII, 103.

321 Kh.: al-Badhbadhun. Podandus of antiquity (Honigmann, index, s.v. Podandos; Minorsky, 220; Zambaur, *Münzprägungen*, 69.

322 Al-Kindi = as-Sakuni (Ibn ‘Asakir, *Tahdhīb*, IV, 371; Ibn Hajar, II, 392; Dh., III, 13).

323 Carthage.

the peninsula[324] for them. [Abu] al-Muhajir came to the springs of Abu l-Muhajir.[325] He conquered Mila,[326] and remained on this raiding expedition for about two years.[327]

'Amr b. Murra al-Juhani[328] conducted a winter land campaign in the land of the Byzantines. There was no naval campaign this year.[329]

In this year, the following died: Sa'id b. al-'As,[330] Jubayr b. Mut'im,[331] Shayba b. 'Uthman,[332] [and] 'Abd Allah b. 'Amir b. Kurayz.[333]

In this year, 'Awf b. Abi Jamila al-A'rabi[334] was born.

Mu'awiya died in Damascus on Thursday 22 *Rajab*/9 May 679. His son, Yazid b. Mu'awiya, recited the prayers for him. Some say Yazid was not present, and that ad-Dahhak b. Qays was the one who recited the prayers for him. [273] Mu'awiya died at 82 years of age. According to some, he was 80; according to others, {216} 86. His reign lasted 19 years, three months, and 20 days. He was born in Mecca, in the house of Abu Sufyan b. Harb. Some say he was born in the house of 'Utba b. Rabi'a.[335]

The following died in the last year of Mu'awiya's reign: Usama

324 The Arabic is *al-jazīra*, which usually means "island."

325 Cf. Abu Bakr al-Maliki, *Riyād*, 21: *al-'uyūn al-ma'rūfa bi-Abī l-Muhājir*, ("the springs known as [the Springs of] Abu l-Muhajir), near Tlemcen; cf. Ibn Khaldun, *Histoire*, I, 211: the "sources de Tlemcen"; cf. ibid., III, 334: "Oioun-el-Mohadjer." Cf. the "Table geographique," ibid., IV, 520, where *'Uyūn Abi l-Muhajir* is identified with 'Ain-el-Hadjer, two miles northwest of Tlemcen.

326 BGA, II, 59, 66, 67; III, 56, 218; VII, 351. Mesnages, 25f., 37, identifies Mila with Milev, a Punic and later Roman city west of Carthage.

327 From "In this year, Abu l-Muhajir Dinar conducted ..." cf. *Dh., II, 266; from "He conquered Mila ..."; cf. IAH, 197, l. 16.

328 Kh.: *al-M-h-r-y* (cf. note 320).

329 From "'Amr b. Murra al-Juhani conducted ..." cf. al-Ya'qubi, II, 286; Tab., II, 188 (al-Waqidi).

330 On the notice of the death of Sa'id b. al-'As cf. *Dh., II, 289 (Khalifa); *Ibn Hajar, IV, 49 (Khalifa).

331 On the notice of the death of Jubayr b. Mut'im cf. #Siyar, III, 65 (Khalifa); #Ibn Hajar, II, 64 (Khalifa). See also GAS, I, 258.

332 On the notice of the death of Shayba b. 'Uthman cf. #Ibn Kathir, VIII, 213 (Khalifa); #Ibn Hajar, IV, 376 (Khalifa). See also *Ṭbq.*, 32; *Istī'āb*, 712; Ibn Sa'd, IV, 448; Ibn Hajar, IV, 376.

333 On the notice of the death of 'Abdallah b. 'Amir b. Kurayz cf. *Dh., II, 301 (Khalifa). See also EI2, I, 43.

334 D. 146/763–764 (*Ṭbq.*, 526; Ibn Sa'd, VII, 258; Ibn Hajar, VIII, 166f.).

335 EI, IV, 1005.

b. Zayd;[336] ʿAmr b. ʿAwf;[337] Safwan b. al-Muʿattal;[338] ʿUthman b. Hunayf;[339] Mujammiʿ b. Jariya;[340] Abu Humayd as-Saʿidi;[341] Khirash b. Umayya;[342] Ibn Bujayna;[343] Qays b. Saʿd b. ʿUbada;[344] Abu Jahm b. Hudhayfa;[345] Maslama b. Mukhallad; Bilal b. al-Harith al-Muzani;[346] al-Harith b. al-Azmaʿ al-Hamdani;[347] Mihjan b. al-Adraʿ,[348] who had contact[349] with Muʿawiya; Fadala b. ʿUbayd; [274] Shaddad b. Aws,[350] who is said by some to have died in 41/661–662.

Baqi[351] < *Yahya b. ʿAbdallah b. Bukayr < al-Layth:
In 59, Junada b. Abi Umayya, ʿAlqama b. Jungda al-Hajari,[352] and ʿAlqama b. al-Akhtham carried out a raid against Rhodes.[353] Muhammad b. Abi Sufyan led the pilgrimage.

[Baqi] < *Bakkar b. ʿAbdallah < Muhammad b. ʿA'idh < al-Walid < a man:
In 59, Junada b. Abi Umayya conducted a winter expedition in the land of the Byzantines.

[Baqi] < *Ibn Numayr:
Abu Hurayra died in 59.

336 EI, IV, 1048.
337 ʿAmr b. ʿAwf b. Zayd (*Ṭbq.*, 87; *Istīʿāb*, 1196; Dh., II, 309; Ibn Hajar, VIII, 85).
338 *Ṭbq.*, 117; *Istīʿāb*, 725; Ibn ʿAsakir, *Tahdhīb*, VI, 438.
339 *Ṭbq.*, 196; *Istīʿāb*, 1033; Ibn Hajar, VII, 112.
340 *Ṭbq.*, 189; *Istīʿāb*, 136; Dh., II, 315; Ibn Hajar, X, 47.
341 ʿAbd ar-Rahman b. ʿAmr (*Ṭbq.*, 217; *Istīʿāb*, 1633; Dh., II, 330; Ibn Hajar, XII, 79).
342 *Istīʿāb*, 445; Dh., II, 278.
343 ʿAbdallah b. Malik al-Azdi (*Ṭbq.*, 23; *Istīʿāb*, 871, 982; Ibn Hajar, V, 381).
344 On the notice of the death of Qays b. Saʿd b. ʿUbada cf. *Ibn Hajar, VIII, 396 (Khalifa). See also *Ṭbq.*, 216; Ibn Saʿd, VI, 52; *Istīʿāb*, 1289; Dh., II, 311; Ibn Hajar, VIII, 395.
345 GAS, I, 263.
346 On the notice of the death of Bilal b. al-Harith al-Muzani cf. #Ibn ʿAsakir, X, 300 (Khalifa). See also *Ṭbq.*, 86; *Istīʿāb*, 183; Ibn ʿAsakir, X, 279; Dh., II, 273; Ibn Hajar, I, 501.
347 *Ṭbq.*, 338; Ibn Saʿd, VI, 119; *Istīʿāb*, 282.
348 *Ṭbq.*, 119; Ibn Saʿd, VII, 12; *Istīʿāb*, 1363; Dh., II, 315; Ibn Hajar, X, 54.
349 The Arabic verb is *adraka*.
350 *Ṭbq.*, 201; Ibn Saʿd, VII, 401; *Istīʿāb*, 694; Ibn ʿAsakir, *Tahdhīb*, VI, 288; Dh., II, 291; Ibn Hajar, IV, 315.
351 Baqi's additions to this chapter begin here. Khalifa's text resumes with the list of judges on page 88.
352 Cf. IAH, 129, l. 7.
353 This sentence parallels *Futūḥ*, 235f.; cf. Tab., II, 188; cf. Ibn ʿAsakir, *Tahdhīb*, III, 409.

[275] Khalifa:[354]

The judges during the caliphate of Mu'awiya

{217} Basra:

'Umayra b. Yathribi ad-Dabbi[355] was appointed by Ibn 'Amir.

'Imran b. Husayn was [then] appointed. He asked to be discharged from his duties, so [Ibn 'Amir] dismissed him.[356]

'Asim b. Fadala, the brother of 'Abdallah b. Fadala al-Laythi, was appointed by Ziyad.

Zurara b. Awfi al-Harashi.[357]

Shurayh[358] served under Ziyad as judge of Basra for a year.

During the caliphate of Mu'awiya, Zurara b. Awfi served as judge for 'Ubaydallah b. Ziyad.

'Abd ar-Rahman b. Udhayna[359] also served as judge for ['Ubaydallah].

Kufa:

Shurayh served as judge in [Kufa] until Ziyad transferred him with himself down to Basra.[360]

Masruq b. Ajda'[361] served as judge after [Shurayh], until Shurayh returned.

[276] Medina:

'Abdallah b. Nawfal b. al-Harith[362] was appointed judge by Marwan. He served as judge until the dismissal of Marwan in 48/668–669.

Sa'id b. al-'As was then appointed as governor.

Abu Salama b. 'Abd ar-Rahman b. 'Awf[363] was appointed as judge by Sa'id. He served as judge until the dismissal of Sa'id b. al-'As.

Marwan b. al-Hakam was then reappointed as governor in 54/673–674. Marwan b. al-Hakam appointed Mus'ab b. 'Abd

354 In the text, the heading "The Judges during the caliphate of Mu'awiya" precedes the citation of Khalifa's name.

355 *Ṭbq.*, 455; Ibn Sa'd, VII, 149.

356 Entry on 'Imran b. Husayn parallels **Istī'āb*, 1208 (Khalifa); *Isaba, III, 27 (Khalifa).

357 D. c. 93/711–712 (*Ṭbq.*, 467; Ibn Sa'd, VII, 150; Dh., III, 368; Ibn Hajar, III, 322; cf. Pellat, 289).

358 Ibn al-Harith, d. between 85 and 99 (GAS, I, 402).

359 *Ṭbq.*, 469; *Jarḥ*, II, II, 210; cf. Pellat, 289.

360 Entry on Shurayh parallels *Dh., III, 76 (Khalifa).

361 D. 63/682–683 (*Ṭbq.*, 338; Ibn Sa'd, VI, 76; Dh., III, 75; Ibn Hajar, X, 109; cf. GAS, I, 179, 632).

362 *Istī'āb*, 999.

363 D. c. 94/712–713 (*Ṭbq.*, 606; *Jarḥ*, II, II, 93; Dh., IV, 76; Ibn Hajar, XII, 115).

ar-Rahman b. 'Awf, who served as judge until the dismissal of Marwan in 57, at the end of *Dhū-l-Qa'da*/September-October 677. Then al-Walid b. 'Utba b. Abi Sufyan was appointed governor. He appointed Ibn Zam'a al-'Amiri, who served as judge until {218} Mu'awiya died.

[Khalifa:]

[Mu'awiya's] Secretary for Correspondence: 'Ubayd b. Aws al-Ghassani.[364]

Chief *Dīwān* Administrator: Sarjun b. Mansur ar-Rumi.[365]

[Mu'awiya's] Chamberlain: Abu Ayyub, his *mawlā*.[366]

Chief of Police:

Yazid b. al-Hurr, his *mawlā*,[367] who died [in office].

Qays b. Humra al-Hamdani was then appointed, but was later dismissed.

Dhuhl b. 'Amr al-'Udhri was then appointed.

[Mu'awiya] was the first to create the office of captain of the guard,[368] and was the first to create the *dīwān* of the seal.[369]

Captain of the Guard: Abu l-Mukhtar, a Himyarite *mawlā*.

Secretary of the Seal: 'Abdallah b. 'Amr al-Himyari.

[277] Mu'awiya died on Thursday 22 *Rajab* 59/9 May 679, may God have mercy on him.

[Khalifa:]

The first to govern Iraq under a unified administration was Ziyad b. Abi Sufyan, who was appointed by Mu'awiya in 50/670–671 and served until his death in 53/672–673.

364 Entry on 'Ubayd b. Aws al-Ghassani parallels Jahshiyari, 24; 31; Tab., II, 837.

365 Entry on Sarjun b. Mansur ar-Rumi parallels *Ansāb*, IV-A, 136 (al-Mada'ini). Cf *Futūḥ*, 193; Ibn 'Asakir, *Tahdhīb*, VI, 71; *Fihrist* (trans.), 583, 1094; Hitti, 195 n. 4; Jahshiyari, index.

366 Entry on Abu Ayyub parallels *Ansāb*, IV-A, 61 (al-Mada'ini).

367 Entry on Yazid b. al-Hurr parallels *Ansāb*, IV-A, 136 (al-Mada'ini).

368 "[Mu'awiya] was the first to create the office of captain of the guard" parallels *Ansāb*, IV-A, 136 (al-Mada'ini); *'Iqd*, IV, 362.

369 The phrase "the first to create the *dīwān* of the seal" parallels Jahshiyari, 24, 1 9.

[278] The Year 60/679–680

Baqi[370] < *Ibn Bukayr < al-Layth:
In 60, Mu'awiya the Commander of the Faithful died on 4 *Rajab*/10 April 680. He designated Yazid b. Mu'awiya as his successor.[371] In this year, the Egyptians carried food to Rhodes. Al-Walid b. 'Utba was dismissed from the governorship of Medina. He was replaced by 'Amr b. Sa'id, who was given {219} jurisdiction over Medina, Mecca, and at-Ta'if. 'Amr b. Sa'id led the pilgrimage in this year. Then he was dismissed at the beginning of *Dhū l-Ḥijja*/September 680, whereupon al-Walid b. 'Utba was reappointed.

Harmala added in his recension < Ibn Bukayr:
Husayn b. 'Ali went out to Iraq, and Ibn az-Zubayr went out to Mecca.

[Baqi] < *Bakkar b. 'Abdallah < Muhammad b. 'A'idh < al-Walid and others, who told us about Mu'awiya's commanders of the summer raids, which I wrote about in accordance with what I heard about it from *Isma'il b. 'Ayyash < Safwan b. 'Amr[372] < Sa'id b. Hanzala:
Mu'awiya b. Abi Sufyan appointed 'Amr b. Mu'awiya [279] al-'Uqayli[373] commander of the summer campaign. When he returned, [Mu'awiya] asked him how much the *khums*[374] amounted to. He informed him, and [Mu'awiya] asked, "Where is it?" 'Amr said, "You are[375] asking me about the *khums*, while I see one of the Emigrants[376] walking on foot. Shouldn't I give him a mount?" Mu'awiya said, "He will not get it[377] as long as I live." ['Amr] said, "Then I don't care!" and recited [the following verses]:

1. The Quraysh in Damascus are given my booty,
   While I abandon my friends. That is unjust.

2. I am not an *amīr* who accumulates money like a merchant,
   And I do not seek a long amirate with miserliness.

370 The first part of this chapter was added by Baqi. Khalifa's text resumes on page 92.

371 From "In 60, Mu'awiya ..." cf. *Istī'āb*, 1419 (Ibn Bukayr < al-Layth).

372 D. 155/771–772 or 158 (*Ṭbq.*, 809; Ibn Sa'd, VII, 467; Ibn 'Asakir, *Tahdhīb*, VI, 437).

373 Cf. *Futūḥ*, 205; Tab., I, 2284f.; *'Uyūn*, I, 116; ibid., III, 175.

374 The fifth of the booty set aside for the central government.

375 Z: He is.

376 The Emigrants (*Muhājirūn*) were those Meccans who supported Muhammad and emigrated with him from Mecca to Medina at the time of the *Hijra* (cf. Hitti, *History of the Arabs*, 116, 140).

377 The feminine pronoun object -*hā* is puzzling. Perhaps it refers to *dābba* (mount), to be understood.

3. So if the *Shaykh* of Damascus withholds his wealth, fine;
But I do not wish to lock up my wealth.[378]

Muhammad b. ‘A’idh < *Isma‘il b. ‘Ayyash < Safwan b. ‘Amr < {220} Abu Hisba:[379]
While ‘Amr b. Mu‘awiya al-‘Uqayli was commander of the army, he used to dismount and participate with his companions in leading the prisoners, the cattle destined for slaughter, and the horses taken as booty, with his clothes rolled up over his legs.

Muhammad < *Marwan b. Muhammad < Rishdin b. Sa‘d[380] < al-Hasan b. Thawban[381] < Yazid:
[On the expedition to] Sicily,[382] ‘Abdallah b. Qays al-Fazari was in command of the Syrians, ‘Awwam al-Yahsubi[383] was in command of the Egyptians, and ‘Abd al-‘Aziz b. Marwan was in command of the Medinese. ‘Awwam was commander-in-chief.

Muhammad < *Marwan b. Muhammad < Rishdin b. Sa‘d < al-Hasan b. Thawban < Yazid:
‘Abdallah b. Qays al-Fazari conquered Sicily[384] during the caliphate of Mu‘awiya. [280] The booty they acquired on that day amounted to 100 *dīnār*s, an ounce of gold, and a brass bottle.[385]

[Muhammad]:
I did not ask Marwan [b. Muhammad] concerning these commanders whom he mentioned in the first report, whether they all participated in this [second] raid, or whether this was an earlier raid.

378 Meter: *ṭawīl*. At-Tabari offers a report in which Mu‘awiya describes himself as one skilled in business and in gathering money from youth to old age (Tab., II, 201).

379 A marginal notation in the manuscript states that Abu Hisba was Muslim b. Ukays, a *mawlā* of ‘Abdallah b. ‘Amir b. Kurayz, and a Syrian. Cf. Ibn Sa‘d, VII, 452, where the name is given as Abu Ḥ-s-n-h Muslim b. Kabis/Kubays.

380 D. 183/803–804 (*Ṭbq.*, 765; Ibn Sa‘d, VII, 517; Ibn Hajar, III, 277; cf. R. Guest, page 33 of his introduction to al-Kindi).

381 D. 145/763 (Ibn Hajar, II, 259; R. Guest, page 35 of his introduction to al-Kindi).

382 The text here seems garbled. The meaningless *m-n-q-l-b-h* should be read Siqiliyya. Arabic *Ṣiqiliyya* (which Khalifa consistently spells with an initial *ṣād*) is almost identical to *m-n-q-l-b-h* when the diacritical points are missing. Cf. the report that follows, and the parallel in the *Futūḥ*, 235.

383 Cf. IAH, 144, l. 9.

384 Kh.: *m-n-q-l-b-h* (cf. note 382).

385 From "‘Abdallah b. Qays al-Fazari conquered Sicily …" cf. *Futūḥ*, 235.

Muhammad < *al-Walid b. Muslim:
The last thing that Mu'awiya charged them to do was, "Tighten the noose around the Byzantines, for then you will have other nations in your power."

Al-Walid:
Mu'awiya died in *Rajab* 60/April–May 680. His reign lasted 19 and a half years.

Muhammad < al-Waqidi:
Mu'awiya died at the age of 78.

{221} Muhammad < al-Walid b. Muslim:
Yazid b. Mu'awiya made a [military] appointment, and in that year Malik[386] raided Suriya.[387]

[Baqi] < *Ibn Numayr:
Bilal b. al-Harith al-Mazini died in 60. Mu'awiya died in *Rajab* 60/ April–May 680. Yazid b. Mu'awiya received the pledge of allegiance. He appointed 'Amr b. Sa'id b. al-'As over Medina, and 'Amr led the pilgrimage in 60/680. Al-Husayn b. 'Ali was killed on 10 *al-Muḥarram* 61/10 October 680. Then[388] 'Amr was dismissed from the governorship of Medina in 60.

Khalifa:
In this year al-Husayn b. 'Ali b. Abi Talib sent his paternal cousin, Muslim b. 'Aqil [281] b. Abi Talib to the people of Kufa [to induce them] to pledge allegiance to [al-Husayn].[389] Many people did so. Yazid b. Mu'awiya consolidated the administration of Iraq under 'Ubaydallah b. Ziyad. The people of Iraq revolted. Muslim b. 'Aqil and Hani' b. 'Urwa al-Muradi[390] were killed. Al-Husayn b. 'Ali departed Mecca for Kufa.

Al-Farazdaq:
{222} I went out intending to make the pilgrimage. When I reached Dhat 'Irq,[391] I saw some tents which had been set up. I inquired, "To whom do

386 Ibn 'Abdallah (see note 89).

387 For a parallel to the phrase "in that year Malik raided Suriya" cf. al-Ya'qubi, II, 302; Tab., II, 196. Wellhausen identifies Suriya with Isauria ('Die Kämpfe der Araber', 437).

388 If al-Hasan was killed in 61, and 'Amr was dismissed in 60, the word "then" seems puzzling. There seems to have been a scribal error. In fact, according to the at-Tabari, 'Amr b. Sa'id was not dismissed from Medina until the end of 61/August 681 (Tab., II, 395).

389 On the revolt of al-Husayn cf. Wellhausen, *Arab Kingdom*, 146f.

390 Kh.: Hani' b. 'Amr al-Muradi (EI2, III, 164).

391 Dhat 'Irq is mentioned frequently, and in all volumes of BGA (see indices).

these belong?" and was told, "They belong to al-Husayn b. 'Ali." I turned to him and said, "Son of the Prophet, what has called you away from the pilgrimage?" He said, "These people – meaning the Kufans – wrote to me about their situation." Then he asked me, "How did you leave the people behind you?" I said, "May my father and mother be a ransom for you! I left the hearts of the people with you, the swords with the Umayyads, and victory in heaven."[392]

In 60, the following were born: Qatada b. Di'ama as-Sadusi,[393] Hisham b. 'Urwa,[394] Sulayman b. Mihrhan al-A'mash,[395] Isma'il b. Abi Khalid.[396]

[Khalifa:]
Yazid b. Mu'awiya sent his *mawlā*, Ruzayq to al-Walid b. 'Utba.

*Wahb b. Jarir < *my father < Muhammad <*Ruzayq, Mu'awiya's *mawlā*: When Mu'awiya died, Yazid b. Mu'awiya sent me to al-Walid b. 'Utba, the governor over Medina, [with a letter] he had written [informing] him about the death of Mu'awiya, and [instructing him] to send a command to these individuals[397] to pledge allegiance to Yazid. I reached Medina [282] at night and said to the chamberlain, "Obtain permission for me to enter." He said, "[Al-Walid] has already retired, and there is no way to reach him." I said, "I have brought him a command." So he went in and informed [Al-Walid] of my arrival. [Al-Walid] gave him permission to allow me to enter while he was in bed. When he read Yazid's letter concerning the death of Mu'awiya and the succession of Yazid, he became very grieved over the death of Mu'awiya. He started to get up, but threw himself back onto his bed. Then he sent a message to Marwan, who arrived wearing a white shirt and a rose-colored robe.[398] [Al-Walid] informed him of Mu'awiya's death, and told him that Yazid had sent him orders to induce these individuals to pledge allegiance to Yazid. Marwan prayed for God's mercy on Mu'awiya, and prayed for his happiness. He said, "Send to these individuals immediately, and call on them to pledge

392 From "I went out intending …" cf. Din., 245, l. 9; Tab., II, 278; cf. Ibn A'tham, V, 120; Ibn A'tham, V, 124; (*) *'Iqd*, IV, 384; cf. Ibn 'Asakir, *Tahdhīb*, IV, 332, l. 5; cf. *Aghānī*, XIX, 34, l. 12; cf. *Aghānī*, XIX, 47, l. 28; cf. *Ta'rīkh al-Khulafā*, 78a, l. 15.

393 D. 117/735–736 (EI2, IV, 748; GAS, I, 31).

394 D. 146/763–764 (GAS, I, 88).

395 D. 148/765–766 (EI2, I, 431).

396 D. 145/763 (*Ṭbq.*, 389; Ibn Sa'd, VI, 344; Ibn Hajar, I, 291; cf. GAS, I, index).

397 Sc. The Qurashite leaders of the Medinese opposition.

398 The Arabic is *milāya* (cf. Dozy, 408–411).

allegiance. If they give the pledge, [fine]. But if they refuse, kill them."[399] {223} [Al-Walid] said, "God be praised! Am I to kill al-Husayn b. 'Ali and Ibn az-Zubayr?" Marwan said, "That is what I am telling you."[400]

*Wahb < *Juwayriya b. Asma' < *an innumerable number of our Medinese *shaykh*s:
At the time of Mu'awiya's death, al-Walid b. 'Utba b. Abi Sufyan was in Medina. When he heard of Mu'awiya's death, he sent word of it to Marwan b. al-Hakam and others of the Banu Umayya. Marwan said, "Send immediately to al-Husayn and Ibn az-Zubayr. If they pledge allegiance, [fine]. If not, kill them."[401] 'Abd ar-Rahman b. Abi Bakr had died before that. Ibn az-Zubayr came to [al-Walid], who announced to him Mu'awiya's death. He prayed for God's mercy and blessing on him. [Al-Walid] said to him, "Pledge allegiance." He responded, "This is not the time for the pledge of allegiance. I am not the kind of person who would give the pledge to you here. You should mount the pulpit, and then I and the people will pledge allegiance to you in public, not secretly." Marwan jumped up and said, "Kill him![402] He is a source of evil discord." [Ibn az-Zubayr] said, "You're a disgrace, son of a blue-eyed woman!"[403] The two of them continued to insult each other. Al-Walid said, "Get these two out of here!" He was a gentle, lofty-minded, noble man. The two were removed from his presence. Al-Husayn b. 'Ali arrived just then. Nothing was said to him[404] until the two returned together. Marwan returned to al-Walid, and said, [283] "The next time you see him he will [be in a position to] harm you." He sent spies to follow [Ibn az-Zubayr], who, upon entering his house, did nothing more than call for water for the ritual ablution, align his feet [for prayer], and pray continuously. He ordered his son Hamza[405] to bring his riding camel

399 Literally, "behead them" (see note 169).

400 From "When Mu'awiya died ..." cf. *Ansāb*, IV-B, 22f.; cf. Din., 227ff.; cf. Tab., II, 216ff.; cf. *Imāma*, I, 215; *Dh., II, 268f.

401 Literally, "behead them" (see note 169).

402 Literally, "behead him" (see note 169).

403 A term of abuse among the Arabs (cf. note in Jarrett's translation of as-Suyuti, 202).

404 Or, perhaps, "He said nothing."

405 *Ṭbq.*, 649; *Ma'ārif*, 206, 225, 226; cf. Ibn Hazm, 123.

to al-Hulayfa,[406] a distance of one *barīd*[407] from Medina, toward al-Fur‘.[408] He had a large amount of money in al-Hulayfa. He continued [to pray] with his two feet aligned. At the end of the night, the spies withdrew from him. He sat upon his mount and rode to al-Hulayfa, where he mounted his riding camel and headed for Mecca. Al-Husayn went out on the same night, and the two met in Mecca. Ibn az-Zubayr asked him, "What is keeping you {224} from your partisans and the partisans of your father? If I had partisans like yours I would certainly go to them."[409]

[Wahb:]
Yazid sent ‘Amr b. Sa‘id to replace al-Walid b. ‘Utba as governor over Medina, because he was worried about al-Walid's weakness. When he arrived, ‘Amr mounted the pulpit, praised God, and mentioned Ibn az-Zubayr and what he had done. He said, "He has taken refuge in Mecca. We will launch a military expedition against him. Then if he enters the Ka‘ba,[410] we will burn it down upon him, no matter how disagreeable that will be."[411]

Wahb < Juwayriya < *Musafi‘[412] < *a man of the Quraysh, whose name I have forgotten:
[I] was sitting with ‘Abd al-Malik b. Marwan below the pulpit from which ‘Amr b. Sa‘id said, "no matter how disagreeable that will be," when ‘Abd al-Malik put his finger on his nose [to indicate disagreeableness].[413] Then

406 Cf. BGA, VII, 202, 313; VIII, 245 (Dhu l-Hulayfa). Yaqut, II, 324.

407 The *barīd* was a unit of distance equal to six, 12, or 20 miles (Yaqut, I, 37 = Jwaideh, 53). For Khalifa, the *barīd* is apparently equivalent to six miles, since he states that al-Hulayfa was a *barīd* from Medina, and Yaqut, II, 324, states that al-Hulayfa was about six miles from Medina.

408 BGA, I, 18, 22; II, 26, 28; III, 53, 69, 79; VI, 129, 248; VII, 177; VIII, 244, 249; Yaqut, III, 878; Minorsky, 148.

409 From "At the time of Mu‘awiya's death ..." cf. *Ansāb*, IV-B, 13–15; cf. Din., 227ff; cf. Tab., II, 216–222; cf. *‘Iqd*, IV, 376; *Ibn ‘Asakir, *Tahdhīb*, VII, 407, l. 18; *Dh., II, 268.

410 Kh.: "If he enters Mecca" (*in dakhala Makka*). Both Ibn ‘Asakir (*Tahdhīb*, VII, 408) and adh-Dhahabi (Dh., II, 268), who took the passage from Khalifa, have "If he enters the Ka‘ba" (*la-’in dakhala l-ka‘ba*), which makes more sense.

411 From "Yazid sent ‘Amr b. Sa‘id ..." cf. *‘Iqd*, IV, 376; *Ibn ‘Asakir, *Tahdhīb*, VII, 408, l. 8; *Dh., II, 268.

412 Ibn ‘Abdallah b. Shayba (*Ṭbq.*, 705; *Jarḥ*, IV, I, 432; Ibn Hajar, X, 102).

413 The Arabic expression for "no matter how disagreeable ... to so-and-so" is literally "despite the nose of so-and-so" (*‘alā raghmi anfi fulān*). In the version given in the *‘Iqd* (IV, 376, l. 18), ‘Amr's nose bleeds (*ra‘afa*).

he said, "Oh God! I find it disagreeable that an attack should be made on your sacred House." There is a story concerning this.

'Amr b. Sa'id led the pilgrimage.

[284] The Year 61/680–681

Al-Husayn b. 'Ali b. Abi Talib was killed on Wednesday 10 *al-Muḥarram*, the day of *'Āshūrā'*, in the year 61/10 October 680. Ja'far b. 'Ali b. Abi Talib was killed with him.

Abu 'Ubayda:
Ja'far b. 'Ali b. Abi Talib was killed with him. His mother was Umm al-Banin bint Hizam b. Abi Khalid, of the[414] Banu l-Wahid, of the Banu Kilab.

Abu l-Hasan:
'Uthman b. 'Ali, whose mother was also Umm al-Banin, was killed with him.

Abu 'Ubayda and Abu l-Hasan:
Al-'Abbas the Younger and Muhammad the Younger, sons of 'Ali b. Abi Talib, were killed with him. Their mother was Lubaba bint 'Ubaydallah b. al-'Abbas.

{225} Abu l-Hasan:
His mother was an *umm walad* [a concubine whose children are recognized by their father as his own].

Abu 'Ubayda and Abu l-Hasan:
'Ali b. Husayn b. 'Ali was killed with him. His mother was Layla or Lubna bint Abi Murra b. 'Urwa b. Mas'ud b. 'Amir b. Mu'attib ath-Thaqafi. Her mother was Maymuna bint Abi Zufyan b. Harb b. Umayya.

Abu l-Hasan:
'Ubaydallah b. 'Ali b. Abi Talib was killed with him. His mother was ar-Rabab bint Imri'il-Qays of the Kalb.

[285] The following were also killed with him: Abu Bakr b. al-Qasim b. Husayn b. 'Ali b. Abi Talib; Muhammad b. 'Abdallah b. Ja'far, whose mother was al-Khawsa' bint Khasafa b. Thaqaf b. Rabi'a b. 'A'idh of the

414 Cf. Ibn Hazm, 37f.

Banu Taym Allat b. Tha'laba b. 'Ukaba; Muslim b. 'Aqil b. Abi Talib, whose mother was a slave girl named Halaba; 'Abd ar-Rahman b. Muslim, whose mother was a slave girl;[415] 'Abdallah b. Muslim b. 'Aqil, whose mother was Ruqayya bint Muhammad b. Sa'id b. 'Aqil b. Abi Talib.

*Muhammad b. Mu'awiya < Sufyan < Abu Masa < *al-Hasan al-Basri:
Sixteen men of al-Husayn's family were killed with him. There is no family on the face of the earth today with men like them.[416]

*Al-Hasan b. Abi 'Amr < *Fitr b. Khalifa[417] < *Mundhir ath-Thawri[418] < Ibn al-Hanafiyya:[419]
Seventeen men, all of whom kicked their feet in the womb of Fatima, were killed with al-Husayn b. 'Ali.[420]

The person responsible for killing al-Husayn was Shimr b. Dhi l-Jawshan. The leader of the army was 'Umar b. Sa'd b. Malik.[421]

In this year, Malik b. 'Abdallah[422] al-Khath'ami conducted a raiding expedition in the land of the Byzantines. He fought a battle at Quniya.[423]

[286] Al-Walid b. 'Utba b. Abi Sufyan led the pilgrimage.

In this year, Hamza b. 'Amr al-Aslami[424] died.

'Umar b. 'Abd al-'Aziz {226} and Sa'id b. Iyas al-Jurayri[425] were born.

[Baqi][426] < *Ibn Bukayr < al-Layth:
In 61, al-Husayn b. 'Ali and his companions were killed. Al-Walid b. 'Utba led the pilgrimage.

*Ibn Numayr:
Then 'Amr was removed from the governorship of Medina and was replaced

415 U lacks: whose mother was a slave girl.
416 From "Sixteen men ..." cf. **Istī'āb*, 396.
417 D. 153/770 (*Ṭbq.*, 393; Ibn Sa'd, VI, 364; Ibn Hajar, VIII, 300).
418 Ibn Ya'la (Ibn Sa'd, VI, 310; Ibn Hajar, X, 304).
419 Muhammad b. 'Ali b. Abi Talib (EI, III, 671).
420 From "Seventeen men ..." cf. (*) *Istī'āb*, 396.
421 D. c. 66/685–686 (*Ṭbq.*, 607; Ibn Sa'd, V, 168; *Ma'ārif*, 243f., 401; Dh., III, 52; Ibn Hajar, VII, 450). From "The person responsible ..." cf. **Istī'āb*, 395 (Khalifa).
422 Kh.: Malik b. 'Abd ar-Rahman (cf. notes 39 and 386, and the same report by Baqi < Bakkar b. 'Abdallah on page 98).
423 From "In this year, Malik b. 'Abdallah ..." cf. al-Ya'qubi, II, 302. See also Konya, Ikonion (EI, II, 1053; Honigmann, index, s.v. Ikonion).
424 *Ṭbq.*, 244; Ibn Sa'd, IV, 315; *Istī'āb*, 375; Ibn Hajar, III, 31.
425 D. 143/760–761 (*Ṭbq.*, 526; Ibn Sa'd, VII, 261; Ibn Hajar, IV, 5).
426 The remainder of this chapter was added by Baqi.

by al-Walid b. 'Utba, who led the pilgrimage in 61/681. Al-Husayn b. 'Ali was killed on 10 *al-Muḥarram*/10 October 680.

*Bakkar b. 'Abdallah < Muhammad b. 'A'idh < al-Walid b. Muslim:
In 61, Malik b. 'Abdallah conducted the summer raid against Quniya.

[287] The Year 62/681–682

In this year, Salm[427] b. Ziyad raided Khwarizm. [The inhabitants] made peace with him, paying a great amount of wealth. Then he crossed [the Oxus] to Samarqand, [the inhabitants of which] also made peace with him.[428]

'Ubaydallah b. Ziyad appointed al-Mundhir b. al-Jarud commander over the frontier of Qandabil. Al-Mundhir died there.[429] Al-Hakam b. al-Mundhir b. al-Jarud went out and conquered Qandabil. Ibn Ziyad [then] sent Sinan b. Salama [on a raiding expedition, in the course of which] he conquered al-Buqan.[430] After that Yazid b. Mu'awiya sent 'Abd ar-Rahman b. Yazid al-Hilali there.

The people of Kabul rebelled, and imprisoned Abu 'Ubayda b. Ziyad b. Abi Sufyan. Yazid b. Ziyad b. Abi Sufyan went [to Kabul] and attacked the enemy. They fought him and {227} he was killed. The following were killed with him: Zayd b. Jud'an, the father of the jurist 'Ali b. Zayd b. Jud'an;[431] Abu s-Sahba' Sila b. Ushaym al-'Adawi,[432] and his son; 'Amr b. Qutayba; Budayl b. Nu'aym al-'Adawi; 'Uthman b. Adam al-'Adawi; and some [other] excellent men.[433]

427 U: Salim. Salm is the name recorded in all the other sources (cf. Ibn 'Asakir, VI, 235).

428 From "In this year, Salm b. Ziyad raided Khwarizm …" cf. *Futūḥ*, 413; cf. al-Ya'qubi, II, 300f.; Tab., II, 395 (al-Mada'ini); *Dh., II, 353.

429 From "'Ubaydallah b. Ziyad appointed al-Mundhir b. al-Jarud …" cf. *Isaba, III, 458 (Khalifa).

430 Kh.: al-Muqan. From "'Ubaydallah b. Ziyad appointed al-Mundhir b. al-Jarud …" cf. *Futūḥ*, 434, al-Ya'qubi, II, 281, and BGA, VI, 56, all of which have al-Buqan. It does not appear in the works of Idrisi or the author of the *Ḥudūd al-'Ālam* (Minorsky). Textual overlap begins at the beginning of paragraph.

431 On the son, d. 131/748–749, see *Ṭbq.*, 517; Ibn Sa'd, VII, 252; Dh., V, 283; cf. GAS, I, 71.

432 *Ṭbq.*, 456; Ibn Sa'd, VII, 134; Dh., III, 19.

433 From "The people of Kabul rebelled …" cf. *Futūḥ*, 397f.; cf. Tab. II, 488; *Dh., II, 353 (Khalifa).

[288] ʻAbdallah b. Asad b. Kurz al-Qasri raided Caesarea, which is near al-Hadath.[434]

Husayn b. Numayr as-Sakuni conducted the summer campaign against Suriya.[435]

In this year, ʻAlqama b. Qays an-Nakhaʻi[436] died.[437]

ʻUthman b. Muhammad b. Abi Sufyan led the pilgrimage.

[289] The Year 63/682–683

In this year occurred the affair of the Harra.[438]

Abu l-Yaqzan:
ʻUthman b. Muhammad led the pilgrimage in 62/682. Then he proceeded to Medina, where he stayed for a month. Then he sent a delegation to Yazid b. Muʻawiya, among whom were the following: ʻAbdallah b. Abi ʻAmr b. Hafs b. al-Mughira al-Makhzumi; Muhammad b. ʻAmr b. Hazm al-Ansari;[439] a man of the Banu Suraqa of the Banu ʻAdi b. Kaʻb; with men of the Quraysh. They went [back] to Medina, publicly reviled Yazid, disavowed [allegiance to] him, and repudiated him.[440]

*Wahb b. Jarir < *Juwayriya b. Asma < *some *shaykh*s of Medina:
Among those who were sent to Yazid b. Muʻawiya were ʻAbdallah b. Hanzala[441] and eight of his sons. [Yazid] {228} gave him 100,000 *dirham*s, and 10,000 *dirham*s to each of his sons, in addition to clothing and mounts. Then, when ʻAbdallah b. Hanzala arrived in Medina, the people came to him and asked, "What news do you bring?"[442] He said, "I come to you from a man against whom I would wage war even if I had only these sons of mine to help me." They said, "We have heard that he rewarded you, honored you, and gave you gifts." He said, "That he did, but I accepted

434 EI2, II, 19; cf. Honigmann, index s.v. Adata; Ramsay, 301, and index s.v. Adata.

435 This sentence parallels *Ibn ʻAsakir, *Tahdhīb*, IV, 372 (Khalifa).

436 *Ṭbq.*, 334, Ibn Saʻd, VI, 86; Dh., III, 50; Ibn Hajar, VII, 276; cf. GAS, I, 398.

437 This sentence parallels *Dh., III, 52 (Khalifa).

438 A *ḥarra* is an area covered with black volcanic rocks. The *ḥarra* at which the battle took place was Harrat Waqim, to the east of Medina (EI2, III, 226f.).

439 *Ṭbq.*, 595; Ibn Saʻd, V, 69; Dh., III, 68; Ibn Hajar, IX, 370.

440 From "ʻUthman b. Muhammad led the pilgrimage …" cf. *Ansāb*, IV-B, 31; cf. Tab., II, 402f. (Abu Mikhnaf).

441 EI2, I, 45.

442 Literally, "What is behind you?" (*mā warā'aka*).

that from him only in order to gain strength against him." [Ibn Hanzala] encouraged the people and they pledged allegiance to him.[443]

Abu l-Yaqzan:
A council was called to [elect] an acceptable [leader]. They put 'Abdallah b. Muti' al-'Adawi[444] in command of the Quraysh, 'Abdallah b. Hanzala al-Ghasil [290] in command of the Ansar, and Ma'qil b. Sinan al-Ashja'i[445] in command of the tribes of the Emigrants.[446] They expelled 'Uthman b. Muhammad b. Abi Sufyan from Medina, and all the Banu Umayya who were there.[447]

*Wahb < *my father < Ayyub[448] < 'Ikrima:[449]
Ibn 'Abbas asked about them when he was in at-Ta'if. He was told that they had appointed 'Abdallah b. Muti' to lead the Quraysh and 'Abdallah b. Hanzala over the Ansar. He said, "Two chiefs! The people are doomed."[450]

Wahb < *my father:
When the Banu Umayya and Marwan were expelled by the people of Medina, they encamped at Hafir.[451] Marwan wrote to Yazid [informing him] about the people's views. [Yazid] ordered a tent set up for him outside his castle, and had military forces levied upon the Syrians, with Muslim b. 'Uqba al-Murri. Three [days] did not pass before he finished.[452] Then on the third morning he showed [Muslim] the letter and said:

1. Inform Abu Bakr[453] when the army gets ready,
   When the army reaches Wadi l-Qura;[454]

443 From "Among those who were sent to Yazid b. Mu'awiya ..." cf. *Ansāb*, IV-B, 43 (Wahb); Tab., II, 422f. (Wahb); **'Iqd*, IV, 387f.; *Ibn 'Asakir, *Tahdhīb*, VII, 372, l. 7; *Dh., II, 354.

444 D. 73/692–693 (EI2, I, 50).

445 *Ṭbq.*, 110; Ibn Sa'd, IV, 282; Dh., III, 83; Ibn Hajar, X, 233.

446 See note 376.

447 From "A council was called ..." cf. *Ansāb*, IV-B, 35; cf. Tab., II, 413; (*) *'Iqd*, IV, 388, l. 12–15; *Dh., II, 354 (Khalifa).

448 See note 172.

449 Perhaps the *mawlā* of Ibn 'Abbas (EI2, III, 1081).

450 From "Ibn 'Abbas asked ..." cf. **'Iqd*, IV, 388, l. 15–17; *Ibn 'Asakir, *Tahdhīb*, VII, 374, l. 7.

451 U: *J-f-y-l*; Z: *Ḥ-f-y-l*. On Hafir and Hufayr cf. BGA, III, 109, 251; VI, 146, 190; VII, 180; Yaqut, II, 296f.

452 From "Marwan wrote to Yazid ..." cf. **'Iqd*, IV, 388, l. 18.

453 Abu Bakr was the *kunya* of 'Abdallah b. az-Zubayr.

454 EI, IV, 1077.

2. {229} Do you think it is an assembly of women?[455]

[Wahb] < *Juwayriya b. Asma' < *shaykh*s of Medina:
When Mu'awiya was on his deathbed, he summoned Yazid and said to him, "There is in store for you a day [of battle] with the people of Medina. When they make their move, send Muslim b. 'Uqba against them. He is a man whose sincerity we have come to know."[456] So when the people of Medina did what they did, he sent Muslim [291] b. 'Uqba against them. The Medinese dispatched to every watering place between Medina and Syria [agents] who poured a skin [filled with] tar into it, and thereby blocked [them] up.[457] But God caused it to rain upon [the Syrians], and they were not compelled to draw water with a bucket before they reached Medina.[458]

Abu l-Yaqzan and others:
Yazid gave a command to Muslim b. 'Uqba, who was complaining [because of his illness]. [Yazid] said, "If anything should happen to you, appoint Husayn b. Numayr [to take your place]."[459]

Wahb < Juwayriya:
The Medinese went out in a great throng, the like of which had never before been seen. When the Syrians saw them, they became frightened and were loath to battle them. Muslim commanded that his chair be placed between the two ranks. Then he ordered his herald [to announce]: "Battle in defense of me or give up!" He thus encouraged the people to fight. The Medinese heard the cry of "God is Great" behind them, from within Medina. The Banu Haritha had allowed the Syrians to penetrate against [the Medinese] who were [fighting] in earnest,[460] and [the latter] were put to rout. 'Abdallah b. Hanzala was leaning on one of his sons, in a deep sleep. His son woke

455 Meter: *rajaz*. The versions in Tab. and *Ansāb* have three full verses each. The versions in all the other works have "a drunken assembly" or "the assembly of a drunkard" (apparently an allusion to Yazid's supposed use of wine), in place of Khalifa's "an assembly of women" (*jam' sakrān*, *jam' as-sakrān*, *jam' an-niswān*). For parallels to this quotation of Yazid's words, see, Cf. *Ansāb*, IV-B, 33; cf. Din., 265; cf. Tab., II, 408; cf. Ibn A'tham, V, 293; cf. *Murūj*, V, 161; cf. *Tanbīh*, 304f.; cf. Ibn Kathir, VIII, 219.

456 From "When Mu'awiya was on his deathbed ..." cf. *Ansāb*, IV-B, 43, l. 16 (Wahb); Tab., II, 422 (Wahb); **'Iqd*, IV, 387, l. 18.

457 For another example of blocking up wells to hinder an enemy army, cf. Tab., II, 1896.

458 From "So when the people of Medina ..." cf. *Ansāb*, IV-B, 44, l. 3 (Wahb); Tab., II, 423; **'Iqd*, IV, 388, l. 20; *Dh., II, 354.

459 From "Yazid gave a command ..." cf. **'Iqd*, IV, 389, l. 1.

460 Kh.: *wa-hum 'alā l-jidd* (cf. Lane, 386b); Tab. = Kh.; *Ansāb*: *wa-hum fī ajaddi mā kāna fī-hi min al-qitāl*; *'Iqd*: *wa-hum 'alā l-judr* (?); Ibn 'Asakir and Dh.: *wa-hum 'alā l-ḥarra*.

him. When he opened his eyes {230} and saw what had been done, he commanded his eldest son, who advanced boldly [against the enemy] until he was killed. One by one, he continued to order his sons to attack the enemy, until the last of them was killed. Then he broke the scabbard of his sword, and battled until he fell.[461] When Muslim b. ʻUqba entered Medina, he called on the people to pledge allegiance to Yazid b. Muʻawiya as his subjects,[462] on whose families, lives, and property he had the right to pass judgment as he saw fit.[463] Then ʻAbdallah b. Zamaʻa,[464] a sincere friend of Yazid b. Muʻawiya, was brought [to Muslim], who said to him, "Pledge allegiance as a subject of the Commander of the Faithful, who has the right to pass judgment on your life, your family, and your property." Ibn Zamʻa said, "I pledge allegiance to you as the paternal cousin of the Commander of the Faithful, who has the right to pass judgment on my life, my family, and my [292] property." [Muslim] said, "Kill him."[465] Marwan jumped up and embraced him, and said, "He pledged allegiance to you as you wanted." [Muslim] said, "I will never forgive him this [faux pas].[466] If [Marwan] does not step aside, kill them both." Marwan left him, and Ibn Zamʻa was put to death.[467]

461 From "The Medinese went out in a great throng ..." cf. *Ibn ʻAsakir, *Tahdhīb*, VII, 372, l. 12; *Dh., II, 356.

462 The Arabic *khawal* actually means "servants," "property," or "slaves." Perhaps one of these words should have more accurately conveyed the meaning of *khawal* here than "subjects." This is particularly compelling in light of some of the other versions. *Ansāb*, IV-B, 38 and al-Yaʻqubi, II, 298 have *ʻabd qinn* ("slave"). Din., 265 has "Pledge allegiance on the basis that you are booty (*fay'*) belonging to the Commander of the Faithful." *Imāma*, II, 10 has "You are booty which God has enabled him (Yazid) to take by means of the swords of the Muslims. If it please him, he can give (you away), free you, or make (you) slaves." (*[antum] khawal la-hu [sc. li-Yazid] mimmā afāʼa llāh ʻalay-hi bi-asyāfi l-muslimīn, wa-'in shāʼa aʻtaqa, wa-'in shāʼa istaraqq*), III, 70 has "The people (of Medina) pledged allegiance as slaves (*ʻabīd*) belonging to Yazid." Even in Khalifa's version it is not that they object to being considered "subjects" – that is, that Yazid would have power over their persons and their property – they objected to being considered chattel, *khawal*.

463 From "The Medinese went out in a great throng ..." cf. Tab., II, 423 (Wahb).

464 *Ṭbq.*, 32; *Istīʻāb*, 910; Ibn Hajar, V, 218.

465 See note 402. From "The Medinese went out in a great throng ..." cf. *Ansāb*, IV-B, 44 (Wahb).

466 Kh.: *lā uqīlu-hā iyyāhu abadan*; cf. Tab., II, 419: *lā uqīlu-kum hādhā abadan*; Tab., II, 420.

467 From "The Medinese went out in a great throng ..." cf. **ʻIqd*, IV, 389. From "When Muslim b. ʻUqba entered Medina ..." cf. Tab., II, 418f. (Hisham b. al-Kalbi < ʻAwana); cf. Tab., II, 420 (Hisham < ʻAwana); **Istīʻāb*, 911f.; *Dh., II, 358.

Abu l-Hasan and 'Awana:
Yazid b. 'Abdallah b. Zam'a[468] was brought to Muslim, who said, "Pledge allegiance." He answered, "I pledge allegiance on the basis of God's holy Book and the Law of His Prophet." [Ibn 'Uqba] ordered him to be put to death.[469]

*Wahb < *my father < *al-Hasan:
The two sons of Zaynab[470] were killed on the day of the Harra, and they were carried to her. She said, "We belong to God and to Him we shall return.[471] How terrible is the affliction their death has brought upon me! My grief for one son is more terrible than my grief for the other. One came forward and battled until he was killed. I fear for him. The other one held himself back until he was killed. I hope for him."[472]

*Wahb b. Jarir < *Abu 'Aqil ad-Dawraqi[473] < Abu Nadra:[474]
Abu Sa'id al-Khudri[475] entered a cave on the day of the Harra. A man came upon him, then left and told a Syrian, "I will lead you to a man whom you will kill." {231} When the Syrian reached the mouth of the cave, he said to Abu Sa'id, who was carrying his sword on his neck,[476] "Come out here to me." Abu Sa'id said, "No. And if you come in after me I will kill you." The Syrian went in to him, but Abu Sa'id laid down his sword, and said, "Add your sin against me to your [other] sins, and join the inhabitants of hell! That is the reward of evil-doers."[477] [The Syrian] said, "Are you Abu

468 *Ṭbq.*, 584.

469 From "Yazid b. 'Abdallah b. Zam'a was brought to Muslim …" cf. *Ansāb*, IV-B, 38, l. 12; Din., 265 (=275 Guirgass); Tab., II, 418f. (Hisham b. al-Kalbi < 'Awana); cf. *Imāma*, II, 9f.

470 Zaynab bint Abi Salama was the wife of 'Abdallah b. Zam'a, and the mother of his children (*Ansāb*, IV-B, 38); *Istī'āb*, 1854; Dh., III, 155; Ibn Hajar, XII, 421).

471 Cf. Qur'ān 2:151.

472 As explicitly stated in the version quoted by Ibn 'Abd al-Barr (*Istī'āb*, 1855), what Zaynab is referring to with respect to her sons is Paradise. Apparently she was not quite sure that the son who had joined the rebellion and had died fighting had done the right thing, so she feared that he might be barred from Paradise for his actions. From "The two sons of Zaynab …" cf. *Istī'āb*, 1855f. ('Abdallah b. al-Mubarak < Jarir); (*) Dh., II, 355.

473 Bashir b. 'Uqba (*Ṭbq.*, 532; Ibn Sa'd, VII, 279; Ibn al-Athir, *al-Lubāb*, I, 428; as-Sam'ani, 291a; Ibn Hajar, I, 465).

474 Al-Mundhir b. Malik al-'Abdi, d. 108/726–727 (*Ṭbq.*, 500; Ibn Sa'd, VII, 208; Ibn Hajar, X, 302).

475 Sa'd b. Malik b. Sinan, d. 74/693–694 (*Ṭbq.*, 215; *Istī'āb*, 602, and 1671; Ibn 'Asakir, *Tahdhīb*, VI, 108; Dh., III, 220; Ibn Hajar, III, 479; cf. GAS, I, index).

476 What is probably meant is that he wore his sword in a kind of halter strapped around his shoulder.

477 Cf. Qur'ān 5:29. What Abu Sa'id is saying is that if the Syrian should kill him, he

Sa'id al-Khudri?" He answered, "Yes." [The Syrian] said, "Then ask God's pardon for me." He said, "May God forgive you."[478]

[293] A list of those killed on the day of the Harra [omitted from the translation][479]

{244}[313] The total number of the Ansar who were killed came to 173 men. [314] The total number of the Quraysh and the Ansar who were killed came to 306 men.[480]

Abu l-Hasan:
The battle of the Harra took place on 26 *Dhū-l-Ḥijja* {245} 63/26 August 683.[481]

The following were put to death in bonds [as prisoners]: Ma'qil b. Sinan al-Ashja'i, Muhammad b. Abi Hudhayfa al-'Adawi,[482] [and] Muhammad b. Abi l-Jahm b. Hudhayfa.[483]

In 63, Salm b. Ziyad sent Talha b. 'Abdallah b. Khalaf al-Khuza'i as governor over Sijistan, with orders to ransom his brother, Abu 'Ubayda b. Ziyad.[484] He ransomed him for 500,000 *dirhams*. [Abu 'Ubayda] joined up with his brother, and [Talha] remained in Sijistan.[485]

---

would be doing an evil deed which would contribute toward his being consigned to the Fire on the Day of Judgment. The narrator of the report assumed that the audience was familiar with the preceding two verses of *Sūra* 5 (cf. Qur'ān 5:27–28), knowledge of which is essential for understanding verse 29. Qur'ān 5:27–29 is the story of Cain and Abel.

478 From "Abu Sa'id al-Khudri entered a cave…" cf. *Ansāb*, IV-B, 44, l. 22 (Wahb); cf. *Ansāb*, IV-B, 37, l. 12; cf. Din., 268, l. 19 (In Din.'s version, the Syrians enter Abu Sa'id's house, and pluck out his beard.); cf. Tab., II, 418 (Abu Mikhnaf); * *'Iqd*, IV, 389f.; *Ibn 'Asakir, *Tahdhīb*, VI, 112, l. 15; *Dh., III, 220f.

479 There follows in the text a list, broken down by tribal and family affiliation, of the names of the casual ties of the battle of the Harra, among the Quraysh and the Ansar. The list extends from page 147 to 155 in the manuscript, and from page 293 to 313 in Zakkar's edition. I know of no such extensive list in any of the other sources. Al-Baladhuri (*Ansāb*, IV-B, 42) lists six "nobles" (*ashrāf*), all of whom are included in Khalifa's list. Most of the individuals listed by Khalifa were not significant enough to merit an entry in his *Ṭabaqāt*.

480 In the preceding list, Khalifa names 166 casualties among the Ansar and 149 among the Quraysh. From "The total number of the Ansar …" cf. *Dh., II, 357 (Khalifa).

481 This sentence parallels *Dh., II, 357 (Khalifa).

482 Cf. *Istī'āb*, 1369 (?).

483 For this list of executions cf. *Istī'āb*, 1368. Cf. Tab., II, 419; * *'Iqd*, IV, 390.

484 Cf. Kh., 287, and Bosworth, 44, 45.

485 From "In 63, Salm b. Ziyad sent Talha …" cf. *Futūḥ*, 398; *Ibn 'Asakir, *Tahdhīb*, VII, 66, l. 3 (Khalifa); (*) Ibn Hajar, V, 17 (Khalifa).

In this year, ‘Uqba b. Nafi‘ conducted a raiding expedition, and left Zuhayr b. Qays al-Balawi[486] as his lieutenant over Kairouan. He went to as-Sus al-Quswa,[487] took booty, was unharmed, and returned. Kusayla b. M-k-y-z-m/k-y-z-m,[488] a Christian, confronted him. ‘Uqba b. Nafi‘, Abu l-Muhajir [Dinar] of the Ansar, and many of his companions were killed. Then Kusayla marched on, and was confronted by Zuhayr b. Qays at a distance of a *barīd* from Kairouan. Kusayla and his companions were promptly killed.[489]

In 63/683, ‘Abdallah b. az-Zubayr led the pilgrimage. According to some, the people agreed upon ‘Abd ar-Rahman b. Zayd b. al-Khattab,[490] who led the people in prayer. According to others, no one led the pilgrimage [in this year].

[315] *‘Uthman b. ‘Uthman[491] < *Hisham b. ‘Urwa[492] < his father:
‘Abd ar-Rahman b. Zayd b. al-Khattab delivered a sermon during the pilgrimage. He mentioned a story concerning the observation of the crescent moon.

{246} Shayba b. ‘Uthman had contact with Yazid b. Mu‘awiya.[493] Rabi‘a b. Ka‘b al-Aslami[494] and Nawfal b. Mu‘awiya ad-Di’li[495] participated in the battle of the Harra.

The following died during the reign of Yazid b. Mu‘awiya: Rabi‘a b. Ka‘b al-Aslami[496] [and] ‘Abd al-Muttalib b. Rabi‘a b. al-Harith b. ‘Abd al-Muttalib b. Hashim.[497]

486 Ibn ‘Asakir, V, 393; Dh., III, 154.

487 The place is more commonly known as as-Sus al-Aqsa (EI, IV, 568; cf. Julien, 8–10; cf. Minorsky, index)

488 EI, II, 1157; cf. Julien, 10f., and 16f. The information on Kusayla – whose father’s name is written “Lemzem” in the article in EI – is somewhat contradictory in the different sources, and within the same sources (cf. Kh., 318 and 359; IAH, 198f.).

489 From “In this year, ‘Uqba b. Nafi‘ conducted a raiding expedition …” cf. IAH, 198f.; (*) *Istī‘āb*, 1076f.; cf. IA, IV, 107f.; *Dh., II, 353f.

490 *Ṭbq.*, 588; Ibn Sa‘d, V, 49; *Istī‘āb*, 833; Ibn Hajar, VI, 179.

491 Ibn Hajar, VII, 137.

492 See note 394.

493 The verb is *adraka*. Shayba b. ‘Uthman died in 59/678–679 (Kh., 272).

494 *Ṭbq.*, 245; Ibn Sa‘d, IV, 313; *Istī‘āb*, 494; Dh., III, 15; Ibn Hajar, III, 262.

495 *Ṭbq.*, 76; *Istī‘āb*, 1513; Dh., III, 89; Ibn Hajar, X, 492.

496 EI2, I, 1313.

497 On the notice of the death of ‘Abd al-Muttalib b. Rabi‘a b. al-Harith b. ‘Abd al-Muttalib b. Hashim cf. *Ṭbq.*, 13; Ibn Sa‘d, IV, 57; Dh., III, 46; Ibn Hajar, VI, 383. See also #Dh., III, 46 (Khalifa).

During the governorship of Ibn Ziyad over Iraq the following died: Ma‘qil b. Yasar al-Muzani,[498] a companion of the Prophet; ‘A'idh b. ‘Amr al-Muzani;[499] Abu Barza al-Aslami.[500] All of the preceding died in Basra.

The following died after the battle of the Harra: Masuq b. al-Ajda‘[501] [and] Abu Bashir al-Mazini.[502]

Abu l-Hasan < a man from Mecca < Salih b. Kaysan[503] < ‘Abd al-‘Aziz b. Marwan:

Yazid sent Ibn ‘Idat al-Ash‘ari to Ibn az-Zubayr, to summon him to pledge allegiance to him. He brought with him a chain of silver, and a burnoose of silk. He came to Ibn az-Zubayr, who was in al-Abtah,[504] sitting with Ayyub b. ‘Abdallah b. Zuhayr b. Abi Umayya al-Makhzumi. The governor of Mecca at that time was al-Harith b. Khalid b. al-‘As b. [316] Hisham b. al-Mughira. Ibn ‘Idat addressed him, while Ibn az-Zubayr's head was lowered in thought. Ayyub said to him, "Abu Bakr! Everybody is waiting for you."[505] Ibn az-Zubayr raised his head and said, "You said that [Yazid] had sworn that he would not accept my pledge of allegiance until I am brought to him on a chain. May God not fulfill his oath!" Ibn az-Zubayr quoted the following:

> I shall not yield to any injustice which is requested of me
> Until rock yields to the tooth of one who bites it.[506]

Then he said, "I will not pledge allegiance to Yazid, and I will not be obedient to him."[507]

498 *Ṭbq.*, 84; Ibn Sa‘d, VII, 14; *Istī‘āb*, 1432; Dh., III, 85; Ibn Hajar, X, 235.

499 *Ṭbq.*, 84; Ibn Sa‘d, VII, 31; *Istī‘āb*, 799; Ibn Hajar, V, 89.

500 See note 221.

501 See note 361.

502 On the death of Abu Bashir al-Mazini cf. *Ṭbq.*, 190; *Istī‘āb*, 1610; Dh., III, 96; Ibn Hajar, XII, 21. See also **Istī‘āb*, 1611 (Khalifa).

503 D. after 140/757–758 (*Ṭbq.*, 658; *Jarḥ*, II, I, 410; Ibn ‘Asakir, *Tahdhīb*, VI, 378.

504 Cf. BGA, III, 75; al-Bakri, *Mu‘jam*, 97; Yaqut, I, 92. Cf. al-Batha', mentioned in EI, III, 438a, 439a, and 441a.

505 Literally: "Do I not consider you an object of the people's desire?"

506 Meter: *basīṭ*. The verse is by al-Farazdaq, and is the fifth verse of a five-verse poem. The first hemistich of al-Farazdaq's verse reads as follows: *amma l-‘adūwu fa-'inna lā yalīnu la-hum* (*Dīwān*, p. 182, l. 3). For parallels cf. *Imāma*, II, 32; cf. Dh., III, 172; cf. al-Farazdaq, *Dīwān*, 182, l. 3; cf. *'Iqd*, II, 215, l. 19, second hemistich.

507 From "Yazid sent Ibn ‘Idat al-Ash‘ari …" cf. *Ansāb*, IV-B, 20f.; cf. Tab., II, 397f. (‘Abd al-‘Aziz b. Marwan, through a different *isnād*); cf. Ibn ‘Asakir, *Tahdhīb*, VII, 410f.; cf. Din., 262 (= 273 Guirgass).

*Al-Ansari[508] and *Ghundar < *Ibn Jurayj:[509]
Ibn az-Zubayr used {247} the mosque as a fortress. Inside, a camp of tents was set up. A Syrian set fire to the Bani Jumah Gate,[510] and the fire spread until it reached the door of the Ka'ba, which was consumed in the conflagration.

Ibn Jurayj < *Ibn Abi 'Ammar:[511]
One of the Syrians, standing at the edge of the well Zamzam, called out, "The *Furqān*[512] has been destroyed!" – or "Both factions have been destroyed! – by the One in Whose hand is Muhammad's soul!"

Ibn Jurayj < Ibn Abi Mulayka:[513]
Ibn az-Zubayr withdrew into the area of the Dar an-Nadwa[514] and said, "Oh Lord! Oh Lord! Would that I had known that this would happen![515] The Ka'ba was vulnerable, and her construction weak to the point that if a bird should alight on it, its stones would be scattered."

*Abu l-Hasan < Baqiyya b. 'Abd ar-Rahman < his father:
When Yazid b. Mu'awiya heard that the Meccans were urging Ibn az-Zubayr to pledge allegiance and that he refused, he sent an-Nu'man b. Bashir al-Ansari[516] and Hammam b. Qabisa an-Numayri[517] to Ibn az-Zubayr to urge him to pledge allegiance to Yazid in return for the governorship of the Hijaz, and whatever [317] he desired in the way of offices for members of his family. The two of them approached Ibn az-Zubayr and presented Yazid's offer to him. Ibn az-Zubayr said, "Are you ordering me to pledge allegiance to a man who drinks wine, neglects his prayers, and goes hunting?" Hammam said, "Your words more aptly describe yourself than

508 Muhammad b. 'Abdallah, d. 215/830–831 (*Ṭbq.*, 545; *Ma'ārif*, 520; adh-Dhahabi, *Tadhkirat al-ḥuffaz*, I, 337; Ibn Hajar, IX, 274.

509 'Abd al-Malik b. 'Abd al-'Aziz b. Jurayj, d. 150/767–768 (GAS, I, 91).

510 BGA, VII, 44–48, 51–53, 310; cf. EI, III, 439a.

511 'Ammar b. Abi 'Ammar (*Ṭbq.*, 507; *Jarḥ*, III, I, 389; Ibn Hajar, VII, 404).

512 *Al-Furqān* is an epithet of the Qur'ān (cf. EI2, II, 949). The word for "the two sides" is *al-farīqān*. The chance for confusion between the two words would probably be greater in written than in oral transmission.

513 'Abdallah b. 'Ubaydallah b. Abi Mulayka, d. c. 117/735–736 (*Ṭbq.*, 704; Ibn Sa'd, V, 472; Ibn Hajar, V, 306).

514 EI2, II, 128.

515 Z adds here: "Oh Lord! Oh Lord!"

516 EI, III, 952; GAS, II, 354.

517 Dh., III, 89; cf. *Ansāb*, V, index.

him." A man of the Quraysh punched him.[518] The envoys returned to Yazid, who became angry and swore that he would not accept [Ibn az-Zubayr's] pledge of allegiance unless his hands were in manacles.[519]

[318] The Year 64/683–684

[Baqi:] [520]

*Ibn Bukayr <al-Layth:
Yazid, Commander of the Faithful, died in 64, on the night of the full moon in *Rabī'* I/November 683. {248} In this year, the Ka'ba was burned, on Saturday 3 *Rabī'* 11/29 November 683. The Commander of the Faithful, Marwan [b. al-Hakam], received the pledge of allegiance in *Dhū-l-Qa'da*/June–July 684, in al-Jabiya.[521] The battle of [Marj] Rahit[522] took place in this year in *Dhū-l-Ḥijja*, two days after the day of Sacrifice/31 July 684. Zuhayr [b. Qays al-Balawi] took control of the Maghrib on the day that Kusayla[523] was killed.

Harmala[524] added in his recension Ibn Bukayr:
Ibn az-Zubayr led the pilgrimage.

Ibn 'Ayyash:
When Yazid b. Mu'awiya died, the Syrians departed [from Mecca] with Husayn [b. Numayr], and some of the companions of Ibn az-Zubayr departed also. The Kharijites said to each other, "Should you not ask [Ibn az-Zubayr] concerning his opinion about 'Uthman?"[525] They came to him and asked him, "What do you have to say concerning 'Uthman?" He turned and, when he saw that he had few supporters left, he said, "Come back this

518 U: *fa-lakama-hu*; Z: "slapped him" (*fa-laṭama-hu*).

519 From "When Yazid b. Mu'awiya heard …" cf. *Ansāb*, IV-B, 19ff. (al-Waqidi); cf. Tab., II, 397f. (Abu Mikhnaf).

520 The first part of this chapter was added by Baqi. Khalifa's text resumes on page 110.

521 EI2, IV, 360.

522 EI, III, 277.

523 Kh.: *'-k-s-y-l*.

524 Ibn Yahya, d. 244/858–859 (adh-Dhahabi, *Tadhkirat al-ḥuffaz*, II, 63; Ibn Hajar, II, 229; Guest, introduction to al-Kindi, 25.

525 The Kharijites considered most of 'Uthman's reign to have been so bad as to constitute unbelief. Certain Kharijites customarily used an individual's opinion of 'Uthman as a test of whether he was a true Muslim by their standards (cf. Brunnow, 155ff., and 159ff.; cf. Wellhausen, *Religio-Political Factions*, 24 n. 4, and 27).

evening." He ordered his followers to be present. The Kharijites arrived and asked, "What do you have to say about 'Uthman?" He answered, "I acknowledge him as caliph[526] living or dead." They said, "May God have nothing to do with you," and departed. Najda [b. 'Amir] revolted in al-Yamama, Nafi' b. al-Azraq revolted in Basra, and the Kharijites split up.[527]

[319] *Bakkar < Muhammad b. 'A'idh:
Yazid b. Mu'awiya died in the middle of *Rabī'* I 64/November 683. His reign lasted three years and eight months.

Muhammad < *'Abd al-A'la:
Yazid b. Mu'awiya was 38 years old when he died.

Muhammad b. 'A'idh:
Yazid b. Mu'awiya sent Yazid b. Asad on a raiding expedition in the land of the Byzantines.

{249} *Muhammad b. 'Abdallah b. Numayr:
Yazid appointed 'Amr b. Sa'id b. al-'As as governor over Medina, and 'Amr led the pilgrimage in 60/680. Yazid received the pledge of allegiance in *Rajab* 60/April–June 680. Then Yazid dismissed 'Amr, and appointed al-Walid b. 'Utba as governor over Medina. Al-Walid led the pilgrimage in 61/681, and again in 62. Then Yazid dismissed him and appointed 'Uthman b. Muhammad b. Abi Sufyan, whom the people of Medina expelled with all the Umayyads who were in Medina. 'Abdallah b. az-Zubayr led the pilgrimage in 63/683, before he received the pledge of allegiance.

*Ibn Numayr:
Yazid b. Mu'awiya died on 14 *Rabī'* I/10 November 683. His reign lasted three years and nine months.

*Ibn Numayr:
Then the Syrians pledged allegiance to Marwan, who died after nine months.

*Ibn Numayr:
Ibn az-Zubayr received the pledge of allegiance in 64/683–684. [320] The

526 The Arabic is *atawallā-hu*.

527 From "The Kharijites said to each other …" cf. Tab., II, 514–517 (Hisham b. al-Kalbi < Abu Mikhnaf).

Ka'ba was burned on Saturday 3 *Rabī'* I 64/30 October 683. 'Abdallah b. az-Zubayr led the pilgrimage eight years in a row, from 64/684 to 71/691.

Khalifa:
In this year, Muslim b. 'Uqba al-Murri died, may God not have mercy on him, and may He curse him. He had led the march toward Mecca while he was weak and near death. When he went out from al-Abwa'[528] he became gravely ill. When he realized that he was dying, he summoned Husayn b. Numayr al-Kindi and said, "I have summoned you not knowing whether to appoint you commander over the army or to send you forward and put you to death." {250} [Husayn] said, "May God grant you success. Do with me as you wish."[529] [Muslim] said, "You are a rough, uncivilized Bedouin. No one has ever allowed himself to listen to this clan of the Quraysh without being won over to their point of view. So lead this army, and when you confront [those] people be careful not to listen to them. Take your stand, do battle, then depart."[530] Husayn b. Numayr proceeded with his army, and they besieged the Meccans without letup until Yazid had died.[531] Ibn az-Zubayr received word of Yazid's death before Husayn.[532] Ibn az-Zubayr called out to them, "Why are you fighting when your leader is dead?" They answered, "We are fighting in the service of his successor." [Ibn az-Zubayr] said, "His designated successor has died." They said, "We are fighting in the service of the designated successor of the successor." [Ibn az-Zubayr] said, "He did not designate anyone as his successor." Husayn said, "If what you say be true, how swift is the news!"[533]

Muslim b. 'Uqba died in *Ṣafar* 64/September–October 683. Husayn's siege lasted 50 days, until Yazid died. Husayn set up mangonels against the Ka'ba, [321] and burned it on Tuesday 5 *Rabī'* II 64/1 December 683.[534] In

528 EI2, I, 169.

529 Literally: "Throw [or shoot] me wherever you wish." There is a play on words here. The previous expression, "May God grant you success," is literally "May God make your lot successful." The word for lot, *sahm*, also means "arrow." Thus the meaning could also be "may God make your arrow [sc. me] successful. Shoot me [i.e. your arrow] wherever you wish."

530 From "In this year, Muslim b. 'Uqba al-Murri died …" cf. Ibn 'Asakir, *Tahdhīb*, IV, 372, l. 21; (*) Dh., II, 361f.

531 From "In this year, Muslim b. 'Uqba al-Murri died …" cf. **'Iqd*, IV, 390f.; cf. Ibn 'Asakir, *Tahdhīb*, VII, 412.

532 From "In this year, Muslim b. 'Uqba al-Murri died …" cf. *Ansāb*, IV-B, 45 (Wahb).

533 From "In this year, Muslim b. 'Uqba al-Murri died …" cf. (*) Ibn 'Asakir, *Tahdhīb*, IV, 372, l. 15 (Khalifa).

534 From "Muslim b. 'Uqba died …" cf. **'Iqd*, IV, 391.

the course of the siege, al-Miswar b. Makhrama[535] was killed, and Mus'ab b. 'Abd ar-Rahman b. 'Awf died.

In this year, Yazid b. Mu'awiya died in Huwwarin,[536] near Homs. His son, Mu'awiya b. Yazid b. Mu'awiya, recited the prayers for him on the night of the full moon in the month of *Rabī'* I/November 683. His mother was Maysun bint Bahdal, a Kalbite woman. He died at the age of 38. Some say he was forty-odd years old. His reign lasted three years, nine months, and 22 days. He designated as his successor his son, Mu'awiya b. Yazid b. Mu'awiya, who retained his father's governors and made no appointments of his own. He remained sickly until he died at the age of 21 or, according to some, 20. Al-Walid b. 'Utba b. Abi Sufyan recited the prayers for him. His reign lasted about a month and a half. It is said that Mu'awiya died 40 days after his father Yazid, at the age of 18.[537]

{251}[322] The Judges during the Caliphate of Yazid

Khalifa:

Basra: 'Abd ar-Rahman b. Udhayna al-'Abdi,[538] until the civil strife occurred.

Kufa: Shurayh [b. al-Harith].

Medina: 'Abdallah b. 'Uthman at-Taymi, appointed by 'Amr b. Sa'id.

During the governorship of Ziyad over Iraq there occurred the affair of Mirdas b. Udayya. He was Mirdas b. Hudayr, of the Banu Rabi'a b. Hanzala. He revolted with 40 men, but did not kill anyone and did not concern himself with means [for survival] or with money until their provisions and money had been exhausted. They became destitute, and eventually [people] began to give [them] charity. Ibn Ziyad sent an army against them led by 'Abdallah b. Hisn ath-Tha'labi,[539] but [Mirdas] routed

535 *Ṭbq.*, 35; *Istī'āb*, 1399; Dh., III, 79; Ibn Hajar, X, 151.

536 EI2, IV, 645.

537 From "In this year, Yazid b. Mu'awiya died ..." cf. (*) *'Iqd*, IV, 391.

538 See note 359

539 Z: 'Abdallah b. Husayn at-Taghlibi; U: 'Abdallah b. Hisn at-Taghlibi. At-Tabari (e.g., II, 436) and al-Baladhuri (*Ansāb*, IV-A, 188) have Hisn, and both report that he belonged to the Banu Tha'laba. Cf. Tab., II, 187, which has Ibn Hisn at-Tamimi.

them and killed some of ['Abdallah's] companions.[540] Then [Ibn Ziyad] sent 'Abbad b. Akhdar,[541] who killed them all[542] on the banks of Maysan.[543]

He[544] < *a man who was in a caravan heading for Fars:
We encountered them while their horses were being led. Abu Bilal [Mirdas b. Udayya] spoke. He said, "You see what has come upon us. Perhaps, now that we have been afflicted by indigence, patience would be best for us. But give [us] alms, for surely God will reward those who give alms."[545] The merchants brought bags of money and put them in front of him. He said, "We need only 2 *dirhams* for each man. Perhaps we will not be able to spend even that much before we are killed." He took 80 *dirhams* for himself and his companions.[546] The Basrans sent against them an army which killed them.

Nafi' b. al-Azraq revolted. {252} He engaged in indiscriminate massacre.[547] Ibn 'Ubays went out against him. [323] Both Nafi' and Ibn 'Ubays were killed. We[548] killed five of their commanders, and they killed five of ours. Ibn 'Ubays was killed, so the Basrans made Rabi'a as-Saliti commander. Ibn al-Azraq was killed, so the Kharijites made 'Abdallah b. Mahuz chief. But [again] both leaders were killed. So the Basrans put Haritha b. Badr al-Ghudani in command, while the Kharijites az-Zubayr

540 From "During the governorship of Ziyad ..." cf. Tab., II, 187 (Wahb < Jarir < Yunus b. 'Ubayd).

541 *Ṭbq.*, 530; *Jarḥ*, III, I, 77.

542 From "During the governorship of Ziyad ..." cf. *Dh., II, 359, l. 10 (Yunus b. 'Ubayd).

543 Maysan is in Iraq (EI, III, 146). Most of the other sources state that Mirdas's death took place in Fars or al-Ahwaz. Yaqut, IV, 712, lists a place called *M-y-j-'-s*, in al-Ahwaz, where, according to Yaqut, Mirdas was killed.

544 Khalifa neglected to cite his source for this report, or else it was lost in the course of the *Ta'rīkh*s transmission. Adh-Dhahabi states that the report is from Ghassan b. Mudar < Sa'id b. Yazid < the man in the caravan. It would seem that this report is part of Wahb b. Jarir's report on the Kharijites, which was related from Ghassan and Sa'id, the last previous excerpt of which is on page 79 (Kh., 264). Adh-Dhahabi's account was probably taken from Khalifa's *Ta'rīkh*. The *isnād* for this report fell out of Baqi's recension, but was apparently preserved in that of at-Tustari.

545 This is an allusion to Qur'ān 12:88.

546 From "We encountered them ..." cf. *Ansāb*, IV-A, 158; cf. al-Mubarrad, 586; cf. *'Iqd*, I, 255; cf. *''Iqd*, II, 399; *Dh., II, 359, l. 14 (Ghassan b. Mudar < Sa'id b. Yazid).

547 The verb here is *i'tarada*, which is used with the same meaning as *ista'raḍa* (Cf. EI2, IV, 269 s.v. *isti'rāḍ*; cf. note 263).

548 Khalifa seems to have neglected to name the narrator of this report. Perhaps it is Mu'awiya b. Qurra al-Muzani, a member of the Basran army, who is indicated as the narrator of the following report.

b. Mahuz in command. Haritha withdrew with his troops, while az-Zubayr proceeded to al-Mada'in.[549]

Mu'awiya b. Qurra al-Muzani:[550]
We went out with Ibn 'Ubays with about 20,000 men. Ibn 'Ubays delivered a sermon to us in which he said, "People! We have come forth to seek God's reward. Whoever of you agrees with our point of view, let him go with us. Those who are not in agreement with us are free to refrain from going out with us." Two thousand of us turned out. We confronted [Nafi' b. al-Azraq] in Dastuwa'[551] and gave battle. Five of our leaders were killed, and we killed five of theirs. My father, Qurra, was killed. I attacked my father's slayer and killed him.[552] By evening a small band [of us] remained. The Harurites were about 500 men. Ibn al-Azraq had been killed, as had Ibn 'Ubays.[553] We got up and they got up. They looked at us and we looked at them. No man among us wanted to stretch out his hand in battle, because of fatigue. The people said, "We ought to keep away from them until it is dark." Someone said, "Do not forgive them." But the people preferred to keep quiet. Then reinforcements reached [the Harurites] from al-Yamama and we were unable to restrain ourselves from running in flight until we reached Basra. [The Harurites] were then victorious, and pledged allegiance to Ibn al-Mahuz. They took possession of al-Ahwaz and Fars, and levied taxes.[554]

In this year, the following died: Hammam b. al-Harith[555] [and] Abu Maysara.[556]

In 64, Ibn az-Zubayr claimed the caliphate for himself. That was after the death of Yazid b. Mu'awiya. He received the pledge of allegiance on 7 *Rajab* 64/29 February 684. He did not call for it, and was not asked [to receive it], until [after] the death of Yazid.

549 From "Nafi' b. al-Azraq revolted…" cf. Din., 270; cf. Tab., II, 580f.

550 *Ṭbq.*, 493; Ibn Sa'd, VII, 221; Ibn Hajar, X, 216.

551 Zambaur, *Münzprägungen*, 117.

552 From "My father, Qurra …" cf. Ibn Sa'd, VII, 32.

553 From "We went out with Ibn 'Ubays …" cf. Tab., II, 580f. (Wahb < … < Mu'awiya b. Qurra).

554 From "We went out with Ibn 'Ubays …" cf. Tab., II, 581f. (Hisham b. al-Kalbi < Abu Mikhnaf).

555 *Ṭbq.*, 336; Ibn Sa'd, VI, 118; Dh., III, 212; Ibn Hajar, XI, 66.

556 'Amr b. Shurahbil (*Ṭbq.*, 338; Ibn Sa'd, VI, 106; Ibn Hajar, VIII, 47).

He:[557]

[324] Abu Hurra, [known as] the Owner of the Cloak,[558] a *mawlā*, was a poet and brave {253} warrior. He said, "Ibn az-Zubayr, we have not shed blood and have not killed people except for your rulership." [Ibn az-Zubayr] asked, "To whom would you pledge allegiance besides me?" He said, "You should wait until we ourselves are summoning you." He departed from him,[559] and then composed the following:

1. The clients[560] at night are berating
   The master, complaining of hunger and war.

2. What are we up against? What has been causing us to suffer?
   Which king has control over what he bestows?[561]

3. We have with God a covenant which we shall not break.
   We will never seek a council after he is gone.[562]

However, before that Ibn az-Zubayr had been calling for a council to be convened among members of the community. Three months after the death of Yazid b. Mu'awiya, he called for the pledge of allegiance for the caliphate on 9 *Rajab* 64/2 March 684.

['Ubaydallah] b. Ziyad was delivering a sermon to the people, in which he announced the death of Yazid.[563] He said, "Choose [an *amīr*] for yourselves." Al-Ahnaf [b. Qays] said, "We will accept you until the people reach an agreement." Ibn Ziyad said, "Come tomorrow for your stipends." He opened the *dīwān* and disbursed the stipends. Salama b. Dhu'ayb ar-Riyahi revolted in the area of al-Mirbad, calling for the

557 "He" may refer to Wahb b. Jarir, as the ascription of this tradition in the *Ansāb* (IV-B, 58) indicates.

558 Cf. *Ansāb*, V, 188, l. 9: Abu Hurra, a *mawlā* of the Khuza'a; *Murūj*, V, 174: Abu Hurra, *mawlā* of az-Zubayr.

559 From "Abu Hurra, [known as] the Owner of the Cloak ..." cf. *Ibn 'Asakir, *Tahdhīb*, VII, 414.

560 "The clients" is *al-mawālī*, and "the master," in the following verse, is *al-muwālī*. This use of two different words of the same root is a technique of poetry known as *jinās* (cf. Arberry, 21f.).

561 From "Abu Hurra, [known as] the Owner of the Cloak ..." cf. *Ansāb*, IV-B, 58 (Wahb).

562 Meter: *basīṭ*. Cf. *Ansāb*, IV-B, 159 (al-Mada'ini; verses 1 and 3, plus two additional); cf. *Ansāb*, V, 188 (verses 1 and 3, plus two additional); cf. *Murūj*, V, 174 (verses 1 and 2).

563 On the events that follow, cf. Wellhausen's analysis of at-Tabari (*Arab Kingdom*, 401–411).

pledge of allegiance to Ibn az-Zubayr.[564] Ibn Ziyad revoked the stipend. He took counsel with his brothers and the members of his family, concerning whether he should do battle against anyone who should resist or oppose him. They advised him to refrain from that, so he withdrew. He betook himself to Mas'ud [b. 'Amr] in *Jumādā* II 64/January–February 684, and remained with him more than two months. However, in *Sha'bān*/March–April 684 he proceeded to the governor's residence. Some reports have it that Ibn Ziyad remained with Mas'ud for 40 days. Others say that he remained three months. [325] The governor's residence was plundered. Al-Ahnaf came saying, "No one shall enter the residence of Ibn Ziyad while I am alive," and guarded it. He sent [agents] to the treasury, to the jail, and to the *arwān*, which he made inaccessible. The Basrans gathered together to appoint a new *amīr*, and agreed upon 'Abdallah b. al-Harith {254} b. Nawfal b. 'Abd al-Muttalib,[565] whose mother was the daughter of Abu Sufyan b. Harb b. Umayya. Malik b. Misma'[566] and Suwayd b. Manjuf[567] proceeded to Mas'ud b. 'Amr to ally themselves with him, and to return ['Ubaydallah] b. Ziyad to the governor's residence. Ibn Ziyad said to 'Abbad b. Ziyad, "Strengthen the alliance with them." They wrote a document between them. Mas'ud sealed it with his seal. He wrote a letter to Malik b. Misma' and sealed it with his seal. He gave the two letters to Dhira', father of Harun b. Dhira' an-Numayri.[568] They put the two [documents] in his care. Then they said to Ibn Ziyad, "Set out so we may return to you to the governor's residence." Ibn Ziyad said to them, "You set out, with Mas'ud as your leader. If you are victorious, you will then have your way." Mas'ud and his companions headed for the residence. Mas'ud's companions entered the mosque, and they killed a fuller who was in the courtyard of the mosque. As soon as al-Ahnaf received news of this, he sent a message to the Banu Tamim, who came. A man of the Banu Tamim went to Mas'ud while he was sitting on a mule in the compound of the Banu Sulaym, and killed him. The Asawira[569] shot

564 Al-Mirbad was the main public square of Basra (cf. al-Ya'qubi, II, 464; *Futūḥ*, 349; Wellhausen, *Arab Kingdom*, 407; Pellat, index; BGA, I, 80; II, 160).

565 He was called Babba, and died c. 84 (*Ṭbq.*, 451; *Istī'āb*, 885; Dh., III, 263; Ibn 'Asakir, *Tahdhīb*, VII, 346; Ibn Hajar, V, 180; cf. Wellhausen, *Arab Kingdom*, 404ff., index).

566 Dh., III, 207; cf. Kh., 471.

567 D. 72/691–692 (Dh., III, 159; Kh., 341).

568 U: Abu Harun b. Dhira' an-Numayri.

569 On the Asawira, a people of Iranian origin, cf. Pellat, 35, and index; Wellhausen, *Arab Kingdom*, 397, 410.

arrows, and they were killed in the mosque. Malik b. Misma' fled to the Banu 'Adi, and the people were routed.[570]

Tawwaf b. al-Mu'alla as-Sadusi[571] revolted as a Kharijite[572] at the castle of Aws.[573] The people threw rocks at him. His horse carried him away and threw him in the river of Basra.[574]

'Abdallah b. az-Zubayr sent 'Abdallah b. Yazid al-Khatmi[575] as leader of the prayer in Kufa. He appointed Ibrahim b. Muhammad b. Talha b. 'Ubaydallah[576] as finance secretary. That was in *Ramaḍān* 64/April–May 684. He retained 'Abdallah b. al-Harith as governor over Basra for 40 days, {255} then he wrote to Anas b. Malik,[577] appointing him as leader of the prayer.[578]

[326] The people pledged allegiance to Marwan b. al-Hakam in the middle of *Dhū-l-Qa'da* 64/July 684. His mother was Amina bint 'Alqama b. Safwan al-Kinani.

In this year, the battle of [Marj] Rahit took place in Syria. The Syrians had pledged allegiance to Ibn az-Zubayr, except for the people of al-Jabiya, the members of the Umayyad family and their clients, and ['Ubaydallah] b. Ziyad, [all of whom] pledged allegiance to Marwan b. al-Hakam, and to Khalid b. Yazid b. Mu'awiya as his successor. That was in the middle of *Dhū-l-Qa'da*/July 684. Then they marched against ad-Dahhak [b. Qays al-Fihri] and met at Marj Rahit. They battled for 20 days, until the rout of ad-Dahhak b. Qays, [in which] ad-Dahhak and his companions were killed. Marwan had 13,000 troops while ad-Dahhak had 60,000. They battled every day for 20 days. Ibn Ziyad said to Marwan, "Ad-Dahhak has on his side cavalry composed of Qaysites, and we will not be able to

570 From "['Ubaydallah] b. Ziyad was delivering a sermon to the people ..." cf. Tab., II, 435–528; from "Mas'ud and his companions headed for the residence ..." cf. *Dh., II, 364 (Khalifa < Abu l-Yaqzan).

571 In the *Ansāb* (IV-A, 154) his name is Tawwaf b. 'Allaq. Cf. Wellhausen, *Religio-Political Factions*, 40, and 42 n. 3, where the name is Tawwaf b. Ghallaq.

572 The Arabic is *kharaja ... fa-ḥakkama* (cf. note 241).

573 Cf. *Futūḥ*, 355, l. 2; BGA, V, 191; Pellat, 153, 172.

574 From "Tawwaf b. al-Mu'alla as-Sadusi revolted ..." cf. *Ansāb*, IV-A, 154, especially l. 21–22); (*) Dh., II, 360.

575 *Istī'āb*, 1001; Dh., III, 40; Ibn Hajar, VI, 78.

576 D. 110/728–729 (*Ṭbq.*, 639; *Jarḥ*, I, I, 124; Ibn 'Asakir, *Tahdhīb*, II, 257; Ibn Hajar, I, 153).

577 D. 93/711–712 (EI2, I, 482; cf. GAS, I, index).

578 From "he wrote to Anas b. Malik ..." cf. (*) Dh., III, 341f. (Khalifa); (*) Siyar, III, 269 (Khalifa).

take what we want from them unless we employ a stratagem. So ask them to make peace. Hold back from battling, but prepare the cavalry. [Then], when they put down their arms, unleash [the cavalry] against them." The ambassadors went between them, and ad-Dahhak refrained from battling. Then Marwan and his cavalry attacked them, and they retreated to their flag in disarray. Ad-Dahhak was killed, as were many of his Qaysite cavalry.[579]

On that day three sons of Zufar b. al-Harith[580] were killed. Zufar had the following to say about this:

1. {256} By my life! The battle of Rahit has left
   A wide cleft which separates us from Marwan. [327]

2. Show me, [woman], my arms, damn you!
   I see that the war only will increase in duration.

3. After [the death], one after the other, of Ibn ʿAmr and Ibn Maʿn,[581]
   And the killing of Hammam,[582] do I have any hopes left?

4. The Kalb go away, our lances not reaching them,
   And the dead of Rahit are left as they are.

5. Before this I was never seen to shrink from anything; [Imagine!]
   Me fleeing, and abandoning my two companions behind me!

6. In the evening when I rush on the high ground[583] I do not see
   Anyone except those who are against me; [I see] no one on my side.

7. Should a single day, if I handle it badly, take away
   My well-being and the excellence of my bravery?

579 From "The Syrians had pledged allegiance to Ibn az-Zubayr …" cf. *Dh., II, 364, l. 20 (az-Zubayr b. al-Khirrit < Abu Labid); Ibn ʿAsakir, *Tahdhīb*, VII, 9.

580 GAS, II, 339.

581 Kh.: Banu ʿAmr b. Maʿn. Ibn Maʿn may be Thawr b. Maʿn as-Sulami (cf. *Ansāb*, V, 136, l. 11; Ibn ʿAsakir, *Tahdhīb*, III, 383), and Ibn ʿAmr may be Ziyad b. ʿAmr b. Muʿawiya al-ʿUqayli (cf. *Ansāb*, V, 136, l. 4). Cf. the commentary by at-Tibrizi (*Sharh Dīwān al-Hamasa*, I, 153).

582 Hammam is Hammam b. Qabisa, who was killed at Marj Rahit (cf. *Ansāb*, V, 136, l. 17; ibid., 143, l. 7; and note 517, above).

583 Kh. and *Murūj*: *bi-l-farīqayn*, "[I rush] with/among the two sides," which does not seem right. Yaqut: *bi-l-qarīnayn*, "with the two companions." Tab.: *bi-l-qirān*, "on the peaks [of mountains]." At-Tabrizi: *bi-ṣ-ṣaʿīd*, "on the high ground." Ibn ʿAsakir: *bi-l-firār*, "in flight, retreat."

8. There will be no peace until the horses snort amidst the spears,
   And until my women take revenge on the women of the Kalb.

9. The grass will sprout forth on the soil of the [deserted] dung heaps,
   While the rancor in the souls will remain as it is.[584]

In the year 64, Ibn az-Zubayr demolished the Ka'ba, then rebuilt it. He incorporated into it about seven cubits of the *ḥijr*.[585]

{257}[328] After the death of Yazid b. Mu'awiya, the people of ar-Rayy revolted. 'Amir b. Mas'ud,[586] the governor over Kufa, sent Muhammad b. 'Umayr b. 'Utarid,[587] but they routed him. Then he sent 'Attab b. Warqa' ar-Riyahi.[588] Al-Farrukhan[589] was killed, and the infidels were routed.[590]

584 Meter: *ṭawīl*. The verses of this poem are arranged in a different order in each of the different versions. The following list shows the various verse orders:

Kh./Yaqut	Tab.	*'Iqd*	*Murūj*	*Tanbīh*	Tibrizi	Ibn 'Asakir
1	7	1	1	1	-	1
2	1	-	3	4	1	3
3	8	-	8	-	-	8
4	6	4	4	2	-	9
5	9	2	5	5	2	5
6	10	-	6	-	3	6
7	11	3	7	-	4	4
8	12	6		-		7
9	5	5	2	3	;	2

There are many minor variations in the verses of the various versions.
From, "Zufar had the following to say about that ..." cf. *Ansāb*, V, 141, l. 21 (verses 2, 4, 5, 9; plus three); *'Uyūn*, III, 111 (verse 9); Tab., II, 483f. (plus four); *Murūj*, V, 203 (lacks verses 2, 3, 6); *'Iqd*, V, 499 (verse 9); *Aghānī*, VII, 176 (verse 9); *Aghānī*, XVII, 112 (verses 1, 3, 4, 9); Ibn 'Asakir, *Tahdhīb*, V, 377; Ibn 'Asakir, *Tahdhīb*, VII, 412 (verses 1, 2, 9); at-Tibrizi, *Sharḥ al-Ḥamāsa*, I, 153; *Yaqut, II, 744; *Tanbīh*, 309f. (lacks verses 3, 6, 7, 8; plus one additional verse).

585 Cf. EI2, IV, 317ff. s.v. Ka'ba.

586 *Istī'āb*, 798; Ibn Hajar, V, 80.

587 *Ma'ārif*, 425, l. 4–5; Dh., III, 302.

588 *Ma'ārif*, 415.

589 Kh.: *B-r-j-'-n*. The name – or title – al-Farrukhan is attested in other sources. Al-Farrukhan appears in Tab. several times. In at least one instance, he is said to have been the *iṣbahbadh* (provincial military governor) of Khurasan in the year 22/642–643 (Tab., I, 2659). Al-Baladhuri states that al-Farrukhan had a castle, which was besieged during the conquest of ar-Ray and Qumis (*Futūḥ*, 317f.). Cf. EI2, II, 809 s.v. Farrukhan; cf. EI2, IV, 207 s.v. Ispahbadh.

590 From "After the death of Yazid b. Mu'awiya ..." cf. (*) IA, IV, 144; *Dh., II, 365 (Abu 'Ubayda).

In this year, Yunus b. 'Ubayd was born.[591]

Marwan had the pledge of allegiance renewed for himself, and for his son 'Abd al-Malik b. Marwan after him, and then for 'Abd al-'Aziz b. Marwan [after 'Abd al-Malik]. That was in the beginning of 65/August–September 684.

[329] The Year 65/684–685

[Baqi:][592]

*Yahya b. Bukayr < al-Layth:
In 65, Marwan entered Egypt at the beginning of *Rabī'* II/15 November 684. He left Egypt in *Jumādā* II/January–February 685, and died at the beginning of *Ramaḍān*/April–May 685. The Commander of the Faithful 'Abd al-Malik became caliph in Iliya'[593] in the month of *Ramaḍān*/April–May 685. In this year Hubaysh b. Dalja[594] was killed. The Commander of the Faithful, 'Abd al-Malik, celebrated the feast of the Sacrifice[595] in Homs. Ibn az-Zubayr led the pilgrimage.

*Bakkar < Muhammad b. 'A'idh < al-Walid:
'Abd al-Malik b. Marwan received the pledge of allegiance, then encamped at Butnan Habib.[596]

*Ibn Numayr:
The Syrians pledged allegiance to 'Abd al-Malik b. Marwan.

Ibn 'Ayyash < *Muhammad b. al-Muntashir[597] < *al-Muhallab b. Abi Sufra, who often used to tell us about that battle of ours – that is, the battle against Qatari [b. al-Fuja'a], or the battle of the parties – told us, "I do not[598] doubt [330] that 'Abd al-Malik will indeed rule." We would say to

591 D. 139/756–757 (*Ṭbq.*, 525; Ibn Sa'd, VII, 260; Ibn Hajar, XI, 442; GAS, I, 88).

592 The first part of this chapter was added by Baqi. Khalifa's text resumes on page 120.

593 Jerusalem. The name Iliya' comes from the Roman name for Jerusalem, Aelia Capitolina (EI, II, 1094; cf. the *Encyclopaedia Judaica*, II, 319).

594 Ibn 'Asakir, *Tahdhīb*, IV, 40.

595 The Feast of Sacrifice (*'Īd al-Adḥā*) is celebrated on 10 *Dhū l-Ḥijja*.

596 Cf. *Futūḥ*, 149; EI2, I, 1348f.; Wellhausen, *Arab Kingdom*, 188ff.; Dixon, 123f., 128.

597 Dh., IV, 201; Ibn Hajar, IX, 471.

598 Kh. lacks the negative.

him, "May God make the *amīr* [i.e., you] prosper. What does he [i.e., you] know?" Al-Muhallab would say:

Salm[599] b. Ziyad sent me from Khurasan to Yazid b. Mu'awiya {258} in Syria. I came to him, and I was standing beside his chair at his head, with my hand on his cushions. Then the chamberlain came in and said to him, "'Abd al-Malik b. Marwan is here, and seeks permission to enter." Yazid b. Mu'awiya said, "Haven't we fulfilled his needs and the needs of his father?" [The chamberlain] said, "But he [only] asks to speak with you standing, without sitting down." Yazid said, "Let him come in." There entered a brownish-reddish man with large black eyes, and not much flesh in his cheeks, good-looking, wearing a black turban which he let hang over in front and in back[600] as the Qurra' do. He spoke to him. Yazid said, "Yes, of course." As he left, Yazid's gaze followed him. Then he turned to me and said, "Muhallab." I said, "At your service, Commander of the Faithful." He said, "The people of the books[601] claim that this man shall be made ruler." I said, "God knows best. If he should become ruler [it would be fine]. He is a decent Muslim, and he is one of the best men of his tribe."

[Ibn 'Ayyash:]
'Abd al-Malik heard about al-Muhallab [and his conversation with Yazid]. He thanked him for it, and eventually wrote him what he wrote. After that he made him governor of Khurasan.

Khalifa:
In this year, Marwan sent 'Ubaydallah b. Ziyad to Iraq with 60,000 troops in *Rabī'* II/November–December 684.

In this year, the following were killed: Sulayman b. Surad,[602] al-Musayyab b. Najaba,[603] and 'Abdallah at-Taymi of the Taym Allat b. Tha'laba.

Ibn az-Zubayr called upon Muhammad b. 'Ali b. Abi Talib, [known as] Ibn al-Hanafiyya, to pledge allegiance to him. He refused, so Ibn az-Zubayr imprisoned him in the Shi'b of the Banu Hashim[604] with a number of

599 U: Salim (see note 427).

600 On the turban (*'imāma*) cf. Dozy, 305–311. The end which is allowed to hang down is known as the *'adhaba* (ibid., 307f.). Adh-Dhahabi relates that al-Hajjaj threw the end (*'adhaba*) of his turban between his shoulders (Dh., III, 117, l. 20).

601 I.e. people versed in books [of wisdom, future events], prognosticators (cf. note 204).

602 EI, IV, 521; cf. Dixon, index.

603 *Ansāb*, V, index; Dh., III, 82; Ibn Hajar, X, 154.

604 Cf. BGA, VIII, 233, l. 3.

his companions, one of whom was Abu t-Tufayl ‘Amir b. Wathila.[605] He threatened them with terrible consequences,[606] until al-Mukhtar [b. Abi ‘Ubayd ath-Thaqafi] sent Abu ‘Abdallah {259} al-Jadali,[607] who freed them from their captivity.[608]

[331] Then ‘Abd al-Malik b. Marwan b. al-Hakam received the pledge of allegiance. His mother was ‘A’isha bint al-Mughira b. Abi l-‘As.

Marwan b. al-Hakam died in Damascus on 3 *Ramaḍān* 65/13 April 685,[609] at the age of 63. His son, ‘Abd al-Malik b. Marwan, recited the prayers for him. His reign lasted nine months and 18 days. Marwan was born in Mecca in the house of Abu l-‘As, which was called the house of Umm Abi l-Hakam. Other reports say he was born in at-Ta’if.

[Marwan’s Officers]

Chief of police: Yahya b. Qays al-Ghassani.

Secretary: Sarjun b. Mansur ar-Rumi.

Chamberlain: Abu Sahl[610] al-Aswad, his *mawlā*.’[611]

According to some, he died on the last day of *Sha‘bān*/10 April 685, at the age of 64.

[332] The Year 66/685–686

[Baqi:][612]

*Ibn Bukayr < al-Layth:

In 66, the first raid in Butnan was made. ‘Ubaydallah b. Ziyad and his companions were killed in al-Khazir.[613] Natil [b. Qays al-Judhami][614] and his companions were killed in Palestine. The Commander of the Faithful

605 D. between 100/718–719 and 107 (*Ṭbq.*, 68, 698; Ibn Sa‘d, V, 457; ibid., VI, 64; *Istī‘āb*, 798; Ibn Hajar, V, 82).

606 From “Ibn az-Zubayr called upon Muhammad b. ‘Ali b. Abi Talib …” cf. (*) Dh., II, 367, l. 8.

607 *Ṭbq.*, 324; Ibn Sa‘d, VI, 228; Ibn Hajar, XII, 148.

608 From “Ibn az-Zubayr called upon Muhammad b. ‘Ali b. Abi Talib …” cf. Ibn Hajar, XII, 149.

609 From “Marwan b. al-Hakam died …” cf. *Ibn Kathir, VIII, 260 (Khalifa).

610 Kh.: Abu Nahshal; *‘Iqd*: Abu Sahl.

611 From “Marwan b. al-Hakam died in Damascus …” cf. (*) *‘Iqd*, IV, 398.

612 The first part of this chapter was added by Baqi. Khalifa’s text resumes on page 122.

613 Yaqut, II, 388; cf. Wellhausen, *Arab Kingdom*, index; Dixon, index.

614 Ibn Hajar, X, 398; cf. Dixon, 121, 123; cf. Wellhausen, *Arab Kingdom*, index.

celebrated the Feast of the Sacrifice in Salamiyya.[615] Egypt was struck by the plague. The battle of Ajnadayn[616] took place. Ibn az-Zubayr led the pilgrimage.

Khalifa:
In this year, al-Mukhtar b. Abi 'Ubayd conquered Kufa. The following were killed at Jabbanat as-Sabi':[617] Rifa'a b. Shaddad,[618] Habib b. Suhban,[619] 'Abdallah b. Sa'd b. Qays. The following were also killed: 'Umar b. Sa'd b. Abi Waqqas[620] and his son, Hafs b. 'Umar b. Sa'd.

{260} In this year, Ibrahim b. al-Ashtar[621] killed ['Ubaydallah] b. Ziyad in al-Khazir, near Mosul, as well as Husayn b. Numayr as-Sakuni, Shurahbil b. Dhi l-Kala',[622] and some Syrians. Among the companions of Ibn al-Ashtar who were killed was Hubayra b. Yarim,[623] from whom Abu Ishaq as-Sabi'i[624] related [traditions].

[333] Najda b. 'Amir made the pilgrimage. Ibn al-Hanafiyya stood [at 'Arafat] with his companions, Najda with his, and Ibn az-Zubayr with the majority of the people.

In this year, the following died: Zayd b. Arqam al-Ansari,[625] Asma' b. Kharija b. Badr al-Fazari.[626]

In this year, the jurist 'Abdallah b. 'Awn b. Artuban[627] was born.

615 EI, IV, 93.

616 EI2, I, 208.

617 Cf. *Futūḥ*, 280, l. 21; Yaqut, II, 16, s.v. *jabbana*; Ibn Hazm, 395; Dixon, index. The vocalization given in the editions of the *Futūḥ* and Ibn Hazm is as-Sabi'.

618 On the notice of the death of Rifa'a b. Shaddad cf. *Ṭbq.*, 345; *Jarḥ*, I, II, 493; Ibn Hajar, III, 281 (Khalifa).

619 *Ṭbq.*, 325, 358; Ibn Sa'd, VI, 166; Ibn Hajar, II, 187.

620 See note 421. On the notice of the death of 'Umar b. Sa'd b. Abi Waqqas cf. *Ibn Hajar, VII, 451 (Khalifa).

621 On the activities of Ibrahim b. al-Ashtar, see Dixon, chapter two; EI2, III, 987.

622 Cf. *Ansāb*, V, index; Ibn Hazm, 434. On his father, see cf. *Istī'āb*, 471; Ibn 'Asakir, *Tahdhīb*, V, 266.

623 *Ṭbq.*, 339; Ibn Sa'd, VI, 170; Dh., III, 89; Ibn Hajar, XI, 23.

624 'Amr b. 'Abdallah (*Ṭbq.*, 375; Ibn Sa'd, VI, 313; Ibn Hajar, VIII, 63), d. 127/744–745.

625 On the notice of the death of Zayd b. Arqam al-Ansari cf. *Ṭbq.*, 212, 305; *Istī'āb*, 535; Ibn Hajar, III, 394–395; #Dh., III, 17 (Khalifa); #Ibn Hajar, III, 395 (Khalifa).

626 On the notice of the death of Asma' b. Kharija b. Badr al-Fazari cf. Dh., II, 385 (Khalifa).

627 *Ṭbq.*, 528; Ibn Sa'd, VII, 261; Ibn Hajar, V, 246.

Ibn al-Kalbi:
'Adi b. Hatim at-Ta'i[628] died during the time of al-Mukhtar.

[334] The Year 67/686–687

[Baqi:][629]

*Ibn Bukayr < al-Layth:
In 67, [the following took place]: the raid in Butnan, the killing of al-Mukhtar b. Abi 'Ubayd, [and] the killing of 'Umar b. Sa'd. The Commander of the Faithful celebrated the Feast of Sacrifice in Damascus.

Harmala added in his recension:
Ibn az-Zubayr led the pilgrimage.

Khalifa:
In this year, the battle of al-Madhar[630] took place. 'Umar b. 'Ali b. Abi Talib and Muhammad b. al-Ash'ath b. Qays[631] were killed. Al-Mukhtar b. Abi 'Ubayd was killed. Tarif and Tarraf,[632] two brothers of the Banu Hanifa, entered upon him in his castle and killed him.[633] They brought his head to Mus'ab [b. az-Zubayr], who gave them {261} 30,000 [*dirhams*].[634]

In this year, Abu l-Kanud,[635] whose name was 'Abdallah b. 'Amir, the companion of Ibn Mas'ud, was killed.

Al-Ahnaf b. Qays died in Kufa. Mus'ab b. az-Zubayr recited the prayers for him and walked in his funeral procession without a cloak. It is said that he was the first person to walk in a funeral procession without a cloak.[636]

628 EI2, I, 195.

629 The first part of this chapter was added by Baqi. Khalifa's text resumes on the same page, below.

630 Cf. Minorsky, 76, 218; Wellhausen, *Religio-Political Factions*, 33, 36 n. 13; Dixon, 71–74; EI, III, 154b–155a.

631 *Ṭbq.*, 33[illegible]; *Jarḥ*, III, II, 206; Ibn Hajar, IX, 64.

632 Cf. *Ansāb*, V, 262; Tab., II, 738, for different versions of the killing of al-Mukhtar, and variations on the names of his killers.

633 From "Al-Mukhtar b. Abi 'Ubayd was killed ..." cf. *Ansāb*, V, 262, l. 5; cf. Tab., II, 738.

634 From "Al-Mukhtar b. Abi 'Ubayd was killed ..." cf. (*) Dh., II, 377.

635 *Ṭbq.*, 343; Dh., III, 224, 322; Ibn Sa'd, VI, 177; Ibn Hajar, XII, 213.

636 The Arabic is *radā'*. Cf. Dozy, 280, l. 8, where a passage is quoted stating that it was the custom of chamberlains to walk in funeral processions without a *ṭaylasān*.

[335] The Year 68/687–688

[Baqi:][637]

*Ibn Bukayr < al-Layth:
In 68, there was the raid of ar-Rayyan with the clients in Yemen. The Commander of the Faithful remained [in Damascus] in this year. 'Abis b. Sa'id[638] died. The Commander of the Faithful celebrated the Feast of Sacrifice in Damascus. Ibn az-Zubayr led the pilgrimage.

*Bakkar < Muhammad b 'A'idh:
There was a famine, so the Syrians did not undertake a raiding expedition in 68. In this year ['Abdallah] b. 'Abbas [b. 'Abd al-Muttalib] died in at-Ta'if.

Khalifa:
In this year, Jabir b. al-Aswad az-Zuhri wanted Sa'id b. al-Musayyab[639] to pledge allegiance to Ibn az-Zubayr, but he refused, so he gave him 60 lashes with a whip.[640]

In this year, the following died: Jabir b. 'Abdallah al-Ansari,[641] Zayd b. Khalid al-Juhani,[642] Abu Waqid al-Laythi,[643] [and] Abu Shurayh al-Khuza'i,[644] a companion of the Prophet.

637 The first part of this chapter was added by Baqi. Khalifa's text resumes below, on the same page.

638 Al-Kindi, 311–313. Cf. IAH, 234, l. 16.

639 D. 93/711–712, or 94 (GAS, I, 76).

640 This sentence parallels *Ma'ārif*, 437, l. 18; *Dh., II, 381 (Khalifa); *Ibn Taghribirdi, I, 181 (Khalifa).

641 GAS, I, 85. Cf. Kh., 357 (256); *Dh., III, 17 (Khalifa).

642 On the notice of the death of Zayd b. Khalid al-Juhani cf. *Ṭbq.*, 264; *Istī'āb*, 549; Dh., III, 155; Ibn Hajar, III, 410. Cf. Kh., 357 (256); *Dh., III, 17 (Khalifa).

643 *Ṭbq.*, 64; *Istī'āb*, 296 and 1774; Dh., III, 106; Ibn Hajar, XII, 270.

644 *Ṭbq.*, 237; Ibn Sa'd, IV, 295; ibid., V, 459; *Istī'āb*, 1688; Dh., III, 101; Ibn Hajar, XII, 125.

{262}[336] The Year 69/688–689

[Baqi:][645]

*Yahya b. ‘Abdallah [b. Bukayr] < al-Layth:
In 69, there was the second expedition in Butnan, and the raid of Hassan [b. an-Nu‘man] in the Awras.[646] The companions of Ibn Muhriz were put in fetters [?].[647] The Commander of the Faithful celebrated the Feast of Sacrifice in Damascus.

*Bakkar < Muhammad b. ‘A’idh:
In 69, ‘Abd al-Malik encamped at Butnan Habib, in the Year of the Mud. The Syrians did not undertake a raiding expedition, so a fifth of their wages was withheld in 70.

Khalifa:
In this year, there was a violent plague, from which many of the children of Anas b. Malik died.[648]

In this year, ‘Abdallah b. al-‘Abbas died in at-Ta’if. Ibn al-Hanafiyya recited the prayers for him.

[337] The Year 70/689–690

[Baqi:][649]

*Ibn Bukayr < al-Layth:
In the year 70, the Commander of the Faithful remained [in Damascus]. ‘Umayr b. al-Hubab[650] was killed. The Commander of the Faithful celebrated the Feast of Sacrifice in Damascus. Ibn az-Zubayr led the pilgrimage.

645 The first part of this chapter was added by Baqi. Khalifa’s text resumes below, on the same page.

646 On the phrase “the raid of Hassan [b. an-Nu‘man] in the Awras” cf. EI2, I, 770;, IA, IV, 370.

647 The Arabic is *ūthiqa* (*awthaqa*?). Perhaps the meaning is “…were reinforced”.

648 This sentence parallels *Ibn ‘Asakir, *Tahdhīb*, III, 150 (Abu l-Yaqzan); *Dh., III, 343 (Khalifa < Abu l-Yaqzan); *Ibn Taghribirdi, I, 182 (Khalifa).

649 The first part of this chapter was added by Baqi. Khalifa’s text resumes on page 126.

650 Cf. Tab., II, 708, 711–714; *Ansāb*, V, index; Din., 293–295, 297.

*Bakkar < Muhammad b. 'A'idh:
The Syrians refused to go on the raiding expedition in {263} the Year of the Mud, so a fifth of their wages was withheld in 70.

Khalifa:
In this year, 'Amr b. Sa'id b. al-'As staged a *coup d'état* against 'Abd al-Malik b. Marwan. He expelled 'Abd ar-Rahman b. Umm al-Hakam from Damascus, and became caliph there. 'Abd al-Malik went to him, and they made peace on condition that 'Amr would be designated heir to the caliphate after 'Abd al-Malik, and that 'Amr would appoint a governor beside each of 'Abd al-Malik's governors. So ['Amr] opened [the gates of] the city, and 'Abd al-Malik entered. Then 'Abd al-Malik betrayed him and killed him.[651] He said, "If I knew that you would allow my kinsmen to live and prosper, I would ransom you with the blood of [my] eyes. But when there are two stallions among the herd of camels, one usually expels the other, then kills him."[652] He recited the following:

1. I drew him near me in order to be safe from his trickery.
   Then I attack with the fury of one resolute and confident in his power,
2. Angrily defending my Faith.
   The way of the one who does evil is not that of the one who does good.[653]

[338] _______[654] wrote the poem, but 'Abd al-Malik quoted it.

In this year, Abu Fudayk ['Abdallah b. Thawr][655] killed Najda b. 'Amir. Rashid b. 'Amr sent {264} Abu Hashim against him, but [Abu Fudayk] killed him.

651 From "In this year, 'Amr b. Sa'id b. al-'As staged a *coup d'état* ..." cf. Din., 286 (= 294 Guirgass); *Dh., III, 59, l. 4 (Khalifa).

652 From "He said, 'If I knew ...'" cf. *Ansāb*, IV-B, 142 l. 20; cf. Din., 286, l. 11 (= 294 Guirgass); al-Ya'qubi, II, 323, l. 8; cf. Tab., II, 789 (Hisham b. al-Kalbi < 'Awana); **'Iqd*, IV, 409, l. 4; *Dh., III, 59, l. 7 ([Khalifa] < Abu l-Yaqzan).

653 Meter: *kāmil*. On the verses themselves cf. al-Jahiz, IV, 161; cf. *Ansāb*, IV-B, 142 (plus one verse); cf. *Ansāb*, IV-B, 146; cf. Al-Ya'qubi, II, 323 (verse 1); cf. Tab., II, 795; cf. *Murūj*, V, 237.

654 Z: *al-B-h-b-y*; U: *al-B-h-y*. Cf. the parallels to page 149, line 16 of al-Baladhuri, *Ansāb*, IV-B, on page 42 of Schloessinger's annotations, where variations on the poet's name are cited.

655 EI2, I, 120; Dixon, 173–176. Cf. Wellhausen, *Religio-Political Factions*, index s.v. Abu Fudayk.

In this year 'Asim b. 'Umar b. al-Khattab died.
Abu Ashhab Ja'far b. Hayyan al-'Utaridi[656] was born.

[339] The Year 71/690–691

[Baqi:][657]

*Ibn Bukayr < al-Layth:
In 71, the raid against F-r-s-t-a[658] took place. The Commander of the Faithful celebrated the Feast of Sacrifice in Damascus. Ibn az-Zubayr led the pilgrimage.

Khalifa:
Abu Fudayk 'Abdallah b. Thawr b. Qays b. Tha'laba betook himself to Bahrain.[659] Mus'ab b. az-Zubayr sent 'Abd ar-Rahman b. al-Iskaf against him. They met [in battle] at Ju'atha',[660] where 'Abd ar-Rahman and the Basrans were routed.[661]

[340] The Year 72/691–692

[Baqi:][662]

*Yahya b. 'Abdallah b. Bukayr < al-Layth:
In 72, the Commander of the Faithful conducted a raiding expedition against Kufa. Mus'ab[663] b. az-Zubayr was killed in Maskin. Hassan

656 D. 162/778–779 (*Ṭbq.*, 536; Ibn Sa'd, VII, 274; Ibn Hajar, II, 88).

657 The first part of this chapter was added by Baqi. Khalifa's text resumes below, on the same page.

658 The place is spelled *Qarṭaṣa* in most of the sources (e.g., BGA, II, 91; VI, 81, 84, 220, 247; VII, 339; IAH, 83; al-Kindi, 191). According to G. Wiet (EI2, II, 105b, s.v. Damanhur), the city of Damanhur in Egypt is on the site of Qartasa.

659 Cf. EI2, I, 941ff.

660 BGA, V, 30; VI, 152, 249; VIII, 392; *Futūḥ*, 83–85, 92; Yaqut, II, 136.

661 From "Abu Fudayk 'Abdallah b. Thawr b. Qays b. Tha'laba betook himself …" cf. *Dh., III, 107.

662 The first part of this chapter was added by Baqi. Khalifa's text resumes below, on the next page.

663 Kh.: al-Mus'ab b. az-Zubayr.

b. an-Nu'man[664] raided and conquered the Awras. Al-Hajjaj b. Yusuf led the pilgrimage. He battled {265} Ibn az-Zubayr while he was undertaking the pilgrimage.

Ibn 'Ayyash:
When 'Abd al-Malik went to an-Nukhayla and Mus'ab [b. az-Zubayr] was killed, he appointed Khalid b. 'Abdallah b. Khalid b. Asid b. Abi l-'As b. Umayya as governor over Basra. He said to him, "Be generous to your *Jufriyya*" – that is, those who fought with him during the battle at al-Jufra,[665] and helped him attain victory over the supporters of Ibn az-Zubayr. So he gave them offices and was generous to them. He removed al-Muhallab [b. Abi Sufra] from fighting the Azraqites, and installed him as governor over al-Ahwaz and the districts of the Tigris. He appointed al-Mughira b. al-Muhallab over Fasa[666] and Darabjird,[667] and Sa'id b. al-Muhallab over Arrajan[668] and Sabur.[669]

[341] Khalifa:
In this year, Mus'ab b. az-Zubayr was killed. During the governorship of Mus'ab b. az-Zubayr the following were killed: al-Bara' b. 'Azib[670] [and] 'Abdallah b. Abi. Hadrad.[671] Mus'ab was killed at the age of 40.

In this year, the following died: Qabisa b. Jabir al-Asadi,[672] Sila b. Zufar al-'Absi,[673] 'Abdallah b. Samit al-Laythi,[674] Suwayd b. Manjuf as-Sadusi,[675] 'Ubayda b. Qays as-Salmani.[676] According to some, 'Ubayda died during the time of al-Mukhtar b. Abi 'Ubayd.

In this year, Hisham b. 'Abd al-Malik was born.

'Abd al-Malik appointed his brother, Bishr b. Marwan, as governor over

664 Kh.: Hassan b. Nu'man.

665 Cf. Dixon, 130.

666 EI2, II, 823.

667 EI2, II, 135.

668 EI2, I, 659.

669 EI, IV, 341, s.v. Shapur; Minorsky, 379; Zambaur, 135.

670 EI2, I, 1025.

671 On the notice of the death of 'Abdallah b. Abi. Hadrad cf. *Ṭbq.*, 242; Ibn Sa'd, IV, 309; *Istī'āb*, 887; Ibn 'Asakir, *Tahdhīb*, VII, 349; Dh., III, 166. #*Istī'āb*, 887 (Khalifa).

672 *Ṭbq.*, 319, 347; Ibn Sa'd, VI, 145; *Jarḥ*, III, II, 125; Ibn Hajar, VIII, 344.

673 On the notice of the death of Sila b. Zufar al-'Absi cf. *Ṭbq.*, 323; Ibn Sa'd, VI, 195; Dh., III, 163; Ibn Hajar, IV, 437. #Ibn Hajar, IV, 437 (Khalifa).

674 *Ṭbq.*, 452; Ibn Sa'd, VII, 212; cf. Ibn Hajar, V, 264.

675 On the notice of the death of Suwayd b. Manjuf as-Sadusi cf. *Dh., III, 159 (Khalifa).

676 *Ṭbq.*, 332; Ibn al-Athir, *al-Lubāb*, I, 552; Ibn Hajar, VII, 84; cf. GAS, I, index.

Kufa.[677] Tariq b. 'Amr, a *mawlā* of 'Uthman b. 'Affan, conquered Medina and called for the pledge of allegiance to 'Abd al-Malik. He expelled Talha b. 'Abdallah b. 'Awf,[678] Ibn az-Zubayr's governor, from Medina.[679]

{266} 'Abd al-Malik sent al-Hajjaj b. Yusuf to Mecca to battle Ibn az-Zubayr. The first battle between them took place in *Dhū l-Qa'da*/ March–April 692. Al-Hajjaj set up mangonels against the Ka'ba.

[342] The Year 73/692–693

In this year, 'Abdallah b. az-Zubayr was killed on Tuesday 16 *Jumādā* 11/2 November 692, at the age of 73. He was born the year of the *Hijra*.

In 73, the following died: 'Awf b. Malik al-Ashja'i,[680] [and] Asma' bint Abi Bakr as-Siddiq. 'Abdallah b. Safwan b. Umayya was killed while clinging to the curtains of the Ka'ba.[681] 'Abdallah b. Muti' was hit by a stone from a mangonel and killed.[682]

When Mus'ab [b. az-Zubayr] was killed, Humran b. Aban[683] conquered Kufa, and called for the pledge of allegiance to 'Abd al-Malik b. Marwan.

Al-Hajjaj b. Yusuf led the pilgrimage.

[343] The judges [under Ibn az-Zubayr]

Basra: Hisham b. Hubayra b. Fadala al-Laythi.[684]

Kufa: When Shurayh retired, Mus'ab appointed Sa'id b. Nimran al-Hamdani.[685] Then he dismissed him and appointed 'Abdallah b. 'Utba b. Mas'ud,[686] who served as judge until Mus'ab was killed and the people agreed upon 'Abd al-Malik [as caliph].

677 This sentence parallels *Ibn 'Asakir, X, 113 (Khalifa).

678 D. 97/715–716 (*Ṭbq.*, 607, 623; Ibn Sa'd, V, 160; Ibn 'Asakir, *Tahdhīb*, VII, 69; Dh., IV, 16; Ibn Hajar, V, 19).

679 From "Tariq b. 'Amr, a *mawlā* ..." cf. *Ibn 'Asakir, *Tahdhīb*, VII, 40, l. 19 (Khalifa).

680 On the notice of the death of 'Awf b. Malik al-Ashja'i cf. *Ṭbq.*, 108, 775; *Istī'āb*, 1226; Dh., III, 199; Ibn Hajar, VIII, 168; #Dh., III, 201 (Khalifa).

681 This sentence parallels #Dh., III, 177 (Khalifa); #Ibn Hajar, V, 266 (Khalifa).

682 This sentence parallels *Dh., III, 185f.

683 *Ṭbq.*, 476, 486; Ibn Sa'd, VI, 148; Ibn 'Asakir, *Tahdhīb*, IV, 435; Dh., III, 152 and 245; Ibn Hajar, III, 24.

684 *Ṭbq.*, 452.

685 Ibn 'Asakir, *Tahdhīb*, VI, 177.

686 *Ṭbq.*, 320, 325, 595; Ibn Sa'd, VI, 120; Dh., III, 177; Ibn Hajar, V, 211.

'Abdallah b. az-Zubayr led the pilgrimage {267} from 64/684 to 72/692. [In 73] Ibn az-Zubayr led the pilgrimage, but the people did not stand [at 'Arafat]. Al-Hajjaj led the Syrians in the pilgrimage, but they did not perform the circumambulation of the Ka'ba.[687]

Ibn az-Zubayr's chamberlain: 'Abdallah b. Sa'd, *mawlā* of Hatib b. Abi Balta'a.

Chief of staff:[688] 'Abdallah b. Safwan b. Umayya b. Khalaf.

The reign of Ibn az-Zubayr lasted nine years, two months, and several days before he was killed. He was born in the house of Abu Bakr, in as-Sunh,[689] in *Jumādā* I 2/October–November 623.

[Baqi:][690]

In 73 [the following occurred]:

*Ibn Bukayr < al-Layth:
In 73, 'Abdallah b. az-Zubayr was killed in *Jumādā* I/September–October 692. Kurayb b. Abraha[691] went down to Alexandria. [344] Abrad b. Habbar went to the army in Ifriqiya. 'Abd ar-Rahman b. Mu'awiya went down to Rashid[692] by boat. Al-Hajjaj b. Yusuf led the pilgrimage.

*Bakkar < Ibn 'A'idh:
In 73, Muhammad b. Marwan conducted a raid against S-b-y-s-ta.[693] He battled the Byzantines, and routed them.[694]

*Ibn Numayr:
Ibn az-Zubayr was killed on Tuesday 17 *Jumādā* I 73/October–November 692.

Khalifa:
Al-Hajjaj b. Yusuf led the pilgrimage in 73/693.

687 From "[In 73] Ibn az-Zubayr led the pilgrimage ..." cf. *Dh., III, 172 (Khalifa).

688 The Arabic is: *'alā amri-hi kulli-hi.*

689 Cf. al-Ya'qubi, II, 142; Yaqut, III, 163.

690 The remainder of this chapter, except for the very last statement, was added by Baqi.

691 D. 75/694–695 or 98/716–717 (Dh., III, 204; *Ṭbq.*, 703; *Jarḥ*, III, II, 168; cf. IAH, index; cf. al-Kindi, index).

692 Rosetta (EI, III, 1165).

693 Sebaste, or Sebastopolis, in Cilicia, is where the battle took place (cf. Wellhausen, "Die Kämpfe der Araber," 431f.; Bury, II, 322).

694 From "In 73, Muhammad b. Marwan conducted a raid ..." cf. Tab., II, 853.

[345] The Year 74/693–694

[Baqi:][695]

*Ibn Bukayr < al-Layth:
In 74, 'Abd al-'Aziz b. Marwan went down to Alexandria. The Kahina[696] was killed. Sufyan b. Wahb[697] went to Ifriqiya. Muhammad b. Marwan battled the Byzantines {268} at the Zab.[698] Al-Hajjaj b. Yusuf led the pilgrimage.

*Bakkar < Muhammad b. 'A'idh:
In 74, Muhammad b. Marwan raided Dorylaion [?].[699]

Khalifa:
'Abd al-Malik consolidated [the administration of] Iraq under the governorship of his brother, Bishr b. Marwan, who went to Basra in *Dhū l-Ḥijja* 74/April–May 694.[700]

In this year, al-Hajjaj tore down the wall of the Ka'ba adjacent to the *ḥijr*. He removed [346] the *ḥijr* from the Ka'ba, blocked the door at the back of the Ka'ba, and rebuilt the wall which was adjacent to the *ḥijr*. He led the pilgrimage.

In this year, the following died: Rafi' b. Khadij,[701] 'Abdallah b. 'Umar b. al-Khattab,[702] Abu Sa'id al-Khudri, [and] Salama b. al-Akwa'.[703] 'Abdallah b. Sa'd b. Khaythama[704] died after 'Abdallah b. az-Zubayr was killed.

695 The first part of this chapter was added by Baqi. Khalifa's text resumes below, on the same page.

696 M. Talbi, in EI2, IV, 422, gives a comprehensive account of the Kahina and her activities. Cf. also Julien, 11ff.

697 D. 82/701–702 (Ibn 'Asakir, *Tahdhīb*, VI, 185; Dh., III, 251; cf. IAH, index).

698 A tributary of the Tigris (EI, IV, 1180; cf. Honigmann, 179).

699 Kh.: *'-n-d-r-l-y-h*. It is possible that this is a corruption of Darawliya, which is the Arabic form of Dorylaion (cf. Minorsky, 220). Cf. the following similar-sounding names in some other sources: *'-n-d-w-l-y-h* (IA, IV, 373); *'-dh-r-w-l-y-h*, raided in 89/708 (Tab., II, 1179); *'-d-r-w-l-y-h*, raided in 88/707 (al-Ya'qubi, II, 350); *'-r-w-l-y-h*, raided in 107/725 (Kh., 493). See IA, IV, 373 for quotation.

700 This sentence parallels *Ibn 'Asakir, X, 113 (Musa b. Zakariyya' < Khalifa).

701 *Ṭbq.*, 185; *Istī'āb*, 479; Dh., III, 153; Ibn Hajar, III, 229.

702 On the notice of the death of 'Abdallah b. 'Umar b. al-Khattab cf. #Dh., III, 184 (Khalifa); #Siyar, III, 156 (Khalifa).

703 *Ṭbq.*, 243; Ibn Sa'd, IV, 305; *Istī'āb*, 639; Ibn 'Asakir, *Tahdhīb*, VI, 230; Dh., III, 158; Ibn Hajar, IV, 150. He is also known as Salama b. 'Amr b. al-Akwa'.

704 *Ṭbq.*, 191; Ibn Sa'd, IV, 382; *Istī'āb*, 917; Dh., III, 175.

[347] The Year 75/694–695

[Baqi:][705]

*Ibn Bukayr < al-Layth:
In 75, 'Abd al-'Aziz b. Marwan left [Egypt] for Syria. Khabbab b. Marthad[706] went down to Alexandria. Ziyad b. Hunata[707] died. [Then] al-Asbagh b. 'Abd al-'Aziz[708] was appointed *amīr*.[709] The Commander of the Faithful, 'Abd al-Malik b. Marwan, led the pilgrimage. 'Umayr b. 'Ubayd al-Khawlani arrived with his army in Ifriqiya.

*Bakkar < Muhammad b. 'A'idh:
In 75, {269} Muhammad b. Marwan conducted the summer raiding campaign. The Byzantines went out to al-A'maq[710] in *Jumādā* I/August–September 694. Aban b. al-Walid b. 'Uqba b. Abi Mu'ayt[711] and Dinar b. Dinar confronted them, and God routed them.[712]

[Khalifa:]
In 75, ...[713] Then al-Hajjaj left Kufa and urged the people to battle the Azraqites. He went out and encamped at Rustaqabadh.[714] [The people of Iraq] renounced him, and pledged allegiance to 'Abdallah b. al-Jarud.[715]

705 The first part of this chapter was added by Baqi, although he did not indicate it by adding his own name; nor did he add Khalifa's name where the original text resumes below, on the same page.

706 Cf. Janab b. Marthad, in al-Kindi, 49, 51, 53.

707 Cf. IAH, 124; al-Kindi, 42, 44, 49, 51. Ziyad b. Hunata was a nobleman of Egypt, of the Banu Tujib (IAH, 124). When 'Abd al-'Aziz b. Marwan, the governor over Egypt, went to visit his brother ('Abd al-Malik) in 75, he left Ziyad b. Hunata as his lieutenant over Egypt. Ziyad died in *Shawwāl*/January–February 695, so 'Abd al-'Aziz appointed al-Asbagh b. 'Abd al-'Aziz to take his place. The preceding is reported by adh-Dhahabi (Dh., III, 117) and al-Kindi, 51.

708 D. 86/705 (cf. IAH, index; al-Kindi, 51, 54–57; Ibn 'Asakir, *Tahdhīb*, III, 83; *Ma'ārif*, 362; *Ansāb*, V, 185; Yaqut, IV, 674f.).

709 From "In 75, 'Abd al-'Aziz b. Marwan left ..." cf. Al-Kindi, 51.

710 Cf. EI2, I, 446f. s.v. 'Amq.

711 Ibn 'Asakir, *Tahdhīb*, II, 133.

712 From "In 75, Muhammad b. Marwan conducted the summer raiding campaign ..." cf. *Futūḥ*, 188, l. 17; al-Ya'qubi, II, 336f.; Ibn 'Asakir, *Tahdhīb*, II, 133 (Muhammad b. 'A'idh).

713 According to U and Z, several words were obliterated here

714 Cf. *Futūḥ*, 281, l. 13; *Ma'ārif*, 339; BGA, VI, 6, 13, 235, 238; Tab., index. All but Kh. and the *Futūḥ* spell it without an *alif* between the *qāf* and the *bā'*.

715 On 'Abdallah b. al-Jarud and his revolt, cf. Dixon, 143–147; cf. Wellhausen, *Arab Kingdom*, 244 n. 3.

They battled,[716] and Ibn al-Jarud and 'Abdallah b. Hakim al-Mujashi'i were killed. Al-Ghadban b. al-Qaba'thari and [348] 'Ikrima b. Rib'i al-Fayyad, of the Banu Taym Allat, fled to Syria with [some] men of Iraq. There is a story about them.

Abu 'Ubayda:
In this year, Dawud b. an-Nu'man,[717] of the Banu Mazin b. 'Abd al-Rays, revolted in Mawqu',[718] in the area of the Taff[719] of Basra. He was the first person to use it as a place of *hijra*.[720] {270} Al-Hakam b. Ayyub ath-Thaqafi,[721] the governor of Basra, was dispatched against him and killed him.[722]

*[Abu l-Yaqzan] 'Amir b. Hafs:
Dawud, who was from Bahrain, revolted. His father said to him, "Give up this point of view, and you can have this garden of mine, of 100 *jarīb*s." He said, "My father, there is a bug in your garden. I want a garden in which there is no bug."[723] Then he went to Basra, and came to Mawqu'. Al-Hakam b. Ayyub dispatched against him 'Abbad b. Husayn with cavalry, and Dawud was killed.[724] About that he[725] said the following:

Remember Dawud! He sold himself,[726]

716 From "In 75, …" cf. *Futūḥ*, 281; cf. *Ma'ārif*, 338f.; cf. Tab., II, 873f. (Hisham b. al-Kalbi < Abu Mikhnaf).

717 On Dawud b. an-Nu'man and his revolt, cf. Dixon, 197.

718 Cf. Yaqut, IV, 688.

719 Cf. *Futūḥ*, index; BGA, V, 187; Yaqut, III, 539; EI, IV, 603.

720 The expression *dār hijra* connotes emigration from an unfriendly place to a place where the reception would be more favorable, alluding to the Prophet's experiences in Mecca, and his flight with his supporters to Medina. In the case of Dawud b. an-Nu'man, the "unfriendly place" might correspond to his home of Bahrain, and the "friendly place" to Mawqu', which had been the site of a previous Khajirite rebellion led by a certain Abu Ma'bad ash-Shanni. The chronology of the events varies somewhat in the different sources (cf. Dixon, 197).

721 Ibn 'Asakir, *Tahdhīb*, IV, 389.

722 From "In this year, Dawud b. an-Nu'man …" cf. (*) Dh., III, 120.

723 Dawud seems to be rejecting worldly wealth (the garden with the bug in it) for Paradise in the hereafter (the garden without the bug). "The Garden" is a frequent Qur'ānic designation for Paradise. On other aspects of the symbology of "garden" in Islam, cf. EI2, I, 1345ff., s.v. *bustān*.

724 From "Dawud, who was from Bahrain …" cf. *Ansāb*, quoted in *Shi'r*, 142f.

725 According to Ihsan 'Abbas, *Shi'r al-Khawārij*, the poet was a certain Ziyad al-A'sam (cf. *Shi'r*, 142, 142f., #39).

726 The expression "sell oneself [to God]" was used frequently in connection with the Kharijites. They are often called the Shurat, "those who sell themselves [to God]" (cf.

And gave of himself generously, seeking Paradise through noble deeds.[727]

Ibn al-Kalbi:
In this year, Muhammad b. Marwan conducted the summer campaign against the Byzantines, when they went out to al-'Amq,[728] in the region of Mar'ash.[729]

'Abd al-Malik b. Marwan led the pilgrimage.

Abu 'Asim[730] < Ibn Jurayj < his father:
'Abd al-Malik b. Marwan led us in the pilgrimage in 75/695, two years after the death of Ibn az-Zubayr. He delivered a sermon in which he said:

[349] "The caliphs who preceded me used to consume this wealth and let others consume it. I shall not cure the diseases of the Community except by means of the sword. I am not a weak caliph – meaning 'Uthman – and I am not a devious caliph – meaning Mu'awiya.[731] People! We will endure all the troubles for you, as long as there is no flag-raising {271} or attacking the pulpit.[732] This man, 'Amr b. Sa'id, had his rights and his family. He said one thing with his head, but we said another with our sword."[733]

*Al-Walid b. Hisham < his father < his grandfather:
Bishr b. Marwan was appointed governor of Iraq in 74/693–694. He died at the beginning of 75/May 694, at forty-odd years of age.[734]

During the governorship of Bishr, the following died: Jabir b. Samura

Brunnow, 178f.; Wellhausen, *Religio-Political Factions*, 22f., and 25 n. 7; L. Massignon in EI, IV, 392, s.v. *shurāt*; cf. Qur'ān 9:111, which is the supposed inspiration for the "selling" terminology).

727 Meter: *ṭawīl*. Al-Baladhuri has five additional verses, quoted by 'Abbas (*Shi'r*, 65f.), although al-Baladhuri does not have the verse Khalifa quotes (cf. 'Abbas, *Shi'r*, 170, #125, citing the sources). On the content of the verse, cf. Qur'ān 9:111 and note 726, above. For parallel quotations of the verse cf., *Dh., III, 120; 'Abbas, *Shi'r*, 66.

728 EI2, I, 446.

729 From "In this year, Muhammad b. Marwan conducted the summer campaign ..." cf. *Futūḥ*, 188; cf. Tab., II, 863; *IA, IV, 391; *Dh., III, 120.

730 Ad-Dahhak b. Makhlad, d. *Dhū l-Ḥijja* 212/February–March 828 (Ṭbq., 545; Ibn Sa'd, VII, 295; Ibn 'Asakir, *Tahdhīb*, VII, 24; Ibn Hajar, IV, 450).

731 From "'Abd al-Malik b. Marwan led us in the pilgrimage ..." cf. *IA, IV, 391; from "I am not a weak caliph ..." cf. al-Jahiz, II, 245; cf. *'Iqd*, IV, 90f.

732 I.e., either military or civilian rebellion. For a similar expression, cf. Kh., 365.

733 From "'Abd al-Malik b. Marwan led us in the pilgrimage ..." cf. *Dh., III, 120; from "He said one thing with his head ..." cf. *'Iqd*, IV, 421; cf. Dh., III, 281; cf. Dh., IV, 65.

734 From "Bishr b. Marwan was appointed ..." cf. *Ibn 'Asakir, X, 127 (Musa b. Zakariyya' < Khalifa); *Dh., III, 142 (Khalifa).

as-Suwa'i,[735] a companion of the Prophet; Abu Juhayfa Wahb as-Suwa'i;[736] Kharasha b. al-Hurr al-Fazari;[737] Aws b. Dam'aj;[738] [350] 'Ubayd b. Nadla,[739] a Khuza'i; 'Asim b. Damra as-Saluli;[740] Shaddad b. al-Azma';[741] 'Abdallah b. 'Utba b. Mas'ud; [and] Abu 'Abd ar-Rahman as-Sulami.[742]

{272}[351] The Year 76/695–696

In this year, Salih b. Musarrah[743] revolted in al-Jazira, in *Ṣafar*/May–June 695. Muhammad b. Marwan b. al-Hakam sent 'Adi b. 'Adi b. 'Umayra al-Kindi[744] against him, but he was routed. So Muhammad b. Marwan sent Khalid b. 'Abdallah as-Sulami and al-Harith b. Ja'wana al-'Amiri. They fought bitterly. Salih b. Musarrah withdrew to Iraq, and they did not pursue him. Then Muhammad b. Marwan sent al-Ash'ath b. 'Umayra al-Hamdani against him. They met in Jukha',[745] where they fought bitterly. Salih was wounded, and died on Tuesday 16 *Jumādā* II 76/1 October 695. Salih designated Shabib b. Yazid[746] as his successor. Shabib confronted Sawra b. Abjar, then marched on. [352] He confronted Sa'id b. 'Amr al-Kindi, and they fought bitterly. Then Shabib departed for Kufa, and entered [the city]. There he killed Abu Sulaym, a *mawlā* of 'Anbasa b. Abi Sufyan and father of al-Layth b. Abi Sulaym.[747] He also killed 'Adi b. 'Amr and Azhar b. 'Ubaydallah al-'Amiri. Ghazala[748] entered the {273} mosque of Kufa,

735 *Ṭbq.*, 132, and 296; Ibn Sa'd, VI, 24; *Istī'āb*, 224; Ibn 'Asakir, *Tahdhīb*, III, 385.

736 Ibn 'Abdallah (*Ṭbq.*, 132, and 296; Ibn Sa'd, VI, 63; *Istī'āb*, 1561; Ibn Hajar, XI, 164).

737 *Ṭbq.*, 324, and 349; Ibn Sa'd, VI, 147; Dh., III, 153; Ibn Hajar, III, 138.

738 *Ṭbq.*, 330; Ibn Sa'd, VI, 213; Dh., III, 139; Ibn Hajar, I, 383.

739 *Ṭbq.*, 342; Ibn Sa'd, VI, 117; Dh., III, 190; Ibn Hajar, VII, 75.

740 *Ṭbq.*, 323; Ibn Sa'd, VI, 222; Dh., III, 163; Ibn Hajar, V, 45.

741 *Ṭbq.*, 338; Ibn Sa'd, VI, 196.

742 'Abdallah b. Habib b. Rubayi'a (*Ṭbq.*, 349; Ibn Sa'd, VI, 172; Dh., III, 222; Ibn Hajar, V, 183).

743 On the revolt of Salih b. Musarrah, see Wellhausen, *Religio-Political Factions*, 69f., and index; Dixon, 182ff. Cf. also Ibn Hazm, 214, on his geneaology.

744 D. 120/737–738 (*Ṭbq.*, 821; Ibn Sa'd, VII, 480; Ibn Hajar, VIII, 168).

745 Kh.: *J-w-kh-'-y*. Cf. BGA, VII, 95; VIII, 36, 40, 54; Wellhausen, *Religio-Political Factions*, index. EI, IV, 244a, s.v. Shabib b. Yazid.

746 On Shabib and his revolt, see Wellhausen, *Religio-Political Factions*, 70–79; K. V. Zettersteen in EI, IV, 243; Dixon, 183–191.

747 Al-Layth d. 143/760–761 (*Ṭbq.*, 388; Ibn Sa'd, VI, 349; *Ma'ārif*, 477; Ibn Hajar, VIII, 465).

748 Ghazala was Shabib's wife (see the references given in note 746, above).

and recited her *wird*[749] from the pulpit. She had made a vow to do so.[750] Concerning this, 'Itban b. Wasila ash-Shaybani[751] said the following:

Ghazala, one of our praiseworthy women, made a vow.
She has a share in the destiny of the Muslims.[752]

'Imran b. Hittan as-Sadusi,[753] censuring al-Hajjaj, said the following:

1. A lion against me, but in combat an ostrich,
   Weak-winged, who jumps with fright at the chirp of a sparrow.
2. Why did you not go out against Ghazala in the battle?
   No, your heart was in the rib cage of a bird.
3. Ghazala tore apart his heart with knights
   Who left his appearance like yesterday which has passed.[754]

Then Shabib departed from Kufa. Al-Hajjaj sent Za'ida b. Qudama ath-Thaqafi[755] against him with an army. They met far down on the lower Euphrates, and Za'ida was killed. Then al-Hajjaj sent 'Abd ar-Rahman b. Muhammad b. al-Ash'ath, but he did not engage Shabib in battle. Then he sent 'Uthman b. Qatan al-Harithi. They met in *Dhū l-Ḥijja* 76/March–April 696. 'Uthman b. Qatan was killed, and his troops were routed.[756]

In 76, 'Abdallah b. Umayya b. 'Abdallah penetrated deeply into Sijistan. His way was obstructed [by some people]. He paid [them] money and they let him pass. 'Abd al-Malik b. Marwan dismissed him, and sent Musa b. Talha b. 'Ubaydallah to replace him.[757]

749 The *wird* includes the reading of a seventh of the Qur'ān (cf. EI, IV, 1139).

750 From "Salih was wounded, and died ..." cf. *Dh., III, 122, l. 2–6, 9–11.

751 Cf. 'Abbas, *Shi'r*, 142, #37. Cf. also ibid., 124, #122 on the ascription of the verses to a different poet.

752 Meter: *ṭawīl*. On other quotations of the verse, cf. *Ansāb*, quoted by Ihsan 'Abbas in *Shi'r*, 64 (plus nine additional verses); cf. *Murūj*, V, 441 (plus six additional verses).

753 EI2, III, 1175; GAS, II, 352.

754 Meter: *kāmil*. On other quotations of the verse, cf. *Ansāb*, quoted by 'Abbas, *Shi'r*, 25 (plus one additional verse); cf *Ma'ārif*, 411 (verses 1 and 2); cf. al-Mubarrad, 450 (verse 2); cf. *Murūj*, V, 367 (verses 1 and 2); cf. *Aghānī*, XVI, 155; cf. Dh., III, 160 (verses 1 and 2).

755 D. 161/777–778 (*Ṭbq.*, 396; Ibn Sa'd, VI, 378; Ibn 'Asakir, *Tahdhīb*, V, 346; Ibn Hajar, III, 306).

756 From "Then Shabib departed from Kufa ..." cf. *Dh., III, 122, l. 6–9, and 11–12.

757 From "In 76, 'Abdallah b. Umayya b. 'Abdallah penetrated ..." cf. *Futūḥ*, 399; *Dh., III, 126.

Muhammad b. Marwan conducted a raiding expedition in the land of the Byzantines near Malatya.[758]

[353] In this year, the following died: al-Aswad b. Yazid;[759] Murra b. Sharahil al-Hamdani;[760] Sa'id {274} b. Wahb al-Khaywani;[761] [and] 'Amr b. Maymun al-Awdi,[762] who, according to some, died in 74/693–694.

[354] The Year 77/696–697

In this year, al-Hajjaj sent 'Attab b. Warqa' ar-Riyahi against Shabib [b. Yazid]. He confronted him in the Sawad of Kufa. 'Attab was killed and his troops were routed. On that day, Zuhra b. Huwayya al-A'raji,[763] an important *shaykh*, was trampled to death by the horses. A man of the Banu Taghlib named Qabisa, said to have been a companion of the Prophet, was [also] killed. Al-Hajjaj then sent al-Harith b. Mu'awiya b. Abi Zur'a b. Mas'ud ath-Thaqafi against Shabib. They met at Zurara.[764] Al-Harith was killed, and his army was routed. Then Shabib crossed the Euphrates. He encamped at as-Sabakha[765] and built a mosque. Al-Hajjaj did not go out against him for three days. But on the fourth day he went out. He sent Abu l-Ward, a *mawlā* of the Banu Nasr, but Shabib killed him. Then he sent Tahman, a *mawlā* of 'Uthman, but Shabib killed him [too]. So al-Hajjaj himself went out against him, and he forced Shabib from his mosque. They fought bitterly, and Ghazala was killed. When night fell, Shabib crossed the Euphrates, and al-Hajjaj cut the bridge. Then al-Hajjaj sent Habib b. 'Abd ar-Rahman b. Zayd al-Hakami with 3,000 troops. He confronted Shabib at al-Anbar, where the two sides [battled and] persevered until night separated them. Then Shabib marched to al-Ahwaz, where Muhammad b. Musa b. Talha b. 'Ubaydallah was. He ventured to battle [355] Shabib, demanding a duel. Shabib came out to him and killed him. Then Shabib went to Kirman, remained there about two months, and returned to

758 This sentence parallels *IA, IV, 418.

759 *Ṭbq.*, 335; Ibn Sa'd, VI, 70; Dh., III, 137; Ibn Hajar, I, 342; cf. GAS, I, index.

760 Cf. *Ṭbq.*, 339; Ibn Sa'd, VI, 116; Ibn Hajar, X, 88.

761 *Ṭbq.*, 339; Ibn Sa'd, VI, 170; Dh., III, 156; Ibn Hajar, IV, 95.

762 *Ṭbq.*, 333; Ibn Sa'd, VI, 117; Dh., III, 197; Ibn Hajar, VIII, 109.

763 *Ṭbq.*, 463.

764 Cf. *Futūḥ*, 274, 282; Tab., index; BGA, V, 182; Yaqut, II, 921.

765 Cf. Tab., II, 966, and index; Yaqut, III, 30. Wellhausen, *Religio-Political Factions*, index.

al-Ahwaz. Al-Hajjaj sent Habib b. 'Abd ar-Rahman b. Zayd al-Hakami and Sufyan b. al-Abrad al-Kalbi[766] against him. Shabib confronted them at the bridge of the Dujayl,[767] and they battled until night separated them.

{275} In the morning, Shabib departed. When he was on the bridge, it was cut and Shabib drowned.[768] Al-Batin,[769] his successor, requested safety, which Sufyan granted him, but al-Hajjaj later put him to death.

Aban b. 'Uthman b. 'Affan led the pilgrimage.

Ibn al-Kalbi:
Al-Walid b. 'Abd al-Malik conducted a raiding expedition in the land of the Byzantines. He reached [the area] between Malatya and al-Massisa.[770]

[356] The Year 78/697–698

In this year, al-Muhallab b. Abi Sufra went to al-Hajjaj after he had driven out the Azraqites. Al-Hajjaj sent Sufyan b. al-Abrad al-Kalbi, who killed Qatari b. al-Fuja'a.

Abu l-Yaqzan:
Sawra b. Abjar ad-Darimi and Badhan, a *mawlā* of Ibn al-Ash'ath, carried out the killing of Qatari.

In this year, 'Abd Rabbihi, *mawlā* of the Banu Qays b. Tha'laba, was killed.

Al-Hajjaj appointed 'Ubaydallah b. Abi Bakra governor over Sijistan. He appointed al-Muhallab [b. Abi Sufra] over Khurasan.[771] 'Ubaydallah b. Abi Bakra sent his son, Abu Bardha'a, [on a raiding mission]. His[772] way was obstructed at a narrow mountain pass. Shurayh b. Hani' al-Harithi[773]

766 Kh.: Sufyan b. Burd al-Kalbi. *Ma'ārif*, 411; Tab., index; Ibn Hazm, 457; Ibn 'Asakir, *Tahdhīb*, VI, 180.

767 A river, now called Karun (EI2, IV, 673, s.v. Karun).

768 From "Then Shabib marched to al-Ahwaz ..." cf. *Dh., III, 124f.

769 Cf. *'Uyūn*, II, 155; *Murūj*, V, 441; *Ma'ārif*, 100 (al-Batin b. Zayd); Ibn Hazm, 322 (al-Batin b. Thawr).

770 From "Al-Walid b. 'Abd al-Malik conducted a raiding expedition ..." cf. al-Ya'qubi, II, 337; cf. Tab., II, 1032.

771 This sentence parallels *Dh., III, 126, l. 11 (Khalifa).

772 According to al-Baladhuri (*Futūḥ*, 399), it was 'Ubaydallah's way that was blocked, and his son succeeded to the command when his father died (cf. Bosworth, 53–56).

773 *Ṭbq.*, 337; Ibn Sa'd, VI, 128; Ibn 'Asakir, *Tahdhīb*, VI, 316; Dh., III, 162; Ibn Hajar, IV, 330.

was killed.[774] The Muslims were worn out and very hungry. A large number of that army perished.[775] Also killed was ‘Abdallah b. ‘Abbas b. Rabi‘a b. al-Harith b. ‘Abd al-Muttalib.[776]

In this year, al-Hajjaj sent Sa‘id b. Aslam b. Zur‘a to Mukran. He was killed by Muhammad b. al-Harith al-‘Ilafi and Mu‘awiya b. al-Harith al-‘Ilafi,[777] of the Banu Sama b. Lu’ayy.[778]

Ibn al-Kalbi:
Muhriz b. Abi Muhriz conducted a raiding expedition in the land of the Byzantines, [in the course of which] he conquered ’-z-q-l-h.[779] On returning, they encountered heavy rain beyond Darb al-Hadath.[780] Many were killed in the rains.[781]

{276} Hassan b. an-Nu‘man al-Ghassani returned from Kairouan, and went to ‘Abd al-Malik, who returned him to Ifriqiya, adding Tripoli [to his jurisdiction].[782] [357] He proceeded to ‘Abd al-‘Aziz b. Marwan in Egypt, but ‘Abd al-‘Aziz did not send him on. [Instead], he appointed Musa b. Nusayr. So Hassan returned to ‘Abd al-Malik, who ordered him to remain at home.[783]

Al-Walid b. ‘Abd al-Malik led the pilgrimage.

In this year, the following died: Zayd b. Khalid al-Juhani,[784] a

774 This sentence parallels #Ibn Hajar, IV, 330 (Khalifa).

775 From “Al-Hajjaj appointed ‘Ubaydallah ...” see *Futūḥ*, 399; *Dh., III, 126, l. 6 (Khalifa); (*) Dh., III, 163 (Khalifa).

776 This sentence parallels. *Ṭbq.*, 587; Ibn Sa‘d V, 28; Ibn Hazm, 230; Dh., III, 184 (Khalifa). All of the preceding have ‘Abdallah b. ‘Ayyash. Adh-Dhahabi points out the discrepancy between Khalifa’s *Ta’rīkh* and his *Ṭabaqāt* (Dh., III, 184). This sentence from *Dh., III, 184 (Khalifa).

777 On the ‘Ilafis (or ‘Alafis), cf. the brief mention by R. N. Frye in EI2, I, 1005b, s.v. Balučistan.

778 From “In this year, al-Hajjaj sent Sa‘id ...” cf. *Futūḥ*, 435.

779 *’-z-q-l-h* may be a misreading of *’-r-q-l-h*, which may be distorted form of Hiraqla (cf. BGA, VI, 99, 100, 113; VII, 98; VIII, 58; Yaqut, IV, 961; Tab., II, 1198), one of the several Herakleias of antiquity (cf. Ramsay, index, s.v. Herakleia; and Zambaur, *Münzprägungen*, 43, s.v. Erekli).

780 Cf. EI2, II, 19f., s.v. Hadath; and note 434.

781 From “Muhriz b. Abi Muhriz conducted a raiding expedition ...” cf. *Dh., III, 126.

782 This sentence parallels *Dh., III, 151 (Khalifa).

783 From “Hassan b. an-Nu‘man al-Ghassani returned from Kairouan ...” cf. IAH, 203; cf. al-Kindi, 52; cf. *Imāma* II, 64.

784 On the notice of the death of Zayd b. Khalid al-Juhani cf. Kh., 335 (261).

companion of the Prophet [and] 'Abd ar-Rahman b. Ghanm al-Ash'ari.[785] In this year, the following were killed: Shurayh b. Hani' al-Harithi; 'Abdallah b. 'Abbas b. Rabi'a b. al-Harith b. 'Abd al-Muttalib, with Ibn Abi Bakra, in Sijistan;[786] [and] 'Amr b. Hurayth al-Makhzumi,[787] a companion of the Prophet.[788] In this year, al-Hajjaj killed Sulayman b. Kindir al-Qushayri.[789]

[358] The Year 79/698–699

In this year, al-Hajjaj appointed Mujja' b. Si'r,[790] of the Banu Murra b. 'Ubayd, over Mukran, and ordered him to seek out the two 'Ilafis [Muhammad b. al-Harith and Mu'awiya b. al-Harith]. They fled and Mujja' died.[791]

Al-Hajjaj {277} appointed Muhammad b. Sa'sa'a al-Kilabi over Bahrain, and included Oman [under his jurisdiction]. He dismissed Ziyad b. ar-Rabi' al-Harithi. Muhammad b. Sa'sa'a appointed [as deputy ?] 'Abd al-Malik b. 'Abdallah b. Abi Raja' al-'Awdhi, the master of the castle of Abu Raja', near Basra. Ar-Rayyan an-Nukri[792] revolted against them in a town called Tab,[793] in [the region of] al-Khatt,[794] in Bahrain. Maymun the Harurite[795] proceeded to him from Oman. 'Abd al-Malik was put to rout, and Muhammad b. Sa'sa'a fled by sea to al-Hajjaj. Al-Hajjaj had sent Yazid b. Abi Kabsha[796] with reinforcements for Muhammad b. Sa'sa'a. But Muhammad had fled before Yazid b. Abi Kabsha reached him.[797]

785 On the notice of the death of 'Abd ar-Rahman b. Ghanm al-Ash'ari cf. *Ṭbq.*, 786; Ibn Sa'd, VII, 441; Dh., III, 188; Ibn Hajar, VI, 250. #Ibn Hajar, VI, 251.

786 On the notice of the death of "'Abdallah b. 'Abbas b. Rabi'a b. al-Harith b. 'Abd al-Muttalib, with Ibn Abi Bakra, in Sijistan" cf. *Dh., III, 184. (Khalifa).

787 *Ṭbq.*, 44, 283; Ibn Sa'd, VI, 23; *Istī'āb*, 1172; Dh., III, 196 and 289; Ibn Hajar, VIII, 17.

788 On the notice of the death of 'Amr b. Hurayth al-Makhzumi cf. #Dh., III, 196 (Khalifa); #Ibn Hajar, VIII, 18 (Khalifa).

789 This sentence parallels Ibn Hajar, IV, 216; *Dh., III, 126.

790 Al-Baladhuri spells his name with a final *tā' marbūṭa*: Mujja'a (*Futūḥ*, 435; also Tab., II, 1140).

791 From "In this year, al-Hajjaj appointed Mujja' …" cf. *Futūḥ*, 435.

792 On Rayyan and his revolt, cf. Dixon, 196.

793 Cf. Yaqut, III, 485.

794 EI, II, 930.

795 On Maymun, cf. Dixon 196.

796 Ibn Hajar, XI, 354; cf. Ibn Hazm, 432.

797 From "Al-Hajjaj appointed Muhammad …" cf. (*) Dh., III, 126f. (brief summary).

Al-Hajjaj appointed Harun b. Dhira‘ an-Numayri over the frontier of al-Hind, [359] and ordered him to seek out the two ‘Ilafis. He killed one of them, and the other fled.[798]

Ibn al-Hakam[799] led a raiding expedition in the land of the Byzantines. He obtained mounts at Marj ash-Shahm.[800] Al-Walid b. ‘Abd al-Malik conducted a raid in the vicinity of Malatya. He acquired booty and prisoners.[801]

In this year, Musa b. Nusayr raided the Maghrib.

*Bakr b. ‘Atiyya < ‘Awana:
The first tribe of the Berbers against whom Musa b. Nusayr conducted a raid were those who killed ‘Uqba b. Nafi‘. He marched against them himself, killing and taking prisoners. Their king, Kusayla, fled.[802]

Muhammad b. Sa‘id:[803]
Musa engaged in killing and took prisoners until he reached Tubna[804] and the Sanhaja.[805] Their prisoners amounted to 20,000.[806] That was in 81/700–701.[807]

Aban b. ‘Uthman led the pilgrimage.

{278} In 79, ‘Ubaydallah b. Abi Bakra died in Sijistan.[808]

In this year, ‘Abd ar-Rahman b. ‘Abdallah b. Mas‘ud[809] died.[810]

Between 70/689–690 and 80/699–700 the following died: Hisham b. Hubayra al-Laythi, the judge; Hittan b. ‘Abdallah ar-Raqashi;[811] ‘Ubaydallah b. ‘Ubaydallah b. Ma‘mar at-Taymi;[812] Safwan b. Muhriz

798 From “Al-Hajjaj appointed Harun …” cf. *Futūḥ*, 435; *Dh., III, 127.

799 Yahya b. al-Hakam (cf. Tab., II, 1035; cf. Dh., III, 213).

800 From “Ibn al-Hakam led a raiding expedition …” cf. al-Ya‘qubi, II, 337; Tab., II, 1035; BGA, VI, 108; Yaqut, III, 264; Ramsay, 445.

801 From “Al-Walid b. ‘Abd al-Malik conducted a raid …” cf. *Dh., III, 127.

802 Cf. note 488. From “The first tribe of the Berbers …” cf. Yaqut, III, 515; *Dh., III, 127.

803 Perhaps he was the administrator in Egypt mentioned by al-Kindi, 77, 110, 365, 366.

804 EI, IV, 805, s.v. Tobna.

805 Cf. G. Marcais in EI, IV, 152.

806 For “Their prisoners amounted to 20,000” see *Dh., III, 127.

807 From “Musa engaged in killing …” cf. *Imāma*, II, 70f.; Yaqut, III, 515.

808 This sentence parallels *Dh., III, 190 (Khalifa).

809 Dh., III, 186; Ibn Hajar, VI, 215.

810 This sentence parallels *Ibn Hajar, VI, 216 (Khalifa).

811 *Ṭbq.*, 484; Ibn Sa‘d, VII, 128; Dh., III, 151; Ibn Hajar, II, 396.

812 Kh.: ‘Abdallah b. ‘Ubaydallah b. Ma‘mar; Z: al-Laythi; U: at-Taymi. Cf. *Ṭbq.*, 452, 431: ‘Ubaydallah b. ‘Abdallah b. Ma‘mar (more than one individual?).

al-Mazini;[813] [and] Habba b. Juwayn al-'Urani,[814] when al-Hajjaj first came to Iraq.[815]

[360] The Year 80/699–700

In this year, al-Muhallab b. Abi Sufra raided Kashsh[816] and Nasaf,[817] in Khurasan. He besieged [the inhabitants] until he received a letter from ['Abd ar-Rahman b. Muhammad] b. al-Ash'ath, inviting him to renounce al-Hajjaj. That was in 81/700–701, and al-Muhallab departed from them, and returned [to Iraq].[818]

Yazid b. Abi Kabsha confronted ar-Rayyan an-Nukri in Bahrain. Ar-Rayyan was with a woman of al-Azd whose name was Jayda'. They met [in battle] at _____ az-Zara.[819] Ar-Rayyan, Jayda', and many of ar-Rayyan's companions were killed. Then Yazid departed and returned [to Iraq].[820]

Al-Hajjaj appointed Qatan b. Ziyad b. ar-Rabi' al-Harithi over Bahrain. Dawud b. 'Amir b. al-Harith revolted against him, and he killed Dawud.

A severe plague struck the people of Syria, so they undertook no raiding campaign this year.[821]

Aban b. 'Uthman led the pilgrimage.

In 80, the following died: as-Sa'ib b. Yazid,[822] son of the sister of an-Namir; Junada b. Abi Umayya; [361] Abu Idris al-Khawlani;[823] Jubayr

813 On the death notice for Safwan b. Muhriz al-Mazini cf. *Ṭbq.*, 458; Ibn Sa'd, VII, 147; Ibn Hajar, IV, 430. #Ibn Hajar, IV, 431 (Khalifa).

814 *Ṭbq.*, 344; Ibn Sa'd, VI, 177; Ibn Hajar, II, 176.

815 For the phrase "Habba b. Juwayn al-'Urani, when al-Hajjaj first came to Iraq" cf. #Ibn Hajar, II, 177 (Khalifa).

816 EI, II, 786, s.v. Kash; cf. Gibb, *passim.*

817 EI, III, 840, s.v. Nakhshab; cf. Gibb, *passim*; cf. Minorsky, 352.

818 From "In this year, al-Muhallab b. Abi Sufra raided Kashsh …" cf. *Futūḥ*, 417.

819 Kh.: *M-n-d-'-n* az-Zara. Cf. *Futūḥ*, 85, 86; BGA, V, 30; VI, 128, note f, 152; VIII, 392; Yaqut, II, 907. According to Yaqut, the place is also known as 'Ayn az-Zara. It is not inconceivable that the word 'Ayn became mutated in the course of transmission, to *M-s-d-'-n*. It is also interesting to find the word *marzubān* (which in Arabic looks much more like *M-s-d-'-n* than 'Ayn) associated with the name az-Zara (cf. BGA, VI, 128, note f).

820 From "Yazid b. Abi Kabsha confronted ar-Rayyan …" cf. *Dh., III, 128.

821 This sentence parallels Tab., II, 1036.

822 *Ṭbq.*, 21; *Istī'āb*, 576; Ibn 'Asakir, *Tahdhīb*, VI, 61; Dh., III, 369; Ibn Hajar, III, 450.

823 Known as 'A'idh Allah b. 'Abdallah (*Ṭbq.*, 789; Ibn Sa'd, VII, 448; Ibn 'Asakir, *Tahdhīb*, VII, 203, and 205; Dh., III, 215; Ibn Hajar, V, 85). Cf. #Ibn 'Asakir, *Tahdhīb*, VII, 205 (Khalifa); #Dh., III, 216 (Khalifa).

b. Nufayr;[824] {279} 'Abd ar-Rahman b. 'Abd al-Qari;[825] [and] 'Abdallah b. Ja'far b. Abi Talib.[826]

Abu l-Hasan:
'Abdallah b. Ja'far died in 84/703–704.

[362] The Year 81/700–701

In this year, Ibn al-Ash'ath revolted in Sijistan, and moved against al-Hajjaj.

*Abu l-Hasan and *Abu l-Yaqzan:
When Ibn al-Ash'ath decided to march against Iraq, he summoned Dharr [b. 'Abdallah],[827] the father of 'Umar b. Dharr al-Hamdani.[828] He clothed him, gave him presents, and ordered him to urge the people on. Every day he preached, denouncing al-Hajjaj. Then they marched in revolt against al-Hajjaj, but making no mention of revolt against 'Abd al-Malik.[829]

Umayya b. Khalid:
When Ibn al-Ash'ath marched, he quoted the following:

1. A splendid, noble man of the Araqim,
   Fair of brow, accustomed to daring attack,

2. Repudiated kings. Under his flag marched
   Men strong as trees and the illustrious chiefs of the peoples.[830]

He also quoted the following:

1. Ask the neighbor of the Jarm. Have I incited them to a
   War, which would cause division between neighbors?

824 On the notice of the death of Jubayr b. Nufayr cf. *Ṭbq.*, 788; Ibn Sa'd, VII, 440; Dh. III, 145; Ibn Hajar, II, 64; *Dh., III, 146 (Khalifa).

825 *Ṭbq.*, 591; Ibn Sa'd, V, 57; Dh., III, 186.

826 EI2, I, 44.

827 Dharr b. 'Abdallah b. Zurara (Dh., III, 247; Ibn Hajar, III, 218; cf. Ibn Hazm, 396).

828 Kh.: 'Amr b. Dharr al-Hamdani, died between 150/767 and 157 (*Ṭbq.*, 394; Ibn Sa'd, VI, 362; Ibn Hajar, VII, 444).

829 From "When Ibn al-Ash'ath decided to march …" cf. *Dh., III, 226.

830 Meter: *kāmil*. The order of the two verses has been reversed in the translation in accordance with the suggestions of a marginal annotation in the manuscript. This seems to make better sense. However, it is remarkable that only the second verse (i.e. the first in the text), is found standing alone in other source. From "Repudiated kings …" cf. Din., 317 (= 323 Guirgass); cf. al-Mubarrad, 155; cf. *Murūj*, V, 303.

2. Did I leave the women of the tribe outside,
In the courtyard of the house, kindling a fire with (the wood of) saddles?[831]

{280} La'y b. Shaqiq b. Thawr as-Sadusi came to al-Hajjaj and informed him [of Ibn al-Ash'ath's moves]. He immediately dispatched him to 'Abd al-Malik, who sent him back to al-Hajjaj, with orders to get ready in earnest until the armies reached him.[832] Al-Hajjaj marched, and they met at Tustar,[833] on the day of the Feast of Sacrifice, according to some. [363] Al-Hajjaj withdrew to Basra, pursued by Ibn al-Ash'ath.

Abu l-Yaqzan:
Zadhanfarrukh advised al-Hajjaj, "Leave Basra to him, for when the Basrans who are with him smell their women and children, they will leave him." So he left for the Taff of Basra. Ibn al-Ash'ath entered Basra, and many of the Basrans who were with him left him.[834]

*Muhammad b. Mu'adh[835] < his father < his grandmother:
I heard one of Ibn al-Ash'ath's heralds call out, "Where are those who pledged allegiance at ar-Rukhkhaj?"

*Someone < Quraysh b. Anas[836] < ['Abdallah] b. 'Awn:
I saw Ibn al-Ash'ath sitting cross-legged on the pulpit making terrible threats to those who would not follow him.[837]

In 81, Musa b. Nusayr went to Tubna, where he killed [many] and took prisoners.[838]

Sulayman b. 'Abd al-Malik led the pilgrimage.

831 Meter: *basīṭ*. According to at-Tabari (II, 1058), the verses were written by al-Harith b. Wa'la. Al-Bakri indicates that the author was al-Wa'la al-Jarmi (*Simt al-la'ali'*, 750). For the verses from "Ask the neighbor of the Jarm ..." cf. al-Mubarrad, 155 (plus an additional verse); cf. Tab., II, 1058 (plus an additional verse); cf. *Aghānī*, XIX, 140 (plus an additional verse).

832 From "La'y b. Shaqiq b. Thawr as-Sadusi came to al-Hajjaj ..." cf. *Ibn 'Asakir, *Tahdhīb*, III, 81 (Khalifa).

833 EI, IV, 393, s.v. Shuster. Cf. Zambaur, *Münzprägungen*, 88, 162.

834 From "Zadhanfarrukh advised al-Hajjaj ..." cf. *Ansāb*, cited in Wellhausen, *Arab Kingdom*, 235 n. 1; cf. Tab., II, 1059.

835 Ibn Hajar, IX, 462. His father, Mu'adh b. Mu'adh b. Nasr, d. 196/811–812 (Ṭbq., 546; Jarḥ, III, II, 142; Ibn Hajar, VIII, 374).

836 D. c. 202/817–818 (Ṭbq., 546; Jarḥ, III, II, 142; Ibn Hajar, VIII, 374).

837 This sentence parallels *Dh., III, 226.

838 This sentence parallels *Dh., III, 226.

[364] The Year 82/701–702

In this year, the battle of az-Zawiya[839] [took place] in *al-Muḥarram*/February–March 701.[840]

*Abu l-Hasan and *Abu l-Yaqzan:
Ibn al-Ash'ath went out and confronted {281} al-Hajjaj at az-Zawiya. They fought bitterly. On that day the following were killed: Abu l-Jawza' ar-Raba'i;[841] 'Uqba b. 'Abd al-Ghafir al-'Awdhi;[842] 'Uqba b. Wassaj al-Bursani;[843] [and] 'Abdallah b. Ghalib al-Jahdami.[844]

*Salm b. Qutayba[845] < Sallam b. Miskin:[846]
'Abdallah b. Ghalib was killed on the day of az-Zawiya.

*Yahya b. Muhammad < Ghassan b. Mudar < Sa'id b. Yazid:
The following were killed on the day of az-Zawiya: Abu l-Jawza'; 'Abdallah b. Ghalib; [and] 'Uqba b. 'Abd al-Ghafir.

*Sulayman b. Harb[847] < *Hammad b. Zayd[848] < *al-Mu'alla b. Ziyad[849] < Murra b. Dabbab:
On the day of az-Zawiya, I passed 'Uqba b. 'Abd al-Ghafir, who had been wounded in the battle and was lying on the ground. He called out to me, "This world and the hereafter are gone."[850]

On that day, 'Abd ar-Rahman b. 'Awsaja an-Nihmi,[851] of the Hamdan,

839 Cf. BGA, VII, 315; *Murūj*, IV, 309, 313; Tab., index; Yaqut, II, 911; Dixon, 158, 159.

840 This sentence parallels *Ibn Hajar, VI, 244 (Khalifa).

841 Aws b. 'Abdallah (*Ṭbq.*, 488; Ibn Sa'd, VII, 223; *Ma'ārif*, 469; Dh., III, 316; Ibn Hajar, I, 383).

842 On the notice of the death of 'Uqba b. 'Abd al-Ghafir al-'Awdhi cf. *Ṭbq.*, 488; Ibn Sa'd, VII, 225; Ibn Hajar, VII, 246.

843 On the notice of the death of 'Uqba b. Wassaj al-Bursani cf. *Ṭbq.*, 488; *Jarḥ*, III, I, 318; Ibn Hajar, VII, 251. #Ibn Hajar, VII, 252 (Khalifa).

844 *Ṭbq.*, 487; Ibn Sa'd, VII, 225; cf. Ibn al-Athir, *al-Lubāb*, I, 283f.; Ibn Hajar, V, 354.

845 Ash-Sha'iri; d. 201 (Ṭbq., 572; Ibn Sa'd, VII, 302; Jarḥ, II, I, 266; Ibn Hajar, IV, 133).

846 D. 167/783–784 (Ṭbq., 538; Ibn Sa'd, VII, 283; Ibn Hajar, IV, 286).

847 D. 224/838–839 (Ṭbq., 574; Ibn Sa'd, VII, 300; Ibn Hajar, IV, 178; cf. *Ma'ārif*, 526).

848 D. 179/795–796 (Ṭbq., 540; Ibn Sa'd, VII, 286; Ibn Hajar, III, 9).

849 Ibn Hajar, X, 237.

850 'Uqba is apparently expressing the fear that, because of what he did, he will not go to Paradise. For parallels from "On the day of az-Zawiya…" cf. Ibn Sa'd, VII, 164; *Dh., III, 284.

851 *Ṭbq.*, 340; Ibn Sa'd, VI, 230; Ibn Hajar, VI, 244.

was killed. He had been commander of Ibn al-Ash'ath's right flank. 'Imran b. 'Isam ad-Duba'i[852] was brought to al-Hajjaj, who executed him.

'Ali b. Muhammad < 'Ubaydallah b. 'Umar al-Bakrawi:[853]
[365] 'Abd al-Malik wrote to al-Hajjaj: "Summon the people to pledge allegiance. Release those who acknowledge [their lapse into] disbelief,[854] except those who raised a flag or reviled the Commander of the Faithful."[855] He summoned the people to pledge allegiance in accordance with these [instructions].[856] When the Banu Dubay'a arrived, he read the letter to them. 'Imran b. 'Isam rose, and al-Hajjaj called him and said, "Do you testify that you are a disbeliever?" He answered, "I have never disbelieved in God since I first came to believe in him." Then al-Hajjaj killed him.[857]

Ibn al-Ash'ath was put to flight, and he left his army behind. The people battled on al-Mirbad for three days. 'Abd ar-Rahman b. al-'Abbas b. Rabi'a b. al-Harith b. 'Abd al-Muttalib assumed command over them. Matar b. Najiya attacked and conquered Kufa. Ibn al-Ash'ath came to him, and Matar b. Najiya pledged allegiance to him. Al-Hajjaj pursued him, and they met at Dayr al-Jamajim.[858]

{282} *Umayya b. Khalid < 'Awana:
There were 81 clashes between them at al-Jamajim. All of them went against al-Hajjaj, except the last one, which went against Ibn al-Ash'ath, who was put to rout.[859]

Among the *qurrā'*, the following were killed at Dayr al-Jamajim: Abu l-Bakhtari Sa'd, a *mawlā* of Hudhayfa [and] Abu l-Bakhtari at-Ta'i.[860]

852 *Ṭbq.*, 485; *Jarḥ*, III, I, 300; Dh., III, 286; *Istī'āb*, 1209 ('Imran b. 'Asim ad-Duba'i); Ibn Hajar, VIII, 134; cf. *Aghānī*, XVI, 60. Ibn Hajar questions whether 'Imran b. 'Isam ad-Duba'i is the same person as 'Imran b. 'Isam al-'Anazi (cf. Kh., 366).

853 Z: *al-B-k-r-w-'-y*; U: *al-B-k-r-w-'-n-y*. He is unidentified.

854 The use of the word *kufr*, "disbelief," is significant in that it reveals how closely bound were religious and political notions in a society that equated political opposition with religious backsliding or heresy. Cf. note 21.

855 Cf. note 732. What the narrator seems to be saying here is that 'Abd al-Malik was ordering al-Hajjaj to release all the rebels who repented, except for the ringleaders.

856 From "'Abd al-Malik wrote to al-Hajjaj ..." cf. *'Iqd*, II, 177, l. 2; cf. *'Iqd*, V, 53, l. 10.

857 From "'Imran b. 'Isam rose ..." cf. *'Iqd*, II, 177, l. 11; cf. *'Iqd*, II, 464f.; cf. *'Iqd*, V, 55, l. 7; *Dh., III, 286.

858 EI2, II, 196.

859 From "There were 81 clashes ..." cf. *Dh., III, 231, l. 8.

860 *Ṭbq.*, 350; Ibn Sa'd, VI, 292; Dh., III, 316; Ibn Hajar, IV, 72.

*Ghundar < *Shu‘ba[861] < ‘Amr b. Murra:[862]
On the day of Dayr al-Jamajim, the *qurrā’* came to Abu l-Bakhtari at-Ta’i to make him their commander. He said, “I am a *mawlā*. Make a full-blooded Arab your commander.” So they gave command to Jahm b. Zahr b. Qays.[863]

[366] *Someone < Sufyan < Aban b. Taghlib[864] < Salama b. Kuhayl:[865]
I saw Abu l-Bakhtari at Dayr al-Jamajim while a man attacked him with his lance, and stabbed him with it.[866]

Ibn al-Ash‘ath withdrew from Dayr al-Jamajim to Basra, pursued by al-Hajjaj. He left Basra for Maskin, in the region of the Dujayl, near al-Ahwaz, pursued by al-Hajjaj. They met at Maskin, where Ibn al-Ash‘ath was put to rout, and many of his companions were killed or drowned.[867]

*Umayya b. Khalid < * Shu‘ba [b. al-Hajjaj] < ‘Amr b. Murra:
The following were lost at Maskin on the night of the Dujayl: ‘Abd ar-Rahman b. Abi Layla,[868] ‘Abdallah b. Shaddad b. al-Had,[869] [and] Abu ‘Ubayda b. ‘Abdallah b. Mas‘ud.[870]

‘Ali b. ‘Abdallah < *Sufyan < *Abu Farwa:[871]
Ibn Abi Layla was lost at S-w-r-a-’.[872]

Al-Hajjaj took many prisoners, among whom were the following:

861 Ibn al-Hajjaj, d. *Rajab* 160/April–May 777 (GAS, I, 92).

862 Al-Jamali, d. 118/736–737 or 120 (*Ṭbq.*, 377; Ibn Sa‘d, VI, 315; Ibn Hajar, VIII, 102)

863 According to a note in the margin of the manuscript, his name was Jabala b. Zahr, rather than Jahm (cf. Tab., index, s.v. Jabala b. Zahr; Ibn Hazm, 409). From “On the day of Dayr al-Jamajim …” cf. *Dh., III, 231, l. 10.

864 D. after 141/758 (*Ṭbq.*, 385; Ibn Sa‘d, VI, 360; Ibn Hajar, I, 93; cf. GAS, I, 24).

865 D. 122/739–740 (*Ṭbq.*, 377; Ibn Sa‘d, VI, 316; Ibn Hajar, IV, 155).

866 This sentence parallels *Dh., III, 231, l. 12.

867 From “Ibn al-Ash‘ath withdrew from Dayr al-Jamajim to Basra …” cf. *Dh., III, 231, l. 13.

868 EI2, III, 687; cf. GAS, I, index.

869 *Ṭbq.*, 348; Ibn Sa‘d, VI, 126; Dh., III, 255; Ibn Hajar, V, 251.

870 ‘Amir (*Ṭbq.*, 348; Ibn Sa‘d, VI, 210; Dh., III, 320; Ibn Hajar, V, 75). On this list of the dead cf. #Dh., III, 231, l. 16; Ibn Hajar, V, 75.

871 Cf. *Ṭbq.*, 387; Ibn Sa‘d, V, 12 (Ibn Sa‘d has Abu Qurra).

872 Cf. the indices to all volumes of BGA, Yaqut, III, 184; Yaqut IV, 840 (Nahr Sura); cf. Minorsky, 77, 140. This sentence parallels *Dh., III, 231, l. 17.

'Imran b. 'Isam al-'Anazi,[873] 'Abd ar-Rahman b. Tharwan,[874] A'sha Hamdan,[875] [and] Fayruz Husayn.[876]

Abu l-Yaqzan < *Salm b. al-Jarud b. Abi Sabra al-Hudhali:
'Imran b. {283} 'Isam al-'Anazi was brought to al-Hajjaj, who said, "'Imran?" He said, "Yes." [Al-Hajjaj] said, "Did I not come to Iraq and send you as an ambassador to the Commander of the Faithful, even though someone like you is not sent out as an ambassador?"[877] He answered, "Yes." [Al-Hajjaj] said, "And did I not marry you to the chief lady of her people, Mawiya bint Misma', even though you were not worthy of her?" He answered, "Yes." [Al-Hajjaj] said, "So what made you revolt with the enemy of God, Ibn al-Ash'ath?" He answered, "Bādhān made me revolt."[878] [Al-Hajjaj] said, "And why were you away from the nuptial chamber of your wife?"[879] He answered, "Bādhān made me go." [Al-Hajjaj] said, "And why were you away from the ruin of Basra?" He answered, [367] "Bādhān made me go." Then a man removed the turban from ['Imran's] head, and behold! his head was shaven. [Al-Hajjaj] said, "And shaven head, too? May God not forgive me if I forgive you." Then al-Hajjaj ordered him to be beheaded.[880]

[Abu l-Yaqzan:]
'Abd al-Malik b. Marwan afterwards inquired about 'Imran b. 'Isam al-'Anazi. He was told, "Al-Hajjaj had him put to death." He asked, "Why?" and was told, "He revolted with Ibn al-Ash'ath." He said, "He should not have killed him after [the following] words of his:

1. You sent from the children of the noble Mu'attib[881]

873 Cf. note 852.

874 D. 120/737–738 (Ibn Hajar, VI, 152).

875 EI2, I, 690; GAS, II, 345. From "Al-Hajjaj took many prisoners…" cf. *Dh., III, 231, l. 18.

876 Cf. *Futūḥ*, 396; Tab., index; Wellhausen, *Arab Kingdom*, 247, 257, 414 n. 1; Ibn Hazm, 209.

877 Al-Hajjaj had sent 'Imran to 'Abd al-Malik in order to persuade him to designate his son, al-Walid b. 'Abd al-Malik, as his successor to the caliphate. 'Imran was the leader of the delegation, and recited a poem in praise of al-Walid (Tab., II, 1166f.; cf. *Aghānī*, XVI, 60).

878 "Bādhān" is unidentified. Perhaps the meaning of this and the following sentences is "He [Ibn al-Ash'ath] made me [revolt] with a call to prayer [*adhān*]." The significance of the entire passage is obscure.

879 *'Iqd*, V, 54 has *h-j-h*; Khalifa has *ḥajala*.

880 From "'Imran b. 'Isam al-'Anazi was brought to al-Hajjaj …" cf. *'*Iqd*, V, 54.

881 Mu'attib b. Malik, of the Thaqif, was an ancestor of al-Hajjaj (cf. Ibn 'Asakir, *Tahdhīb*, IV, 48; *Ma'ārif*, 395).

A falcon, whose dove takes refuge in the *'awsaj* tree.

2. If you cook in his fire, you will cook us well.
   If you cook in another fire, you will not cook [us] well.

3. He is a lion. If he wants to seize an animal as prey,
   Loud screaming will not rescue it from him."[882]

Then Ibn al-Ash'ath headed for Khurasan, followed by the remnants of his army. But he abandoned them, and went to [the] Zunbil in Sijistan. 'Abd ar-Rahman b. al-'Abbas b. Rabi'a b. al-Harith b. 'Abd al-Muttalib assumed command of the people. At Harat he was confronted and put to rout by al-Mufaddal b. al-Muhallab, the governor for his brother, Yazid [b. al-Muhallab]. [Al-Mufaddal] took some of his companions as prisoners, among whom were Muhammad b. Sa'd b. {284} Malik[883] and al-Hilqam b. Nu'aym.[884]

*'Amir b. Salih b. Rustam[885] < *Abu Bakr al-Hudhali:[886]
Among the prisoners were the following: Yazid b. Talha b. 'Abdallah b. Khalaf [known as Talha] at-Talahat; an-Nadr b. Anas b. Malik;[887] 'Abdallah b. Fadala az-Zahrani;[888] Sa'd b. Najd; and many Yemenites. Yazid b. al-Muhallab released them and clothed them, but sent the Mudarites to al-Hajjaj. The first one to speak to him was al-Hilqam b. Nu'aym, who said, "May God curse you, Hajjaj, if [368] this Mazuni[889] – that is, Yazid [b. al-Muhallab] – escapes from you." [Al-Hajjaj] asked, "Why?" He said:

1. Because he was deceitful in releasing his family,
   While he led the Mudar toward you in chains.

2. He preserved his family from the heat of death by means of your people.

882 Meter: *kāmil*. From "'Abd al-Malik b. Marwan afterwards inquired …" cf. Aa-Jahiz, I, 48; **'Iqd*, V, 54; cf. *Aghānī*, XVI, 60 (verses 1 and 2).

883 *Ṭbq.*, 608; Ibn Sa'd, V, 167; Ibn Hajar, IX, 183 (Malik = Abu Waqqas).

884 From "Then Ibn al-Ash'ath headed for Khurasan …" cf. Tab., II, 1109, 1111, 1121; Ibn Hazm, 233; *Dh., III, 232, l. 4.

885 D. 182/798–799 (Ibn Hajar, V, 70).

886 Sulmi b. 'Abdallah (*Ṭbq.*, 533, 538; *Jarḥ*, II, I, 538).

887 *Ṭbq.*, 501; Ibn Sa'd, VII, 191; Ibn Hajar, X, 435.

888 *Ṭbq.*, 451; *Jarḥ*, II, II, 135; Ibn Hajar, V, 357.

889 Mazun was a name of the natives of Oman (BGA, V, 35f.) On the Omani origin of the Muhallabids, see *Ma'ārif*, 399.

Your tribe was considered by them to be less important than themselves.[890]

[Al-Hajjaj] said, "You're a liar," and ordered him to be put to death.

['Amir b. Salih:]
Al-Hajjaj said to Muhammad b. Sa'd b. Malik, "Shadow of Satan,[891] you most conceited person! [But] you were willing to be a muezzin for a slave of the Banu Nasr." – that is, 'Amr[892] b. Abi s-Salt b. Kinnara. Then he ordered him to be put to death.[893]

The first battle between them, the day of Tustar, was on the Feast of Sacrifice [10 *Dhū l-Ḥijja*], at the end of 81/25 January 701. The second battle, at az-Zawiya, was in *al-Muḥarram* at the beginning of 82/February–March 701. The third battle, at al-Mirbad, was on a Sunday, in *Ṣafar* 82/March–April 701. The fourth battle, at-Dayr al-Jamajim, was the rout on 14 *Jumādā* {285} 82/26 June or 26 July 701. The fifth battle, the night of the Dujayl, was in *Sha'bān* 82/September–October 701.[894]

Abu 'Ubayda < Abu Na'ama 'Amr b. 'Isa al-'Adawi:[895]
I was coming from Mecca in *al-Muḥarram*, while the people were at az-Zawiya. I came to al-Harish,[896] who was sitting on the skin of a lion, wearing his garment thrown over his shoulder. I greeted him and he returned [the greeting]. He asked my name, and recognized me. Then a man came. He said, [369] "Al-Hajjaj has removed the squadrons from the trench." He lifted his head and looked at the sun, and said, "This is not the time for battle."[897] Then another man came, and he said the same thing. When still another came, he said to someone, "Stand on this stump and look." He said, "I see the squadrons leaving." The two armies had gotten ready. He said, "Get me my horse and my arms." He put on his armor,

890 Meter: *basīṭ*. According to the report in at-Tabari (II, 1121), the verses were recited by 'Abdallah b. 'Amir, who was brought to al-Hajjaj after al-Hilqam had already been put to death, and he said to al-Hajjaj, "May your eyes never see Paradise, Hajjaj, if you forgive Ibn al-Muhallab for what he did." Al-Hajjaj asked what he had done, and Ibn 'Amir answered with the two verses. On quotation of the verse cf. Tab., II, 1121.

891 According to Ibn Hajar (IX, 183), Zill ash-Shaytan was Muhammad b. Sa'd's nickname.

892 Tab., II, 1120; 'Umar b. Abi s-Salt.

893 From "Al-Hajjaj said to Muhammad b. Sa'd b. Malik ..." cf. Tab., II, 1120.

894 From "The first battle between them ..." cf. *Dh., III, 232, l. 1 (Khalifa).

895 Ibn Sa'd, VII, 256; Ibn Hajar, VIII, 87; ibid., XII, 257.

896 Cf. Tab., index, s.v. al-Harish b. Hilal as-Sa'di; cf. *'Iqd*, I, 117, J. 7.

897 Cf. the battle preparations of Sinan b. Salama, and his observation of the sun (Kh., 249f.).

and his forearm seemed to me the forearm of a lion. Then he sat down on a chair. The knights came down. The first to come to him was Abu l-'Ilj, a *mawlā* of the Banu Taym of the Taym of the Quraysh, and his son. Then Mujahid b. Bal'a' al-'Anbari and Jahdam b. 'Abbad b. Husayn came. Then the knights of the Banu Tamim came down, until I counted 60 of them. [Al-Harish] mounted up. I followed them, observing what they were doing. A column of the Azd came. He incited them, mentioned what they had done, and spoke abusively of the Syrians. He said to his companions, "Attack!" and they broke the column. He did that several times, and continued to do it until evening. I returned to my house. That was on Wednesday, at the end of *al-Muḥarram*. I was listening to their voices part of the night. Then the voices died away, and [the armies] separated from each other. Then on Thursday morning they fought bitterly. The two sides persevered until night separated them. Then they met in the afternoon of the third day, and battled with thrusts and blows.[898] Al-Hajjaj ordered 'Abd ar-Rahman b. Muslim to take possession of the dam so that he might reach Basra. The Iraqis heard of this, and al-Harish offered them resistance. They met at the bridge. Thirty of al-Harish's companions were killed. {286} Abu Bakr b. al-Hantaf b. as-Sijf[899] advanced. A Syrian dealt al-Harish [370] a blow to the head. He was carried to Basra. They said, "Al-Harish has been killed." The two sides persevered. The following, all of whom were companions of Ibn al-Ash'ath, were killed: 'Abd ar-Rahman b. 'Awsaja, commander of Ibn al-Ash'ath's right flank; 'Abdallah b. Razam; Ziyad b. Muqatil; [and] Tufayl b. 'Amir.[900] Sufyan b. al-Abrad attacked. The people moved around, while enduring and steadfast people remained. The following were killed: 'Abdallah b. 'Abd al-Ghafir, with many of the *qurrā'*; 'Abdallah b. 'Amir b. Misma', with about 300 men; Abu 'Umar Kuthayyir, owner of the linen cloth,[901] a *mawlā* of the 'Anaza, with 200 *mawālī*. The army was routed. Sufyan b. al-Abrad pursued them until they entered Basra, and killed them. Then he returned. All he encountered – 400 or more – were killed before his eyes.

898 The Arabic *iqtatalū ṭa'nan wa-ḍarban* might perhaps be the equivalent of "they fought tooth and nail."

899 On his father, al-Hantaf b. as-Sijf, cf. *Ṭbq.*, 460; *Ma'ārif*, 416f., and 587; Ibn Hazm, 228.

900 Cf. Ibn Hazm, 183.

901 Sahib al-Kattan (unidentified).

[371] A List of the *Qurrā'* who revolted with Ibn al-Ash'ath
Muslim b. Yasar,[902] a Muzani, said by some to be a *mawlā* of Abu Bakr, and by others a *mawlā* of 'Uthman b. 'Affan; 'Uqba b. 'Abd al-Ghafir al-'Awdhi, who was killed in combat; 'Uqba b. Wassaj al-Bursani, killed in combat; 'Abdallah b. Ghalib al-Jahdami, killed in combat; an-Nadr b. Anas b. Malik; Abu l-Jawza', killed in combat; 'Imran b. 'Isam ad-Duba'i, killed in bonds [as a prisoner]; Abu l-Minhal Sayyar b. Salama ar-Riyahi;[903] Malik {287} b. Dinar;[904] Murra b. Dabbab al-Hadadi; Abu Nujayd al-Jahdami; Abu Shaykh al-Huna'i;[905] al-Hasan b. Abi l-Hasan [al-Basri], who was forced to revolt, was not killed.[906]

[372] *Umayya b. Khalid < *Hammad b. Zayd < Ayyub [b. Abi Tamima]: Ibn al-Ash'ath was told, "If you want them to be killed around you as they were killed around the camel of 'A'isha, make al-Hasan join the revolt."[907]

Among the Kufans [who revolted with Ibn al-Ash'ath were the following]: Sa'id b. Jubayr;[908] 'Amir ash-Sha'bi;[909] 'Abdallah b. Shaddad b. al-Had, who was lost on the night of the Dujayl; 'Abd ar-Rahman b. Abi Layla, also lost on the night of the Dujayl; –

*Ghundar < * Shu'ba < Husayn:
I saw Ibn Abi Layla during the night of al-Jamajim urging the people on.[910]

– Abu 'Ubayda b. 'Abdallah b. Mas'ud; al Ma'rur b. Suwayd;[911] Muhammad b. Sa'd b. Malik, killed in bonds [as a prisoner]; Talha b. Musarrif al-Iyami;[912] Zubayd b. al-Harith al-Iyami;[913] 'Ata' b. as-Sa'ib,[914] a *mawlā* of the Thaqif; Abu l-Bakhtari at-Ta'i, killed in combat.[915]

902 D. 100/718–719 (*Ṭbq.*, 491, 751; Ibn Sa'd, VII, 186; Ibn Hajar, X, 140).

903 D. 129/746–747 (*Ṭbq.*, 509; Ibn Sa'd, VII, 236; Ibn Hajar, IV, 290).

904 D. c. 130/747–748 (GAS, I, 634).

905 D. after 100/718–719 (*Ṭbq.*, 489; 503; Ibn Sa'd, VII, 155; Ibn Hajar, XII, 129).

906 For the entire list, including the title, cf. *Dh., III, 232, l. 9–14 (Khalifa).

907 The Battle of the Camel was proverbial for slaughter (cf. Abbot, 160 n. 211). The number of dead according to one report exceeded 6,000 (Tab., I, 3231). This sentence parallels Ibn Sa'd, VII, 163; *Dh., III, 232, l. 15.

908 D. 95/713–714 (GAS, I, 28).

909 D. between 104/722–723 and 109 (EI, IV, 242; GAS, I, 277).

910 This sentence parallels Tab., II, 1086.

911 *Ṭbq.*, 347; Ibn Sa'd, VI, 118; Ibn Hajar, X, 230.

912 D. 113/731–732 (*Ṭbq.*, 374; Ibn Sa'd, VI, 308; Ibn Hajar, V, 25).

913 D. 122/739–740 (*Ṭbq.*, 374; Ibn Sa'd, VI, 309; Ibn Hajar, III, 310).

914 D. 136/753–754 (*Ṭbq.*, 381; Ibn Sa'd, VI, 338; Ibn Hajar, VII, 203).

915 From "Among the Kufans [who revolted with Ibn al-Ash'ath …" cf. *Dh., III, 232, l. 16–19.

*‘Abd ar-Rahman [b. Mahdi] < *Hammad < Ayyub:
There was none of Ibn al-Ash‘ath’s [companions] who fell whose death was not regretted, and there was not one who escaped whose salvation by God did not evoke praise of God.[916]

[373] Muhammad b. Talha:[917]
Zubayd [b. al-Harith] saw me laughing with al-‘Ala’ b. ‘Abd {288} al-Karim.[918] He said, “If you had been present at al-Jamajim, you would not laugh. I would prefer that my hand”– or perhaps he said “my right hand” –”were cut off from my forearm, rather than to have been present.”

Abu l-Hasan < ‘Awana:
At Maskin, al-Hajjaj killed 5,000 or 4,000 prisoners.[919]

[Al-Mada’ini] < al-Hasan al-Jufri[920] < Malik b. Dinar:
Five hundred of the *qurrā’* revolted with Ibn al-Ash‘ath, all of whom participated in the fighting. Tufayl b. ‘Amir b. Wathila was killed.

al-Asma‘i < *‘Uthman ash-Shahham:[921]
When ash-Sha‘bi was brought to al-Hajjaj, he scolded him. Ash-Sha‘bi said, “Our land has become dry and our abode rugged. We are in continuous fear. We have been troubled by civil war with respect to which we were neither innocent and pious, nor wicked and strong.”[922] [Al-Hajjaj] said, “You have spoken well.”[923]

In 82, the following died, after al-Jamajim: Suwayd b. Ghafla[924] [and] Zirr b. Hubaysh.[925] According to some, Zirr died before the battle of

916 This sentence parallels *Dh., III, 232, l. 19; (*) Dh., III, 284.

917 D. 167/783–784 (*Ṭbq.*, 394; Ibn Sa‘d, VI, 376; Ibn Hajar, IX, 238).

918 D. c. 150/767–768 (Ibn Hajar, VIII, 188).

919 This sentence parallels *Dh., III, 232, l. 21.

920 U: *al-Ḥ-f-r-y* (unidentified).

921 Ibn al-Athir, *al-Lubāb*, II, 13 (= as-Sam‘ani, 330b); Ibn Hajar, VII, 160.

922 Ibn ‘Asakir (*Tahdhīb*, VII, 151) provides a commentary on some of the usual vocabulary of ash-Sha‘bi’s speech.

923 From “When ash-Sha‘bi was brought to al-Hajjaj …” cf. *‘Uyūn*, I, 104 (al-Asma‘i < ‘Uthman ash-Shahham); cf. Tab., II, 1112f.; cf. *‘Iqd*, II, 177, 464; cf. *‘Iqd*, V, 55; *Murūj*, V, 334f.; cf. Ibn ‘Asakir, *Tahdhīb*, VII, 151, l. 1; Ibn ‘Asakir, *Tahdhīb*, VII, 151, l. 4 (al-Asma‘i < ‘Uthman ash-Shahham).

924 *Ṭbq.*, 333; Ibn Sa‘d, VI, 68; Dh., III, 252; Ibn Hajar, IV, 278.

925 *Ṭbq.*, 317; Ibn Sa‘d, VI, 104; *Jarḥ*, I, II, 622; Ibn ‘Asakir, *Tahdhīb*, V, 374; Dh., III, 249; Ibn Hajar, III, 321.

al-Jamajim. Abu Wa'il;[926] Zadhan;[927] Rib'i b. Hirash';[928] Zayd b. Wahb;[929] Hudhayl b. Shurahbil; Abu sh-Sha'tha';[930] [and] Maymun b. Abi Shabib[931] [died] at al-Jamajim.

[374] In this year, al-Hajjaj killed Kumayl b. Ziyad an-Nakha'i.[932] Al-Muhallab b. Abi Sufra died in Marw. Qutayba b. Muslim killed the following: 'Amr b. Abi s-Salt b. Kinnara; Abu s-Salt; as-Salt b. Abi s-Salt; Musa b. Kuthayyir al-Harithi; Bukayr b. Abi Harun al-Bajali.[933]

In this year, 'Abd al-Malik sent his brother Muhammad to Armenia. The inhabitants confronted him, but he routed them. {289} Then they sought to make peace with him. He appointed Abu Shaykh b. 'Abdallah al-'Anazi[934] over them, but they betrayed him, and killed him.[935]

['Abdallah b.] 'Abd al-Malik b. Marwan[936] conquered Hisn Sinan[937] in the land of the Byzantines, near al-Massisa.[938]

Musa b. Nusayr sent al-Mughira b. Abi Burda al-'Abdi on a raiding expedition against the Sanhaja.[939]

Aban b. 'Uthman led the pilgrimage.

926 On the death notice of Abu Wa'il cf. Shaqiq b. Salama al-Asadi (*Ṭbq.*, 356; Ibn Sa'd, VI, 96 and 180; Ibn 'Asakir, *Tahdhīb*, VI, 334; Ibn Hajar, IV, 361–2).

927 *Ṭbq.*, 364; Ibn Sa'd, VI, 178; Ibn 'Asakir, *Tahdhīb*, V, 344; Dh., III, 248; Ibn Hajar, III, 302. On the death notice of Zadhan cf. *Ibn Hajar, III, 303 (Khalifa).

928 *Ṭbq.*, 349; Ibn Sa'd, VI, 127; Ibn 'Asakir, *Tahdhīb*, V, 297; Dh., IV, 111; Ibn Hajar, III, 236.

929 *Ṭbq.*, 364; Ibn Sa'd, VI, 102; Dh., III, 251; Ibn Hajar, III, 427.

930 On the death notice of Abu sh-Sha'tha' cf. Sulaym b. Aswad al-Muharibi (*Ṭbq.*, 349; Ibn Sa'd, VI, 195; Dh., III, 318; Ibn Hajar, IV, 165).

931 *Ṭbq.*, 366; *Jarḥ*, IV, I, 234; Dh., III, 308; Ibn Hajar, X, 389.

932 This sentence parallels *Ṭbq.*, 335; Ibn Sa'd, VI, 179; Dh., III, 293; Ibn Hajar, VIII, 447; #Ibn Hajar, VIII, 448 (Khalifa).

933 From "Qutayba b. Muslim killed the following …" cf. *Dh., III, 233, l. 1 (Khalifa).

934 Kh.: *N-b-y-ḥ* b. 'Abdallah al-'Anazi. The *nisba* should probably be read al-Ghanawi (Kh., 376).

935 From "In this year, 'Abd al-Malik sent his brother …" cf. *Dh., III, 233, l. 2.

936 Al-Baladhuri (*Futūḥ*, 165) gives the correct name.

937 Cf. BGA, VI, 99; Yaqut, II, 277; cf. E. Honigmann in EI, III, 526b, s.v. Missis.

938 This sentence parallels *Futūḥ*, 165; *Dh., III, 233, l. 4.

939 This sentence parallels *Imāma*, II, 70, 71; (*) Dh., III, 233, l. 5.

[375] The Year 83/702–703

In this year, al-Hajjaj appointed Muhammad b. al-Qasim over Fars, and ordered him to kill the Kurds.[940]

Al-Hajjaj sent 'Umara b. Tamim al-Qayni to [the] Zunbil in connection with the matter of Ibn al-Ash'ath. [The] Zunbil came to terms, and gave him a free hand with respect to Ibn al-Ash'ath. He bound him and a number of his kinsmen in iron fetters, and set out for al-Hajjaj. A man named Abu l-'Anz was joined [in bonds] with [Ibn al-Ash'ath]. When he came to ar-Rukhkhaj, he threw himself from the top of the citadel, and the two of them died together. Ibn al-Ash'ath's head was carried to al-Hajjaj.[941]

*Abu l-Hasan:
When the head was brought to al-Hajjaj, he quoted the following:

1. His misfortune and stupidity destined him to rush headlong to destruction,
   Which he encountered; thick-armed, contemptible,
2. Unpleasant of face, grim like a lion, aggressive,
   Rapacious, biting and breaking the necks of the brave.
3. {290} So good riddance to the son of the castratress;[942]
   Worthy of blame he met the Merciful One.[943]

Then he sent the head to 'Abd al-Malik, who sent it to 'Abd al-'Aziz [b. Marwan] in Egypt.[944]

'Abd al-Malik b. Marwan sent his brother Muhammad to Armenia, [the inhabitants of which] [376] made peace with him. He appointed Abu Shaykh b. 'Abdallah al-Ghanawi[945] and 'Amr b. as-Sudayy al-Ghanawi over them. But [the Armenians] betrayed the two [governors], and killed them.[946]

'Abdallah b. 'Abd al-Malik b. Marwan conducted a raiding expedition

940 The Kurds are said to have rallied to Ibn al-Ash'ath when he fled to Sabur, after the battle of Dayr al-Jamajim (Tab., II, 1101). This sentence parallels *Dh., III, 233; l. 16.

941 From "Al-Hajjaj sent 'Umara b. Tamim al-Qayni to [the] Zunbil …" cf. Din., 320 (= 325 Guirgass); al-Ya'qubi, II, 334; *Dh., III, 233, l. 17.

942 The Arabic *ibn wāhiṣat al-khuṣā*, a term of abuse, may approximate the English expression "son of a bitch."

943 Meter: *ṭawīl*.

944 For the phrase "who sent it to 'Abd al-'Aziz [b. Marwan] in Egypt" cf. (*) Dh., III, 233.

945 Cf. Kh., 374.

946 From "'Abd al-Malik b. Marwan sent his brother …" cf. Kh., 374.

in the land of the Byzantines. He confronted the Byzantines in Syria and Lu'lu'a,[947] and the Byzantines were routed.[948]

Hisham b. Isma'il al-Makhzumi led the pilgrimage.

[377] The Year 84/703–704

In this year, 'Abd al-'Aziz b. Marwan died in Egypt, and 'Abd al-Malik designated his sons, al-Walid and Sulayman, as the heirs to the caliphate. Hisham b. Isma'il b. Ibrahim summoned Sa'id b. al-Musayyab to pledge allegiance to al-Walid and Sulayman, but he refused to pledge allegiance to two princes, so [Hisham] gave him 100 lashes.[949]

Abu l-Yaqzan:
Sa'id b. al-Musayyab said to Hisham b. Isma'il, "If 'Abd al-Malik wants me to pledge allegiance to al-Walid, let him resign."[950] [Hisham b. Isma'il] said to him, "Enter from this door, and go out from this door," in order that the people might think he had pledged allegiance. But he refused, saying, "No one should be deceived by me." Therefore [Hisham] gave him 100 lashes, dressed him in hairy pants,[951] and indicated that he would gibbet him.

Abu l-Yaqzan < *Abu l-Miqdam:[952]
They passed by us with Sa'id b. al-Musayyab while we were in school.[953] He had been given 100 lashes, and was wearing hairy pants. While taking him along, they threatened him with [the prospect of] being gibbeted. Sa'id said afterwards, "If I had known that they were not going to gibbet me, {291} I would not have put on the hairy pants for them."[954]

947 EI, III, 41; cf. Ramsay; Honigmann, indices, s.v. Loulon.

948 From "'Abdallah b. 'Abd al-Malik b. Marwan conducted a raiding expedition ..." cf. al-Ya'qubi, II, 337.

949 From "In this year, 'Abd al-'Aziz b. Marwan died in Egypt ..." cf. *Ma'ārif*, 437; cf. Tab., II, 1169 (al-Mada'ini); cf. Tab., II, 1171 (al-Waqidi); cf. *'Iqd*, IV, 421.

950 Cf. Ibn az-Zubayr's unwillingness to pledge to both Mu'awiya and Yazid at one time (Kh., 252). This sentence parallels cf. Tab., II, 1169; cf. *'Iqd*, IV, 421.

951 The Arabic is *tubban sha'r*. At-Tabari (II, 1169) uses the word *musūḥ*, "hair-shirt." On the *tubbān*, cf. Dozy, 93; on the *musūḥ*, cf. ibid., 405ff.

952 Thabit b. Hurmuz al-Haddad (*Ṭbq.*, 372; Ibn Hajar, II, 16).

953 A similar expression is found in Dh., III, 307, l. 18, in an unrelated story (*kāna ... yamurru bi-nā wa-naḥnu fī l-kuttāb*).

954 From "They passed by us with Sa'id b. al-Musayyab ..." cf. Tab., II, 1169f.; cf. Tab., II, 1171; (*) *'Iqd*, IV, 421; (*) Dh., III, 310.

When news of what Hisham had done to Sa'id reached 'Abd al-Malik, he said, "What Hisham did is wrong. Someone like Sa'id should not be scourged with a whip. He should have been either beheaded or released."[955]

Hisham b. Isma'il al-Makhzumi led the pilgrimage.

[378] Musa b. Nusayr raided Sh-k-w-m-',[956] in Ifriqiya. He attacked the Awraba,[957] who battled him. Then God granted him victory, and he killed [many] and took prisoners.[958]

*Abu Khalid b. Sa'id[959] < Abu Bara' an-Numayri:
The Byzantines marched against Muhammad b. Marwan in Armenia. God put them to rout. This was the Year of the Fire. It was so called because after the people had been routed, Muhammad b. Marwan sent Ziyad b. al-Jarrah, a *mawlā* of 'Uthman b. 'Affan, and Hubayra b. al-A'raj al-Hadrami, who set fire to them in their churches, their houses of worship,[960] and their villages. The fire was in an-Nashawa[961] and as-S-f-r-jān.[962]

955 From "When news of what Hisham had done ..." cf. Tab., II, 1170; cf. Tab., II, 1171; (*) *'Iqd*, IV, 421.

956 Al-Bakri, *Description*, 117f. spells the name of this place *S-q-w-m'*; the *Imāma*, II, 71, spells it *S-j-w-m-'*; Ibn al-'Idhari, *al-Bayān*, 41, – quoting "Ibn Qutayba" – spells it *S-j-w-m-h*. Cf. the *table géographique* in Ibn Khaldun, *Histoire des Berbères*, IV, 526, where the name is written as Sekiouma or Segouma. According to al-Bakri, *Description*, 117f., *S-q-w-m-'* was a fortress (*qal'a*) near Fez.

957 A Berber tribe (cf. Gautier, index s.v. Aureba; cf. Julien, index).

958 From "Musa b. Nusayr raided Sh-k-w-m-' ..." cf. *Imāma*, II, 71f.; (*) Dh., III, 234; cf. al-Bakri, *Description*, 117f.

959 If the "Abu Khalid" from whom Khalifa learned so many traditions is actually Yusuf b. Khalid as-Samti, then there may be a scribal error here; or perhaps Yusuf b. Khalid is not the right person (cf. introduction, page 33).

960 The Arabic is *fī kanā'isi-him wa-biya'i-him*. The conjunction of those two words is reminiscent of the same expression which is found in the account of a treaty between Habib b. Maslama and the people of Dabil, in which Christians, Jews, and Magians were guaranteed their rights (*Futūḥ*, 200). In view of this, *biya'* might here be translated "synagogues."

961 EI, III, 839, s.v. Nakhchuwan; cf. Zambaur, *Münzprägungen*, 255, s.v. Nakhdjuwan.

962 The province of Waspurakan (Aspourakan, Asprakania, Basprakania, Asfarajan, Asfurjan). It is spelled al-Basfurjan in most of the Arabic works (cf., e.g., *Futūḥ*, 194, 195; al-Ya'qubi, I, 203; Tab., III, 1410; BGA, V, 287, 288; VI, 122, 246; Yaqut, I, 624). Cf. Honigmann, index, s.v. Waspurakan. On the revolt of the Armenians, and the attempt of the Byzantines to retake Armenia, see Bury, II, 355; Wellhausen, "Die Kämpfe der Araber," 433, A.M. 6195. For a parallel from "The Byzantines marched against Muhammad b. Marwan ..." cf. (*) Dh., III, 234.

Abu Bara':
In that raid, the mother of Yazid b. Asid[963] was captured from as-Sisajan.[964] She was the daughter of the *bitrīq*[965] in as-Sisajan.[966]

{292} Ibn al-Kalbi:
In this year, 'Abdallah b. 'Abd al-Malik b. Marwan conducted a raiding expedition, and reached Taranda.[967]

In this year, 'Abdallah b. 'Abd al-Malik rebuilt al-Massisa.[968]

[379] The Year 85/704–705

In this year, Muhammad b. Marwan conducted a raiding expedition in Armenia throughout the summer and the winter.[969]

*Abu Khalid < Abu Bara' an-Numayri:
Muhammad b. Marwan returned, and appointed 'Abdallah b. Hatim b. an-Nu'man al-Bahili [over Armenia]. 'Abdallah b. Hatim died, so Muhammad b. Marwan appointed his brother, 'Abd al-'Aziz b. Hatim. He rebuilt the cities of Dabil,[970] an-Nashawa, and Bardha'a.[971]

Ibn al-Kalbi:
In 85, 'Abdallah b. 'Abd al-Malik, while at al-Massisa, sent Yazid b. Hunayn,[972] who was confronted by the Byzantines with a large army.

963 Cf. Ibn Hazm, 262.

964 Kh.: *as-S-y-j-sān*. Cf. *Futūḥ*, 194, 195; al-Ya'qubi, I, 203 (translation in Dunlop, 20f.); BGA, I, 193; II, 252; V, 286–288; VI, 122, 246; VII, 98, 106; Yaqut, III, 216.

965 On the title *biṭrīq*, cf. I. Kawar, in EI2, I, 1249.

966 From "In that raid, the mother …" cf. *Futūḥ*, 205.

967 Z: *Ṭ-r-b-n-dh-h*. Cf. Honigmann, index, s.v. Taranta; cf. Ramsay, 71, 309 (Derende, Dalanda); cf. Wellhausen, "Die Kämpfe der Araber," 433, A.M. 6193. For a parallel from "In that raid, the mother …" cf. *Futūḥ*, 205.

968 This sentences parallels *Futūḥ*, 165; cf. Tab., II, 1127 (al-Waqidi).

969 This sentences parallels *IA, IV, 515; *Dh., III, 235.

970 EI2, II, 678, s.v. Dwin.

971 EI2, I, 1040. For parallels from "Muhammad b. Marwan returned …" cf. *Futūḥ*, 205; (*) Dh., III, 235.

972 Cf. the *Azidos ho tou Khounei* of Theophanes (Wellhausen, "Die Kämpfe der Araber," 33f., A.M. 6169).

The people were attacked at M-y-s-w-s-n-h.[973] Maymun al-Jurjumani[974] was killed at Tuwana,[975] with about 1,000 men from Antioch.[976]

[380] Hisham b. Isma'il b. Ibrahim al-Makhzumi led the pilgrimage.

In 85, the following died: Wathila b. al-Asqa' al-Laythi[977] [and] 'Abdallah b. 'Amir b. Rabi'a,[978] who learned traditions from the Prophet.

{293}[381] The Year 86/705

In this year, Qutayba b. Muslim b. 'Amr arrived in Khurasan as governor.[979] The *dihqāns*[980] of Balkh met him, and proceeded with him. The king of as-Saghaniyan[981] brought him gifts and a key of gold, and delivered his country over to him.[982]

Ibn al-Kalbi:
In 86, Maslama b. 'Abd al-Malik conducted a raiding expedition in the land of the Byzantines. He conquered Hisn T-w-l-q[983] and Hisn al-Akhram[984] before the death of 'Abd al-Malik.[985]

Musa b. Nusayr sent al-Mughira b. Abi Burda al-'Abdi on a naval

973 Tab., II, 1185, and 1235: Susana, which Honigmann, in EI, III, 522a, s.v. Missis, identifies with Sis (cf. EI, IV, 453ff., s.v. Sis). Cf. Wellhausen, "Die Kämpfe der Araber," 433f., A.M. 6196. For parallels from "In 85 …" cf. Tab., II, 1185; (*) Dh., III, 235.

974 On the Jarajima (singular: Jurjumani), also known as Mardaites, see M. Canard, in EI2, II, 456, s.v. Djaradjima. On Maymun al-Jurjumani, cf. ibid., 457a. Cf. Wellhausen, "Die Kämpfe der Araber," 436f.

975 Cf. Honigmann; Ramsay, indices, s.v. Tyana; Wellhausen, "Die Kämpfe der Araber," 436f.

976 This sentence parallels *Futūḥ*, 160f.; cf. Tab., II, 1185; *Dh., III, 235.

977 *Ṭbq.*, 69, 273, 411, 773; Ibn Sa'd, VII, 407; *Istī'āb*, 1563; Dh., III, 310; Ibn Hajar, XI, 101.

978 *Ṭbq.*, 52, 146, 590; Ibn Sa'd, V, 9; *Istī'āb*, 930; Ibn Hajar, V, 270.

979 On the conquests of Qutayba, cf. Gibb, 29–59; K. V. Zettersteen in EI, II, 1165.

980 On the term *dihqān*, see EI2, II, 253.

981 Kh.: *as-S-gh-'-n-y-n*. EI2, II, 1, s.v. Caghaniyan.

982 From "In this year, Qutayba b. Muslim b. 'Amr arrived in Khurasan …" cf. *Futūḥ*, 419f.; Tab., II, 1180; *Dh., III, 236, l. 3.

983 Tab., II, 1185: Hisn *B-w-l-q* (unidentified).

984 Unidentified.

985 From "In 86 …" cf. Tab., II, 1185; cf. Tab, II, 1194; *Dh., III, 236, l. 5.

expedition. He conquered '-w-l-y-h,[986] which is the first of the cities of Sicily, in the Maghrib.[987]

In 86, 'Abd al-Malik b. Marwan died.

*Al-Walid b. Hisham < his father < his grandfather; and *'Abdallah b. Mughira < his father:
'Abd al-Malik died in Damascus, in the middle of *Shawwāl* 86/October 705. He was 63 years old. Al-Walid b. 'Abd al-Malik recited the prayers for him. 'Abd al-Malik was born in Medina, in the house of Marwan, in [the quarter of] the Banu Hudayla, in the year 23/643–644. Some say he was born in 26/646–647. [382]

In this year, the following died: Qabisa b. Dhu'ayb al-Khuza'i;[988] Abu Umama al-Bahili,[989] a companion of the Prophet; 'Abdallah b. Abi Awfa al-Aslami,[990] a [294] companion of the Prophet; [and] Mutarrif {294} b. 'Abdallah b. ash-Shikhkhir.[991]

During the reign of 'Abd al-Malik b. Marwan, the following died: Busr b. Artat,[992] [a companion of the Prophet]; 'Umar b. Abi Salama,[993] a companion of the Prophet;[994] 'Alqama b. Waqqas al-Laythi;[995] Ghunaym b. Qays al-Mazini;[996] [and] Umayya b. 'Abdallah b. Khalid b. Asid.[997]

986 Perhaps this is an error for Syracuse (cf. Amari, *Biblioteca*, 354 n. 1: *Q-w-s-h* is written for Syracuse). Cf. Ghaluliya, mentioned in EI, IV, 398, s.v. Sicily. Cf. Ghalwaliya, which appears in Amari, *Storia dei Musulmani di Sicilia*, I, 421.

987 From "Musa b. Nusayr sent al-Mughira ..." cf. *Imāma*, II, 75; cf. Ibn 'Idhari, in Amari, 353f.

988 GAS, I, 403.

989 Sudayy b. 'Ajlan (*Ṭbq.*, 106; Ibn Sa'd, VII, 411; *Istī'āb*, 736; Ibn 'Asakir, *Tahdhīb*, VI, 417; Ibn Hajar, IV, 420). On the death of Abu Umama al-Bahili cf. #Dh., III, 315 (Khalifa); #Ibn Hajar, IV, 420 (Khalifa).

990 *Ṭbq.*, 242, 308; Ibn Sa'd, IV, 301, and VI, 21; *Istī'āb*, 870; Dh., III, 260; Ibn Hajar, V, 151. On the death of 'Abdallah b. Abi Awfa al-Aslami cf. #Dh., III, 261 (Khalifa).

991 *Ṭbq.*, 467; Ibn Sa'd, VII, 141; Dh., IV, 56; Ibn Hajar, X, 173. On the death of Mutarrif b. 'Abdallah b. ash-Shikhkhir cf. #Dh., IV, 57 (Khalifa).

992 See note 51.

993 *Ṭbq.*, 43, 448; *Istī'āb*, 1159; Dh., III, 194 and 286; Ibn Hajar, VII, 455.

994 On the deaths of Busr b. Artat and 'Umar b. Abi Salama cf. *Ibn 'Asakir, X, 15 (Khalifa).

995 *Ṭbq.*, 592; Ibn Sa'd, V, 60; Ibn Hajar, VII, 280.

996 *Ṭbq.*, 458; Ibn Sa'd, VII, 123; Ibn Hajar, VIII, 251.

997 On the death of Umayya b. 'Abdallah b. Khalid b. Asid cf. Ibn 'Asakir, *Tahdhīb*, III, 128; Dh., III, 242; Ibn Hajar, I, 371; *Ibn Hajar, I, 372 (Khalifa).

[383] A List of ‘Abd al-Malik’s Governors

Medina:

Tariq b. ‘Amr, a *mawlā* of ‘Uthman b. ‘Affan, seized control in 72/691–692, upon the death of Mus‘ab b. az-Zubayr, and called [for the pledge of allegiance] to ‘Abd al-Malik.[998]

Al-Hajjaj b. Yusuf was appointed by ‘Abd al-Malik over Mecca, Medina, and at-Ta’if, upon the death of ‘Abdallah b. az-Zubayr in 73/692–693.

‘Abdallah b. Qays b. Makhrama was appointed lieutenant over Medina while al-Hajjaj was in Mecca.

Al-Hajjaj was then made governor over Iraq, so he went there.

Yahya b. al-Hakam b. Marwan was appointed by ‘Abd al-Malik b. Marwan in 75/694–695.[999] He later went to Syria.

Aban b. ‘Uthman was designated by Yahya b. al-Hakam, and was retained by ‘Abd al-Malik, but dismissed in 83/702–703.

Hisham b. Isma‘il al-Makhzumi served until ‘Abd al-Malik died.

Mecca:

Al-Hajjaj went [to Iraq] in 75/694–695.

Qays b. Makhrama was designated by al-Hajjaj [when he left for Iraq in 75], but was dismissed by ‘Abd al-Malik.

[384] Nafi‘ b. ‘Alqama[1000] served until ‘Abd al-Malik died.

Yemen:

Muhammad b. Yusuf served until ‘Abd al-Malik died.

{295} Basra:

Khalid b. ‘Abdallah b. Khalid b. Asid[1001] was appointed by ‘Abd al-Malik after the death of Mus‘ab b. az-Zubayr, and arrived at the end of 72/April-May 692. [‘Abd al-Malik later] dismissed him.

Bishr b. Marwan b. al-Hakam was then given jurisdiction [in addition to his authority over Kufa], and he arrived in *Dhū l-Ḥijja* 74/April 694,[1002] but he died after a month.[1003]

998 This sentence parallels *Ibn ‘Asakir, *Tahdhīb*, VII, 40 (Khalifa).

999 Cf. Kh., 390, where the year is given as 76/695–696.

1000 *Ṭbq.*, 700; Ibn Sa‘d, V, 464.

1001 Ibn ‘Asakir, *Tahdhīb*, V, 63.

1002 For the entry on Bishr b. Marwan b. al-Hakam cf.*Ibn ‘Asakir, X, 113 (Khalifa).

1003 Z: several months.

Khalid b. 'Abdallah b. Khalid b. Asid was designated by Bishr, but dismissed by 'Abd al-Malik.

Al-Hajjaj was appointed, and went to Iraq in *Rajab* 75/October–November 694.

Al-Hakam b. Ayyub ath-Thaqafi was appointed over Basra in 75/694–695, and served until Ibn al-Ash'ath revolted and went to Basra at the beginning of 82/February–March 701, at which time he [left and] joined up with al-Hajjaj.[1004]

'Abdallah b. Ishaq b. al-Ash'ath was appointed by Ibn al-Ash'ath, who then dismissed him.

A certain Ghamidi, from the family of 'Abdallah b. Mughaffal, was then appointed, according to Hatim [385] b. Muslim.

Al-Hakam b. Ayyub was reappointed by al-Hajjaj after the rout of Ibn al-Ash'ath.

Kufa:

Qatan b. 'Abdallah al-Harithi was appointed by 'Abd al-Malik upon the death of Mus'ab [b. az-Zubayr], but he dismissed him after several months.

Bishr b. Marwan served for about {296} two months. Then Basra was added to his jurisdiction, and he went [there].[1005]

'Amr b. Hurayth al-Makhzumi was designated by Bishr.

Al-Hajjaj arrived in 75/694–695.

'Urwa b. al-Mughira b. Shu'ba,[1006] or, according to others, Hawshab b. Ruwaym ash-Shaybani, was appointed by al-Hajjaj upon his arrival in 75/694–695, and was later dismissed.

Al-Bara' b. Qabisa ath-Thaqafi was [then] appointed, and later dismissed.

'Abd ar-Rahman b. 'Abdallah b. 'Amir al-Hadrami was then appointed, but was expelled by Matar b. Najiya ar-Riyahi, who called for allegiance to Ibn al-Ash'ath. Ibn al-Ash'ath then arrived.

'Abdallah b. Ishaq b. al-Ash'ath was appointed by Ibn al-Ash'ath when he went out to Dayr al-Jamajim.

1004 From "Al-Hajjaj was appointed, and went to Iraq ..." cf. (*) Dh., III, 360 (Khalifa).

1005 From "Qatan b. 'Abdallah al-Harithi ..." cf. *Ibn 'Asakir, X, 113 (Khalifa). Entry on Bishr b. Marwan cf. *Ibn 'Asakir, X, 127 (Khalifa).

1006 'Urwa b. al-Mughira b. Shu'ba named by *Ṭbq.*, 358; Ibn Sa'd, VI, 269; Dh., III, 283; Ibn Hajar, VII, 189; *Ibn Hajar, VII, 189 (Khalifa).

Al-Hajjaj arrived when Ibn al-Ash'ath was put to rout at al-Jamajim. He then went to Basra.

'Umayr b. Hani',[1007] a Damascene, was [then] appointed, and later dismissed.

Al-Mughira b. 'Abdallah b. Abi 'Aqil[1008] was appointed to lead the prayer.

Ziyad b. Jarir b. 'Abdallah served as chief of police until the death of 'Abd al-Malik.

[386] Khurasan:

In the year of Mus'ab's death, 'Abd al-Malik wrote to 'Abdallah b. Khazim concerning his governorship over Khurasan.[1009] He sent the letter with Sawra b. Abjar ad-Darimi. Ibn Khazim said to him, "If I did not abhor sowing dissension between the Banu Tamim and the Sulaym, I would kill you. But I am going to make you eat your letter." So he [was forced to] eat it.[1010] Then 'Abd al-Malik wrote to Bukayr b. Wishah[1011] as-Sarimi: "If you kill him or expel him from Khurasan, {297} you shall be the [new] *amīr*." Bukayr killed ['Abdallah b. Khazim], and served as governor until the arrival of Umayya b. 'Abdallah b. Khalid b. Asid, when he was dismissed.

Umayya [b. 'Abdallah] was appointed, but later dismissed. Al-Muhallab b. Abi Sufra was appointed in 79/698–699.[1012] He died in 82/701–702.

Yazid b. al-Muhallab b. Abi Sufra was designated by his father, and was retained by 'Abd al-Malik for two years or more.

Al-Hajjaj then had Khurasan added to his jurisdiction.

Qutayba b. Muslim, appointed by al-Hajjaj, arrived in 86/705, before the death of 'Abd al-Malik.

1007 Ibn Hajar, VIII, 149.

1008 Ibn Hajar, X, 263.

1009 'Abdallah b. Khazim had been a supporter of Ibn az-Zubayr. 'Abd al-Malik offered to grant him the governorship for seven years if he would pledge allegiance to him (Tab., II, 832). On 'Abdallah b. Khazim, cf. EI2, I, 47; Shaban, *'Abbasid Revolution*, 42ff.; Wellhausen, *Arab Kingdom*, 416ff.

1010 From "In the year of Mus'ab's death ..." cf. Tab., II, 831f. (al-Mada'ini).

1011 EI2, I, 1293

1012 From "Then 'Abd al-Malik wrote to Bukayr ..." cf. *Ibn 'Asakir, *Tahdhīb*, III, 129, l. 3.

Sijistan:[1013]

'Abdallah b. 'Ali b. 'Adi b. Haritha b. Rabi'a b. 'Abd al-'Aziz b. 'Abd Shams[1014] was appointed by 'Abd al-Malik, and later dismissed.

[387] Umayya b. 'Abdallah b. Khalid b. Asid was given jurisdiction over [Sijistan] together with Khurasan in 73/692–693.

'Abdallah b. Umayya was appointed by his father, then dismissed by 'Abd al-Malik after about three years.

Muhammad b. Musa b. Talba b. 'Ubaydallah was [then] appointed, but was killed by Shabib the Harurite at al-Ahwaz in 77/696–697, before he reached Sijistan.

Al-Hajjaj was given jurisdiction over [Sijistan] upon the dismissal of Umayya [b. 'Abdallah].[1015]

'Ubaydallah b. Abi Bakra was appointed by al-Hajjaj in 78/697–698. He died in 79.

Abu Bardha'a, the son of 'Ubaydallah b. Abi Bakra, was designated by his father.

Waki' b. Bakr b. Wa'il al-Azdi was sent by al-Muhallab [b. Abi Sufra], upon the orders of al-Hajjaj, who wrote to him: "Send one of your men to Sijistan."

'Abd ar-Rahman b. Muhammad b. al-Ash'ath was appointed by al-Hajjaj in 80/699–700. Then he revolted against al-Hajjaj, and marched to Iraq at the end of 81/January-February 701, leaving [someone over Sijistan].

'Umara b. Tamim al-Qayni or al-Lakhmi was appointed by al-Hajjaj, and later dismissed.

{298} 'Abd ar-Rahman b. Sulaym was appointed in 84/703–704.

Misma' b. Malik was appointed by al-Hajjaj on written orders from 'Abd al-Malik, and served until he died.

Muhammad b. Shayban, the son of the brother of [Misma'], was appointed [by Misma'], but dismissed by al-Hajjaj.

[388] Ash'ath b. Bishr al-Kalbi was [then] appointed, and later dismissed.

Qutayba b. Muslim was given jurisdiction over [Sijistan].

'Amr b. Muslim was appointed by his brother, Qutayba. Qutayba then went to Sijistan, and later departed.

1013 For a detailed discussion of the activities of the governors over Sijistan, cf. Bosworth, chapter III.

1014 Cf. Bosworth, 51.

1015 Passage from the heading "Sijistan" cf. *Ibn 'Asakir, *Tahdhīb*, III, 129, l. 6.

'Abd Rabbihi b. 'Abdallah b. 'Umar al-Laythi was then appointed by Qutayba. All that was in 86/705 and part of 87. He served as governor until dismissed by Qutayba in 93/711–712.

[389] The Judiciary [of Basra, Kufa, Medina, and Syria]

Basra:

'Abd al-Malik b. Marwan appointed Khalid b. 'Abdallah [b. Khalid] b. Asid [as governor] over Basra in 72/691–692, upon the death of Mus'ab b. az-Zubayr.

'Ubaydallah b. Abi Bakra was appointed judge by Khalid, and retained by al-Hajjaj b. Yusuf when the latter arrived.

Hisham b. Hubayra al-Laythi was appointed by al-Hajjaj. 'Abd ar-Rahman b. Udhayna al-'Abdi was then appointed.

Kufa:

Shurayh was returned by 'Abd al-Malik when the people rallied to the latter upon the death of Mus'ab. Then al-Hajjaj arrived and retained him as judge. He later asked to be dismissed, and [al-Hajjaj] dismissed him.

Abu Burda b. Abi Musa al-Ash'ari[1016] was then appointed. He asked to be dismissed after [the battle of] al-Jamajim, and [al-Hajjaj] dismissed him.

Abu Bakr b. Abi Musa al-Ash'ari[1017] was then appointed, and served as judge until he died.

'Amir b. Sharahil ash-Sha'bi was then appointed.

Medina:

Tariq b. 'Amr, a *mawlā* of 'Uthman b. 'Affan, seized control in 72/691–692, upon the death of Mus'ab [390] b. az-Zubayr, and called [for the pledge of allegiance] to 'Abd al-Malik.[1018] Then 'Abd al-Malik appointed {299} al-Hajjaj b. Yusuf [as governor] in 73/692–693.

'Abdallah b. Qays b. Makhrama[1019] was appointed by al-Hajjaj, and

1016 'Amir b. 'Abdallah, d. c. 103/721–722 (EI2, I, 693; GAS, I, index).

1017 D. 106/724–725 (*Ṭbq.*, 365; Ibn Sa'd, VI, 269; Dh., IV, 216; Ibn Hajar, XII, 40).

1018 This sentence parallels Kh., 383 (294); *Ibn 'Asakir, *Tahdhīb*, VII, 40 (Khalifa); (*) Ibn Hajar, V, 7 (Khalifa).

1019 Dh., III, 269; Ibn Hajar, V, 363.

served as judge until al-Hajjaj went to Iraq,[1020] and appointed him [governor] over Medina. Then 'Abd al-Malik appointed his paternal uncle Yahya b. al-Hakam [governor] over Medina in 76/695–696. [Yahya] designated Aban b. 'Uthman b. 'Affan to take his place, and 'Abd al-Malik retained him.

Nawfal b. Musahiq al-'Amiri[1021] was appointed judge by Aban, and served until Aban was dismissed in 83/702–703.

Then 'Abd al-Malik appointed Hisham b. Isma'il b. Ibrahim al-Makhzumi [governor] over Medina.

'Umar b. Khalda az-Zuraqi[1022] was appointed judge by Hisham, and served until 'Abd al-Malik died.

Syria:

Abu Idris al-Khawlani served as judge for 'Abd al-Malik.

[The governors (continued)]

Sind:

Sa'id b. Aslam al-Kilabi was appointed by al-Hajjaj b. Yusuf in 78/697–698. The two 'Ilafis, Muhammad b. al-Harith and Mu'awiya b. al-Harith, of the Banu Sama b. Lu'ayy, killed him.

Mujja' b. Si'r, of the Banu Murra b. 'Ubayd,[1023] was appointed by al-Hajjaj in 79/698–699. [391] He later died.

Muhammad b. Harun b. Dhira' an-Numayri was appointed by al-Hajjaj in 80/699–700, and he served until 'Abd al-Malik died.

Bahrain:[1024]

'Umar b. 'Ubaydallah was sent by 'Abd al-Malik, and he killed Abu Fudayk.

Ibn Asid b. al-Akhnas b. Shariq ath-Thaqafi was then appointed by 'Abd al-Malik.

1020 From "'Abdallah b. Qays b. Makhrama was appointed ..." cf. Ibn Hajar, V, 364 (Khalifa).

1021 Dh. III, 309; Ibn Hajar, X, 491.

1022 *Ṭbq.*, 643; Ibn Sa'd, V, 279; Ibn Hajar, VII, 442.

1023 Z: Murra b. *'-b-'-d*.

1024 In Zakkar's edition, the heading "Bahrain" comes between Ibn Asid b. al-Akhnas and Sinan b. Salama. Since Abu Fudayk was killed in Bahrain (cf. Dixon, 175f.), al-'Umari's reading must be correct. Cf. note 1025.

Sinan b. Salama b. al-Muhabbaq al-Hudhali[1025] was appointed by al-Hajjaj, and he died [in office].
Musa b. Sinan b. Salama was designated by his father.
Sa'id b. Hassan al-Asidi was appointed by al-Hajjaj.
Ziyad b. ar-Rabi' al-Harithi was [then] appointed [by al-Hajjaj], who dismissed him in {300} 79/698–699.
Muhammad b. Sa'sa'a al-Kilabi was appointed.
'Abd al-Malik b. 'Abdallah al-'Awdhi was appointed by Muhammad b. Sa'sa'a [as his lieutenant]. Ar-Rayyan an-Nukri revolted against him, and 'Abd al-Malik and Muhammad fled. Al-Hajjaj sent Yazid b. Abi Kabsha, who killed ar-Rayyan, gibbeted him, and then returned.
Qatan b. Ziyad b. ar-Rabi' al-Harithi was appointed by al-Hajjaj, and he served until al-Hajjaj and al-Walid died.

Oman:

Musa b. Sinan b. Salama was sent by al-Hajjaj in the seventies.
Then Sa'id b. 'Abbad[1026] and Sulayman b. 'Abbad seized control. Al-Hajjaj sent Tufayl b. Husayn al-Bahrani, who expelled the two from [Oman]. Al-Hajjaj sent him written orders to appoint a governor and return.
Hajib b. Shayba was appointed [by Tufayl]. He died there.
[392] Then Ibn 'Abbad [again] seized control.
Mujja' b. Si'r[1027] was sent by al-Hajjaj, who then removed him.
Muhammad b. Sa'sa'a was then appointed, and was killed by Ibn 'Abbad.
Sawra b. Abjar was then sent by al-Hajjaj, and he killed Ibn 'Abbad.
Sa'id b. Hassan al-Asidi was then appointed by al-Hajjaj.

Egypt:

'Abd al-'Aziz b. Marwan was appointed, and died in 84/703–704.

1025 Cf. note 100. Since Khalifa states that Sinan died in office before the year 79 (Ziyad b. ar-Rabi' was appointed to the post in 79/698–699), the statement that he died at the end of al-Hajjaj's regime (Kh., 412) must be a mistake. In the *Ṭabaqāt* (*Ṭbq.*, 453) Khalifa correctly places his death at the beginning of al-Hajjaj's regime.

1026 On Sa'id and Sulayman, the sons of 'Abbad, and their rebellion, see Dixon, 149–151; Ibn 'Asakir, *Tahdhīb*, VI, 167f.

1027 Cf. note 793. Cf. the Mujja'a b. Sha'wa of other sources, discussed by Dixon, 150. Ibn 'Asakir, *Tahdhīb*, VI, 168, l. 13, has Mujja' b. Si'r.

'Abdallah b. 'Abd al-Malik was appointed by his father, and he served as governor until 'Abd al-Malik died in 86/705.

Ifriqiya:[1028]

Hassan b. an-Nu'man was appointed by 'Abd al-Malik in 74/693–694. He left [Ifriqiya], returning [to Syria] in 78/697–698.

Sufyan b. Malik al-Fahmi was designated [by Hassan] to take his place when he went to 'Abd al-Malik. 'Abd al-Malik sent Hassan back, but 'Abd al-'Aziz did not allow him to proceed [to his post].

Badr b. Sufyan b. Malik was appointed by Musa b. Nusayr in 79/698–699.

Musa b. Nusayr was appointed in 79/698–699, and served until 'Abd al-Malik died. 'Abd al-Malik had appointed Hassan b. {301} an-Nu'man al-Ghassani before Musa, [393] but 'Abd al-'Aziz, the governor over Egypt, did not let him take office, and [instead] sent out Musa b. Nusayr.

al-Jazira:

Muhammad b. Marwan was appointed by his brother 'Abd al-Malik, and he served until 'Abd al-Malik and al-Walid died.

Armenia and Azerbaijan:

Muhammad b. Marwan was given jurisdiction over [Armenia and Azerbaijan] in 83, [and continued to hold jurisdiction over them] until 'Abd al-Malik died. Muhammad b. Marwan withdrew [from Armenia and Azerbaijan] in 85/704–705.

'Abdallah b. Hatim b. an-Nu'man al-Bahili was appointed [by Marwan b. Muhammad] as his lieutenant over Armenia and Azerbaijan. He died [in office].

'Abd al-'Aziz b. Hatim b. an-Nu'man was [then] appointed by Muhammad b. Marwan

al-Yamama:

Yazid b. Hubayra.

Ibrahim b. 'Arabi al-Laythi [was then appointed, and served] until 'Abd al-Malik died.

1028 In the editions of both Z and U, the heading "Ifriqiya" comes between Badr b. Sufyan and Musa b. Nusayr. However, during the reign of 'Abd al-Malik, only 'Abd al-'Aziz b. Marwan and 'Abdallah b. 'Abd al-Malik were governors over Egypt (cf. Zambaur, *Manuel de généalogie*, 25).

The Summer Raid:

Malik b. 'Ubaydallah al-Hanafi.
Al-Walid b. 'Abd al-Malik was appointed by [his father].
Muhammad b. Marwan b. al-Hakam.
'Amr b. Muhriz al-Ashja'i.

The Syrian districts:

[394] Palestine: Sulayman b. 'Abd al-Malik, ['Abd al-Malik's] son.
Homs: 'Abdallah b. 'Abd al-Malik, his son.
Jordan: Abu 'Uthman b. Marwan b. al-Hakam.
al-Balqa': Muhammad b. 'Umar ath-Thaqafi, the brother of Yusuf b. 'Umar.

The Pilgrimage:

73/693 and 74/694 – al-Hajjaj b. Yusuf
75/695 – 'Abd al-Malik b. Marwan
76/696 and 77/697 Aban b. 'Uthman
78/698 – al-Walid b. 'Abd al-Malik
79/699 and 80/700 – Aban b. 'Uthman {302}
81/701 – Sulayman b. 'Abd al-Malik
82/702 – Aban b. 'Uthman
83/December 702–January 703, 84/December 703–January 704, 85/704, and 86/705 – Hisham b. Isma'il al-Makhzumi

Chief of Police:

Yazid b. Abi Kabsha as-Saksaki, later dismissed.
[395] Abu Natil Riyah b. 'Abda al-Ghassani, later dismissed.
'Abdallah b. Zayd al-Hakami, later dismissed.
Ka'b b. Hamid al-'Absi served until 'Abd al-Malik died.

Secretary for Correspondence:

Abu z-Zu'ayzi'a,[1029] his *mawlā*.

Finance [Secretary]:[1030]

Sarjun b. Mansur ar-Rumi, who died [in office].
Sulayman b. Sa'd,[1031] a *mawlā* of the Khushayn, [which is] a clan

1029 Cf. Ibn 'Asakir, *Tahdhīb*, VI, 57, s.v. Salim.
1030 Arabic: *al-kharāj wa-l-jund*, literally: "taxation and army" (disbursements).
1031 Cf. al-Jahshiyari, index; Ibn 'Asakir, *Tahdhīb*, VI, 276.

of the Quda'a. He was the first to use Arabic for the records of the Syrian *dīwān*.[1032]

The official seal, the treasuries, and the warehouses:

Qabisa b. Dhu'ayb al-Khuza'i, who died [in office].

'Umar b. al-Harith.

Chamberlain:

Abu Yusuf, ['Abd al-Malik's] *mawlā*.

[Captain of] the Guard:

'Adi b. 'Ayyash, a *mawlā* of Himyar.

Abu z-Zu'ayzi 'a, in addition [to his position as secretary for correspondence].

Ar-Rayyan b. Khalid b. ar-Rayyan,[1033] a *mawlā* of the Banu Muharib. He died [in office].

[396] Khalid b. ar-Rayyan, son of [the preceding], who served until 'Abd al-Malik died.

The reign of 'Abd al-Malik, from the time he received the pledge of allegiance, lasted 13 years, three months, and 28 days. Then al-Walid b. 'Abd al-Malik received the pledge of allegiance in the middle of *Shawwāl* 86/October 705. Al-Walid's mother was Wallada bint al-'Abbas b. Jaz'[1034] b. al-Harith b. Zuhayr b. Jadhima, of the Banu 'Abs b. Baghid. {303} Al-Walid was born in Medina, in the house of 'Abd al-Malik, in [the quarter of] the Bana Judayla,[1035] in 52/672. Some say that it was earlier than that.

The following died during the caliphate of 'Abd al-Malik b. Marwan: 'Umar b. Abi Salama al-Makhzumi, who reported [traditions] from the Prophet; 'Alqama b. Waqqas al-Laythi; Zurara b. Awfa al-Jurashi; 'Abd ar-Rahman b. Udhayna; 'Abdallah b. 'Itban al-Asadi; 'Utba b. an-Nudr as-Sulami.[1036]

1032 Entry on "Sulayman b. Sa'd, a *mawlā* of Khushayn" cf. al-Jahshiyari, 40; Ibn 'Asakir, *Tahdhīb*, VI, 276, l. 7.

1033 From the heading "Chief of Police" cf. (*) *'Iqd*, IV, 399.

1034 Cf. Ibn Hazm, 91.

1035 Z: Banu Hudayla.

1036 *Ṭbq.*, 120, 775; Ibn Sa'd, VII, 413; Ibn Hajar, VII, 102.

[397] The Year 87/705–706

In this year, Nayzak Tarkhan went to Qutayba b. Muslim, made peace with him, and released the prisoners he had taken.[1037] Qutayba raided Baykand, near Bukhara. [The inhabitants] sought the help of the Soghdians, who came to them with a large army. But God put the polytheists to rout, and the Muslims pursued them, killing many, and taking prisoners. People took refuge in the city, and asked for peace. [Qutayba] made peace with them, appointed one of the Banu Qutayba over them, then departed. [But the inhabitants rebelled and] killed most of his companions. When Qutayba returned, they [again] asked to make peace, but he refused. He conquered the city forcibly, killed all the warriors in the city, and obtained many vessels of gold and silver.[1038]

In this year, Musa b. Nusayr sent his son, 'Abdallah b. Musa b. Nusayr,[1039] on a raiding expedition against Sardinia, in the Maghrib.[1040] He conquered Q-w-l-h.[1041] In this year, {304} Musa also sent 'Abdallah b. Hudhayfa al-Azdi on a raid against Sardinia. He acquired booty and prisoners.

In this year, al-Walid b. 'Abd al-Malik built the Mosque of Damascus.[1042]

Al-Walid b. 'Abd al-Malik ordered 'Umar b. 'Abd al-'Aziz to rebuild the Mosque of the Prophet.[1043] He added [extensions] to it.

In this year, a plague struck the young girls in Basra, in the month of *Shawwāl*/September–October 706.[1044]

Maslama b. 'Abd al-Malik conducted a raiding expedition. He conquered F-y-'-m[1045] and Buhayrat al-Fursan, [398] and his army reached Claudiopolis.[1046] He killed [many] and took prisoners.[1047]

1037 This sentence parallels *Futūḥ*, 420; Tab., II, 1184 (al-Mada'ini); *Dh., III, 236f.

1038 From "Qutayba raided Baykand ..." cf. *Futūḥ*, 420; Tab., II, 1185–1188 (al-Mada'ini); (*) Dh., III, 237.

1039 EI2, I, 50.

1040 This sentence parallels cf. *Imāma*, II, 75; (*) Dh., III, 237.

1041 Unidentified.

1042 This sentence parallels *Ibn 'Asakir, II, 19 (Khalifa); *Dh., III, 236.

1043 This sentence parallels *Dh., III, 236.

1044 This sentence parallels *IA, IV, 530.

1045 Cf. *Q-m-q-m* (Tab., II, 1185). Unidentified.

1046 Z: *Q-l-w-dh-y-m-'-n-l-s*; U: *Q-l-w-dh-y-m-'-th-l-s*. Claudiopolis was the name of several different places (cf. Ramsay, index; Honigmann, 44). Cf. also Honigmann, 88ff., and index, s.v. Kalcudia.

1047 From "Maslama b. 'Abd al-Malik conducted a raiding expedition ..." cf. Tab., II, 1185; (*) Dh., III, 237.

'Umar b. 'Abd al-'Aziz b. Marwan led the pilgrimage.

In 87, the following died: Shurayh, the judge; al-Miqdam b. Ma'dikarib;[1048] –

Abu Nu'aym:[1049]
Shurayh died in 76.
– 'Utba b. 'Abd as-Sulami,[1050] a companion of the Prophet.

In this year, the following were born: Shu'ba b. al-Hajjaj; 'Umar b. Hubayra al-Fazari, the governor of Iraq.

[399] The Year 88/706–707

In this year, Qutayba b. Muslim raided Tumushkath,[1051] the inhabitants of which received him and made peace with him. Then {305} he marched to '-r-m-th-n-a,[1052] the inhabitants of which made peace with him, and he departed. The Turks, together with the Soghdians and the people of Farghana, marched against him, and opposed the Muslims. They were led by the son of the sister of the king of China, and it is said that they had 200,000 [troops]. God granted the Muslims victory, and scattered most of the infidels.[1053]

Muhammad b. Marwan led a raiding expedition in Armenia, spending the summer and the winter there.

Maslama b. 'Abd al-Malik and al-'Abbas b. al-Walid b. 'Abd al-Malik conducted a raiding expedition. They stationed [the army] in Antioch and spent the winter there. The Byzantines raised a large army, and marched against them. God put the Byzantines to rout, and caused many of them

1048 On the death of al-Miqdam b. Ma'dikarib cf. *Ṭbq.*, 165, 780; Ibn Sa'd, VII, 451; Dh., III, 306; Ibn Hajar, X, 287; #Dh., III, 307 (Khalifa).

1049 Al-Fadl b. Dukayn, d. 219/834 (EI2, I, 143; GAS, I, 101).

1050 *Ṭbq.*, 120, 774; Ibn Sa'd, VII, 413; Dh., III, 282; Ibn Hajar, VII, 98.

1051 Cf. Gibb, 34; Minorsky, 352; R. N. Frye, in EI2, I, 1293, s.v. Bukhara.

1052 In their parallel accounts, al-Baladhuri has Karminiya (*Futūḥ*, 420), and at-Tabari has Ramithana. Without the diacritical points, the Arabic forms of all three are practically identical. Karminiya is found in volumes I, II, III, V, and VI of BGA (see indices). Cf. Minorsky, 113, 352, s.v. Karmina. Cf. note 275, and Gibb, 34. Cf. EI2, I, 1295a, s.v. Bukhara.

1053 From "In this year, Qutayba b. Muslim raided Tumushkath …" cf. *Futūḥ*, 420; Tab., II, 1194f. (al-Mada'ini); (*) Dh., III, 237.

to be killed. It is said that 50,000 were killed. God [granted the Muslims] conquest of Jurjuma.[1054] And Tuwana.[1055]

'Umar b. al-Walid b. 'Abd al-Malik led the pilgrimage.

In this year, 'Abdallah b. Busr as-Sulami,[1056] a companion of the Prophet, died.

[400] The Year 89/707–708

In this year, Qutayba b. Muslim conducted a raid against Wardan Khudah, the king of Bukhara. [But] he was unable [to vanquish] them, and returned.[1057]

Musa b. Nusayr sent his son, 'Abdallah b. Musa, on a raiding expedition. He went to Mallorca and Menorca, two islands between Sicily and Spain, and conquered them. This expedition was called the "Raid of the Nobles" because among his troops were many nobles.[1058]

Musa b. Nusayr sent his son, Marwan b. Musa, on a raiding expedition to as-Sus al-Aqsa. The captives he took amounted to 40,000.[1059]

Maslama b. 'Abd al-Malik raided 'Ammuriya.[1060] He confronted an army of the polytheists, {306} whom God put to rout.[1061]

'Umar b. 'Abd al-'Aziz b. Marwan led the pilgrimage.

Khalid b. 'Abdallah al-Qasri was appointed governor over Mecca.[1062]

In 89, 'Abdallah b. Tha'laba b. Su'ayr[1063] died.[1064]

The following died after 80/699 and before 90/709: Zurara b. Awfa,

1054 Kh.: Jurthuma. Cf. M. Canard, in EI2, II, 456a, s.v. Djaradjima.

1055 From "Maslama b. 'Abd al-Malik and al-'Abbas b. al-Walid b. 'Abd al-Malik conducted a raiding expedition ..." cf. Tab., II, 1191f.; *Dh., III, 237.

1056 *Ṭbq.*, 120, 774; Ibn Sa'd, VII, 413; Ibn 'Asakir, *Tahdhīb*, VII, 307; Ibn Hajar, V, 158

1057 From "In this year, Qutayba b. Muslim conducted a raid ..." cf. Tab., II, 1198f. (al-Mada'ini); *Dh., II, 239.

1058 From "Musa b. Nusayr sent his son, 'Abdallah b. Musa ..." cf. *Imāma*, II, 75f.; cf. IA, IV, 539f.; *Dh., III, 239.

1059 From "Musa b. Nusayr sent his son, Marwan b. Musa ..." cf. *Futūḥ*, 230; *Imāma*, II, 76; *Dh., III, 239.

1060 EI2, I, 449 (The city of Amorion); cf. Bury, II, 378ff.

1061 From "Maslama b. 'Abd al-Malik raided 'Ammuriya ..." cf. Tab., II, 1198; *Dh., III, 239; *Dh., IV, 302.

1062 This sentence parallels *Dh., III, 239; *Dh., V, 64 (Khalifa).

1063 *Ṭbq.*, 52, 597; *Jarḥ*, II, II, 19; *Istī'āb*, 876; Ibn Hajar, V, 165; cf. GAS, I, index.

1064 This sentence parallels #Dh., III, 262 (Khalifa).

'Abd ar-Rahman b. Udhayna, [401] Ma'bad al-Juhani,[1065] Humayd b. 'Abd ar-Rahman al-Himyari,[1066] Abu Ghallab Yunus b. Jubayr,[1067] Abu Ayyub al-Azdi,[1068] Qusama b. Zuhayr,[1069] Abu s-Sawwar al-'Adawi,[1070] Nasr b. 'Asim al-Laythi,[1071] Yahya b. Ya'mar,[1072] 'Abd ar-Rahman b. Abi Bakra,[1073] Muslim b. Abi Bakra,[1074] Khaythama b. 'Abd ar-Rahman.[1075]

[402] The Year 90/708–709

In this year, Qutayba b. Muslim made a second raid against Wardan Khudah. Wardan Khudah sent [messages] to the Soghdians and the Turks and those around them, seeking their assistance. Qutayba confronted them, and God put them to rout, scattering them.[1076]

Maslama b. 'Abd al-Malik raided Syria, and conquered five fortresses in that territory.[1077]

Al-'Abbas b. al-Walid b. 'Abd al-Malik conducted a raiding expedition. He reached Arzan,[1078] then returned.[1079]

'Umar b. 'Abd al-'Aziz b. Marwan led the pilgrimage.

1065 On the death of Ma'bad al-Juhani cf. *Ṭbq.*, 503; *Jarḥ*, IV, I, 280; Ibn Hajar, X, 225. See also *Ibn Hajar, X, 226 (Khalifa).

1066 *Ṭbq.*, 487; Ibn Sa'd, VII, 147; Ibn Hajar, III, 46; cf. note 198.

1067 Abu Ghallab (*Ṭbq.*, 483; Ibn Sa'd, VII, 153; Ibn Hajar, XI, 436).

1068 On the death of Abu Ayyub al-Azdi cf. *Ṭbq.*, 487; Ibn Sa'd, VII, 226; Ibn Hajar, XII, 16. See also #Ibn Hajar, XII, 16 (Khalifa).

1069 On the death of Qusama b. Zuhayr cf. *Ṭbq.*, 458 (the name is mistakenly written Usama); Ibn Hajar, VIII, 378. See also # Ibn Hajar, VIII, 378 (Khalifa).

1070 *Ṭbq.*, 482, 495; Ibn Sa'd, VII, 151; Ibn Hajar, XII, 123.

1071 On the death of Nasr b. 'Asim al-Laythi cf. *Ṭbq.*, 485, 492; *Jarḥ*, IV, I, 464; Ibn Hajar, X, 427; cf. GAS, I, 4, 24; #Ibn Hajar, X, 427 (Khalifa).

1072 *Ṭbq.*, 484, 831; Ibn Sa'd, VII, 368; Ibn Hajar, XI, 305; cf. GAS, I, index.

1073 See note 139. On the death of 'Abd ar-Rahman b. Abi Bakra cf. #Ibn Hajar, VI, 148 (Khalifa).

1074 On the death of Muslim b. Abi Bakra cf. *Ṭbq.*, 484; Ibn Sa'd, VII, 190; Ibn Hajar, X, 123; *Ibn Hajar, X, 123 (Khalifa).

1075 *Ṭbq.*, 361, 364; Ibn Sa'd, VI, 286; Ibn Hajar, III, 178.

1076 From "In this year, Qutayba b. Muslim made a second raid …" cf. Tab., II, 1201ff. (al-Mada'ini); *Dh., III, 240.

1077 This sentence parallels Tab., II, 1200 (al-Waqidi); *Dh., IV, 302.

1078 EI2, I, 679.

1079 Tab., II, 1200.

{307} In this year, the following died: 'Abd ar-Rahman b. Miswar b. Makhrama[1080] [and] Abu Zabyan al-Janbi.[1081]

[403] The Year 91/709–710

In this year, al-Walid b. 'Abd al-Malik dismissed Muhammad b. Marwan from [the governorship of] al-Jazira, Armenia, and Azerbaijan, and appointed Maslama b. 'Abd al-Malik over them. In 91, Maslama conducted a raiding expedition against the Turks until he reached al-Bab,[1082] in the territory of Azerbaijan. He conquered cities and fortresses,[1083] and subjugated the inhabitants of the region beyond al-Bab.[1084]

Al-Walid b. 'Abd al-Malik led the pilgrimage.

In this year, Sahl b. Sa'd as-Sa'idi,[1085] a companion of the Prophet, died.

[404] The Year 92/710–711

In this year, Muhammad b. al-Qasim b. Abi 'Aqil ath-Thaqafi conquered the city of Fannazbur.[1086] He also conquered the city of Armabil[1087] by peace agreement.[1088]

Qutayba conquered Shuman,[1089] Kashsh, and Nasaf. Al-Hajjaj wrote to him, [ordering him] to march against [the] Zunbil. So he marched, and [the] Zunbil made peace with him.[1090]

1080 *Ṭbq.*, 609; *Jarḥ*, II, II, 283; Dh., III, 274; Ibn Hajar, VI, 269.

1081 Husayn b. Jundub (*Ṭbq.*, 364; Ibn Sa'd, VI, 224; Ibn al-Athir, *al-Lubāb*, I, 239; Dh., III, 319; Ibn Hajar, II, 379).

1082 EI2, I, 835.

1083 From "In this year al-Walid b. 'Abd al-Malik dismissed Muhammad b. Marwan ..." cf. (*) IA, IV, 555; from "In 91, Maslama conducted a raiding expedition ..." cf. Tab., II, 1217.

1084 From "In this year, al-Walid b. 'Abd al-Malik dismissed Muhammad b. Marwan ..." cf. *Dh., III, 323; *Dh., IV, 302.

1085 *Ṭbq.*, 217; *Istī'āb*, 664; Dh., IV, 11; Ibn Hajar, IV, 252.

1086 Minorsky, 373; Idrisi, 83, and index, s.v. Firbuz; cf. Gabrieli, 284.

1087 Kh.: Arma'il. Idrisi, 77, and index; cf. Gabrieli, 284, n. 17.

1088 From "In this year, Muhammad b. al-Qasim b. Abi 'Aqil ath-Thaqafi conquered ...' cf. *Futūḥ*, 436; al-Ya'qubi, II, 345; *Dh., III, 324.

1089 Shuman is mentioned numerous times in the first three volumes of BGA (see index); also BGA, VI, 34, 211; VII, 291; Minorsky, 115, 120, 337.

1090 From "Qutayba conquered Shuman ..." cf. Tab., II, 1227–1230 (al-Mada'ini).

Musa b. Nusayr sent his *mawlā* Tariq[1091] [on an expedition]. He went to Tangier on the sea shore, and crossed over to Spain, where he was confronted by the king.[1092] He killed [many], and took captives and prisoners. He killed the prisoners and their king.[1093]

Abu Nu'aym:
In this year, 'Ali b. Husayn b. 'Ali b. Abi Talib died.[1094] {308} According to some, he died in 94/712–713.

[405] The Year 93/711–712

In this year, Muhammad b. al-Qasim b. 'Aqil ath-Thaqafi conquered ad-Daybul.[1095] Then he marched to Nirun.[1096] He received a letter from al-Hajjaj [saying]: "You are governor over whatever [territory] you conquer."[1097]

Abu 'Ubayda:
Al-Hajjaj gave [Muhammad b. al-Qasim] command at 17 years of age. Concerning that, Yazid b. al-Hakam[1098] said the following:

1. Bravery, forbearance, and generosity
   Are (virtues) of Muhammad b. al-Qasim b. Muhammad.
2. He led armies at seventeen years of age.
   How close was leadership here to birth![1099]

1091 EI, IV, 666.

1092 The king was named Roderick (cf. E. Levi Provencal, in EI, IV, 666, s.v. Tarik; Wellhausen, "Die Kämpfe der Araber." 438f.; Hitti, 494; E. Gibbon, V, 503ff.

1093 From "Musa b. Nusayr sent his *mawlā* Tariq ..." cf. IAH, 204ff.; cf. *Futūḥ*, 230f.; Tab., II, 1235; cf. *Imāma*, II, 78ff.; cf. IA, IV, 556ff.

1094 This sentence parallels #Dh., IV, 39 (Khalifa).

1095 EI2, II, 188.

1096 Z: *T-y-r-w-n*; U: *B-y-r-w-n*. Minorsky, 372; Idrisi, 98, and index; Gabrieli, 286 n. 24.

1097 From "In this year, Muhammad b. al-Qasim b. 'Aqil ath-Thaqafi conquered ad-Daybul ..." cf. *Futūḥ*, 436ff.; al-Ya'qubi, II, 345f.; *Dh., III, 324.

1098 D. 105/723–724 (GAS, II, 332).

1099 Meter: *kāmil*. According to al-Baladhuri (*Futūḥ*, 441), the author of the verses was Hamza b. Bayd al-Hanafi; according to al-Ya'qubi (II, 347), it was Ziyad al-A'jam. Both were famous poets of the Umayyad period. From "Al-Hajjaj gave [Muhammad b. al-Qasim] ..." cf. *Dh., III, 326; from "Bravery, forbearance, and generosity ..." cf. *Futūḥ*, 441; cf. al-Ya'qubi, II, 347.

He [?] < *['Awn] b. Kahmas b. al-Hasan[1100] < *my father [Kahmas b. al-Hasan:][1101]
I was with Muhammad b. al-Qasim when Dahir[1102] came against us with a large army, including 27 elephants. We crossed over[1103] to them. God put them to rout, and Dahir fled.[1104]

My father:
Then we crossed over to them. A band of Muslims pursued the enemy, killed them, then returned to the army. When night fell, Dahir and a large army attacked with drawn swords. Dahir and most of his companions were killed, and the rest were routed. Muhammad b. al-Qasim pursued them until he reached the city of B-r-h-m-'.[1105] Many of them came out to battle them. [406] He forced them back into their city, then besieged them until he conquered the city. Then he marched to al-K-y-r-j,[1106] and conquered it.[1107]

In 93, Musa b. Nusayr conducted a raiding expedition in the Maghrib.

*Bakr b. 'Atiyya < 'Awana:
Musa b. Nusayr conducted a raiding expedition in *al-Muḥarram* 93/ October–November 711. He went to Tangier, then crossed over [to Spain]. Every city he came upon he either conquered, or the inhabitants submitted to him. Then he marched to Córdoba. Then he marched west. He conquered the {309} city of Baja,[1108] which is near the sea, and conquered the city of al-Bayda'.[1109] He sent armies, which proceeded to conquer and take booty.[1110]

In this year, Qutayba b. Muslim raided Khwarizm, [the inhabitants of which] made peace with him on payment of 10,000 head. Then he marched

1100 Ibn Hajar, VIII, 173.
1101 D. 149/766–767 (*Ṭbq.*, 531; Ibn Sa'd, VII, 270; Ibn Hajar, VIII, 450).
1102 On the Indian king Dahir, cf. Gabrieli, *passim*.
1103 The Indus (Mihran) was crossed (cf. *Futūḥ*, 438; Gabrieli, 286).
1104 From "I was with Muhammad b. al-Qasim …" cf. *Futūḥ*, 438; al-Ya'qubi, II, 346; cf. Tab., II, 1200; cf. Tab., II, 1275; *Dh., III, 326.
1105 I.e. Brahmannabadh, discussed by Minorsky, 372f; cf. Idrisi, 80, s.v. Bamiraman; cf. Gabrieli, 287; cf. EI, III, 257, s.v. Mansura.
1106 Jarrett, 229, suggests identification with Karachi; cf. LeStrange, 400; cf. Gabrieli, 289 n. 39.
1107 From "Then we crossed over to them …" cf. *Futūḥ*, 438f.; *Dh., III, 326.
1108 Cf. EI2, I, 862.
1109 Cf. BGA, VI, 90.
1110 From "Musa b. Nusayr conducted a raiding expedition in *al-Muḥarram* …" cf. IAH, 207ff.; *Dh., III, 326.

to Samarqand, [whose inhabitants] fought him bitterly. He besieged them until they made peace, on condition that they pay 2,200,000 *dirhams*, and that they give him 30,000 head that year. He was satisfied with that.[1111]

In this year, al-'Abbas b. al-Walid b. 'Abd al-Malik conducted a raiding expedition in the land of the Byzantines, and [God][1112] granted him the conquest of a fortress. Marwan b. al-Walid also conducted a raiding expedition, and went as far as Khanjara.[1113] Maslama b. 'Abd al-Malik conducted a raiding expedition. He conquered the two gates of Hisn al-Hadid[1114] in the territory of Malatya.[1115]

'Abd al-'Aziz b. al-Walid b. 'Abd al-Malik led the pilgrimage.

In 93, Anas b. Malik died.[1116]

Abu l-Yaqzan:
Qatan b. [407] Mudrik al-Kilabi recited the prayers for him. Anas had reached the age of 103.

In this year, the following died: Sa'id b. al-Musayyab; 'Urwa b. az-Zubayr;[1117] Abu Salama b. {310} 'Abd ar-Rahman b. 'Awf;[1118] Abu Bakr b. 'Abd ar-Rahman b. al-Harith b. Hisham;[1119] Mahmud b. Labid;[1120] Khubayb b. 'Abdallah b. az-Zubayr;[1121] Jabir b. Zayd,[1122] in Basra; Tamim

1111 From "In this year, Qutayba b. Muslim raided Khwarizm ..." cf. *Futūḥ*, 422 (Abu 'Ubayda); *Dh., III, 326 (Khalifa).

1112 Tab., II, 1236, and Dh., III, 326 (< Khalifa), have *fataḥa llāh 'alā yaday-hi*.

1113 Kh.: Hanjara. Cf. Changri, Gangra (Minorsky, 220; Ramsay, index, s.v. Gangra), which could have been transmogrified in the Arabic annals to Khanjara. Cf. note 1401.

1114 Kh.: Hisn al-Jadid. Hisn al-Hadid, "the Iron Fortress," is an Arabic translation of the Greek *tò Sidēroun kástron* (Wellhausen, "Die Kämpfe der Araber," 444, A.M. 6230). Cf. note 1130, below. Cf. Ramsay, index, s.v. Sidēropalos; Honigmann, index, s.v. Sidērogéphuron, and Sidērópalos.

1115 From "In this year, al-'Abbas b. al-Walid b. 'Abd al-Malik conducted a raiding expedition in the land of the Byzantines ..." cf. al-Ya'qubi, II, 350; Tab., II, 1236; *Dh., III, 326 (Khalifa).

1116 This sentence parallels #*Istī'āb*, 110 (Khalifa); #Dh., III, 343 (Khalifa); #Ibn Hajar, I, 378 (Khalifa).

1117 EI, IV, 1047; GAS, I, 278.

1118 On the death of Abu Salama b. 'Abd ar-Rahman b. 'Awf cf. *Dh., IV, 77 (Khalifa).

1119 On the death of Abu Bakr b. 'Abd ar-Rahman b. al-Harith b. Hisham cf. *Ṭbq.*, 611; Ibn Sa'd, V, 207; Dh., IV, 72; Ibn Hajar, XII, 30; Dh., IV, 73 (Khalifa); *Ibn Hajar, XII, 31 (Khalifa).

1120 *Ṭbq.*, 596; Ibn Sa'd, V, 77; Ibn Hajar, X, 65.

1121 GAS, I, 265.

1122 EI2, II, 359; GAS, I, 586.

b. Tarafa,[1123] in al-Kara; Ibrahim b. Yazid at-Taymi,[1124] in Wasit, imprisoned by al-Hajjaj. Some say [Ibrahim] died in 94/712–713.

[408] The Year 94/712–713

In this year, Qutayba b. Muslim raided Kabul. He besieged the inhabitants until he conquered it.[1125] Qutayba raided Farghana, besieged its inhabitants, and conquered its fortresses. He sent cavalry which conquered ash-Shash.[1126]

Musa b. Nusayr went from Spain to report to al-Walid b. 'Abd al-Malik, and inform him about the conquests God had granted him, and about the wealth and crowns[1127] he had in his possession. He sent the [customary] fifth [of the booty] to [al-Walid].[1128]

Muhammad b. al-Qasim killed Sassa.[1129]

Maslama b. 'Abd al-Malik conducted a raiding expedition in the land of the Byzantines, and conquered S-n-d-r-h.[1130]

Al-'Abbas b. al-Walid conducted a raiding expedition in the land of the Byzantines. He conquered Antioch,[1131] and Q-'-r-t-h[1132] on the sea shore.[1133]

In 94, 'Abd al-'Aziz b. al-Walid conducted a raiding expedition in the

1123 *Ṭbq.*, 365; Ibn Sa'd, VI, 288; Ibn Hajar, I, 513.

1124 *Ṭbq.*, 358; Ibn Sa'd, VI, 285; Ibn Hajar, I, 176.

1125 From "In this year, Qutayba b. Muslim raided Kabul …" cf. *Dh., III, 327.

1126 EI, IV, 687, s.v. Tashkent. From "Qutayba raided Farghana …" cf. Tab., II, 1256f. and 1267f. (al-Mada'ini). *Dh., III, 327.

1127 Cf. IAH, 207, where it is reported that the table and crown belonging to Solomon were captured in Spain. Cf. IAH, 208, where mention is made of the crown belonging to the king of Spain.

1128 From "Musa b. Nusayr went from Spain …" cf. IAH, 210f.; cf. *Imāma*, II, 80f.

1129 On the Indian king Sassa, cf. Gabrieli, *passim*. For parallels to this sentence cf. *Futūḥ*, 442; Tab., II, 1200. *Dh., III, 327.

1130 Wellhausen believes that *S-n-d-r-h* should be read Sidara, and identifies it with *tò Sidēroun kástron*, which also appears in Arabic works in the guise of Hisn al-Hadid ("Die Kämpfe der Araber," 444, A.M. 6230). Cf. note 1114. For a parallel to this sentence cf. *Dh., IV, 302.

1131 From "Al-'Abbas b. al-Walid conducted a raiding expedition …" cf. Tab., II, 1255.

1132 Unidentified. It is written *Q-'-n-ṭ-h* in the edition of Ibn 'Asakir, *Tahdhīb*, VII, 271.

1133 From "Al-'Abbas b. al-Walid conducted a raiding expedition …" cf. *Ibn 'Asakir, *Tahdhīb*, VII, 271; (*) Dh., III, 327.

land of the Byzantines and reached Ghazala.[1134] Maslama b. 'Abd al-Malik led the pilgrimage.

{311}[409] The Year 95/713–714

In this year, Muhammad b. al-Qasim conquered Multan.[1135]

In this year, Musa returned [to Syria] from Ifriqiya, leaving his son, 'Abdallah b. Musa b. Nusayr to take his place. He carried the booty on carts and the backs [of animals]. Included in the booty were 30,000 head. He went to al-Walid.[1136]

Maslama b. 'Abd al-Malik conquered the city of al-Bab in Armenia. He demolished the city and left it in ruins. Then Maslama rebuilt it nine years later.[1137]

*Abu Khalid < Abu Bara' < *Yazid b. Asid:[1138]
Maslama went on a raiding expedition and conquered Sharwan,[1139] J-m-r-'-n, '-l-b-r-'-n,[1140] and the city of Sul,[1141] until he reached al-Bab.

[Abu Khalid < Abu Bara'] < *Abu Marwan al-Bahili < a man of the Bahila who was with Maslama:
Maslama was attacking the city of al-Bab when a man came to him and asked him to grant him safety for himself and his family. [In return], he would show [Maslama] a weak spot in [410] the city. [Maslama] granted his request. When the Muslims entered the city, the enemy was on guard

1134 Cf. Gazala, Gazelon (Ramsay, 323), and Gazelonitis (Ramsay, index). Tab., II, 1256; *Dh., III, 327.
1135 EI, III, 721; Idrisi, 96f. For parallels to this sentence cf. *Futūḥ*, 339f.; *Dh., III, 328 (Khalifa).
1136 From "In this year, Musa returned [to Syria] ..." cf. IAH, 210f.; (*) Dh., III, 328 (Khalifa).
1137 From "Maslama b. 'Abd al-Malik conquered the city of al-Bab ..." cf. *Dh., III, 328.
1138 A certain Yazid b. Usayd, who took part in raiding expeditions in Armenia, is mentioned by al-Baladhuri (*Futūḥ*, 240, 246). Cf. Dunlop, index, s.v. Yazid b. Usayd as-Sulami.
1139 Kh.: *S-r-w-'-n*. EI, IV, 382, s.v. Shirwan; cf. Minorsky, 403ff.; Dunlop, index, s.v. Shirwan.
1140 *J-m-r-'-n* is unidentified, but cf. Hayzan (note 1311); cf. also Minorsky, 448–449 (*Kh-n-dān*, *Jaydān*, *Kh-y-zān*, *H-m-r-y-n*]; Hamzin, (Dunlop, 63 n. 30, and index. *'-l-b-r-'-n* could possibly be identified with *K-y-r-'-n* (cf. note 1583). Cf. *L-y-z-'-n* discussed in Minorsky, 406–410, and index, s.v. Layzan.
1141 Cf. BGA, VI, 123 (Bab, Sul); Dunlop, 18, 19 n. 77, and index.

against them. They fought bitterly. At dawn the *shaykh* of the Muslims called out "God is great!" and God granted Maslama[1142] victory.[1143]

In this year, Qutayba raided ash-Shash for the second time. When news of the death of al-Hajjaj reached him, {312} he returned to Marw.[1144]

In this year, al-Hajjaj b. Yusuf killed Sa'id b. Jubayr.

In this year, al-Hajjaj died at the age of 53.

*Al-Walid b. Hisham < his father < his grandfather; *'Abdallah b. Mughira < his father; *Abu l-Yaqzan; and others:
[The administration of] Iraq was consolidated under [the administration of] al-Hajjaj, who arrived in *Rajab* 75/October–November 694.

[Al-Hajjaj's Officers]

Chief of Police:

Kufa:

'Abd ar-Rahman b. 'Ubayd as-Sa'di, before he took up residence in Wasit. He was also given charge of the police of Basra.

Mawdud, the son of his brother, was left to take his place when he went down to Basra. When he left Basra, he left his predecessor to take his place. Then al-Hajjaj dismissed him.

Ziyad b. Jarir b. 'Abdallah al-Bajali was [then] appointed.

Kufa:

'Amir b. Misma' b. Malik.

[Khurasan:]

Al-Muhallab b. Abi Sufra was appointed by 'Abd al-Malik.

Yazid b. 'Umayr al-Usaydi was appointed [by al-Muhallab].

'Umar b. Yazid b. 'Umayr, his son.

Ziyad b. 'Amr al-'Ataki.

[411] Then [al-Hajjaj] built Wasit. He was the founder of the city. He had four Syrians as chief of police:

Musa b. Wajih al-Himyari.

Muhasir b. Suhaym at-Ta'i.

'Ikrima b. al-Awsafi, a Himyarite.

Abu 'Ulafa as-Saksaki, who later returned to Syria

1142 U: the Muslims.

1143 From "Maslama was attacking the city of al-Bab ..." cf. *Dh., III, 328.

1144 From "In this year, Qutayba raided ash-Shash ..." cf. Tab., II, 1267f. (al-Mada'ini); *Dh., III, 328.

Sufyan b. Sulaym al-Azdi was then appointed.

*Al-Walid b. Hisham < *Bishr b. 'Isa < his grandfather:
Al-Hajjaj passed us in Wasit – I was at that time but a lad – and before him were Sufyan b. al-Abrad and another man, both of whom were in charge of his spear.[1145]

*'Abdallah b. al-Mughira < his father:
In charge of his spear was Abu s-Sakan, {313} a *mawlā* of the Khushayn, a clan of the Quda'a, of Himyar.

[Al-Walid, et al.:]
Finance Secretary:
Zadhanfarrukh, who died [in office].
Yazid b. Abi Muslim was then appointed by al-Hajjaj.

[412] Secretary for Correspondence:
Nafi', his *mawlā*.

Al-Hajjaj died at the age of 53.

The following died at the end of the governorship of al-Hajjaj: al-'Ala b. Ziyad b. Matar al-'Adawi;[1146] Sinan b. Salama b. al-Muhabbaq; Hakim b. Jabir;[1147] Malik b. al-Harith;[1148] [and] 'Uqba b. Suhban,[1149] after [the year] 90/708–709.

The following died during the caliphate of al-Walid: Rabi'a b. 'Abbad ad-Du'ali;[1150] 'Abbas b. Sahl b. Sa'd as-Sa'idi;[1151] 'Abdallah b. Abi Qatada;[1152] Ja'far b. 'Amr b. Umayya ad-Damri,[1153] at the end of al-Walid's

1145 Cf. S. D. Goitein, in EI2, II, 593a, s.v. *djum'a*, where it is stated that the *imām* held a rod, sword, or lance when delivering the Friday sermon. Cf. G. C. Miles, in EI2, I, 482, s.v. *'anaza*, which is synonymous with *ḥarba*, the word Khalifa uses. Cf. Tab., II, 1268, where it is stated that Yazid b. Abi Kabsha was appointed *'alā l-ḥarb* (not *harba*) *wa-ṣ-ṣalat*. A similar expression is found in Tab., II, 1305.

1146 On the death of al-'Ala b. Ziyad b. Matar al-'Adawi cf. *Ṭbq.*, 482; Ibn Sa'd, VII, 217; Ibn Hajar, VIII, 181; #Ibn Hajar, VIII, 182 (Khalifa).

1147 *Ṭbq.*, 350, 364; Ibn Sa'd, VI, 288; Ibn Hajar, II, 444.

1148 Ibn Hajar, X, 12.

1149 *Ṭbq.*, 488; Ibn Sa'd, VII, 146; Dh., III, 193; Ibn Hajar, VII, 242.

1150 *Ṭbq.*, 76; *Istī'āb*, 492.

1151 On the death of 'Abbas b. Sahl b. Sa'd as-Sa'idi cf. *Ṭbq.*, 622; Ibn Sa'd, V, 271; Ibn Hajar, V, 118; *Ibn Hajar, V, 118 (Khalifa).

1152 *Ṭbq.*, 631; Ibn Sa'd, V, 274; Ibn Hajar, V, 360.

1153 *Ṭbq.*, 620; Ibn Sa'd, V, 247; Ibn Hajar, II, 100.

reign; ‘Ubaydallah b. ‘Adi b. al-Khiyar;[1154] Abu Sa‘id al-Maqbari;[1155] [and] Thabit b. Abi Qatada.[1156]

Bishr b. al-Walid b. ‘Abd al-Malik b. Marwan led the pilgrimage.[1157]

[413] The Year 96/714–715

In this year, al-Walid b. ‘Abd al-Malik b. Marwan died.

*Al-Walid b. Hisham < his father < his grandfather; * ‘Abdallah b. al-Mughira < his father; *Abu l-Yaqzan; and others:
Al-Walid died on Saturday in the middle of *Rabī‘* I – some say *Rabī‘* II – 96/ November or December 714, at the age of 44. Sulayman b. ‘Abd al-Malik recited the prayers for him.

‘Aziz b. ‘Imran[1158] < Muhammad b. ‘Abdallah b. al-Mu’ammil al-Makhzumi:[1159]
Al-Walid was born in Medina in 45/665–666. He died at the {314} age of 51.[1160]

Hatim b. Muslim:
[He died] at 49 years of age. Sulayman b. ‘Abd al-Malik recited the prayers for him. His reign lasted nine years, five months, and several days.

Then Sulayman b. ‘Abd al-Malik b. Marwan received the pledge of allegiance.[1161] His mother was Wallada bint al-‘Abbas, who was also the mother of al-Walid b. ‘Abd al-Malik.

[414] A List of the Governors of al-Walid b. ‘Abd al-Malik and al-Hajjaj

Basra:

Al-Hakam b. Ayyub, governor when al-Walid came to power, was dismissed.

1154 On the death of ‘Ubaydallah b. ‘Adi b. al-Khiyar cf. *Ṭbq.*, 582; Ibn Sa‘d, V, 49; Ibn Hajar, VII, 36; *Ibn Hajar, VII, 36 (Khalifa).
1155 Kaysan (*Ṭbq.*, 619; Ibn Sa‘d, V, 85; Ibn Hajar, VIII, 453; *Riyād an-Nufūs*, 80.
1156 *Ṭbq.*, 631; Ibn Sa‘d, V, 275.
1157 This sentence parallels *Ibn ‘Asakir, X, 132 (Khalifa).
1158 D. 197/812–813 (Ṭbq., 692; Ibn Sa‘d, V, 436; Ibn Hajar, VI, 350).
1159 On his father, ‘Abdallah b. al-Mu’ammil, cf. Ṭbq., 712; Ibn Hajar, VI, 46.
1160 This sentence parallels *Dh., IV, 67 (Khalifa).
1161 This sentence parallels *Ibn ‘Asakir, *Tahdhīb,* IV, 377 (Khalifa).

Talha b. Sa'id al-Juhani, a Damascene, was appointed, and later dismissed.
'Amr b. Sa'id al-'Awdhi, a Damascene, was appointed, and later dismissed.
Muhasir b. Suhaym at-Ta'i,[1162] an Emesan, later dismissed.
Qatan b. Mudrik al-Kilabi, later dismissed.
Al-Jarrah b. 'Abdallah al-Hakami,[1163] served until al-Hajjaj and al-Walid died.

Kufa:

'Urwa b. al-Mughira b. Shu'ba ath-Thaqafi, in 95/713–714.[1164]
Ziyad b. Jarir b. 'Abdallah served as chief of police until al-Hajjaj died.
Harmala b. 'Umayr al-Lakhmi, appointed by Yazid {315} b. Abi Kabsha, served until al-Walid died.

Khurasan:

Qutayba b. Muslim served until al-Hajjaj and al-Walid died.
[415] Sijistan:
It was under the jurisdiction of Qutayba b. Muslim.
'Abd Rabbihi b. 'Abdallah b. 'Umayr al-Laythi was appointed by Qutayba, and later dismissed.
An-Nu'man b. 'Awf al-Yashkuri was appointed during the reign of al-Walid, and served until al-Hajjaj and al-Walid died.

Bahrain:

Qatan b. Ziyad b. ar-Rabi' al-Harithi was appointed in 79/698–699, and served as a governor until 'Abd al-Malik, al-Walid, and al-Hajjaj died.

Oman:

'Abd ar-Rahman b. Sulaym al-Kalbi.
'Abd al-Jabbar b. Sabara al-Mujashi'i served until al-Hajjaj died.

Sind:

Muhammad b. al-Qasim b. Abi 'Aqil, in 95/713–714.

1162 U: al-Kinani; cf. Kh., 411; at-Ta'i.
1163 EI2, II, 482.
1164 Entry on 'Urwa b. al-Mughira b. Shu'ba ath-Thaqafi cf. *Ibn Hajar, VII, 189 (Khalifa).

Mecca:

Nafi' b. 'Alqama b. Safwan, governor under 'Abd al-Malik at the time of his death, was retained by al-Walid for two years, then dismissed.[1165]

Khalid b. 'Abdallah al-Qasri was appointed in 89/707–708, and served as governor until al-Walid died.[1166]

[416] Medina:

Hisham b. Isma'il al-Makhzumi, governor under 'Abd al-Malik at the time of his death, was retained by al-Walid for two years, then dismissed.

'Umar b. 'Abd al-'Aziz b. Marwan was appointed at the beginning of 87/December 705–January 706,[1167] or at the end of 86/November–December 705. He served until 93/711–712, when he was dismissed.

Abu Bakr b. Hazm was designated by 'Umar b. 'Abd al-'Aziz to take his place, but dismissed by al-Walid.

'Uthman b. Hayyan al-Murri was then appointed, and served until al-Walid died.

al-Yamama:

Ibrahim b. 'Arabi,[1168] governor under 'Abd al-Malik at the time of his death, was retained by al-Walid.

al-Jazira:

Muhammad b. Marwan b. al-Hakam was retained [by al-Walid] until he died. Jurisdiction over Armenia and Azerbaijan were included.

{316} Egypt:

'Abdallah b. 'Abd al-Malik, governor for his father, 'Abd al-Malik, at the time of his death, was retained by al-Walid, and later dismissed.

Qurra b. Shurayk al-'Absi was one of al-Walid's governors over Egypt.

[417] Ifriqiya:

Musa b. Nusayr, governor under 'Abd al-Malik at the time of his

1165 This sentence parallels *Ibn Hajar, III, 102 (Khalifa); *Dh., V, 64 (Khalifa).

1166 From "Nafi' b. 'Alqama b. Safwan, governor ..." cf. *Dh., V, 64 (Khalifa).

1167 Kh.: "*until* the beginning of 87," which must be a scribal error.

1168 Z: Ibrahim b. 'Adi; (cf. Kh., 393: Ibrahim b. 'Arabi).

death, remained for two years,[1169] then returned to al-Walid in 95/713–714.

'Abdallah b. Musa was appointed by his father to take his place when he went to al-Walid, and served until al-Walid died.

Yemen:

Muhammad b. Yusuf, [governor under 'Abd al-Malik], was retained by al-Walid, and served until [al-Walid] died.

The Syrian Districts:

Damascus: 'Abd al-'Aziz b. al-Walid b. 'Abd al-Malik, until al-Walid died.

Jordan: 'Umar b. al-Walid, his son, until al-Walid died.

Palestine: Sulayman b. 'Abd al-Malik.

Homs. Al-'Abbas b. al-Walid, until al-Walid died.

The Pilgrimage:

86/705 – Hisham b. Isma'il.

87/706 – 'Umar b. 'Abd al-'Aziz.

88/707 – 'Umar b. al-Walid b. 'Abd al-Malik.

[418] 89/708 and 90/709 – 'Umar b. 'Abd al-'Aziz.

91/710 – al-Walid b. 'Abd al-Malik.

92/711 – 'Umar b. 'Abd al-'Aziz.

93/712 – 'Abd al-'Aziz b. al-Walid b. 'Abd al-Malik.

94/713 – Maslama b. 'Abd al-Malik.

95/714 – Bishr b. al-Walid b. 'Abd al-Malik.

{317} The Summer Raid:

Maslama b. 'Abd al-Malik.

'Abbas, [al-Walid's] son.

'Umar, [al-Walid's] son.

Chief of Police:

Riyah b. 'Abda, later dismissed.

Ka'b b. Hamid al-'Absi served until al-Walid died.[1170]

Secretary for Correspondence:

Janah, his *mawlā*.

1169 Perhaps the "two years" is in reference to Musa's stay in Spain, which was reported to have been for two years (cf. IAH, 210).

1170 From the heading "Chief of Police …" cf. (*) *'Iqd*, IV, 422.

Finance Secretary:[1171]

Sulayman b. Sa'd, a *mawlā* of 'Amir b. Lu'ayy, who died [in office].
Janah, his *mawlā*.

[Secretary of] the official seal:

'Amr b. al-Harith, a *mawlā* of 'Amir b. Lu'ayy, who died [in office].
[419] Janah, his *mawlā*.

Secretary of the Treasury:[1172]

'Abdallah b. 'Amr.

Captain of the Guard:

Khalid b. ar-Rayyan.

His Chamberlain:

Sa'id, his *mawlā*.
Muhammad b. Abi Sahl,[1173] according to some.

All of the preceding was reported to me by *al-Walid [b. Hisham] < his father < his grandfather; *'Abdallah b. al-Mughira < his father; and others.

[420] The Judges

Medina:

Al-Walid b. 'Abd al-Malik appointed 'Umar b. 'Abd al-'Aziz governor over Medina at the end of 86/November–December 705 or at the beginning of 87/December 705–January 706.
'Abd al-Rahman b. Yazid b. Jariya[1174] was appointed judge by 'Umar b. 'Abd al-'Aziz, and was later dismissed.
Abu Bakr b. Muhammad b. 'Amr b. Hazm[1175] was appointed judge, and later dismissed by al-Walid.
'Uthman b. Hayyan al-Murri[1176] was then appointed [as governor over Medina].

1171 Literally, "taxation and military [registers]."

1172 Literally, "treasuries and warehouses" (*buyūt al-amwāl wa-l-khazā'in*).

1173 U: Muhammad b. Abu Suhayl.

1174 *Ṭbq.*, 190; Ibn Sa'd, VI, 52; *Istī'āb*, 855; Ibn Hajar, VI, 298.

1175 D. 120/737–738 (*Ṭbq.*, 643; *Ma'ārif*, 466, 599; Ibn Hajar, XII, 38; cf. GAS, I, index).

1176 Dh., IV, 149; Ibn Hajar, VIII, 113.

Abu Bakr [b. Muhammad b. 'Amr] b. Hazm was then appointed [as governor] over Medina in 93/711–712.[1177]

Kufa:

'Amir ash-Sha'bi.

In 96, Sulayman b. 'Abd al-Malik put Kufa under the jurisdiction of Yazid b. al-Muhallab b. Abi Sufra, who appointed Salih b. 'Abd ar-Rahman as Secretary of Finance.

{318} In this year, Yazid b. al-Muhallab appointed al-Ash'ath b. 'Ubaydallah b. al-Jarud governor over Bahrain. Mas'ud b. Abi Zaynab al-Muharibi revolted against him, al-Ash'ath withdrew, and Mas'ud seized control Bahrain.[1178]

[421] In this year, Qutayba b. Muslim was killed in Khurasan.

*'Abdallah b. al-Mughira < *my father < 'Abdallah b. Abi Hadir al-Usaydi:

I came to Hudayn b. al-Mundhir[1179] when the people moved against Qutayba. He asked me, "What have the people done?" I said, "I think that they will certainly kill him if they are able to kill him." He bowed his head in silence for a long time. Then he said, "Ibn Abi Hadir, in this army, how many horses, mounts, mules, and asses do you think there are?" I said, "One hundred thousand." He said, "If they chose 10,000 from that, then chose 1,000 from the 10,000, and sent each one in a different direction trying to find [another] like Qutayba, they would not succeed."

In 96, the following died: Ibrahim an-Nakha'i,[1180] at the age of 53; Ibrahim b. 'Abd ar-Rahman b. 'Awf;[1181] Mahmud b. ar-Rabi' al-Khazraji.[1182]

Sulayman b. 'Abd al-Malik sent Maslama b. 'Abd al-Malik in command of the summer raid.[1183]

Abu Bakr b. Muhammad b. 'Amr b. Hazm led the pilgrimage.

1177 Entry on 'Uthman b. Hayyan al-Murri cf. Kh., 416 (315); cf. Tab., II, 1255; cf. Ibn Hajar, VII, 113, l. 15–17.

1178 From "In this year, Yazid b. al-Muhallab appointed al-Ash'ath ..." cf. IA, V, 118f.; cf. Yaqut, I, 570f.; cf. Kh., 430, 488. A somewhat fuller account of Mas'ud and his revolt is given by Ibn al-Athir, V, 118f., and includes several verses of poetry. Cf. Yaqut, I, 570f.

1179 EI2, III, 540.

1180 GAS, I, 403.

1181 *Ṭbq.*, 606; Ibn Sa'd, V, 55; Ibn Hajar, I, 139.

1182 *Ṭbq.*, 230, 596; *Jarḥ*, IV, I, 289; Ibn Hajar, X, 63.

1183 This sentence parallels *Dh., III, 329.

In this year, al-'Abbas b. al-Walid raided and conquered T-b-r-s[1184] and al-Marzubanayn.[1185] Bishr b. al-Walid conducted a raiding expedition, and returned after al-Walid died.[1186]

In this year Jidar,[1187] who was with him in the land of the Byzantines, was killed.[1188]

{319}[422] The Year 97/715–716

In this year, Yazid b. al-Muhallab raided Jurjan.

*Abu l-Hasan:
Yazid raided Jurjan during the caliphate of Sulayman b. 'Abd al-Malik. It was at that time not a [walled] city, but was walled in by mountains.[1189] Sul[1190] transferred to al-Buhayra, an island in the sea, and encamped there.[1191] Yazid entered Jurjan with 30,000 [troops], and obtained booty. Then he went out to al-Buhayra and besieged Sul, who would come out [with his army] during the daytime and battle them. They continued to do that for several months. [Yazid] departed in the month of *Ramaḍān*/April–May, 716.[1192]

*Al-Walid b. Hisham < his father < his grandfather:
Yazid made peace with them against payment of 500,000 *dirhams* annually.[1193]

1184 Unidentified. Cf. Tab., II, 1267: *T-w-l-s*. Perhaps Tarsus should be read (cf. E. Honigmann in EI, IV, 201b, s.v. Sebastiya, #3).

1185 This sentence parallels Tab., II, 1267. Z: *al-M-r-z-b-'-s*. Cf. E. Honigmann, in EI, IV, 201b, s.v. Sebastiya #3. Cf Nahr Marsban, which branches westward from the Euphrates, and appears on the map "Fines Orientales … 960" in Honigmann's *Ostgrenze*.

1186 This sentence parallels *Ibn 'Asakir, X, 132 (Khalifa).

1187 Dh., III, 329: Jidar al-'Udhri ash-Sha'mi.

1188 This sentence parallels *Dh., III, 329.

1189 Al-Mada'ini's statement (also in Tab., II, 1324) gives the impression that Jurjan had a natural defense perimeter formed by mountains, but no man-made wall. On the other hand, al-Baladhuri's account, also allegedly from al-Mada'ini, states that there was a wall of baked brick around the city (*Futūḥ*, 336). Cf. EI2, II, 1141, s.v. Gurgan.

1190 On the Turkish leader, Sul, see Minorsky, 311.

1191 On the basis of the parallel texts of at-Tabari and adh-Dhahabi, Khalifa's *taḥawwala ilā Ṣūl* has been translated ignoring the word *ilā*.

1192 From "Yazid raided Jurjan …" cf. *Futūḥ*, 335f. (partially from al-Mada'ini); Tab., II, 1323ff. (al-Mada'ini); *Dh., III, 329.

1193 This sentence parallels *Dh., III, 329.

*Hatim b. Muslim < Yunus b. Abi Ishaq,[1194] who was present there with Yazid b. al-Muhallab:
He made peace with them against payment of 500,000 *dirhams*, [ten] weighing five [*mithqāls*].[1195] They also sent him cloths, *ṭaylasāns*, and 1,000 head.[1196]

In this year, the following died: Talha b. 'Abdallah b. 'Awf[1197] [and] Sa'id b. Marjana.[1198]

[423] Maslama b. 'Abd al-Malik raided Barjama,[1199] and the fortress which al-Waddah had conquered – that is, Hisn Ibn 'Awf. Maslama also conquered Hisn al-Hadid and S-r-d-w-s-l[1200] in the outskirts of the land of the Byzantines.[1201]

{320} 'Umar b. Hubayra conducted a winter naval expedition.[1202]

Sulayman b. 'Abd al-Malik led the pilgrimage.

[424] The Year 98/716–717

In this year, Yazid b. al-Muhallab raided Tabaristan. The Isbahbadh sought to make peace with him, but he refused. So the Isbahbadh sought help from the inhabitants of the mountains and the Daylamites. They met at the slope of the mountain, and fought bitterly. Then God put the polytheists to rout, and they fled up the mountain. Yazid sent Hayyan an-Nabati, who made peace with the Isbahbadh against payment of 700,000 *dirhams*, 400 loads of saffron or its value in cash, and 400 men, each bearing a burnoose,[1203]

1194 D. 159/775–776 (Ṭbq., 393; Ibn Sa'd, VI, 363; Ibn Hajar, XI, 433).

1195 See note 285.

1196 From "He made peace ..." cf. *Dh., III, 329.

1197 On the death of Talha b. 'Abdallah b. 'Awf cf. #Ibn 'Asakir, *Tahdhīb*, VII, 69 and 71 (Khalifa).

1198 *Ṭbq.*, 620; Ibn Sa'd, V, 285; Ibn Hajar, IV, 78.

1199 Pergamus (cf. Wellhausen, "Die Kämpfe der Araber," 440, A.M. 6208; cf. Bury, II, 389 and 401).

1200 Perhaps Sardes is meant (cf. Wellhausen, "Die Kämpfe der Araber," 440, A.M. 6208). *S-r-d-w-s-l* might be another Arabic corruption of Sideropalos (cf. note 1130, and 1114).

1201 From "Maslama b. 'Abd al-Malik raided Barjama ..." cf. Tab., II, 1305; cf. Tab., II, 1306 (al-Waqidi); *Dh., III, 329 (Khalifa).

1202 This sentence parallels Tab., II, 1306.

1203 On the *burnus*, cf. Dozy, 73ff.

a *taylasān*, a silver drinking cup, silk cloth, and a suit of clothes. Yazid accepted that and departed.[1204]

Abu l-Hasan:
The inhabitants of Jurjan betrayed and killed the governor and the Muslims whom Yazid had left behind. When he had finished pacifying Tabaristan, he marched against them. They took up a fortified position with their leader, the Marzuban. Yazid battled them for several months. Then they surrendered, and put themselves at his mercy. He put their warriors to death, and took their women and children as captives. He gibbeted the warriors [one after the other] for a distance of two *parasangs*. He led {321} 12,000 of them to al-Andar,[1205] the river of Jurjan, and killed them. Then water was made to flow over [425] the blood in the river bed, over which mills [had been set up] to grind [grain] with their blood. He ground [the grain], baked bread, and ate it. He had vowed to do that.[1206]

In 98, Maslama conducted a winter campaign in the outlying districts of the land of the Byzantines. 'Umar b. Hubayra conducted a winter naval expedition. Maslama set out from his winter quarters [and proceeded] by sea and land until he reached Constantinople. He crossed the Straits and conquered the city of the Slavs.[1207] Maslama was attacked by mounted troops of the Bulgarians,[1208] but God put them to rout. Maslama laid waste to the area between the Straits and Constantinople.[1209]

In this year 'Abdallah b. Sharahil was killed.

'Abd al-' b. 'Abdallah b. Khalid b. Asid led the pilgrimage.

In 98, the following died: Kurayb,[1210] *mawlā* of Ibn 'Abbas; Abu 'Ubayd,[1211] *mawlā* of Ibn Azhar; 'Abd ar-Rahman b. Yazid b. Jariya;[1212]

1204 From "In this year, Yazid b. al-Muhallab raided Tabaristan ..." cf. *Futūḥ*, 336f.; Tab., II, 1327ff. (al-Mada'ini); *Dh., III, 330.

1205 Tab., II, 1327: Andar Haz, which Minorsky identifies with the Hirand, a river which flows through Jurjan (cf. Minorsky, 29, 218, 385, and index, s.v. Hirand).

1206 From "The inhabitants of Jurjan betrayed and killed the governor ..." cf. Tab., II, 1330ff. (al-Mada'ini); *Dh., III, 330.

1207 Medinat as-Saqaliba. On the Arab siege of Constantinople in this year, cf. Wellhausen, "Die Kämpfe der Araber," 440f.; Bury, II, 401–405; Hitti, 203.

1208 The Arabic is *Burjān*. Cf. references in note 1207.

1209 From "In 98, Maslama conducted a winter campaign ..." cf. Tab., II, 1317 (al-Waqidi); *Dh., III, 330 (Khalifa).

1210 *Ṭbq.*, 703, *Jarḥ*, III, II, 168; Ibn Hajar, VIII, 433.

1211 Sa'd b. 'Ubayd (*Ṭbq.*, 609; Ibn Sa'd, V, 86; Ibn Hajar, III, 477).

1212 On the death of 'Abd ar-Rahman b. Yazid b. Jariya cf. #Ibn Hajar, VI, 299 (Khalifa).

Qays b. Abi Hazim;[1213] 'Abd ar-Rahman b. Ka'b b. Malik,[1214] during the caliphate of Sulayman b. 'Abd al-Malik;[1215] 'Abdallah b. Muhammad b. al-Hanafiyya,[1216] during the caliphate of Sulayman.

[426] The Year 99/717–718

In this year, the Khazars attacked Armenia and Azerbaijan. 'Abd al-'Aziz b. Hatim {322} b. an-Nu'man al-Bahili was governor at the time. God caused most of the Khazars to be killed. 'Abd al-'Aziz wrote about that to 'Umar b. 'Abd al-'Aziz when ['Umar] began his reign.[1217] 'Umar sent 'Adi b. 'Adi [b. 'Umayra] to Armenia. 'Adi dug a canal which to this day is called 'Adi's Canal [*Nahr 'Adī*].

In this year, Sulayman b. 'Abd al-Malik died in Dabiq.[1218]

*Al-Walid b. Hisham < his father < his grandfather; *'Abdallah b. Mughira < his father:
Sulayman died in Dabiq on Friday 10 *Ṣafar* 99/22 September 717. He was 43 years old. 'Umar b. 'Abd al-'Aziz recited the prayers for him.

'Abd al-'Aziz [b. 'Imran]:
He died at the age of 33.

Hatim b. Muslim:
He was 45 years old.

His reign lasted two years and ten and a half or nine and a half months. Sulayman was born in the house of 'Abd al-Malik, in Medina, in the quarter of the Banu Hudayla. He died in Dabiq in the district of Qinnasrin.

[427] Then 'Umar b. 'Abd al-'Aziz b. Marwan received the pledge of allegiance. His mother was Umm 'Asim bint 'Asim b. 'Umar b. al-Khattab.

1213 On the death of Qays b. Abi Hazim cf. *Ṭbq.*, 344; Ibn Sa'd, VII, 67; Ibn Hajar, VI, 259; #Dh., IV, 47 (Khalifa); #Ibn Hajar, VIII, 388 (Khalifa).

1214 *Ṭbq.*, 630; Ibn Sa'd, V, 274; Ibn Hajar, VI, 259.

1215 Death of 'Abd ar-Rahman b. Ka'b b. Malik reported in #Ibn Hajar, VI, 259 (Khalifa).

1216 Abu Hashim (EI2, I, 124).

1217 From "In this year, the Khazars attacked Armenia and Azerbaijan…" cf. Tab., II, 1346; *Dh., III, 333.

1218 EI2, II, 72.

{323} *Al-Walid b. Hisham < his father < his grandfather; *'Abdallah b. Mughira < his father; *Abu l-Yaqzan; and others:
[The administration] of Iraq was consolidated under the governorship of Yazid b. al-Muhallab in 96/714–715.

Chief of Police:

Kufa: Ziyad b. Jarir b. 'Abdallah al-Bajali was retained [by Yazid].
Basra: 'Uthman b. al-Hakam b. Tha'laba al-Huna'i.
Wasit: Harb b. 'Abdallah.

Then [Yazid b. al-Muhallab] went to Khurasan and left al-Jarrah b. 'Abdallah al-Hakami as his lieutenant over Iraq. He appointed Muhammad b. 'Alqama b. 'Abd ar-Rahman al-Hakami as his chief of police in Wasit, and retained the incumbent chiefs of police in Basra and Kufa. Yazid's secretaries were Kawthar and al-Mughira b. Abi Qurra, a *mawlā* of the Banu Sadus.

Yazid was killed at the age of 49.

[428] A List of the Governors (and other Officials) of Sulayman b. 'Abd al-Malik

Mecca:

Khalid b. 'Abdallah al-Qasri was retained, and later dismissed.
Dawud b. Talha was appointed and later dismissed. 'Abd al-'Aziz b. 'Abdallah served until Sulayman died.

Medina:

'Uthman b. Hayyan al-Murri, governor under al-Walid at the time of his death, was dismissed by Sulayman.
Abu Bakr [b. Muhammad b. 'Amr] b. Hazm was appointed in *Ramaḍān* 96/May–June 715, and served until Sulayman died.

Yemen:

'Urwa b. Muhammad b. 'Atiyya as-Sa'di, of the Banu Sa'd b. Bakr b. Mu'awiya.

Basra:

Sufyan b. 'Umayr al-Kindi was appointed by Yazid b. al-Muhallab during the caliphate of Sulayman. He dismissed al-Jarrah in 100/718–719.
Yazid b. 'Abdallah b. Bilal al-Kilabi was appointed, then dismissed. [429]
Marwan b. al-Muhallab was appointed and served until Sulayman died.

{324} Kufa:

Harmala b. 'Umayr, the governor under al-Walid at the time of his death, was retained for several months by Yazid b. al-Muhallab, then dismissed.

Bishr b. Hassan al-Mahri was then appointed, and later dismissed.

Sufyan b. Harish al-Khawlani was appointed and served until Sulayman died.

Khurasan:

Qutayba b. Muslim, governor under al-Walid at the time of his death, did not pledge allegiance to Sulayman. He was killed.

Waki' b. Abi Sud al-Ghudani assumed control, but was dismissed by Yazid b. al-Muhallab.

Makhlad b. Yazid was appointed by his father, [Yazid b. al-Muhallab]. Then Yazid arrived. Then he departed, leaving his son, Makhlad, who served until Sulayman died.

Sijistan:

Mudrik [b. al-Muhallab] was appointed by his brother, Yazid, who later dismissed him.

Mu'awiya b. Yazid, his son, was then appointed, and served until Sulayman died.

Sind:

Sulayman b. 'Abd al-Malik wrote to Salih b. 'Abd ar-Rahman[1219] ordering him to apprehend the family of the Banu 'Aqil and to demand an accounting from them.[1220]

Habib b. al-Muhallab was appointed by Salih as military commander.

Yazid b. Abi Kabsha was appointed Finance Secretary. He [430] served less than a month, then died.[1221]

'Ubaydallah b. Abi Kabsha was designated by his brother to take his place, but Salih dismissed him.

1219 Cf. *Fihrist* (trans.), 581–583, 1091; Ibn 'Asakir, *Tahdhīb*, VI, 371; al-Jahshiyari, index.

1220 Muhammad b. al-Qasim and al-Hajjaj b. Yusuf were descendants of Abu 'Aqil (cf. Gabrieli, 282 n. 3). Enmity had developed between Sulayman b. 'Abd al-Malik and the family and protégés of al-Hajjaj, who included Muhammad b. al-Qasim. When caliphs desired to remove frontier commanders from their posts, they frequently demanded an accounting of the booty that had been gained, of which a fifth (the *khums*) was supposed to be sent to the caliph. On the recalling of Muhammad b. al-Qasim, cf. Gabrieli, 290.

1221 From the heading "Sind ..." cf. *Futūḥ*, 440f.

'Imran b. an-Nu'man al-Kala'i was then appointed. Then [Salih] consolidated the military command and the secretariat of finance under Habib b. al-Muhallab.

Bahrain:

Al-Ash'ath b. 'Abdallah b. al-Jarud was appointed by Yazid b. al-Muhallab. Mas'ud b. Abi Zaynab al-'Abdi, of the Banu Muharib, expelled him, and took control of Bahrain in 96/714–715.

Ifriqiya:

'Abdallah b. Musa b. Nusayr was retained, then dismissed in 97/715–716.

Muhammad b. Yazid, a *mawlā* of Rayhana bint Abu l-'As, was appointed in 97, according to some reports.

Oman:

'Abd ar-Rahman b. Qays al-Laythi was appointed by Salih b. 'Abd ar-Rahman.

{325} Ziyad b. al-Muhallab was then appointed by his brother, Yazid b. al-Muhallab.

al-Yamama:

Sufyan b. 'Amr al-'Uqayli was appointed by Sulayman.

Nuh b. Hubayra [was appointed later].

[431] Armenia:

'Abd al-'Aziz b. Hatim b. an-Nu'man was in command of the Armenian frontier until Sulayman died.

The Pilgrimage:

96/715 – Abu Bakr b. 'Amr b. Hazm.

97/716 – Sulayman b. 'Abd al-Malik.

98/717 – 'Abd al-'Aziz b. 'Abdallah b. Khalid b. Asid.

The Summer Raid:

Ayyub b. Sulayman b. 'Abd al-Malik.

Maslama b. 'Abd al-Malik.

Chief of Police:

Ka'b b. Hamid al-'Absi.

Secretary for Correspondence:

Layth b. Abi Ruqayya,[1222] a *mawlā* of Umm al-Hakam.

Finance Secretary:

Sulayman b. Sa'd.

Secretary of the Official Seal:

Nu'aym b. Abi Salama,[1223] a *mawlā* of the Yemenites.

[432] The treasuries, warehouses, slaves, and expenditures:

'Abdallah b. 'Amr b. al-Harith,[1224] a *mawlā* of the Banu 'Amir b. Lu'ayy.

Captain of the Guard:

Khalid b. ar-Rayyan, a *mawlā* of the Banu Muharib.

[Sulayman's] Chamberlain:

Abu 'Ubayd, his *mawlā*.

During the caliphate of Sulayman, the following were born: Sufyan b. Sa'id ath-Thawri;[1225] [and] Malik b. Anas.[1226]

'Abd ar-Rahman:
I asked those two about their ages, and they confirmed that.

In 99, al-Walid b. Hisham and 'Amr b. Qays al-Kindi, the father of 'Isa b. 'Amr, conducted a raiding expedition. Ibn al-Ja'd, one of the companions of 'Amr b. Qays, was killed with some people from Antioch. Al-Walid b. Hisham attacked some mounted troops in the outlying area of the Byzantine territory, {326} and took many captives.[1227]

In this year 'Umar b. 'Abd al-'Aziz had food and mounts brought to Maslama b. 'Abd al-Malik in the land of the Byzantines. He ordered that everyone who had relatives there be sent to them, and he [also] sent troops with them, thus relieving the people. Then he gave them permission to return.[1228]

1222 Position of Layth b. Abi Ruqayya cf. Jahshiyari, 48.
1223 Position of Nu'aym b. Abi Salama cf. Jahshiyari, 48.
1224 Position of 'Abdallah b. 'Amr b. al-Harith cf. Jahshiyari, 49.
1225 D. 162/778–779 (EI, IV, 500; GAS, I, 518).
1226 D. 179/795–796 (EI, III, 205; GAS, I, 457).
1227 From "In 99, al-Walid b. Hisham and 'Amr b. Qays al-Kindi ..." cf. Tab., II, 817 (al-Waqidi).
1228 From "In this year 'Umar b. 'Abd al-'Aziz had food ..." cf. Tab., II, 1346; *Dh., III, 333.

In this year, the Turks raided Azerbaijan.

*Abu Khalid < Abu Bara'; and others:
The Turks inflicted casualties on the people. 'Abd al-'Aziz b. Hatim b. an-Nu'man al-Bahili marched against them, and God killed [most of] [433] the Turks. Only a remnant escaped. ['Abd al-'Aziz b. Hatim] went to 'Umar while he was at Khunasira.[1229]

In this year, Yazid b. al-Muhallab left Khurasan. Hardly had he crossed the bridge,[1230] than he found himself dismissed [from his governorship]. 'Adi b. Artat arrived as governor over Basra, appointed by 'Umar b. 'Abd al-'Aziz.[1231] Yazid [b. al-Muhallab] went to greet him, but he put him in irons and sent him to 'Umar b. 'Abd al-'Aziz. 'Umar put him in prison,[1232] [where he remained] until ['Umar] died.[1233]

'Umar b. 'Abd al-'Aziz sent al-Jarrah b. 'Abdallah al-Hakami as governor over Khurasan. 'Umar wrote to him: "Do not undertake any raids. Hold on to what you already have in your possession."

Abu Bakr b. Muhammad b. 'Amr b. Hazm led the pilgrimage.

In 99, the following died: 'Ubaydallah b. 'Abdallah b. 'Utba;[1234] 'Abdallah b. Muhammad b. al-Hanafiyya, at the end of Sulayman's reign. Before 100/718–719, 'Abd ar-Rahman b. al-Aswad b. Yazid an-Nakha'i[1235] died.[1236] Abu Sasan Hudayn b. al-Mundhir died at the beginning of the caliphate of Sulayman b. 'Abd al-Malik.[1237] {327} During Sulayman's reign, Salim b. Abi l-Ja'd[1238] died.

This sentence parallels (*) Dh., III, 333 (Khalifa). This report probably refers to the Arabs who were besieging Constantinople (cf. Wellhausen, "Die Kämpfe der Araber," 441f).

1229 From "In this year, the Turks raided Azerbaijan ..." cf. Tab., II, 1346. Khunasira is a town in northern Syria (BGA, I, 13, 61, 67; II, 17, 119, 126; III, 54, 154; Minorsky, 81, 149; cf. Wellhausen, *Arab Kingdom*, 311.)

1230 "The Bridge," according to the account of Abu Mikhnaf (Tab., II, 1350), was the Bridge of Basra, at the Ma'qil canal (*Nahr Ma'qil*: BGA, I, 81; II, 160; III, 117; V, 191; VI, 59, 194; VII, 185).

1231 This sentence parallels *Ibn Hajar, VIII, 164 (Khalifa).

1232 From "'Adi b. Artat arrived as governor ..." cf. *Dh., IV, 150 (Khalifa).

1233 From "In this year, Yazid b. al-Muhallab left Khurasan ..." cf. Tab., II, 1349ff (Abu Mikhnaf); *Dh., III, 333.

1234 *Ṭbq.*, 609; *Jarḥ*, II, II, 319; Ibn Hajar, VII, 23.

1235 *Ṭbq.*, 362; Ibn Sa'd, VI, 289; Ibn Hajar, VI, 140.

1236 This sentence parallels *Ibn Hajar, VI, 140 (Khalifa).

1237 This sentence parallels #Ibn Hajar, II, 395 (Khalifa).

1238 *Ṭbq.*, 359; Ibn Sa'd, VI, 291; Ibn Hajar, III, 432.

[434] The Year 100/718–719

Abu Bakr b. Muhammad b. 'Amr b. Hazm led the pilgrimage.[1239]

In this year, the following died: Kharija b. Zayd b. Thabit;[1240] Abu Umama b. Sahl b. Hunayf;[1241] Abu Bakr b. Muhammad b. 'Amr b. Hazm;[1242] Busr b. Sa'id,[1243] a *mawlā* of the Hadramis; Abu 'Uthman an-Nahdi,[1244] in Basra; Muslim b. Yasar,[1245] in Basra; Tamim b. Salama,[1246] in Kufa; Shahr b. Hawshab,[1247] in Syria.

In this year, Hammad b. Zayd[1248] was born.

{328}[461] The Year 101/719–720

In this year, 'Umar b. 'Abd al-'Aziz died.

*Al-Walid b. Hisham < his father < his grandfather; *'Abdallah b. Mughira < his father:
'Umar b. 'Abd al-'Aziz died on Friday 25 *Rajab*/10 February 720, at Dayr Sam'an,[1249] near Homs. Yazid b. 'Abd al-Malik b. Marwan recited the prayers for him. He was 39 and a half years old.

*'Uthman b. 'Uthman < *'Ali b. Zayd b. Jud'an:[1250]
I heard 'Umar b. 'Abd al-'Aziz say, "God's proof is completed against him who is 40 years old," and he died at [that age].[1251]

1239 This sentence parallels *Ibn Hajar, XII, 39 (Khalifa).

1240 *Ṭbq.*, 627; Ibn Sa'd, V, 262; Ibn 'Asakir, *Tahdhīb*, V, 24; Ibn Hajar, III, 74; cf. GAS, I, 396.

1241 On the death of Abu Umama b. Sahl b. Hunayf cf. #Ibn Hajar, I, 264 (Khalifa). *Ṭbq.*, 625; Ibn Sa'd, V, 82; Ibn Hajar, I, 263.

1242 On the death of Abu Bakr b. Muhammad b. 'Amr b. Hazm cf. *Ibn Hajar, XII, 39 (Khalifa).

1243 *Ṭbq.*, 622, 636; Ibn Sa'd, V, 281; Ibn Hajar, I, 437; cf. GAS, I, index.

1244 *Ṭbq.*, 489; Ibn Sa'd, VII, 97; Ibn al-Athir, *al-Lubāb*, III, 247f; Ibn Hajar, VI, 277.

1245 On the death of Muslim b. Yasar cf. #Dh., IV, 55 (Khalifa).

1246 *Ṭbq.*, 365; Ibn Sa'd, VI, 287; Ibn Hajar, I, 512.

1247 On the death of Shahr b. Hawshab cf. #Dh., IV, 14 (Khalifa). *Ṭbq.*, 798; Ibn Sa'd, VII, 449; Ibn 'Asakir, *Tadhīb*, VI, 343; Ibn Hajar, IV, 369.

1248 See note 848.

1249 There are a number of places bearing this name (EI2, II, 198).

1250 D. 131/748–749 (*Ṭbq.*, 517; Ibn Sa'd, VII, 252; Ibn Hajar, VII, 322).

1251 This sentence parallels **'Iqd*, IV, 432. 'Umar predicted that he would die at the age of 40, and did so (cf. the anecdote in Yaqut, II, 671, l. 10).

Al-Asma'i < Ibn Abi z-Zinad[1252] < 'Abd al-'Aziz b. 'Umar b. 'Abd al-'Aziz: My father died before reaching 40 years of age.

'Umar was born in Egypt in 61/680–681. He died at Dayr Sam'an in 101/719–720.

'Abd al-'Aziz:
He was born in 59/678–679.[1253]

[462] Abu l-Yaqzan:
'Umar was born in Egypt in 61/680–681, and died at Dayr Sam'an, near Homs. Yazid b. 'Abd al-Malik recited the prayers for him.

Yazid b. 'Abd al-Malik b. Marwan received the pledge of allegiance. His mother was 'Atika bint Yazid b. Mu'awiya.

In 101, Yazid b. al-Muhallab entered Basra on the night of the full moon in *Ramaḍān*/31 March 720. 'Adi b. Artat, the governor of Basra, engaged him in battle.

{329}[463] A List of the Governors of 'Umar b. 'Abd al-'Aziz

Basra:

'Adi b. Artat al-Fazari [served] until 'Umar died.

Kufa:

'Abd al-Hamid b. 'Abd ar-Rahman b. Zayd b. al-Khattab [served] until 'Umar died.

Khurasan:

Al-Jarrah b. 'Abdallah al-Hakami.

Then he wrote to him, and he left 'Abd ar-Rahman b. Nu'aym al-Ghamidi to take his place.

Sijistan:

Al-Jarrah b. 'Abdallah.

Then [Sijistan] was added to the jurisdiction of 'Abd ar-Rahman b. Nu'aym in the year 100/718–719.

When he revolted, Yazid b. al-Muhallab sent his brother, Mudrik.

1252 'Abd ar-Rahman, d. 174/790–791 (Ṭbq., 689, 851; Ibn Sa'd, V, 415; ibid., VII, 324; Ibn Hajar, VI, 170).

1253 Note that in the previous report from al-Asma'i, 'Abd al-'Aziz is quoted as saying that his father died before the age of 40. If he was born in 59/680–681, and died in 101/719–720, he would have been at least 41.

But 'Abd ar-Rahman [b. Nu'aym] prevented him from entering [Sijistan] until Yazid was killed.

Sind:

'Abd al-Malik b. Misma' b. Malik b. Misma' was appointed by 'Adi b. Artat, and late dismissed.

[464] 'Amr b. Muslim al-Bahili served until 'Umar died.

Bahrain:

Salt b. Hurayth sent Kharijites to 'Adi from [Bahrain].[1254] Then 'Adi dismissed him.

'Abd al-Karim b. al-Mughira, who I think, was a Bahili, was then appointed.

Oman:

Sa'id b. Mas'ud was appointed by 'Adi.

'Amr b. 'Abdallah b. Abi Talha al-Ansari was appointed by 'Umar b. 'Abd al-'Aziz.

al-Yamama:

Zurara b. 'Abd ar-Rahman.

Mecca:

'Abd al-'Aziz b. 'Abdallah b. Khalid b. Asid was retained, and served until he died.

Medina:

Abu Bakr b. Muhammad b. 'Amr b. Hazm was retained by 'Umar, and served until he died.

'Uthman b. 'Uthman:

Muhammad b. Qays was governor over Medina for 'Umar b. 'Abd al-'Aziz.

Yemen:

'Urwa b. Muhammad was retained by 'Umar, and served until he died.

al-Jazira, Armenia, and Azerbaijan.

'Abd al-'Aziz b. Hatim b. an-Nu'man was appointed over [465] Armenia.

{330} Then 'Adi b. 'Adi was appointed.

1254 The meaning is not clear.

Sawada, the father of as-Sabbah b. Sawada al-Kindi, was appointed over al-Jazira.

The Syrian Districts:

Damascus: 'Ubayd b. al-Hashas al-'Udhri.
Jordan: 'Ubada b. Nusayy, a Kindi.
Palestine: An-Nadr b. Yarim b. Abraha b. as-Sabbah.
Homs: Yazid b. Husayn as-Sakuni.
Qinnasrin: Al-Walid b. Hisham b. al-Walid b. 'Uqba.
al-Balqa': Al-Harith b. 'Amr, a Ta'i.

Egypt:

Ayyub. B. Shurahbil b. Abraha b. as-Sabbah.

[466] Ifriqiya:

Muhammad b. Yazid was dismissed.
'Abdallah b. Muhajir al-Ansari, one of their *mawālī*, was appointed.
Isma'il b. 'Ubaydallah,[1255] a *mawlā* of the Banu Makhzum, was then appointed. He arrived in 100/718–719. Many of the Berbers became Muslims during his governorship. His conduct was good.[1256] He served until 'Umar died.[1257]

[467] The Judges

Basra:

*[Abu l-Yaqzan] 'Amir b. Hafs:

'Umar b. 'Abd al-'Aziz wrote to 'Adi b. Artat [the following]: "Gather the people around you, and ask their opinion about Iyas b. Mu'awiya[1258] and al-Qasim b. Rabi'a al-Jawshani.[1259] Then appoint {331} one of those two as judge." So 'Adi gathered the people. Al-Qasim swore that "Iyas is more knowledgeable, and better qualified for the judgeship than I am." So 'Adi appointed [Iyas].[1260]

1255 *Ṭbq.*, 806; Ibn 'Asakir, III, 25; Dh., V, 226; Ibn Hajar, I, 317; *Riyād an-Nufūs*, 75.
1256 From "Many of the Berbers …" cf. *Dh., V, 226 (Khalifa); from the beginning of the entry on Isma'il b. 'Ubaydallah cf. *Ibn 'Asakir, *Tahdhīb*, III, 27, l. 12; *Ibn Hajar, I, 318 (Khalifa).
1257 This whole entry on Isma'il b. 'Ubaydallah cf. IAH, 213, l. 16; *Futūḥ*, 231, l. 7.
1258 D. 120/737–738 (EI2, IV, 291).
1259 *Ṭbq.*, 496; Ibn Sa'd, VII, 152; Ibn Hajar, VIII, 312.
1260 From "'Umar b. 'Abd al-'Aziz wrote to 'Adi b. Artat …" cf. *'Iqd*, I, 19; Ibn 'Asakir, *Tahdhīb*, III, 180, l. 5; *Ibn Hajar, VIII, 313 (Khalifa).

*Sahl b. Yusuf[1261] < Khalid b. al-Hadhdha':[1262]

Iyas b. Mu'awiya said to me, "This man was sent to me and I went with him." [Iyas] went in to 'Adi, then came out with a bodyguard. [Iyas] said, "He refused to excuse me." He went to the mosque and [468] prayed, performing two *rak'as*.[1263] Then he said to the bodyguard, "Present [the cases]." He did not get up until he had made 70 judgments. Then Iyas left Basra because of something that had happened, and 'Adi appointed al-Hasan b. Abi l-Hasan.[1264]

Kufa:

Al-Qasim b. 'Abd ar-Rahman b. 'Abdallah b. Mas'ud.[1265]

Medina:

Abu Tuwala, whose name was 'Abdallah b. 'Abd ar-Rahman b. Hazm[1266] served until 'Umar died.

The Pilgrimage:

99/718 and 100/719 – Abu Bakr [b. Muhammad] b. 'Amr b. Hazm.

The Summer Raid:

['Umar] divided command between al-Walid b. Hisham and 'Amr b. Qays as-Sakuni.

Chief of Police:

Yazid b. Bishr b. Yazid b. Bishr al-Kalbi.

['Umar's] Secretary:

Layth b. Abi Ruqayya, a *mawlā* of Umm al-Hakam bint Abi Sufyan.[1267]

Finance Administrator:

Salih b. Jubayr al-Ghudani.

[Secretary of] the Official Seal:

Nu'aym b. Salama.

1261 D. c. 190/805–806 (Ibn Hajar, IV, 259).

1262 D. 142/759–760 or 143 (*Ṭbq.*, 525; Ibn Sa'd, VII, 259; *Ma'ārif*, 501; Ibn Hajar, III, 120).

1263 A *rak'a* consists of a bending and prostration in the Muslim prayer ritual.

1264 From "Iyas b. Mu'awiya said to me …" cf. *Ibn 'Asakir, *Tahdhīb*, III, 180, l. 16; *Dh., V, 45f.

1265 *Ṭbq.*, 368; Ibn Sa'd, VI, 303; Dh., IV, 293; Ibn Hajar, VIII, 321.

1266 *Ṭbq.*, 661; *Jarḥ*, II, II, 64; Ibn Hajar, V, 297.

1267 On this entry for 'Umar's secretary cf. Jahshiyari, 53.

[469] Captain of the Guard:
Ibn 'Ayyash al-Alhani, who was later dismissed.
'Umar b. al-Muhajir, a *mawlā* of the Ansar, was then appointed.

{332} His Chamberlain:
Hubaysh, his *mawlā*.[1268]

During the caliphate of 'Umar b. 'Abd al-'Aziz, the following died: Muhammad b. Jubayr b. Mut'im;[1269] al-Qasim b. Mukhaymira,[1270] a Hamdani;[1271] 'Isa b. Talha b. 'Ubaydallah;[1272] 'Alqama b. 'Abdallah al-Muzani;[1273] Abu d-Duha Muslim b. Subayh;[1274] 'Abdallah b. Murra,[1275] a Hamdani from Kufa; al-Hasan b. Muhammad b. al-Hanafiyya;[1276] Yusuf b. 'Abdallah b. Sallam;[1277] Abu t-Tufayl 'Amir b. Wathila,[1278] who had contact with 'Umar.

In 101, the following died: Muqsim,[1279] a *mawlā* of 'Abdallah b. al-Harith; Abu Salih Dhakwan;[1280] [470] Muhammad b. Marwan b. al-Hakam; [and] 'Abdallah b. Rafi' b. Khadij.[1281]

In this year, Yazid b. 'Abd al-Malik consolidated [the administration] of Iraq under the governorship of Maslama b. 'Abd al-Malik, and ordered him to battle Yazid b. al-Muhallab.

'Abd ar-Rahman b. ad-Dahhak b. Qays al-Fihri led the pilgrimage.

1268 From the heading "Chief of Police …" cf. (*) *'Iqd*, IV, 432.

1269 On the death of Muhammad b. Jubayr b. Mut'im cf. #Ibn Hajar, IX, 91f. (Khalifa). *Ṭbq*., 602; Ibn Sa'd, V, 205; Ibn Hajar, IX, 91; cf. GAS, I, 258.

1270 *Ṭbq*., 363, 797; Ibn Sa'd, IV, 303; Ibn Hajar, VIII, 337.

1271 On the death of al-Qasim b. Mukhaymira cf. #Ibn Hajar, VIII, 337 (Khalifa).

1272 On the death of 'Isa b. Talha b. 'Ubaydallah cf. #Ibn Hajar, VIII, 215 (Khalifa). *Ṭbq*., 335, 610; Ibn Sa'd, V, 164; *Jarḥ*, III, 1, 279; Ibn Hajar, VIII, 215.

1273 *Ṭbq*., 454, 493; Ibn Sa'd, VII, 209; Ibn Hajar, VII, 275.

1274 *Ṭbq*., 363; Ibn Sa'd, VI, 288; Ibn Hajar, X, 132.

1275 *Ṭbq*., 363; Ibn Sa'd, VI, 290; Ibn Hajar, VI, 24.

1276 On the death of al-Hasan b. Muhammad b. al-Hanafiyya cf. #Ibn Hajar, II, 320f (Khalifa). *Ṭbq*., 598; Ibn Hajar, II, 320.

1277 On the death of Yusuf b. 'Abdallah b. Sallam cf. *Ibn Hajar, XI, 416 (Khalifa). *Ṭbq*., 18, 315; *Istī'āb*, 1590; Ibn Hajar, XI, 416.

1278 On the death of Abu t-Tufayl 'Amir b. Wathila cf. #Dh., IV, 79 (Khalifa); #Ibn Hajar V, 82 (Khalifa).

1279 *Ṭbq*., 703; Ibn Sa'd, V, 471; Ibn Hajar, X, 288.

1280 *Ṭbq*., 620; Ibn Sa'd, V, 301; Ibn Hajar, III, 219; cf. GAS, I, index.

1281 *Ṭbq*., 626; Ibn Sa'd, V, 256.

[471] The Year 102/720–721

In this year, Yazid b. al-Muhallab was killed on Friday 12 *Ṣafar* 102/22 August 720.[1282] Also in *Ṣafar* 102, Mu'awiya b. Yazid killed 'Adi b. Artat and al-Qasim b. Muslim, a *mawlā* of the Banu Ghubar, and the father of Rawh b. al-Qasim and Hisham b. al-Qasim.

*Shihab < *'Abdallah b. al-Mughira < his father:
I was present {333} at the governor's residence in Wasit on the day the news of the killing of Yazid b. al-Muhallab arrived. Mu'awiya b. Yazid was sitting, and the following were brought to him: 'Adi b. Artat, his son Muhammad b. 'Adi, Malik b. Misma', 'Abd al-Malik b. Misma', al-Qasim b. Muslim, and 'Abdallah b. 'Umar an-Nasri. He cut off their heads.[1283]

In this year, Yazid b. Abi Muslim, while in Ifriqiya, sent Muhammad b. Aws al-Ansari with the people on a naval raiding expedition to Sicily, in the Maghrib. He acquired booty, and returned safely.[1284]

In this year, the army revolted against Yazid b. Abi Muslim and killed him.

*Abu l-Yaqzan < al-Waddah b. Khaythama < *Dawud b. Abi Hind[1285] < Muhammad b. Yazid al-Ansari:
When 'Umar b. 'Abd al-'Aziz came to power, [472] he sent me to release everyone who had been imprisoned by Sulayman, and I did so, except for Yazid b. Abi Muslim. He vowed to take my life in revenge. When 'Umar died, Yazid b. 'Abd al-Malik made [Yazid b. Abi Muslim] governor over Ifriqiya, while I was there. I was seized and brought to him in *Ramaḍān*, at night. He said, "Muhammad b. Yazid?" I said, "Yes." He said, "Praise God, who has enabled [me] to get my hands on you without agreement and obligation! For a long time I have begged God to allow me to get my hands on you." I said, "And how often I have begged God to save me from you!" He said, "May God not protect you from me. If the Angel of Death vied with me to reach you first, I would win!" The evening prayer was begun,

1282 This sentence parallels *Ibn Khallikan, VI, 306 (Khalifa).
1283 From "the news of the killing of Yazid b. al-Muhallab …" cf. Tab., II, 1409.
1284 From "In this year, Yazid b. Abi Muslim, while in Ifriqiya …" cf. Ibn 'Idhari, in Amari, 354 (trans., II, 3).
1285 D. end of 139/757 or beginning of 140 (*Ṭbq*., 525; Ibn Sa'd, VII, 255; Ibn Hajar, III, 204; cf. GAS, I, 595).

and after he had prayed just one *rak'a*, the soldiers revolted against him and killed him. They said [to me], "Go wherever you wish."[1286]

Abu Khalid:
Muhammad b. Yazid returned from his raiding expedition after Yazid b. Abi Muslim had been killed, and wrote to Yazid b. 'Abd al-Malik informing him of that. Yazid [b. 'Abd al-Malik] wrote to Bishr b. Safwan al-Kalbi, his governor in Egypt, appointing him [governor over Ifriqiya]. Bishr arrived in Ifriqiya in *Shawwāl* 102/April–May 721.[1287]

{334} In this year, Maslama b. 'Abd al-Malik sent Hilal b. Ahwaz al-Mazini to Qandabil in pursuit of the Muhallabids. During their encounter, al-Mufaddal b. al-Muhallab was killed, and the people were put to rout. Hilal slew some of the Muhallabids. He did not inspect or show any interest in the women. He sent the women and children and the prisoners to Yazid b. 'Abd al-Malik.[1288]

*Hatim b. Muslim:
When they entered upon Yazid b. 'Abd al-Malik, Kuthayyir b. Abi Jam'a[1289] – who is called Kuthayyir 'Azza – stood up and recited [the following]:

1. [473] A man of forbearance, whenever he gets [the opportunity] he either summarily punishes
   Most severely, or he forgives, without a harsh reprimand.

2. Forgiveness, Commander of the Faithful! [Divine] reckoning!
   Whatever good you will do in the hope of divine reward will be credited to you.

3. They did evil. If you forgive – for you are able [to forgive];
   And the greatest forbearance that can be imagined
   Is the forbearance of an angry man –

4. The Quraysh will drive them from the valleys of Mecca,
   As will Yemenites, with the striped *mashrafī* sword.[1290]

1286 From "When 'Umar b. 'Abd al-'Aziz came to power …" cf. IAH, 214; cf. Tab., II, 1435; *'Iqd*, IV, 427; Jahshiyari, 56f.
1287 From "Muhammad b. Yazid returned …" cf. *Ibn 'Asakir, X, 92 (Khalifa).
1288 From "In this year, Maslama b. 'Abd al-Malik sent Hilal …" cf. *Futūḥ*, 442; cf. Tab., II, 1412ff.; **'Iqd*, IV, 442f.; *Dh., IV, 86 (Khalifa).
1289 EI, II, 1169; GAS, II, 408.
1290 Meter: *ṭawīl*.

Yazid said, "You are swayed by family considerations.[1291] There is no possibility of that. Whoever has a blood claim against the Muhallabids, let him step forth."[1292] He handed them over to them until about 200[1293] had been killed.[1294]

{335} In 102, Maslama b. 'Abd al-Malik sent Sa'id b. 'Abd al-'Aziz to Khurasan. He conducted raids but did not conquer anything. The Soghdians battled him, and some of the Banu Tamim were killed, among whom were the following: al-Mughira b. Habra'; Shu'ba b. Zuhayr an-Nahshali; 'Abdallah b. Zuhayr al-'Adawi. Some say that this was in 103/721–722.

In this year, al-'Abbas b. al-Walid b. 'Abd al-Malik conducted a raiding expedition in which he conquered D-b-s-h,[1295] in the land of the Byzantines.[1296]

'Abd ar-Rahman b. ad-Dahhak b. Qays al-Fihri led the pilgrimage.

At the end of 102/June 721 or the beginning of 103/July 721, Maslama b. 'Abd al-Malik was dismissed from the governorship of Iraq.

*Al-Walid b. Hisham < his father < his grandfather; *'Abdallah b. Mughira < his father; *Abu l-Yaqzan; and others:
[474] Yazid b. 'Abd al-Malik consolidated [the administration of] Iraq under the governorship of his brother, Maslama, at the end of 101/June–July 720 or at the beginning of 102/July–August 720. He dismissed him at the end of the year/June 721, or at the beginning of 103/July 721.

Maslama's Chiefs of Police

Kufa:

Qatan b. Habba al-Kalbi.
Al-'Uryan b. al-Haytham b. al-Aswad an-Nakha'i.

Basra:

'Abd ar-Rahman b. Sulaym al-Kalbi.

1291 The Muhallabids had acted as patrons to Kuthayyir 'Azza (EI, II, 1169).
1292 *Dh., IV, 86.
1293 *'Iqd*, IV, 443; 80.
1294 From "When they entered upon Yazid b. 'Abd al-Malik ..." cf. *Dīwān*, II, 147 (verses 1, 2, and 3); **'Iqd*, IV, 443; (*) Azdi, 15 (verses 1, 2, and 3); (*) IA, V, 87 (verses 1, 2, and 3).
1295 Cf. Tab., II, 1437; *R-s-l-h*, which Wellhausen was unable to identify ("Die Kämpfe der Araber," 443). *D-b-s-h* appears in Tab., III, 709. Ramsay identifies Dabesa with Thebasa (Ramsay, 340, and note on 354; cf. Ramsay, 339, and Honigmann, 47).
1296 This sentence parallels Tab., II, 1437.

[475] The Year 103/721–722

In this year, Yazid b. ‘Abd al-Malik consolidated [the administration of] Iraq under the governorship of ‘Umar b. Hubayra al-Fazari. He dismissed [Sa‘id b.] ‘Abd al-‘Aziz b. al-Harith b. al-Hakam b. Abi l-‘As, and appointed Sa‘id b. ‘Amr al-Harashi[1297] [as governor over Khurasan]. The Soghdians revolted, and went with their families and property. Sa‘id b. ‘Amr al-Harashi marched against them. They asked him to make peace on the condition that they return to their homes, and pay the poll tax. {336} Some of them went out, while others remained.[1298] Then they went out against the people, smiting them right and left. Sa‘id killed them to the last man, and took the women and children as captives.[1299]

In this year, Ma‘laq b. Saffar al-Bahrani raided Armenia.

Abu Khalid < Abu Bara’:
The Khazars confronted Ma‘laq b. Saffar at Marj al-Hijara. There were many casualties among the Muslims. That was in *Ramaḍān* 103/February–March 722, during a bitter winter, and the Khazars overpowered the army.[1300]

Muhammad b. Safwan led the major summer raid. ‘Uthman b. Hayyan led the smaller summer raid.[1301] Al-‘Abbas b. al-Walid conducted a raiding expedition in the land of the Byzantines.[1302]

‘Abd ar-Rahman b. ad-Dahhak b. Qays al-Fihri led the pilgrimage.

In *al-Muḥarram*/July 721, Bishr b. Safwan sent Yazid b. Masruq al-Yahsubi on a raiding expedition against Sardinia, in the Maghrib. He took booty, and returned safely.[1303]

[476] In 103, the following died: Yahya b. Waththab,[1304] a *mawlā* of the Banu Asad, a Kufan; Mus‘ab b. Sa‘d b. Malik;[1305] ‘Ata’ b. Yasar,[1306] a

1297 Ibn ‘Asakir, *Tahdhīb*, VI, 162.

1298 Z: *baqiya*; U: illegible word in the manuscript.

1299 From “In this year, Yazid b. ‘Abd al-Malik consolidated [the administration of] Iraq …” cf. Tab. II, 1436, 1438, 1439ff (al-Mada’ini). From “The Soghdians revolted…” cf. *Ibn ‘Asakir, *Tahdhīb*, VI, 163, l. 4 (Khalifa).

1300 From “The Khazars confronted Ma‘laq …” cf. IA, V, 110f.

1301 This sentence parallels al-Ya‘qubi, II, 378; (*) Ibn Hajar, VII, 113 (Khalifa).

1302 This sentence parallels al-Ya‘qubi, II, 378.

1303 From “In *al-Muḥarram*/July 721 …” cf. *Ibn ‘Asakir, X, 92 (Khalifa).

1304 *Ṭbq*., 357, Ibn Sa‘d, VI, 299; Ibn Hajar, XI, 294.

1305 *Ṭbq*., 608; Ibn Sa‘d, V, 169; Ibn Hajar, X, 160.

1306 *Ṭbq*., 618; Ibn Sa‘d, V, 173; Ibn Hajar, VII, 217.

mawlā of Maymuna; 'Abd al-'Aziz b. Hatim b. an-Nu'man al-Bahili, in Armenia.

In this year, Yazid b. Zuray'[1307] was born.

{337}[477] The Year 104/722–723

In this year, Yazid b. 'Abd al-Malik dismissed Ma'laq b. Saffar from his post in Armenia, and appointed al-Jarrah b. 'Abdallah al-Hakami. Al-Jarrah raided and conquered Balanjar[1308] on Monday 3 *Rabī'* I 104/21 August 722. Then al-Jarrah confronted the son of the Khaqan two *parasang*s from al-Bab, at the river of Arran.[1309] They fought bitterly, and the son of the Khaqan [and his army] were put to rout. The Muslims pursued them, killing many, and taking [many] captives.[1310]

*Abu Khalid < Abu l-Bara':
[Certain] inhabitants asked al-Jarrah to make peace on condition that he transfer them and settle them at Rustaq Hayzan.[1311] So he transferred them. Then he marched [478] to Rustaq Targhu,[1312] and remained there for several days. [The inhabitants] asked him to make peace on condition that he transfer them to Rustaq F-y-l-h.[1313]

Abu Bara' < *Sawada, who was an honest *shaykh*:
We were with al-Jarrah at Balanjar. One of the Muslims stepped forth and said, "Who will sell himself for God?"[1314] A group whose number did not amount to 30 men answered him. They broke the scabbards of their swords, and attacked the carts at the walls [of the city].[1315] They kept the men away. They seized one of the carts. The carts had been connected to each other, so when the one [they had seized] rolled down [away from the

1307 *Ṭbq.*, 541; Ibn Sa'd, VII, 289; *Ma'ārif*, 508; Ibn Hajar, XI, 325; cf. GAS, I, index.
1308 EI2, I, 985.
1309 The "river of Arran" is probably the Kura (Kur).
1310 From "In this year, Yazid b. 'Abd al-Malik dismissed Ma'laq ..." cf. *Futūḥ*, 206; cf. Tab., II, 1453; IA, V, 111f; (*) Dh., IV, 87.
1311 Cf. the variants discussed by Minorsky, 448f. Cf. the first part of note 1140.
1312 Z: *B-z-gh-w-'*; U: *Y-z-'-w-'*; IA, V, 112: *U-r-gh-w-'*. On Targhu (Tarqu, Tarkhu), see Minorsky, 452; Dunlop, 64.
1313 From "[Certain] inhabitants asked al-Jarrah to make peace..." cf. *Futūḥ*, 206; IA, V, 112. Cf. Kh., 524; Filan. Cf. Minorsky, 454 n. 1; C. Bosworth, in EI2, IV, 343a, s.v. Kabk.
1314 Cf. note 726.
1315 Cf. Dunlop, 64f.

fortress], the rest of the carts followed it, until they were all in the camp of the Muslims. There were about 300 carts. Then [the Muslims] attacked the inhabitants of Balanjar. The people went out through the gate. The lord of Balanjar escaped on the back of his horse, and al-Jarrah captured Balanjar. Then al-Jarrah marched against the Turks, who were 40[1316] families. They asked him to make peace on condition that {338} they join him against the Khazars. He accepted that from them, then marched to Warthan.[1317]

In this year, 'Uthman b. Hayyan al-Murri and 'Abd ar-Rahman b. Sulayman al-Kalbi conducted a raiding expedition. They attacked and conquered S-y-b-r-h.[1318] They also conquered Qaysara, a Byzantine fortress.[1319] [479] Bishr b. Safwan, the governor over Ifriqiya, sent 'Amr b. Fatik al-Kalbi on a naval raiding expedition. He acquired booty and returned safely. That was in 104.[1320]

'Abd al-Wahid b. 'Abdallah an-Nasri,[1321] of the [Banu] Nasr b. Mu'awiya, led the pilgrimage.

In 104, the following died: Sulayman b. Yasar,[1322] a *mawlā* of Maymuna; Yahya b. 'Abd ar-Rahman b. Hatib b. Abi Balta'a;[1323] Mujahid b. Jabr;[1324] Abu Ma'bad,[1325] a *mawlā* of Ibn 'Abbas; Abu Qilaba al-Jarmi;[1326] 'Amir b. Sa'd b. Malik,[1327] Yazid b. al-Asamm.[1328]

*Hatim b. Muslim < 'Uthman b. Muwahhib:[1329]
The following died: ['Amir] ash-Sha'bi; Musa b. Talha b. 'Ubaydallah;[1330]

1316 IA, V, 112: 40,000.

1317 From "We were with al-Jarrah at Balanjar ..." cf. IA, V, 112f. See also Cf. Minorsky, index, s.v. Vartan; cf. Dunlop, index, s.v. Warathan.

1318 Cf. Ramsay, index, s.v. Sibora, and Honigmann, 51.

1319 From "In this year, 'Uthman b. Hayyan al-Murri and 'Abd ar-Rahman b. Sulayman al-Kalbi conducted a raiding expedition ..." cf. al-Ya'qubi, II, 378; (*) Ibn Hajar, VII, 113f. (Khalifa).

1320 From "Bishr b. Safwan, the governor over Ifriqiya ..." cf. *Ibn 'Asakir, X, 92 (Khalifa).

1321 *Ṭbq.*, 805; Ibn Hajar, VI, 436.

1322 On the death of Sulayman b. Yasar cf. *Dh., IV, 122 (Khalifa). See note 145.

1323 See note 119.

1324 GAS, I, 29.

1325 Nafidh (*Ṭbq.*, 703; *Jarḥ*, IV, I, 507; Ibn Hajar, X, 404).

1326 'Abdallah b. Zayd (*Ṭbq.*, 503; Ibn Sa'd, VII, 183; Ibn Hajar, V, 224; cf. GAS, I, index).

1327 *Ṭbq.*, 607; Ibn Sa'd, V, 167; Ibn Hajar, V, 63.

1328 On the death of Yazid b. al-Asamm cf. *Ibn Hajar, XI, 314 (Khalifa); Ibn Hajar XI, 313.

1329 He is 'Uthman b. 'Abdallah b. Muwahhib, d. 160/776–777 (*Ṭbq.*, 685; *Jarḥ*, III, I, 155; Ibn Hajar, VII, 132).

1330 *Ṭbq.*, 355, 610; Ibn Sa'd, V, 161., VI, 211; Ibn Hajar, X, 350.

Abu Burda b. Abi Musa al-Ash'ari, on the last Friday of 103/June 722, or at the beginning of 104.

Abu Nu'aym:
They died in 104.

'Ikrima b. 'Abd ar-Rahman b. al-Harith {339} b. Hisham[1331] died during the caliphate of Yazid b. 'Abd al-Malik.

[480] The Year 105/723–724

In this year, the Khaqan[1332] marched with a large army of Turks toward Armenia. Al-Jarrah b. 'Abdallah al-Hakami moved [against him]. They met in *Ramaḍān*/February–March 724, at a place called _____,[1333] between the Kura and the Arax. They battled for several days, then God put the infidels to rout.[1334]

Abu Khalid < Abu l-Bara' < Malik b. Adham:
We were with al-Jarrah. We battled them until night separated us, and God gave victory to the Muslims.[1335]

Ibn al-Kalbi:
In this year, al-Jarrah b. 'Abdallah conducted a raiding expedition against the Alans, reaching cities beyond Balanjar. He conquered some of them, and drove away [the inhabitants of] some. He killed [many] and acquired booty. That was in 105.[1336]

Ibn al-Kalbi:
[481] Marwan b. Muhammad led the summer raid of the right flank, and conquered a city in the land of the Byzantines near Kamakh.[1337]

In 105, Yazid b. 'Abd al-Malik b. Marwan died.

1331 *Ṭbq.*, 611; Ibn Sa'd, V, 209; Ibn Hajar, VII, 260.

1332 Kh.: Jaban; Azdi, 22, and Dh., IV, 88: Khaqan.

1333 U: *ar-R-m*; Z: az-Z-m; (unidentified).

1334 From "In this year, the Khaqan marched …" cf. (*) Azdi, 22; *Dh., IV, 88/

1335 From "We were with al-Jarrah …" cf. *Azdi, 22 (Khalifa).

1336 From "In this year, al-Jarrah b. 'Abdallah conducted a raiding expedition against the Alans …" cf. al-Ya'qubi, II, 378; Tab., II, 1462; (*) Azdi, 23, (Khalifa). Cf. Dunlop, 65f.

1337 This sentence parallels IA, V, 125. Kh.: *'-n-j*, which could be confused with Kamakh in Arabic script. Cf. Honigmann, 56 n. 12, and index, s.v. Kamacha; cf. Ramsay, index, s.v. Kamakha.

{340} *Al-Walid b. Hisham < his father < his grandfather; *'Abdallah b. Mughira < his father; and others:
The mother of Yazid b. 'Abd al-Malik was 'Atika bint Yazid b. Mu'awiya. He was born in Damascus in 71/690–691 or 72. He died in ______,[1338] in the district of al-Balqa', on Friday 24 *Sha'bān* 105/26 January 724. His brother, Hisham b. 'Abd al-Malik, recited the prayers for him. He was 34 or 33 years old. His reign lasted four years and a month.[1339]

Jarir[1340] said the following [in praise of Yazid]:

You were clothed in the garment of sovereignty
not forcibly snatched,
Before the age of 30. Sovereignty usually
is of impure origin.[1341]

Hisham b. 'Abd al-Malik received the pledge of allegiance. His mother was Umm Hashim bint Isma'il b. Hisham al-Makhzumi.

[482] A List of the Governors of Yazid b. 'Abd al-Malik

Medina:

He dismissed Abu Bakr [b. Muhammad b. 'Amr] b. Hazm.

'Abd ar-Rahman b. ad-Dahhak b. Qays al-Fihri was appointed in 101/719–720, and later dismissed.

'Abd al-Wahid b. 'Abdallah, of the Banu Nasr b. Mu'awiya, was appointed in 104/722–723, and served until [Yazid] died.

Mecca:

He dismissed 'Abd al-'Aziz b. 'Abdallah b. Khalid b. Asid.

'Abd ar-Rahman b. ad-Dahhak b. Qays was then given jurisdiction over Mecca and at-Ta'if [as well as Medina] in 103/721–722. He was later dismissed.

'Abd al-Wahid b. 'Abdallah an-Nasri was then given jurisdiction over Mecca and at-Ta'if [as well as Medina] in 104/722–723, and he served until Yazid died.

{341} Yemen:

'Urwa b. Muhammad was retained [by Yazid].

1338 U: *'-b-l*; Z: *'-r-b-d*. On Abil, the name of a number of places in Syria, cf. BGA, VI, 78; VII, 329 n. c; Tab., index; Yaqut, I, 56.

1339 From "The mother of Yazid b. 'Abd al-Malik was 'Atika …" cf. *'Iqd*, IV, 441.

1340 Ibn 'Atiyya, d. 110/728–729 (EI2, II, 479; GAS, II, 356).

1341 From "You were clothed …" cf. *Dīwān*, 66; *'*Iqd*, IV, 441. Meter: *basīṭ*.

Basra:

Yazid b. al-Muhallab revolted, and reached Basra on the night of the full moon in *Ramaḍān* 101/February 724. 'Adi b. Artat was in Basra. Yazid took control of the city and imprisoned 'Adi, then marched to Wasit. [Yazid b. al-Muhallab] left his brother, Marwan b. al-Muhallab, as his lieutenant over Basra.

[483] Shabib al-Mazini was chosen by the people of Basra upon the death of Yazid [b. al-Muhallab] in *Ṣafar* 102/August 720.

Then Maslama b. 'Abd al-Malik, who was governor over Iraq, sent 'Abd ar-Rahman b. Sulaym al-Kalbi to the frontier.[1342]

'Abd al-Malik b. Bishr b. Marwan was then appointed by Maslama [b. 'Abd al-Malik].

Then Yazid b. 'Abd al-Malik appointed 'Umar b. Hubayra al-Fazari over Iraq, and he arrived in 103/721–722.

Sa'id b. 'Umar al-Harashi was appointed over Basra.

Hassan b. 'Abd ar-Rahman b. Mas'ud al-Fazari, a Damascene, [was then appointed].

Firas b. Sumayy al-Fazari, the husband of the mother of 'Umar b. Hubayra, [was then appointed] and served until Yazid died.

Kufa:

'Abd al-Hamid b. 'Abd ar-Rahman b. Zayd b. al-Khattab, the governor under 'Umar b. 'Abd al-'Aziz at the time of his death, was retained by Yazid b. 'Abd al-Malik. He was dismissed by Maslama b. 'Abd al-Malik, the governor over Iraq.

Muhammad b. 'Amr b. al-Walid b. 'Uqba b. Abi Mu'ayt was appointed by Maslama b. 'Abd al-Malik, but dismissed by ['Umar] b. Hubayra in 103/721–722.

As-Sa'ir b. 'Abdallah, of the Murra of the Ghatafan, was then appointed by 'Umar b. Hubayra, and he served until Yazid b. 'Abd al-Malik died.

Khurasan:

'Abd ar-Rahman b. Nu'aym al-Ghamidi was there. When Yazid

1342 The Arabic is *al-Maslaḥa*, and probably refers to the Byzantine frontier. In 102/720–721, 'Abd ar-Rahman b. Sulaym was named chief of police in Basra by Maslama b. 'Abd al-Malik (cf. Kh., 474; Zambaur, *Manuel de généalogie*, 40). Then, still in 102, before the end of Maslama's governorship over Iraq, 'Abd ar-Rahman was sent by Maslama – possibly at the request of the caliph, Yazid II – to take command of the summer raid (cf. Kh., 487; al-Ya'qubi, II, 378).

b. al-Muhallab revolted, he sent his brother, Mudrik, but 'Abd ar-Rahman prevented him from entering.

[484] Sa'id b. 'Abd al-'Aziz b. al-Harith b. al-Hakam b. Abi l-'As was sent by Maslama [b. 'Abd al-Malik] when he arrived in Iraq [as governor]. He was retained by Ibn Hubayra, but later dismissed.

Sa'id b. 'Amr al-Harashi was then appointed in 103/721–722, but was later dismissed.

Muslim b. Sa'id b. Aslam b. Zur'a al-Kilabi was then appointed [by Ibn Hubayra] in 104/722–723.

Sijistan:

Al-Qa'qa' b. Suwayd, of the Banu Minqar {342} b. 'Ubayd, was appointed by Yazid b. 'Abd al-Malik, but later dismissed by Ibn Hubayra.

As-Sayyal b. al-Mundhir b. 'Awf b. an-Nu'man was then appointed [by Ibn Hubayra].

Sind:

'Amr b. Muslim was governor when 'Umar died.

A certain as-Saba'i was appointed by Yazid b. al-Muhallab when Yazid b. Wida' b. Humayd al-Azdi seized control of Basra. He served until 102/720–721, when Hilal b. Ahwaz arrived, sent by Maslama b. 'Abd al-Malik.

'Ubaydallah b. 'Ali as-Sulami was then appointed by Ibn Hubayra in 103/721–722, but was later dismissed.

'Abd al-Hamid b. 'Abd ar-Rahman, of the Murra of the Ghatafan, was then appointed [by Ibn Hubayra], and served until Yazid b. 'Abd al-Malik died.

[485] Bahrain and al-Yamama.

Ibrahim b. 'Arabi was returned.

Armenia:

Ma'laq b. Saffar b. Falhas b. Janb al-Jammar b. Muqid an-Nar al-Bahrani, an Emesan, was appointed by Yazid b. 'Abd al-Malik in 103/721–722. He dismissed him in 104.

Al-Jarrah b. 'Abdallah al-Hakami was then appointed.

al-Jazira:

Fayid b. Muhammad al-Kindi.

Al-'Urs b. Qays b. Shu'ba b. al-Arqam al-Kindi.

Ifriqiya:

Yazid b. Abi Muslim [was appointed] in *Dhū l-Qa'da* 101/May–June 720. He was killed there.
Bishr b. Safwan was appointed by Yazid b. 'Abd al-Malik in 102. Bishr then left to report to Yazid b. 'Abd al-Malik.
Yahya b. Na'isa al-Kalbi was left by Bishr b. Safwan as his lieutenant [when he went to report to Yazid b. 'Abd al-Malik] in 105/723–724.
When [Bishr] arrived [in Syria], Yazid had already died.

Egypt:

Bishr b. Safwan al-Kalbi, who was later appointed over Ifriqiya.[1343]

{343}[486] The Judges [and other officials]

Basra:

Maslama b. 'Abd al-Malik appointed 'Abd al-Malik b. Bishr b. Marwan as governor over Basra.
An-Nadr b. Anas b. Malik was appointed as judge by 'Abd al-Malik b. Bishr.
Musa b. Anas b. Malik[1344] was appointed by Maslama b. 'Abd al-Malik in 102/720–721.
Then ['Umar] b. Hubayra arrived.
'Abd al-Malik b. Ya'la[1345] was appointed by Ibn Hubayra in 103/721–722.

Kufa:

Al-Qasim b. 'Abd ar-Rahman b. 'Abdallah b. Mas'ud was retained, but later dismissed in 103/721–722.
Al-Husayn b. al-Hasan al-Kindi was then appointed.[1346]

Medina:

Yazid [b. 'Abd al-Malik] appointed 'Abd ar-Rahman b. ad-Dahhak b. Qays as governor.
Maslama b. 'Abdallah b. Salama al-Makhzumi was appointed as judge [by 'Abd ar-Rahman b. ad-Dahhak]. Then 'Abd al-Wahid

1343 For the entry on Egypt cf. (*) Ibn 'Asakir, X, 92 (Khalifa).
1344 *Ṭbq.*, 501; Ibn Sa'd, VII, 192; Ibn Hajar, X, 335.
1345 *Ṭbq.*, 492; Ibn Sa'd, VII, 217; Ibn Hajar, VI, 429.
1346 For the entry on Kufa cf. *Dh., IV, 293 (Khalifa).

b. 'Abdallah an-Nasri was made governor over Medina[1347] in 104/722–723.

Sa'd b. Ibrahim b. 'Abd ar-Rahman b. 'Awf[1348] was appointed judge by 'Abd al-Wahid, but he was later dismissed.

Sa'id b. Sulayman b. Zayd b. Thabit[1349] was then appointed, and served until Yazid died.

[487] The Pilgrimage:

101/720, 102/721, and 103/722 – 'Abd ar-Rahman [b. ad-Dahhak] b. Qays al-Fihri.

104/723 – 'Abd al-Wahid an-Nasri.

The Summer Raid:

'Abd ar-Rahman b. Sulaym al-Kalbi, until Yazid died.

Chief of Police:

Ka'b b. Hamid al-'Absi, until [Yazid] died.

Secretary of Finance and Correspondence:

Salih b. Jubayr al-Ghudani, who was later dismissed.

Usama b. Zayd, a *mawlā* of the Yemenites.[1350]

Administrator of the Official Seal, the Warehouses, and the Treasuries:

Mutayr, his *mawlā*.

Hatim b. Muslim:

Usama b. Zayd was in charge of the official seal.

{344} Captain of the Guard:

Ghaylan, the son-in-law of Abu Ma'n.

Hatim [b. Muslim]:

Abu Malik as-Saksaki was captain of the guard.

His Chamberlain:

Khalid, his *mawlā*.[1351]

1347 Kh.: over Basra.

1348 D. 127/744–745 (*Ṭbq.*, 651; *Jarḥ*, II, I, 79; Ibn Hajar, III, 463).

1349 *Ṭbq.*, 662; *Jarḥ*, II, I, 25; Ibn Hajar, IV, 42.

1350 For the entry on the Secretary of Finance and Correspondence cf. *Dh., IV, 253 (Khalifa).

1351 From the heading "Chief of Police" cf. (*) *'Iqd*, IV, 441.

[488] *'Abdallah b. al-Mughira < his father; *al-Walid b. Hisham < his father < his grandfather; and others:
Iraq was consolidated under the administration of 'Umar b. Hubayra al-Fazari at the beginning of 103/July 721.

Chief[s] of Police:
Wasit: Suwayd al-Murri, the father of Ziyad b. Suwayd.
Hawthara b. Suhayl.[1352]
Kufa: Muhammad b. Manzur al-Asadi.
Basra: Ibn Riyat.

[Ibn Hubayra's] Secretary:
A Syrian named 'Uthman.
Sa'd b. 'Atiyya.

Ibn Hubayra died at fifty-odd years of age.

During the governorship of Ibn Hubayra, the following died: Sa'd b. 'Ubayda as-Sulami,[1353] a Kufan; Abu Mijlaz;[1354] Muwarriq al-'Ijli;[1355] [and] Abu s-Salil.[1356]

During the governorship of Ibn Hubayra, Mas'ud b. Abi Zaynab revolted. He took control of Bahrain and al-Yamama. Sufyan b. 'Amr al-'Uqayli killed him.

[489] In 105, the following also died: Humayd b. 'Abd ar-Rahman b. 'Awf;[1357] 'Umara b. Khuzayma b. Thabit;[1358] Sinan b. Abi Sinan ad-Di'li;[1359] 'Ikrima,[1360] a *mawlā* of Ibn 'Abbas; Abu Raja' al-'Utaridi;[1361] [and] al-Musayyab b. Rafi'i;[1362] ad-Dahhak b. Muzahim.[1363]

During the caliphate of Yazid b. 'Abd al-Malik, the following died:

1352 Z: Hawthara b. Sahl.
1353 *Ṭbq.*, 359; Ibn Sa'd, VI, 298; Ibn Hajar, III, 478.
1354 Lahiq b. Humayd (*Ṭbq.*, 499, 831; Ibn Sa'd, VII, 216 and 368; Ibn Hajar, XI, 171).
1355 *Ṭbq.*, 500; Ibn Sa'd, VII, 213; Ibn Hajar, X, 331.
1356 Durayd b. Nuqayr (*Ṭbq.*, 511; Ibn Sa'd, VII, 222; Ibn Hajar, IV, 457).
1357 On the death of Humayd b. 'Abd ar-Rahman b. 'Awf cf. #Ibn Hajar, III, 45 (Khalifa). *Ṭbq.*, 606; Ibn Sa'd, V, 153; Ibn Hajar, III, 45.
1358 *Ṭbq.*, 621, 627; *Jarḥ*, III, I, 365; Ibn Hajar, VII, 416.
1359 *Ṭbq.*, 619; Ibn Sa'd, V, 249; Ibn Hajar, IV, 242.
1360 EI2, III, 1081.
1361 'Imran b. Tamim (*Ṭbq.*, 464; Ibn Sa'd, VII, 138; Ibn Hajar, VIII, 140).
1362 *Ṭbq.*, 357; Ibn Sa'd, VI, 293; Ibn Hajar, X, 153.
1363 GAS, I, 29.

Aban b. ‘Uthman[1364] [and] ‘Ubayd b. Hunayn,[1365] a *mawlā* of the family of Zayd b. al-Khattab.

{349}[490] The Year 106/724–725

In this year, Muslim b. Sa‘id b. Aslam b. Zur‘a raided Farghana. He was confronted by the army of the Turks. The son of the brother of the Khaqan was killed, along with many of the polytheists. That was during the governorship of Ibn Hubayra.[1366]

Then Khalid b. ‘Abdallah al-Qasri went to Iraq as governor. Khalid appointed his brother, Asad b. ‘Abdallah,[1367] as governor over Khurasan. He met Muslim b. Sa‘id, and returned with the army in *Rabī‘* II 106/ August–September 724.[1368]

In this year, al-Jarrah b. ‘Abdallah al-Hakami conducted a raiding expedition in Armenia.

*Abu Khalid < Abu Bara’ an-Numayri:
Al-Jarrah b. ‘Abdallah al-Hakami penetrated deep into the land of the Khazars. The Alans made peace with him, and paid him the *jizya* and the *kharāj*.[1369] He was the first to return from Bab al-Lan.[1370]

Bishr b. Safwan, the governor of Ifriqiya, sent Muhammad b. Abi Bakr, a *mawlā* of the Banu Jumah, on a raiding expedition. He attacked Corsica and Sardinia.[1371]

[491] Sa‘id b. ‘Abd al-Malik conducted a raiding expedition in the land of the Byzantines.

Hisham b. ‘Abd al-Malik led the pilgrimage.

1364 On the death of Aban b. ‘Uthman cf. *Ibn Hajar, I, 97 (Khalifa). GAS, I, 277; EI2, I, 2.

1365 *Ṭbq*., 617, 624; Ibn Sa‘d, V, 285; Ibn Hajar, VII, 63.

1366 From “In this year, Muslim b. Sa‘id b. Aslam b. Zur‘a raided Farghana …” cf. Tab., II, 1477ff (al-Mada’ini); (*) Dh., IV, 88.

1367 D. 120/737–738 (EI2, I, 684).

1368 From “Then Khalid b. ‘Abdallah al-Qasri went to Iraq …” cf. (*) Dh., IV, 88.

1369 From “Al-Jarrah b. ‘Abdallah al-Hakami penetrated deep …” cf. al-Ya‘qubi, II, 394; Tab., II, 1472; (*) Azdi, 23 (Khalifa) and (*) Azdi, 22 (the report is broken up into two parts in al-Azdi); *Dh., IV, 88. On the *jizya*, cf. EI2, II, 559; Dennett, *passim*; on the *kharāj*, cf. note 138.

1370 On Bab al-Lan, cf. EI2, I, 837; On the Alans, cf. EI2, I, 354.

1371 From “Bishr b. Safwan, the governor of Ifriqiya …” cf. *Ibn ‘Asakir, X, 92 (Khalifa).

In 106, Tawus b. Kaysan[1372] died in Mecca. Hisham b. 'Abd al-Malik recited the prayers for him, before he set out for Mina.[1373]

In this year, Muslim b. Jundub al-Hudhali[1374] died.

Mu'awiya b. Hisham led the summer raid.

{350} Khalid b. 'Abdallah al-Qasri assumed the governorship of Iraq.[1375]

[492] The Year 107/725–726

In this year, Hisham b. 'Abd al-Malik dismissed al-Jarrah b. 'Abdallah al-Hakami from the governorship of Armenia and Azerbaijan, and replaced him with Maslama b. 'Abd al-Malik. Maslama sent al-Harith b. 'Amr at-Ta'i [on a raiding expedition].[1376]

Abu Khalid < Abu Bara':
Al-Harith conducted a raiding expedition. He conquered a district called Kh-sh-d-'-n,[1377] in the region of the Kura.[1378]

Abu Bara':
In that same year, Maslama conducted a raiding expedition. He invaded from Malatya, [through the mountain passes]. He halted at Caesarea, and conquered it by force.[1379] That was on 4 *Ramaḍān* 107/13 January 726.

Ibn al-Kalbi:
In this year, Mu'awiya b. Hisham conducted a raiding expedition in the land of the Byzantines. He reached his encampment, and sent al-Waddah,

1372 *Ṭbq*., 732; Ibn Sa'd, V, 537; Dh., IV, 126; Ibn Hajar, V, 8.

1373 From "In 106, Tawus b. Kaysan died in Mecca ..." cf. *Azdi, 24.

1374 *Ṭbq*., 642; *Jarḥ*, IV, I, 182; Ibn Hajar, X, 124.

1375 This sentence parallels *Ibn Hajar, III, 102 (Khalifa).

1376 From "In this year, Hisham b. 'Abd al-Malik dismissed al-Jarrah ..." cf. *Azdi, 25; IA, V, 137f; (*) Dh., IV, 89.

1377 Cf. BGA, I, 187; *J-sh-m-d-'-n*; cf. *Futūḥ*, 206: *Ḥ-s-m-d-'-n*. Cf. the variants (*Kh-n-d-'-n*, *Kh-y-z-'-n*, etc.) in Minorsky, 448f., which may look fairly similar to *Kh-sh-d-'-n* in Arabic script.

1378 From "Al-Harith conducted a raiding expedition ..." cf. *Futūḥ*, 206; *Azdi, 25; IA, V, 137f.

1379 From "In that same year, Maslama conducted a raiding expedition ..." cf. Tab., II, 1491; *Azdi, 26; (*) Dh., IV, 89.

the leader of the Waddahiyya. He burned the villages and crops, and cut down the trees.[1380]

Ibn al-Kalbi:

In this year, a severe plague struck Syria. It even afflicted the riding animals and the cattle.[1381]

[493] Asad b. ‘Abdallah raided Gharshistan.[1382] He sent Ibn Salim al-Azdi in command of the cavalry. A throng of the enemy confronted him, and some of the Muslims were killed. The people were afflicted by famine, and they returned exhausted.[1383]

{351} Mu‘awiya b. Hisham conducted a raiding expedition in the land of the Byzantines. He reached ’-r-w-l-y-h.[1384]

Ibrahim b. Hisham b. Isma‘il al-Makhzumi led the pilgrimage.

In 107, the following died: Salim b. ‘Abdallah b. ‘Umar,[1385] at the beginning of the year; al-Qasim b. Muhammad b. Abi Bakr,[1386] at the end of the year;[1387] ‘Ata’ b. Yazid al-Laythi.[1388]

In this year, the following were born: al-Mu’tamir b. Sulayman;[1389] Sufyan b. ‘Uyayna.[1390]

At the beginning of the caliphate of Hisham, the following died: Yazid b. Talha b. Rukana;[1391] Muhammad b. Talha b. Rukana;[1392] Muslim b. Jundub.

1380 From “In this year, Mu‘awiya b. Hisham conducted a raiding expedition …” cf. al-Ya‘qubi, II, 394; cf. Tab., II, 1492 (al-Waqidi).

1381 From “In this year, a severe plague struck Syria …” cf. Tab., II, 1488.

1382 EI2, II, 1010, s.v. Ghardjistan.

1383 From “Asad b. ‘Abdallah raided Gharshistan …” cf. (*) Dh., IV, 89.

1384 This could be a misreading of Darawliya, Dorylaion (cf. note 699).

1385 On the death of Salim b. ‘Abdallah b. ‘Umar cf. #Ibn Hajar, III, 438 (Khalifa]. *Ṭbq.*, 614; Ibn Sa‘d, V, 195; Ibn Hajar, III, 436.

1386 *Ṭbq.*, 609; Ibn Sa‘d, V, 187; Ibn Hajar, VII, 333.

1387 The phrase “al-Qasim b. Muhammad b. Abi Bakr, at the end of the year” is also found in #Dh., IV, 185 (Khalifa); #Ibn Hajar, VIII, 335 (Khalifa). That is, he died at the end of 106 (or the beginning of 107; cf. *Ṭbq.*, 609).

1388 *Ṭbq.*, 619; Ibn Sa‘d, V, 249; Ibn Hajar, VII, 217.

1389 *Ṭbq.*, 541; Ibn Sa‘d, VII, 290; al-Bukhari, *at-Ta’rīkh al-kabīr*, IV, II, 49; Ibn Hajar, X, 227; d. 187/803

1390 D. 198/813–814 (GAS, I, 96).

1391 *Ṭbq.*, 601.

1392 *Ṭbq.*, 600; *Jarḥ*, III, II, 291; Ibn Hajar, IX, 239.

[494] The Year 108/726–727

In this year, Asad b. 'Abdallah raided Ghur.[1393] [The inhabitants] confronted him with a large army. They fought bitterly, then God put the enemy to rout.[1394]

Maslama b. 'Abd al-Malik led the summer raid to the right flank. 'Asim b. 'Abdallah b. Yazid al-Hilali led the summer raid to the left flank.

In this year, the son of the Khaqan marched into Azerbaijan.

Abu Khalid < Abu Bara':
Martik,[1395] the son of the Khaqan, marched into Azerbaijan in 108. He besieged the city of Warthan, and employed mangonels against it. News [of this] reached al-Harith b. 'Amr, who set out, and crossed the Arax above Warthan. The son of the Khaqan heard [of this], and he moved against al-Harith. They met [in battle], and God put the son of the Khaqan and his companions to rout, and killed many of them. Al-Harith b. 'Amr was also killed,[1396] may God have mercy on him.[1397]

Bishr b. Safwan sent Qutham b. 'Awana al-Kalbi from Ifriqiya on a raiding expedition. He acquired booty and [returned] safely.[1398]

Ibrahim b. Hisham b. Isma'il led the pilgrimage.

{352}[495] 'Abbad the Harurite revolted in Yemen, and was killed by Yusuf b. 'Umar.[1399]

1393 EI2, II, 1096.

1394 From "In this year, Asad b. 'Abdallah raided Ghur ..." cf. Tab., II, 1489, 1493f (al-Mada'ini); *Azdi, 27; *Ibn 'Asakir, *Tahdhīb*, II, 459 (Khalifa); (*) Dh., IV, 89.

1395 The name is found as "Barjik," and other spellings, in al-Bal'ami (cf. Dunlop, 63 n. 29, and index, s.v. Barjik). Ibn 'Asakir, *Tahdhīb*, III, 453, renders Khalifa's "Martik" as *D-'-r-y-n-d* (or at least it was read as such by the editor).

1396 Cf. page 227 below, where he is alive and well in the year 112/730–731. Ibn 'Asakir commented on the discrepancy in Khalifa's reports (*Tahdhīb*, III, 453). Cf. Dunlop, 67, 68, and 76.

1397 From "Martik, the son of the Khaqan, marched into Azerbaijan ..." cf. *Azdi, 27; (*) Ibn 'Asakir, *Tahdhīb*, III, 453; IA, V, 140f.; *Dh., IV, 89.

1398 From "Bishr b. Safwan sent Qutham ..." cf. *Ibn 'Asakir, X, 92 (Khalifa).

1399 This sentence parallels Tab., II, 1487. His name was 'Abbad ar-Ru'ayni (cf. Wellhausen, *Religio-Political Factions*, 89 n. 3). At-Tabari dates the revolt of 'Abbad in 107/725–726. Ibn al-Athir (IA, V, 141) has the same report as at-Tabari, but includes it under the events of the year 108, which corresponds to Khalifa's account. Perhaps Ibn al-Athir did that while consulting Khalifa's *Ta'rīkh*.

Mu'awiya b. Hisham conducted a raiding expedition in the land of the Byzantines. He sent al-Battal[1400] to Khanjara,[1401] which he conquered.[1402]

In 108, the following died: Abu l-'Ala' Yazid b. 'Abdallah b. ash-Shikhkhir al-Harashi,[1403] Bakr b. 'Abdallah al-Muzani,[1404] Abu l-Mulayh al-Hudhali,[1405] Abu Nadra al-'Abdi,[1406] Abu Harb b. Abi l-Aswad ad-Di'li,[1407] [and] Khalid b. Ma'dan ash-Sha'mi.[1408]

After the year 100/718–719 the following died: Abu Shaykh al-Huna'i,[1409] 'Abdallah b. Shaqiq al-'Uqayli,[1410] Sa'id b. Abi l-Hasan,[1411] [and] Abu l-Mutawakkil an-Naji.[1412]

[496] The Year 109/727–728

In this year, Bishr b. Safwan sent Hassan b. Muhammad b. Abi Bakr, a *mawlā* of the Banu Jumah, from Ifriqiya on a raiding expedition to Sardinia. He acquired booty and [returned] safely.[1413]

1400 EI2, I, 1102.

1401 Kh.: Hanjara. Cf. note 1113. M. Canard, in EI2, I, 1102, s.v. al-Battal, states that Gangra, in Paphlagonia, was captured by al-Battal in 109/728.

1402 For the last two sentences from "Mu'awiya b. Hisham conducted a raiding expedition" cf. *Dh., IV, 89.

1403 On the death of Abu l-'Ala' Yazid b. 'Abdallah b. ash-Shikhkhir al-Harashi cf. #Ibn Hajar, XI, 341 (Khalifa). *Ṭbq.*, 497; Ibn Sa'd, VII, 155; Ibn Hajar, XI, 341.

1404 *Ṭbq.*, 493; Ibn Sa'd, VII, 209; Ibn Hajar, I, 484.

1405 On the death of Abu l-Mulayh al-Hudhali cf. #Dh., IV, 224 (Khalifa). *Ṭbq.*, 494; Ibn Sa'd, VII, 219; Ibn Hajar, XII, 246.

1406 On the death of Abu Nadra al-'Abdi cf. #Ibn Hajar, X, 303 (Khalifa). Al-Mundhir b. Malik (see note 474).

1407 On the death of Abu Harb b. Abi l-Aswad ad-Di'li cf. #Ibn Hajar, XII, 70 (Khalifa). *Ṭbq.*, 492; Ibn Sa'd, VII, 226; Ibn Hajar, XII, 69.

1408 On the death of Khalid b. Ma'dan ash-Sha'mi cf. #Ibn Hajar, III, 119 (Khalifa). *Ṭbq.*, 794; Ibn Sa'd, VII, 455; Ibn 'Asakir, *Tahdhīb*, V, 86; Ibn Hajar, III, 118; cf. M. Sharon, in EI2, IV, 446a, s.v. Kahtaba.

1409 On the death of Abu Shaykh al-Huna'i cf. #Ibn Hajar, XII, 129 (Khalifa).

1410 On the death of 'Abdallah b. Shaqiq al-'Uqayli cf. #Ibn Hajar, V, 254 (Khalifa). *Ṭbq.*, 466, 496; Ibn Sa'd, VII, 126; Ibn Hajar, V, 253.

1411 *Ṭbq.*, 502; Ibn Sa'd, VII, 187; Ibn Hajar, IV, 16.

1412 *Ṭbq.*, 491; Ibn Sa'd, VII, 225; Ibn Hajar, VII, 318.

1413 From "In this year, Bishr b. Safwan sent Hassan ..." cf. *Ibn 'Asakir, X, 93 (Khalifa).

Bishr b. Safwan died in Ifriqiya, and designed _____[1414] b. Qurt al-Kalbi to succeed him.[1415]

Maslama b. 'Abd al-Malik conducted a raiding expedition. The armies roamed freely in Azerbaijan, where they spent the winter.[1416] Mu'awiya b. Hisham led a raiding expedition in the land of the Byzantines, and conquered a fortress called al-Gh-ṭ-'-s-y-n.[1417]

{353} Ibrahim b. Hisham b. Isma'il led the pilgrimage.

In 109, the following died: Abu Najih,[1418] the father of 'Abdallah b. Abi Najih;[1419] Dufayf,[1420] a *mawlā* of Ibn 'Abbas; [and] 'Abd ar-Rahman b. Sa'id b. Yarbu'.[1421]

[497] The Year 110/728–729

In this year, Maslama b. 'Abd al-Malik conducted a raiding expedition against the Khazars. It was called the Campaign of the Mud.

Abu Khalid < Abu Bara' an-Numayri:
Maslama was heading for T-l-m-y-s,[1422] and encountered the *ṭāghiya*[1423] of

1414 U: *N-'-ās*; Z: *Q-'-ās*; IAH, 216: *N-gh-āsh*; Ibn 'Asakir, X, 94: *Q-'-āsh*; Dh., IV, 93: *Q-'-ās*; cf. Kh., 539 (376): *N-'-ās*.

1415 This sentence parallels IAH, 216; *Ibn 'Asakir, X, 94 (Khalifa); *Dh., IV, 93.

1416 From "Maslama b. 'Abd al-Malik conducted a raiding expedition ..." cf. (*) Azdi, 29; (*) Dh., IV, 89.

1417 From "Mu'awiya b. Hisham led a raiding expedition ..." cf. Tab., II, 1495; (*) Azdi, 28; (*) Dh., IV, 89. Compare with the Kastron Ateous of Theophanes (Wellhausen, "Die Kämpfe der Araber," 443, A.M. 6219); perhaps the initial *ghayn* of Khalifa's *Gh-ṭ-'-s-y-n* should be read as an *'ayn*. Cf. Ramsay, 143f. Cf. also Getasa (Ramsay, 308). In his account of this expedition, at-Tabari has *Ṭ-y-b-h* (Tab., II, 1495).

1418 Yasar ath-Thaqafi (Ibn Hajar, XI, 377).

1419 D. 131/748–749 (*Ṭbq.*, 707; Ibn Sa'd, V, 483; Ibn Hajar, VI, 54; cf. GAS, I, index).

1420 *Ṭbq.*, 703: Dhufayf; *Jarḥ*, I, II, 443.

1421 *Ṭbq.*, 613; *Jarḥ*, II, II, 239; Ibn Hajar, VI, 187.

1422 Perhaps Tiflis is meant (cf. note 1442).

1423 The word *ṭāghiya* is used frequently in connection with the leaders of the Byzantines. The word may possibly be traced to the Greek *tagós*, "commander" (cf. *tagé*, "commanders," and *tageía*, "office of *tagós*/commander"). The first two consonants of the Greek word correspond to an Arabic root, *ṭ-gh-y*, meaning "to be impious, tyrannical" (cr. Hebrew *ṭā'āh*, Syriac *ṭa'ā*, "wander," "deviate"). Through a process of folk etymology, the Greek *tagós*, "commander," became the Arabic *ṭāghiya*, "impious tyrant." The *tā' marbūṭa*, which usually serves to indicate the feminine of a noun, may have been added as a sign of contempt; (but cf. al-Mubarrad, 535, l. 11, for a different explanation of the feminine ending of this word.).

the Khazars at the head of a large army, near al-Bab. They battled for many days. Then God put [the Khazars] to rout. That was on Thursday 7 *Jumādā* II 110/17 September 728.[1424]

Abu Bara' < *'Abdallah b. Asid al-Kilabi:
Maslama was returning from Bab al-Lan, when the Khazars confronted him. They skirmished with him until night separated them. Maslama returned safely.[1425]

Ibn al-Kalbi:
Maslama's battle against them lasted about a month, in heavy rain. Then God put them to rout.[1426]

In this year, Mu'awiya b. Hisham conducted a raiding expedition in the land of the Byzantines. He conquered two of their fortresses, Ṣ-m-l-h[1427] and '-l-m-w-h.[1428]

[498] Abu Khalid:
In this year 'Ubayda b. 'Abd ar-Rahman adh-Dhakwani[1429] of the Banu Sulaym arrived in Ifriqiya. He sent 'Uthman b. Abi 'Ubayda in command of 700 [men] on a {354} raiding expedition, and he headed for Syracuse,[1430] the city of Sicily. He was confronted [by the inhabitants], but he captured their *bitrīq* and God put them to rout.[1431]

Ibrahim b. Hisham b. Isma'il al-Makhzumi led the pilgrimage.

In 110, al-Hasan b. Abi l-Hasan died in *Rajab*/October–November 728. An-Nadr b. 'Amr al-Muqri'i, a Himyarite from Syria, recited the

1424 From "In this year, Maslama b. 'Abd al-Malik conducted a raiding expedition against the Khazars ..." cf. (*) Dh., IV, 90.

1425 From "Maslama was returning from Bab al-Lan ..." cf. Tab., II, 1506.

1426 From "Maslama's battle against them ..." cf. Tab., II, 1506.

1427 Cf. *Futūḥ*, 170: Ṣamalu (written with initial *ḍād*, rather than *ṣād*), Samalu; al-Ya'qubi, I, 177; *Ṣ-m-l-h*; BGA, VI, 108: *Ṣ-m-l-h*. It is identified with Semalouos kastron (cf. Minorsky, 220; E. Honigmann, in EI, III, 526b, s.v. Missis; Ramsay, 278, 355).

1428 From "In this year, Mu'awiya b. Hisham conducted a raiding expedition ..." cf. Tab., II, 1506; (*) Dh., IV, 90. Unidentified. A marginal manuscript annotation has *al-B-w-h*, also unidentified.

1429 Kh.: 'Ubayda b. 'Abd ar-Rahman *al-B-r-kānī*; IAH, 216: al-Qaysi; al-Maqrizi (Amari, 661: adh-Dhakwani (adh-Dhakuni?); cf. Amari, trans., II, 572 n. 3.

1430 The spelling here is *S-r-'-q-s*.

1431 From "In this year 'Ubayda b. 'Abd ar-Rahman adh-Dhakwani of the Banu Sulaym arrived in Ifriqiya ..." cf. IAH, 216; (*) Dh., IV, 90; cf. al-Maqrizi, in Amari, 661f (trans., II, 572f.).

prayers for him. In this year, Muhammad b. Sirin[1432] died in *Shawwāl*/January–February 729, and an-Nadr b. 'Amr recited the prayers for him. In this year, al-Farazdaq[1433] died, followed by Jarir several months later.[1434]

Ibn al-Kalbi:
In this year, the following died: 'Abd al-Malik b. [499] Yasar,[1435] the brother of 'Ata', [and] [499] Sulayman b. Yasar.

In this year, the following died: Wahb b. Munabbih[1436] [and] Ibrahim b. Muhammad b. Talha b. 'Ubaydallah.[1437]

[500] The Year 111/729–730

In this year, Ashras b. 'Abdallah as-Sulami sent [a message] to the kings of Tokharistan,[1438] and they came to him.[1439] They had no military activity.[1440]

Hisham b. 'Abd al-Malik dismissed his brother, Maslama, from [the governorship of] Armenia and Azerbaijan, and reappointed al-Jarrah b. 'Abdallah al-Hakami.[1441]

Abu Khalid < Abu l-Khattab:
Al-Jarrah was reappointed to his governorship in 111. He went to Tiflis,[1442] and raided a Khazar city called al-Bayda',[1443] which he conquered. Then he departed. The Khazars gathered a large army, [led by] the son of the

1432 EI2, III, 947; GAS, I, 633.
1433 EI2, II, 788; GAS, II, 359.
1434 This sentence parallels *Ibn Kathir, IX, 265.
1435 *Ṭbq.*, 618; Ibn Sa'd, V, 175; Ibn Hajar, VI, 429.
1436 EI, IV, 1084; GAS, I, 305.
1437 On the death of Ibrahim b. Muhammad b. Talha b. 'Ubaydallah cf. #Ibn Hajar, I, 154 (Khalifa).
1438 EI, IV, 807.
1439 On Ashras and his administration in Khurasan, see Gibb, 69ff. and Wellhausen, *Arab Kingdom*, 456ff. According to the report in at-Tabari, II, 1507, the "message" Ashras sent was an invitation to convert to Islam in return for being relieved of the *jizya*.
1440 From "In this year, Ashras b. 'Abdallah as-Sulami sent [a message] …" cf. Tab., II, 1507.
1441 From "Hisham b. 'Abd al-Malik dismissed his brother …" cf. *Azdi, 30; *Dh., IV, 225 (Khalifa); IA, V, 158.
1442 Z: *T-l-m-y-s*. Cf. Kh., 497.
1443 Cf. Minorsky, 452f.; Dunlop, index, s.v.

Khaqan, {355} and they entered Armenia. The son of the Khaqan marched against Ardabil[1444] and besieged its inhabitants.[1445]

Ibn al-Kalbi:
Mu'awiya b. Hisham led the summer raid to the left flank.[1446] He departed, meeting no resistance.[1447]

Sa'id b. Hisham also conducted a summer raid in the territory near al-Jazira. He reached [501] Caesarea.

Abu Khalid:
'Ubayda b. 'Abd ar-Rahman sent al-Mustanir b. al-Harith from Ifriqiya on a raiding expedition with 180 ships. He disembarked, and besieged [the people of Sicily].[1448] When winter set in, he sailed for home with a good wind. When he was in the middle of the sea, there was a storm, and their ships sank. All but 17 ships were lost.[1449]

Ibrahim b. Hisham led the pilgrimage.

In this year, the following died: Tamim b. Aws, who had been a judge, [and] 'Ubaydallah b. Rafi' b. Khadij.[1450]

[502] The Year 112/730–731

In this year, Ashras b. 'Abdallah as-Sulami raided Farghana. The Turks marched, confronted him, and surrounded him. Hisham b. 'Abd al-Malik heard about that, and appointed al-Junayd b. 'Abd ar-Rahman al-Murri,[1451] of the Murra of the Ghatafan, [over Khurasan].[1452]

1444 EI2, I, 625.

1445 From "Al-Jarrah was reappointed ..." cf. *Azdi, 30 (Khalifa); IA, V, 158; *Dh., IV, 225f (Khalifa).

1446 This sentence parallels Tab., II, 1526.

1447 On the expression *lam yalqā kayd*, cf. *Futūḥ*, glossary, 95f.

1448 The parallel accounts state that Sicily was the object of this raid.

1449 From "'Ubayda b. 'Abd ar-Rahman sent al-Mustanir ..." cf. IAH, 216; cf. IA, V, 174; *Dh., IV, 226; al-Maqrizi, in Amari, 662 (trans., II, 573).

1450 *Ṭbq.*, 626; Ibn Sa'd, V, 256.

1451 Cf. Ibn 'Asakir, *Tahdhīb*, III, 412.

1452 From "In this year, Ashras b. 'Abdallah as-Sulami raided Farghana ..." cf. *Ibn 'Asakir, *Tahdhīb*, III, 412, l. 23 (Khalifa); *Dh., IV, 226.

In 112, al-Jarrah marched from Bardha'a[1453] to Azerbaijan. He encamped with his army at Marj Sabalan.[1454] There was a river over which he built a bridge. To this day it is called al-Jarrah's Bridge [*Jisr al-Jarrāḥ*].[1455]

Abu Khalid < Abu Bara':
In 112, al-Jarrah marched against the son of the Khaqan, who was besieging the inhabitants of Ardabil. They fought bitterly. Al-Jarrah was killed – may God have mercy on him – on 22 *Ramaḍān* 112/8 December 730, and {356} the Khazars took control of Azerbaijan. Their cavalry roamed about unopposed, [even] getting close to Mosul.[1456] They set up mangonels against Ardabil while the inhabitants of Ardabil were battling them. When the siege against them had lasted too long, they surrendered the city, and the Khazars entered it. They killed the warriors and took the women and children captive.

Abu Khalid < Abu l-Khattab < *a man of the Banu Sulaym:
Al-Jarrah was killed in Arshaq.[1457]

[503] Abu l-Khattab:
When al-Jarrah was killed, Hisham b. 'Abd al-Malik sent Sa'id b. 'Amr al-Harashi with Arab knights riding post-horses. Sa'id b. 'Amr went to Bardha'a.[1458]

Abu l-Khattab < *Abu 'Alqama ath-Thaqafi < a *shaykh* of Homs < *Thubayt al-Bahrani:[1459]
Al-Harashi [and his companions] came to us in Bardha'a riding post-horses. We went with them to al-Baylaqan,[1460] and they went toward Azerbaijan. A Khazar army was advancing. They had many carts on which they were carrying the Muslim prisoners and the booty taken from the inhabitants of Ardabil.

1453 For the phrase "In 112, al-Jarrah marched from Bardha'a" cf. *Dh., IV, 226; *Dh., IV, 238 (Khalifa).
1454 Cf. Minorsky, 66, 202; Dunlop, 69.
1455 From "In 112, al-Jarrah marched from Bardha'a ..." cf. *Futūḥ*, 206.
1456 From "In 112, al-Jarrah marched against the son of the Khaqan ..." cf. IA, V, 159; *Dh., 226; *Dh., IV, 238 (Khalifa).
1457 Cf. *Futūḥ*, 329, l. 13: cf. Yaqut, I, 208.
1458 From "When al-Jarrah was killed ..." cf. Tab., II, 1531; *Ibn 'Asakir, *Tahdhīb*, VI, 163; (*) Dh., IV, 226.
1459 Thubayt was an Arab general who took part in the Khazar wars (cf. Dunlop, 62, citing IA, V, 110; cf. p. 207, above).
1460 EI2, I, 1134.

Thubayt:
Al-Harashi sent me on a scouting mission. I came upon the Khazar camp while they were sleeping, then I departed and informed him [of what I had found]. He roused his men and marched against the Khazars, and rescued the carts and their contents.[1461]

Thubayt:
He sent me to the city of al-Baylaqan. He wrote to Hisham b. ‘Abd al-Malik about the victory, and informed him of the many carts in the region of Warthan, carrying the prisoners and booty. He attacked them at night, and killed all the enemy troops within reach. He brought the carts into the city of Warthan, {357} and wrote to Hisham about the victory. Then he marched and confronted the *ṭāghiya* of the Khazars. God put them to rout, the *ṭāghiya* fled, and al-Harashi rescued the Muslim prisoners and their booty.[1462]

Abu Khalid < Abu Bara’ < *‘Abdallah b. ‘Abdallah al-‘Amiri:
Sa‘id b. ‘Amr al-Harashi confronted the son of the Khaqan, attacked them at night, and killed a great many of them. The *ṭāghiya* of the Khazars fled. [Sa‘id] wrote of the victory to Hisham b. ‘Abd al-Malik.[1463]

[504] Ibn al-Kalbi:
Al-Jarrah and those who were with him were martyred on the steppes of Ardabil. He had designated his brother al-Hajjaj b. ‘Abdallah, as his successor.[1464] [Sa‘id b. ‘Amr] al-Harashi went to them. God put [the enemy] to rout, and rescued what they had [taken].

Ibn al-Kalbi:
In *Shawwāl* 112/December 730–January 731, Maslama b. ‘Abd al-Malik went out in pursuit of the Turks, in driving rain and snow, until he passed al-Bab. He left at-Ta‘i[1465] to rebuild and fortify al-Bab.[1466] He assigned a

1461 From “Al-Harashi [and his companions] …” cf. Tab., II, 1531; cf. IA, V, 160f.; (*) Dh., IV, 226.

1462 From “He sent me to the city of al-Baylaqan …” cf. IA, V, 161f.

1463 From “Sa‘id b. ‘Amr al-Harashi confronted the son of the Khaqan …” cf. *Ibn ‘Asakir, *Tahdhīb*, VI, 163.

1464 From “Al-Jarrah and those who were with him were martyred …” cf. Tab., II, 1530f.

1465 I.e. al-Harith b. ‘Amr al-Ta‘i; cf. note 1396, above.

1466 From “In *Shawwāl* 112/December 730–January 731 …” cf. Tab., II, 1532; IA, V, 162.

detachment for that. Then he sent the armies, and conquered cities and fortresses. The enemies of God burned themselves in their cities.[1467]

In 112 –

Abu Khalid:
'Ubayda b. 'Abd ar-Rahman sent Thabit b. Khaytham of Jordan from Ifriqiya on a raiding expedition to Sicily. He acquired captives and booty, and [returned] safely.[1468]

Ibn al-Kalbi:
Mu'awiya b. Hisham conducted the summer raid. He conquered Kharshana,[1469] in the vicinity of Malatya.[1470]

Ibrahim b. Isma'il al-Makhzumi led the pilgrimage.

In this year, the following died: Raja' b. Haywa,[1471] [and] 'Abd ar-Rahman b. Abi Sa'id al-Khudri.[1472]

{358}[505] The Year 113/731–732

In this year, al-Junayd b. 'Abd ar-Rahman, of the Murra of the Ghatafan, went out on a raiding expedition, and headed for Tukharistan. The Turks took up arms in Samarqand. Al-Junayd marched until he was four parasangs from Samarqand, when he was confronted by the Khaqan. They fought bitterly until nightfall, and then separated. Al-Junayd wrote to Sawra b. Abjar, of the Banu Aban b. Darim, who was his lieutenant in Samarqand, and ordered him to come to him. So he went, but was confronted by the Turks before he reached al-Junayd, and Sawra b. Abjar and most of his army were killed. Among the dead was Mujahid b. Bal'a' al-'Anbari. Then

1467 From "In *Shawwāl* 112/December 730–January 731 …" cf. *Dh., IV, 226; *Dh., IV, 302f. From "He assigned a detachment for that …" cf. Tab., II, 1560.

1468 From "'Ubayda b. 'Abd ar-Rahman sent Thabit …" cf. (*) Dh., IV, 226; al-Maqrizi, in Amari, 662.

1469 *Tò Kharsianòn kástron*, in Cappadocia (cf. Wellhausen, "Die Kämpfe der Araber," 443, A.M. 6222; cf. Ramsay, 343; cf. EI, III, 271a, s.v. Mar'ash; cf. Honigmann, index, s.v. Charsianon Festung; cf. Minorsky, 420f.).

1470 From "Mu'awiya b. Hisham conducted the summer raid …" cf. Tab., II, 1530; *Dh., IV, 227.

1471 On the death #Ibn 'Asakir, *Tahdhīb*, V, 315 (Khalifa); #Ibn Hajar, III, 266 (Khalifa). *Ṭbq.*, 793; Ibn 'Asakir, *Tahdhīb*, V, 312; Ibn Hajar, III, 265; cf. Shaban, *Islamic History*, and *'Abbasid Revolution*, index.

1472 *Ṭbq.*, 633; Ibn Sa'd, V, 267; Ibn Hajar, VI, 183.

al-Junayd confronted [the Turks], God put them to rout, and al-Junayd entered Samarqand.[1473]

In 113, Hisham appointed his brother, Maslama, governor over Armenia and Azerbaijan. Sa'id b. 'Amr al-Harashi was dismissed. Maslama appointed 'Abd al-Malik b. Muslim [as his lieutenant], and marched off. He apprehended Sa'id b. 'Amr [al-Harashi], put him in fetters, and threw him in prison.[1474] But Hisham sent [orders for his release], so he released him.[1475]

Abu Khalid < Abu Bara':
Maslama marched against Hayzan, and sought the peaceful surrender of the inhabitants, but they refused, so he battled them. Then they asked him for [a declaration of] safety [for themselves]. He swore that he would not kill a man and would not kill a dog. So they came down [from their positions]. He put them all to death except for one man and one dog, and took over the fortress. Then he marched to the land of S-w-rān,[1476] whose king sought to make peace with him. He made a peaceful settlement with them.[1477] He also made peaceful settlements with the people of Masqat[1478] and the people of Lakz.[1479] Then Maslama confronted the Khaqan, and they fought bitterly. Then Maslama departed, [506] and went to Ghazala, where he was surrounded by the Khazar armies. They fought bitterly. God put the Khazars to rout, and the Khaqan fled.

{359} Abu Khalid < Abu l-Khattab:
When Maslama advanced, the Khazars returned to him. Maslama was unaware of this until they came upon him. He battled them until night separated them. The Muslims spent the night awake, while the Khazars departed. Maslama returned [home], and designated Marwan b. Muhammad to take his place. All that was in 113.

Abu Khalid:
In 113, 'Ubayda b. 'Abd ar-Rahman sent 'Abd al-Malik b. Qatan from

1473 From "In this year, al-Junayd b. 'Abd ar-Rahman, of the Murra of the Ghatafan, went out ..." cf. Tab., II, 1532–1544 (al-Mada'ini); *Ibn 'Asakir, *Tahdhīb*, III, 412, l. 25 (Khalifa); *Dh., IV, 227.

1474 Cf. Dunlop, 74f.

1475 From "In 113, Hisham appointed his brother ..." cf. *Futūḥ*, 206f.; cf. al-Ya'qubi, II, 381 (*) Dh., IV, 227.

1476 Cf. Minorsky, 454f. – *S-w-r*.

1477 From "Maslama marched against Hayzan ..." cf. *Dh., IV, 227.

1478 Cf. Minorsky, 454–456; cf. EI, III, 393, s.v. Maskat, #3.

1479 Kh.: *'-l-k-r*. Cf. Minorsky, 454f. and index, s.v. Lakz; cf. Dunlop, 85.

Ifriqiya on a raiding expedition. He went to Sicily, where he acquired booty, and [returned] safely.

In this year, he also sent Abu ʻImran al-Hudhali on a raiding expedition. He took booty and [returned] safely.

Sulayman b. Hisham b. ʻAbd al-Malik led the pilgrimage.

In 113, the following died: Makhul ash-Sha'mi, in Syria; Talha b. Musarrif al-Iyami, in Kufa; Yusuf b. Mahak,[1480] in Mecca; ʻAbdallah b. ʻUbayd b. ʻUmayr,[1481] in Mecca; Haram b. Saʻd b. Muhaysa.[1482]

*Someone < *al-Walid b. Muslim[1483] < ʻAbd ar-Rahman b. Yazid b. Jabir:[1484]
Makhul died in 113.

[507] The Year 114/732–733

In this year, Hisham b. ʻAbd al-Malik dismissed Maslama b. ʻAbd al-Malik from the governorship of Armenia, Azerbaijan, and al-Jazira, and appointed Marwan b. Muhammad b. Marwan at the beginning of *al-Muḥarram* 114/ March 732.[1485]

Abu Khalid < Abu l-Bara':
In 114, Marwan marched until he crossed the river ʻ-l-r-m.[1486] He killed [many] and took captives. He conducted a raid against the Slavs.[1487]

Abu Khalid:
In this year, ʻUbayda b. ʻAbd ar-Rahman sent ʻAbd {360} al-Malik[1488] b. Qatan from Ifriqiya on a raiding expedition to Sicily. He acquired booty

1480 On the death of Yusuf b. Mahak cf. #Ibn Hajar, XI, 421 (Khalifa). *Ṭbq.*, 704; Ibn Saʻd, V, 470; Ibn Hajar, XI, 421.

1481 *Ṭbq.*, 705; Ibn Saʻd, V, 474; Ibn Hajar, V, 308.

1482 *Ṭbq.*, 626; Ibn Saʻd, V, 258; Ibn Hajar, II, 223.

1483 D. 194/809–810 (GAS, I, 293).

1484 D. 153/770 (*Ṭbq.*, 801, and 808; Ibn Saʻd, VII, 466; Ibn Hajar, VI, 297).

1485 From "In this year, Hisham b. ʻAbd al-Malik dismissed Maslama ..." cf. *Dh, IV, 228.

1486 Unidentified: cf. Kh., 480. Adh-Dhahabi (< Khalifa), has Nahr ar-Rum in one instance (Dh., V, 298), and Nahr *az-Z-m* in another (Dh., IV, 228); cf. Dunlop, 83f. and Dunlop, *Arab Civilization*, 93 n. 151.

1487 From "In 114, Marwan marched until he crossed the river ʻ-l-r-m ..." cf. *Azdi, 34; *Dh., IV, 228; *Dh., V, 298 (Khalifa).

1488 Kh.: ʻAbdallah; cf. al-Maqrizi (Amari, 662), and Kh., 506.

and [returned] safely. He also sent 'Abdallah b. Ziyad al-Ansari on a raiding expedition to Sardinia. He acquired booty and [returned] safely.[1489]

Al-Junayd b. 'Abd ar-Rahman raided as-Saghaniyan, meeting no resistance, then departed.[1490]

Ibn al-Kalbi:
Mu'awiya b. Hisham conducted a raiding expedition in the land of the Byzantines. 'Abdallah al-Battal confronted Constantine with an army. God put the enemy to rout, and Constantine[1491] was taken prisoner.[1492]

[508] Sulayman b. Hisham conducted a raiding expedition in the land of the Byzantines, in territory near al-Jazira, until he reached Caesarea.[1493]

Khalid b. 'Abd al-Malik b. al-Harith b. al-Hakam b. Abi l-'As led the pilgrimage.

In 114, al-Hakam b. 'Utayba[1494] died.

[509] The Year 115/733–734

In this year, al-Harith b. Surayj[1495] revolted, taking control of al-Juzajan[1496] and Marw. Hisham b. 'Abd al-Malik sent 'Asim b. 'Abdallah b. Yazid al-Hilali, who confronted al-Harith b. Surayj. They fought bitterly, then made peace on the condition that al-Harith b. Surayj remain in Balkh, and that he and 'Asim would each send a representative to Hisham.[1497] Khalid [b. 'Abdallah al-Qasri] sent his brother, Asad b. 'Abdallah as governor over Khurasan, and dismissed 'Asim. Al-Harith crossed the river of Balkh, and Asad marched [against him]. They met [in battle], and al-Harith was put to rout and fled to the Turks. Asad b. 'Abdallah apprehended some of

1489 From "In this year, 'Ubayda b. 'Abd ar-Rahman sent 'Abd {360} al-Malik …" cf. Al-Maqrizi, in Amari, 662.

1490 This sentence parallels *Dh., IV, 228.

1491 Possibly Constantine V Copronymous (cf. Wellhausen, "Die Kämpfe der Araber," 444, A.M. 6229; M. Canard in EI2, I, 1103a, s.v. al-Battal).

1492 From "Mu'awiya b. Hisham conducted a raiding expedition …" cf. al-Ya'qubi, II, 395; Tab., II, 1561; (*) Dh., IV, 228 (Khalifa).

1493 This sentence parallels Tab., II, 1561.

1494 *Tbq.*, 376; *Jarh*, I, II, 123; Ibn Hajar, II, 432.

1495 Kh.: al-Harith b. Shurayh (throughout the text); al-Jahiz, I, 199, Ibn Hazm, 231, and *Ta'rīkh al-khulafā'*: Shurayh. On al-Harith b. Surayj, see EI2, III, 223.

1496 EI2, IV, 608, s.v. Dhuzdjan.

1497 From "In this year, al-Harith b. Surayj revolted …" cf. *Ibn 'Asakir, *Tahdhīb*, VII, 124, l. 15.

his companions, killed some of them, and cut off the hands and feet of others.[1498]

{361} Mu'awiya b. Hisham conducted a raiding expedition in *Ramaḍān*/October–November 733, and went as far as [510] Paphlagonia.[1499]

Abu Khalid:
In 115, 'Ubayda b. 'Abd ar-Rahman sent Bakr b. Suwayd from Ifriqiya on a raiding expedition. He reached Sicily and _____.[1500] He was confronted by the Byzantines, who bombarded his ships with [Greek] fire.[1501]

Muhammad b. Hisham b. Isma'il led the pilgrimage.

In 115, 'Ata' b. Abi Rabah[1502] died. Some say he died in 116/734–735.

[511] The Year 116/734–735

In this year, Hisham b. 'Abd al-Malik wrote to his governor in Egypt, 'Ubaydallah[1503] b. al-Habhab, a *mawlā* of the Banu Salul, appointing him governor over Ifriqiya. He went there in 116. 'Abd al-A'la b. Hudayj,[1504] a Sufrite and a *mawlā* of Musa b. Nusayr, revolted in Tangier. 'Amr b. 'Abdallah al-'Absi, one of Ibn al-Habhab's governors, went out against him, but was killed, and his companions were routed.[1505]

Ibn al-Habhab sent 'Abd ar-Rahman b. Habib b. Abi 'Ubayda b. 'Uqba b. Nafi' on a raiding expedition to as-Sus and Sudan. He conquered [many places], and acquired much gold.[1506]

1498 From "In this year, al-Harith b. Surayj revolted ..." cf. Tab., II, 1565–1591 (al-Mada'ini); (*) Dh., IV, 228.
1499 Kh.: Aflajuniya. Cf. Wellhausen, "Die Kämpfe der Araber," 444, A.M. 6224; Bury, II, 405 n. 1; Minorsky, 420.
1500 Z: *D-w-b-'-n-h*; U: *D-r-b-'-n-h*. Al-Maqrizi's version of this account, although otherwise corresponding to Khalifa's word for word, lacks *D-w/r-b-'-n-h*.
1501 From "In 115, 'Ubayda b. 'Abd ar-Rahman sent Bakr ..." cf al-Maqrizi, in Amari, 662. On Greek fire, cf. Gibbon, VI, 10–13; Bury, II, 319.
1502 EI2, I, 730; GAS, I, 31.
1503 Khalifa sometimes records his name as 'Ubayda, and sometimes as 'Ubaydallah. Cf. Dh., V, 273; IAH, index; al-Kindi, 73–76, 341, 342; al-Ya'qubi, II, 382; all of which have 'Ubaydallah.
1504 IAH, 218, l. 3: 'Abd al-A'la b. Jurayj.
1505 From "In this year, Hisham b. 'Abd al-Malik wrote to his governor ..." cf. Kh., 525 (368); cf. IAH, 217f.; *Azdi, 36 (Khalifa); *Dh., IV, 229.
1506 From "Ibn al-Habhab sent 'Abd ar-Rahman ..." cf. IAH, 217; *Futūḥ*, 231f.; *Azdi, 36; IA, V, 185; *Dh., IV, 229.

{362} In this year, Ibn al-Habhab also sent ‘Uthman b. Abi ‘Ubayda on a raiding expedition. He raided a part of Sicily, then set out for home. He was confronted at sea by Byzantine ships, and God put them to rout. [However,] they killed some of the Muslims, and captured the two sons of ‘Uthman [b. Abi ‘Ubayda], ‘Amr and Abu r-Rabi‘ Sulayman, as well as ‘Abd ar-Rahman b. Ziyad b. An‘am[1507] and his brother, al-Mughira b. Ziyad. They remained in the hands of the Byzantines until ‘Abd ar-Rahman b. Habib became governor and ransomed his two paternal cousins and other Muslim captives, including ‘Abd ar-Rahman b. Ziyad, in 121/738–739.[1508]

[512] Al-Walid b. Yazid b. ‘Abd al-Malik led the pilgrimage. Some say that ‘Isa b. Miqsam, a *mawlā* of al-Walid, led the pilgrimage, at al-Walid’s behest.

In this year, Maymun b. Mihran[1509] died in al-Jazira.[1510]

[513] The Year 117/735–736

In this year, the Turks took up arms in Khurasan. Al-Harith b. Surayj was with them. The Khaqan, accompanied by al-Harith, went to al-Juzjan. The Turks carried out raids, ultimately reaching Marw ar-Rudh.[1511]

*Someone < *Abu dh-Dhayyal:
Asad b. ‘Abdallah marched against them and engaged them in battle. God put them to rout, and the Muslims slaughtered them.[1512]

Abu Khalid < Abu Bara’:
Marwan b. Muhammad, who was governor over Armenia and Azerbaijan, sent two detachments to Jabal al-Qabq.[1513] One of the detachments conquered three fortresses of the Alans. The other attacked the Tuman Shah, who surrendered to Marwan b. Muhammad. Marwan sent him to

1507 *Ṭbq.*, 762; *Jarḥ*, II, II, 234; *Riyād an-Nufūs*, 96; Ibn Hajar, VI, 173 (d. c. 156/772–773).
1508 From “In this year, Ibn al-Habhab also sent ‘Uthman …” cf. *Azdi, 36f.; IA, V, 185; (*) Dh., IV, 229.
1509 *Ṭbq.*, 820; al-Azdi, 37; Ibn Hajar, X, 390.
1510 This sentence parallels #Ibn Hajar, X, 392 (Khalifa).
1511 From “In this year, the Turks took up arms …” cf. *Azdi, 37; *Ibn ‘Asakir, *Tahdhīb*, II, 460, l. 2 (Khalifa); *Dh., IV, 229.
1512 From “Asad b. ‘Abdallah marched …” cf. *Azdi, 38 (Khalifa); *Ibn ‘Asakir, *Tahdhīb*, II, 460; (*) Dh., IV, 229.
1513 The Caucasus (cf. C. Bosworth in EI2, IV, s.v. Kabk).

Hisham b. 'Abd al-Malik, who returned him to Marwan, and Marwan returned him to his kingdom.[1514]

[514] Abu Khalid:
'Ubayda b. al-Habhab sent Habib b. Abu 'Ubayda on a raiding expedition. He raided a village in Sardinia, slaughtering many, and taking many captives.[1515]

Ibn al-Kalbi:
In this year, Mu'awiya b. Hisham conducted a raiding expedition in the land of the Byzantines.[1516] He reached {363} S-y-b-r-h.[1517] His troops reached S-r-d-h,[1518] and they took prisoners.

Khalid b. 'Abd al-Malik b. al-Harith b. al-Hakam led the pilgrimage.

In 117, the following died: 'Abd ar-Rahman b. Hurmuz al-A'raj,[1519] a *mawlā* of Rabi'a b. al-Harith b. 'Abd al-Muttalib; Sa'id b. Yasar,[1520] a *mawlā* of al-Hasan b. 'Ali; Muhammad b. Ka'b al-Qurazi;[1521] 'A'isha bint Sa'd b. Malik;[1522] Sukayna bint al-Husayn b. 'Ali;[1523] – all [of the preceding] in Medina – [and] Qatada b. Di'ama, in Wasit.

In this year, Mu'adh b. Mu'adh[1524] was born.

[515] The Year 118/736–737

In this year, Marwan b. Muhammad went on a raiding expedition from Armenia, and entered the land of Wartanis, from three points. Wartanis fled to the Khazars, abandoning his citadel. Marwan set up mangonels against [the citadel]. The inhabitants of Kh-m-r-y-n[1525] killed Wartanis and

1514 From "Marwan b. Muhammad, who was governor …" cf. *Futūḥ*, 208; Tab., II, 1573; *Azdi, 38 (Khalifa); (*) Dh., IV, 229.

1515 From "'Ubayda b. al-Habhab sent …" cf. *Azdi, 38; IA, V, 191; (*) Dh., IV, 229.

1516 This sentence parallels Tab., II, 1573.

1517 Perhaps Sibora, or Sipylos. Cf. Kh., 478, and note 1318.

1518 Perhaps Sardes (cf. Ramsay, index, s.v. Sardis).

1519 *Ṭbq*., 600; Ibn Sa'd, V, 283; Ibn Hajar, VI, 290.

1520 *Ṭbq*., 638; Ibn Sa'd, V, 284; Ibn Hajar, IV, 102.

1521 On the death of Muhammad b. Ka'b al-Qurazi cf. #Dh., IV, 201 (Khalifa). *Ṭbq*., 661; *Jarḥ*, IV, I, 67; Ibn al-Athir, *al-Lubāb*, II, 254; Ibn Hajar, IX, 420.

1522 Ibn Hajar, XII, 436.

1523 EI, IV, 508.

1524 D. 196/811–812 (*Ṭbq*., 544; Ibn Sa'd, VII, 293; Ibn Hajar, X, 194).

1525 Perhaps this should be read Hamzin (cf. Dunlop, 63 and n. 30, 64, 77; cf. Minorsky, 448f.; cf. note 1140, first part).

sent his head to Marwan, who set it up within sight of the inhabitants of the citadel. [The inhabitants] surrendered to Marwan, and he put their warriors to death, and took captive the women and children.[1526]

Abu Khalid:
Ibn al-Habhab sent Qutham b. 'Awana al-Kalbi on a raiding expedition. He attacked '-w-l-y-h in Sicily. [The inhabitants] surrounded him, then let him go.

Mu'awiya b. Hisham conducted a raiding expedition in the land of the Byzantines.

Muhammad b. Hisham b. Isma'il led the pilgrimage.

In 118, the following died: Abu Ja'far Muhammad b. 'Ali b. Husayn b. 'Ali b. Abi Talib,[1527] in Medina; 'Ali b. 'Abdallah b. 'Abbas,[1528] in Syria; [516] 'Abd ar-Rahman b. Sabit al-Jumahi,[1529] in Mecca; 'Amr b. Shu'ayb b. Muhammad b. 'Abdallah b. 'Amr b. al-'As,[1530] in at-Ta'if; 'Abdallah b. Abi Mulayka,[1531] in Mecca; 'Ubada {364} b. Nusayy,[1532] in Syria; 'Amr b. Murra al-Jamali,[1533] in Kufa.

In this year, Muhammad b. 'Abdallah al-Ansari[1534] was born.

[517] The Year 119/737

In this year, Marwan b. Muhammad conducted a raiding expedition, roaming [far] in Armenia. He entered from Bab al-Lan, and passed all the way through the land of the Alans until he left it [and entered] the land of the Khazars. He passed Balanjar and Samandar,[1535] and reached al-Bayda', where the Khaqan was. The Khaqan fled.[1536]

1526 From "In this year, Marwan b. Muhammad went on a raiding expedition ..." cf. IA, V, 198; (*) Dh., IV, 230.
1527 EI, III, 670.
1528 EI2, I, 381
1529 *Ṭbq.*, 704; Ibn Sa'd, V, 472; Ibn Hajar, VI, 180.
1530 On the death of 'Amr b. Shu'ayb b. Muhammad b. 'Abdallah b. 'Amr b. al-'As cf. #Ibn Hajar, VIII, 51 (Khalifa). *Ṭbq.*, 726; *Jarḥ*, III, I, 238; Ibn Hajar, VIII, 48.
1531 See note 513.
1532 *Ṭbq.*, 794; Ibn Sa'd, VII, 456; Ibn 'Asakir, VII, 214; Ibn Hajar, V, 113.
1533 *Ṭbq.*, 377; Ibn Sa'd, VI, 315; Ibn Hajar, VIII, 102.
1534 D. 215/830–831 (*Ṭbq.*, 545; Ibn Sa'd, VII, 294; Ibn Hajar, IX, 274).
1535 Cf. Minorsky, 162, 452, 454; Dunlop, index, s.v.
1536 From "In this year, Marwan b. Muhammad conducted a raiding expedition ..." cf. *Azdi, 39f.; IA, V, 215; *Dh., IV, 230.

Ibn al-Habhab sent Qutham b. 'Awana on a raiding expedition. He raided a fortress in Sardinia, in the Maghrib. Qutham was drowned, and some of the Muslims' ships sank, while some [returned] safely.[1537]

Mu'awiya b. Hisham conducted a raiding expedition in the land of the Byzantines. He reached B-l-w-n-y-h.[1538] Sulayman b. Hisham also conducted a raiding expedition in the land of the Byzantines, from al-Jazira.

'Abd al-Malik b. Marwan b. Muhammad killed Hazar Tarkhan[1539] and many of his companions in Armenia.[1540]

Abu Shakir Maslama b. Hisham b. 'Abd al-Malik led the pilgrimage.

In 119, the following died: Sulayman b. Musa,[1541] in Syria; Abu Ma'shar,[1542] in Kufa; [518] Habib b. Abi Thabit,[1543] in Kufa; Qays b. Sa'd,[1544] in Mecca; Iyas b. Salama b. al-Akwa',[1545] in Medina; 'Abd ar-Rahman b. Sa'id, b. Yarbu', in Medina; 'Abdallah b. Waqid b. 'Abdallah b. 'Umar b. al-Khattab.[1546]

[519] The Year 120/727–728

In this year, Hisham b. 'Abd al-Malik dismissed Khalid b. 'Abdallah al-Qasri from the governorship of Iraq, and appointed Yusuf b. 'Umar [ath-Thaqafi].

{365} Muhammad b. Hisham b. Isma'il led the pilgrimage.

Maslama b. Hisham raided the land of the Byzantines.

In 120, the following died: al-Jarud b. Abi Sabra al-Hudhali,[1547] in Basra; 'Asim b. 'Umar b. Qatada al-Ansari,[1548] in Medina; Abu Bakr b. Muhammad

1537 From "Ibn al-Habhab sent Qutham b. 'Awana on a raiding expedition …" cf. (*) Dh., IV, 230.

1538 Cf. Apollonia, the name of several places (cf. Ramsay, index). Cf also, Balaneos (Baniyas), Honigmann, index.

1539 Cf. Dunlop, 83, 191.

1540 This sentence parallels *Azdi, 40.

1541 On the death of Sulayman b. Musa cf. #Ibn Hajar, IV, 227 (Khalifa). *Ṭbq.*, 799; Ibn Sa'd, VII, 457; Ibn 'Asakir, *Tahdhīb*, VI, 284; Ibn Hajar, IV, 226.

1542 *Ṭbq.*, 372; Ibn Sa'd, VI, 330; Ibn Hajar, III, 382.

1543 *Ṭbq.*, 369; Ibn Sa'd, VI, 320; Ibn Hajar, II, 178.

1544 *Ṭbq.*, 706; Ibn Sa'd, V, 483; Ibn Hajar, VIII, 397.

1545 *Ṭbq.*, 621, 660; Ibn Sa'd, V, 248; Ibn Hajar, I, 388.

1546 *Ṭbq.*, 641, 827; *Jarḥ*, II, II, 190; Ibn Hajar, VI, 65.

1547 *Ṭbq.*, 508; *Jarḥ*, II, II, 190; Ibn Hajar, VI, 65.

1548 GAS, I, 279.

b. ‘Amr b. Hazm, in Medina; Hammad b. Abi Sulayman,[1549] in Kufa; ‘Adi b. ‘Adi, in al-Jazira; Asad b. ‘Abdallah, in Khurasan;[1550] Maslama b. ‘Abd al-Malik b. Marwan,[1551] on Wednesday in *al-Muḥarram*/December 737–January 738, in Syria; Abu Qays ‘Amr b. Muslim al-Bahili;[1552] Muhammad b. ‘Abd ar-Rahman b. al-Harith al-______.[1553]

[520] In this year, Yahya b. Sa‘id al-Qattan[1554] was born.

Abu Khalid:
There were no raiding expeditions in Ifriqiya in 120.

Sulayman b. Hisham led the summer raid.

Hisham b. ‘Urwa went to Basra during the governorship of Khalid b. ‘Abdallah al-Qasri.

*Al-Walid b. Hisham < his father < his grandfather; *‘Abdallah b. Mughira < his father; *Abu l-Yaqzan ‘Amir b. Hafs; and others:
[The administration of] Iraq was consolidated under the governorship of Khalid b. ‘Abdallah b. Yazid b. Asad b. Kurz al-Bajali in 106/724–725. He was dismissed in 120.

Chief[s] of Police:

{366} Wasi: ‘Amr b. ‘Abd al-A‘la al-Hakami.

Kufa: Al-‘Uryan b. al-Haytham an-Nakha‘i.[1555]

Basra: Malik b. al-Mundhir b. al-Jarud al-‘Abdi, who was later dismissed.

Bilal b. Abi Burda b. Abi Musa al-Ash‘ari[1556] was then appointed, and later served also as prayer leader and judge.

Khalid’s Secretary for Correspondence:

Dawud b. Sa‘id al-Katib.

1549 GAS, I, 404.

1550 On the death of “Asad b. ‘Abdallah, in Khurasan” cf. *Ibn ‘Asakir, *Tahdhīb*, II, 463 (Khalifa); *Dh., IV, 232 (Khalifa); *Ibn Hajar, I, 260 (Khalifa).

1551 On the death of Maslama b. ‘Abd al-Malik b. Marwan cf. *Dh., IV, 303 (Khalifa); *Ibn Hajar, X, 144 (Khalifa).

1552 Cf. Ibn Hajar, VIII, 105.

1553 Z: at-Taymi; U: al-Laythi; (cf. manuscript marginal annotation, X, 519 n. 1).

1554 D. 198/813–814 (*Ṭbq.*, 542; Ibn Sa‘d, VII, 293; *Ma‘ārif*, 514; Ibn Hajar, XI, 216; cf. GAS, I, index).

1555 *Ṭbq.*, 336; *Jarḥ*, III, I, 233; Ibn Hajar, VII, 190.

1556 Ibn Hajar, I, 500; cf. EI2, I, 694a.

Finance Secretary:
Al-Hajjaj b. 'Umayr.

[521] [Secretary] in charge of _____[?]:[1557]
Harun b. Mayyas, a *mawlā* of the Banu Layth.

Khalid was killed in 126/743–744 at the age of about 60.

During the governorship of Khalid b. 'Abdallah over Iraq, which lasted about 14 years, the following died: Nu'aym b. Abi Hind,[1558] at the beginning of Khalid's governorship; Shimr b. 'Atiyya,[1559] at the beginning of [his governorship]; 'Abd ar-Rahman b. al-Isbahani;[1560] al-'Ayzar b. Hurayth;[1561] Abu s-Safar;[1562] – all [of the last three] in the middle of [his governorship]; Humayd b. Hilal al-'Adawi;[1563] Anas b. Sirin;[1564] al-Azraq b. Qays;[1565] [522] 'Ammar b. Abi 'Ammar,[1566] a *mawlā* of the Banu Hashim, in the middle of Khalid's governorship; Muharib b. Dithar adh-Dhuhli;[1567] al-Qasim b. 'Abd ar-Rahman b. 'Abdallah b. Mas'ud;[1568] Wabara b. 'Abd ar-Rahman;[1569] 'Abd al-Malik b. Maysara;[1570] Abu 'Awn ath-Thaqafi;[1571] 'Adi b. Thabit;[1572]

1557 Z: *'alā t-tajwīz*; U: *'alā t-tajwīn. Tajwīn* does not seem to have any applicable meaning. The verb *jawwaza* can mean "to make, declare, anything lawful," "to execute [a design]," "to give currency to money" (these definitions are from Hava's dictionary). Perhaps it means mint master.

1558 *Ṭbq.*, 359; Ibn Sa'd, VI, 306; Ibn Hajar, X, 468.

1559 Ibn Hajar, IV, 364.

1560 *Ṭbq.*, 361, 378; Ibn Hajar, VI, 217.

1561 *Ṭbq.*, 360; Ibn Sa'd, VI, VIII, 203.

1562 Sa'id b. Yuhmid (*Ṭbq.*, 374; Ibn Sa'd, VI, 299; Ibn Hajar, IV, 96).

1563 *Ṭbq.*, 509; Ibn Sa'd, VII, 231; Ibn Hajar, III, 51.

1564 *Ṭbq.*, 513; Ibn Sa'd, VII, 207; Ibn Hajar, I, 374.

1565 *Ṭbq.*, 514; Ibn Sa'd, VII, 235; Ibn Hajar, I, 200.

1566 See note 511.

1567 On the death of Muharib b. Dithar adh-Dhuhli cf. #Ibn Hajar, X, 50 (Khalifa). *Ṭbq.*, 372; Ibn Sa'd, VI, 307; Ibn Hajar, X, 49.

1568 On the death of al-Qasim b. 'Abd ar-Rahman b. 'Abdallah b. Mas'ud cf. *Ibn Hajar, VIII, 322 (Khalifa).

1569 On the death of Wabara b. 'Abd ar-Rahman cf. *Ibn Hajar, XI, 111 (Khalifa). *Ṭbq.*, 368; Ibn Sa'd, VI, 312; Ibn Hajar, XI, 111.

1570 *Ṭbq.*, 368; Ibn Sa'd, VI, 319; Ibn Hajar, VI, 426.

1571 *Ṭbq.*, 368; Ibn Sa'd, VI, 312; Ibn Hajar, IX, 322 (Muhammad b. 'Ubaydallah).

1572 *Ṭbq.*, 373; Ibn Sa'd, VI, 308; Ibn Hajar, VII, 165.

'Alqama b. Marthad;[1573] 'Awn b. Abi Juhayfa,[1574] at the end of Khalid's governorship;[1575] 'Atiyya b. Sa'd al-'Awfi.[1576]

{367}[523] The Year 121/738–739

In this year, Marwan b. Muhammad conducted a raiding expedition in Armenia while he was governor. He came to the fortress of Bayt as-Sarir,[1577] killing [many] and taking captives. Then he came to a second fortress, and killed [many] and took captives. Then he entered Ghumiq,[1578] a fortress which was the residence of the king of as-Sarir. The king fled to a fortress called Kh-th-r-j,[1579] in which was a throne of gold. Marwan remained there winter and summer, [besieging them]. He made peace with [the king] against payment of 1,000 head every year, as well as 10,000 *modii*[1580] [of grain]. Marwan marched on, and entered the land of Tuman. Tuman, the king, made peace with him. Marwan marched on and entered the land of Zirikaran,[1581] whose king made peace with him. Then Marwan came to Kh-m-r-y-n, but its king refused to make peace with him. [Marwan] battled [the inhabitants of] one of the fortresses of Kh-m-r-y-n for a month. He laid the land of Kh-m-r-y-n in ruins. Then [the inhabitants of] Kh-m-r-y-n asked him to make peace, which he did. Then Marwan came to the land of M-s-d-'-r,[1582] which he conquered [524] by peace agreement. Then Marwan

1573 On the death of 'Alqama b. Marthad cf. #Ibn Hajar, VII, 279 (Khalifa). *Ṭbq.*, 378 Ibn Sa'd, VI, 331; Ibn Hajar, 278.

1574 *Ṭbq.*, 367, Ibn Sa'd, VI, 319; Ibn Hajar, VIII, 170.

1575 On the death notice "'Awn b. Abi Juhayfa, at the end of Khalid's governorship" cf. #Ibn Hajar, VIII, 170 (Khalifa).

1576 GAS, I, 30.

1577 Cf. Minorsky, 447ff., and index, s.v. Sarir; Dunlop, 95f and index; EI2, IV, 343a, s.v. Kabk.

1578 Kh.: *Gh-w-m-s-k*; cf. Qumiq, Minorsky, 450 and n. 2.

1579 Cf. Minorsky, 448 (*H-m-r-j*, *H-y-r-j*, *Kh-n-d-kh*, *Kh-n-z-kh*).

1580 The Arabic is *mudā* (from Latin *modius*).

1581 Z: *Z-r-w-b-k-r-'-n*; U: *Z-r-w-b-k-z-'-n*; cf. *Futūḥ*, 206: Zirikaran. Cf. also Zirigaran, Zirihgaran, Zirihkaran (Minorsky, 450; Dunlop, 257 n. 122. Bosworth, in EI2, IV, 343a, s.v. Kabk, identifies Zirihkaran with Kubači; cf. *Murūj*, II, 40f., and 443).

1582 Cf. *Futūḥ*, 208; al-Bal'ami, IV, 292: Sandan. It is unidentified.

encamped at Kiran.[1583] [The people of] Tabarsaran[1584] and Filan[1585] made peace with him.[1586]

In 121, Maslama b. Hisham[1587] led the summer raid, and reached Malatya.[1588]

There was no raiding in Ifriqiya.

Muhammad b. Hisham b. Isma'il led the pilgrimage.

In this year, al-Battal was killed in the land of the Byzantines.[1589]

{368} In 121, the following died: Muhammad b. Ibrahim at-Taymi;[1590] Muhammad b. Yahya b. Habban al-Ansari;[1591] 'Amir b. 'Abdallah b. az-Zubayr.[1592]

In this year, Abu 'Asim ad-Dahhak b. Makhlad[1593] was born.[1594]

[525] The Year 122/739–740

Abu Khalid:

In this year, 'Abd al-A'la b. Hudayj, a Sufrite and *mawlā* of Musa b. Nusayr, revolted in Tangier in the Maghrib. 'Amr b. 'Abdallah al-'Absi, Ibn al-Habhab's deputy, went out against him. 'Amr was killed, and his men were put to rout. 'Abd al-A'la killed them, and took their women captive.[1595]

1583 Cf. *L-y-zān*, in Minorsky, 144, 402, 404, 406–410. Cf. BGA, I, index, s.v. *L-y-ran*; cf. BGA, VI, 124: Bab Liranshah.

1584 Kh.: *Ṭ-b-r-s-t-'-n*. Cf. Minorsky, 450; cf. Dunlop, 21 (a translation of al-Ya'qubi, II, 204f.); cf. Bosworth, in EI2, IV, 343a, s.v. Kabk.

1585 Cf. note 1313.

1586 From "In this year, Marwan b. Muhammad conducted a raiding expedition …" cf. *Futūḥ*, 208f.; cf. al-Ya'qubi, II, 381f.; cf. Tab., II, 1667; *Azdi, 42f.; IA, V, 240; *Dh., V, 26.

1587 Kh.: "Maslama b. 'Abd al-Malik … accompanied by Hisham." Cf. the parallel accounts.

1588 This sentence parallels al-Ya'qubi, II, 395; cf. Tab., II, 1667; *Dh., V, 26.

1589 This sentence parallels Tab., II, 1716; *Azdi, 43; *Dh., IV, 273 (Khalifa); *Dh., V, 26 (Khalifa); *Ibn Kathir, IX, 334 (Khalifa); *Ibn Taghribirdi, I, 286 (Khalifa).

1590 On the death of Muhammad b. Ibrahim at-Taymi cf. #Ibn Hajar, IX, 6 (Khalifa); #an-Nawawi, I, I, 77 (Khalifa). *Ṭbq.*, 639, *Jarḥ*, III, II, 184; Ibn Hajar, IX, 5.

1591 *Ṭbq.*, 644; *Jarḥ*, IV, I, 122; Ibn Hajar, IX, 509. (Kh.: Hayyan).

1592 *Ṭbq.*, 648; *Jarḥ*, III, I, 325; Ibn Hajar, V, 74; cf. Kh., 532.

1593 D. *Dhū l-Ḥijja* 212/February–March 828 (*Ṭbq.*, 545; Ibn Sa'd, VII, 295; Ibn 'Asakir, VII, 24; Ibn Hajar, IV, 450; cf. GAS, I, index).

1594 This sentence parallels *Ibn 'Asakir, *Tahdhīb*, VII, 25 (Khalifa).

1595 From "In this year, 'Abd al-A'la b. Hudayj, a Sufrite …" cf. Kh., 511 (361); (*) Dh., V, 27.

Maysara b. al-Haqir, who had been a water-seller in Kairouan, also revolted in this year.[1596] The revolts of the two [i.e., 'Abd al-A'la and Maysara] were at a prearranged time, in the middle of *Ramaḍān* 122/August 740. Isma'il b. 'Ubaydallah b. al-Habhab sent an army against Maysara al-Haqir and his companions, and he put them to rout. Then Maysara al-Haqir attacked the camp of Isma'il b. 'Ubaydallah at night, killing [many] and taking captives. Then he sent a general against al-Haqir, and he killed 'Abd al-A'la b. Hudayj.[1597] When ['Ubaydallah] b. al-Habhab heard about the killing of his son, Isma'il, he went out and confronted Maysara at a river called Nahr al-K-d-r. Abu l-Asamm Khalid b. Abi Habib was in command of Ibn al-Habhab's men. The following were killed: Khalid [b. Abi Habib], and his son; 'Uthman b. Abi 'Ubayda b. 'Uqba b. Nafi', and his son Ibrahim b. 'Uthman; Musa b. 'Abd al-Rahman; [526] 'Abd al-Karim b. _____[1598] b. _____[1599] b. Dirar b. al-Khattab; Zurara b. 'Amr, one of the sons of Abu 'Aziz b. 'Umayr, of the Banu 'Umayr, of the Banu 'Abd ad-Dar b. Qusayy. It was called the Raid of the Nobles.[1600] They were killed at the end of the year/October–November 740, or in *al-Muḥarram* 123/November–December 740.

{369} Abu Khalid:
When [word of] their deaths reached Ibn al-Habhab, he sent 'Abd ar-Rahman b. al-Mughira al-'Abdi to be governor over Tlemcen. He initiated [a campaign] to kill the Sufrites, and [for that] he was called "The Butcher." They revolted against 'Abd ar-Rahman b. al-Mughira, who fled. Habib b. Abi 'Ubayda returned from his naval expedition, and Ibn al-Habhab sent him [against the Sufrites]. He encamped at the *wādī* of Tlemcen, but did not cross it before the governorship of Ibn al-Habhab had come to an end.

In this year, Zayd b. 'Ali b. Husayn b. 'Ali b. Abi Talib was killed in Kufa.[1601]

1596 On Maysara and his revolt, see EI, III, 155.

1597 U: Then Maysara al-Haqir sent a general, who killed 'Abd al-A'la b. Hudayj (?).

1598 U: *M-s-j-l*; Z: *M-s-h-l*.

1599 U: 'Uqba; Z: 'Utba.

1600 From "Maysara b. al-Haqir, who had been a water-seller in Kairouan ..." cf. IAH, 217f.; cf. IA, V, 191f.; (*) Dh., V, 27.

1601 On the abortive revolt of Zayd b. 'Ali, see R. Strothmann, in EI, IV, 1193; Shaban, *Islamic History*, 143, 179; Wellhausen, *Arab Kingdom*, 337f. and index; Wellhausen, *Religio-Political Factions*, 163f., 166f.

*Abu l-Yaqzan:
In this year, Mu'awiya b. Hisham and Sulayman b. Hisham conducted raiding expeditions in the land of the Byzantines. The two together besieged the Byzantines. But the Muslims were faced with great lack of food and high prices.

In this year, al-Hakam b. 'Awana was killed in Sind. Yusuf b. 'Umar appointed 'Amr b. Muhammad b. al-Qasim [as a governor over Sind].[1602]

Muhammad b. Hisham led the summer raid.

[527] Muhammad b. Hisham b. Isma'il led the pilgrimage.

In this year, the following died: Yazid b. 'Abdallah b. Qusayt,[1603] in Medina; Iyas b. Mu'awiya b. Qurra al-Muzani,[1604] in Wasit; Zubayd b. al-Harith b. 'Abd al-Karim al-Iyami; Bukayr b. 'Abdallah b. al-Ashajj;[1605] Salama b. Kuhayl,[1606] in Kufa; [and] Ya'qub b. 'Abdallah b. al-Ashajj.[1607]

In this year, Muhammad b. Sulayman b. 'Ali b. 'Abdallah b. 'Abbas b. 'Abd al-Muttalib[1608] was born in al-Humayma,[1609] in Syria.

[528] The Year 123/740–741

In this year, Kulthum b. 'Iyad arrived in Ifriqiya as governor at the beginning of *Sha'bān*/June 741, and proceeded {370} to Tlemcen Yazid b. Hisham b. 'Abd al-Malik, who was called al-Afqam,[1610] led the pilgrimage.

Sulayman b. Hisham led the summer raid.

In this year, [Muhammad b. Muslim] az-Zuhri made the pilgrimage.

1602 From "In this year, al-Hakam b. 'Awana was killed …" cf. al-Ya'qubi, II, 389.

1603 *Ṭbq.*, 658; Ibn Hajar, XI, 342; cf. Kh., 599.

1604 On the death of Iyas b. Mu'awiya b. Qurra al-Muzani cf. *Ibn Hajar, I, 390 (Khalifa).

1605 GAS, I, 405.

1606 See note 865.

1607 *Ṭbq.*, 671; Ibn Hajar, XI, 390.

1608 Cf. Tab., index.

1609 EI2, III, 574.

1610 Al-Afqam means "having crooked teeth, or a crooked jaw." Ibn Qutayba, in the section of the *Ma'ārif* listing persons with various defects, has one entry under those who were afflicted with *al-fuqm*, "crookedness of the teeth, or jaw." The individual listed is a certain Yazid b. Yazid b. Hisham b. 'Abd al-Malik, which may be a scribal error for Yazid b. Hisham b. 'Abd al-Malik (al-*Ma'ārif*, 586).

[529] The Year 124/741–742

In this year, Maysara al-Haqir, the Sufrite, died in the Maghrib.[1611] The Sufrites divided into two groups, one faction led by Khalid b. Humayd, the other by Abu Yusuf Salim al-Azdi. Kulthum b. ʻIyad marched against them. Then the two factions joined together again, and confronted Kulthum at a river of Tangier. The following were killed: Kulthum, Muhammad b. ʻUbaydallah al-Azdi, Yazid b. Saʻid b. ʻAmr al-Harashi, [and] Habib b. Abi ʻUbayda. They proclaimed it lawful to kill the army of Kulthum, and they took the women and children captive.

Balj b. Bishr, the paternal cousin of Kulthum, was routed with the people. Abu Yusuf [and] Ibn Humayd pursued them. Hassan b. _____[1612] was in the rear of the army of Balj b. Bishr. When they came against him, he battled them, persevered, and put them to rout. Abu Yusuf and many of the Sufrites were killed, and the Sufrites went away in defeat. Balj and his companions went and encamped at the fortress.[1613] He declared his allegiance to Abu l-Khattar al-Kalbi[1614] as commander of the people, and called on them to fight. But the people refused, [530] saying, "Make ʻAbd ar-Rahman b. ʻUqba al-Ghifari commander." So he did so. He confronted ʻUkasha al-Fazari at al-Fahs al-Abyad. ʻAbd ar-Rahman put [ʻUkasha] to rout, and killed many of the Berbers. ʻAbd ar-Rahman marched and encamped at the Zab,[1615] where he spent the month of *Ramaḍān*/July–August 742 fasting. {371} After his rout, [ʻUkasha] al-Fazari went to Tangier, where he was met by ʻAbd al-Wahid b. Yazid al-Hawari, whom Khalid b. Humayd, the leader of the Sufrites, had sent to battle the people

1611 On the events in North Africa in this year, see EI, II, 1114, s.v. Kulthum b. ʻIyad; EI2, I, 990, s.v. Balj b. Bishr b. ʻIyad; EI2, III, 169, s.v. Hanzala b. Safwan; EI2, I, 134, s.v. Abu l-Khattar (by E. Levi-Provencal); EI2, III, 601, s.v. al-Husam b. Dirar (by A. Huici Miranda; al-Husam b. Dirar is the same person as Abu l-Khattar. The second article somehow slipped by the editors). Cf. also Julien, 21f. Khalifa's text dealing with these events is unclear in the extreme. Names are thrown in one after another, without adequately identifying them, and sometimes they seem to be confused with each other. There are contradictions in the report, and it seems that Khalifa (or his source) combined several differing traditions, without ascribing them to anyone.

1612 Z: Gh-naca; U: ʻ-naba; Ibn ʻAsakir, X, 264: Ghassan b. ʻAtaqa.

1613 From "Balj b. Bishr, the paternal cousin of Kulthum …" cf. *Ibn ʻAsakir, X, 264 (Khalifa).

1614 U: Abu l-Khattab; cf. EI2, I, 134; EI2, III, 601, s.v. al-Husam b. Dirar; cf. Ibn Hazm, 457, l. 1.

1615 EI, IV, 1181f.

of Ifriqiya. He made al-Fazari return with him. Hanzala [b. Safwan] wrote to 'Abd ar-Rahman b. 'Uqba b. Nafi', ordering him to battle 'Abd al-Wahid b. Yazid. 'Abd ar-Rahman went out with the people of az-Zab. They met in battle on Thursday, in the middle of *Dhū l-Qa'da* 124/September 742. The following were killed: 'Abd ar-Rahman b. 'Uqba, Marwan b. 'Uthman al-Ghassani, [and] Muhammad b. Yusuf b. _____ [?].[1616] The remnants of the army went to Hanzala [b. Safwan] in Kairouan. 'Abd al-Wahid captured the women and children of Tubna. Hanzala made Thabit b. Khaytham[1617] commander. 'Abd al-Wahid marched on 1 *Ṣafar* 125/4 December 742, and they met in battle. Ibn Khaytham was killed and the people were routed. Hanzala wrote to al-Mustanir b. al-Harith [531] al-Harashi, his governor in Tunis [the following]: "If you are able to fight the people, [then do so]. If not, come [to me]." So he went with the women and children. Khalid b. Humayd, chief of the Sufrites in Tangier, heard that 'Abd al-Wahid had been acknowledged as caliph [by the Sufrites]. 'Abd al-A'la sent Zurzur, a *mawlā* of Musa b. Nusayr, with cavalry, and ordered him to unfurl the flag of 'Abd al-Wahid [b. Yazid al-Hawari], and he gave him command over his men. He reached 'Abd al-Wahid, who marched against Kairouan, where they were confronted by the cavalry of Hanzala. 'Abd al-Wahid was killed, the Berbers were put to rout, and many of them were killed. Hanzala's herald proclaimed safety [for those who surrendered]. 'Ukasha al-Fazari fled in defeat. He was apprehended by some people who put him in chains and sent him to Hanzala. Hanzala was requested to grant safety, but he put him to death. The Sufrites went away, and the region was quiet.

In 124, the Berbers revolted in Spain, and 'Ukasha b. al-Fazari revolted in Qabis,[1618] in Ifriqiya, without making propaganda for any particular sectarian views. The governor over Ifriqiya at that time was 'Abd ar-Rahman b. 'Uqba al-Ghifari, the successor of Kulthum [b. 'Iyad]. He sent Muslim b. Sawada al-Fihri [against 'Ukasha]. 'Ukasha put him to rout, and pursued him until he entered Kairouan. 'Ukasha went to the city of Qabis, where 'Abd al-A'la b. 'Uqba and Sa'id b. Bajra al-Ghassani were. He besieged them, and set up {372} mangonels against the city, but he did not reach them. Then he went to Qafsa[1619] and besieged it. The remnant of Kulthum's army went to 'Abd ar-Rahman b. 'Uqba, who joined

1616 Kh.: *fī b-sh-r*. Perhaps it should be read as Muhammad b. Yusuf b. Bishr; in Arabic script, the words *fī* and *ibn* without initial *alif* could look practically identical.
1617 U: Khuthaym. Cf. Kh., 504.
1618 Gabes EI2, IV, 335, s.v. Kabis.
1619 Gafsa EI2, IV, 414, s.v. Kafsa.

forces with them. He designated 'Abd al-Hamid b. Dhu'ayb as-Sahmi as his lieutenant over Kairouan. [532] 'Ukasha marched against him. They met in battle in *Ṣafar* 124/December 741–January 742. 'Ukasha al-Fazari was put to rout, and went to Tubna. 'Abd ar-Rahman [b. 'Uqba] returned to Kairouan. Hisham b. 'Abd al-Malik appointed Hanzala b. Safwan al-Kalbi as governor, and he arrived there in the middle of *Jumādā* I 124/ March–April 742.

Muhammad b. Hisham b. Isma'il led the pilgrimage.

In 124, the following died: Muhammad b. Muslim b. 'Ubaydallah b. Shihab az-Zuhri, on Monday night 17 *Ramaḍān*/25 July 742;[1620] Muhammad b. 'Ali b. 'Abdallah b. 'Abbas b. 'Abd al-Muttalib,[1621] in Syria; al-Qasim b. Abi Bazza,[1622] in Mecca; Abu Jamra ad- Duba'i,[1623] in Basra; Muhammad b. 'Abd ar-Rahman, a descendant of Sa'd b. Zurara, in Medina; 'Amir b. 'Abdallah b. az-Zubayr b. al-'Awamm, at the end of Hisham's caliphate.

[533] The Year 125/742–743

In this year, Hisham b. 'Abd al-Malik b. Marwan died – may God have mercy on him – in ar-Rusafa.[1624]

*Al-Walid b. Hisham < his father < his grandfather < 'Abdallah b. Mughira < his father; *Abu l-Yaqzan; and others:
Hisham b. 'Abd al-Malik died in ar-Rusafa on Wednesday 3 *Rabī'* II 125/3 February 743, at the age of 53. Al-Walid b. Yazid b. 'Abd al-Malik recited the prayers for him.

Hatim b. Muslim:
He died at the age of 61. His reign lasted 19 years, seven months, and 11 days.

{373} Then al-Walid b. Yazid b. 'Abd al-Malik received the pledge of

1620 On the death of "Muhammad b. Muslim b. 'Ubaydallah b. Shihab az-Zuhri, on Monday night 17 *Ramaḍān*/25 July 742" cf. *Dh., V, 152 (Khalifa).

1621 He was the father of the first two 'Abbasid caliphs, 'Abdallah al-Saffah and Abu Ja'far al-Mansur *Ṭbq.*, 799; Ibn Hajar, IX, 355.

1622 *Ṭbq.*, 705; Ibn Sa'd, V, 479; Ibn Hajar, VIII, 310.

1623 On the death of Abu Jamra ad-Duba'i cf. Nasr b. 'Imran *Ṭbq.*, 512; Ibn Sa'd, VII, 235; Ibn Hajar, X, 431. See also Ibn Hajar, X, 432 (Khalifa).

1624 A town near Palmyra. See EI, III, 1183.

allegiance. His mother was Umm al-Hajjaj, the daughter of Muhammad b. Yusuf, who was the brother of al-Hajjaj b. Yusuf.

[534] A List of the Governors of Hisham b. 'Abd al-Malik

Mecca, Medina, and at-Ta'if:

Ibrahim[1625] b. Hisham b. Isma'il al-Makhzumi, [was appointed] in *Jumādā* I 106/September–October 724, and served over Mecca until Hisham died.

Medina:

Ibrahim b. Hisham b. Isma'il was appointed over [both Medina] and Mecca, but was dismissed from [the governorship over Medina] in 114/732–733.

Khalid b. 'Abd al-Malik b. al-Harith b. al-Hakam was then appointed, and dismissed in 119/737. [Then] he wrote to Abu Bakr b. Muhammad b. 'Amr b. Hazm, who served as prayer leader until the arrival[1626] in 119/737 of-Muhammad b. Hisham, who served until Hisham died.

Yemen:

Yusuf b. 'Umar ath-Thaqafi was appointed by Hisham, and he arrived on 27 *Ramaḍān* 106/15 February 725. He served until [Hisham] wrote to him in 120/737–738, appointing him over Iraq, and he went.

As-Salt b. Yusuf was left by his father to take his place.[1627]

Al-Qasim b. 'Umar was then appointed by his brother [Yusuf], and served until Hisham died.

[535] Basra:

When Khalid b. 'Abdallah al-Qasri became governor over Iraq, he appointed Aban b. {374} Dabara b. 'Ufayr b. Sayf b. Dhi Yazan, an Emesan.

Chief of Police [in Basra]:

'Uqba b. 'Abd al-A'la al-Kala'i, a Damascene.

1625 Kh.: Muhammad. Cf. Tab., II, 1487; Kh., 540, 544; Zambaur, *Manuel de généalogie*, 19, 24. (This note applies as well to the first name in the list of governors over Medina, below).

1626 According to al-Waqidi, he served as governor or prayer leader for six days, until Muhammad b. Hisham arrived Tab., II, 1592.

1627 From the heading "Yemen" to this point cf. *Dh., V, 191 (Khalifa).

Malik b. al-Mundhir b. al-Jarud al-'Abdi was then appointed, and arrived in *Dhū l-Qa'da* 106/March–April, 725. He was later dismissed.

Bilal b. Abi Burda was then appointed, [and served] for a year.

Prayer Leader:

An-Nadr b. 'Amr al-Muqri'i al-Himyari, a Damascene, was appointed, then dismissed at the end of 110/ March–April 729.

The duties of prayer leader, chief of police, and judge were then given to Bilal b. Abi Burda, who served until Khalid [b. 'Abdallah] was dismissed from [the governorship of] Iraq in 120/737–738. [Then Hisham] appointed Yusuf b. 'Umar ath-Thaqafi over Iraq. He sent al-Wazi' b. 'Abbad al-Kalbi to arrest Bilal.

Kuthayyir b. 'Abdallah as-Sulami, whose *kunya* was Abu l-'Ajj, was then appointed by Yusuf, who later dismissed him in 122/739–740.

Al-Qasim b. Muhammad was then appointed, and served as governor until Hisham died.

Kufa:

'Abd al-Malik b. Jaz' b. Hadrujan [?] al-Azdi, a man from Palestine, was appointed by Khalid b. 'Abdallah, who later dismissed him.

[536] Isma'il b. Awsat al-Bajali, later dismissed.

'Abdallah b. 'Amr al-Bajali, later dismissed.

'Asim b. 'Amr, the brother of the preceding, later dismissed.

Dabis b. 'Abdallah al-Bajali, later dismissed.

Nawf al-Ash'ari, later dismissed.

Ziyad b. 'Ubaydallah al-Harithi.

Then [Hisham] dismissed Khalid in 120/737–738, and appointed Yusuf b. 'Umar [over Iraq].

Al-Hakam b. as-Salt ath-Thaqafi, later dismissed.

Yusuf b. Muhammad b. al-Qasim ath-Thaqafi, later dismissed.

Muhammad b. 'Ubaydallah ath-Thaqafi, later dismissed.

Ziyad b. Sakhr al-Lakhmi, later dismissed.

'Ubaydallah b. al-'Abbas al-Kindi, later dismissed.

Abu Umayya b. al-Mughira b. 'Abdallah b. Abi 'Aqil ath-Thaqafi served for one week, until Yusuf b. 'Umar fled.

{375}[537] Khurasan:

Asad b. 'Abdallah was appointed by his brother Khalid b. 'Abdallah. He was dismissed by Hisham in 108/726–727.

Ashras b. 'Abdallah as-Sulami was then appointed, and was dismissed in 113/731–732.

Al-Junayd b. 'Abd ar-Rahman, of the Murra of the Ghatafan, was then appointed, and later dismissed in 115/733–734.

'Asim b. 'Abdallah b. Yazid al-Hilali was then appointed. Then Khalid b. 'Abdallah was given jurisdiction over Khurasan for the second time.

Asad b. 'Abdallah was appointed by his brother. Asad died in 120/737–738, shortly before Khalid was dismissed.

Ja'far b. Hanzala al-Bahrani was designated to take his place.

Nasr b. Sayyar al-Laythi was then appointed by Hisham, and he served until Hisham died.

Sijistan:

Yazid b. al-Ghurayf al-Hamdani was appointed by Khalid b. 'Abdallah.

Al-Asfah al-Kindi, the father of Khalid b. al-Asfah al-Kindi.

'Abdallah b. Abi Burda b. Abi Musa al-Ashtari served until Khalid was dismissed.

[538] Yusuf b. 'Umar [then] became governor over Iraq.

Muhammad b. Hijr b. Qays al-'Abdi was then appointed by Yusuf b. 'Umar.

Ibrahim b. 'Asim al-'Uqayli, who died [in office].

Harb b. Qatan b. Qabisa b. Mukhariq al-Hilali was then appointed by Yusuf, and served until Hisham died.

Sind:

Al-Junayd b. 'Abd ar-Rahman, of the Murra of the Ghatafan, was retained for two years by Khalid b. 'Abdallah, then dismissed.

Tamim b. Zayd al-Qayni, later dismissed.

Al-Hakam b. 'Awana was appointed, and killed by al-Maydh.[1628]

Muhammad b. 'Azar al-Kalbi was designated to succeed him, but was dismissed by Yusuf in 122/739–740.

'Amr b. Muhammad b. al-Qasim was then appointed, and served until Hisham died.

1628 The vocalization and spelling are uncertain. The Maydh (Mayd, Mand) were a people of India. See V. Minorsky, in EI, III, 236, s.v. Mand; cf. Idrisi, 145, and index, s.v. al-Mayd.

Bahrain:

Khalid's governors:

Muhammad b. Ziyad b. Jarir b. 'Abdallah al-Bajali.

Hazzan[1629] b. Sa'id.

[539] Yahya b. Isma'il.

Yahya b. Ziyad b. al-Harith al-Harithi.

Yusuf's governors over Bahrain:

'Abdallah b. Shurayk an-Numayri.

Muhammad {376} b. Hassan b. Sa'd al-Usayyidi.

Al-Musayyab b. Fadala seized control, [which he held] for about three years.

al-Yamama:

Al-Muhajir b. 'Abdallah, of the Banu Bakr b. Kilab, was appointed by Hisham. Al-Muhajir died [in office]. His son was then appointed, and served until al-Walid was killed.

Egypt:

Muhammad b. 'Abd al-Malik b. Marwan was appointed by Hisham 'Ubaydallah b. al-Habhab a *mawlā* of the Banu Salul was then appointed.

Ifriqiya:

Bishr b. Safwan was governor over [Ifriqiya], and he went to report to Yazid b. 'Abd al-Malik, leaving Yahya b. Na'isa al-Kalbi to take his place. Hisham returned Bishr b. Safwan to his post, and he arrived in 106/724–725. He served until he died in 109/727–728.

Na''as b. Qurt al-Kalbi was designated to succeed him, [540] but he was dismissed by Hisham.

'Ubayda b. 'Abd ar-Rahman as-Sulami was then appointed, and arrived in 110/728–729.[1630] He later departed.

'Uqba b. 'Abdallah b. Qudama at-Tujibi was designated to take his place.

'Ubaydallah b. al-Habhab was then given jurisdiction over [Ifriqiya] as well as Egypt, and he arrived in 110/728–729. He was dismissed in 123/740–741.

Kulthum b. 'Iyad was then appointed.

Hanzala b. Safwan al-Kalbi was then appointed, and he arrived

1629 U: Hazzaz.

1630 From the heading "Ifriqiya" cf. IAH, 216, 1.4; *Ibn 'Asakir, X, 93 (Khalifa).

in the middle of *Jumādā* I 124/March–April 742. He served until 129/746–747.

The Pilgrimage:

105/724 – Hisham b. Isma'il al-Makhzumi.
106/725 – Hisham b. 'Abd al-Malik.
107/726–112/731 – Ibrahim b. Hisham b. Isma'il.
113/732 – Sulayman b. Hisham b. 'Abd al-Malik.
114/733 – Khalid b. 'Abd al-Malik b. al-Harith b. al-Hakam b. Abi l-'As. {377}
115/734 – Muhammad b. Hisham b. Isma'il.
116/735 – Al-Walid b. Yazid. –

*Al-Walid b. Hisham and *Abu l-Yaqzan:

[541] 'Isa b. Miqsam, a *mawlā* of al-Walid b. Yazid, led the pilgrimage in 116/735.
– 117/735–736 – Khalid b. 'Abd al-Malik b. al-Harith b. al-Hakam.
118/736 – Muhammad b. Hisham b. 'Abd al-Malik.
119/737 – Maslama b. Hisham b. 'Abd al-Malik.
120/738–122/740 – Muhammad b. Hisham b. Isma'il.
123/741 – Yazid b. Hisham b. 'Abd al-Malik.
124/742 – Muhammad b. Hisham b. Isma'il.

The Summer Raid:

Maslama b. 'Abd al-Malik.
Mu'awiya b. Hisham, [Hisham b. 'Abd al-Malik's son]. Sulayman b. Hisham [b. 'Abd al-Malik].
We have already reported that under [the appropriate] years in [the present] history.

Armenia:

Al-Jarrah b. 'Abdallah al-Hakami, governor under Yazid [b. 'Abd al-Malik] at the time of his death, was retained by Hisham, who dismissed him in 107/725–726.
Maslama b. 'Abd al-Malik was then appointed, and dismissed in 109/727–728.
Al-Jarrah was reappointed. He was killed in 112/730–731.
[542] Sa'id b. 'Amr al-Harashi was then appointed, but dismissed in 113/731–732.
Maslama b. 'Abd al-Malik was [re]appointed. Maslama returned [to Syria].

Marwan b. Muhammad was designated to take his place, and was appointed at the beginning of 114/March 732.

[543] The Judges during the Reign of Hisham b. ‘Abd al-Malik

Basra:

Thumama [b. ‘Abdallah] b. Anas b. Malik[1631] was appointed by Khalid b. ‘Abdallah, and was dismissed in 109/727–728.
Bilal b. Abi Burda was then given the judgeship, and he served as judge until the arrival of Yusuf b. ‘Umar in 120/737–738.[1632]
{378} ‘Abdallah b. Burayda al-Aslami[1633] was then appointed,[1634] but soon died.
‘Amir b. ‘Ubayda al-Bahili[1635] was then appointed, and served as judge until the deaths of Hisham and al-Walid, and the outbreak of the civil war.

Kufa:

Al-Husayn b. al-Hasan al-Kindi was retained by Khalid, who later dismissed him.
Said b. Ashwa‘ al-Hamdani.[1636]
Muharib b. Dithar was appointed in 113/731–732.
Al-Hakam b. ‘Utayba al- ‘Ijli.
[544] Ibn Ashwa‘ was then reappointed, and served as judge until he died.
‘Isa b. al-Musayyab al-Bajali was then appointed. Then Yusuf b. ‘Umar arrived [as governor], and dismissed ‘Isa b. al-Musayyab.
‘Abdallah b. Shubruma ad-Dabbi[1637] was then appointed, but later dismissed, and given charge of the treasury.
Muhammad b. ‘Abd ar-Rahman b. Abi Layla[1638] was then appointed, and served until the deaths of Hisham and al-Walid.

1631 *Ṭbq.*, 513; Ibn Sa‘d, VII, 239; *Jarḥ*, I, I, 466; Ibn Hajar, II, 28.

1632 From the heading “Basra” cf. *Ibn Hajar, I, 500 (Khalifa).

1633 D. 115/733–734 (*Ṭbq.*, 504, 831; *Jarḥ*, II, I, 102; Ibn Sa‘d, VII, 221; Ibn ‘Asakir, *Tahdhīb*, VII, 306; Ibn Hajar, V, 157).

1634 From the heading “Basra” cf. *Ibn ‘Asakir, X, 382 (Khalifa).

1635 Ibn Hajar, V, 79.

1636 Sa‘id b. ‘Amr b. Ashwa‘, d. 120/737–738 (*Ṭbq.*, 374; Ibn Sa‘d, VI, 327; Ibn Hajar, IV, 67).

1637 D. 144/761–762 (*Ṭbq.*, 388; Ibn Sa‘d, VI, 350; Ibn Hajar, V, 250).

1638 D. 148/765–766 (EI2, III, 687; GAS, I, 518).

Medina:

Hisham appointed Ibrahim b. Hisham b. Isma'il over Medina.
Muhammad b. Safwan al-Jumahi[1639] was appointed as judge.
As-Salt b. Zubayd b. as-Salt was then appointed as judge, and was dismissed by Ibrahim b. Hisham in 114/732–733.
[Hisham] then appointed Khalid b. 'Abd al-Malik b. al-Harith b. al-Hakam b. Abi l-'As over Medina.
Abu Bakr b. 'Abd ar-Rahman b. Huwaytib, of the Banu 'Amir b. Lu'ayy, was then appointed as judge by Khalid, and later dismissed.
Muhammad b. Safwan al-Jumahi was then [re]appointed as judge.
Hisham dismissed Khalid [b. 'Abd al-Malik] in {379} 119/737.
Abu Bakr [b. Muhammad] b. 'Amr b. Hazm then received a letter of appointment, and he served as judge until he died.

Hisham's Chief of Police:

Ka'b b. Hamid al-'Absi was retained for 13 years, then appointed over Armenia.
Yazid b. Ya'la b. Dakhm al-'Absi was then appointed.

[545] Secretary for Correspondence:

Salim, a *mawlā* of Sa'id b. 'Abd al-Malik.

Finance Secretary:

Usama b. Zayd,[1640] who was later dismissed.
'Ubaydallah b. al-Habhab, *mawlā* of the Banu Salul, was then appointed, and later appointed over Egypt.
Sa'id b. 'Uqba, a *mawlā* of the Banu l-Harith b. Ka'b, was appointed to replace him.

Secretary of the Official Seal:

Ar-Rabi' b. Shabur, a *mawlā* of the Banu l-Harith.

Administrator of the warehouses and treasuries:

'Abdallah b. 'Amr b. al-Harith.

Captain of the Guard:

Nusayr, his *mawlā*, who was later dismissed.
Ar-Rabi' b. Ziyad, in addition to his charge of the official seal.[1641]

1639 Ibn Hajar, IX, 232.
1640 Ibn 'Asakir, *Tahdhīb*, II, 399; Ibn Hajar, I, 207.
1641 Cf. above, al-Rabi' b. Shabur.

Secretary of the Minor Seal and the Inner Circle [?]:
Abu z-Zubayr Istakhr, his *mawlā*.

[546] [Hisham's] Chamberlain:
Ghalib b. Mas'ud, his *mawlā*.[1642]

In 125, al-Walid b. Yazid wrote to Yusuf b. 'Umar, and ordered him to come to him. He handed over to him Khalid b. 'Abdallah al-Qasri, Muhammad b. Hisham b. Isma'il al-Makhzumi and Ibrahim b. Hisham b. Isma'il al-Makhzumi, and ordered him to put them to death.[1643]

*Isma'il b. Ibrahim ash-Shu'ayrawi al-'Ataki < *as-Sari b. Muslim, the father of Bishr b. as-Sari:[1644]
I saw them when Yusuf b. 'Umar brought them to al-Hira. Khalid was wearing a cloak, [seated] on one side of a camel litter. [Yusuf b. 'Umar] tortured them until he killed them.[1645]

Al-Ghamr b. Yazid b. 'Abd al-Malik led the summer raid.[1646]

{380} Yusuf b. 'Umar led the pilgrimage.

In this year, the following died: Salih b. Nubhan,[1647] a *mawlā* of at-Taw'ama bint Umayya b. Khalaf, in Medina; Abu Bishr Ja'far b. Abi Wahshiyya,[1648] in Wasit; Budayl b. Maysara al-'Uqayli,[1649] in Basra; Adam b. 'Ali ash-Shaybana,[1650] in Kufa; [and] Muhammad b. 'Amr b. 'Ata',[1651] in Medina.

[547] During the governorship of Yusuf b. 'Umar over Iraq, the following died: Zubayd [b. al-Harith] al-Iyami, Simak b. Harb adh-Dhuhli,[1652] Jabala b. Suhaym al-Shaybani,[1653] [and] Ash'ath b. Abi sh-Sha'tha'.[1654]

1642 From the heading "Hisham's Chief of Police" cf. *'Iqd*, IV, 445.
1643 From "In 125, al-Walid b. Yazid wrote to Yusuf …" cf. Tab., II, 1768; * *'Iqd*, IV, 452.
1644 On Bishr, the son of as-Sari, see *Ṭbq.*, 720; Ibn Hajar, I, 450.
1645 From "I saw them when Yusuf b. 'Umar brought them to al-Hira …" cf. Tab., II, 1822; * *'Iqd*, IV, 452.
1646 This sentence parallels al-Ya'qubi, II, 395; cf. Tab., II, 1728; cf. Tab., II, 1769.
1647 *Ṭbq.*, 657; *Jarḥ*, II, I, 416; Ibn Hajar, IV, 405.
1648 On the death of Abu Bishr Ja'far b. Abi Wahshiyya cf. *Ṭbq.*, 845; *Jarḥ*, I, I, 473; Ibn Hajar, II, 83–84.
1649 *Ṭbq.*, 510; Ibn Sa'd, VII, 240; Ibn Hajar, I, 424.
1650 *Ṭbq.*, 373; Ibn Sa'd, VI, 322; Ibn Hajar, I, 197.
1651 *Ṭbq.*, 657; *Jarḥ*, IV, I, 29; Ibn Hajar, IX, 373.
1652 *Ṭbq.*, 373; Ibn Sa'd, VI, 323; Ibn Hajar, IV, 232.
1653 On the death of Jabala b. Suhaym al-Shaybani cf. *Ṭbq.*, 373; Ibn Sa'd, VI, 312; Ibn Hajar, II, 61–62; cf. *Dh., V, 54 (Khalifa); *Ibn Hajar, II, 62 (Khalifa).
1654 *Ṭbq.*, 371; Ibn Sa'd, VI, 319; Ibn Hajar, I, 355.

[548] The Year 126/743–744

In this year, al-Walid b. Yazid b. 'Abd al-Malik b. Marwan was killed.

*Al-Walid b. Hisham < his father < his grandfather; * 'Abdallah b. Mughira < his father; *Abu l-Yaqzan; and others:
Al-Walid was killed in al-Bakhra',[1655] some miles from Tadmur,[1656] on Thursday 27 *Jumādā* II 126/16 April 744. He was 35 or 36 years of age.[1657]

*Yahya b. Muhammad < 'Abd al-'Aziz b. Abi 'Imran:
He was killed at the age of 45 or 44.

Hatim b. Muslim:
He was 45 and several months.[1658]

Al-Walid was born in Damascus in 90/708–709. Some say 92/710–711. His reign lasted one year, two months, and 22 days.

{381} *Isma'il b. Ibrahim < 'Abdallah b. Waqid al-Jarmi, who was a witness to the killing of al-Walid:
When they agreed to murder al-Walid, they entrusted the leadership to Yazid b. al-Walid b. 'Abd al-Malik b. Marwan. 'Abd al-'Aziz b. al-Hajjaj b. 'Abd al-Malik, a member of his family, pledged allegiance to him. Yazid b. al-Walid went out one night to his brother, al-'Abbas, to ask his advice about killing al-Walid. He advised him against it. Yazid set out at night and entered Damascus with 40 men. They broke [549] the door of the *maqṣūra*,[1659] entered, and bound the officer in charge of it. Yazid carried the valuables on carts to Bab al-Midmar. He put 'Abd al-'Aziz b. al-Hajjaj b. 'Abd al-Malik in command [of the army]. His herald called out, "Whoever joins [the movement] against al-Walid[1660] shall receive

1655 EI2, I, 952.

1656 EI, III, 1020, s.v. Palmyra.

1657 From "Al-Walid was killed …" cf. *'*Iqd*, IV, 452. On "36 years of age" cf. *Dh., V, 178 (Khalifa).

1658 This sentence parallels *'*Iqd*, IV, 452.

1659 *Maqṣūra* generally means the enclosed area in the mosque reserved for the caliph or ruler, to keep him separated, and protected, from the people. *Maqṣūra* in the present narrative seems to mean "storage place," or "treasury." Perhaps the later writers, at-Tabari and Abu l-Faraj al-Isbahani, did not realize that the word was being used in that sense, since in their versions of the story, the rebels went to the mosque, a detail they may have added to the narrative, in order to explain the usage of the word *maqṣūra*.

1660 The Arabic is *man intadaba ilā l-Walīd*. Cf. Dh., II, 360, l. 4, where the expression *intadaba li-* has the same meaning, "to join up *against* [someone]."

2,000 [*dirhams*]." Two thousand men responded.[1661] [Yazid] associated Ya'qub b. 'Abd ar-Rahman b. Sulaym and Mansur b. Jumhur with 'Abd al-'Aziz b. al-Hajjaj [as commanders]. [News of what was transpiring] reached al-Walid b. Yazid, who left al-Balqa' and went to Homs. He wrote to al-'Abbas b. al-Walid b. 'Abd al-Malik, and ordered him to come to him with an army of Emesans, since he was nearby. Al-Walid set out, and ultimately went to al-Bakhra', a castle in desert and sand, several miles from Tadmur. In the morning, the cavalry came to al-Walid at al-Bakhra'. Al-'Abbas b. al-Walid arrived without cavalry, [and was seized] by 'Abd al-'Aziz, and held prisoner behind him. 'Abd al-'Aziz's herald called out [to the troops with al-Walid], "Whoever comes over to al-'Abbas b. al-Walid will be safe. He is between us and you."[1662] The people, supposing that al-'Abbas [had joined] with 'Abd al-'Aziz, defected from al-Walid.[1663] Then the people attacked [al-Walid]. The first to pounce on him were as-Sari b. Ziyad b. Abi Kabsha as-Saksaki and 'Abd as-Salam al-Lakhmi. As-Sari fell upon him with his sword, while 'Abd as-Salam struck him in the face. Thus he was killed.[1664]

{382} Isma'il < *'Abdallah b. Waqid al-Jarmi:
They entered upon al-Walid, who was wearing a pair of cuirasses.[1665] In his hand was his drawn sword, and they drew back from him. Their herald called out, "Kill the sodomite the way sodomites should be killed!" Thus he was killed.[1666]

1661 From "When they agreed to murder al-Walid ..." cf. *Dh., V, 176 (Khalifa).
1662 It does not seem that this should be taken literally. The Arabic *huwa bayna-nā wa-bayna-kum* may mean something like "He [al-'Abbas] is a *link* between us and you; [and since he is now on our side, you should join us, and you will be safe]."
1663 'Abd al-'Aziz b. al-Hajjaj received word of the march of al-'Abbas b. al-Walid (the brother of Yazid b. al-Walid) in support of the caliph al-Walid b. Yazid b. 'Abd al-Malik. He sent Mansur b. Jumhur with orders to ambush al-'Abbas and seize him. Mansur ambushed al-'Abbas and his sons, and ordered him to pledge allegiance to his brother, Yazid b. al-Walid b. 'Abd al-Malik, the ringleader of the revolt, and to come with him to 'Abd al-'Aziz b. al-Hajjaj. Al-'Abbas complied, under threats against him. They raised a flag, saying that it was the flag of al-'Abbas b. al-Walid b. 'Abd al-Malik, who had pledged allegiance to the (new) Commander of the Faithful, Yazid b. al-Walid b. 'Abd al-Malik. Al-'Abbas said, "A devilish deception!" (*khud'a min khuda' ash-shayṭān*). The people defected from al-Walid, and joined al-'Abbas. This is how at-Tabari explains the event (Tab., II, 1798f.; cf. EI2, I, 57, s.v. 'Abd al-'Aziz).
1664 From "When they agreed to murder al-Walid ..." cf. Tab., II, 1784–1800 (al-Mada'ini); * *'Iqd*, IV, 461; (*) Azdi, 54 (Khalifa); cf. *Aghānī*, VI, 136–140.
1665 The Arabic is *wa-qad ẓāhara bayna dir'ayn*.
1666 From "They entered upon al-Walid ..." cf. Tab., II, 1799 (al-Mada'ini); *Azdi,

[550] Isma'il < *'Abdallah b. Waqid < *Yazid b. Abi Farwa, a *mawlā* of the Umayyads:
When the head of al-Walid b. Yazid was brought to Yazid b. al-Walid, he said, "Set it up before the people." I said, "Don't do that. Only the heads of the Kharijites are [customarily] set up."[1667] [But] he vowed that he would surely set it up, [saying], "I myself and nobody else will do it."[1668] It was put on a lance and planted at the steps of the mosque of Damascus. Then he said, "Go and walk with it around the city of Damascus."[1669]

*Al-Walid b. Hisham < his father:
When they surrounded al-Walid, he took a copy of the Qur'ān and said, "I shall be murdered the same way my paternal cousin 'Uthman was murdered."[1670]

*Isma'il b. Ibrahim < *my father, Ibrahim b. Ishaq:
Yazid b. al-Walid rose to deliver a sermon. He praised God, then he said [the following]:

People! I have revolted not out of arrogance or pride, nor out of greed for material things, or appetite for power. I have not come here to praise myself, or to justify my actions. I have done myself wrong if my Lord does not have mercy on me. But [rather], I revolted in defense of God and His religion, appealing for a return to His Book and the Law [*sunna*] of His Prophet, at a time when the signs of true guidance were obliterated;

---

54 (Khalifa); *Aghānī*, VI, 139, l. 11. The word for "sodomite" in Arabic is *lūṭī*, "Lotite." The name of Sodom is not mentioned in the Qur'ān, only the name of Lot, one of the few righteous people in the city, who is, in fact, considered to be a prophet. Since in the Qur'ān the people of Sodom are always called the people of Lot, the name of Lot became associated with the practices ascribed to the people of Sodom. Thus the word *lūṭī* was erroneously used to describe one who engages in sodomy. Lot and "the people of Lot" are mentioned frequently in the Qur'ān (e.g., 7:80–84, 11:77–83, 29:28–33, 54:33–34). The "people of Lot" were destroyed in a rain of stones sent by God. In other versions of the account of al-Walid's murder, an additional detail is added. After the cry, "Kill the sodomite, etc.," the crier is said to have added, "Pelt him with stones!" (e.g. Tab., I, 1799).

1667 In the version of at-Tabari, Yazid b. Abi Farwa protests, adding the warning that the people might feel sorry for al-Walid, and that his family might be angered (Tab., II, 1807).

1668 Or: He vowed that he would set it up, and that no one would set it up but me.

1669 From "When the head of al-Walid b. Yazid ..." cf. Tab., II, 1807 (al-Mada'ini); *'Iqd*, IV, 461; *Azdi, 55 (Khalifa).

1670 This sentence parallels Tab., II, 1800 (al-Mada'ini); *'Iqd*, IV, 462 (Khalifa); *Aghānī*, VI, 139, l. 25; *Dh., V, 176 (Khalifa). 'Uthman was the paternal cousin of al-Walid II's great-grandfather, Marwan I. According to tradition, 'Uthman was murdered while reading the Qur'ān.

when the light of the pious was extinguished; when the willful tyrant had appeared, permitting that which is prohibited, engaging in [heretical] innovations, and altering the *sunna*. When I saw that, I became worried, since you had fallen into darkness, from which you could not be released because of your many sins and the hardness of your hearts. I feared that he would invite many of the people to join him in his iniquities, {383} and that some of you would consent. I asked God for guidance in my affairs. I asked him not to entrust me to myself. I called upon my family and friends who obey me to do likewise. [Al-Walid] was my paternal cousin, my kinsman, and my equal in nobility of descent. God delivered mankind from him, and cleansed [551] the land of him. [That came about] through God's patronage and help, not through any power or strength we might have, but through the power, the strength, the patronage, and the help of God.

"People! If I assume authority, you will have in me a man who will not lay brick upon brick, or stone upon stone, or transfer wealth from one region to another until I have secured the frontiers and distributed among the garrisons of the region enough of it to give them strength. If there is anything left over, I will send it to a neighboring region that is more in need of it, so that the standard of living among the Muslims may be in good condition, and so that you will [all] be equal with respect to it. I shall not keep your troops cantoned in the land of the enemy, [a hardship] which rouses you and your families to rebellion. If you wish to pledge allegiance to me on the conditions I have offered you, I am at your service. If I show bias in any way, allegiance to me is not binding upon you. If you are of the opinion that someone else is more capable of the task than I, and you wish to pledge allegiance to him, I shall be the first to pledge allegiance and obedience to him. While saying this, I ask God's forgiveness for myself and for you."[1671]

1671 From "Yazid b. al-Walid rose to deliver a sermon ..." cf. al-Jahiz, II, 141f.; *'Uyūn*, II, 248f.; Tab., II, 1834f. (al-Mada'ini); Tab., II, 2009 (This is a version of the speech of the Kharijite Abu Hamza, in which some of the vocabulary and turns of phrase resemble portions of Yazid's speech.); **'Iqd*, IV, 95f. (Baqi b. Makhlad < Khalifa); **'Iqd*, IV, 462f.; *Azdi, 57f. (Khalifa); *Dh., V, 189 (Khalifa).

Yazid's speech, from as-Suyuti's *Ta'rīkh al-khulafā'*, has been translated into English by Jarrett, 257f. As-Suyuti used Khalifa's version of the speech, through adh-Dhahabi. It has been translated into German by Weil, *Geschichte der Chalifen*, from at-Tabari. On Yazid III's coup and its consequences, see Shaban, *Islamic History*, 155–160.

{384}[552] A List of the Governors of al-Walid b. Yazid

Medina:

Al-Walid wrote to Muhammad b. Hisham b. Isma'il, the governor of Mecca under Hisham b. 'Abd al-Malik, and he went [to report] to al-Walid. He left Muhammad b. Abi Bakr b. Muhammad b. 'Amr b. Hazm as his lieutenant over Medina, but al-Walid dismissed him. Yusuf b. Muhammad b. Yusuf was then given jurisdiction over [Medina] along with Mecca and at-Ta'if. He served until al-Walid was killed.

Yemen:

Ad-Dahhak b. Zaml, who served until al-Walid was killed.

Basra:

Al-Qasim b. Muhammad b. al-Qasim served until Hisham died. He was retained by al-Walid, and served until [al-Walid] was killed.

Kufa:

'Ubaydallah b. al-'Abbas al-Kindi, who was later dismissed by Yusuf [b. 'Umar].

[553] Abu Umayya b. al-Mughira b. 'Abdallah b. Abi 'Aqil ath-Thaqafi was then appointed, and served for a week, until Yusuf [b. 'Umar] fled after the murder of al-Walid.

Khurasan:

Nasr b. Sayyar al-Laythi was retained, and he served until al-Walid was killed.

Sijistan:

Harb b. Qatan b. Qabisa al-Hilali served until al-Walid was killed.

Sind:

'Amr b. Muhammad b. al-Qasim ath-Thaqafi served until al-Walid was killed.

Bahrain:

Muhammad b. Hassan b. Sa'id al-Usayyidi served until al-Walid was killed. According to some, Bishr b. Sallam al-'Abdi killed al-Musayyab b. Fadala, and remained [in control of Bahrain] until the arrival of [Yazid b. 'Umar] b. Hubayra.

al-Yamama:

Al-Muhajir b. 'Abdallah al-Kilabi served until al-Walid was killed.

{385} Ifriqiya:

Hanzala b. Safwan, governor under Hisham at the time of his death, continued to serve as governor until al-Walid was killed. He left in 129/746–747.

Oman:

Al-Fayd b. Muhammad b. Kardam b. Bayhas was appointed by Yusuf b. ʿUmar.

[554] The Judiciary:

Basra:

ʿAmir b. ʿUbayda served until al-Walid was killed, and the civil war broke out, at which time he retired.

Kufa:

[Muhammad b. ʿAbd ar-Rahman] b. Abi Layla served until al-Walid was killed.

Medina:

Saʿd b. Ibrahim was appointed by Yusuf b. Muhammad b. Yusuf, who later dismissed him.

Yahya b. Saʿid[1672] was then appointed, and he served until al-Walid was killed.

The Pilgrimage:

Yusuf b. Muhammad b. Yusuf, in 125/743.

Al-Jazira, Armenia, and Azerbaijan:

Marwan b. Muhammad b. Marwan b. al-Hakam served until al-Walid was killed. Then, when Marwan left and went to Syria, he left ʿAsim b. ʿAbdallah b. Yazid al-Hilali over Armenia and Azerbaijan.

The Summer Raid:

Al-Ghamr b. Yazid b. ʿAbd al-Malik b. Marwan.

[555] Chief of Police:

ʿAbd ar-Rahman b. Hanbal al-Kalbi, who was later dismissed.

ʿAbdallah b. ʿAmir al-Kalaʿi was then appointed.

1672 D. 143/760–761 (GAS, I, 407).

Secretary for Correspondence

Salim, a *mawlā* of Sa'id b. 'Abd al-Malik.
'Abdallah b. Salim, his son.

Finance Secretary:

'Abd al-Malik b. Muhammad b. al-Hajjaj b. Yusuf.
Al-Hajjaj b. 'Umayr, was then appointed.

Administrator of the Official Seal, the Warehouses, and the Treasuries:

'Abd ar-Rahman b. Hanbal al-Kalbi, in addition to his duties as chief of police.

Secretary of the Minor Seal:

Rabah b. Abi 'Umara.[1673]

{386} [Al-Walid's] Chamberlain:

'Isa b. Miqsam.

Captain of the Guard:

Ghaylan, the son-in-law of Ibn Ma'n.

[556] The Governorship of Yusuf b. 'Umar over Iraq

*Al-Walid b. Hisham < his father < his grandfather; *'Abdallah b. Mughira < his father; *Abu l-Yaqsan; and others:
Hisham b. 'Abd al-Malik b. Marwan consolidated [the administration of] Iraq under the governorship of Yusuf b. 'Umar ath-Thaqafi in 120/737–738.

Chief of Police:

al-Hira: al-'Abbas b. Sa'd b. Murra, of the Murra of the Ghatafan.
Basra and Kufa: Yusuf allowed his governors to appoint whomever they wished.

Finance Secretary:

Qahdham b. Sulayman,[1674] a *mawlā* of the family of Bakra.

Secretary for Correspondence with the Caliph:

Rishdin, his *mawlā*.

1673 From the heading "Secretary for Correspondence ..." cf. Jahshiyari, 68.
1674 Qahdham b. Sulayman was the grandfather of al-Walid b. Hisham, who is the source of a large amount of material in Khalifa's *Ta'rīkh*, most of which was compiled by Qahdham, and related to his son, Hisham, who passed it on to his son, al-Walid.

Secretary for Correspondence with the Governors:
'Uqba.

Yusuf was killed in 127/744–745, in his sixties.[1675]

During the governorship of Yusuf b. 'Umar, Jabala b. Suhaym died.[1676]

In 126, the following died: 'Amr b. Dinar,[1677] a *mawlā* of the family of Badhan, in Mecca; Sa'id b. Abi Sa'id al-Maqburi,[1678] in Medina; [557] 'Abd ar-Rahman b. al-Qasim b. Muhammad b. Abi Bakr,[1679] in Medina; [and] Sulayman b. Habib,[1680] who had been a judge, in Syria.

During the reign of al-Walid b. Yazid, the following died: Nubayh b. Wahb;[1681] Muhammad b. Qays,[1682] a *mawlā* of Abu Sufyan b. Harb; [and] al-Husayn b. 'Abd ar-Rahman b. 'Amr b. Sa'd b. Mu'adh.[1683]

Yazid b. al-Walid b. 'Abd al-Malik received the pledge of allegiance at the beginning of *Rajab*/April 744. His mother was the daughter of {387} Yazdajird b. Kisra.[1684]

In this year, Yazid b. al-Walid b. 'Abd al-Malik b. Marwan, who was called Yazid an-Naqis,[1685] died.

1675 This sentence parallels *Dh., V, 193 (Khalifa).

1676 This sentence parallels *Dh., V, 54 (Khalifa); Ibn Hajar, II, 62 (Khalifa).

1677 *Ṭbq.*, 706; Ibn Sa'd, V, 479; Ibn Hajar, VIII, 28; cf. GAS, I, index.

1678 On the death of Sa'id b. Abi Sa'id al-Maqburi cf. *Ṭbq.*, 643; Ibn al-Athir, *al-Lubāb*, III, 168; Ibn Hajar, IV, 38–39. Cf. #Ibn Hajar, IV, 39 (Khalifa).

1679 On the death of 'Abd ar-Rahman b. al-Qasim b. Muhammad b. Abi Bakr cf. *Ṭbq.*, 670; *Jarḥ*, II, II, 278; Ibn Hajar, VI, 254; cf. Kh., 603. Cf. #Ibn Hajar, VI, 254 (Khalifa).

1680 *Ṭbq.*, 799; Ibn Sa'd, V, 456; Ibn 'Asakir, *Tahdhīb*, VI, 246; Ibn Hajar, IV, 177.

1681 *Ṭbq.*, 605; Ibn Hajar, X, 418.

1682 On the death of Muhammad b. Qays cf. *Ṭbq.*, 648; *Jarḥ*, IV, I, 64; Ibn Hajar, IX, 413–414. Cf. #Ibn Hajar, IX, 414 (Khalifa).

1683 Ibn Hajar, II, 380.

1684 It is noteworthy that Yazid III, whose mother was of Iranian origin, intended to put into effect policies which would benefit the Muslims, regardless of their ethnic heritage. In his speech, he promised that he would endeavor to equalize the standard of living among the Muslims, which would include those of Iranian origin. Yazid III was the first caliph who did not have an Arab lineage through both of his parents.

1685 He was called *an-Nāqiṣ*, "the Decreaser," because he reduced the military stipends, which his predecessor had increased (cf. Wellhausen, *Arab Kingdom*, 367). Adh-Dhahabi reports a tradition which portrays Yazid III as somewhat of a fanatic about the evils of money. Yazid is quoted as follows, warning the Umayyads against the evils of riches: "Umayyads! Be on guard against [the evils of] wealth. Wealth diminishes [*yanquṣ*] modesty, increases the appetites, and destroys manliness [*murūwa*]. Wealth is like wine, and has the effect of intoxicating [drink]. If you must handle wealth [*in kuntum lā budda fā'ilīn*], at least keep it away from the women, for wealth leads to fornication" (Dh., V, 189, l. 19 < Abu 'Uthman al-Laythi).

*Al-Walid b. Hisham < his father < his grandfather; *'Abdallah b. Mughira < his father; *Abu l-Yaqzan; and others:
Yazid b. al-Walid b. 'Abd al-Malik died in Damascus on 19 *Dhū l-Ḥijja* 126/2 October 744, at 35 or 36 years of age. His brother, Ibrahim b. al-Walid b. 'Abd al-Malik, recited the prayers for him.

Hatim b. Muslim:
He was 46 years old.

'Abd al-'Aziz [b. 'Imran]:
He received the pledge of allegiance when he was 39, and died before reaching the age of 40.

Yazid was born in Damascus in 96/714–715.

[558] The Syrians pledged allegiance to Ibrahim b. al-Walid b. 'Abd al-Malik, except the people of Homs, who refused to pledge allegiance to him.[1686]

*Al-'Ala' b. Burd b. Sinan < *my father [Abu l-'Ala' Burd b. Sinan]:[1687]
I was present with Yazid b. al-Walid when he was dying. Qatan came to him and said, "I am a messenger from the people outside. They ask you to appoint your brother, Ibrahim, to be their ruler." He frowned, and with his hand on his forehead, said, "I should appoint Ibrahim?" Then he said to me, "Abu l-'Ala', whom do you think I should designate to succeed me?" I said, "I shall not advise you now at the end of an affair which I advised you not to enter upon in the first place." He lost consciousness, and I thought that he had died. He did that more than once. Qatan sat down and forged a document of succession in the name of Yazid b. al-Walid, and summoned people to witness it. [However,] Yazid did not indicate anything [with respect to the succession] to him or anyone else.[1688]

{388}[559] A List of the Governors of Yazid b. al-Walid

Iraq:

[Yazid] appointed Mansur b. Jumhur al-Kalbi. According to some, he forged a document of appointment in [Yazid's] name. He served

1686 This sentence parallels Jahshiyari, 70.

1687 D. 135/752–753 (*Ṭbq.*, 807; *Jarḥ*, II, I, 422; Ibn Hajar, I, 428).

1688 From "I was present with Yazid b. al-Walid when he was dying ..." cf. **'Iqd*, IV, 465; Jahshiyari, 69f.; *Azdi, 59f.; *Ibn 'Asakir, *Tahdhīb*, II, 303, l. 14; *Ta'rīkh al-Khulafā'*, 231b–232a (= Jahshiyari's version); *Dh., V, 41; *Dh., V, 224.

for about 40 days. His chief of police was al-Hajjaj b. Artat,[1689] the jurist.[1690]

Mecca, Medina, and at-Ta'if:

'Abd al-'Aziz b. 'Abdallah b. 'Amr b. 'Uthman b. 'Affan was appointed by Yazid b. al-Walid, who later dismissed him.

'Abd al-'Aziz b. 'Umar b. 'Abd al-'Aziz was then appointed.

Basra:

Muhammad b. al-Qasim b. Muhammad, governor under al-Walid, fled when he was killed.

'Abdallah b. 'Abdallah b. Umayya, who was called al-Afwah, was chosen by the people of Basra, and he served as prayer leader for a week.

Jarir b. Yazid b. Jarir b. 'Abdallah al-Bajali[1691] then arrived.

[Yazid] then appointed 'Abdallah b. 'Umar b. 'Abd al-'Aziz over Iraq. He wrote to 'Abdallah b. Abi 'Uthman, who led the people in prayer until the arrival of ['Amr] b. Suhayl.

It is said: Sa'id b. 'Amr b. Ja'da b. Hubayra al-Makhzumi was appointed by 'Abdallah b. 'Umar, after 'Abdallah b. Abi 'Uthman, but the people of Basra drove him out.

[560] 'Amr b. Suhayl b. 'Abd al-'Aziz b. Marwan was then appointed.

When ad-Dahhak b. Qays the Kharijite took control, he sent 'Umara.[1692]

Kufa:

'Ubaydallah b. al-'Abbas was appointed by Mansur b. Jumhur, but was dismissed by Ibn 'Umar.

'Asim b. 'Umar was then appointed by his brother, 'Abdallah b. 'Umar.

Sijistan[1693]:

Harb b. Qatan was governor at the time of the death of al-Walid.

1689 *Ṭbq.*, 290; Ibn Sa'd, VI, 359; Ibn Hajar, II, 196.

1690 For the entry on Iraq cf. *Dh., V, 303 (Khalifa).

1691 Ibn Hajar, II, 77.

1692 The meaning of this sentence is unclear, and the translation may not be correct.

1693 On events in Sijistan under Yazid III, see Bosworth, 75–77.

Muhammad b. '-z-'r[1694] was appointed by Mansur b. Jumhur, but was dismissed by ['Abdallah] b. 'Umar.
Harb b. Qatan was then [re]appointed. {389} He served for a month, then departed from [Sijistan], leaving Sawwar b. al-Ash'ar[1695] al-Mazini to take his place. But the Bakr b. Wa'il were dissatisfied, and they battled the Tamim.
Sa'id b. 'Amr,[1696] of the family of Sa'id b. al-'As, was sent by Ibn 'Umar, but neither the Tamim nor the Bakr were satisfied.

Khurasan:

Nasr b. Sayyar served until the downfall of the Umayyads.

Sind:

When Mansur b. Jumhur was dismissed from [the governorship] of Iraq, he went to Sind and took control over it. [561] The army encamped, and he called [the place] al-Mansuriyya.[1697]

Ifriqiya:

'Abd ar-Rahman b. Habib took control over it.

[562] The Judges

Basra:

'Amir b. 'Ubayda retired during the civil war.

Kufa:

[Muhammad b. 'Abd ar-Rahman] b. Abi Layla.

Medina:

Sa'd b. Ibrahim was appointed by 'Abd al-'Aziz b. 'Abdallah b. 'Amr b. 'Uthman. Yazid [b. al-Walid] then dismissed 'Abd al-'Aziz b. 'Abdallah, and appointed 'Abd al-'Aziz b. 'Umar b. 'Abd al-'Aziz [over Medina]. He dismissed Sa'd b. Ibrahim.
'Uthman b. 'Umar at-Taymi was then appointed as judge.

Yazid b. al-Walid's Chief of Police:

Bukayr b. Shammakh al-Lakhmi served until Yazid died.[1698]

1694 For several variations in his name, cf. Bosworth, 75.

1695 Z: al-As'ar.

1696 The name is also found as Sa'id b. 'Umar (Bosworth, 75, 76).

1697 It is usually called al-Mansura (EI, III, 257; cf. Idrisi, 93 and index; Minorsky, 372 and index).

1698 For the entry on Yazid b. al-Walid's Chief of Police cf. *Ibn 'Asakir, X, 257 (Khalifa).

Secretary for Correspondence:
Layth b. Abi Sulayman b. Sa'd.

Administrator of Finance, the Military Registers, and the Minor Seal, and Captain of the Guard:
An-Nadr b. 'Amr, a Yemenite.

Secretary of the Official Seal of the Caliphate:
'Abd ar-Rahman b. Hanbal al-Kalbi.
According to some: Qatan, [Yazid's] *mawlā*.[1699]
[563] In 126 'Amr b. Suhayl {390} b. 'Abd al-'Aziz b. Marwan b. al-Hakam was made commander [?].[1700]

*Abu 'Ubayda:
At his accession, Yazid b. al-Walid sent 'Abdallah b. 'Umar b. 'Abd al-'Aziz to Iraq.

In 126, Sa'id b. Bahdal, of the [Banu] n-Namir b. Qasit, revolted in al-Jazira, in *Sha'bān* 126/May–June 744.[1701] Then he crossed the Tigris, proceeding toward Qarda.[1702] Then he marched and encamped at al-Marj,[1703] a district of Mosul, on 1 *Ramaḍān*/17 June 744. He encountered [a certain] Abu Karib, a man of Himyar, who had revolted with many followers, and was called "Commander of the Faithful." Their respective revolts were examined, and it was ascertained that Sa'id had revolted before Abu Karib. Abu Karib acknowledged that to him, yielded the leadership to him, and went home. His followers dispersed. About 500 men joined with Sa'id, and accompanied him to the city of Mosul, where he encamped for several days. They asked him to depart. They pledged allegiance to him,[1704] and he departed. He marched to Shahrazur,[1705] where he encountered Shayban b. 'Abd al-'Aziz al-Yashkuri, who had gathered a following and was called

1699 From the heading "Yazid b. al-Walid's Chief of Police" cf. *'Iqd*, IV; 464; cf. Jahshiyari, 69.

1700 According to Khalifa (Kh., 560), 'Amr was appointed governor over Basra by Yazid III.

1701 At-Tabari (II, 1897) spells the name Bahdal with a *hā'* rather than a *ḥā'*. Cf. Wellhausen, *Religio-Political Factions*, 80; Rotter, "The Umayyad Fulūs of Mosul," 192f.

1702 On Qarda, cf. BGA, II, 145; V, 132, 136; VI, 76, 95, 245, 251; VII, 106, 195; VIII, 52; *Futūḥ*, 176; Yaqut, IV, 56.

1703 On al-Marj, cf. *Futūḥ*, 331; BGA, II, 145, 146; V, 128, 131; VII, 106; VIII, 52.

1704 The Arabic is *a'ṭaw-hu r-riḍā*. Khalifa uses also this expression with the same meaning elsewhere (Kh. 571, l. 10).

1705 EI, IV, 344, s.v. Shehrizur.

"Commander of the Faithful." Their respective revolts were examined, and it was ascertained that Sa'id had revolted first. So Shayban yielded the leadership, and marched with him. Before that, Shayban had battled a Syrian named Nusayr, with cavalry, killed him, and put his companions to rout.[1706]

{391}[564] The Year 127/744–745

In this year, the civil war broke out.

Isma'il b. Ibrahim:
When al-Walid b. Yazid was killed, Marwan b. Muhammad was governor in Armenia. When news of al-Walid's murder reached him, he called on the people to pledge allegiance to whomever the Muslims would approve of. They pledged allegiance to him. When news of the death of Yazid b. al-Walid reached him, he called on the Qays and the Rabi'a. He enrolled 26,000 of the Qays and 7,000 of the Rabi'a in the *dīwān*, and paid them their stipends. He appointed Ishaq b. Muslim al-'Uqayli commander over the Qays, and al-Musawir b. 'Uqba as commander over the Rabi'a. Then he marched toward Syria, leaving his brother, 'Abd al-'Aziz b. Muhammad b. Marwan, as his lieutenant in al-Jazira.[1707] He was met by the leaders of the Qays, among whom were al-Wathiq b. al-Hudhayl b. Zufar, Yazid b. 'Umar

1706 From "In 126, Sa'id b. Bahdal, of the [Banu] n-Namir b. Qasit, revolted ..." cf. *Azdi, 60.

1707 A comparison of Khalifa's account of the following events with that reported by at-Tabari might prove useful. Marwan left al-Jazira, and went on to Qinnasrin, where he confronted Bishr and Masrur, the sons of al-Walid b. 'Abd al-Malik, and took them prisoner (Tab., II, 1876f.; cf. EI2, I, 1244, s.v. Bishr b. al-Walid). Marwan then went to Homs, and received the Emesans' pledge of allegiance. 'Abd al-'Aziz b. al-Hajjaj fled when Marwan arrived (Tab., II, 1877; cf. EI2, I, 57, s.v. 'Abd al-'Aziz b. al-Hajjaj). Marwan proceeded to 'Ayn al-Jarr. Ibrahim b. al-Walid sent Sulayman b. Hisham to confront Marwan, who, according to at-Tabari's narrative, was "an experienced master of wile" (*kāna Marwān mujarraban mukāyidan*). He summoned three of his generals and ordered them to go with 3,000 cavalry troops (Khalifa gives the figure as 300] behind his own lines. They slipped away, crossed the river that was between the two armies, and attacked the enemy camp by surprise, from behind, putting them to rout. After the battle, Marwan received the pledge of allegiance for al-Hakam and 'Uthman, the sons of al-Walid II, from the prisoners, then released them, giving everyone one *dīnār* (Tab., II, 1877f.; cf. EI2, III, 990, s.v. Ibrahim al-Walid; cf. Ibn 'Asakir, *Tahdhīb*, VI, 286, s.v. Sulayman b. Hisham). Sulayman b. Hisham and the remnant of his army went to Damascus. Marwan's army entered the city. Ibrahim b. al-Walid fled and hid. Sulayman b. Hisham cleaned out the treasury, divided the money

b. Hubayra al-Fazari, Abu l-Ward b. al-Hudhayl b. Zufar, and 'Asim b. 'Abdallah b. Yazid al-Hilali. With them were 4,000 or 5,000 Qaysites. They marched with him until he reached Aleppo, where Bishr and Masrur, the sons of al-Walid b. 'Abd al-Malik, had been sent by Ibrahim b. al-Walid when he received word of Marwan's march. The people drew themselves up in battle formation. Abu l-Ward b. al-Hudhayl b. Zufar went out with 300 men. They shouted "God is great!" and charged toward Marwan, until they were close to him. Then they turned around and reversed [the direction of] their shields, and joined up with Marwan. Marwan and those who were with him attacked. Masrur and Bishr were put to flight [565] without a fight. Marwan apprehended them and imprisoned them, and imprisoned {392} many of their companions, but then released them. Then Marwan marched to Homs. He invited [the Emesans] to join him and to pledge allegiance to the two designated heirs, al-Hakam and 'Uthman, the sons of al-Walid b. Yazid, who were being held prisoner in Damascus by Ibrahim b. al-Walid. They pledged allegiance, and went out with him. He reached the camp of Sulayman b. Hisham b. 'Abd al-Malik after a fierce battle. Marwan took over his army. 'Abd al-'Aziz b. al-Hajjaj b. 'Abd al-Malik received word of what Sulayman had encountered, while he was camped with his army in another place. He marched toward Damascus. Ibrahim b. al-Walid went out from Damascus, encamped at Bab al-Jabiya, and prepared for battle. He had [brought] valuables with him on carts. He called to the people, but they deserted him. 'Abd al-'Aziz b. al-Hajjaj and Sulayman b. al-Walid went to Damascus, and entered the city with the intention of killing al-Hakam and 'Uthman, the sons of al-Walid [b. Yazid], who were in jail. Yazid b. Khalid b. 'Abdallah al-Qasri went, and entered the prison. He killed Yusuf b. 'Umar [ath-Thaqafi], and al-Hakam and 'Uthman, the sons of al-Walid b. Yazid. [Al-Hakam and 'Uthman] were [called] al-Hamalan.[1708]

Isma'il < *'Abdallah b. Waqid al-Jarmi:
Yazid b. Khalid [b. 'Abdallah al-Qasri] killed them. It is said that the killing of them was entrusted to a *mawlā* of Khalid b. 'Abdallah named

---

among his companions, and fled (Tab., II, 1878f.). 'Abd al-'Aziz b. al-Hajjaj was killed in Damascus (Tab., II, 1890f.).

1708 From "When news of the death of Yazid b. al-Walid reached him ..." cf. *'Iqd*, IV, 466f. (Khalifa) *Azdi, 61f. Ibn Qutayba reports that al-Hakam and 'Uthman were called *al-Ḥamalān* (*Ma'ārif*, 366). At-Tabari calls them *al-ghulāmān*, "the two youths" (Tab., II, 1879). *Al-Ḥamalān* means "the two lambs, or young rams."

Abu l-Asad, who beat them [to death] with a club. A messenger from Ibrahim came to them. 'Abd al-'Aziz b. al-Hajjaj went to his house in order to remove his family. But the people of Damascus fell upon him and killed him. They cut off his head, and brought it to Abu Muhammad b. 'Abdallah b. Yazid b. Mu'awiya, who had been imprisoned with Yusuf b. 'Umar and his companions. They brought him out and put him on the pulpit, still in his chains, and with the head of 'Abd al-'Aziz in front of him. They loosened his fetters when he was on the pulpit. Then he delivered a sermon to them, and pledged allegiance to Marwan. He reviled Yazid b. al-Walid and Ibrahim b. al-Walid and their supporters. Orders were given for the body of 'Abd al-'Aziz to be gibbeted upside down at Bab al-Jabiya. His head was sent to Marwan [566] b. Muhammad. [Word] reached Ibrahim, who {393} fled. Abu Muhammad requested safety for the people of Damascus. Marwan granted them safety, and was pleased with them.[1709] Then the following came to Marwan: Yazid b. Khalid b. Yazid b. Mu'awiya, Abu Muhammad b. 'Abdallah b. Yazid b. Mu'awiya, Muhammad b. 'Abd al-Malik b. Marwan, Abu Bakr b. 'Abdallah b. Yazid. He granted them permission to enter. The first to speak was Abu Muhammad b. 'Abdallah b. Yazid b. Mu'awiya, who greeted him as caliph, and consoled him on the death of al-Walid and his two sons, al-Hakam b. al-Walid and 'Uthman b. al-Walid.[1710] He said, "And the two young men were killed – verily we belong to God! They were the two lambs, who were eaten and put down."[1711] Then they pledged allegiance to him. Then [Marwan] went to Damascus and ordered [the body] of Yazid b. al-Walid to be disinterred and gibbeted. [Marwan] received the pledge of allegiance from the people of Syria. Ibrahim b. al-Walid went to Marwan b. Muhammad in al-Jazira. He abdicated, and pledged allegiance to Marwan, who accepted it, and granted him safety. Ibrahim went and encamped at ar-Raqqa,[1712] on the banks of the Euphrates. Then [Marwan] received a letter from Sulayman b. Hisham requesting safety, which he granted. [Sulayman b. Hisham] went to him, and pledged allegiance to him. [The affairs of] Marwan b. Muhammad were going well.[1713]

1709 From "Yazid b. Khalid [b. 'Abdallah al-Qasri] killed them …" cf. *'Iqd*, IV, 467f. (Khalifa).

1710 From "Yazid b. Khalid [b. 'Abdallah al-Qasri] killed them …" cf *Azdi, 62f.

1711 The meaning is not clear. Perhaps there is a confusion between the word *ḥamal*, "lamb," and *ḥiml* or *ḥaml*, "load, burden."

1712 EI, III, 1108.

1713 From "Ibrahim b. al-Walid went to Marwan b. Muhammad in al-Jazira …" cf. **'Iqd*, IV, 468; *Azdi, 64.

The reign of Ibrahim b. al-Walid, who was deposed, lasted several months.

Abu l-Hasan:
[The reign of Ibrahim b. al-Walid lasted] two and a half months.[1714]

Yazid b. Khalid b. ʻAbdallah al-Qasri was killed in the Ghuta,[1715] by a man of the Banu Tamim, named Saʻsaʻa. Zamil b. ʻAmr, acting on orders from Marwan, killed al-Walid and Khalid, the sons of Yazid b. al-Walid b. ʻAbd al-Malik.[1716]

In this year, Thabit b. Nuʻaym renounced [Marwan]. He said, "I am al-Aṣqar al-Qahtani."[1717]

The people of Homs and Damascus renounced Marwan. Marwan marched against Homs, [567] and overpowered [the inhabitants]. He killed some of their leaders, and ordered a portion of their city to be demolished. [Then] he proclaimed safety for the people.[1718]

Then [Marwan] sent al-Walid b. Muʻawiya b. Marwan against Thabit b. Nuʻaym in Tiberias. He besieged the inhabitants [of Tiberias]. Thabit was put to flight, and many of his companions were killed. {394} Thabit fled to Palestine in order to hide himself there. Marwan sent ʻAmr b. al-Waddah and Abu l-Ward in pursuit of him. His hideout was discovered, and he was apprehended. He was sent to Damascus, to Marwan, who cut off his hands and feet.[1719]

1714 From "The reign of Ibrahim b. al-Walid …" cf. *ʻ*Iqd*, IV, 468.

1715 EI2, II, 1104.

1716 This sentence parallels *Azdi, 66, l. 8.

1717 On Thabit b. Nuʻaym, cf. *Futūḥ*, 209, Tab., II, 1871ff., 1892ff.; Wellhausen, *Arab Kingdom*, index; Ibn ʻAsakir, *Tahdhīb*, III, 372; al-Azdi, 66. Thabit was a leader of the Yemenites, and the title *al-Qaḥṭānī* indicated his position (Qahtan was the legendary ancestor of the South Arabian tribes). Ibn al-Ashʻath had assumed the title in order to appeal to the many Yemenites among his supporters (cf. *Tanbīh*, 314; Dixon, 168). The title was also used by Yazid b. al-Muhallab, who revolted during the reign of Yazid b. ʻAbd al-Malik (Dh., IV, 150, l. 13). The first part of Thabit's title is unclear. Z reads "al-Aqṣar"; U and al-Azdi, 66 read "al-Aṣfar." Al-Aṣqar, or al-Aṣfar, may have been Thabit's *laqab*. Al-Azdi adds that Thabit was urged to revolt by several verses by a *mawlā* of the Kalb, named ʻAtiyya al-Aṣfar (Azdi, 66). Al-Aṣfar may be the correct reading, and it is possible that Thabit took the name from ʻAtiyya; however, this cannot be proven. Another dubious possibility is "al-Aṣghar" – that is, "al-Qahtani junior." Perhaps Thabit fancied himself, or was considered by his followers, a younger version of Ibn al-Ashʻath or Yazid b. al-Muhallab, who had years earlier used the title al-Qahtani.

1718 From "The people of Homs and Damascus …" cf. *Azdi, 66, l. 8.

1719 From "Then [Marwan] sent al-Walid …" cf. Tab., II, 1894f.

In 127, the people of Kufa pledged allegiance to 'Abdallah b. Mu'awiya b. 'Abdallah b. Ja'far Dhi l-Jinahayn.[1720] With him were his two brothers, al-Hasan b. Mu'awiya and Yazid b. Mu'awiya.[1721]

*Isma'il b. Ibrahim:
'Abdallah b. Mu'awiya b. 'Abdallah b. Ja'far and his two brothers, al-Hasan and Yazid, came to 'Abdallah b. 'Umar b. 'Abd al-'Aziz in Kufa during the reign of Yazid b. al-Walid. He honored them, gave them mounts, and 300 *dirham*s every day. When Yazid died and Ibrahim b. al-Walid pledged allegiance to Marwan, some Shi'ites revolted, calling for the pledge of allegiance to ['Abdallah] b. Mu'awiya. The one who did that [i.e., the instigator] was Hilal b. al-Ward, a *mawlā* of the Banu 'Ijl.[1722] They brought ['Abdallah b. Mu'awiya] into the citadel. The people of Kufa, Isma'il b. 'Abdallah, and the Syrians who were in Kufa pledged allegiance to him. He entered [the citadel], and remained several days, during which time the people pledged allegiance to him. Pledges of allegiance came to him from al-Mada'in, and from everywhere. On Wednesday he went out, heading for ['Abdallah] b. 'Umar. But they did not do battle. Then, in the morning the people began to do battle. M-k-b-r b. al-Hawari and many of the Yemenites who were with Ibn Mu'awiya were killed. He was put to rout, and entered the citadel. But the Zaydites remained, and fought bitterly. They stuck to the entrances of the roads until [a promise] was made that 'Abdallah b. Mu'awiya and his two brothers could go [568] wherever they wished and would not be pursued. ['Abdallah] b. 'Umar sent [word] to 'Umar b. {395} al-Ghadban al-Qan'athra', ordering him to attack the citadel and to evict Ibn Mu'awiya. So 'Umar b. al-Ghadban was sent against him, and he drove [Ibn Mu'awiya] away, and also drove away his partisans and followers, composed of people of al-Mada'in, the Sawad, and Kufa. Agents of 'Umar [b. al-Ghadban] accompanied them until they expelled them from the Bridge.[1723] 'Umar [b. al-Ghadban] took

1720 On the revolt of 'Abdallah b. Mu'awiya, see EI2, I, 48, s.v. 'Abdallha b. Mu'awiya; Wellhausen, *Religio-Political Factions*, 164f., 167 n. 13; Wurtzel, "The Coinage of the Revolutionaries"; GAS, II, 349.

1721 From "In 127, the people of Kufa pledged allegiance …" cf. *Azdi, 66, l. 12.

1722 From "'Abdallah b. Mu'awiya b. 'Abdallah b. Ja'far and his two brothers …" cf. *Azdi, 66, l. 13.

1723 "The Bridge" refers to the bridge over the Euphrates at Kufa (Yaqut, II, 81).

up residence at the citadel.[1724] Then ['Abdallah] b. 'Umar sent Isma'il b. 'Abdallah as commander.[1725]

In 127, Sa'id b. Bahdal the Kharijite died.[1726]

*Isma'il b. Ibrahim:
When Sa'id b. Bahdal lay dying in Shahrazur, his generals gathered before him. He had summoned them in order to name one of them as his successor. They had entrusted that to him. He said to us,[1727] "Choose from among yourselves ten men." Then he narrowed the ten down to four, and said to the four, "Choose from among yourselves." They chose ad-Dahhak b. Qays al-Muhallimi[1728] and Shayban b. 'Abd al-'Aziz al-Yashkuri. Sa'id said to them, "Make a choice for the Muslims and for yourselves." Shayban said, "I choose ad-Dahhak, for myself and for the people." Ad-Dahhak said, "My choice is Shayban, for myself and for the people." But Shayban insisted on ad-Dahhak. The followers of both were satisfied with that, so they pledged allegiance to ad-Dahhak. Ad-Dahhak recited the following line of poetry:

> I shall lead men down, if I am their master,
> To a piercing which will [make blood] flow like water spouts![1729]

Isma'il b. Ibrahim < *al-Walid b. Sa'id ash-Shaybani:[1730]
Sa'id b. Bahdal convoked a council [*shūra*] from among six, among whom were ad-Dahhak, al-Khaybari, Shayban [b. 'Abd al-'Aziz], and 'Ubayda b. Sawwar at-Taghlibi, who was away in Azerbaijan. They pledged allegiance to ad-Dahhak. Then 'Ubayda arrived, and declared that he would not accept ad-Dahhak. But he was told by the others, "You had better go along with [569] the rest of us, or else we will let you know [about it

1724 From "'Abdallah b. Mu'awiya b. 'Abdallah b. Ja'far and his two brothers …" cf. Tab., II, 1881–1887.

1725 This sentence parallels *Azdi, 67, l. 2.

1726 This sentence parallels *Azdi, 67, l. 3.

1727 Khalifa and Isma'il b. Ibrahim neglected to name the original source for this report. It would seem to have been a Kharijite general, since he narrates in the first person (unless Isma'il himself was a participant in these events).

1728 On Ad-Dahhak's genealogy, cf. Ibn Hazm, 322; EI2, II, 90, s.v. ad-Dahhak b. Qays ash-Shaybani; Wellhausen, *Religio-Political Factions*, 80f.; Rotter, "The Umayyad Fulūs of Mosul," 193.

1729 Meter: *basīṭ*. From "When Sa'id b. Bahdal lay dying …" cf. *Azdi, 67, l. 3 (Khalifa).

1730 Perhaps this was a son of Sa'id b. Bahdal, or perhaps it was a grandson of ad-Dahhak, whose *kunya* was Abu Sa'id, according to al-Jahiz, III, 265.

with] our lances." So he pledged allegiance. Then ad-Dahhak sent Habna' b. 'Isma ash-Shaybani with mounted troops to Tikrit,[1731] {396} which he conquered, and he sent Abu r-Rish Khalid b. al-Rish to Hawlayya[1732] and its surrounding area.[1733] He confronted Jumay' b. Muqarrin al-Kalbi and Hurayth b. Abi l-Jahm. Jumay' was killed and Hurayth was put to flight. [Abu r-Rish] continued on to al-Mada'in. 'Abdallah b. 'Umar sent al-Asbagh b. Dhu'ala, who encamped at al-Mada'in. Abu r-Rish, 'Abthal, and Habna' b. 'Isma advanced, and they all met together at al-Mada'in. Al-Asbagh b. Dhu'ala crossed the Bridge and departed for Kufa. Ad-Dahhak b. Qays advanced toward Kufa, and encamped at Dayr ath-Tha'alib[1734] with 3,000 troops. At most, according to some, there were 4,000. 'Abdallah b. 'Umar sent 'Ubaydallah b. al-'Abbas al-Kindi with 10,000 troops. They came together, with the Euphrates between them. Miskin[1735] said, "'Ubaydallah! We offer you a choice. If you wish, cross over to us, and you have our guarantee that we will not attack you until everyone who is with you has crossed over. Or, we will cross over to you, under the same conditions." 'Ubaydallah refused [the proposal], and departed for Kufa. Miskin crossed the Euphrates. Ad-Dahhak advanced, and encamped on the bank of the Euphrates. The people set up pontoon bridges, and crossed over. Miskin advanced, and he found ['Abdallah] b. 'Umar with the Syrians and Kufans holding the entrances of the roads. They had dug trenches and prepared themselves for battle. [570] That was on a Wednesday in the first few days of *Sha'bān* 127/May 745. Miskin's troops stormed the trenches. Seventeen of them were killed, men and women. [Word of] that reached ad-Dahhak, who sent Habna' b. 'Isma with troops, but he decided against doing battle that night. Ad-Dahhak advanced against them with his troops. When he was within arrow shot, he sent down from each squadron a band which went eagerly into battle. It was not {397} long before the Syrians were put to rout. They crossed the trenches and entered Kufa.[1736] Then they returned immediately. That was on Thursday. They returned to their positions. Some of them attacked them. 'Asim b. 'Umar b. 'Abd al-'Aziz

1731 EI, IV, 632.

1732 Kh.: Hawlan; a marginal annotation suggests Hawlayya (cf. Yaqut, II, 366).

1733 From "Then ad-Dahhak sent Habna' …" cf. *Azdi, 67, l. 13.

1734 Cf. Yaqut, II, 650.

1735 Miskin is unidentified. Ibn Hazm, 322, mentions a Kharijite named Sukayn.

1736 In several of the following lines it is unclear to which antecedents some of the pronouns refer.

and Ja'far b. al-'Abbas were killed, and the Syrians were put to rout. Then, on Friday morning, Ibn 'Umar urged [his] troops on. He sent al-Asbagh b. Dhu'ala with 10,000 troops. He set out as though he were heading for Syria. Ad-Dahhak and his troops remained in position. He had intended to get to their camp when they had left. [But word of] that [plan] had reached them, so they left Shayban [b. 'Abd al-'Aziz] behind in the camp, while al-Asbagh and his troops proceeded until, when they were face to face with him, ad-Dahhak attacked them and Ibn 'Umar. Not one of them stuck to the man next to him [i.e., their ranks collapsed]. When night fell, the Syrians went out from Kufa,[1737] [scattering] in every direction. No one remained in the city. In the morning, Ibn 'Umar set out for Wasit. Ad-Dahhak's herald called out, "Do not pursue anyone who turns his back, and do not harm anyone. We have granted you a respite, Syrians, for three [days]. Whoever joins us shall have what we have. Those who prefer to go wherever they wish may go in safety."[1738] Those who came forward, they admitted to their ranks. They paid no attention to those who chose to depart. Habna' b. 'Isma was sent to the citadel of Kufa. He sold the booty, and obtained many stores, arms, and valuables. On 1 *Ramaḍān*/6 June 745 ad-Dahhak marched against Wasit, leaving Milhan as his lieutenant over Kufa. Ad-Dahhak marched against Ibn 'Umar, confronted him [571] in Wasit, and battled him. The hero of the Syrians in that battle was Mansur b. Jumhur. Jahshana, Mansur's nephew, was killed in that battle. Mansur attacked 'Ikrima,[1739] and killed him.

Isma'il [b. Ibrahim] b. Ishaq < *al-Walid b. Sa'id:
Mansur went out one day, and attacked 'Abd al-Malik b. 'Alqama, and struck him. The lance went right through him and came out his back, killing him. Ad-Dahhak's ranks collapsed, as they went off mourning for him. It is said that the fighting lasted six months. Some say it lasted a year, until Ibn 'Umar made peace with [ad-Dahhak]. Ibn 'Umar sent [word] to ad-Dahhak {398} that he would pledge allegiance to him, and give him free reign in the area under his authority.[1740]

Isma'il < *'Awn b. Yazid al-Bahili:
I was in Wasit, and I saw 'Abdallah b. 'Umar go to ad-Dahhak and pledge

1737 Khalifa's text, *kharaja ilā ahli sh-sha'm*, seems not to be correct. The word *ilā* has been omitted in the translation, and the phrase read as *kharaja ahlu sh-sha'm*.

1738 From "Ad-Dahhak's herald called out..." cf. (*) Azdi, 67, l. 16.

1739 According to at-Tabari's account he was 'Ikrima b. Shayban (Tab., II, 1906).

1740 From "Mansur went out ..." cf. (*) Azdi, 67, l. 18.

allegiance to him. Concerning that, Shubayl b. 'Azra ad-Duba'i[1741] said the following:

> Do you not see that God has granted victory to His Religion,
> And that the Quraysh pray behind the Bakr b. Wa'il?[1742]

In 127, 'Abd al-'Aziz b. 'Umar b. 'Abd al-'Aziz led the pilgrimage.

In 127, the following died: Abu Ishaq ['Amr b. 'Abdallah b. 'Ubayd] al-Hamdani, on the day, it is said, that ad-Dahhak b. Qays entered Kufa; Abu Hasin;[1743] Sa'id b. Masruq ath-Thawri;[1744] [572] Jabir b. Yazid al-Ju'fi;[1745] –

Abu Nu'aym:
[Jabir b. Yazid died] in 128.

– 'Asim b. Bahdala,[1746] a *mawlā* of the Banu Asad; Isma'il b. 'Abd ar-Rahman as-Suddi;[1747] Jami' b. Shaddad;[1748] – all [of the above] in Kufa; Muhammad b. Wasi' al-Azdi,[1749] in Basra; Yazid b. Abi Habib,[1750] in Egypt; [and] Wahb b. Kaysan,[1751] a *mawlā* of the family of az-Zubayr.

[573] The Year 128/745–746

In this year, ad-Dahhak b. Qays went to Mosul, whose governor went out against him. {399} Ad-Dahhak killed him, and took control of the

1741 D. before 131/748–749 (*Ṭbq.*, 522; *Jarḥ*, II, I, 381; 'Abbas, *Shi'r*, 144, #51; cf. GAS, II, 174, 437).

1742 Meter *ṭawīl*. Cf. Wellhausen, *Arab Kingdom*, 390; Wellhausen, *Religio-Political Factions*, 80. The first hemistich of the verse as found in al-Mas'udi, *Tanbīh*, 326, reads *alam tara anna llāh anzala naṣra-hu*. Cf. al-Jahiz, I, 343, and III, 265; Tab., II, 1913; Azdi, 68; al-Mas'udi, cf. *Tanbīh*, 326; Ibn Hazm, 322; Ibn 'Asakir, *Tahdhīb*, VI, 286; Dh., V, 33; 'Abbas, *Shi'r*, 74 (< volume VIII, unpublished, of the *Ansāb al-Ashrāf*).

1743 On the death of Abu Hasin cf. Ibn Hajar, VII, 128; 'Uthman b. 'Asim (*Ṭbq.*, 369; Ibn Sa'd, VI, 321; Ibn Hajar, VII, 126).

1744 *Ṭbq.*, 371; Ibn Sa'd, VI, 327; Ibn Hajar, IV, 82.

1745 GAS, I, 307.

1746 On the death of 'Asim b. Bahdala cf. Ibn Hajar, V, 39 (Khalifa); EI2, I, 706; GAS, I, 7.

1747 On the death of Isma'il b. 'Abd ar-Rahman as-Suddi cf. #Dh., V, 43 (Khalifa); GAS, I, 32.

1748 On the death of Jami' b. Shaddad cf. #Ibn Hajar, II, 57 (Khalifa); *Ṭbq.*, 369; Ibn Sa'd, VI, 318; Ibn Hajar, II, 56.

1749 On the death of Muhammad b. Wasi' al-Azdi cf. #Dh., V, 32 (Khalifa); #Ibn Hajar, IX, 499–500 (Khalifa); *Ṭbq.*, 515; Ibn Sa'd, VII, 241.

1750 GAS, I, 341.

1751 *Ṭbq.*, 651; Ibn Hajar, XI, 166.

city.[1752] [News of this] reached Marwan, who wrote to his son 'Abdallah b. Marwan, who at that time was governor over al-Jazira, ordering him to encamp at Nasibin. Ad-Dahhak marched against him, and besieged him for about two months at Nasibin, but was unable to gain any advantage over him. He sent his cavalry raiding in al-Jazira, and they eventually went as far as ar-Raqqa. The Syrian kings, of the Quraysh and other [tribes], who were fleeing from Marwan, rallied to ad-Dahhak. Marwan marched toward Nasibin. He departed from 'Ayn al-Warda,[1753] and encamped at al-Akdar,[1754] with his army prepared for combat. His infantry went on foot, and his cavalry were clad in armor. He was at the center of the army. He confronted ad-Dahhak at about two *parasangs* from ad-Dahhak's camp, close to the time of the noon prayer.[1755]

Isma'il < *as-Sari b. Muslim and *al-Walid b. Sa'id:
When the two armies approached each other, the Syrian nobles who were with ad-Dahhak approached him and said, "Since the beginning of Islam, no one who has espoused[1756] this view has gathered a following to compare with yours. So stay behind, and send some of your cavalry and infantry to confront this tyrant." He said, [574] "I have no need of anything in this world of yours. I only want this tyrant. I have made it my duty before God that when I see him, I shall attack him [and battle him] until God decides for me or for them. I have a debt of 7 *dirhams*, of which I have 3 *dirhams* in my sleeve.[1757] Then Marwan approached. They met and battled until the sun went down. Ad-Dahhak was killed in the battle, but no one realized it. Night separated them, and the two sides returned to their camps. The dead numbered about {400} 6,000, most of them followers of ad-Dahhak. About 800 of the slain *shurāt* were women. In the morning, Marwan ordered a flag to be raised [signaling] quarter, and he called [on the people] to take note of it. Al-Khaybari went out and called to his *shurāt*, "Whoever desires Paradise and death, let him present himself, [and make a stand] with me!" Three hundred and fifty horsemen presented themselves [and joined] with him. They attacked Marwan in the center of the army. He withdrew and

1752 Cf. Rotter, "The Umayyad Fulūs of Mosul," 193.
1753 Cf. EI2, I, 789; cf. EI, III, 1119, s.v. Ra's al-'Ayn.
1754 Unidentified.
1755 From "In this year, ad-Dahhak b. Qays went to Mosul …" cf. Tab., II, 1938f.
1756 Apparently, they are referring to Kharijitism, the ideology of which is rather unclear, as regards the so-called Kharijites of the late Umayyad period.
1757 From "When the two armies approached each other …" *Azdi, 70, l. 12 (Khalifa); (*) Dh., V, 34.

abandoned the center. One of the Kharijites attacked Marwan and struck him on the shoulder with his sword, cutting his sword belt so that the scabbard fell. Marwan struck him, and cut off his hand. He turned his back and fled.

Ismail < *as-Sari, who was present on that day:
On that day there was a dense fog, and a man could not see the mane of his horse, or his whip. The remnant of Marwan's army scattered in every direction. His son, 'Abdallah b. Marwan, remained with the right flank, and Ishaq b. Muslim remained with the left flank. In their positions, they were unaware of Marwan's situation. Al-Khaybari went and entered Marwan's camp. He cut the tent ropes of his living quarters, and sat down on his bed. His companions scattered around the room taking booty and killing. Their motto was "Oh Khaybari!" The rest of al-Khaybari's companions did not know what was happening, because of the dense fog. They did not see al-Khaybari until he had been killed. When those in Marwan's camp saw how few [the Kharijites] were, a *mawlā* of Muhammad b. Marwan – a man in his guard named Sulayman b. Masruh, a Berber – became excited, and called out to the slaves, "Whoever follows me will be free!" About 3,000 or 4,000 men, slaves and non-slaves, [575] rallied around him. Al-Khaybari was killed. The fog dissipated from the two flanks of Marwan's army, which were led by 'Abdallah b. Marwan and Ishaq b. Muslim, and they saw the flags of the Kharijites in Marwan's place. They said, "Al-Khaybari has been killed." His companions carried him away and buried him, so [Marwan's men] could not find his head or his body.[1758] One of Marwan's *mawālī*, named Ghazwan, went out and rode his horse at a gallop {401} to Marwan, and informed him of the news. Marwan returned to his camp. The Kharijites retraced their steps, and Shayban prepared to turn back. He encamped at the two Zabs,[1759] in the region of Mosul, and entrenched himself. Marwan battled them for ten months. Every day Marwan's flag was put to rout. Then Shayban abandoned the trenches, and went out to Shahrazur. Then he went down to Mah,[1760] then to as-Saymara.[1761] Then he

1758 From "On that day there was a dense fog …" cf. (*) Azdi, 72, l. 4 (Khalifa).

1759 Az-Zab is the name of two tributaries of the Tigris (cf. EI, IV, 1180f.).

1760 Mah al-Basra was a designation of Nihawand, and Mah al-Kufa was a designation of Dinawar (cf. Zambaur, *Münzprägungen*, 222). The old Persian province of Mada was called Mah (cf. ibid., 223, s.v. Mahi).

1761 As-Saymara is found mentioned in all volumes of the BGA (see indices); cf. Yaqut, III, 443; cf. Minorsky, 52, 132.

went to Kirman. Then he went to the island of Barkawan.[1762] Then he went to Oman, where they battled him, and he was killed.[1763]

Isma'il < *'Asim b. al-Hadthan < *Habib b. Jadara al-Hilali:[1764]
I never saw a woman suffer greater grief than a [certain] woman of the Banu Shayban. Her father, her brother, her husband, her mother, and her paternal and maternal aunts were killed with ad-Dahhak. Her eyes never ceased to flow with tears. I never saw her laugh or smile. She said:

1. Who is there to give comfort to a heart racked by sadness,
   Or to a soul that has no peace?

2. The pious ones have departed and gone away;
   The best family there is has departed;

3. [576] A family that is [now] dead.
   Whatever they did was good;

4. They faced the swords in battle
   Unflinchingly, and were no cowards.

5. Youths who sold themselves,[1765]
   And, by the Lord of the Ka'ba, were not defrauded.

6. They pursued the pleasure of their Lord,
   When Religion and Law had died.

7. {402} This people attained what they sought:
   God's blessing unprecedented![1766]

In 128, Bistam b. Layth at-Taghlibi, one of the Banu Zayd, revolted in Azerbaijan. He held the views of the Bayhasiyya.[1767] He killed one of

1762 The island is also known as Lafit, and is today known as Qishm (see Minorsky, 190). Khalifa spells the name Abarakawan elsewhere (Kh., 586).
1763 Cf. below, pages 284–285; cf. Tab., III, 78. On Shayban b. 'Abd al-'Aziz, see Wellhausen, *Religio-Political Factions*, 82. From "On that day there was a dense fog ..." cf. Tab., II, 1940f., 1943–1949; (*) Dh., V, 34.
1764 Cf. Habib b. Khadara or Khidra (al-Jahiz, *al-Bayān*, III, 264; al-Mubarrad, 709, l. 10; 'Abbas, *Shi'r*, 144, #56).
1765 Cf. note 726.
1766 Meter: *madīd*. The verses are not in Ihsan 'Abbas's *Shi'r al-Khawārij*. From "I never saw a woman suffer greater grief ..." cf. * *'Iqd*, III, 260 (Khalifa; lacking sixth verse).
1767 On the Bayhasiyya, cf. EI2, I, 113, s.v. Abu Bayhas. On Bistam b. Layth, see Rotter, "The Umayyad Fulūs of Mosul," 192.

Marwan's governors, then went to Balad[1768] with some 40 men. Yahya b. Abi l-Hurr marched against him with men from Mosul, but he put them to rout. Then he went to Qarda. A band of more than 1,000 Syrians passed him. He attacked them at night, and caused some casualties among them. Then he departed for Nasibin,[1769] where he killed a man of the Shaybanids named Tariq al-Ahdab. Then he went to Armenia and Azerbaijan. 'Asim b. Yazid sent his brother, 'Abd al-Malik, against him with 6,000 troops. With about 200 men, [Bistam] killed 'Abd al-Malik and the chiefs among his men.[1770] Then he marched to Shahrazur, where Jidar b. Qays ash-Shaybani, Marwan's governor, [577] fortified himself against him. {403} Then Bistam proceeded to Iraq, where he confronted 'Aziz b. Abi l-Mutawakkil who had about 2,000 men, and he defeated them. News of [Bistam's exploits] reached ad-Dahhak, who sent Shajara b. Zuhayr ash-Shaybani and al-Khaybari against him. Al-Khaybari confronted him and attacked him at night. Bistam and most of his companions were killed. In the morning, [al-Khaybari] pursued those of them who remained in the vineyards and the gardens. He sold the booty [*fay'*], then departed. Then Shajara arrived, and departed.

In 128, the following died: Bukayr b. 'Abdallah al-Ashajj; Abu 'Imran al-Jawni;[1771] Sa'd b. Ibrahim.[1772]

'Abd al-'Aziz b. 'Umar b. 'Abd al-'Aziz led the pilgrimage.

[578] The Governorship of 'Abdallah b. 'Umar b. 'Abd al-'Aziz in Iraq

*Al-Walid b. Hisham < his father < his grandfather; *'Abdallah b. Mughira < his father; *Abu l-Yaqzan; and others:
Abdallah b. 'Umar b. 'Abd al-'Aziz assumed the governorship of Iraq in 126/743–744, appointed by Yazid b. al-Walid.

His Chief of Police:

Al-Hajjaj b. Artat the jurist, who later went to Wasit.

A man of the Kalb was then appointed, and served for the duration of 'Abdallah's governorship.

1768 Cf. Minorsky, 76, 140; Zambaur, *Münzprägungen*, 77.

1769 From "In 128, Bistam …" cf. (*) Dh., V, 34, l. 27.

1770 U: He killed 'Abd al-Malik, and took his men as prisoners.

1771 'Abd al-Malik b. Habib (*Ṭbq*., 515; Ibn Sa'd, VII, 238; Ibn Hajar, VI, 389).

1772 On the death of Sa'd b. Ibrahim cf. Ibn Hajar, III, 464 (Khalifa).

Chief of Police in Basra and Kufa: He left their appointment to his lieutenants in those cities.

Finance Secretary: Ruzbihan.

Secretary for Correspondence: Al-Hakam b. an-Nu'man, one of their *mawālī*.

Ibn 'Umar was dismissed when he was less than 40 years of age.

In 128, Marwan sent Yazid b. 'Umar b. Hubayra as governor over Iraq. That was before the death of ad-Dahhak. He marched, and encamped at Hit.[1773] The news reached al-Muthanna b. 'Imran al-'A'idhi of the Quraysh, [579] ad-Dahhak's lieutenant in Kufa, who sent Mansur b. Jumhur and his Kharijite followers against him. {404} Mansur encamped at al-Anbar. Ibn Hubayra marched. He left the al-Anbar road, and went out to 'Ayn at-Tamr.[1774] Mansur b. Jumhur went back. They met at Gh-m-r[1775] and joined in battle. Mansur and his companions were put to rout, and fled to Kufa. Ibn Hubayra proceeded to ar-R-w-h-'.[1776] Then al-Muthanna b. 'Imran went out against him, but Ibn Hubayra put them to rout, and killed many of them. On the same night, they went out from Kufa. Ibn Hubayra encamped at an-Nukhayla. 'Ubayda b. Sawwar at-Taghlibi marched against him, with al-Mantuf b. Sawwar in command of his vanguard. He put him to rout, and he fled to as-Sarat[1777] and crossed the bridge. 'Ubayda was opposite as-Sarat. Muta'in b. Muta'in[1778] approached from Kaskar[1779] with his *shurāt*. He encamped at as-Sib.[1780] Ibn Hubayra sent a man named 'Atiyya at-Taghlibi against him. Muta'in was killed at as-Sib. His army remained as it was, led by a man named Shayban. 'Ubayda b. Sawwar marched toward Shayban's camp. Ibn Hubayra approached, and they fought bitterly. 'Ubayda and the *shurāt* who stood firm with him were killed. [580] Mansur b. Jumhur went

1773 EI2, IV, 510.

1774 EI2, I, 788.

1775 Unidentified.

1776 Cf. Yaqut, II, 829.

1777 Cf. BGA, I, 84, 85; II, 165; III, 120, 124 (Nahr as-Sarat). Cf. *Futūḥ*, 246, 259, 287, 295; al-Ya'qubi, II, 449; Yaqut, III, 377.

1778 Muta'in had been sent by ad-Dahhak as governor over Kufa, replacing Milhan, who had been killed (Tab., II, 1938).

1779 EI, II, 800.

1780 Cf. BGA, III, 53, 110, 134; cf. Sib Bani Kuma (BGA, VI, 193; VII, 186; VIII, 367); cf. BGA, VII, 267. Cf. also *Futūḥ*, 291; Yaqut, III, 208.

to Hulwan, and remained there.[1781] Then he went from place to place, and eventually reached Sind. Abu Talut al-Khasi went to Basra, remained there for several days, then joined Shayban b. 'Abd al-'Aziz al-Yashkuri.[1782]

In 128, al-Harith b. Surayj took refuge with al-Kirmani [Juday' b. 'Ali], governor of the Azd. He said, "Come, let us battle this tyrant" – meaning Nasr b. Sayyar. They battled Nasr, and put him to rout. When night fell, Nasr went out in the direction of Abrashahr.[1783] Al-Harith hoped that the Tamim would rally to him, so he made contact with them. They said, "We are with you," so he showed favor to them. The Mudar joined al-Harith, and pledged allegiance to him. The Yemen and the Rabi'a sided with al-Kirmani. They battled. Al-Harith was killed – by whom, it is not known – and the Tamim were put to rout. Al-Kirmani conquered {405} Marw, and appointed lieutenants.[1784] In this connection, concerning the killing of al-Harith b. Surayj, Nasr said [the following]:

1. [581] Bringer of disgrace on your people,
   Away with you, who are doomed to perdition!
2. The Azd and their partisans did not
   Desire 'Amr or Malik.[1785]

'Abd al-'Aziz b. 'Umar b. 'Abd al-'Aziz led the pilgrimage.

[582] The Year 129/746–747

Isma'il b. Ishaq:
After Ibn Hubayra had killed 'Ubayda b. Sawwar and his companions, he marched to Wasit. The inhabitants of the city rose up and blocked the gate of the citadel against Ibn 'Umar with bricks, until Ibn Hubayra came. Bishr b. 'Abd al-Malik b. Bishr b. Marwan came to him.[1786] He took away

1781 Mansur b. Jumhur joined the movement of 'Abdallah b. Mu'awiya, and seized and held parts of al-Jibal for a short time, before he fled to Sind (cf. Tab., II, 1883, 1946, 1977).

1782 From "In 128, Marwan sent Yazid ..." cf. Tab., II, 1945ff.

1783 Cf. EI2, I, 3; cf. EI, III, 928, s.v. Nisapur; cf. Zambaur, *Münzprägungen*, 36.

1784 The Arabic is *wa-kataba l-'uhūd*. On Juday' b. 'Ali al-Kirmani, see Shaban, *'Abbasid Revolution*, index; Wellhausen, *Arab Kingdom*, index; 'Abd al-'Aziz Hamid, 26–28.

1785 Meter: *sarī'*. Ibn al-Athir explains that 'Amr and Malik were clans (*buṭūn*) of the Tamim (IA, V, 347). The Tamim had joined al-Harith, and the Azd were al-Kirmani's people. On the verse cf. Tab., II, 1935 (Tab.'s version has an additional verse after each of Kh.'s).

1786 The mention here of Bishr b. 'Abd al-Malik b. Bishr is puzzling. The impression one

his sword, and ordered him [to be confined] in one of the rooms of the citadel. Ibn Hubayra did not want to have anything further to do with this matter, and wrote to Marwan concerning that. Marwan wrote back to him, ordering him to assassinate him, but Ibn Hubayra did not wish to do that. So Marwan wrote to him, ordering him to send [Bishr] to him. So he sent [Bishr] to Marwan, who imprisoned him in Harran with Ibrahim [b. Muhammad] b. ‘Ali.[1787]

In 129, ‘Abdallah b. Yahya al-A‘war {406} al-Kindi, who was called Talib al-Haqq [Seeker of the Truth], revolted in Hadramawt, and expelled the governor there, Ibrahim b. Jabala b. Makhrama al-Kindi, without a fight. The Ibadites and many of his Basran companions joined him and pledged allegiance to him. Then he went out to San‘a’, whose governor was al-Qasim b. ‘Umar ath-Thaqafi, with 2,000 of the *shurāt*. Al-Qasim b. ‘Umar went out with about 30,000 [men]. [583] They met at Lahj,[1788] a village of Abyan,[1789] and fought bitterly, until al-Qasim was put to rout, and fled to San‘a’. Most of the dead were from among his men. ‘Abdallah b. Yahya advanced. Al-Qasim entrenched himself. [‘Abdallah b. Yahya] attacked him at the crack of dawn, and al-Qasim fled. As-Salt b. Yusuf b. ‘Umar was killed in the battle, as were many others. [‘Abdallah b. Yahya] entered San‘a’, and seized the stores and valuables, with which he increased his power. He remained [there] several months, then he sent an Azdite of Basra, named Balj b. al-Muthanna, to Mecca. Then he sent Abu Hamza al-Mukhtar b. ‘Awf al-Azdi with 10,000 [troops], and ordered him to remain in Mecca.[1790]

Isma‘il b. Ishaq:
Balj [b. al-Muthanna] went forth during the pilgrimage season. The people, being at ‘Arafat, were unaware of them, until the cavalry appeared suddenly

---

gets from this report is that Bishr is the one who is locked up, then sent to Marwan, and imprisoned in Harran with Ibrahim b. Muhammad. However, it is known that ‘Abdallah b. ‘Umar was imprisoned in Harran with Ibrahim (cf. Tab., III, 43f.). There is practically no mention of Bishr b. ‘Abd al-Malik b. Bishr in any of the literature. Cf. Tab., III, 68f., parts of which bear some superficial resemblances to the present narrative in Khalifa. Al-Azdi, 77, quotes part of the account from Khalifa, but omits mention of Bishr b. ‘Abd al-Malik.

1787 On Ibrahim b. Muhammad b. ‘Ali, see EI2, III, 988; Shaban, *‘Abbasid Revolution*, 164. From “After Ibn Hubayra had killed ‘Ubayda …” cf. (*) Azdi, 77, l. 2.

1788 Z: al-Janih; U: al-Jalih. On Lahij (or Lahj), cf. EI, III, 5. On the revolt of ‘Abdallah b. Yahya and Abu Hamza, see Wellhausen, *Religio-Political Factions*, 85–91.

1789 EI2, I, 169.

1790 From “In 129, ‘Abdallah b. Yahya al-A‘war …” cf. Tab., II, 1942f.; cf. *Aghānī*, XX, 97–99 (= Tab., in part); (*) Azdi, 77, l. 4 and 101, l. 12; (*) Dh., V, 36.

from the hill on the at-Ta'if road. The people rallied to 'Abd al-Wahid b. Sulayman b. 'Abd al-Malik b. Marwan, the governor over Mecca and Medina. 'Abd al-Wahid did not wish to do battle with them, so 'Abdallah b. Hasan b. Hasan b. 'Ali b. Abi Talib went between them, cutting them off from each other, so that they would not cause any incident until the pilgrimage was finished. They observed [that]. 'Abd al-Wahid stood with the people [at 'Arafat], and Balj stood with his companions at 'Arafat, both at the same time. They remained for several days at Mina. On *Yawm an-Nafr*, 'Abd al-Wahid left Mina and went to Mecca. Then Abu Hamza came to Mecca, and delivered a sermon from the pulpit.[1791] He said, "People of Mecca![1792] You reproach me because of my companions. You claim that they are youths."

{407}[584] Abu Hamza's Sermon

People of Mecca! You reproach me because of my companions. You claim that they are youths. What were the companions of the Prophet if not youths? Indeed, I am aware of your headlong rush [into vice], which will cause you harm in the hereafter. If I were not occupied with other affairs, I would not forego taking control of you. Yes, they are youths, mature in their youth, serious, their eyes ignorant of evil, their feet slow to commit any deception. They have been observed in the middle of the night, their spines bent [as they pore] over the Qur'an. When one of them comes upon a verse in which Paradise is mentioned, he weeps, longing for it. When he comes upon a verse in which the Fire is mentioned, he moans as if the groans of Hell were in his ears. They exhaust themselves continually, night and day, [with their religious devotions]. The earth has worn out their foreheads, their hands, and their knees. Their [skin] color has turned yellow, and their bodies have become emaciated from their constant worship and the frequency of their fasting. They consider that little on God's behalf. They fulfill God's covenant in expectation of His reward. When they see the arrows of the enemy notched [and poised for shooting]; when they see their lances aimed, and their swords unsheathed; when they behold the squadron, terrifying, flashing with the thunderbolts of death, they consider the threat of the squadron as naught in comparison to God's threat. A youth among them went forward until his feet slid from the neck of his horse. His

1791 From "Balj [b. al-Muthanna] went forth ..." cf. al-Ya'qubi, II, 406; cf. Tab., II, 1981ff.; cf. *Aghānī*, XX, 99f. (= Tab., in part).

1792 There is some difference of opinion in the sources as to whether the following speech was delivered in Mecca or Medina.

beautiful face was sprinkled with blood, and his brow was covered with the dust of the ground. The predatory creatures of the land hastened to him. How many an owner of an eye, now being nibbled by birds, used to weep for fear of God! How many an owner of a hand, which has been separated at its wrist, used to lean on it while prostrating himself in prayer to God in the middle of the night![1793] And how many soft cheeks {408} and noble brows have been torn by shafts of iron! May God have mercy on bodies such as those, and may He admit their souls to Paradise.[1794]

[585] Then he said:

We are all one people, on the same side, except for the worshipers of graven images, the infidel people of the Book, tyrannical princes, or anyone who supports them.[1795]

*Isma'il b. Ishaq < az-Zanji b. Khalid:[1796]
Abu Hamza delivered a sermon to us in Mecca. He raised doubts among the insightful, and the skeptics increased.[1797] He praised God, and said:

"People! We have asked you about these governors[1798] of yours. You said what we are aware of concerning them. You said, 'They have taken wealth to which they were not entitled, and have put it where it does not belong. They have ruled despotically, and have taken exclusive possession of what rightfully belongs to us, including our booty [gained in raids]. They have passed it around among their rich and their possessors of worldly rank. They have used our portions, and that which rightfully belongs to us, as dowries for women and for [the purchase of] slave girls for sexual intercourse.' We said to you, 'Go after those who have oppressed us and

1793 From "People of Mecca! …" cf. al-Jahiz, II, 124f.; cf. *'Uyūn*, II, 250.

1794 On the obsession with death which most of the Kharijites seemed to have had, see Wellhausen, *Religio-Political Factions*, 22f.; cf. also note 726. See also the asceticism of Dawud b. an-Nu'man, who gave up worldly wealth for Paradise (Kh., 348). Nearly all of the Kharijite leaders whose activities Khalifa treats, died quick and violent deaths. From "People of Mecca! …" cf. Tab., II, 2010f.; **'Iqd*, IV, 144; cf. *Aghānī*, XX, 104, l. 20; *Aghānī*, XX, 107, l. 21; (*) Azdi, 105, l. 14 (Khalifa – see Azdi, 103, l. 13).

1795 This sentence parallels Tab., II, 2010; **'Iqd*, IV, 144; (*) Azdi, 106; cf. *Aghānī*, XX, 104, l. 15 (= Tab.).

1796 Muslim b. Khalid, d. 180/796–797 (*Ṭbq.*, 719; Ibn Sa'd, V, 499; *Ma'ārif*, 511, 596; Ibn Hajar, X, 128; cf. GAS, I, 38).

1797 This statement is credited to Malik b. Anas in the *'Iqd*, IV, 54 and 144. Portions of Abu Hamza's sermon, quoted by al-Jahiz and Ibn 'Abd Rabbihi, but absent from Khalifa's version, have been translated by Williams, 215–219. From "Abu Hamza delivered a sermon…" cf. *'Iqd*, IV, 54, l. 14 (Malik b. Anas); cf. *'Iqd*, IV, 144, l. 22 (Malik b. Anas).

1798 The Arabic is *wulāt*. The Umayyads are meant.

you; those who have ruled as tyrants, governing without regard to God's revealed Law.' You replied, 'We are unable to do that. But we would like to find a person who would help us.' We said, 'We can help you. Then God is a shepherd over us.' If we are victorious, we shall surely give to every man what rightfully belongs to him. We have come and have braved the lances with our faces, and the swords with our breasts. We have taken God as our shepherd and guarantor that if we are victorious, we shall surely give to each person that which he justly deserves. [But] you disregarded them, and battled us,[1799] damn you! If you say, 'We do not know what you are talking about, and we are not acquainted with it,' it would be a better excuse, even though there is no excuse for ignorance. But God wanted to speak the truth by relying on your own statements, and he will hold you responsible for it in the hereafter."[1800]

In 129, Ibn Hubayra sent Nubata b. Hanzala, of the Banu Bakr b. Kilab, against Sulayman b. Habib b. al-Muhallab, who had gone to al-Ahwaz when Shayban b. 'Abd al-'Aziz withdrew, and was with him.[1801] Sulayman sent Dawud b. Hatim [to confront Nubata]. They met [in battle] at al-Madhiyar, which is also known as [586] Manadhir.[1802] Dawud and his companions were put to rout {409} and killed.[1803] The following were killed: Dawud b. Hatim, Qabisa b. 'Umar[1804] b. al-Muhallab b. Qabisa b. al-Muhallab, [and] Makhlad b. Mu'awiya b. al-Muhallab.

In this year, Ibn Hubayra sent 'Amir b. Dubara, of the Murra of the Ghatafan, against Shayban b. 'Abd al-'Aziz al-Yashkuri, after Shayban had withdrawn from Marwan. Shayban sent al-Jawn ash-Shaybani [to confront him], and they met at as-Sinn.[1805] Al-Jawn and his companions were killed. Shayban went down to Shahrazur. Marwan wrote to Ibn Hubayra, "Do not engage him in battle, but whenever he departs [from a camp], encamp

1799 That is, "You disregarded the real enemy, and battled us instead." This section of the speech must have been delivered after Abu Hamza battled the Medinese at Qudayd (cf. Kh. 592f.).

1800 From "People! We have asked ..." cf. al-Jahiz, II, 124; cf. Tab. II, 2008; *'*Iqd*, IV, 146, l. 5; cf. *Aghānī*, XX, 103, l. 23 (= Tab.).

1801 Sulayman b. Habib also joined the rebellion of 'Abdallah b. Mu'awiya (cf. Tab., II, 1947, 1978).

1802 Cf. *Futūḥ*, 377, 378, 385; BGA, I, 89, 95; II, 171, 177; III, 52, 406; VI, 42; VII, 188, 248, 274, 361; Zambaur, *Münzprägungen*, 249.

1803 From "In 129, Ibn Hubayra sent Nubata ..." cf. Tab., II, 1946 (Hisham b. al-Kalbi < Abu Mikhnaf).

1804 Z: Qabisa b. 'Amr.

1805 Cf. Minorsky, 76, 141; cf. EI2, II, 249b, s.v. Dijla; EI2, III, 1252a, s.v. 'Irak.

there." [Shayban's] companions began to disperse from him, and he eventually went to Mah.

Isma'il b. Ishaq:
Then he went to as-Saymara, then to the island of Abarkawan.[1806] Then he crossed over to Oman, where he was killed.[1807]

Ibn Hubayra wrote to 'Amir b. Dubara, ordering him to march against 'Abdallah b. Mu'awiya al-Hashimi, and he confronted him in Istakhr. His two brothers, al-Hasan b. Mu'awiya and Yazid b. Mu'awiya, were with him. Ibn Dubara put him to rout, and he fled to Khurasan, where Abu Muslim, who had appeared in *Ramaḍān* 129/May–June 747, imprisoned al-Hashimi and his two brothers.[1808]

In 129, al-Kirmani marched to Marw ar-Rudh. Salm b. Ahwaz al-Mazini, governor under Nasr b. Sayyar, marched against him. They met [in battle], and [587] al-Kirmani was routed. The Tamim fell upon the camp for plundering. Al-Kirmani turned around and attacked them, and put them to rout. That was at night. They returned to their camp, and agreed a truce for three days. Al-Kirmani set out at night from behind the mountain. In the morning they pursued him and engaged him in battle. Then they made peace on condition that al-Kirmani reside in the village of Bab 'Abd al-Qays until they examined their views, and Ibn Ahwaz [would remain] in the city of Marw ar-Rudh.[1809] Nasr b. Sayyar marched against them. They battled for six months, into the middle of winter, and the [horses'] shanks became emaciated. Al-Kirmani sent [word of the situation] to his son, who was in control of Marw. His son sent about 1,000 men to him, along with clothes and commodities {410} sufficient for a year. 'Abd al-Jabbar b. Shu'ayb, a man of the Banu Huna'a, was in command of them. Cavalry of the Banu Tamim confronted them, put them to rout, and took what they were conveying. Then they returned to Marw. The Banu Tamim who were in Marw, led by 'Arfaja b. al-Ward as-Sa'di, attacked the son of al-Kirmani, and besieged him in the city. They received word that Nasr and al-Kirmani had made peace. They expelled Ibn al-Kirmani from the city. Nasr and al-Kirmani returned to Marw. Al-Kirmani remained for

1806 See note 1762.

1807 From "In this year, Ibn Hubayra sent 'Amir ..." cf. Tab., II, 1945–1949; *Ibn 'Asakir, *Tahdhīb*, VII, 155 (Khalifa).

1808 From "Ibn Hubayra wrote to 'Amir b. Dubara ..." cf. *Ibn 'Asakir, *Tahdhīb*, VII, 155, l. 3.

1809 The translation of this sentence is uncertain.

several days, then he withdrew from Nasr, and went out on the same night. When Nasr had performed the morning prayer, he went out to them. The ambassadors went between them, and proceeded to prohibit the people from doing battle. While they were in this situation, al-Harith b. Surayj[1810] attacked with the Banu Hanzala, and fighting broke out. Al-Kirmani was put to flight, and they caught up with him and killed him. A man of the Banu Mujashi', named Muharib b. Hilal b. 'Ulaym, brought his head. Ibn al-Kirmani, the Rabi'a, and the [Banu] l-Asad went to Sarakhs, where they joined, and pledged allegiance to, Shayban b. Maslama of the Banu Sadus, a Harurite who had taken control of Sarakhs, Tus, and part of Abrashahr with about 30,000 Kharijites. When the Basran Kharijites who were with him saw that, they said, "He is putting his trust in this world, and is engaging in partisanship." [588] Mishkan, a *mawlā* of the Banu Sulaym, seceded with 5,000 men. 'Abdallah b. as-Simt, a *mawlā* of the Mudar, separated from him with about 1,000[1811] men. 'Abd ar-Rahman b. Ziyad, a *mawlā* of the Quraysh, and one of their chiefs, [withdrew], remaining in his house. Shayban marched with the Harurites who remained with him, in two directions. He sent Ibn al-Kirmani, with 5,000 or 6,000 men, to cross over to Marw. Shayban also marched to Marw. Nasr b. Sayyar marched with an army of Mudarites against Ibn al-Kirmani, and confronted him in Qar, a village of Marw. They fought bitterly until the Harurites were put to rout. They killed about 300 of them. Ibn al-Kirmani departed on the same night. He encamped at a village called '-b-z-n, which was below [Nasr's] position.[1812] In the morning, Nasr and his companions engaged him in battle, put them to rout, and slaughtered them, [although] Ibn al-Kirmani escaped. Shayban entered from the other side. He came to where the Azd were and dug a trench. {411} The Rabi'a and the [Banu] l-Asad pledged allegiance to him. Nasr besieged them, and [also] entrenched himself. They fought in those two trenches for about a year and a half.

In 129, there was an uprising by the Ibadites in the Maghrib. 'Abd ar-Rahman b. Habib al-Fihri attacked, killed, and gibbeted their chief, Sa'd b. Mas'ud. The Ibadites revolted, led by 'Abd al-Jabbar b. Ma'n. Yazid b. Safwan al-Ma'afiri confronted them in *Ṣafar* 129/October–November 746. The chiefs were killed, and Ibn Habib's companions were put to rout.

1810 According to a previous report, al-Harith b. Surayj had been killed in 128/745–746 (Kh., 580). Perhaps al-Harith's son, al-Hatim b. al-Harith b. Surayj is meant (cf. Tab., II, 1970, 1975).

1811 Z: 2,000.

1812 Z: *asfal min makāni-hi*; U: *asfal min Mukrān* (?).

Abu Qurra the Sufrite went from Tlemcen in *Ṣafar*/October–November 746 also. Ibn Habib sent Sulayman b. ʿUthman against him. Sulayman, ʿAbdallah, and ʿUthman were killed, along with [other] nobles of Ifriqiya. Abu Qurra departed, and returned to Tlemcen.[1813]

ʿAbd al-Wahid b. Sulayman b. ʿAbd al-Malik b. Marwan led the pilgrimage.

[589] In 129, the following died: Abu ʿAmr Bishr b. Harb[1814] [and] ʿAmr b. Malik an-Nukri.[1815]

The following died before 130/747–748: Ghaylan b. Jarir,[1816] ʿAbdallah b. Abi Ishaq an-Nahwi al-Hadrami,[1817] Matar b. Tahman al-Warraq,[1818] ʿAsim al-Jahdari,[1819] Wasil al-Ahdab,[1820] Abu l-Minhal Sayyar b. Salama ar-Riyahi, Tariq b. ʿAbd ar-Rahman,[1821] Ziyad b. Fayyad,[1822] Firas,[1823] [and] Qabus b. Abi Zabyan.[1824]

[590] The Year 130/747–748

In this year, Nasr b. Sayyar and Ibn al-Kirmani made peace. Al-Kirmani's name was Juday' b. ʿAli b. Shabib b. ʿAmir b. Nuwari b. Duyaym b. Mulayh b. Shurtan {412} b. Maʿn b. Malik of the Azd.[1825] They made peace on condition that they would battle Abu Muslim [together]. When they finished, they would examine their affairs. Abu Muslim intrigued with ʿAli, the son of al-Kirmani, [and said], "I am on your side." Ibn al-Kirmani made peace with him, and pledged allegiance to him, and they marched

1813 From "In 129, there was an uprising ..." cf. IAH, 224, l. 5; cf. IA, V, 313.
1814 *Ṭbq.*, 514; Ibn Saʿd, VII, 233; Ibn Hajar, I, 446.
1815 *Ṭbq.*, 513; *Jarḥ*, III, I, 259; Ibn Hajar, VIII, 96.
1816 *Ṭbq.*, 514; Ibn Saʿd, VII, 240; Ibn Hajar, VIII, 253.
1817 *Ṭbq.*, 515; *Jarḥ*, II, II, 4; Ibn Hajar, V, 148; EI2, I, 42.
1818 *Ṭbq.*, 515; Ibn Saʿd, VII, 254; Ibn Hajar, X, 167.
1819 *Ṭbq.*, 513; Ibn Saʿd, VII, 235.
1820 On the death of Wasil al-Ahdab cf. Ibn al-Hayyan (*Ṭbq.*, 370; Ibn Saʿd, VI, 318; Ibn Hajar, XI, 103).
1821 *Ṭbq.*, 373; Ibn Saʿd, VI, 323; Ibn Hajar, V, 4.
1822 *Ṭbq.*, 374; *Jarḥ*, I, II, 542; Ibn Hajar, III, 381.
1823 Ibn Yahya (*Ṭbq.*, 375; Ibn Saʿd, VI, 344; Ibn Hajar, VIII, 259).
1824 *Ṭbq.*, 379; Ibn Saʿd, VI, 339; Ibn Hajar, VIII, 305.
1825 Cf. Ibn Hazm, 381, for variants in the names of some of his ancestors. It should be kept in mind that it is the son of al-Kirmani, ʿAli b. Juday' b. ʿAli, who is the subject of the following passage, not his father, Juday' b. ʿAli, who had been killed in 129/746–747 (cf. Kh., 587).

together against Nasr. Abu Muslim sent [a message] to Ibn al-Kirmani, saying, "Cause fighting to break out between the two of you." [Ibn al-Kirmani and Nasr] battled day and night. In the morning, Abu Muslim came toward them from behind. When Nasr saw that, he sent [a message] to Abu Muslim, [saying], "I am on your side. I am more worthy of you than Ibn al-Kirmani. I will pledge allegiance to you." Abu Muslim marched with more than 10,000 [men] to the [governor's] residence. He sent his companions to strike the leading members of the Azd and the Banu Tamim. They departed, and the people made peace. Abu Muslim sent [a message] to Nasr, ordering him to render himself obedient. [Nasr] said, "Let me perform the ritual ablution," and went out from another door. He mounted a horse, [and rode away], leaving Abu Muslim's messengers sitting [waiting]. That was after the afternoon prayer. They sent word to Abu Muslim, informing him that [Nasr] had fled, and that his companions had fled right and left. Abu Muslim marched on the same night, until he reached the place where Nasr's household was, [591] in the farthest corner of Marw. He seized his wives and young children, but his older children fled. Nasr went to Sarakhs, where he remained. Abu Muslim sent Ibrahim b. Bassam,[1826] a *mawlā* of the Banu Layth, to Sarakhs. Shayban the Harurite and the Rabi'a who were there battled him. He put them to rout, and killed Shayban,[1827] as well as a large number of the Rabi'a. The people of Tus sent a message to Nasr saying, "We are with you," and pledged allegiance to him. Nasr sent his son Tamim to them with nearly 3,000 [troops], as reinforcements. Abu Muslim sent Qahtaba, whose name was Ziyad b. Shabib – Qahtaba being his nickname.[1828] Qahtaba came from the upper Tus. Troops from Abiward[1829] marched against them. Al-Qasim b. Mujashi' marched against them with the Musawwida from Sarakhs. 'Asim b. 'Umayr marched with most of the people against Qahtaba, but Qahtaba put him to rout. 'Asim b. 'Umayr went {413} and joined up with Nasr, who departed, encamping at Qumis.[1830]

1826 Cf. Tab., II, 1996; and *Ma'ārif*, 371: Bassam b. Ibrahim.

1827 From "In this year, Nasr b. Sayyar and Ibn al-Kirmani made peace ..." cf. (*) Dh., V, 37 (Khalifa).

1828 For a clear, concise account of Qahtaba's march from Khurasan to Iraq, see M. Sharon, in EI2, IV, 445–447, s.v. Kahtaba b. Shabib.

1829 Kh.: Abi l-Ward; (cf. Tab., II, 2000). On Abiward, see EI2, I, 99.

1830 From "In this year, Nasr b. Sayyar and Ibn al-Kirmani made peace ..." cf. Tab., II, 1995–2003.

*'Amr b. 'Ubayda < *Qaza'a, a *mawlā* of Nasr b. Sayyar:
Abu Muslim sent [a message] to Nasr, [ordering him to] render himself obedient. Nasr went out from another door, and left the city. Salm b. Ahwaz, Nasr's chief of police, was seized and put to death.

*Muhammad b. Mu'awiya < *Bayhas b. Habib '-l-r-'-m:
Abu Muslim appeared in *Ramaḍān* 129/May–June 747. He imprisoned 'Abdallah b. Mu'awiya and his two brothers, then he killed him, but freed his two brothers, in 130. Nasr b. Sayyar fled. Abu Muslim sent Qahtaba b. Shabib, who confronted Nubata b. Hanzala of the Banu Abi [592] Bakr b. Kilab in Jurjan in *Dhū l-Ḥijja* 130/August 748. Nubata and his son Habba were killed.

Abu dh-Dhayyal:
On that day, the people of Khurasan and Jurjan killed the Banu Tamim and the people of the mosques there. When Nasr heard about this, he retreated from Qumis, and wrote to Ibn Hubayra and to Marwan requesting that they send help.

In 130, the battle of Qudayd[1831] took place.

*'Ali b. Muhammad < Ishaq b. Ibrahim al-Azdi:
When the people went out from Mecca at the end of 129/August–September 747, 'Abd al-Wahid b. Sulayman went to Medina. He wrote to Marwan informing him of the Meccans' desertion. Marwan dismissed him, and wrote to 'Abd al-'Aziz b. 'Umar, his governor in Medina, and ordered him to send an army. Abu Hamza set out for Medina at the beginning of 130/September–October 747, leaving Abraha[1832] b. as-Sabbah al-Himyari as his lieutenant over Mecca. He made Balj b. 'Uqba as-Sa'di commander of his vanguard. {414} The Medinese went out, and they met at Qudayd on Thursday 9 *Ṣafar* 130/19 October 747. Balj had 30,000 horsemen. He said to [the Medinese], "Get out of our way, so we can go to [battle] those who have treated us unjustly, and have ruled despotically. Do not [make us] put our swords against you. We do not wish to do battle with you." But [the Medinese] refused, and engaged them in battle. The Medinese were put to rout. Abu Hamza came to them, and was told by 'Ali b. al-Husayn b. al-Hurr, "Pursue them and finish off [593] their wounded. Every period has its judgment. The massacre of those people is appropriate." [But Abu

1831 BGA, VI, 129, 131, 187; VII and VIII, index; cf. Yaqut, IV, 42; Wellhausen, *Religio-Political Factions*, 86.
1832 In Z, Abraha sometimes appears as Ibrahim.

Hamza] said, "I do not agree. I do not think my behavior should be different from that of my predecessors."[1833]

Abu Hamza went to Medina, and entered the city on Monday 13 *Ṣafar* 130/23 October 747.[1834]

Abu l-Hasan < A *shaykh* of the Ansar; < al-Mus'abi, and others:
'Abd al-'Aziz b. 'Umar b. 'Abd al-'Aziz appointed 'Abd al-'Aziz b. 'Abdallah b. 'Amr b. 'Uthman b. 'Affan [as commander]. The flag of the Quraysh was with Ibrahim b. 'Abdallah b. Muti'.[1835] Abu Hamza advanced, and encamped opposite them. They battled, and the two sides persevered. Three hundred of the Quraysh were killed. On that day, the family of az-Zubayr proved its courage. Twelve of them were killed.

[594] A List of Those Killed at Qudayd

From the family of az-Zubayr: Hamza b. Mus'ab b. az-Zubayr; his son, 'Umara b. Hamza;[1836] Mus'ab b. 'Ukasha b. Mus'ab; 'Atiq b. 'Amir b. 'Abdallah b. az-Zubayr; his son, 'Amr b. 'Atiq; Salih b. 'Abdallah b. 'Urwa b. az-Zubayr; al-Hakam b. Yahya b. 'Urwa b. az-Zubayr; [and] al-Mundhir b. 'Abdallah b. al-Mundhir [died]. Four of the offspring of Khalid b. az-Zubayr were killed: Sa'id b. Muhammad b. Khalid, a son of Musa b. Khalid, one of them named B-h-b-n-dh-', [and] another man. Forty men of the Banu Asad were killed. {415}[595] Umayya b. 'Abdallah b. 'Amr b. 'Uthman b. 'Affan[1837] was killed on that day.[1838] 'Abd al-'Aziz b. 'Abdallah, the commander of the people, fled. Sumayy,[1839] a *mawlā* of Abu Bakr b. 'Abd ar-Rahman b. al-Harith b. Hisham, was killed on that day.[1840]

1833 From "When the people went out from Mecca ..." cf. Tab., II, 2007ff.; *Azdi, 108, l. 8 (Khalifa); *Aghānī*, XX, 100, l. 24-102 (al-Mada'ini); (*) Dh., V, 38, l. 5.

1834 This sentence parallels *Azdi, 109, l. 1.

1835 This sentence parallels *Aghānī*, XX, 101, l. 29.

1836 "From the family of az-Zubayr: Hamza b. Mus'ab b. az-Zubayr; his son, 'Umara b. Hamza" also in *Ma'ārif*, 589, l. 11.

1837 According to Ibn 'Asakir, *Tahdhīb*, III, 130f., his name was Umayyad b. 'Abdallah b. 'Umar b. 'Uthman b. Abi l-'As b. Umayya, and his *kunya* was Abu 'Uthman. *Aghānī* and Dh., V, 44 agree with Khalifa with respect to his name.

1838 This sentence parallels *Ibn 'Asakir, *Tahdhīb*, III, 131, l. 14 (Khalifa); *Dh., V, 44, l. 12 (Khalifa).

1839 *Ṭbq*., 654; *Jarḥ*, II, I, 315; Ibn Hajar, 238.

1840 From "'Abd al-'Aziz b. 'Umar b. 'Abd al-'Aziz appointed 'Abd al-'Aziz ..." cf. *Azdi, 109, l. 3; *Dh., V, 38, l. 11 (Khalifa – l. 15).

*Isma'il b. Ibrahim < *Juwayriya b. Asma':
When 'Abd al-'Aziz b. 'Abdallah went out to Qudayd, his flag fell, and the people considered that an evil omen.[1841]

Isma'il < *Ghassan b. 'Abd al-Hamid:[1842]
Umayya b. 'Abdallah b. 'Amr b. 'Uthman went out on the day of Qudayd, wearing an iron helmet. Without turning or speaking to anyone, he advanced intently[1843] until he was killed.[1844]

Abu l-Hasan:
The people never heard weeping women more heartrending than the weeping women of Qudayd. There was weeping in every household in Medina. A mourning woman lamenting them said:

1. What is the matter with this time and with me?
   Qudayd has destroyed my men.[1845]

2. So I shall weep in private,
   And I shall weep in public.[1846]

*Isma'il b. Ishaq:
Marwan b. Muhammad b. Marwan sent Muhammad b. 'Atiyya as-Sa'di,[1847] of the Sa'd b. Bakr, with 4,000 of his troops,[1848] most of them frontier troops. They imposed a condition on Marwan, [saying], "When we kill al-A'war we shall turn back.[1849] You have no authority over us." He conceded that

1841 This sentence parallels Absab, V, 112, l. 1; cf. Tab., II, 2006; *Azdi, 109, l. 13 (Khalifa); cf. *Aghānī*, XX, 100, l. 7 (=Tab.).

1842 Cf. *Fihrist* (trans.), 277, 989.

1843 Kh.: *muqbilan 'alā baththi-hi*; al-Azdi: *muqbilan 'alā niyyatin.*

1844 From "Umayya b. 'Abdallah b. 'Amr b. 'Uthman went out ..." cf. *Azdi, 109, l. 15 (Khalifa); *Aghānī*, XX, 102, l. 11, (al-Mada'ini); *Ibn 'Asakir, *Tahdhīb*, III, 131 (Khalifa).

1845 From "The people never heard..." cf. *Azdi, 109, l. 18.

1846 Meter: *kāmil.* On the verse cf. Tab., II, 2012 (plus an additional verse); al-Mas'udi, *Tanbīh*, 327; cf. *Aghānī*, XX, 102 (plus two additional verses); (*) Dh., V, 38 (verse 1).

1847 This should be 'Abd al-Malik b. Muhammad b. 'Atiyya (cf. Kh., 618, 619; Tab., II, 2012; Dh., V, 104; Wellhausen, *Religio-Political Factions*, 90 n. 11).

1848 From "Marwan b. Muhammad b. Marwan sent Muhammad ..." cf. *Azdi, 110, l. 14 (Khalifa).

1849 Although there is no further mention of this condition in Khalifa's account, al-Mada'ini, in *Aghānī*, XX, 113, states that the Jazirans returned to al-Jazira when Ibn 'Atiyya marched toward Yemen

to them, and Ibn 'Atiyya advanced.[1850] At Wadi l-Qura he confronted Balj, who had been marching toward {416} Syria. They battled, and Balj and many of his companions were killed. [Ibn 'Atiyya] continued [pursuing them and] killing them, until they entered Medina. He caught up with about 1,000 of them, led by one of them named as-Sabbah, of the Hamdan, who fortified himself in one of the mountains of Medina. He battled them there for three [596] days. Then he withdrew at night with about 300 men, went over the mountains, and eventually reached Mecca.[1851] Ibn 'Atiyya entered Medina, then marched to Mecca, and confronted Abu Hamza with 15,000 [troops] at al-Abtah. Ibn 'Atiyya divided the cavalry against him. [One division of] cavalry attacked him from below Mecca, while [another division of] cavalry attacked him from Mina. [Ibn 'Atiyya] himself attacked from above the mountain pass, and they battled until the day was half over. The cavalry went out against them on the low ground of al-Abtah, and drove them back to their camp. Abraha b. as-Sabbah was killed at Bi'r Maymun,[1852] with his wife. Abu Hamza was also killed. They proclaimed it lawful to kill the soldiers, and a great many of them were killed.[1853] [News about the fate of his army] reached 'Abdallah b. Yahya al-A'war, and he marched with about 30,000 men. Ibn 'Atiyya encamped at Tabala,[1854] and al-A'war encamped at Sa'da.[1855] Then they met [in battle]. Al-A'war was put to rout, and fled to Jurash.[1856] Ibn 'Atiyya advanced, and they met. They battled until night separated them. In the morning, Ibn 'Atiyya remained in his position. Al-A'war attacked with about 1,000 Hadramis, and battled until he and his men were killed.[1857] Al-A'war's head was sent to Marwan. Ibn 'Atiyya marched on, eventually reaching San'a'. A man of Himyar, named Yahya b. 'Abdallah b. 'Umayr b. as-Sabbaq, revolted there, seizing al-Janad.[1858] Ibn 'Atiyya sent his nephew, 'Abd ar-Rahman b. Yazid, against him. Yahya b. 'Abdallah was put to rout, and some of his companions were

1850 From "Marwan b. Muhammad b. Marwan sent Muhammad ..." cf. *Aghānī*, XX, 108, l. 9 (al-Mada'ini).

1851 From "At Wadi l-Qura he confronted Balj ..." cf. *Aghānī*, XX, 108, l. 25.

1852 EI2, I, 1232.

1853 From "Ibn 'Atiyya entered Medina ..." cf. *Aghānī*, XX, 109, l. 20 (al-Mada'ini).

1854 EI, IV, 575.

1855 EI, IV, 33; (Kh.: *K-'-d-h*).

1856 BGA, indices; cf. Minorsky, 146; Yaqut, II, 59; cf. EI, IV, 1155b, s.v. Yemen.

1857 From "[News about the fate of his army] reached 'Abdallah ..." cf. *Azdi, 113, l. 16 (Khalifa).

1858 BGA, III, 53, 70, 90, 105, 113; VI, 140, 143, 144; VII, 318, 320; cf. Yaqut, II, 127; cf. EI, IV, 1155a, s.v. Yemen.

killed. Yahya went to 'Adan Abyan, where he raised an army of about 2,000 [men]. Ibn 'Atiyya himself marched against him, and confronted him at one of their *wādīs*. Yahya and those with him were killed, and Ibn 'Atiyya returned to San'a'. Then a man {417} named Yahya b. Harb,[1859] of Himyar, revolted at the sea [597] shore. Ibn 'Atiyya sent a man of the Kinda, named Abu Umayya, the commander of the Waddahiyya, against him. Yahya and some of his companions were killed. Then Ibn 'Atiyya marched against 'Abdallah b. Sa'id,[1860] al-A'war's successor, who had a large army of Hadramis. Ibn 'Atiyya battled them in the morning, until night gave him shelter. Then he received a letter from Marwan with orders to lead the pilgrimage. He called on the Hadramis to make peace with him, which they did. Ibn 'Atiyya departed with 15 prominent men from among his companions. Leaving his nephew, 'Abd ar-Rahman b. Yazid, as his lieutenant, Ibn 'Atiyya hastily departed. He encamped at one of the *wādīs* of the Murad, at a village called Shibam,[1861] where he and his companions were attacked and killed.[1862] His head was cut off.[1863] Some people of the Hamdan came and buried his body in a village called Khaywan,[1864] on the pilgrimage road of Yemen. [News of what had happened] reached 'Abd ar-Rahman b. Yazid, who sent a man of the Waddahiyya named Shu'ayb al-Bariqi with mounted troops, and ordered him to kill all the people he found. Shu'ayb killed the men, and cut open the women. He also killed the children, took the property of value, cut down the date palms, and burned the villages. Then he departed, and returned to 'Abd ar-Rahman.[1865]

Muhammad b. 'Abd al-Malik b. Muhammad b. 'Atiyya as-Sa'di led the pilgrimage.[1866]

[598] In *Ramaḍān* 130/May–June 748, as-Saqr b. Ayyub al-Fazari went {418} with a large army to Tlemcen. 'Abd ar-Rahman b. Habib went out against him. As-Saqr b. Ayyub was killed, and the Berbers were routed. Sulayman b. Dharraq al-Murhibi, a Sufrite, arrived. Ibn Habib went out against him, and Sulayman departed without a battle.

1859 *Aghānī*, XX, 113, l. 12: Yahya b. Karib.

1860 *Aghānī*, XX, 113, l. 15: 'Abdallah b. Ma'bad.

1861 EI, IV, 358ff.

1862 From "Marwan b. Muhammad b. Marwan sent Muhammad ..." cf. Tab., II, 2012–2015.

1863 From "Then he received a letter from Marwan ..." cf. (*) Azdi, 114, l. 2.

1864 BGA, I, 23, 25; II, 32; III, 88, 111; VI, 136, 137, 189, 192; VII, 317; Yaqut, II, 512; cf. EI, IV, 1156b, s.v. Yemen.

1865 From "Ibn 'Atiyya marched on ..." cf. *Aghānī*, XX, 113, l. 4 (al-Mada'ini).

1866 Cf. note 1347, and Kh. 622. Ibn 'Atiyya never reached Mecca, but was killed on his way from Yemen.

In 130, the following died: Muhammad b. al-Munkadir, in Medina; _____[1867] b. ʻAmr b. Hazm, in Medina; Yazid b. Ruman;[1868] Abu z-Zinad;[1869] Ismaʻil b. Abi Hakim[1870] – all [of the above] in Medina – Malik b. Dinar;[1871] Shuʻayb b. al-Habhab;[1872] Yazid ar-Rishk;[1873] Abu t-Tayyah;[1874] Kulthum b. Jabr;[1875] Habib al-Muʻallim;[1876] Yahya al-Bakka'[1877] – all of these in Basra – ʻAbd al-ʻAziz b. Suhayb;[1878] [599] ʻAsim al-Ahwal;[1879] ʻAli b. al-Hakam al-Bunani;[1880] Humayd b. Qays al-Aʻraj;[1881] Yazid b. ʻAbdallah b. Qusayt, in Medina; Abu Wajza as-Saʻdi.[1882]

[600] The Year 131/748–749

In this year, Qahtaba b. Shabib left Jurjan after the killing of Nubata, [word of which] reached Ibn Hubayra. ʻAmir b. Dubara went down to Istakhr. [Ibn Hubayra] sent his son, Dawud b. Yazid b. ʻUmar b. Hubayra, who marched with ʻAmir from Istakhr to Isbahan. Ibn Hubayra also sent Malik b. Adham al-Bahili with a large mounted force, as well as al-Musʻab b. Sahsah al-Asadi, and Ghutayf as-Sulami, each under a separate banner.[1883] One [corps] encamped at Mah, another at Hamadhan. Qahtaba sent his son, al-Hasan, against those armies. [News of] al-Hasan's march

1867 Z: Muhammad; U: ʻAbdallah (unidentified).
1868 GAS, I, 284.
1869 On the death of Abu z-Zinad cf. #Ibn Hajar, V, 204 (Khalifa); ʻAbdallah b. Dhakwan (GAS, I, 405). Cf. #Ibn Hajar, V, 204 (Khalifa).
1870 *Ṭbq*., 649; *Jarḥ*, I, I, 164; Ibn Hajar, I, 289.
1871 On the death of Malik b. Dinar cf. #Ibn Hajar, X, 15 (Khalifa).
1872 *Ṭbq*., 519; Ibn Saʻd, VII, 253; Ibn Hajar, IV, 350.
1873 On the death of Yazid ar-Rishk cf. #Ibn Hajar, XI, 372 (Khalifa); Yazid b. Abi Yazid ad-Dubaʻi (*Ṭbq*., 518; Ibn Saʻd, VII, 245; Ibn Hajar, XI, 371). Cf. #Ibn Hajar, XI, 372 (Khalifa).
1874 On the death of Abu t-Tayyah cf. Yazid b. Humayd ad- Dubaʻi (*Ṭbq*., 519; Ibn Saʻd, VII, 238; Ibn Hajar, XI, 320).
1875 Ibn Saʻd, VII, 244; Ibn Hajar, VIII, 442.
1876 Ibn Zayd (*Ṭbq*., 519; *Jarḥ*, I, II, 101).
1877 Ibn Muslim (*Ṭbq*., 518; Ibn Saʻd, VII, 245; Ibn Hajar, XI, 278).
1878 *Ṭbq*., 519; Ibn Saʻd, VII, 245; Ibn Hajar, VI, 341.
1879 ʻAsim b. Sulayman al-Ahwal (*Ṭbq*., 523; Ibn Saʻd, VII, 256; Ibn Hajar, V, 42). Z: ʻAmir; ʻAhim. Cf. ʻAmir b. ʻAbd al-Wahid al-Ahwal (Ibn Hajar, V, 77).
1880 *Ṭbq*., 520; Ibn Saʻd, VII, 256; Ibn Hajar, VI, 311.
1881 *Ṭbq*., 707; Ibn Saʻd, V, 486; Ibn Hajar, III, 46.
1882 Yazid b. ʻUbayd (Ibn Hajar, XI, 349).
1883 The Arabic is *mutasānidīn* (cf. Lane, 1443b, 1444b).

reached them, and they joined forces at Nihawand. Al-Hasan encamped there and besieged them.[1884]

*Muhammad b. Mu'awiya < Abu Habib Bayhas b. Habib:
Qahtaba marched, and confronted 'Amir b. Dubara and Dawud. They met [in battle] at Jabalq,[1885] a district belonging to Isbahan, {419} on Saturday 23 *Rajab* 131/18 March 749. 'Amir was killed, and Dawud was put to rout and joined up with his father. Qahtaba joined up with his companions, and together with his son, al-Hasan b. Qahtaba, besieged the people of Nihawand.[1886]

In 131, 'Amir [b. Dubara] was killed. Nasr b. Sayyar wrote to Marwan and Ibn Hubayra requesting reinforcements. But support did not reach him before Qahtaba [601] had already marched, so Nasr withdrew. He encamped at ar-Rayy, where he became ill. Then he proceeded [further], but died at Hamadhan.[1887]

*'Amr b. 'Ubayda < Qaza'a, Nasr b. Sayyar's *mawlā*:
Nasr died in Sawa,[1888] in the environs of ar-Rayy. We buried him and caused water to flow over his grave.[1889]

Qaza'a:
When he was dying, [Nasr] summoned his sons, and said, "Beware of the cities. Stay in Syria.[1890] If the Marwanids still have time, so do you. If that is not the case, whatever befalls them is in store for you also." He recited to me the following verses [composed] by Nasr b. Sayyar when the reinforcements had been delayed:

1. Through the ashes I see the sparkle of burning coal.
   It is only natural that it should [soon] have a flame.

2. The fire is kindled by means of the fire-drill,
   And the word precedes the deed.

1884 From "In this year, Qahtaba ..." cf. Tab., III, 4ff. (al-Mada'ini); (*) Azdi, 116, l. 1.
1885 BGA, VI, 21; VII, 273; Yaqut, II, 2.
1886 From "Qahtaba marched, and confronted 'Amir ..." cf. *Azdi, 116, l. 7 (Khalifa); cf. Tab., III, 4ff.
1887 From "so Nasr withdrew ..." cf. *Azdi, 116, l. 11.
1888 EI, IV, 182.
1889 From "Nasr died ..." cf. (*) Azdi, 116, l. 12.
1890 This sentence parallels (*) Dh., V, 199, l. 3.

3. I speak in astonishment; I wish I knew –
   Are the Umayyads awake, or are they sleeping?[1891]

Bayhas b. Habib:
Ibn Hubayra wrote to Marwan, informing him of the death of Ibn Dubara. He sent al-Hawthara b. Suhayl al-Bahili, of the Banu Farras, with 10,000 special Qaysites.[1892] The troops gathered at Nihawand. Ibn Hubayra {420} appointed Malik b. Adham as their commander.[1893]

Bayhas:
Qahtaba besieged the people of Nihawand for about four months.[1894]

'Amr b. 'Ubayda < Qaza'a:
We were besieged there until we had eaten our mounts, and were afflicted by starvation and exhaustion.[1895]

Bayhas:
Then Malik b. Adham made peace with Qahtaba, and the city was opened [602] in *Shawwāl* 131/May–June 749. Qahtaba put to death the Khurasanis who had fled with Nasr b. Sayyar.[1896] He said, "I did not make peace on condition [that I spare] the Khurasanis, but only the Syrians." Malik [b. Adham] claimed that he had made peace on condition [that he spare] both the Khurasanis and the Syrians.[1897]

Abu dh-Dhayyal:
He granted safety to the Syrians, except for two men, a Qurashite named

1891 Meter: *wāfir*. The verses were translated by Nicholson, 251; by Browne, I, 242; by Barbier de Maynard, *Murūj*, VI, 62; by MacGuckin de Slane, *Ibn Khallikan's Biographical Dictionary*, II, 104. On the verses themselves cf. al-Jahiz, I, 158; cf. *'Uyūn*, I, 128 (plus an additional verse); cf. Din., 357 (plus two additional verses); cf. al-Ya'qubi, II, 408; cf. Tab., II, 1973; cf. *'Iqd*, I, 94; cf. *'Iqd*, IV, 478 (plus three additional verses); Azdi, 106 (lacks all but second hemistich of third verse); cf. *Murūj*, VI, 62 (plus three additional verses); cf. *Aghānī*, VI, 128; cf. *Imāma*, II, 148 (plus two additional verses); cf. IA, V, 365f.; cf. Ibn Khallikan, III, 150 (plus two additional verses); cf. Dh., V, 199 (plus one additional verse).

1892 The Arabic is *('asharat ālāf) min Qays khāṣṣa*. Cf. Tab., III, 13: *wa-nās min wujūhi ahli sh-Sha'm*. Perhaps Khalifa's description could be translated "distinguished Qaysites."

1893 From "Ibn Hubayra wrote to Marwan ..." cf. Tab., III, 6ff; *Azdi, 116, l. 13; (*) Dh., V, 199, l. 9.

1894 This sentence parallels Tab., III, 7; *Azdi, 116, l. 15; *Dh., V, 199, l. 11.

1895 This sentence parallels cf. (*) Dh., V, 199, l. 11.

1896 From "Then Malik b. Adham made peace with Qahtaba ..." cf. *Azdi, 116, l. 15.

1897 From "Then Malik b. Adham made peace with Qahtaba ..." cf. Tab., III, 7f.

Abu l-Bakhtari, and a man of the Banu Sulaym named Sufyan, both of whom he put to death in bonds [as prisoners].[1898]

Qaza'a:
Qahtaba stationed men at the gates of the city. There was no Khurasani of eminence whom he let go [through the gates] whom he did not put to death.[1899] He seized the sons of Nasr b. Sayyar, and killed them.[1900]

Abu l-Hasan:
He conquered [the city] by peace agreement on the first day of *Dhū l-Qa'da*/22 June 749. The following were killed: Sa'id b. al-Hurr b. 'Ubaydallah b. 'Umar b. al-Khattab, of al-Jazira; Hatim b. al-Harith b. Surayj at-Tamimi; 'Asim b. 'Amr as-Samarqandi, whose name was Hazar Mard; [and] 'Umara b. Sulaym.[1901]

Bayhas b. Habib:
When Qahtaba finished in Nihawand, he headed for Ibn Hubayra. Ibn Hubayra set out, with 'Ubaydallah b. al-'Abbas al-Laythi[1902] in command of his vanguard, and {421} encamped at [603] Baraz ar-Ruz,[1903] between Hulwan and al-Mada'in.[1904]

Bayhas:
Hawthara b. Suhayl eventually reached us, at a river called Tamarra.[1905] We were joined by those who there were of the companions of 'Amir b. Dubara, and those who left Nihawand. There were 53,000 of us altogether receiving [military] pay. Al-Hasan b. Qahtaba, in command of the vanguard of his father's army, marched to Hulwan, where he encamped. His father came to him, and all the people gathered together. Ibn Hubayra marched to Jalula' – of the [famous] battle[1906] – and encamped there. Qahtaba encamped at

1898 From "He granted safety to the Syrians …" cf. Tab., III, 7.
1899 From "Qahtaba stationed men at the gates …" cf. Tab., III, 8.
1900 Sentence parallels cf. Tab., III, 7; (*) Azdi, 116, l. 17; (*) Dh., V, 199, l. 13.
1901 On the list of the dead cf. Tab., III, 7; *Dh., V, 199, l. 13.
1902 Cf. the 'Ubaydallah b. al-'Abbas al-Kindi, who served as governor over Kufa for al-Walid II (Kh., 552).
1903 BGA, VI, 6, 235, 239; VII, 186; Yaqut, I, 534.
1904 From "When Qahtaba finished in Nihawand …" cf. Tab., III, 10; *Azdi, 116, l. 17; (*) Dh., V, 199, l. 14.
1905 Kh.: *B-'-m-r-'*. Cf. BGA, I, 84, 86; II, 165, 167; VI, 6, 175, 235; VII, 90, 269; VIII, 53. Yaqut, I, 812f.
1906 Cf. EI2, II, 406, s.v. Djalula'. The "famous battle" was in the year 16/637. According to Khalifa, it was in 17 (Kh., 127ff.).

Khaniqin.[1907] There were four *parasang*s between the two armies. That was at the end of *Dhū l-Qa'da* 131/July 749. Our front ranks and theirs were face to face for several days. Each side held its position.[1908]

In this year, Basra was stricken by the plague.

*'Ali b. Muhammad:
The plague began in *Jumādā* II/January-February 749. Many were dying from it. It continued in *Rajab*/February–March, and got worse in *Sha'bān*/March–April. It reached the peak of its virulence in *Ramaḍān*/April–May and *Shawwāl*/ May–June. Then it decreased in severity, and returned to the way it began, until the end of the year. The following died in the plague: Ayyub [b. Abi Tamima] as-Sakhtiyani [and] 'Ali b. Zayd b. Jud'an.[1909]

In this year, the following died: 'Abdallah b. Abi Najih al-Makki [and] 'Abd ar-Rahman b. al-Qasim [b. Muhammad] b. Abi Bakr.[1910]

Al-Walid b. 'Urwa b. Muhammad b. 'Atiyya, of the [Banu] Sa'd b. Bakr, led the pilgrimage.

[604] The following died after the year 130: 'Abd al-'Aziz b. Hakim al-Hadrami,[1911] 'Abd al-'Aziz b. Rufay',[1912] ar-Rukayn b. ar-Rabi',[1913] Abu l-Aswad Muhammad b. 'Abd ar-Rahman,[1914] [and] 'Umara {422} b. 'Abdallah b. Dubara.[1915]

During the caliphate of Marwan, Abu l-Huwayrith died. His name was 'Abd ar-Rahman b. Mu'awiya, a Muradi, and ally of the Banu Nawfal b. 'Abd Manaf.

1907 EI, II, 901.
1908 From "Hawthara b. Suhayl eventually reached us ..." cf. Tab., III, 10; *Azdi, 117, l. 2; (*) Dh., V, 199, l. 16.
1909 On the death of 'Ali b. Zayd b. Jud'an cf. #Dh., V, 284 (Khalifa); #Ibn Hajar, VII, 324 (Khalifa).
1910 On the death of 'Abd ar-Rahman b. al-Qasim [b. Muhammad] b. Abi Bakr cf. #Dh., V, 198, l. 8 (Khalifa).
1911 *Ṭbq*., 386; Ibn Sa'd, VI, 323.
1912 *Ṭbq*., 384; Ibn Sa'd, VI, 323; Ibn Hajar, VI, 337.
1913 *Ṭbq*., 382; Ibn Sa'd, VI, 325; Ibn Hajar, III, 287.
1914 GAS, I, 284.
1915 Cf. 'Umara b. 'Abdallah b. Sayyad (Ibn Hajar, VII, 418).

[605] The Year 132/749–750

In this year, Qahtaba b. Shabib confronted Yazid b. ʿUmar b. Hubayra.[1916]

*Muhammad b. Muʿawiya < Bayhas b. Habib:
When Ibn Hubayra received word that Qahtaba had left, and was heading for Mosul, he asked his companions, "Why have the people left us?" He was told, "They are heading for Kufa." Ibn Hubayra gave orders to march, and he did not stop until he reached Baraz ar-Ruz, six *parasangs* from our trench. [While] we left our provisions and foodstuffs, Qahtaba came and encamped at our trench. We encamped in the open country. He remained about 20 days, until [his horses] became fat and rested, then he marched off in the direction of the north wind, eventually crossing the Tigris from Bahamsha.[1917] That was in the summer. The unripe dates had turned red, and the water [level] was low,[1918] so he crossed over on horseback. He and we, together, advanced toward Kufa, until we reached the Euphrates. He encamped in the open country, and we encamped at the dam of the Euphrates, in the area of al-Falluja al-ʿUlya.[1919] That was on Tuesday 8 [606] *al-Muḥarram* 132/27 August 749. Then Qahtaba crossed the Euphrates with about 700 men. We had about that [number of men too]. He came to Ibn Hubayra, unnoticed. They were on the dam, and we were below them. We thrust at them [with our weapons], but they drove us about 200 cubits from our position. Then we attacked them again, and put them to rout, until they came to the dam. {423} Qahtaba received a blow to the face, and fell in the Euphrates and died, although we and they were unaware of what had happened.[1920]

1916 This sentence parallels *Azdi, 118, l. 10. On the following events, see M. Sharon, in EI2, IV, 445ff., s.v. Kahtaba b. Shabib. Cf. Wellhausen, *Arab Kingdom*, 541.

1917 BGA, III, 134; VI, 93, 214; VII, 256; Yaqut, I, 458.

1918 The Arabic is *qallat al-miyāh*; cf. al-Yaʿqubi, II, 412: *fī ayyām al-madd wa-kathrat al-māʾ*, "in the days of high, abundant water." If these events were taking place in the summer, as Khalifa's account states, the water level would probably be low.

1919 EI2, II, 768.

1920 From "When Ibn Hubayra received word ..." cf. Tab., III, 12–18; *Azdi, 118, l. 10 (Khalifa); (*) Dh., V, 200, l. 13.

Abu dh-Dhayyal:
Qahtaba was killed, [but] Ibn Hubayra's men were put to rout,[1921] [and fled], until they reached Fam an-Nil.[1922]

Bayhas:
Each side continued to resist the other until the moon set. That was on 8 *al-Muḥarram*/27 August 749. Then we went, proceeding aimlessly, until we reached the people at Sura. We forded the river at Sura. Many people drowned, and much baggage was lost. The people assembled after we had crossed. Someone called out, "Whoever wants to go to Syria, let's go!" A group of people went with him, without our knowing it. Someone else called out, "Whoever wants to go to al-Jazira, [let's go]!" Another called out, "Whoever wants to go to Kufa, [let's go]!" A group of people went with both. I said, "Whoever wants to go to Wasit, let's go!" In the morning [we found ourselves] at the barrages of as-Sib. Ibn Hubayra approached, and we encamped together at Fam an-Nil. Hawthara b. Suhayl approached, not having entered Kufa [607] before he came to us at Fam an-Nil. Then we departed, and entered Wasit on Friday, the day of 'Ashura' [10 *al-Muḥarram*]/29 August 749. In the morning, the Black Ones[1923] missed their leader. After a search, they found him [dead], with a spear wound in the forehead. They buried him on Wednesday. [Then] they gave command to al-Hasan b. Qahtaba, and marched to Kufa. Ziyad b. Salih fled to us, and they entered Kufa on the day of 'Ashura'. They made Abu Salama al-Khallal governor over Kufa.[1924] Among the companions of Ibn Hubayra killed on the night of [the battle of] the Euphrates were the following: Ziyad b. Suwayd al-Murri, Ibn Hubayra's chief of police [and] 'Asim b. {424} Abi 'Asim, one of Ibn Hubayra's secretaries, a *mawlā* of Abu Sufyan b. Harb. Abu Salama [then] sent al-Hasan b. Qahtaba, with Khazim b. Khuzayma, against Wasit.[1925]

1921 When Marwan b. Muhammad was informed of the rout of Ibn Hubayra's troops, he is reported to have expressed amazement that a dead man (Qahtaba) had routed a living man (Ibn Hubayra; cf. al-Ya'qubi, II, 412; *'Iqd*, IV, 481).

1922 Cf. BGA, III, 27, 53, 114, 121; VI, 233; VII, 322; VIII, 52; Yaqut, IV, 861 (s.v., al-Nil). Cf. Wellhausen, *Arab Kingdom*, 541.

1923 The Arabic is *as-Sūdān*. The term al-Musawwida is more common, and is used as an epithet applied to the pro-'Abbasid revolutionaries, who were supposed to have carried black flags (*al-musawidda* means "those who make black"). The verb *sawwada*, literally "to make black," was used in the sense of "join the revolution of the Musawidda" (cf. note 21).

1924 From "Hawthara b. Suhayl approached …" cf. (*) Azdi, 119, l. 6.

1925 From "We forded the river at Sura …" cf. *Dh., V, 200, l. 17.

Bayhas:
Al-Hasan b. Qahtaba came toward us at the end of *al-Muḥarram* 132/September 749, and encamped at al-Mahuz.[1926] Then he came to us in *Ṣafar*/September–October, not intending to do battle, but looking for a place to encamp. He brought workers to dig a trench. The people said to Ibn Hubayra, "Let us engage [those] people in battle," but he refused. They continued to importune him until he said, "Muslims, open the gates." He appointed his son, Dawud, with Muhammad b. Nubata and Ma'n b. Za'ida, to command the center [of the army], facing al-Hasan b. Qahtaba. Hawthara b. Suhayl went out facing Khazim b. Khuzayma on Wednesday. We battled, and were put to rout. One of us, Hakim b. al-Musayyab, of the Jadilat Qays, was killed, and Yazid b. Qahtaba was killed. In the evening, they returned [to their positions]. In the morning, [608] we buried those of our dead who were at the trench. Then Abu l-'Abbas 'Abdallah b. Muhammad b. 'Ali b. 'Abdallah b. 'Abbas received the pledge of allegiance. He sent his brother, Abu Ja'far, to al-Hasan b. Qahtaba and the people who were with him. The mother of Abu l-'Abbas was Rayta bint 'Ubaydallah b. 'Abdallah b. 'Abd al-Madan al-Harithi. He received the pledge of allegiance on Thursday night, 17 *Rabīʿ* 132/3 November 749, in Kufa, in the quarter of the Banu Awd, in the house of al-Walid b. Sa'd, a *mawlā* of the Banu Hashim. In the morning, he rode off and led the people in the Friday prayer. On that day he received the pledge of allegiance of most of the people.

Bayhas:
When Abu Ja'far came against us, they attacked us all together. We began to battle them, [and continued to battle] until we received word of Marwan's rout. We battled in *Sha'bān*, *Ramaḍān*, and *Shawwāl*/March–June 750. Al-Hasan b. Qahtaba came to us at the end of *Shawwāl*/June and said, "For whom are you exerting yourselves? There is no one left who has not entered into obedience to the Commander of the Faithful. You have God's covenant and document[1927] that you will be completely safe with respect to us." Then, in the morning, Khazim b. Khuzayma came to us and spoke words to the same effect. Then al-Harith b. Nawfal al-Hashimi came to us. Then Ishaq b. Muslim {425} al- 'Uqayli came to us and said, "The people will give you whatever you want." Therefore, we wrote a

1926 Cf. al-Mahuza, near Samarra' (BGA, VII, 266, 267; al-Ya'qubi, II, 601–602; *Futūḥ*, 298; Yaqut, II, 86).
1927 Cf. Qur'ān 13:20, etc.

peace treaty between us and them, stipulating what we wanted.[1928] That was at the beginning of *Dhū l-Qa'da* 132/June 750. What we wanted was that Ibn Hubayra should retain his command, with 500 of his companions, encamped for 50 days at Medinat ash-Sharqiyya,[1929] during which time he would not pledge allegiance. When the time was up, and if he should wish, he could go to a safe place; or, if he wished, he could enter into what the people had entered [sc. pledge allegiance to Abu l-'Abbas]. Whatever possessions we had would remain ours. We opened the gates on Saturday, several days into the month of *Dhū l-Qa'da*/June 750. They entered the city, and roamed around in it, then left. They did the same thing on Sunday. On [609] Monday, one of their barbarians entered with cavalry. He sought every mount bearing the brand "belonging to God,"[1930] and seized it, saying, "This is [for] the government."[1931]

Bayhas:
I informed Abu 'Uthman, and he informed Ibn Hubayra, saying, "The people have been betrayed by the Lord of the Ka'ba!" He said to Abu 'Uthman, "Go to Abu Ja'far, greet him, then say to him, 'If you see fit to allow us to come to you, [we shall come].'" He granted him permission. On Monday, we – about 200 of us – rode with him until we reached the tent [of Abu Ja'far]. Ibn Hubayra, Abu 'Uthman, Sa'id, and I dismounted, and we walked with him. When we reached the door of his chamber, the tent flaps were lifted and there was Abu Ja'far, sitting. Ibn Hubayra said to him, "Greetings, Commander, and the mercy and blessings of God." Then the tent flaps were lowered. I heard Abu Ja'far say, "Yazid, we, the Banu Hashim, forgive evildoers, and are generous. As far as we are concerned, there is no one else like you. You are trustworthy. The Commander of the Faithful is most desirous to favor someone like you. So you can expect to be very pleased [with the treatment you will receive from us]."

1928 Cf. *Imāma*, II, 163–166 for an alleged text of the document guaranteeing safety (*amān*) issued by Abu Ja'far to Ibn Hubayra.

1929 Cf. *Futūḥ*, 295; BGA, VII, 245; Yaqut, III, 279. Ash-Sharqiyya, in Karkh, a part of Baghdad, presumably existed before the foundation of Baghdad, and may be what is meant here.

1930 U: Every mount with fatness for God (?).

1931 The other sources do not mention seizure of horses, but report that Abu Ja'far's troops "sealed the treasuries" and carried off the valuables (cf. Tab., III, 68; *Imāma*, II, 167f.).

Abu l-Hasan:
Ibn Hubayra said to him, "Your position of leadership is new.[1932] Allow the people to taste its sweetness, and spare them its bitterness,[1933] and you will gain their hearts. I am still waiting for this call." Then he rose. Abu Ja'far said, "How astonishing for anyone to order me to kill this man!"[1934]

Bayhas:
On Monday 17 *Dhū l-Qa'da* 132/27 June 750, Abu Ja'far sent Khazim b. Khuzayma to kill Ibn {426} Hubayra. The one who carried out his killing was 'Abdallah b. al-Bakhtari al-Khuza'i. He also killed the following: _____[1935] b. Abi Umara, a *mawlā* of the Banu Umayya; 'Abdallah b. al-Habhab [610] al-Katib. They [also] killed Dawud b. Yazid b. 'Umar b. Hubayra. [Abu] 'Uthman,[1936] Ibn Hubayra's secretary, was sent out to Khazim b. Khuzayma, who killed him, and seized the following: Bishr b. 'Abd al-Malik b. Bishr b. Marwan, Aban b. 'Abd al-Malik b. Marwan, al-Hawthara b. Suhayl, [and] Muhammad b. Nubata. Al-Hasan b. Qahtaba sat down in the mosque of Hassan an-Nabati, by the Tigris, near al-Mada'in. They were brought to him, and he had their heads cut off. Harith b. Qatan al-Hilali was brought to him, and he ordered him to be thrown into prison. He sought Khalid b. Salama al-Makhzumi, but was unable to find him. Their heralds announced, "Khalid b. Salama shall not be harmed." So he came out a day after the people had been put to death, and they killed him too.[1937]

In 132, Sufyan b. Mu'awiya b. Yazid b. al-Muhallab joined the Musawidda in Basra, and called for the pledge of allegiance to the Banu Hashim. Salm b. Qutayba, who was Ibn Hubayra's governor over Basra, sent to him, requesting that he hold back until he saw what Ibn Hubayra would do.

1932 Cf. Tab., III, 68, where Ibn Hubayra is said to have asked Abu Ja'far to forgive him for addressing him as "hey you" (*yā hāhunā* or *yā ayyuhā l-mar'*), since it had only been very recent that he had to address anyone as "commander."

1933 Mu'awiya b. Yazid b. Mu'awiya is also quoted applying the words "bitterness" and "sweetness" to a position of leadership (cf. *'Iqd*, IV, 391; *Murūj*, V, 169).

1934 His brother, Abu l-'Abbas as-Saffah, ordered him to put Ibn Hubayra to death (cf. Tab., III, 67). Ibn 'Abd Rabbihi includes this anecdote in the section "Faithfulness and Treachery" (*al-wafā' wa-l-ghadr*) in the *'Iqd* (I, 79). From "Ibn Hubayra said to him, "Your position ..." cf. al-Ya'qubi, II, 424; cf. al-Mubarrad, 139; *'Iqd*, I, 79, l. 15 (al-Mada'ini); *'Iqd*, II, 157, l. 14.

1935 U: Riyah; Z: Rabah.

1936 Cf. Tab., III, 69: "his chamberlain, Abu 'Uthman." Cf. *Imāma*, II, 168.

1937 From "He sought Khalid b. Salama al-Makhzumi ..." cf. (*) Dh., V, 239, l. 19 (Khalifa).

Abu 'Ubayda; Abu l-Yaqzan; and others:
The following acted as ambassadors between [Salm and Sufyan]: Abu Sufyan b. al-'Ala',[1938] Salama b. 'Alqama al-Mazini,[1939] 'Abbad b. Mansur,[1940] 'Amir b. 'Ubayda al-Bahili, 'Uthman al-Batti,[1941] Isma'il al-Makki, [and] Mu'awiya b. 'Umar al-Ghallabi. [Sufyan] agreed {427} to come to terms, and they made peace. They wrote a document between them, in which it was agreed that Salm would remain in the governor's residence, and that Sufyan would remain in [the quarter of] the Azdites, until they saw what Ibn Hubayra would do. When Abu Salama al-Khallal heard about this, he wrote to Balj b. al-Muthanna b. Makhrama al-'Abdi, saying, "If Sufyan battles against Salm, [fine]. If not, then you will be governor." Sufyan agreed to do battle, and marched against Salm with his son, Mu'awiya, in the vanguard. Mu'awiya was killed, and Sufyan was put to rout.[1942]

[611] In this year, Rawh b. Hatim[1943] killed Ishaq ad-Dabbi, who used to be market supervisor. Salm b. Qutayba sent Ibn R-'-l-'-n[1944] against him, and he put him to rout. Then Rawh fled on the same night. He went to Maysan, and took control of it.

In 132, Abu l-'Abbas sent his paternal uncle, 'Abdallah b. 'Ali b. 'Abdallah b. 'Abbas, to battle Marwan b. Muhammad. Marwan marched with his Syrian and Jaziran troops. The Banu Umayya themselves and their followers rallied around him.

*Bishr b. Bashshar[1945] < *a *shaykh* of al-Jazira:
Marwan went out with 100,000 Syrian and Jaziran horsemen.[1946]

Abu dh-Dhayyal:
Marwan had 150,000 troops. He marched, and eventually encamped at the two Zabs,[1947] below Mosul. 'Abdallah b. 'Ali marched. They met [in battle] on Saturday morning, 11 *Jumādā* II 132/25 January 750, and Marwan was

1938 *Ṭbq.*, 530.
1939 *Ṭbq.*, 527; Ibn Sa'd, VII, 260; Ibn Hajar, IV, 150.
1940 *Ṭbq.*, 532; Ibn Sa'd, VII, 270; Ibn Hajar, V, 103.
1941 *Ṭbq.*, 525; Ibn Sa'd, VII, 257; Ibn al-Athir, *al-Lubāb*, I, 96f.; cf. GAS, I, 410 (d. 143/760–761).
1942 From "In 132, Sufyan b. Mu'awiya b. Yazid b. al-Muhallab …" cf. Tab., III, 21f.
1943 Cf. Ibn 'Asakir, *Tahdhīb*, V, 226.
1944 Ibn Ralan (Ra'lan?) was Salm b. Qutayba's chief of police in Basra (Kh., 623). Ishaq ad-Dabbi is unidentified.
1945 U: Bishr b. Yasar (unidentified).
1946 Sentence parallels *Azdi, 126, l. 9 (Khalifa).
1947 *Azdi, 126, l. 10 (Khalifa).

put to rout. He cut the bridge [behind him] and went to al-Jazira, where he seized the [contents of] the treasuries [*buyūt al-amwāl wa-l-kunūz*], then went to Damascus. 'Abdallah b. 'Ali marched on to al-Jazira, then departed, leaving Musa b. Ka'b at-Tamimi as his lieutenant. 'Abdallah b. 'Ali went to Syria. Abu l-'Abbas sent Salih b. 'Ali, and [their troops] gathered together. Then they marched against Damascus. They besieged [the inhabitants] for several days, then conquered the city. Al-Walid b. Mu'awiya was killed. When 'Abdallah b. 'Ali {428} entered Damascus, he apprehended Yazid b. Mu'awiya b. Marwan and 'Abdallah b. 'Abd al-Jabbar b. Yazid b. 'Abd al-Malik b. Marwan, and sent them to Abu l-'Abbas, who gibbeted them.[1948] 'Abdallah b. 'Ali entered Damascus in *Ramaḍān* 132/April–May 750. At that time Marwan was in Palestine. Then he fled to Egypt.[1949] [612] 'Abdallah b. 'Ali killed more than 80 of the Banu Umayya.

Abu dh-Dhayyal:
Marwan was in Egypt. When he received word of 'Abdallah b. 'Ali's entry into Damascus, he crossed the Nile, cutting the bridge [behind him], then marched in the direction of Ethiopia. 'Abdallah b. 'Ali sent his brother Salih b. 'Ali in pursuit of Marwan. Salih arrived after Marwan had crossed [the Nile]. Salih put 'Amir b. Isma'il, of the Banu l-Harith b. Ka'b, in charge, and sent him against Marwan. He caught up with Marwan at an Egyptian village called Busir,[1950] and killed him in *Dhū l-Ḥijja* 132/July–August 750.[1951]

*Bakr b. 'Atiyya < his father:
I was in Kufa. Marwan's head was brought and set up on a lance at the entrance to the mosque. Thus the hopes of the partisans of the Banu Umayya were crushed.

*Al-Walid b. Hisham < his father < his grandfather; *'Abdallah b. Mughira < his father; *Abu l-Yaqzan; and others:
Marwan was born in al-Jazira in 72/691–692. His mother was a slave girl who belonged to Mus'ab b. az-Zubayr. He was killed in Busir, at the end of *Dhū l-Ḥijja* 132/August 750.

1948 From "Abu l-'Abbas sent Salih …" cf. (*) Azdi, 138, l. 9 (Khalifa).
1949 From "Marwan had 150,000 troops …" cf. (*) Dh., V, 300, l. 3 (Khalifa).
1950 Cf. EI2, I, 1343.
1951 From "Marwan was in Egypt …" cf. (*) Azdi, 136, l. 4 (Khalifa); (*) Dh., V, 300, l. 8.

Hatim b. Muslim:
He was killed in 132. His reign lasted five years, ten months, and ten days before he was killed.[1952]

{429} Dawud b. 'Ali b. 'Abdallah b. 'Abbas led the pilgrimage.[1953]

[613] In 132, the following died: Mansur b. al-Mu'tamir,[1954] Ishaq b. 'Abdallah b. Abi Talha,[1955] Safwan b. Sulaym,[1956] [and] Muhammad b. Abi Bakr b. 'Amr b. Hazm[1957] – all of [the above] in Medina; 'Umara b. Abi Hafsa[1958] [and] Yahya b. Abi Ishaq al-Hadrami[1959] in Basra; Abu Sinn Dirar b. Murra ash-Shaybani[1960] in Kufa; Abu l-Mu'alla al-'Attar[1961] in Basra; [and] Salim al-Aftas, killed in al-Jazira.

During Marwan's reign, the following died: Khubayb b. 'Abd ar-Rahman;[1962] [614] Abu Ja'far Yazid b. al-Qa'qa' al-Qari',[1963] a *mawlā* of Ibn 'Ayyash; Shayba b. Nisah;[1964] Yahya b. Khallad az-Zuraqi;[1965] Abu l-Huwayrith az-Zuraqi; Sa'id b. Sulayman b. Zayd b. Thabit; [and] Isma'il b. Muhammad b. Sa'd b. Malik.

[615] A List of the Governors of Marwan b. Muhammad

Basra:

> There was civil war until the arrival of [Yazid b. 'Umar] b. Hubayra, in 129/746–747. He wrote to al-Miswar b. 'Abbad b. Husayn, ordering him to serve as prayer leader. [Al-Miswar] took up lodgings in the governor's residence, but he was rejected by the Banu Sa'd.

1952 From "Marwan was born in al-Jazira ..." cf. Kh., 622 (433); (*) *'Iqd*, IV, 469.

1953 This sentence parallels *Dh., V, 243 (Khalifa).

1954 On the death of Mansur b. al-Mu'tamir cf. *Ṭbq.*, 381; Ibn Sa'd, VI, 337; Ibn Hajar, X, 312, 315; cf. GAS, I, 404; cf. *Ibn Hajar, X, 315.

1955 *Ṭbq.*, 662; *Jarḥ*, I, I, 226; Ibn Hajar, I, 239.

1956 On the death of Safwan b. Sulaym cf. *Ṭbq.*, 653; *Jarḥ*, II, I, 423; Ibn Hajar, IV, 425–426.

1957 *Ṭbq.*, 660; *Jarḥ*, III, II, 212; Ibn Hajar, IX, 80.

1958 On the death of 'Umara b. Abi Hafsa cf. *Ṭbq.*, 520; Ibn Sa'd, VII, 257; Ibn Hajar, VII, 415; cf. *Dh., V, 285 (Khalifa); *Ibn Hajar, VII, 415 (Khalifa).

1959 *Ṭbq.*, 518; Ibn Sa'd, VII, 254; Dh., V, 312; Ibn Hajar, XI, 177.

1960 On the death of Abu Sinn Dirar b. Murra ash-Shaybani cf. *Ṭbq.*, 383; *Jarḥ*, II, I, 465; Ibn Hajar, IV, 457. Cf. #Dh., V, 263 (Khalifa); #Ibn Hajar, IV, 457 (Khalifa).

1961 Yahya b. Maymun (*Ṭbq.*, 521; Ibn Sa'd, VII, 271; Dh., V, 312; Ibn Hajar, XI, 292).

1962 Ibn Hajar, III, 136.

1963 On the death of Abu Ja'far Yazid b. al-Qa'qa' al-Qari' cf. *Ṭbq.*, 654; Dh., V, 188; Ibn Hajar, XII, 58; cf. GAS, I, 9.

1964 *Ṭbq.*, 654; *Jarḥ*, II, I, 335; Ibn Hajar, IV, 377; cf. GAS, I, 5.

1965 *Ṭbq.*, 221; Ibn Sa'd, V, 72; Ibn Hajar, XI, 204.

'Abbad b. Mansur, a judge, was accepted by the people, and served as prayer leader.

It is said that Ibn Hubayra wrote to 'Abdallah b. Abi 'Uthman, who served as prayer leader until the arrival of {430} Salm b. Qutayba b. Muslim b. 'Amr al-Bahili as governor over Basra for Ibn Hubayra. Sufyan b. Mu'awiya joined the Musawwida and battled Salm, but was defeated. [616] Salm later left Basra when Ibn Hubayra surrendered. Muhammad b. Ja'far al-Hashimi, of the Banu Nawfal, remained as his successor.

Asad b. 'Abdallah b. Malik al-Khuza'i was then sent by Abu l-'Abbas, and served as leader of the Friday prayer.

Sufyan b. Mu'awiya was then appointed by Abu Salama.

Kufa:

Milhan ash-Shaybani was appointed by ad-Dahhak b. Qays, and was [later] killed.

Sa'd al-Khasi – who was called al-Khasi ["the eunuch"] because he had no beard – an Azdite, was then appointed, but was later dismissed.

Al-Muthanna b. 'Imran al-'Ai'dhi, of the Quraysh, was then appointed, and served until ['Abdallah] b. 'Umar made peace with ad-Dahhak, who then marched against Marwan.

'Umar b. 'Abd al-Hamid[1966] was appointed over Kufa by Ibn 'Umar, who later dismissed him.

Isma'il b. 'Abdallah was then appointed, and was later dismissed.

'Abd as-Samad b. Aban b. an-Nu'man b. Bashir al-Ansari was then appointed.

Then Ibn Hubayra arrived. He appointed Ziyad b. Salih al-Harithi over Kufa. [Ziyad] served until the arrival of Qahtaba.[1967] Muhammad b. Khalid b. 'Abdallah al-Qasri joined the Musawidda, expelled Ziyad b. Salih, and called for the pledge of allegiance to the Banu Hashim.

Hawthara b. Suhayl al-Bahili was sent by Ibn Hubayra, but he did not reach Kufa, so he returned to Ibn Hubayra.

1966 He was the son of 'Abd al-Hamid b. 'Abd ar-Rahman, who had served as governor over Kufa for 'Umar b. 'Abd al-'Aziz, the father of 'Abdallah b. 'Umar (cf. Tab., II, 1902; Zambaur, *Manuel de généalogie*, 43).

1967 Qahtaba himself never reached Kufa, but was killed crossing the Euphrates (Kh., 606). His son, al-Hasan b. Qahtaba, did finally reach Kufa (cf. *Ma'ārif*, 371).

When al-Hasan b. Qahtaba entered Kufa, he yielded [authority] to Abu Salama al-Khallal, [617] who retained Muhammad b. Khalid b. 'Abdallah.

Then Abu l-'Abbas 'Abdallah b. Muhammad b. 'Ali emerged [as caliph].

Khurasan:

Nasr b. Sayyar served until he was driven out by Abu Muslim.

Sijistan[1968]:

Bujayr b. as-Salhab held control until the arrival of Ibn Hubayra [in Iraq].

'Amir b. Dubara al-Murri was [then] appointed [by Ibn Hubayra].

Malik b. al-Haytham, a Khurasani, was sent by Abu Muslim.

{431} 'Umar b. al-'Abbas b. 'Umayr b. 'Utarid b. Hajib b. Zurara was then sent [by Abu Muslim].

Isma'il b. 'Imran was then sent [by Abu Muslim].

Sind:

Mansur b. Jumhur seized control, and was there at the time Marwan was killed.

Bahrain:

Bishr b. Sallam al-'Abdi was in control at the time of al-Walid's murder. He served until the arrival of Ibn Hubayra [in Iraq]. He was retained [by Ibn Hubyara], and served until he died.

Sayyar b. Bishr was then appointed, but he died [in office].

Salm b. Bishr, the brother [of the preceding] was then appointed, and served until Marwan was killed.

al-Yamama:

Al-Bahi, a man of the Banu Hanifa, took control, and later died.

[618] 'Abdallah b. an-Nu'man al-Hanafi served until Abu l-'Abbas received the pledge of allegiance.

Medina:

'Abd al-'Aziz b. 'Umar b. 'Abd al-'Aziz b. Marwan was retained by Marwan, who later dismissed him in 129/746–747.

'Abd al-Wahid b. Sulayman b. 'Abd al-Malik b. Marwan was then appointed. He withdrew from Abu Hamza, who entered Medina.

1968 Cf. Bosworth, 75–80.

'Abd al-Malik b. Muhammad b. 'Atiyya, of the Banu Sa'd b. Bakr, was then sent by Marwan. He killed Abu Hamza, and Mecca was included in his jurisdiction. 'Abd al-Malik then went out to Yemen, and left al-Walid b. 'Urwa b. Muhammad b. 'Atiyya as his lieutenant.

Yusuf b. 'Urwa b. Muhammad b. 'Atiyya was then appointed by Marwan [b. Muhammad]. He served until Abu l-'Abbas received the pledge of allegiance.

Mecca:

'Abd al-'Aziz b. 'Umar was retained, including jurisdiction over Medina.

'Abd al-Wahid b. Sulayman b. 'Abd al-Malik was then appointed, but he withdrew from Abu Hamza the Kharijite. Abu Hamza the Kharijite remained there, then went out heading for Medina, [619] leaving Abraha b. as-Sabbah as his lieutenant. Abu Hamza then returned [to Mecca], and was killed by 'Abd al-Malik b. Muhammad b. 'Atiyya. [Ibn 'Atiyya] then went out to at-Ta'if.

Rumi b. Ma'iz al-Kilabi was then appointed, but later dismissed.

Muhammad b. 'Abd al-Malik was then appointed. 'Abd al-Malik b. Muhammad was later killed somewhere in Yemen.

Yusuf b. 'Urwa b. Muhammad was appointed by Marwan, and served as governor until Abu l-'Abbas received the pledge of allegiance.

Ifriqiya:

'Abd ar-Rahman b. Habib al-Fihri took control, [and held it] until he was killed in {432} 138/755–756.

Yemen:

When the civil war broke out, 'Abdallah b. Yahya rose up and expelled ad-Dahhak b. Ziml. Marwan sent 'Abd al-Malik b. Muhammad, who killed 'Abdallah b. Yahya. Then ['Abd al-Malik b. Muhammad] went down,[1969] headed for Mecca, but was assassinated somewhere in Yemen.

Yusuf b. 'Urwa was then appointed by Marwan b. [Muhammad], including jurisdiction over Mecca and Medina. He sent his brother, al-Walid b. 'Urwa, who served as governor until Abu l-'Abbas received the pledge of allegiance.

1969 The verb is *inḥadara*, and connotes going down from a mountainous region to a lower region.

[620] [Armenia]:

When al-Walid was killed, Marwan [b. Muhammad] returned from Armenia, leaving 'Asim b. 'Abdallah b. Yazid al-Hilali as his lieutenant. Ad-Dahhak b. Qays sent Musafir b. al-Qassab, who killed 'Asim b. 'Abdallah. News [of this] reached Marwan, who sent 'Abdallah b. Muslim, who died [in office].

Ishaq b. Muslim was then appointed, but [later] left.

Musafir b. Yahya[1970] was chosen by the people of Bardha'a, and served until Abu l-'Abbas came to power.

[621] The Judiciary

Basra:

'Abbad b. Mansur served as judge in the days of ['Amr] b. Suhayl. When Salm b. Qutayba arrived, he dismissed 'Abbad.

Mu'awiya b. 'Umar al-Ghallabi was then appointed. He served as judge for three days, then asked to be discharged, and he was.

'Amir b. 'Ubayda al-Bahili was then appointed, but later asked to be discharged.

'Abbad b. Mansur was then [re]appointed, and served as judge until Abu l-'Abbas received the pledge of allegiance.

Kufa:

[Muhammad b. 'Abd ar-Rahman] b. Abi Layla served [as judge] until ad-Dahhak b. Qays entered the city.

Ghaylan b. Jami' al-Muharibi[1971] was then appointed [by ad-Dahhak].

Then Ibn Hubayra arrived, and appointed al-Hajjaj b. 'Asim al-Muharibi[1972] as judge, but later dismissed him.

Mansur was then appointed, and served until Abu l-'Abbas received the pledge of allegiance.

{433} Medina:

'Uthman b. 'Umar at-Taymi, of the Quraysh, was retained by 'Abd al-Wahid b. Sulayman.

Muhammad b. 'Imran at-Taymi[1973] then served as judge for

1970 U: Musafir b. Bujayr; cf. al-Ya'qubi, II, 429: Musafir b. Kathir.

1971 Ibn Hajar, VIII, 252.

1972 Ibn Hajar, II, 202.

1973 *Ṭbq.*, 682; *Jarḥ*, IV, I, 41; *Ma'ārif*, 232.

al-Walid b. 'Urwa b. Muhammad b. 'Atiyya, at the end of the reign of Marwan.

[622] The Pilgrimage:

127/745 and 128/746 – 'Abd al-'Aziz b. 'Umar b. 'Abd al-'Aziz b. Marwan.
129/747 – 'Abd al-Wahid b. Sulayman b. 'Abd al-Malik.
130/748 – 'Abd al-Malik b. Muhammad b. 'Atiyya.
131/749 – Al-Walid b. 'Urwa b. Muhammad b. 'Atiyya.

Marwan's Chief of Police:

Kawthar b. al-Asad al-Ghanawi.

Administrator of the Army Rolls, Finance, the Treasuries, and Warehouses:

'Imran b. Salih, a *mawlā* of the Hudhayl.

Secretary for Correspondence:

'Abd al-Hamid al-Kabir.[1974]

Secretary of the Small Seal:

'Abd al-A'la b. Maymun b. Mihran.

Secretary of the Official Seal of the Caliphate:

One of his *mawālī*.

[Marwan's] Chamberlain:

S-q-l-'-b, or, according to some, M-q-l-'-s, one of their *mawālī*.[1975]

*Al-Walid b. Hisham < his father < his grandfather; *'Abdallah b. Mughira < his father; *Abu l-Yaqzan; and others:
Marwan was born in al-Jazira in 72/691–692. His mother was a slave girl belonging to Mus'ab b. az-Zubayr. He was killed in an Egyptian village called [623] Busir, on Thursday 23 *Dhū l-Ḥijja* 132/2 August 750. Marwan's reign lasted five years, ten months, and ten days.[1976]

[Marwan] appointed Yazid b. 'Umar b. Hubayra over Iraq, and he arrived there in 129/746–747.

1974 For the entry on Secretary for Correspondence cf. Dh., V, 270; cf. al-Jahshiyari, index, s.v. 'Abd al-Hamid b. Yahya, 72, l. 2.

1975 From the heading "Marwan's Chief of Police ..." cf. (*) *'Iqd*, IV, 469.

1976 From "Marwan was born in al-Jazira ..." cf. Kh., 612 (428).

Chief of Police:

Wasit: Ziyad b. Suwayd al-Murri, who was killed on the night of [the battle of] the Euphrates.

{434} Kufa: 'Abd ar-Rahman b. Bashir al-'Ijli.[1977]

Basra: [He left the selection of chief of police] to the governors over [Basra]. Salm b. Qutayba [appointed] Ibn R-'-l-'-n.

Ibn Hubayra's Finance Secretary:

'Abdallah[1978] b. al-Habhab, a *mawlā* of the Banu Salul, who was killed when Ibn Hubayra was killed.

[Secretary for] Caliphal Correspondence:

Yahya b. Bukayr, the nephew of Rabah[1979] b. Abi 'Umara.

Ibn Hubayra was killed in Wasit on Monday 17 *Dhū l-Qa'da* 132/27 July 750, at about 40 years of age.

In 132, Abu l-'Abbas 'Abdallah b. Muhammad b. 'Ali b. 'Abdallah b. al-'Abbas b. 'Abd al-Muttalib received the pledge of allegiance. His mother was Rayta bint 'Ubaydallah[1980] b. 'Abdallah b. 'Abd al-Madan al-Harithi. He received the pledge of allegiance in Kufa, on Thursday night, 13 *Rabī'a* I 132/9 November 749, in the quarter of the Banu Awd, in the house of al-Walid [624] b. Sa'd, a *mawlā* of the Banu Hashim. In the morning, he rode to the mosque and led the people in the Friday prayer. On that day, he received the pledge of allegiance of the generality [of the people].

*'Abdallah b. Mughira < his father:

I saw Abu l-'Abbas when he went out to the Friday prayer, riding a grey horse, close to the ground,[1981] between his paternal uncle, Dawud b. 'Ali, and his brother, Abu Ja'far. He was a handsome young man, [but] pallid.[1982] He went to the mosque, ascended the pulpit, and spoke. Dawud b. 'Ali ascended and stood two steps up on the pulpit. [Dawud] praised God, then

1977 This sentence parallels Tab., II, 1916.

1978 U: 'Ubaydallah; cf. Dh., V, 273.

1979 U: Riyah.

1980 Kh.: 'Abdallah; cf. Ibn Hazm, 20; Kh.: 608.

1981 For a similar expression, cf. Tab., II, 1078. Perhaps what is meant is a small horse, or a horse afflicted with a severe case of lordosis.

1982 At-Tabari's account states that he seemed nervous and shaky (Tab., III, 30). Ibn Qutayba's account compares the pallor of his face to a sheet of paper of the Qur'ān (*'Uyūn*, II, 252).

said, "People! No one has ascended this pulpit of yours as caliph after 'Ali b. Abi Talib, other than this nephew of mine." He made promises to the people.[1983]

['Abdallah b. Mughira] < my father:
Then I saw him on the next Friday. His face seemed like a shield, and his neck seemed like {435} a silver pitcher. The pallor had disappeared. Only a week had elapsed.[1984]

In this year, 'Abdallah b. 'Ali b. 'Abdallah b. 'Abbas put to death the following: al-Ghamr b. Yazid b. 'Abd al-Malik b. Marwan,[1985] Ishaq b. 'Abdallah b. Abi Talha, 'Abdallah b. 'Abd al-Malik, [and] 'Umar b. Abi Salama b. 'Abd ar-Rahman b. 'Awf.[1986]

Dawud b. 'Ali b. 'Abdallah b. 'Abbas put to death the following: 'Imran b. Musa b. 'Amr b. Sa'id,[1987] Yahya b. Umayya b. 'Amr b. Sa'id, [625] Isma'il b. Umayya b. 'Amr b. Sa'id,[1988] 'Abdallah b. 'Anbasa b. Sa'id b. al-'As,[1989] 'Iyad b. 'Abdallah b. 'Anbasa b. Sa'id b. al-'As, [and] Ayyub b. Musa b. 'Amr b. Sa'id.[1990]

Dawud b. 'Ali led the pilgrimage.[1991]

1983 From "I saw Abu l-'Abbas ..." cf. *'Uyūn*, II, 252; cf. al-Ya'qubi, II, 419f.; cf. Tab., III, 28–33; *Azdi, 123, l. 17 (Khalifa).

1984 From "Then I saw him on the next Friday ..." cf. *Azdi, 124, l. 5.

1985 Cf. *Ma'ārif*, 583; *'Iqd*, IV, 484, 485, 487; cf. Wellhausen, "Die Kämpfe der Araber," 444, 445.

1986 On the death of 'Umar b. Abi Salama b. 'Abd ar-Rahman b. 'Awf cf. *Ṭbq.*, 654; *Jarḥ*, II, I, 164; Ibn Hajar, VII, 456–457. Cf. *Dh., V, 286 (Khalifa); *Ibn Hajar, VII, 457 (Khalifa).

1987 Ibn Hajar, VIII, 141.

1988 *Ṭbq.*, 707; *Jarḥ*, I, I, 159; Ibn Hajar, I, 283.

1989 On his father, and the grandfather of his two sons, 'Anbasa b. Sa'id b. al-'As, cf. Ibn Hajar, VIII, 155.

1990 On the death of Ayyub b. Musa b. 'Amr b. Sa'id cf. *Ṭbq.*, 708; *Jarḥ*, I, I, 257; Ibn Hajar, I, 412–413.

1991 This sentence parallels Kh., 612 (429).

BIBLIOGRAPHY

There have been no specific studies on Khalifa ibn Khayyat since 1977, but for more recent thinking on historiographical issues see T. Khalidi, *Arabic Historical Thought in the Classical Period* (Cambridge, 1994), C. Robinson, *Islamic Historiography* (Cambridge, 2003), and the bibliographies therein [RGH].

'Abbas, Ihsan, *Shi'r al-khawārij*, Beirut, n.d.

Abbot, Nadia, *Aisha*, Chicago, 1942.

'Abd al-'Aziz Hamid, "Dirhām faḍḍī farīd li-abī 'Alī al-Kirmānī," *al-Maskūkāt*, 4 (1973), 26–28.

Amari, Y., ed., *Biblioteca Arabo-Sicula*, Leipzig, 1857; trans. M. Amari, 2 vols, Torino, 1880–1881.

Amari, M., *Storia dei Musulmani di Sicilia*, ed. C. A. Nallino, 3 vols, Catania, 1933.

Arberry, A. J., *Arabic Poetry*, Cambridge, 1965.

al-Azdi, Abu Zakariyya', *Ta'rīkh al-Mawṣil*, Cairo, 1387/1967.

al-Bakri, Abu 'Ubayd, *Description de l'Afrique septentrionale*, ed. MacGuckin de Slane, Algiers, 1857.

—, *Mu'jam mā sta'jam*, ed. M. as-Saga, Cairo, 1945.

—, *Simt al-la'ali'*, Cairo, 1354/1936.

al-Baladhuri, Ahmad b. Yahya, *Ansāb al-ashrāf*, vol. IV-A, ed. M. Schloessinger, Jerusalem, 1971; vol. IV-B, ed. M. Schloessinger, Jerusalem, 1938; vol. V, ed. S. D. Goitein, Jerusalem, 1936.

al-Baladhuri, Ahmad b. Yahya, *Futūḥ al-buldān*, ed. M. J. de Goeje, Leiden, 1866. Trans. in two parts as *The Origins of the Islamic State*, part 1 trans. P. Hitti, New York, 1916; part 2 trans. F. C. Murgotten, New York, 1924.

Bonner, M. R. J., *An Historiographical Study of Abu Hanifa al-Dinawari's Kitāb al-aḫbār aṭ-ṭiwāl*, Oxford, DPhil., 2014.

Bosworth, C. E., *Sistān under the Arabs*, Rome, 1968.

Brockelmann, C., *Geschichte der arabischen Litteratur*, 2 vols, Leiden, 1945–1949; 3 supplementary vols, Leiden, 1937–1942.

Brockelmann, C., *Das Verhältnis von Ibn-el-Atirs Kamil fi-t-ta'rih zu Tabaris Akhbar errusul walmuluk*, Strasbourg, 1890.

Browne, E. G., *A Literary History of Persia*, 2 vols, London, 1902.

Brunnow, R. E., "The Kharijites under the First Omayyads," trans. S. Khuda Bukhsh in *Contributions to the History of Islamic Civilization*, vol. 2, Calcutta, 1930, 153–200.

al-Bukhari, Muhammad b. Isma'il, *aṣ-Ṣaḥīḥ*, ed. O. Houdas, Leiden, 1862–1908.

—, *at-Ta'rīkh al-kabīr*, Hyderabad, India, 1358–1362/1938–1942.

Bury, J. B., *A History of the Later Roman Empire*, 2 vols, Chicago, 1967.

Dennett, D. C., *Conversion and the Poll Tax in Early Islam*, Cambridge, Mass., 1950.

adh-Dhahabi, Shams ad-Din Muhammad b. Ahmad, *al-'Ibar fī khabar man ghabar*, Kuwait, 1960.

—, *Mīzān al-i'tidāl fī naqd ar-rijāl*, no place, n.d., published by 'Isa al-Babi al-Halabi and Co.

—, *al-Mushtabih fī r-rijāl*, Cairo, 1962.

—, *Ṭabaqāt al-ḥuffāẓ*, ed. F. Wuestenfeld, Gottingen, 1833.

—, *Ṭabaqāt al-ḥuffāẓ*, Hyderabad, India, 1333/1914.

—, *Ta'rīkh al-Islām*, 5 vols, Cairo, 1367–1369/1947–1949.

ad-Dinawari, Ahmad b. Dawud, *al-Akhbār aṭ-Ṭiwāl*, ed. 'Abd al-Mun'im 'Amir, Cairo, 1960.

Dixon, A. A., *The Umayyad Caliphate 65–86/684–705*, London, 1971

Dozy, R., *Noms des vêtements chez les Arabes*, Amsterdam, 1845.

Dunlop, D. M., *Arab Civilization to A.D. 1500*, New York, 1971.

—, *The History of the Jewish Khazars*, Princeton, 1954.

ad-Duri, A., *Baḥth fī nash'at 'ilm at-ta'rīkh 'inda l-'arab*, Beirut, 1960.

—, *Muqaddima fī ta'rīkh ṣadr al-Islām*, Beirut, 1961.

Encyclopaedia Islamica 2nd ed., ed. P. Bearman, Th. Bianquis, C. E. Bosworth, E. van Donzel, W. P. Heinrichs, Leiden, III, 838.

Encyclopaedia Judaica, 16 vols, Jerusalem, 1971–1972.

al-Farazdaq, *Dīwān*, ed. Shakir al-Fahham, Damascus, 1385/1965.

Frye, R. N., *The Heritage of Persia*, New York, 1963.

—, *Bukhārā*, Norman, Oklahoma, 1965.

Gabrieli, F., "Muhammad ibn Qasim ath-Thaqafi and the Arab Conquest of Sind," *East and West*, n.s., XV, 3–4 (1965), 281–295.

Gautier, E. F., *Les siècles obscurs du Maghreb*, Paris, 1927.

Gibb, H. A. R., *The Arab Conquests in Central Asia*, London, 1923.

—, "The Evolution of Government in Early Islam," in id., *Studies on the Civilization of Islam*, Boston, 1962, 34–46.

Gibbon, E., *The History of the Decline and Fall of the Roman Empire*, ed. J. Bury, 7 vols, London, 1909–1912.

Haji Khalifa, *Kashf aẓ-ẓunūn*, ed. and with Latin trans. G. Fluegel, 7 vols, London, 1835–1858.

Hinds, M., "Kufan Political Alignments and their Background in the Mid-seventh Century A.D.," *International Journal of Middle East Studies*, 2 (1971), 346–367.

Hitti, P. K., *History of the Arabs*, New York, 1970.

Honigmann, E., *Die Ostgrenze des Byzantinischen Reiches*, vol. 3 of A. A. Vasiliev, *Byzance et les Arabes*, Brussels, 1935.

Hoyland, R., "Arabic, Syriac and Greek Historiography in the First Abbasid Century: An Inquiry into Inter-Cultural Traffic", *Aram* 3 (1991), 215–219.

—, "History and Fiction in Classical Arabic Literature," in Julia Bray ed., *Muslim Horizons: Writing and Representation in Medieval Islam*, London, 2006, 16–46.

Ḥudūd al-ʿĀlam, trans. V. Minorsky, London, 1937.

Ibn ʿAbd al-Barr, Yusuf b. ʿAbdallah, *al-Istīʿāb fī maʿrifat al-aṣḥāb*, ed. ʿAli Muhammad al-Bajawi, 4 vols, Cairo, n.d.

Ibn ʿAbd al-Hakam, ʿAbd ar-Rahman b. ʿAbdallah, *Futūḥ Miṣr wa-akhbāru-hā*, ed. C. C. Torrey, New Haven, Conn., 1922.

Ibn ʿAbd Rabbihi, Ahmad b. Muhammad, *al-ʿIqd al-farīd*, ed. Ahmad Amin et al. 7 vols, Cairo, 1949–1965.

Ibn Abi Hatim ar-Razi, Abu Muhammad ʿAbd ar-Rahman, *al-Jarḥ wa-t-taʿdīl*, 4 vols, Hyderabad, India, 1371/1952.

Ibn al-ʿArabī, Abu Bakr Muhammad b. ʿAbdallah, *al-ʿAwāṣim min al-qawāsim*, Cairo, 1371/1951.

Ibn ʿAsakir, Abu l-Qasim ʿAli b. al-Hasan, *Tahdhīb Taʾrīkh Ibn ʿAsākir*, ed. and abridged by ʿAbd al-Qadir b. Badran, 7 vols, Damascus, n.d.–1351/n.d.–1932.

—, *Taʾrīkh madīnat Dimashq*, vols 1 and 2 ed. Salah ad-Din al-Munajjid, Damascus, 1951–1954; vol. 10 ed. Muhammad Ahmad Dahman, Damascus, 1963.

Ibn Aʿtham al-Kufi, Ahmad, *Kitāb al-futūḥ*, Hyderabad, 1968–.

Ibn al-Athir, ʿIzz ad-Din, *al-Kāmil fī t-taʾrīkh*, ed. C. Tornberg, 13 vols, Beirut, 1965–1967.

—, *al-Lubāb fī tahdhīb al-ansāb*, 3 vols, Cairo, 1356/1936.

Ibn Faqih al-Hamadhani, *al-Buldān*, ed. M. J. de Goeje (Bibliotheca geographorum Arabicorum, vol. 5), Leiden, 1885.

Ibn Hajar al-ʿAsqalani, Ahmad b. ʿAli, *al-Iṣāba fī tamyīz aṣ-ṣaḥāba*, Cairo, 1939.

—, *Tahdhīb at-tahdhīb*, Hyderabad, 1325–1327/1906–1908.

Ibn Hawqal, Abu l-Qasim Muhammad, *al-Masālik wa-l-mamālik*, ed. M. J. de Goeje (Bibliotheca geographorum Arabicorum, vol. 2), Leiden, 1872.

Ibn Hazm, ʿAli b. Ahmad, *Jamharat ansāb al-ʿArab*, ed. ʿA. M. Harun, Cairo, 1391/1971.

Ibn Hibban al-Busti, Muhammad, *Mashāhīr ʿulamāʾ al-amṣār*, Cairo, 1379/1959.

Ibn ʿIdhari al-Marrakushi, *al-Bayān al-mughrib*, ed. G. S. Colin and E. Levi-Provencal, Leiden, 1948. Trans. E. Fagnan as *Histoire de l'Afrique et de l'Espagne*, 2 vols, Algiers, 1901–1914.

Ibn al-ʿImad, Abu l-Fallah ʿAbd al-Hayy, *Shadharāt adh-dhahab fī akhbār man dhahab*, 8 vols, Beirut, n.d.

Ibn Kathir, ʿImad ad-Din Ismaʿil b. ʿUmar, *al-Bidāya wa-n-nihāya*, 14 vols, Cairo, n.d.

Ibn Khaldun, *Histoire des Berbères et des dynasties musulmanes de l'Afrique septentrionale par Ibn Khaldoun*, trans. MackGucken de Slane, 4 vols, Paris, 1925–1956.

Ibn Khallikan, Ahmad b. Muhammad, *Wafāyāt al-a'yān*, Beirut, n.d. Trans. MacGuckin de Slane as *Ibn Khallikan's Biographical Dictionary*, 4 vols, London, 1843–1871.

Ibn Khurdadhbih, 'Ubaydallah b. 'Abdallah, *al-Masālik wa-l-mamālik*, ed. M. J. de Goeje (Bibliotheca geographorum Arabicorum, vol. 6, 3–183), Leiden, 1889.

Ibn an-Nadim, Muhammad b. Ishaq, *al-Fihrist*, ed. G. Fluegel, Beirut, 1964. Trans. B. Dodge as *The Fihrist of al-Nadim*, New York, 1970.

Ibn al-Qaysarani, Abu l-Fadl Muhammad b. Tahir, *al-Jam' bayna kitābay Abī Naṣr al-Kalābādhī wa-Abī Bakr al-Iṣbahānī fī rijāl al-Bukhārī wa-Muslim*, 2 vols, Hyderabad, 1323/1904.

Ibn Qutayba, 'Abdallah b. Muslim, *Kitāb al-ma'ārif*, ed. Tharwat 'Ukasha, Cairo, 1960.

—, *'Uyūn al-akhbār*, 4 vols, Cairo, 1964.

Ibn Rustah, Ahmad b. 'Umar, *al-A'lāq an-nafīsa*, ed. M. J. de Goeje (Bibliotheca geographorum Arabicorum, vol. 7, 1–229), Leiden, 1892.

Ibn Sa'd, Muhammad, *aṭ-Ṭabaqāt al-kubrā*, 9 vols, Beirut, 1957–1968.

Ibn Taghribirdi, Abu l-Mahasin Yusuf, *an-Nujūm az-zāhira*, Cairo, 1963.

al-Idrisi, ash-Sharif Muhammad b. Muhammad, *India and the Neighbouring Territories in the Kitāb Nuzhat al-mushtāq fī 'khtirāq al-āfāq*, trans. S. Maqbul Ahmad, Leiden, 1960.

al-Imāma wa-s-siyāsa, 2 vols, Cairo, 1937.

al-Isbahani, Abu l-Faraj, *Kitāb al-aghānī*, 20 vols, Cairo (Bulaq), 1285/1868.

al-Ishbili, Abu Bakr Muhammad b. Khayr, *Fahrasat mā rawā-hu 'an shuyūkhi-hi*, ed. F. Codera, Baghdad, 1963.

Isma'il Pasha al-Baghdadi, *Hadiyyat al-'ārifīn*, 2 vols, Istanbul, 1951.

al-Istakhri, Abu Ishaq Ibrahim b. Muhammad, *Masālik al-mamālik*, ed. M. J. de Goeje (Bibliotheca geographorum Arabicorum, vol. 1), Leiden, 1870.

al-Jahiz, Abu l-'Uthman 'Amr b. Bahr, *al-Bayān wa-t-tabyīn*, ed. 'A. M. Harun, 4 vols, Cairo, 1968.

al-Jahshiyari, Abu 'Abdallah Muhammad b. 'Abdus, *al-Wuzarā' wa-l-kuttāb*, ed. M. as-Saqa et al., Cairo, 1938.

Jarir b. 'Atiyya, *Dīwān*, Beirut, 1964.

Jarrett, H. S., *History of the Caliphs*, Calcutta, 1881 (a translation of as-Suyuti's *Ta'rīkh al-khulafā'*, see below).

al-Jazari, Abu l-Khayr Muhammad b. Muhammad, *Ghāyat an-nihāya fī ṭabaqāt al-qurrā'*, ed. G. Bergstrasser, Cairo, 1933.

Julien, C.-A., *History of North Africa*, trans. J. Petrie, New York, 1970.

al-Kahhala, 'Umar Rida, *Mu'jam al-mu'allifīn*, 15 vols, Damascus, 1957–1961.

al-Kattani, Muhammad b. Ja'far, *ar-Risāla al-mustaṭrafa*, Damascus, 1383/1964.

Kennedy, H. ed., *Al-Tabari* (Princeton, 2008).

Khalifa b. Khayyat, *aṭ-Ṭabaqāt*, ed. S. Zakkar, Damascus, 1966; ed. A. D. al-'Umari, Baghdad, 1967.

—, *at-Ta'rīkh*, ed S. Zakkar, Damascus, 1967; ed. A. D. al-'Umari, an-Najaf, 1967.

al-Khazraji, Safi ad-Din Ahmad b. 'Abdallah, *Khulāṣat tahdhīb al-kamāl fī asmā' ar-rijāl*, Cairo, 1323/1905.

al-Kindi, Muhammad b. Yusuf, *Kitāb al-wulāt wa-kitāb al-quḍāt*, ed. Rhuvon Guest, Leiden, 1912.

Kuthayyir 'Azza, *Dīwān*, ed. H. Peres, Paris, 1930.

Lammens, H., *Etudes sur le siècle des Omayyades*, Beirut, 1930.

Lane, E. W., *An Arabic English Lexicon*, 8 vols, London, 1863–1893.

Le Strange, G., *The Lands of the Eastern Caliphate*, Cambridge, 1930.

Lewis, B., *The Arabs in History*, Oxford, 1958.

Løkkegaard, F., *Islamic Taxation in the Classic Period*, Copenhagen, 1950.

Lynch, Ryan, *Between the Conquests and the Court: A Critical Analysis of the Futūḥ al-Buldān of al-Balādhurī*, Oxford, DPhil., forthcoming.

al-Maliki, Abu Bakr 'Abdallah b. Abi 'Abdallah, *Riyāḍ an-nufūs*, ed. H. Mu'nis, Cairo, 1951.

Margoliouth, D. S., *Lectures on Arabic Historians*, Calcutta, 1930.

al-Mas'udi, Abu l-Hasan 'Ali b. al-Husayn, *Murūj adh-dhahab wa-madā'in al-jawhar/Les Prairies d'or*, ed. and trans. C. Barbier de Maynard and P. de Courteille, 9 vols, Paris, 1861–1877.

—, *at-Tanbīh wa-l-ishrāf*, ed. M. J. de Goeje (Bibliotheca geographorum Arabicorum, vol. 8), Leiden, 1893.

Mesnage, le Père J., *Romanisation de l'Afrique: Tunisie, Algérie, Maroc*, Paris, 1913.

al-Mubarrad, Abu l-'Abbas Muhammad b. Yazid, *al-Kāmil*, ed. W. Wright, Leipzig, 1864.

al-Muqaddasi, Muhammad b. Ahmad, *Aḥsan at-taqāsīm fī ma'rifat al-aqālīm*, ed. M. J. de Goeje (Bibliotheca geographorum Arabicorum, vol. 3), Leiden, 1877.

Nicholson, R., *A Literary History of the Arabs*, New York, 1969.

Pellat, C., *Annales de l'institut d'études orientales*, Algiers, 1952.

—, *Le Milieu basrien et la formation de Ǧaḥiẓ*, Paris, 1953.

—, *The Life and Works of Jahiz*, Berkeley, 1969.

Petersen, E. L., "'Ali and Mu'awiya: The Rise of the Umayyad Caliphate 656–661," *Acta Orientalia*, 23 (1959), 157–196.

—, "Studies on the Historiography of the 'Ali-Mu'awiyah Conflict," *Acta Orientalia*, 27 (1963), 83–118.

Qudama b. Ja'far, Abu l-Faraj, *Kitāb al-kharāj*, ed. M. J. de Goeje (Bibliotheca geographorum Arabicorum, vol. 6, 184–266), Leiden, 1889.

Ramsay, W. M., *The Historical Geography of Asia Minor*, London, 1890.

Rosenthal, F., *A History of Muslim Historiography*, Leiden, 1968.

Rotter, G., "The Umayyad Fulūs of Mosul," *American Numismatic Society Museum Notes*, 19 (1974), 165–198.

—, "Zur Ueberlieferung einiger historischer Werke Madā'inīs eis in Ṭabarīs Annalen," *Oriens*, 23–24 (1974), 103–133.

as-Sam'ani, 'Abd al-Karim b. Muhammad, *al-Ansāb*, introduction by D. S. Margoliouth, Leiden, 1912.

Sezgin, F., *Geschichte des arabischen Schrifttums*, 5 vols, Leiden, 1967–1975.

Shaban, M. A., *The 'Abbasid Revolution*, Cambridge, 1970.

—, *Islamic History A.D. 600–750*, Cambridge, 1971.

Shboul A., *Al-Mas'udi and His World: A Muslim Humanist and his Interest in Non-Muslims*, Oxford, 1978.

Shoshan, B., *Poetics of Islamic Historiography: Deconstructing Tabari's History*, Leiden, 2004.

as-Suyuti, Jalal ad-Din 'Abd ar-Rahman, *Ta'rīkh al-khulafā'*, Cairo, 1383/1964. Trans. H. S. Jarrett as *History of the Caliphs*, Calcutta, 1881.

at-Tabari, Muhammad b. Jarir, *Ta'rīkh ar-rusul wa-l-mulūk*, ed. M. J. de Goeje, Leiden, 1879–1890. Trans. from an abridged Persian version of al-Bal'ami, as *Chronique de Abou-Djafar ... Tabari*, by M. H. Zotenberg, 4 vols, Paris, 1867–1874.

Ta'rīkh al-khulafā', anonymous, ed. P. Griyaznevitch, Moscow, 1967.

at-Tibrizi, Abu Zakariyya' Yahya, *Sharḥ dīwān al-ḥamāsa*, ed. M. M. 'Abd al-Hamid, 4 vols, Cairo, n.d.

Waki', Muhammad b. Khalaf, *Akhbār al-quḍāt*, Cairo, 1947.

Weil, Gustav, *Geschichte der Chalifen*, 5 vols, Heidelberg and Stuttgart, 1846–1851.

Wellhausen, J., *The Arab Kingdom and its Fall*, trans. M. G. Weir, Beirut, 1963.

—, "Die Kämpfe der Araber mit den Romäern in der Zeit der Umaijiden," *Nachrichten von der Königl. Gesellschaft der Wissenschaften zu Göttingen, Philologisch-historische Klasse, 1901* (Göttingen, 1902), 414–447.

—, *The Religio-Political Factions in Early Islam*, ed. and trans. R. C. Ostle, New York, 1975.

Wensinck, A. J. et al., *Concordance et indices de la tradition musulmane*, 7 vols, Leiden, 1936–1969.

Williams, J. A., *Islam*, New York, 1962.

Wuestenfeld, F., *Die Geschichtschreiber der Araber and ihre Werke*, New York, n.d. (reprint of Göttingen, 1882 edition).

Wurtzel, C., "The Coinage of the Revolutionaries during the Reign of Marwan II," unpublished.

al-Ya'qubi, Ahmad b. Abi Ya'qub, *al-Buldān*, ed. M. J. de Goeje (Bibliotheca geographorum Arabicorum, vol. 7, 231–373), Leiden, 1892.

—, *Ta'rīkh*, ed. M. T. Houtsma, 2 vols, Leiden, 1883.

Yaqut, Shihab ad-Din b. 'Abdallah, *Mu'jam al-buldān*, ed. F. Wuestenfeld, Teheran, 1965 (reprint of Leipzig, 1866–1870 edition). Trans. of the introductory chapters by Wadie Jwaideh as *The Introductory Chapters of Yuqat's Mu'jam al-Buldan*, Leiden, 1959.

Zakkar, S. "Ibn Khayyāt, al-ʿUṣfurī," *Encyclopaedia Islamic* 2nd ed., ed. P. Bearman, Th. Bianquis, C. E. Bosworth, E. van Donzel, W. P. Heinrichs, Leiden, III, 838.

Zambaur, E. von, *Manuel de généalogie et de chronologie pour l'histoire de l'Islam*, Hanover, 1927.

—, *Die Münzprägungen des Islams*, Wiesbaden, 1968.

az-Zirikli, Khayr ad-Din, *al-A'lām*, 10 vols, Cairo, 1373–1378/1954–1959.

INDEX OF PEOPLE AND PLACES